WHEREVER THERE'S A

FIGHT

HOW RUNAWAY SLAVES, SUFFRAGISTS, IMMIGRANTS, STRIKERS, AND POETS SHAPED CIVIL LIBERTIES IN CALIFORNIA

WHEREVER THERE'S A FIGHT

HOW RUNAWAY SLAVES, SUFFRAGISTS, IMMIGRANTS, STRIKERS, AND POETS SHAPED CIVIL LIBERTIES IN CALIFORNIA

ELAINE ELINSON AND STAN YOGI

HEYDAY, BERKELEY, CALIFORNIA

This project was originally made possible by the generous support of the Evelyn and Walter Haas, Jr. Fund and the California Civil Liberties Public Education Program.

©2009 by Elaine Elinson and Stan Yogi
Preface ©2019 by Elaine Elinson and Stan Yogi

Library of Congress Cataloging-in-Publication Data
Names: Elinson, Elaine, author. | Yogi, Stan, author.
Title: Wherever there's a fight : how runaway slaves, suffragists, immigrants, strikers, and poets shaped civil liberties in California / Elaine Elinson and Stan Yogi.
Description: Tenth anniversary edition. | Berkeley, California : Heyday, 2019. | Includes bibliographical references and index.
Identifiers: LCCN 2019021561 | ISBN 9781597144919 (pbk. : alk. paper)
Subjects: LCSH: Minorities--Civil rights--California--History. | Civil rights--History--California--Civil rights--History. | California--Social conditions. | California--Ethnic relations.
Classification: LCC F870.A1 E45 2019 | DDC 305.8009794--dc23
LC record available at https://lccn.loc.gov/2019021561

Original ISBN: 978-1-59714-114-7

Cover Design: Ashley Ingram
Interior Design and Typesetting: Lorraine Rath and Ashley Ingram

Printed in East Peoria, Illinois, by Versa Press, Inc.

Published by Heyday
P. O. Box 9145, Berkeley, California 94709
(510) 549-3564
heydaybooks.com

10 9 8 7 6 5 4 3 2 1

Elaine Elinson dedicates this book to:
Her father, Jack Elinson, who taught her to be curious about the
world, and her mother, May Gomberg Elinson, who encouraged
her to embrace it.

Stan Yogi dedicates this book to his parents:
John Yogi (1924–1970) and Tokiko Kuniyoshi Yogi (1925–1989),
who were incarcerated during World War II and still had faith in
the promise of American freedom and justice.

— CONTENTS —

ACKNOWLEDGMENTS

As we compiled these acknowledgments, we were reminded of the many people we depended on to create this history.

We especially want to thank all those we interviewed (a complete list is in the bibliography), whose life experiences and hard-won battles helped ensure civil liberties for all Californians. We are grateful that they opened their living rooms, hearts, and memories to us—we have learned so much from them, not only about California history, but about tenacity, courage, and in many cases, pure chutzpah!

We have had the great fortune to work with the visionary, skilled, and generous staff of Heyday: publisher Malcolm Margolin, who came up with the idea for this book and gently shepherded us through the demanding process of turning the idea into reality; our deft editor, Jeannine Gendar, who helped us craft a narrative out of voluminous material; our production editor, Diane Lee; and the many others who worked on this lengthy project.

We have both worked for the ACLU and want to give special thanks to our ACLU colleagues for their unwavering support. We could not have completed this work without their expertise, enthusiasm, and ongoing commitment to civil liberties.

At our home base, the ACLU of Northern California, we especially appreciate the help of Michelle Alexander, Wendy Baker, Ann Brick, Cheri Bryant, John Crew, Margaret Crosby, Dorothy Ehrlich, Maya Harris, Shana Heller, Aundré Herron, Sandy Holmes, Francisco Lobaco, Robert Nakatani, Nancy Otto, Gigi Pandian, Leticia Pavon, Stella Richardson, Catrina Roallos, Alan Schlosser, Nigar Shaikh, Valerie Small-Navarro, Jeffrey Vessels, and Cynthia Williams. And thanks go to our colleagues at the ACLU of Southern California: Julianna Alexander, Lois Bader, Heather Carrigan, Sandy Graham-Jones, Hal Gunn, Brenda Maull, Pam Noles, Ramona Ripston, Mark Rosenbaum, and Liz Schroeder. And at the national ACLU, Mariana Bustamante, Joel Engardio, Robin Goldfaden, and Lucas Guttentag.

Some of the most exciting moments in this joint endeavor took place in dusty library stacks and the rich archives of historical societies and museums. For their help in guiding us through this treasure-filled territory, we would like to thank: Mary Morganti, Joe Evans, Debra Kaufman, and Alison Moore at the California Historical Society; Karen Strauss, Charlotte Sanders, Christina Moretta, Jason Baxter, Tami Suzuki, and Tim Wilson at the San Francisco Public Library; Catherine Powell and Conor Casey at the Labor Archives at San Francisco State University; Margaret Kimball at the Stanford Library; Charles L. Miller and Daniel Nealand at the National Archives; Susan Snyder, Jack von Euw, and Corliss Lee at the Bancroft Library; Jeff Crawford at the California State Archives; Vickie Lockhart at the California State Library; Jeff Lanzman, Donna Da Vigo, and Elizabeth Falk at the Colton Hall Museum; Daniel Bao and Rebekah Kim at the GLBT Historical Society; Paul Evans at ONE Institute; Rukshana Singh at the Southern California Library for Social Studies and Research; and Octavio Olvera, Simon Elliott, and Angela Riggio at UCLA Special Collections.

Our heartfelt appreciation goes to the many people who took time to share with us resources, memories, contacts, and encouragement: Lee Adams, Christopher Arriola, Maria Blanco, Nicolie Bolster, Ruth Borenstein, Scot Brown, Jordan Budd, Jorge Bustamante, Joe Chan, LeRoy Chatfield, Jolene Chu, Paul Cox, Bob Egelko, Susan Englander, Julia Epstein, Ann Forfreedom, Eric Paul Fournier, Jo Anne Frankfurt, Marcia Gallo, Susan Greef, Robert Hedin, Susan Henderson, Abe Ignacio, Karen Kai, Linda Kilb, David Kipen, Karen Korematsu-Haigh, Kathryn Korematsu, Azmeena Ladha, Bill Lann Lee, Ian Haney Lopez, Waverly Lowell, Pam Matsuoka, Michael McCone, Sylvia Mendez, Sandra Meucci, Tom Meyers, Hongyu Min, Susan Mizner, Carlos Muñoz, Kathy Murguia, Drew Oetzel, Eva Paterson, Nancy Ramirez, James Rawls, Barbara Rhine, Greg Robinson, Rick Rocamora, John and Reiko Ross, Paul Richards, Margaret Russell, Nina Serrano, Susan Serrano, Steve Stallone, Ken Stein, Barbara Takei, John True, Howard Watkins, C. Todd White, Hayden White, Richard Yarborough, and Silvia Yee.

We offer special bouquets to two people whom we met during the course of our research, and—not knowing what they were getting themselves into—offered to help. Michael Ginsborg is an extraordinary law librarian who volunteered hours and hours of research to help us track down legal cases and histories, from the most obscure sources. Lindsay Kefauver is a talented photo researcher whose vast knowledge of images and archives helped make this book a much richer and more vivid volume.

We offer our gratitude to the California Civil Liberties Public Education Program, which awarded us a grant that enabled us to initiate this project. In addition to its financial support and early endorsement, we are proud to be part of this unique program that ensures the legacy of the internment during World War II will never be forgotten. In particular, we thank Diane Matsuda, Colette Moody, and Elaine Yamaguchi. We also thank the Evelyn and Walter Haas, Jr. Fund for a grant to Heyday Institute that was directed to this book.

We offer deep appreciation to those who shared their expertise and wisdom by reading different chapters of the manuscript and offering their critiques: Robert Allen, Lorraine Bannai, Mary Lou Breslin, Matt Coles, Claire Cooper, Margaret Crosby, Dorothy Ehrlich, Joel Engardio, Julia Epstein, Marcia Gallo, Mary Gerber, Aileen Hernandez, Marshall Krause, Judith Kurtz, Francisco Lobaco, Matthew Markovich, Dale Minami, Susan O'Hara, Catherine Powell, James Rawls, Marcy Rein, Amitai Schwartz, Pat Shiu, Debbie Smith, Jayashri Srikantiah, Peter Sussman, Cecillia Wang, and Charles Wollenberg. Their patience, intelligence, and phenomenal knowledge have greatly enriched this book. Despite their valuable critiques, we accept responsibility for any errors and inaccuracies in the text.

Our gratitude goes as well to those who provided us with generous gifts of time and place: the writing residencies at Anderson Center for Interdisciplinary Studies, Hedgebrook, and Mesa Refuge; Eileen Goldman and Robert Gabriner, and Ron Wong and Mike Tekulsky, who provided havens for writing in San Francisco; and Julie, Mark, Max, and Nicholas Akita, Ellen and Jimmy Bernal, Steve Carroll and Martha Mayo, Teresita CiriaCruz, Joe and Mitzi Nagano, and Kevin Schaeffer and Steve Killam, who offered hospitality during research and writing trips to Los Angeles and Texas.

We are grateful to Heyday for publishing this tenth anniversary edition of *Wherever There's a Fight*. We especially thank publisher Steve Wasserman and editor Emmerich Anklam. We also appreciate Heyday's former publicist extraordinaire Lillian Fleer, who arranged so many readings for us at bookstores, libraries, museums, community centers, and schools around California.

The stories in this book were amplified through several related projects. For those opportunities we thank the following organizations and individuals: For California Humanities' *Wherever There's a Fight* exhibit, Ralph Lewin, Malcolm Margolin, and the Exhibit Envoy team of Adrienne McGraw, Joan Jasper, and Sarah Davis. For the film, *Ain't Gonna Be Treated This Way: The Fight for Social Justice in California*, which regularly screens at Riverside's Center for Social Justice and Civil Liberties, Hal Fisher and Jonathan Crosby. For the exhibit *Art of Survival: Enduring the Turmoil of Tule Lake*, project team Madeleine Blake, Sarah Bone, and Hiroshi Shimizu.

We thank the faculty and staff of the many high schools, community colleges, and universities who invited us to speak, especially Christina Accomando, Wurlig Bao,

ACKNOWLEDGMENTS

and Kumi Watanabe-Schock at Humboldt State University. They were particularly enthusiastic about this book, inviting us to deliver keynote presentations to incoming students, and other talks. Students there and at schools throughout California inspired us with accounts of their own activism. As we shared with them stories from the past, their efforts and dreams gave us hope for the future.

Stan thanks his partner, David Carroll, for his love, support, encouragement, and patience during the long process of birthing this book. And Elaine would like to thank her son, Matthew, for his encouragement, and her husband, Rene Ciria-Cruz, a loving and beloved fellow traveler.

PREFACE TO THE
TENTH ANNIVERSARY EDITION

We wrote in our initial introduction to *Wherever There's a Fight* that we hoped our book would be "part of an ongoing dialogue about justice, freedom, and equality in California."

During the past ten years, that dialogue has flourished, and we have been grateful and exhilarated to be part of it. We have presented at dozens of libraries, schools, bookstores, and cultural institutions throughout California. We were honored to speak at the Manzanar National Historic Site in 2011 to commemorate the day, sixty-nine years earlier, when President Franklin Roosevelt signed Executive Order 9066, authorizing the mass removal of Japanese Americans into camps like Manzanar. We read at San Francisco's City Lights bookstore, whose founder Lawrence Ferlinghetti we feature for standing up to censorship during the 1957 *Howl* trial. We traveled twice to Humboldt State University, where all first-year students were assigned to read our book.

On this journey we've met many people who've shared with us how they've fought for justice. At Northtown Books in Arcata, we met a Native American woman who participated in demonstrations to halt a logging road through sacred land. At Cal State Bakersfield, we were greeted by Lupe Murguia, a United Farm Workers organizer whom police arrested so many times on picket lines that his name is associated with a court procedure that bars selective prosecution for political reasons. At a bookstore in Clayton, Nancy Rowe shared drawings from her father Frank, an art professor fired from San Francisco State University in 1950 for refusing to sign the state's loyalty oath.

Wherever There's a Fight has generated related projects that have broadened understanding of California's civil liberties history. In 2011 California Humanities invited us to create a traveling exhibit based on our book. So far, dozens of sites have hosted the exhibit. We also composed the script for a short documentary film that screens at the Center for Social Justice and Civil Liberties in Riverside. And we wrote text for *Art of Survival: Enduring the Turmoil of Tule Lake*, an exhibit that has been shown throughout the country.

In our initial introduction, we quoted Wallace Stegner—"California is like the rest of the country, only more so"—to point out that the state's diversity has contributed to its being a bellwether for the nation—initiating laws and policies, for better or worse, that other states adopted or that became federal law.

In the past decade, that trend has continued. One of the most significant milestones was securing marriage equality. California progressed from a state in which same-sex relationships were criminal to one in which Gavin Newsom, then San Francisco's Mayor, boldly moved in 2004 to allow gay and lesbian couples to marry. The road to progress took an unfortunate detour with Proposition 8, a successful 2008 initiative amending the state Constitution to deny same-sex couples marriage rights. But lesbian and gay couples fought back, winning positive federal court rulings invalidating Proposition 8. The United States Supreme Court let those decisions stand, two years before ruling that same-sex marriages were legal in all fifty states.

We've seen similar progress in criminal justice. For many years California was infamous for its harsh penal system. Fueled by the war on drugs and the three-strikes law, by the end of the millennium the state's prison population was the largest in the nation. But in the past decade, several criminal justice reforms moved the pendulum in the other direction. The Public Safety Realignment Act of 2011 allowed people convicted of low-level nonviolent felonies—mainly drug and property crimes—to serve time in county jails rather than state prisons. In 2012 two-thirds of California voters approved changes to the state's draconian three-strikes law, reducing some mandatory life sentences. Both of these measures dramatically lowered the number of people held in state prisons.

High-profile killings of unarmed black men—from Oscar Grant on a BART platform in Oakland to Stephon Clark in his grandmother's backyard in Sacramento—spurred the Black Lives Matter movement, as well as the passage of two major laws exposing long-secret records of police abuse and documenting racial profiling by law enforcement agencies.

In one of the most historic changes in the arena of criminal justice, in March 2019 Governor Gavin Newsom issued a moratorium on the death penalty, declaring it racially discriminatory and "broken beyond repair," thus granting a reprieve to all 737 persons on Death Row in the state. Though California has not executed anyone since 2006, it has the largest death row population in the country.

But, unfortunately, current national political leaders are reviving many of the negative policies from California's darker history. The Trump administration's travel ban against people from majority Muslim countries tragically echoes rampant nineteenth-century anti-Asian discrimination in California that resulted in the 1882 Chinese Exclusion Act, the first law denying entry to the US of a specific ethnic group.

Contemporary anti-immigrant sentiment, which has motivated calls for a border wall and the detention of thousands of immigrant children ripped from their parents and housed in cages, recalls the xenophobia underlying the mass deportation from California of Mexican immigrants and American citizens of Mexican ancestry in the early 1930s, as well as the more recent passage of Proposition 187, a 1994 ballot initiative denying public services to undocumented immigrants.

In these difficult times, when our nation's leaders legitimize bigotry and hatred, it is crucial to look back at our history—when Chinese residents were massacred and run out of towns, when enslaved people who came to this free state were kidnapped to be forcibly sent back into bondage, when workers were jailed and killed for trying to form unions, when women couldn't vote, and when 120,000 Japanese Americans were incarcerated in desolate camps simply because of their ethnicity.

It is also important to remember that in each of those instances the targets of violence and repression fought back—in the courts, in legislatures, and in the streets.

We've lived through many setbacks and many victories in the past decade, but above all we've witnessed a powerful, growing resistance. And again California is playing a unique role.

When President Trump announced the first iteration of his Muslim travel ban in January 2017, volunteer lawyers, some with no immigration law experience, rushed to Los Angeles and San Francisco airports to provide assistance. Thousands of activists protested and offered shelter, clothing, food, and transportation.

In response to federal policies targeting immigrants during the past ten years, California's legislators have passed laws providing health care to children, drivers' licenses, and higher education opportunities regardless of immigration status. As of

2018, California is a sanctuary state, limiting local law enforcement officers' cooperation with federal immigration authorities.

The outpouring of women in California cities and small towns during the Women's Marches of recent years draws attention to the threats of rollbacks of women's rights—including reproductive freedom. The #MeToo movement brought to light widespread sexual harassment and assault experienced by so many women now determined to expose it.

This activism has translated into an unprecedented number of women not only voting but running for and winning seats in Congress, including the first Native American women representatives, the first Muslim women, lesbians, wounded war veterans, and the mother of an African American son who was killed by a white man for playing music too loudly. During the 2019 State of the Union address, these pioneering congresswomen wore white, paying homage to the suffragists who a century earlier fought for their right to vote. Those early suffragists probably never imagined that in 2019 California's two senators would be women—one the daughter of immigrants from Jamaica and India, the other a Jew—and that the woman holding the third highest office in the land would be a San Francisco woman.

We hope that our book is playing a part in this wave of resistance, bolstering new readers and activists with inspiring stories from our history. City Lights Books has included *Wherever There's a Fight* on its "Pedagogy of Resistance" reading list.

Many courageous people we featured have received statewide and national recognition in the past decade. National Park ranger Betty Reid Soskin shared with us how racial segregation tainted the "Rosie the Riveter" experience for many black women, stories she later recounted at the White House at the invitation of President Barack Obama. And Fred Korematsu, jailed in 1942 for refusing to obey orders to leave his home and shunned by his community for his stance, now receives recognition annually on January 30, his birthday, through California's Fred Korematsu Day of Civil Liberties and the Constitution. This is the first statewide acknowledgement anywhere in the nation for an Asian American.

These honors remind us of the wisdom of Clinton Lee Scott, a Los Angeles minister we quoted in our initial introduction: "Grandchildren of those who stoned the prophet sometimes gather up the stones to build the prophet's monument."

One final note on terminology: In the past decade, our language has evolved to describe more accurately and justly people who faced and fought against oppression. "Enslaved person" is the term many scholars and others now use instead of "slave," which implies an inherent condition. "Enslaved" reflects how a person was treated and reminds us that slavery is a societally enforced system. Similarly, "internment" is not an accurate term for the World War II mass imprisonment of American citizens of Japanese ancestry, as "internment" applies to foreign nationals imprisoned in another country, not citizens of the country. "Incarceration" is more precise.

We recognize how much words matter, and we acknowledge that we weren't aware of these distinctions ten years ago, so older terminology appears in this book.

Writing *Wherever There's a Fight* made us more optimistic about the future. Sharing these stories and hearing from people who endured difficult times and fought hard fights gave us hope. And we maintain that hope even in these challenging days for civil liberties.

We are honored that our book has illuminated movements that started long before us and has played a role in movements that will continue long after us. We are grateful to help keep the dialogue about justice, freedom, and equality alive.

Elaine Elinson, San Francisco
Stan Yogi, Los Angeles

"*Wherever they's a fight so hungry people can eat, I'll be there. Wherever they's a cop beatin' up a guy, I'll be there....I'll be in the way guys yell when they're mad—an' I'll be in the way kids laugh when they're hungry an' they know supper's ready. An' when our folks eat the stuff they raise an' live in the houses they build—why, I'll be there.*"

—John Steinbeck, *The Grapes of Wrath*

INTRODUCTION

In 1982, sixty-three-year-old Fred Korematsu learned that the U.S. government had lied to justify the incarceration of one hundred and twenty thousand Japanese Americans during World War II. Korematsu had been jailed for defying military orders to leave his hometown of San Leandro to be interned in a concentration camp. He had challenged the government, and his case went to the U.S. Supreme Court, which ruled against him.

Nearly four decades later, when a researcher told him about the government's deception, he said quietly, "They did me a great wrong."

This simple yet profound statement encapsulates the aspects of California history that we examine in this book.

The internment of Japanese Americans (and the long history of anti-Japanese and anti-Asian sentiment that laid the social and political groundwork for the internment) is a touchstone event, key to our examination of California. And that bleak episode fits into a spectrum of civil liberties conflicts that have impacted the lives of millions of Californians from the founding of the state until today.

Vigilante attacks on immigrants during the gold rush, extermination and enslavement of Native Americans, exclusion of and trafficking in Chinese immigrants, suppression of labor organizers on the waterfront and in the field, jailing and deportation of political radicals, segregation of Mexican schoolchildren, banning of books from John Steinbeck's *Grapes of Wrath* to Allen Ginsberg's *Howl*, the hounding of suspected Communists during the Cold War…these and many other shameful incidents have shaped California. Yet for every crisis, there were resonant voices of resistance. Like Fred Korematsu, who challenged the internment order because he was, as he said, "an American" and it was "wrong," many heroes and heroines have stood up against the repressive laws, political oppression, and outright violence that targeted them because of who they were or what they believed.

1

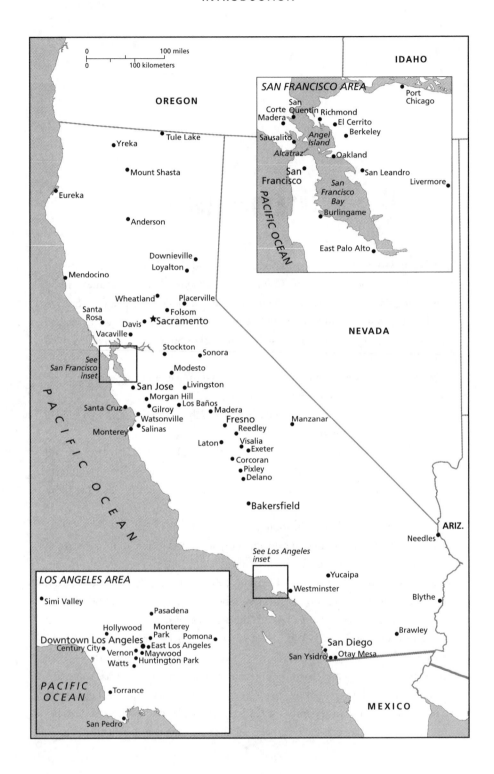

0 100 miles
0 100 kilometers

SAN FRANCISCO AREA

Port Chicago
Corte Quentin Richmond
San
Madera
El Cerrito
Sausalito *Angel Island* Berkeley
Alcatraz Oakland
San Leandro
San Francisco
San Francisco Bay Livermore
Burlingame
PACIFIC OCEAN
East Palo Alto

IDAHO

OREGON

Yreka
Tule Lake
Mount Shasta
Eureka
Anderson

Mendocino

Downieville
Loyalton

Wheatland Placerville
Santa Rosa Folsom
Davis ★Sacramento
Vacaville

See San Francisco inset

Stockton
Sonora
Modesto

PACIFIC OCEAN

San Jose Livingston
Morgan Hill
Los Baños
Santa Cruz Gilroy Madera
Watsonville Fresno
Monterey Salinas Reedley
Laton Visalia
Exeter
Corcoran
Pixley
Delano

NEVADA

Manzanar

Bakersfield

See Los Angeles inset

ARIZ.

Needles

Yucaipa
Westminster

Blythe

LOS ANGELES AREA

Simi Valley

Pasadena
Hollywood Monterey Park
Downtown Los Angeles Pomona
Century City East Los Angeles
Vernon Maywood
Watts Huntington Park

Brawley

San Diego
San Ysidro Otay Mesa

PACIFIC OCEAN

Torrance

San Pedro

MEXICO

2

Runaway slave Archy Lee fought in Sacramento to retain his freedom. Lee Yick, a San Francisco laundryman, demanded equal treatment from a legal system skewed against Chinese immigrants. Charlotte Brown refused to leave when ordered off a San Francisco streetcar in 1863—almost a century before Rosa Parks's similar defiance launched the civil rights movement. Sacramento elementary school student Charlotte Gabrielli faced expulsion for not reciting the Pledge of Allegiance because it violated her religion. Gonzalo and Felicitas Mendez challenged segregation to ensure that their children and other Latino youth could attend good schools in Orange County. Los Angeles Black Panther leader Geronimo Pratt battled for decades against a wrongful murder conviction resulting from an FBI frame-up.

All of these individuals, and the many, many more that they represent, shaped California history with their resistance, their courage, and their tenacity.

Some, like Harry Bridges, leader of the 1934 West Coast maritime strike, rose to prominence—although, as he said, "I'm a working stiff I just happened to be around at the right time, and no one else wanted the job."

Others, like noted author Upton Sinclair, who was arrested in 1923 for reading the Constitution to a group of strikers in San Pedro, purposefully took a stand. He explained, "I intend to do what little one man can do to awake the public conscience....I know that our liberties were not won without suffering, and may be lost again through our cowardice."

Still others, like Selina Solomons, a Jewish suffragist who was, a full decade before the passage of the Nineteenth Amendment, organizing shop girls in San Francisco to win the vote for women, are not as well known.

And for every Bridges, Solomons, or Korematsu, there are many others who crossed borders, defied unjust orders, went to jail, marched, wrote books, read books, and sang out on picket lines. Though we may never know their names, they too have shaped California. Their efforts show us that civil liberties are not bestowed from on high by presidents, governors, and legislators. Rather, people who have fought against inequality and injustice have turned abstract principles into meaningful freedoms and rights.

Their vision and organizing gave rise to the trade union movement, the civil rights and women's movements, and the fights for prison reform, disability rights, and lesbian and gay equality.

They stood up and faced tremendous odds because, in the words of United Farm Workers leader Cesar Chavez, "From the depth of need and despair, the people can work together, can organize themselves to solve their own problems with dignity and respect."

* * *

"California is just like the rest of the United States, only more so," observed Pulitzer Prize–winning writer Wallace Stegner. Even before it became a state, California was a place where people of different races, religions, political beliefs, ethnicities, sexual orientations, and class interests both clashed and harmonized.

Our book is an exploration of historical moments when unpopular and vulnerable groups have been the targets of what we broadly consider vigilante injustice. At times, that injustice took the form of vigilante violence. At other times, it was manifest in unfair legislation or discriminatory enforcement of laws and policies against feared and marginalized people. In some instances, vigilante injustice results from direct democracy in the form of voter initiatives.

The initiative process has been significant in shaping and misshaping civil liberties in California. It began as a progressive tool in the early twentieth century to ensure that legislators controlled by big businesses would not block laws benefiting the majority of Californians. The first initiatives granted women the right to vote, established a limit on working hours for women and children, and set a minimum wage. Through the decades, initiatives were the vehicle to establish labor law coverage for farmworkers and to add an explicit right to privacy to the state constitution. In the latter half of the twentieth century, however, initiatives were used to restrict and deny civil liberties: to people of color, immigrants, lesbians and gay men, and voiceless minorities, like prisoners.

Voters, though, cannot undo constitutional rights and freedoms. Neither can politicians. Brave individuals have resisted vigilante injustice, primarily through the state and federal judicial systems and via political organizing and advocacy. The result has been a steady growth in jurisprudence and traditions protecting civil liberties and civil rights for growing numbers of Californians.

* * *

We interviewed many generous individuals for this book, and we have also drawn on a rich trove of materials, including newspapers, archives of labor and social movements, files of the ACLU affiliates in northern and southern California, and letters and diaries. (In the bibliography, we have listed the individuals who shared with us their experiences, insights, and in many cases, their personal files. We have organized our references by chapter, so that the reader may more easily identify source material on a particular subject.)

The scope of our book is broad, covering more than a century and a half and a range of issues. In some instances, we believed the most effective way to illustrate a constitutional principle was to focus a chapter on a specific civil liberty, such as freedom of religion or the right to dissent. In others, the sweep of how a particular group won freedoms and equal rights was so compelling that we focused on specific populations, such as women and people with disabilities, that have secured civil liberties through long struggles.

Some lawsuits and incidents in this book cover multiple issues and populations. In such cases, we have integrated the topic into the chapter that we believe is most relevant. Similarly, some laws and repressive tactics have been employed against numerous groups. You will find, for instance, examples of police abuse of power in several chapters, not just the chapter focused on criminal justice.

We believe the incarceration of Japanese Americans during World War II crystallizes many of the book's themes and issues—anti-immigrant sentiment, racism, collapse of the criminal justice system, and dissent. For this reason we dedicated a chapter to this tragic episode. We have placed it at the end of the book because our epilogue links the experience of Japanese Americans with the post-9/11 targeting of vulnerable Arab, South Asian, Middle Eastern, and Muslim communities, and with repressive measures like the Patriot Act, which allows for government surveillance of innocent civilians and punishment for voicing dissident ideas.

Our book is not a comprehensive catalogue of the history of civil liberties in California, nor is it a legal text or an encyclopedia. Rather we offer fragments of history, illuminating incidents, and personal stories to illustrate the impact of civil liberties—and the lack of them—on people's lives. We recognize that we have left out many worthy cases and issues. We have done so only because our space and our comprehension were limited. We encourage future researchers, historians, and civil liberties advocates to fill the gaps they see in this book. We hope this volume will be a part of an ongoing dialogue about justice, freedom, and equality in California.

* * *

In 1998 President Bill Clinton awarded Fred Korematsu, by then seventy-nine years old, the Medal of Freedom, the nation's highest civilian honor, comparing him to Rosa Parks.

This recognition, coming more than five decades after Korematsu stood virtually alone in arguing that the mass incarceration of Japanese Americans was unconstitutional, confirms the insight of Los Angeles minister Clinton Lee Scott, who said, "Grandchildren of those who stoned the prophet sometimes gather up the stones to build the prophet's monument. Always it is easier to pay homage to prophets than to heed the direction of their wisdom."

History is dynamic. Consider this statement: "Strange voices today cry throughout the land. We are told that liberty must be suppressed in order for liberty to exist. We are told that labor must abdicate its traditional rights in order to avoid abdication of its traditional rights. We are told that free speech must be limited in order to avoid the limitation of free speech. We are told that classes must be persecuted in order to avoid the persecution of classes. We are told we are already at war in order to avoid war."

Dalton Trumbo, a screenwriter later to be blacklisted during the Cold War, wrote these words in 1941. To know our past enables us to confront and overcome current challenges. Stories that emerge from the paradox of California resonate throughout the country—sometimes as harbingers of what is to come, and sometimes as affirmations of what is both difficult and inspiring in the development of law in this country.

We are happy to share the lessons of Californians. In doing so, we hope to give voice to the hundreds of thousands of people, native to the state or from around the nation and globe, who have fought for their rights in California so that all of us might benefit from their struggle.

California has been transformed from a storm of vigilante injustice into a state where rights are recognized by law.

May we learn from our history and support the civil liberties prophets among us today.

— ONE —

STAKING OUR CLAIM

THE LAW IN EARLY CALIFORNIA

Todos los hombres son por naturaleza libres i independientes y tienen ciertos derechos inajenables, entre los cuales son los de gozar y defender la vida y la libertad, de adquirir, poseer y proteger sus propriedades y de procurer y obtener sus seguridad y felicidad. —Constitución de California, 1849

On the afternoon of Saturday, February 7, 1885, in the foggy northern coastal town of Eureka, Wei Lum, a Chinese immigrant, was visiting Charles Huntington, the Congregationalist minister who had converted him to Christianity. A crowd of angry men led by local resident Sam Kelsey burst into the parsonage and demanded Wei Lum. Kelsey grabbed the frightened man by his queue and pulled him out of the clergyman's home and through the dirt streets to the edge of Eureka's one-block Chinatown, where a gallows had been quickly erected a few hours earlier.

Before hundreds of jeering townspeople, a noose was placed around Wei Lum's neck. He was about to hang when a Methodist minister climbed onto the gallows and firmly stated, "Boys, take that rope off that boy's neck! If you hang him, you'll hang him over my dead body." Perhaps sobered or intimidated by the minister's declaration, the men who minutes earlier were prepared to kill Wei Lum instead took him to the town's wharf, where the other Chinese residents of Eureka waited under guard.

Wei Lum was nearly executed not because he had committed a crime. He almost died simply because he was Chinese.

The violence that Wei Lum and Eureka's more than two hundred other Chinese residents endured that tragic weekend was part of a vigilante rampage to purge the lumber town of all Chinese.

The evening before the aborted hanging, Eureka city council member David Kendall had been caught in crossfire between two Chinese men and killed. Word of the popular politician's death spread quickly. Within twenty minutes, more than six hundred people obeyed the call of a bell ringer who commanded, "Go to Centennial Hall. Go now!" Many were loggers and mill workers who were unemployed or fearful that the depression gripping the country would leave them jobless. They saw the Chinese as unfair competition and believed them to be an inferior race.

Bent on revenge, the crowd deliberated on how to exact it. They rejected the idea of killing every Chinese man in town and vetoed the suggestion of looting and destroying Chinese businesses and homes. But the proposal of forcing every Chinese person to leave Eureka, under threat of violence, appealed to the group. A committee of fifteen volunteered to order all Chinese residents to leave Eureka en masse aboard two steamships that were in the port.

Just hours after the Kendall shooting, nearly two hundred and twenty Chinese were packing their belongings for a hasty exodus. Vigilantes looted Chinese stores and scoured the surrounding countryside, rousting Chinese mill workers, cooks, farm laborers, and lumbermen. Merchants' wives hobbled through the streets on bound feet. The exiles took what they could carry and were herded into a warehouse on the wharf, where they would be forced onto boats headed for San Francisco.

By Sunday morning, less than forty-eight hours after Kendall was shot, all of Eureka's Chinese inhabitants were gone.

* * *

The Eureka purge, one of hundreds of late-nineteenth-century banishments of Chinese residents throughout California, is emblematic of civil liberties violations throughout California history. In Eureka, fear of economic competition and racist beliefs contributed to the expulsion of the entire Chinese community. Even Wei Lum's Christian affiliation could not save him.

The accidental death of a city councilman became the pretext for vengeance. The criminal justice system virtually collapsed. Rather than seeking out the perpetrators of the shooting, Eureka's citizens punished all of their Chinese neighbors.

This targeting of marginalized groups would be repeated on much larger geographic, social, and political stages throughout California history. Fear in its many forms—of economic competition and of racial, religious, gender, political, and sexual difference—has motivated shifting majorities in California to try to strip the less powerful of civil liberties and rights.

By the time of the Eureka purge, California had been a state for thirty-five years and was thus governed by federal and state laws. Nevertheless, expulsions like the one in Eureka were not uncommon. Early in California's statehood, the legislature erected legal barriers to equality and justice for women, immigrants, people of color, and other minorities. Even when laws were in place to protect minority rights, justice in California's raw cities, towns, ranches, and mining communities was unevenly applied.

Legal Limbo and Gold Rush Justice

The Treaty of Guadalupe Hidalgo, which ended the Mexican-American War in 1848, resulted in Mexico officially ceding California to the United States. The transition of political control took place just weeks before tens of thousands of people from around the world began descending on California after learning about the discovery of gold. This sudden mix of nationalities, races, and ethnicities in one region was unprecedented in U.S. history. Sharing dreams of instant wealth, the fortune seekers competed intensely. Among American miners, especially those whose hopes were eroded by unproductive claims, nativism buttressed by the Manifest Destiny philosophy of the era fed tensions and resentments about competitors from other countries.

During the raucous years of the gold rush, the nature of justice in California varied by region and often depended on which group was in the majority and wielded power. Between 1846, the start of the Mexican-American War, and 1850, the region of California operated under a patchwork of military, international, and homegrown laws. Washington provided no legal form of government for California until its admission to the union in 1850.

Under international law, a conquered territory under military occupation, like California, retained the system of local law in effect at the time of the conquest, with any modifications that the military commander of the territory considered necessary. The prevailing system of justice in California under Spanish and Mexican rule was organized around an alcalde—a local, mayor-like official. The title, a legacy of Spain that derives from the Arabic *al-cadi*, or village judge, came with multifaceted executive, legislative, and judicial powers. Under the first few years of American rule, California was overseen by American military commanders who acted as governors, and other military officials acting as alcaldes.

News of gold in California spread quickly throughout the world. Because of their relative proximity to California along the Pacific Ocean, miners from Valparaiso, Chile, and Lima, Peru—two port cities with histories of gold mining and established trade relations with San Francisco—were the first to arrive in the Sierra Nevada in search of gold. Tens of thousands of people from Mexico, Australia, China, Europe, and America soon followed.

As miners raced into California's gold country, only two alcaldes, one in

Sacramento and another in San Joaquin, were located anywhere near the vast and remote mining regions. Without access to established legal systems, miners created their own quasi-governments. At mass meetings, they organized "mining districts" and elected committees to devise rules and regulations. Eventually more than five hundred camps adopted such codes. Each code defined the permissible size of a claim and its use. Each district elected a leader—variously called an alcalde, arbitrator, or chairman. He settled disputes, sometimes with the assistance of a panel of arbitrators or jurors chosen by the contending parties. Civil liberties were often absent in mining camps. Many codes, for example, included "restrictive covenants" barring Mexicans, Asians, and other foreigners from mining. A system of justice based on violence emerged in many camps.

With few jails and law enforcement officers, some miners resorted to extreme punishments, including death, for even relatively minor offenses. Gold rush frontier "justice" administered at the end of a lynch rope was not uncommon. In January 1849, for example, miners in Dry Diggings (now Placerville) tried five non-English-speaking men for attempted robbery and larceny and beat them as punishment. Soon thereafter, three of the same men were charged with murder, and an ad hoc "jury" of the two hundred miners in the camp convicted and hung them. Miners on the Yuba River hanged one Chilean crew leader and cut off the ears of another, simply for attempting to stake claims.

The Bilingual California Constitution of 1849

Following the Bear Flag Revolt and the short-lived California Republic of 1846, San Franciscans began advocating for California's statehood. Civic leaders, seeking order in the rapidly growing region and perhaps some power for themselves, were anxious to create a civil government. The California constitution, drawn up by forty-eight delegates in 1849, tried to impose legal order on the sprawling new territory.

The territorial governor, General Bennett Riley, called the constitutional convention, though whether he had the authority to do so is questionable. Riley had been appointed governor in April 1849, the sixth person to fill the position in a little more than a year. Meanwhile, Congress had been wrestling with the question of slavery in the land ceded by Mexico to the United States. A proviso in the Treaty of Guadalupe Hidalgo banning slavery in the newly acquired lands was defeated; Texas was annexed as a slave territory, and the issue remained an open sore on the body politic.

When Governor Riley learned that Congress had once again adjourned without determining the status of California, he decided to take matters into his own hands. He had the support of President Zachary Taylor, who hoped that California would resolve the thorny question of slavery on its own; Taylor even sent a presidential emissary to encourage the burgeoning population of the mining camps to participate in the constitutional convention. Riley put out the call for delegates on June 3, and from September 1 to October 30, delegates gathered from ten regions throughout the state, mostly the central and northern areas. They were a mixed bunch of men. Half were under thirty-five, and only four were over fifty. Thirty-six were American citizens, more from the northern states than the South. Eight were native Californians, of whom only two were fluent in English. There were even three foreigners—citizens of Scotland, Ireland, and France.

The delegates listed varied pre–gold rush occupations: the single largest group was lawyers, and there were eleven farmers, eight merchants, three soldiers, and two printers. But the majority of the delegates (as well as the majority of the population) were miners. Some familiar figures from early California history participated: Johann (John) Sutter of Sutter's Mill, where gold was first discovered; General Mariano Vallejo, California's official *comandante* under Mexican rule; Edward Gilbert, the editor of the *Alta California* newspaper; and Lewis Dent, brother-in-law of Ulysses S. Grant. One delegate, William Gwin, a Tennessee slaveholder who had served in Congress, came with the express intention of returning to Washington as a senator from California.

They met at Colton Hall in Monterey, California's first capital, on a street lined with adobe buildings. The sidewalks were made of whalebone, a plentiful byproduct of the booming whaling industry on the coast. The building was named for Reverend Walter Colton, Monterey's first American alcalde. According to Colton, the hall was erected "out of the slender proceeds of town lots, the labor of convicts, taxes on liquor shops and fines on gamblers." A fitting

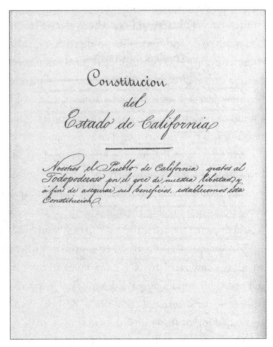

The proceedings of the first constitutional convention in Monterey's Colton Hall were conducted in English and Spanish. The 1849 California constitution was published in both languages.

11

venue to devise a document to bring order to a rambunctious, wildly expanding California.

Inside the wooden hall, on one end of a long, U-shaped wooden table, a well-thumbed Spanish-English dictionary held a place of prominence. The proceedings were conducted in both English and Spanish. Before every vote, the resolution was read in both languages.

Despite the hodgepodge nature of the group, in those autumn weeks of 1849 they accomplished quite a bit. They voted to become a state (as opposed to a territory), determined California's eastern border, and selected El Pueblo de San José as the first state capital. Although many of the California constitution's standard provisions were adopted from the constitutions of Iowa and New York, the delegates also included some innovative proposals and laid the groundwork for key civil liberties in the new state. They granted the right to vote to every "white male citizen of the United States" and "every white male citizen of Mexico" who opted to become a citizen of the United States. They also authorized the legislature to extend the vote to Indians, in the (unlikely) event that two-thirds of that body agreed to do so.

Slavery was forbidden by a unanimous vote. The provision read: "neither slavery nor involuntary servitude, unless for the punishment of crimes, shall ever be tolerated in this state." This vote did not wholly derive from antislavery sentiment, but rather had much to do with preventing competition from slave labor in the goldfields. In the summer prior to the constitutional convention, a mass meeting had been held in the mining camps along the Yuba River. At that meeting, the miners elected William E. Shannon as their delegate and also passed a resolution stating, "No slave or Negro should own claims or even work in the mines." Shannon introduced the antislavery resolution at the constitutional convention.

A delegate who had migrated from Louisiana added, "The labor of the white man brought into competition with the labor of the Negro is always degraded. There is now a respectable and intelligent class of population in the mines; men of talent and education; men digging there in the pit with spade and pick—do you think they would dig with the African? No sir, they would leave this country first."

The delegates also considered a proposal to exclude free blacks from the state, an idea popularized by *The Californian* editor Sam Brannan, the Mormon leader renowned for announcing the discovery of gold to San Franciscans. Just a few months before the constitutional convention, Brannan had spoken at a Sacramento meeting and called for an all-white California.

M. M. McCarver, a delegate from Sacramento by way of Kentucky, proposed the resolution to exclude free blacks. He claimed that southern slaveholders were planning to bring slaves to work the gold mines and grant them "freedom" if they would continue to work for their former owners. He warned the delegates that blacks were "idle in their habits, difficult to be governed by laws," and should be prohibited from entering the state.

He was opposed by Edward Gilbert, editor of the *Alta California*, who argued, "If you insert in your Constitution such a provision or anything like it, you will be guilty of a great injustice—you will do a great wrong to the principles of liberal and enlightened freedom. Are we to attempt here to turn back the tide of human freedom which has rolled across from continent to continent? Are we to say that a free negro or Indian, or any other freeman shall not enter the boundaries of California? I trust not, Sir."

The debate raged for two days, but McCarver could not sway enough delegates. Although some, like Gilbert, opposed the resolution on moral grounds, most rejected the measure because they feared that Congress would consider it a violation of the U.S. Constitution and reject their newly drafted document in its entirety.

Women also benefited from the new constitution, but again, not from the purest of motives. The California delegates did something unprecedented in other state constitutions: they included a provision for separate property for married women. All property of a wife, whether acquired before or during the marriage, could remain in her name. Although this was partly a carryover from the prevailing law in Mexico, and inspired by a newly changed law in New York, delegate Henry Halleck's reasoning probably reflects the more common motive. He claimed this provision would not only attract prospective wives, but *wealthy* prospective wives. The state's population was more than 90 percent male at the time.

A month after the convention, Governor Riley put ratification of the document to a statewide vote. Though there were about 107,000 males of voting age, only 13,000 participated. The constitution was approved by an overwhelming vote of 12,601 to 811 on November 13, 1849. Peter H. Burnett, a Tennessee native who had lived for many years in Mississippi before migrating to California, was elected the first governor.

Legislators were elected as well, and the first legislative session, convened on December 15 in San Jose, selected the senators who would represent California in the U.S. Congress. Gwin had his way. He pulled together a caucus of the Chivalry wing of the Democratic Party, popularly known as "Chivs," who were staunch supporters of the South. Many, like him, still owned slaves in their home states. Other legislators supported him because they thought it would take a southerner to gain congressional acceptance for California's bid for statehood. The other senator elected, John C. Frémont, a veteran of the Bear Flag Revolt and one of the most well-known men in the state, won handily on the first ballot.

A year later, on September 9, 1850, California was the first western state admitted to the union. It had skipped being a territory. California was admitted as a free state, but to appease the South, Congress at the same time passed the Fugitive Slave Law, which allowed the forcible capture and return of slaves who had escaped. Even though California had outlawed slavery, it was not a safe haven for runaway slaves.

One of the reasons California was admitted so quickly—Arizona and New Mexico were not admitted until more than sixty years later—was gold. As historian Carey McWilliams noted, "When a millionaire knocks on the door, you don't keep him waiting too long; you let him in." Another reason was that the delegates to the constitutional convention had resolved the vexing issue of slavery, often a sticking point for the admission of new states.

Indians: Endangered Lives

The constitution's framers and California's first legislature also focused on the state's population of Indians. On March 15, 1848, Sam Brannan ran an editorial in *The Californian* that stated, "We desire only a White population in California; even the Indians among us, as far as we have seen, are more a nuisance to the country, we would like to get rid of them." His attitude reflected popular sentiment.

Before the arrival of Europeans in the 1700s, California was home to many vibrant, diverse, and complex societies: more than one hundred native languages were spoken. Between the sixteenth and nineteenth centuries, during Spanish and Mexican rule, the Indian population dropped by 50 percent, to one hundred and fifty thousand. Native peoples who did not succumb to European-introduced diseases were often forced into labor on Spanish missions. The Spanish, unlike their British counterparts, who actively engaged in displacement and extermination of Native populations in North America, considered Native Californians to be subjects of Spain. They sought to Christianize them and assimilate them into Spanish culture and society. After Mexican independence, the new government considered Indians citizens. Under the 1848 Treaty of Guadalupe Hidalgo, Indians were to become American citizens, but California's new government denied Native people their citizenship rights.

After Americans took control of California, Native people found themselves targeted for relocation and extermination. Some background on land titles will help in understanding the relocation aspect of this formula.

The Treaty of Guadalupe Hidalgo specified that the property rights of Mexicans who owned land in the territory ceded to the U.S. would be "inviolably respected." When the treaty went into effect, a few hundred Mexican landowners controlled thirteen million acres of California land. This angered the many American settlers who believed that the territory ceded to the U.S. should be public by right of conquest.

After conflicting government reports on the validity of Mexican land titles,

Congress adopted a bill establishing a Land Commission to determine whether the titles were valid. The commission heard more than eight hundred cases between 1852 and 1856; nearly all the commission's decisions were appealed to federal courts. On average, it took seventeen years for Mexican property owners, if they were successful, to secure title to their lands. But by that time most were bankrupt, or squatters had settled the lands and refused to leave.

In 1851 Congress declared that all lands occupied by Indian tribes at the time of the Treaty of Guadalupe Hidalgo became public domain, unless individuals presented to the Land Commission verification of prior Mexican legal title. Claimants had two years from the enactment of the law to make their claims. Native Californians, whose ancestors had lived on their lands for centuries, had no concept of land ownership determined by money and deeds. Unsurprisingly, most did not file a claim.

The gold rush threw together populations of white settlers, Indians, and immigrants in a rapid and volatile mix. Armed conflicts between Indians and miners in the Sierra Nevada now spurred the federal government to negotiate treaties with tribes. Between March 1851 and January 1852, three United States commissioners met with 402 California tribal leaders and produced eighteen treaties. Because of the state's enormity and the diversity of tribes, the commissioners met with only a fraction of California's indigenous groups. Further complicating the process were language barriers, as well as Indians' distrust of the government. Nevertheless, the commissioners' understanding was that under the terms of these treaties, the Indians would recognize U.S. government control of the land annexed from Mexico at the conclusion of the Mexican-American War, place themselves under the government's protection, maintain peace, and remove themselves from vast regions of the state. In exchange, the Indians would be granted reservations comprising about 8.5 million acres of land that they could occupy "forever," along with livestock and farming equipment.

When the California legislature learned about these treaties, both houses objected, complaining that reservation lands, which the treaty commissioners considered next to worthless, were some of the most desirable mineral and agricultural areas in the state and had been improved by miners and pioneer farmers. The legislators argued that the land would be wasted on "a few tribes of ignorant barbarians." They recommended that the U.S. Senate reject the treaties and remove the Indians from California.

On July 7, 1852, in a closed session, the Senate rejected the treaties, but not before some Indians had complied with their end of the agreement and vacated their homes. After the Senate vote, the military and volunteer militias moved some Native people to government lands, often forcibly. Even there, white settlers and miners violently evicted many from their new homes. In 1853 Edward F. Beale, superintendent of

Indian Affairs in California, documented that the California Indians were "reduced to despair—their country, and all support, taken away from them; no resting place, where they can be safe, death on one hand from starvation, and on the other by killing and hanging."

Buttressed by their sense of racial superiority over people they denigrated as "grown-up children" and "diggers," a pejorative denoting those who dig in the dirt for bugs and other food, the newcomers engaged in what became a state-funded and state-sanctioned annihilation policy. In 1851 California's governor, Peter H. Burnett, announced in his annual message, "That a war of extermination will continue to be waged between the two races until the Indian race becomes extinct, must be expected; while we cannot anticipate this result with but painful regret, the inevitable destiny of the race is beyond the power and wisdom of man to avert."

During the 1850s, California issued more than one million dollars in bonds to pay for local volunteer militias to hunt and kill Indians. Regular army units, miners, and new settlers joined the militias in murdering Indians. The killers justified their actions as punishment for Indian theft of livestock or revenge for an Indian's killing of a white person (which was often in retaliation for the murder of an Indian). At other times, the murders were merely committed for sport and because the killers knew that they would not be punished.

In July 1852, O. M. Wozencraft, the United States Indian agent in California (and one of the signers of the 1849 California constitution), asked Governor John Bigler for aid in trying a gang of white men for murdering Indians on federal land in the Fresno area. The governor never responded.

Because the state took no action, Wozencraft attempted to bring the murderers to justice in federal court, but the U.S. attorney in San Francisco explained that he lacked jurisdiction to try the case. Pursuing justice in the local court was not an option because, as a discouraged Wozencraft reported to the superintendent of Indian Affairs for California, "The gentleman who commanded the [Indian killing] party in this unfortunate affair was soon after elected county judge; consequently, I did not think it worth while to prosecute him in his own county."

One of the largest massacres occurred on February 26, 1860, in the Humboldt Bay area. Major G. J. Raines, the commander of Fort Humboldt, described the aftermath:

> I have just been to Indian Island, the home of a band of friendly Indians between Eureka and Uniontown, where I beheld a scene of atrocity and horror unparalleled not only in our own Country, but even in history, for it was done by men, self acting and without necessity, color of law, or authority—the murder of little innocent babes and women, from the breast to maturity, barbarously and I can't say brutally—for it is worse—

perpetrated by men who act in defiance of and probably in revenge upon the Governor of the State for not sending them arms and having them mustered in as a Volunteer Company for the murder of Indians....I repaired to the place, but the villains—some 5 in number had gone—and in midst the bitter grief of parents and fathers—many of whom returned—I beheld a spectacle of horror, of unexampled description—babes, with brains oozing out of their skulls, cut and hacked with axes, and squaws exhibiting the most frightful wounds in death which imagination can paint—and this done...without cause, otherwise, as far as I can learn, as I have not heard of any of them losing life or cattle by the Indians.

Raines estimated that 188 Indians had been slaughtered.

Many Native women were kidnapped or forced by starvation, disease, and war into prostitution in mining camps. The rape of Indian women was widespread, and yet because a white person could not be convicted on the basis of Indian testimony, the rapists went unpunished. Some miners traded in kidnapped Indian women and killed those who tried to rescue them.

Historian Albert Hurtado stresses that Indian women faced even more dangers than their male counterparts with the onset of white settlement. Abduction, rape, prostitution, and forced concubinage, he asserts, "endangered their own lives and contributed to the falling population rate because they were removed from the

Yosemite Miwok/Paiute woman and cedar slab house. The population of native Californians dropped dramatically after the U.S. takeover of California. Native Americans were the target of state-sponsored extermination and could be forced into indentured servitude by court order.

reproductive cycle. The hardships on Indian women are reflected in statistics that show their numbers declined in greater proportion than Indian men." The rapid decline in the population of Indian women of childbearing age contributed to the decimation of the Indian population. By 1870, it had declined from an estimated one hundred and fifty thousand to thirty thousand; by 1880 to sixteen thousand.

Native people who survived the toll of disease, malnutrition and starvation, and violence often found themselves between a legal rock and economic hard place. An 1850 law, titled "An Act for the Government and Protection of Indians," allowed a judge to declare an unemployed Indian a vagrant who could be sold to the highest bidder as an indentured servant for up to four months.

The state legislature distinguished between "wild" and "tame" Indians. With legal sanction, white settlers exploited the labor of "tame" Indians, while those considered "wild" or hostile were targeted for extermination.

Indian children faced even more perils than "vagrant" adults. The law allowed an Indian child to be indentured to a white family until the child reached maturity. Since the lure of gold resulted in a scarcity of agricultural and domestic labor, Indians became a convenient source of slave labor, and many Indian children were kidnapped and sold. In 1853 the district attorney of Contra Costa County reported to the superintendent of Indian Affairs in California that:

> Ramon Briones, Mesa, Quiera, and Beryessa of Napa County, are in the habit of kidnapping Indians in the mountains near Clear Lake, and in their capture several have been murdered in cold blood. There have been Indians to the number of one hundred and thirty-six thus captured and brought into this county, and held here in servitude adverse to their will....It is also a notorious fact that these Indians are treated inhumanly, being neither fed nor clothed; and from such treatment many have already died, and disease is now threatening destruction of the remainder.

Newspaper and military accounts from Eureka and the Sacramento Valley recount the kidnapping and sale of Indian children into slavery for $30 and $250 each. In 1861 George Hanson, superintendent of Indian Affairs, wrote to his superiors in Washington, DC, that one of three kidnappers apprehended near Marysville with nine Indian children, ages three to ten, tried to justify his actions as an act of charity, because the children's parents had been killed. When Hanson asked the man how he knew that the parents were dead, his answer was "I killed them myself."

The practice of kidnapping Indian children was so widespread that the *San Francisco Bulletin* editorialized on December 6, 1861:

> It is notorious that there are parties in the northern counties of this State, whose sole occupation has been to steal young children and squaws from

the poor Diggers, who inhabit the mountains, and dispose of them at handsome prices to settlers, who being, in the majority of cases, unmarried but at housekeeping, willingly pay fifty or sixty dollars for a young Digger to cook and wait upon them, or a hundred dollars for a likely young girl.

Although the enslavement of Indians legally ended in 1863 when the state legislature, prompted by Lincoln's Emancipation Proclamation, repealed the law allowing whites to forcibly indenture Indians, this practice set the stage for a dark, century-long history in which wealthy agriculturalists believed it was their right to work their fields with the labor of meagerly paid racial and ethnic groups they considered inferior.

"Greasers," "Slaves," "Diggers," and "Mongolians"

By 1855 the spirit that had unified the Mexican and American delegates at the California constitutional convention had greatly diminished. That year, the legislature passed a law voiding the constitutional requirement to publish all laws in Spanish as well as English.

That same year, the legislature passed what came to be known as the "Greaser law," under the official title of "An Act to Punish Vagrants, Vagabonds and Dangerous and Suspicious Persons." The law encompassed "All persons who are commonly known as 'Greasers' or the issue of Spanish and Indian blood...and who go armed and are not known to be peaceable and quiet persons, and who can give no good account of themselves." They could be arrested and sent to jail with hard labor for up to ninety days.

Loss of their land and hostile treatment in mining camps and the legal system led to declining conditions and influence for the Mexican population, which was diluted by the influx of Europeans, at first in the northern part of the state but eventually throughout California. By 1870 the Mexican population was only 4 percent of the state's total, down from 15 percent during the gold rush era. By the turn of the century, there were more Chinese and Native Americans in California than Mexicans, who comprised only 1 to 2 percent of the population.

California's early governments were hostile to other people of color, as well.

For nearly the first ten years of statehood, the majority of California's congressional representatives were Chiv Democrats. They included the two U.S. Senators William Gwin, who during the Civil War returned to the South to work for the Confederacy, and John Weller, formerly of Ohio, who advocated for the expansion of slavery. The Chivs also exerted power in the state legislature. Although California technically entered the union as a free state, these politicians worked to pass laws stripping African Americans of their rights and liberties.

In 1852 the legislature supplemented federal law by passing a fugitive slave law allowing local law enforcement officers to capture slaves brought into California who had fled their owners. The law was vigorously opposed by David Broderick, an Irish immigrant stonecutter's son and product of New York's infamous Tammany Hall, who became a leading opponent to slavery in his adopted state. The fugitive slave law was allowed to lapse in 1855.

Broderick's nemesis was Governor Peter Burnett, who had advocated denying "free Negroes and persons of color" entry into California during the state's constitutional convention. Broderick politically outmaneuvered him and between 1850 and 1858 prevented five exclusion bills from being enacted. The 1858 bill came so close to passage that many African Americans—perhaps 15 percent of the total population in the state—fled to Canada as a preemptive measure.

But other Chiv-supported bills easily became laws. In 1850 the legislature passed a law denying blacks, mulattoes, and Indians the right to testify in criminal trials involving white people. The next year, following Governor Burnett's statement in his annual message that "the colored races are inferior by nature to the white," the legislature extended the prohibition on testimony to civil cases. In 1855 a black Sacramento resident lamented, "The Statute books and the common law, the great bulwark of society, which should be to us as the rivers of water in a dry place, like the shadow of a great rock in a weary land, where [the] wretched should find sympathy and the weak protection, spurn us with contempt and rule us from their very threshold and deny us a common humanity." The state's small black population campaigned annually to repeal the law because it left them largely defenseless against crimes committed by whites. The legislature ignored their pleas for several years.

In an 1854 appeal of a murder conviction, a state supreme court decision extended the ban on testimony to Chinese. On August 9, 1853, miner George Hall fatally shot a Chinese miner on the Bear River in Nevada County. Hall was convicted of murder, based on the testimony of a Chinese witness. On appeal, Hugh C. Murray, the twenty-nine-year-old chief justice of the state supreme court, ruled that because "Mongolians" were historically considered racially indistinct from Indians, the law barring testimony of Indians extended to Chinese witnesses. In addition, Murray reasoned, granting Chinese the right to testify would initiate a slippery slope towards equal rights of citizenship, voting, and legislative and judicial service. To the justices of the supreme court, that prospect was unacceptable.

It was not until 1862, in the midst of the Civil War and the ascendancy of pro-Union Republicans in the state legislature, that a bill to revoke the ban on African American testimony passed the legislature and was signed by Republican Governor

Chinese gold miners were not an uncommon sight in the Sierra Nevada, but in 1854 the California Supreme Court denied Chinese the right to testify in court, fearing it would lead to "the slippery slope of equal rights of citizenship."

Leland Stanford. Another decade would pass before the law barring Chinese and Indian testimony would be dropped, in deference to the passage of the Fourteenth Amendment and federal civil rights legislation.

Women Wanted

The newly minted miners who flocked to the Golden State were overwhelmingly white and male: the 1850 California census shows that there were more than twelve men for every woman. As the decade wore on, however, more women migrated west, and by 1860 there were two men for every woman.

The paucity of women did not prevent the first legislature from enacting laws that deeply affected women's lives, including an abortion ban in 1850. The law made it a crime, with a penalty of two to five years in prison, to use abortifacients or instruments to "procure miscarriage," except to save the life of the mother. As a result, some of the commonly used practices of early California physicians and midwives to induce abortion before "quickening," the first perceptive signs of movement by the fetus, were outlawed. By 1858 the legislature had passed an additional measure making it a crime to advertise, advise, or "hint" about how to obtain an abortion. This carried a stiff penalty as well: three to ten years in prison.

Some argue that the legislature hastened to pass the anti-abortion laws to save women from infection or death at the hands of unskilled or unsanitary practitioners. Yet at the time, childbirth was also extremely dangerous, so there may have been other underlying causes, including religious influences and a desire to increase the birthrate among whites in the new state.

In 1851 the legislature passed a divorce law, authored by future California and U.S. Supreme Court Justice Stephen Field, which allowed both women and men to sue for divorce for a long list of causes ranging from adultery and extreme cruelty to neglect and fraud. The bill came under scathing criticism, not only from the Catholic Church but the local press. Calling divorce "an insult to the Bible and the principles of Christianity," the *Alta California* editorialized that divorce laws are "all reprehensible, all opposed to good morals, all at variance with the principle of marriage, all tending to encourage immorality…"

California's divorce rate quickly rose higher than in other parts of the country, leading another *Alta California* editorial to bemoan, "California is becoming notorious for the rapid, steam-engine manner in which the family tie is severed."

More women than men took advantage of the divorce law. According to a study of divorce proceedings in San Mateo and Santa Clara Counties in the 1850s and 1860s, three times as many women as men sued their spouses for divorce; 70 percent of the women successfully obtained one. But just as with property rights guaranteed to married women in the 1849 constitution, the basis for the rather simple divorce law was grounded more in demographics than in respect for women's independence. With a dozen men for every woman in the state, male lawmakers put aside their religious and moral beliefs to respond to the drastic situation: under a more liberal divorce law, a man would have better odds of finding a mate.

These laws were written with white women in mind. Native women and other women of color found themselves outside the protection of law. Hawaiian women were forced into prostitution in mining camps. John Sutter himself is said to have kept two Hawaiian and Indian women as concubines.

Trafficking in women from China began soon after the gold rush. Young women and girls were kidnapped or purchased from destitute families in southern China and forced into prostitution in San Francisco and the gold camps. Private commercial contracts that they were forced to sign legalized their status as indentured servants in grimy brothels. Though a few escaped and returned home, most died in bondage before prostitution was outlawed.

"Yet the Blood Stain Lingers"

Adventurers from Mexico and South America comprised the first significant wave of immigrants to California after the discovery of gold. By the time "Americans" arrived, months later, they found the best claims already being worked by Spanish-speaking miners. The American miners—using methods both inside and outside the law—targeted Latino miners with violence and expulsion.

One of the earliest sieges took place during the cold December of 1849 in Calaveras County, when American miners, bolstered by an order from a judge that they had elected, attacked hundreds of Chilean miners and stole their critical winter supplies. This failed to uproot the determined South Americans, so the enraged attackers returned a week later. When the Chileans defended their camp, the local sheriff arrested them for starting a riot. He sent them to prison in Stockton, where they were tortured, shot, and hanged.

American miners convinced the first state legislature in 1850 to pass the Foreign Miners' Tax, requiring all noncitizens, including Mexicans who had lived on the land prior to statehood, to pay a twenty-dollar monthly fee for a mining license. After protests from Canadian, German, British, and Irish miners, the legislature quickly rewrote the law to exempt any "free white person" or individual who could become an American citizen.

Tuolumne County, where Latin American miners were concentrated, was the site of intense confrontation during the summer of 1850. Days after the Foreign Miners' Tax passed, a mob of three hundred armed white men tried to force Latin American miners in the town of Columbia to pay the tax. They refused and instead organized a mass meeting of thousands of Latin American and French miners, taking over the plaza of Sonora, the county seat.

A mob of American miners invaded the meeting. Witnesses reported that the aggressors fired at "every Mexican in sight," burned their camp to ashes, and drove more than a hundred men into a corral. A week of violence followed, and according to historian Carey McWilliams, Americans lynched and killed scores of Mexicans.

White miners posted five hundred notices throughout Tuolumne County demanding that "Peons of Mexico, the renegades of South America, and the convicts of the British Empire [targeted at Australians]…leave the limits of said county within fifteen days." The threats, murder, and destruction had the desired result of driving most Mexicans and Latinos from their gold claims into the southern counties of the state, where the Mexican population was larger and Spanish was still the lingua franca.

In 1851 Josefa Segovia (popularly known as Juanita), a Mexican woman in her early twenties, lived with her husband, José María Loaiza, in a tiny cabin on Main Street in Downieville. The town, nestled in the lush Sierra foothills, was at the center of the Mother Lode and, within two years of the discovery of gold, had grown to five thousand residents—mostly miners.

As in other diggings, the American miners did not allow Mexicans to stake claims in Downieville, so José made his living dealing cards at Craycroft's saloon.

The July 4 Independence Day celebration in Downieville that year was raucous. Hundreds of miners descended from camps in the surrounding hills, and the town was festooned with flags and banners. Whiskey barrels rolled down Main Street and tent saloons greeted revelers.

In the days prior to the celebration, Downieville had hosted a Democratic convention, drawing many politicians. Among them were Colonel John B. Weller, a future senator and California governor, Stephen Field, then alcalde of Marysville, and William Walker, who declared himself president of Nicaragua a few years later.

Though several dignitaries stayed for the festivities in the booming gold rush town, their speeches were overshadowed by brawls and wild drinking that went on well past midnight.

One of the inebriated miners, Jock Cannon, a Scotsman of "Herculean proportions," staggered along Main Street, approached Josefa and José's cabin, broke down the door, and then lumbered off into the night. The next morning he returned to the house; his friends later testified that he intended to apologize, but that is not what transpired. José demanded that Cannon pay for the door and Cannon refused. The two men argued, and when Josefa appeared she also demanded payment. Cannon swore at her, calling her *puta*, whore, and followed her inside her house. In a rage, the diminutive young woman picked up a kitchen knife and stabbed the miner in the heart.

While Cannon's friends carried him next door to the doctor, José and Josefa fled for safety to Craycroft's saloon. When Cannon died, an angry mob, many still hung over from the night before, tracked them down and put Josefa on "trial." When the mob called for her to be hanged, one man jumped to the platform and shouted, "We'll give 'em a fair trial first—and then hang 'em."

The crowd swelled from several hundred to nearly two thousand. A judge and twelve jurors were chosen; prosecutors and defense attorneys were pulled from the crowd.

Several eyewitnesses testified for the prosecution; their testimony was skewed not only because of their friendship with Cannon but because they could not understand Spanish. Finally, the raven-haired Josefa was allowed to take the stand. "I took the knife to defend myself," she said. "I had been told that some of the boys wanted to get into my room to sleep with me…it frightened me so that I used to fasten the door and take a knife to bed."

But the crowd of miners paid little attention to Josefa's claim of self-defense. Their hostility toward Mexicans was embodied in this woman and they were focused on revenge. Their ire was roused even more when Cannon's body was put on public view,

During a raucous Independence Day celebration in the gold mining center of Downieville, Josefa Segovia (popularly known as Juanita) stabbed a white miner who broke into her home. After a kangaroo court trial, she was hanged from a bridge over the Yuba River.

his shirt unbuttoned to show the fatal knife wound. Shouts, lubricated by whiskey, rang out: "Hang her!" A group of men erected a gallows on Jersey Bridge, over the foamy, rushing Yuba River.

Dr. E. C. Aiken was called by the defense to testify that Josefa was pregnant, in an effort to halt the execution. As a final humiliation, Josefa was forced to undergo an examination by three male doctors in a nearby shack. When they emerged, the impromptu medical committee declared that she was not pregnant.

Stephen Field, the Marysville alcalde known for his oratory, climbed on a barrel and pleaded with the crowd: "Gentlemen of Downieville, you cannot hang a woman! Think! I beg you! Our fair California has been one of the sisterhood of states not ten months. Her fame is world wide. Would you have it rolled off the world's tongue that California men are cowards enough to…"

Field could not even complete his sentence before he was pushed off the barrel into the street. No one else spoke up for Josefa. One eyewitness stated that Colonel Weller was seated on the speakers' platform during the trial but made no effort to halt the kangaroo court. As Josefa was led to the makeshift gallows, the riverbank was lined with "the hungriest, craziest, wildest mob that ever I saw anywhere," according to the correspondent from the *Pacific Star.*

Her fate clear, Josefa now said she would defend herself in the same way under similar circumstances. Extending her hand to people she knew in the crowd, she called out, "Adios, señores." Though she must have felt alone and full of fear, she climbed the makeshift scaffold, placed the hangman's noose around her neck, adjusted it, let her luxuriant hair loose, and stepped to her death.

As word of the lynching spread, Downieville met with great condemnation in the press. Newspapers as far away as London chastised the town for its vigilante justice. *The Sacramento Times and Transcript* called it "a blot upon the history of the state."

In 1875 José María Loaiza filed a claim with the U.S.–Mexico Commission against the United States for the lynching of his wife. His claim was denied.

A winter storm destroyed the Jersey Bridge, and George Barton, a local poet who had witnessed the hanging, wrote that "the bridge went down, and yet the blood stain lingers."

The vigilante justice of mining camps and the purges of Latinos from mining areas, though terrifying, were largely ad hoc. In the quickly expanding city of San Francisco, however, leading businessmen were organizing vigilante groups that circumvented the Constitution and the law.

San Francisco's Vigilantes

Chileans were among the first gold rush arrivals in San Francisco. They set up a makeshift tent camp called Chiletown along the slope of Telegraph Hill, overlooking San Francisco Bay. Chiletown was the target of the Hounds, a predatory group of young men who extorted money, food, and drink. Vicente Pérez Rosales, a Chilean, recorded these impressions:

> They were vagrants, gamblers, or drunks, drawn together in a fellowship of crime; and they had as their motto: "We can get away with it." Fear and hatred spread in advance of their appearance, and they deliberately generated these feelings by their provocations. Everywhere they went they established their control by quarrelsomeness and violence.

The Hounds initially coalesced in 1848, when San Francisco merchants paid the young men twenty-five dollars for each runaway sailor that they could track down; the siren song of gold lured thousands of sailors to jump ship, and the local businessmen, dependent on ships' crews for trade, panicked. Though the Hounds' abilities as bounty hunters were no match for the sailors' lust for gold, in the absence of any organized law enforcement, they designated themselves the town police. They set up a tent headquarters, dubbed Tammany Hall, where they were joined by former Australian prisoners and veterans of the New York Volunteers, a regiment recruited by a leader of the real Tammany Hall to fight in the Mexican-American War. They paraded in San Francisco streets with martial music and banners and redubbed themselves the "Regulators."

The Hounds strong-armed San Franciscans, mostly Chilean residents and merchants, for protection "fees," stealing merchandise and tearing down the tents of those who refused to pay. As long as the violence was directed at Spanish-speaking immigrants, most San Franciscans turned a blind eye to the paramilitary group.

On the unusually warm summer Sunday of July 15, 1849, Sam Roberts, field commander of the Hounds, half drunk, went to visit his Chilean mistress. He was outraged to discover her with another man, whom Roberts viciously beat. He returned to the Hounds' tent and recruited others to join him in attacking Chiletown.

The Hounds rampaged into the night, ransacking tents, beating residents with stones and wooden clubs, and stealing money and jewelry. They raped a Chilean woman and assaulted her mother.

The following morning, Sam Brannan, who had amassed a fortune selling mining supplies to gold seekers, climbed to the roof of alcalde Thaddeus Leavenworth's office and exhorted the growing crowd to rid the town of the Hounds. More than two hundred men, calling themselves the Law and Order Party, were deputized to hunt down the marauders. They caught and imprisoned twenty Hounds. The Law and Order Party organized a court and appointed Leavenworth chief judge. Nine of the Hounds

On July 15, 1849, the Hounds, a band of bounty hunters, viciously attacked a settlement of Chilean immigrants in San Francisco.

were convicted, but as the city lacked a functioning jail, the men were sentenced to banishment, which proved unenforceable.

Between 1849 and 1850, five serious fires ravaged San Francisco's main commercial area. Some residents speculated that criminals intentionally set the fires to distract the populace while they robbed stores and homes. The press fanned the flames of public perception that the city was wracked with violent crime. The arrival early that year of 1,648 Australian immigrants proved well timed for scapegoating. San Franciscans considered them exiled British convicts. A depressed local economy and heightened unemployment brought the tense city to the point of eruption.

On the rainy evening of February 19, 1851, prominent merchant C. J. Jansen was closing his store on the corner of Montgomery and Washington Streets when two men beat him and stole two thousand dollars.

Police apprehended Australian immigrants Thomas Berdue and Robert Windred. Though both men claimed their innocence, Jansen, still not fully lucid from the beating, identified them as the thieves. A rumor also circulated that the black-bearded Berdue was actually an infamous ex-convict from Sydney, James Stuart, who was wanted for murder in Marysville.

The day following the arrests, five to six thousand people surged into City Hall, where the two Australians were being arraigned. The mob shouted and broke furniture in the courtroom as sheriff's deputies attempted to protect the accused men. Mayor John Geary called in soldiers to drive the crowd from the building. Leaders of the frustrated mob called a mass meeting for ten o'clock the next morning.

At the appointed hour, hundreds jammed into the city plaza between Kearny, Clay, Washington, and Wentworth Streets. Sam Brannan called for immediate lynching, shouting, "I am very much surprised to hear people talk about grand juries, or recorders, or mayors. I'm tired of such talk. These men are murderers, I say, as well as thieves. I know it, and I will die or see them hung by the neck....I want no technicalities. Such things are devised to shield the guilty."

Two days later, on a chilly Sunday morning, hundreds gathered again at the plaza. William Tell Coleman, a twenty-seven-year-old merchant, proposed that the crowd organize a "people's court." If the court convicted the men, they would hang. When the so-called trial ended in a hung jury, the impatient mob erupted in anger. Coleman persuaded them that the jury's decision should be respected. Eventually, the two Australians were both tried and convicted in a court of law: Windred was sentenced to ten years in prison and Berdue to fourteen.

Spurred by the incident, Brannan called a meeting of merchants in May 1851 to form the "Committee of Vigilance." The group's secret constitution stated that "no thief, burglar, incendiary, or assassin shall escape punishment either by the quibbles of the law, the insecurity of prisons, the carelessness or corruption of the police, or the laxity of those who pretend to administer justice."

The committee was governed by strict secrecy and obedience to its leadership, a twenty-member executive committee comprised, in their own words, of "the most intelligent, best educated, and property owning classes of the city." Membership eventually grew to approximately seven hundred. The pealing of the fire bell at the Monumental Engine Company was their call to gather at their headquarters on Bush and Sansome Streets (which also housed Brannan's real estate office).

On June 10, businessman George Virgin was arriving at his office near the bay when he saw his office safe being carried away by a stranger rowing away from the wharf in a dinghy. Virgin shouted, "Stop, thief!" arousing nearby merchants and boatmen to pursue the man, John Jenkins. The tall Australian heaved the stolen property overboard before being apprehended and taken to the vigilantes' headquarters. The fire bell rang its alert, drawing not only about eighty vigilantes but many curious spectators. A hastily convened "jury" quickly ruled that Jenkins was guilty and sentenced him to death.

At one-thirty in the morning, the vigilantes led Jenkins at gunpoint to the city plaza, where they threw a hangman's rope over a beam of an old adobe building that had served as the Mexican-era customs house. Brannan commanded, with theatrical self-righteousness, "Every lover of liberty and good order, lay hold of this rope!" Several men grabbed the rope and hung Jenkins. He dangled at the edge of the town square until dawn.

After the execution, a coroner's jury identified nine men, including Brannan, as having been directly involved in Jenkins's killing. An outraged Brannan published a statement in the local newspapers categorically denying any involvement. His public denial drew an incredulous response, also published in the San Francisco newspapers, from David Broderick, who had attempted futilely to stop Jenkins's hanging and had witnessed Brannan's leadership of the murderous vigilantes.

The committee closed ranks. They published a notice signed by one hundred and eighty men in the local papers, stating, "We desire that the public will understand that [the nine men named] have been unnecessarily picked from our number, as the coroner's jury had full evidence of the fact that all the undersigned were equally implicated with their above-named associates."

When it became apparent that no legal action would be taken against those involved with Jenkins's killing, the emboldened committee took on the self-appointed mantle of immigration authority and secret police. Committee members boarded ships from Australia to prevent ex-convicts from landing in San Francisco and they issued a public statement that they had the right to enter any home or business where they thought "suspicious characters" or stolen goods were located.

Less than a month after Jenkins's execution, vigilantes arrested a dark-haired, bearded man. They were about to release the handsome, glib stranger, but a vigilante arrived at the committee's headquarters and recognized the prisoner as the infamous criminal James Stuart.

After several others identified Stuart, he made a full confession of his crimes, including the attack on Jansen, for which the hapless Berdue had almost been lynched. Berdue's mistaken identity problems had continued, and he was now in Marysville awaiting execution for a murder believed to have been committed by Stuart. Word of Stuart's arrest was sent to Marysville and a stay of execution was granted to Berdue.

The San Francisco city attorney obtained a writ of habeas corpus compelling the vigilantes to deliver Stuart to court, but they ignored it. On the morning of July 11, San Franciscans again heard the ominous ringing of the bell at the Monumental Engine Company. Committee members gathered to hear Stuart's confession read aloud. He was sentenced to die immediately.

Manacled and surrounded by platoons of nearly four hundred vigilantes ten abreast, Stuart was led to a wharf at the end of Market Street, where a noose awaited him. A crowd witnessed the hangman encircling Stuart's neck with the deadly rope and jerking the victim's body from a derrick on the wharf.

California Governor John McDougall issued a tepid statement after learning of Stuart's execution, reminding San Franciscans that groups such as the Committee of Vigilance posed a danger in acting outside the law. Mayor Charles J. Brenham wrote an open letter to the people of San Francisco imploring them to shift their support from the vigilantes to the proper legal authorities. The most severe criticism came from Judge Alexander Campbell, who convened a grand jury the day after Stuart's killing and instructed them:

> The question has now arisen whether the laws made by the constitutional authorities of the State are to be obeyed and executed, or whether secret societies are to frame and execute laws for the government of the country, to exercise supreme power over the lives, liberty and property of our citizens....Every person who in any manner acted, aided, abetted, or assisted in taking Stuart's life, or counseled or encouraged his death is undoubtedly guilty of murder.

Despite Judge Campbell's exhortation, the grand jury elected not only to dismiss charges against the vigilantes but to praise the Committee of Vigilance. No fewer than seven of the sixteen men on the grand jury were committee members.

By the time it ended its activities in September, a few months after it began, the committee had tried ninety-one people (most of whom were Australian), hung four, whipped one man, sentenced twenty-eight to deportation, remanded fifteen to the lawful authorities for trial, and released forty-one. Scholar Robert M. Senkewicz argues that the fall commercial business season, rather than any decrease in crime, was the major cause for the committee's demise.

The Fort Gunnybags Gallows

In 1856 a second San Francisco vigilance committee emerged. Like its predecessor, the 1856 Committee of Vigilance was led by the city's economic elite. William Tecumseh Sherman, future Civil War general and at the time commander of the San Francisco district of the California militia, wrote that "all the large merchants" were "active controlling members" and that "most of the rich men are contributing means and countenance *sub rosa*." The editor of the *Herald*, the only major San Francisco newspaper to join David Broderick in opposing the committee, called it a "mercantile junta." The committee enlisted between six thousand to eight thousand men, making it the largest vigilante movement in American history.

The formation of the 1856 vigilance committee was precipitated by two sensational killings: the November 1855 shooting of U.S. Marshal William Richardson by a well-known gambler, Charles Cora, and the May 1856 shooting of James King of William by a San Francisco supervisor, James P. Casey. Members of the 1851 Committee of Vigilance held a secret meeting and reactivated the group under the leadership of William Tell Coleman.

James King of William, the anti-Catholic editor of the *Daily Evening Bulletin*, had taken pleasure in journalistically denouncing the political machine of David Broderick, calling the state senator and party leader a "Satan among the fallen angels." He had accused Broderick of bringing Casey from New York to rig elections. When King revealed that Casey had been imprisoned at Sing Sing Penitentiary in New York, the Broderick loyalist stormed into King's newspaper office, demanded a retraction, and threatened the editor. King dismissed the incensed politician. Casey left, but two hours later he accosted King on the street and shot the editor with a revolver.

Leaders of the vigilantes privately agreed that both Casey and Cora, whose trial had ended with a hung jury, would hang. The new committee, like its previous incarnation, would follow a military model, with absolute obedience and absolute secrecy.

Anticipating that the committee would try to seize Casey and Cora, Sheriff David Scannell armed about a hundred men to defend the city jail and the prisoners inside. Alerted by San Francisco Mayor Van Ness of the tension, Governor J. Neely Johnson

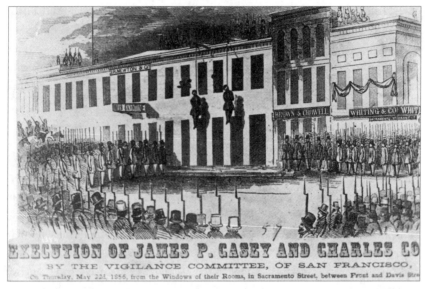

Gambler Charles Cora and County Supervisor James Casey were two of the four men executed by the 1856 San Francisco Committee of Vigilance, which was led by the city's leading businessmen. Cora and Casey were hung from Fort Gunnybags, the committee's fortified downtown headquarters.

traveled from Sacramento to negotiate with Coleman. The governor left the meeting with a promise from Coleman that the vigilantes would not attack the jail to seize Cora and Casey.

But days later, several thousand armed vigilantes, buttressed by a cannon, stormed the jail and kidnapped both men. They spirited them to the committee's Sacramento Street headquarters, dubbed Fort Gunnybags because of the sandbags piled eight to ten feet high in front of the building to fortify it from attack. The committee placed cannons on the roof of Fort Gunnybags and armed sentries guarded the building. While the committee was conducting "tribunals" against Casey and Cora, word arrived that editor King had died. This news all but guaranteed a lynching.

Two days later, as King's funeral party wound its way through San Francisco to the Lone Mountain Cemetery, Casey's and Cora's bodies hung from the roof of Fort Gunnybags.

In response to the vigilance committee, a group of leading citizens, including Mayor Van Ness, Sheriff Scannell, General Sherman, and David Broderick, formed the Law and Order Party, adopting the name of the 1849 group that had defeated the Hounds.

But the committee was not easily silenced. Its constitution, almost identical to that of the 1851 committee, included the additional ominous complaint that "our ballot boxes have been stolen and others substituted, or stuffed with votes that were never polled, and thereby our elections nullified, our dearest rights violated, and no other method left by which the will of the people can be manifested." *Herald* editor John Nugent wrote that the committee's goal was the "resignation of the county and state officers, and the election of the prominent members of the vigilance committee to the offices thus rendered vacant."

The committee specifically targeted Broderick, who had made enemies of its leaders by using his political machine to oppose their anti-immigrant goals. He opposed the Foreign Miners' Tax and voiced concern for the rights of Californios (the non-Indian residents of the state before the American takeover), as well as Mexicans and Europeans. He organized Irish immigrants, another group the nativists reviled. The Chiv wing of Broderick's own Democratic Party opposed his advocacy for the rights of blacks.

The committee methodically tried to dismantle Broderick's political machine, literally nabbing his political allies from the streets, taking them to Fort Gunnybags for "trials" on electoral fraud, and marching the many Irish immigrants among them to the harbor for deportation.

The Law and Order Party asked the governor to call out the state militia to halt the committee's lawlessness. The governor secured the promise of arms from the commandant of the nearby federal arsenal at Benicia, forty miles northwest of San Francisco. State Supreme Court Justice David S. Terry issued an order for the release of the county jail keeper, whom the committee was holding prisoner. The committee defied the order, and Sheriff Scannell telegraphed the governor requesting help from the militia. The governor declared that San Francisco was in a state of insurrection and ordered all members of the volunteer state militia to report to General Sherman.

Only a few hundred responded. Making matters worse, the federal arsenal keeper reneged on his promise of arms. Sherman, unwilling to command a small company of unarmed men, resigned. Justice Terry, now the chief advisor to the Law and Order Party, discovered a federal statute requiring the government to provide arms to the state militia. Compelled by this statute, the federal arsenal keeper finally released 113 muskets and shipped the guns by schooner to San Francisco. The vigilantes, however, learned that the arms were making their way across the bay and intercepted the boat.

When vigilantes later tried to catch the militiamen who transported the arms, in order to prevent them from testifying against the vigilantes on piracy charges, a fight ensued in which Terry stabbed a vigilante. The judge fled to a San Francisco militia armory. When news of the stabbing reached committee headquarters, the familiar ring of the alarm bell called thousands of armed vigilantes to Fort Gunnybags. They surrounded the armory, and Terry surrendered.

Once Terry was in custody, the committee faced a dilemma. Would they dare hang a state supreme court justice and possibly incite civil war? Despite Terry's rash action, the state government stood behind him, if only as a symbol of its sovereignty. The federal government sent the sloop *John Adams* to San Francisco, where it was stationed within shooting distance of Fort Gunnybags.

The committee conducted a "trial" against Terry. Unlike previous tribunals, which were quick, this one dragged on for days because of the vigilantes' ambivalence. Fortunately for Terry, the man he had stabbed did not die. Although the vigilantes convicted Terry of assault with the intent to kill, they released him on August 7. The following day, the committee decided to disband. During its three months of existence, it had hung four men and banished thirty others.

For over a century, historians of California praised the vigilantes. Beginning in the 1970s, however, their views began to change. As historian Kevin J. Mullen argues:

> Part of what created the impression of general lawlessness in San Francisco was that for a long period, beginning almost with the conquest, prominent citizens—at odds first with the military-backed government and later with officials who did not suit their taste—inflated the figures of crime to further their political purposes. The victors write the history—and as things turned out, the victors were those who opposed the established government.

The vigilance committees of 1851 and 1856 acted in defiance of existing legal systems and spurred vigilantes throughout the state. When the Committee of 1856 was at its peak, it received resolutions of support from San Jose, Sacramento, Stockton, Vallejo, Marysville, and Sonora. Historian James Rawls comments that the vigilance committees left a "vicious, dangerous and persistent tradition of contempt for the normal processes of democratic government."

In a bizarre twist of fate, Justice Terry killed his former ally David Broderick in an 1859 duel over slavery. Terry had attacked Broderick's political bloc as "black Republicans" and "negro lovers" who took directions from "the banner of the black Douglass, whose name is Frederick." A friend of Broderick eulogized him at the funeral: "What was his public crime? The answer is in his own words: 'I die because I was opposed to a corrupt administration and the extension of slavery.'"

During the Civil War, Terry returned to the South and became a brigadier general in the Confederate army.

Massacre in L.A.'s Chinatown

San Francisco's history notwithstanding, in the years following the gold rush, Los

Angeles became known as the murder capital of California, and it was not uncommon for angry, armed crowds to storm a jail and hang accused criminals. In 1855 the mayor of Los Angeles temporarily resigned to lead a lynch mob.

In late October 1871, a mob of white and Latino vigilantes in Los Angeles participated in the largest mass lynching in California history. The violence was precipitated by an exchange of gunfire between two rival Chinese syndicates, or tongs. Sam Yuen, leader of the Nin Yung Tong, and Yo Hing, leader of the rival Hong Chow Tong, shot at each other, and a white rancher was killed in the crossfire. The chief of Los Angeles's small police force randomly deputized a large number of men who had gathered near the short and narrow alley, called Calle de los Negros during the Mexican period, that was the nucleus of Los Angeles's small Chinatown. The police chief instructed the men to shoot any Chinese leaving their homes.

Mayor Cristóbal Aguilar, the sheriff, and the rest of the city's police force arrived at the scene but soon left, leaving the angry mob—which had swelled to five hundred—unrestrained. Rumors spread that the Chinese had hidden caches of gold.

The mob rampaged through Chinatown for three to four hours, smashing holes in adobe roofs and firing at terrorized residents. Those who ran from their homes were captured and lynched. The first victim was hung from a corral gate across from Saint Athanasius Episcopal Church.

When the violence ended, the mob had killed nineteen Chinese, fifteen of whom

Los Angeles's early Chinatown was centered in a street called Calle de los Negros when Mexico ruled California. In 1871 a vigilante mob massacred nineteen Chinese residents in the worst mass lynching in California history.

hung from impromptu gallows on an awning, a gutter spout, the beams of a lumber-yard gate, and even the sides of prairie schooners. Looters stole over thirty thousand dollars in cash and personal property.

As news of the mass killing spread throughout the country, Governor Newton Booth condemned the vigilante action. A grand jury excoriated the police as "deplorably inefficient" and indicted dozens of men, but eventually only eleven faced trial. Eight of them were convicted of manslaughter and were sentenced to San Quentin for terms of two to six years. Within months of the sentencing, the state supreme court reversed the verdicts on a technicality, and the convicted men were released.

Sam Yuen sued the city of Los Angeles for recovery of his property, but a jury ruled against him.

The violence of the Los Angeles massacre overshadowed hundreds of forced banishments of Chinese from towns throughout California and foreshadowed the 1889 expulsion from Eureka. In Truckee, which by 1869 had the second largest Chinese population in the state, whites boycotted the businesses of Chinese merchants, and of whites who hired or continued to do business with them, to drive the Chinese away. These purges, whether economic or violent, were clearly violations of the Burlingame Treaty of 1868, which granted Chinese residents in the United States protection from ill treatment and bestowed on them the same rights, privileges, immunities, and exemptions enjoyed by citizens. They were also violations of the state and federal constitutions.

Instead of dealing with this lawless behavior, state officials decided to change the law to legitimize anti-Chinese discrimination.

Rewriting the Constitution

In the quarter-century after the 1849 constitution was written, California's population grew seventeenfold, to 864,500. New cities emerged. Gold mining declined, and agriculture grew exponentially. More people were employed on the docks, in factories, and in the trades. Organized labor spurred new political movements, demanding better conditions for workers. By the 1870s, about the time the mass lynching in Los Angeles took place, unemployment resulting from an economic depression had created the conditions for white labor organizers to scapegoat Chinese immigrants for their troubles.

The Workingmen's Party, led by Irish immigrant Denis Kearney, rallied under the slogan "The Chinese must go!" Members of the party attacked Chinese men in San Francisco streets and cut off their queues. A generation earlier it was Irish immigrants who had been targeted as a threat to society. Blinded by racism and

In bad economic times, white workers blamed Chinese immigrants for unemployment. In July 1877, a mob destroyed many Chinese laundries in San Francisco. A century later, muralist Anton Refregier depicted those days of violence known as the "Sandlot riots."

xenophobia, the nascent labor movement could not recognize it shared a common interest with Chinese workers.

California had not finished debating its constitutional framework. Its early government reflected the chaos and uncertainty of the rapidly growing population. New waves of Californians had amended the constitution many times, and labor was among the groups lobbying for a new constitution that addressed the issues raised by the changing demographics of the developing state.

In 1878, when a second constitutional convention was called, Kearney's Workingmen's Party ran a full slate of delegates from every region in the state. The meeting convened in Sacramento with three times as many delegates as the first (more than one hundred and forty), who remained in session three times longer than the 1849 framers. Unlike their earlier counterparts, most of the delegates were affiliated with political parties—in addition to the Democratic and Republican Parties, fifty-one delegates represented the Workingmen's Party. The delegates came up with one of the longest constitutions in the world, several times longer than U.S. Constitution. This time there was no Spanish-English dictionary on the table.

The new constitution did not improve civil rights for any group. Quite the opposite. At the urging of the Workingmen's Party, it singled out one group for particularly odious treatment: the Chinese. Despite the Burlingame Treaty, the new constitution explicitly denied Chinese the right to vote; prohibited the employment of Chinese by corporations or on public works "except in punishment for crime"; and authorized cities to require Chinese residents to live outside city limits or only in segregated neighborhoods within cities.

On May 17, 1879, California voters ratified the new state constitution. Only through a series of federal court cases were Chinese plaintiffs able to invalidate most of its anti-Chinese provisions and similar laws that followed. It took almost a century for the last of the 1879 anti-Chinese constitutional provisions to be removed from the books by a statewide ballot initiative.

No Return to Eureka

Like Chinese litigants who used courts to strike the discriminatory aspects of the 1879 constitution, the Chinese of Eureka did not passively reconcile themselves to their treatment at the hands of local vigilantes. The afternoon they arrived in San Francisco after being forced from their northern homes, a group of the exiles described their expulsion to the local Chinese community and to the San Francisco press. Then these bold settlers announced plans to seek reparations by suing the city of Eureka.

On January 21, 1886, nearly a year after they were expelled, fifty-two of Eureka's former Chinese residents sued the city in federal court for not protecting them from the mob violence. The lead plaintiff, Wing Hing, a twenty-five-year-old merchant, was joined by dozens of plaintiffs representing every aspect of Eureka's Chinese community, from merchants and domestic servants to prostitutes, cooks, fishermen, construction workers, and vegetable growers. They requested seventy-five thousand dollars in lost property and more than thirty-seven thousand dollars in damages—and an acknowledgement that the purge was illegal.

Colonel Fred Bee, the Chinese consul in San Francisco, hired two respected attorneys, Hall McAllister and Thomas Riordan, to represent the Chinese plaintiffs. *Wing Hing v. City of Eureka* was one of the first legal actions for reparations in United States history.

The city of Eureka flatly denied that any mob violence had occurred and contested the assertion that Chinese had been forced from town. Judge S. E. Buck, Eureka's city attorney, argued that the Chinese had left voluntarily after a few citizens told them to. Buck acknowledged that "a large, unarmed, peaceable and unorganized assemblage, without the slightest indication of insult or menace, witnessed their exodus." If there was no mob forcibly evicting the Chinese, the city had no culpability. Buck further argued that whatever property the Chinese had left behind had no value.

The case reached Judge Lorenzo B. Sawyer of the Ninth Judicial District in March 1886. He quickly ruled that the city of Eureka was not responsible for any mob violence, for any business losses the Chinese had suffered, or for the expulsion.

Although they did not succeed in this litigation, Chinese immigrants continued to access federal and state courts to ensure their rights. In so doing, they would set an example for other immigrants, people of color, and others who were marginalized, attacked, and seemingly powerless to use the legal system to stand up for their rights.

— TWO —

IN A STRANGE LAND

THE RIGHTS OF IMMIGRANTS

The Western styled buildings are lofty; but I have not
  the luck to live in them.

How was anyone to know that my dwelling place
  would be a prison?

*—Poem carved on the wall at Angel Island immigration station by an anony-
mous Chinese immigrant sometime between 1910 and 1940*

In June 1862, merchant Lin Sing paid the San Francisco tax collector five dollars, two
months' worth of "Chinese Police Tax," on behalf of one of his employees. Represented by the respected San Francisco law firm of Hepburn and Dwinelle, Lin Sing then
sued the tax collector for a refund. When *Lin Sing v. Washburn* reached the California
Supreme Court, the high court ruled that the state had overstepped its authority and
legislated in an area—foreign commerce—that was the exclusive sphere of the federal government. The justices stated that singling out a specific group of foreigners
for taxation discouraged immigration and commerce. Consequently, Chinese immigrants could not be targeted for special taxation. *Lin Sing* was the first case in which a
Chinese immigrant challenged a state law as a violation of federal law or the United
States Constitution.

Taxation targeting Chinese had begun a decade earlier, when the California legislature resurrected the Foreign Miners' Tax, which had initially been imposed against
Latinos but lapsed because so few complied with the law. The new iteration of the

41

tax compelled Chinese miners to pay three dollars a month. The following year, the tax increased to four dollars, with an annual two-dollar increase thereafter. An 1854 amendment named Chinese immigrants as the only miners required to pay the tax.

As Chinese workers began migrating from the mines to cities and towns, the state legislature imposed another tax on them. The tax imposed by the 1862 law, formally titled "An Act to Protect Free White Labor against Competition with Chinese Coolie Labor, and to Discourage the Immigration of Chinese into the State of California," was popularly called the Capitation Tax, or Chinese Police Tax. It required all Chinese, except merchants, miners, and those working in the sugar, rice, coffee, or tea business, to pay a tax of two dollars and fifty cents a month.

Chinese immigrants were accustomed to organizing themselves into mutual aid groups, based on the region from which they had immigrated and their surnames. The largest of these groups, the Chinese Consolidated Benevolent Association, known popularly as the Chinese Six Companies, often hired well-known attorneys to bring strategic test cases challenging anti-Chinese laws. As early as 1853, leaders of district associations worked with attorneys to lobby in Sacramento; by 1860 they had hired their own lobbyist.

In 1870 Chinese immigrants successfully promoted federal legislation safeguarding their civil rights. Although Congress passed the 1870 Civil Rights Act mainly to protect newly freed slaves, it included provisions that ensured the right of Chinese immigrants to testify in court, and it prohibited state and local governments from imposing discriminatory taxes, licenses, or penalties on Chinese. Although some rural counties continued to impose the tax, when pressed by federal officials they backed down.

Despite this federal protection, San Francisco, the home of the largest population of Chinese immigrants in the state during the latter half of the nineteenth century, took the category of anti-Chinese laws to a new creative high. San Francisco officials passed numerous laws that appeared neutral on their face—never mentioning the word "Chinese"—but aimed at making the lives of Chinese residents unbearable, in an effort to drive them from the city.

Because many Chinatown buildings were crowded tenements, the city passed an ordinance in 1870 requiring every lodging house to provide at least five hundred cubic feet of air per inhabitant. Though many overcrowded buildings existed in other poor areas of San Francisco, this ordinance was enforced only in Chinatown. The penalty for violating the law was a fine that could only be reduced by jail time. Many of those who were arrested opted to go to jail. In May 1873 the *San Francisco Bulletin* reported, "There was a good deal of difficulty in enforcing this ordinance on account of the number of Chinese who violated it, and their omission to pay the fines imposed. They were arrested in great numbers, and packed in cells where they had not one hundred cubic feet of air to the person. They overcrowded the jails, and it was thought necessary by the authorities of the city to adopt a policy which would compel the Chinese to pay their fines."

This policy came in the form of another ordinance, which mandated, "Each and every male prisoner shall have the hair of his head cut to an inch of his scalp." This meant that jailed Chinese men would forcibly have their queues cut off by a guard. At the time, a Q'ing dynasty law required all Chinese men to wear their hair in queues, and the queues had become a key component of the cultural identity of the immigrants so far from their homeland.

Ho Ah Kow was jailed for violating the air ordinance. When a warden cut his queue, Ho sued the San Francisco sheriff for ten thousand dollars in compensatory damages for mental anguish. Ho charged that the cutting of his queue violated the Fourteenth Amendment to the U.S. Constitution, passed just a few years before, which requires states to provide equal protection under the law to all persons. He argued that the ordinance had a particularly harsh impact on Chinese, to whom the queue was an important cultural symbol.

In an opinion by Circuit Court Justice Stephen Field, Ho was vindicated. Field drew the veil off the thinly disguised anti-Chinese laws, stating:

> The ordinance is known in the community as the "Queue Ordinance" being so designated from its purpose to reach the queues of the Chinese, and it is not enforced against any other persons. The reason advanced for its adoption…is, that only the dread of the loss of his queue will induce a Chinaman to pay his fine. That is to say, in order to enforce the payment of a fine imposed upon him it is necessary that torture should be superadded to the imprisonment.

This was the first federal case to rule clearly that the Fourteenth Amendment applied to noncitizens.

Despite this victory, Chinese Americans remained subject to widespread racism and official discrimination. A determined Chinese immigrant named Lee Yick, backed by his community, initiated a lawsuit that impacted civil liberties nationally.

Washing Dirty Laundry Laws

Recognizing an unfilled economic niche, many Chinese immigrants opened commercial laundries in San Francisco during the gold rush years. By 1870 about thirteen hundred Chinese Americans in San Francisco were in the laundry business. In the tradition of the craft guilds of China, San Francisco's Chinese American laundry-men organized a trade association, known as the Tung Hing Tong, which approved applications from Chinese immigrants for new laundries, resolved disputes among members, and set rules on the location of Chinese-run laundries and the prices that could be charged.

Between 1870 and 1884, the San Francisco Board of Supervisors issued a series of ordinances restricting the operations of laundries. The first such law, the "Sidewalk Ordinance of 1870," imposed the highest laundry license fee (fifteen dollars a quarter, more than seven times the lowest fee) on laundries that did not use horse-drawn vehicles. Not coincidentally, Chinese laundrymen carried finished laundry to their customers on poles as they walked through the streets. A San Francisco County judge invalidated that law as discriminating against poorer (not necessarily Chinese) laundry operators.

Lee Yick had arrived in California from China in 1861 and opened the Yick Wo laundry business. He operated the laundry for twenty-two years from the same wooden building on Third Street, just south of Folsom Street in a sunny area of San Francisco. He secured certification from the San Francisco Board of Fire Wardens that his laundry was fire safe, and from the city health officer that his laundry was properly drained.

In November 1883 a superior court judge upheld an ordinance requiring approval from the board of supervisors for the continued operation of wooden laundries. On its face, the law barring such laundries was reasonable because it was grounded in the public safety goal of preventing fires. In practice, however, enforcement of the law was discriminatory. Lee Yick and two hundred other Chinese immigrant laundry owners petitioned the board for permission to continue operating their businesses in the wooden buildings that many had occupied for more than twenty years. The board denied all of their requests. Yet the board granted, with one exception, the petitions of all eighty non-Chinese laundry owners. With the encouragement of the Tung Hing Tong, Lee Yick and the others continued working out of their wooden laundries in protest.

On August 22, 1885, as on other sunny days, freshly washed clothes hung on the roof of Lee Yick's laundry building. A sheriff entered his business and arrested him for operating an unauthorized wooden laundry. Two days later, the Tung Hing Tong hired attorneys to file a petition for writ of habeas corpus with the California Supreme Court.

Lee Yick's attorneys stressed that the ordinance did not define any standards for approving continued operation of wooden laundries and was therefore open for discriminatory enforcement, in violation of the Fourteenth Amendment.

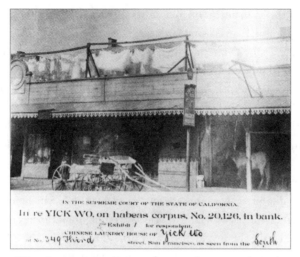

IN THE SUPREME COURT OF THE STATE OF CALIFORNIA.

In re YICK WO, on habeas corpus, No. 20,126, in bank.

Exhibit _I_ for respondent.

CHINESE LAUNDRY HOUSE OF _Yick Wo_

at No. 349 _Third_ street, San Francisco, as seen from the _South_

Nineteenth-century Chinese immigrants were the targets of numerous laws meant to harass them and drive them from San Francisco. The owner of the Yick Wo laundry took his case to the U.S. Supreme Court, which ruled in 1886 that a city ordinance outlawing wooden laundries, unequally enforced against Chinese laundrymen, violated the Constitution.

Alfred Clarke, special counsel to the San Francisco Board of Supervisors, whose sole job was to defend the array of laundry ordinances in court, denied any racial animus in enforcement of the law. Instead, he claimed that no Caucasian laundry owners were arrested for violating the ordinance because, unlike the Chinese laundry operators, they did not use roof scaffolding to dry laundry. But Clarke's brief to the high court betrayed an underlying racism. He contended that all Chinese-run laundries were cheaply constructed firetraps, despite the fact that Lee Yick's laundry, as well as other Chinese laundries, had passed fire inspections. He also attacked the Tung Hing Tong as a sinister, troublemaking "state within a state" determined to prevent the city government from regulating laundries.

On December 29, 1885, the state supreme court upheld the San Francisco wooden laundry ordinance as a valid public safety law that was not discriminatorily enforced.

The next month, Lee Yick's attorneys appealed to the U.S. Supreme Court, where his case was combined with the case of another laundryman, Wo Lee.

On May 10, 1886, the high court issued a unanimous decision that the city was unconstitutionally enforcing the ordinance. The justices ruled that the law was a barrier to the pursuit of a fundamental right—working in a chosen trade or profession—by requiring governmental approval, which could be denied arbitrarily or prejudicially. Justice Stanley Matthews disagreed with the state court ruling that the ordinance was an acceptable application of San Francisco's police power, explaining that the government offered no standards for laundry operators seeking the board's approval. It was clear, Matthews stated, that the ordinance was enforced so oppressively against a specific group as to "amount to a practical denial by the state of that equal protection of the laws which is secured...by the broad and benign provisions of the Fourteenth Amendment." Matthews further pointed out, "Though the law itself be fair on its face and impartial in appearance, yet, if it is applied and administered by public authority with an evil eye and an unequal hand so as to make unjust and illegal discriminations between persons in similar circumstances...the denial of equal justice is still within the prohibition of the Constitution."

Upon hearing news of the decision, Chinatown residents celebrated with fireworks. The white press, however, was not so pleased. The San Francisco *Evening Bulletin* editorialized: "The Delphic oracle at Washington intimates that we can do nothing to bridge the chasm which separates [the Chinese] from the modern races of men. We can do nothing to elevate or reform them, for that would be discrimination, contrary to the Fourteenth Amendment."

The short-term local result of the decision was that the board of supervisors issued a new comprehensive laundry ordinance in October 1887 requiring all laundries to pass inspections by the city's health officer and Board of Fire Wardens. The decision had significant long-term consequences because the Supreme Court had articulated the principle that the discriminatory enforcement of an otherwise neutral law was just as constitutionally suspect as a law that permitted outright discrimination.

Paper Sons and Daughters

Early Chinese immigration was governed by the Burlingame Treaty of 1868, which the United States pressured China into signing. Among other things, the agreement allowed for the free flow of trade and laborers between the two countries, greatly benefiting American railroad companies and large landowners who sought cheap labor in the post–Civil War period.

As the Chinese began establishing their own businesses and permanent homes in California, however, nascent West Coast trade unions, workingmen's associations, legislators, and self-described community leaders pressured the federal government to restrict Chinese immigration.

In the first instance of the U.S. singling out a specific ethnic group for discrimination, Congress in 1882 passed the landmark Chinese Exclusion Act, which suspended all Chinese immigration, except of government officials, merchants, students, teachers, and wives and children of U.S. citizens. The law also instituted a certification process for those Chinese Americans permitted to remain.

California Governor George Perkins declared Saturday, March 4, 1882, a legal holiday to allow "universal demonstration" in support of the new law.

But the Exclusion Act did not satisfy the lobby that was intent on driving out all Chinese from the state and nation. In February 1886 the Anti-Coolie League sponsored a statewide anti-Chinese convention in San Jose. Branches of the league had sprouted up throughout California. Members met over home-baked pies, held dances and brass band concerts, and raised funds to realize their dream of a Chinese-free California.

Their agitation paid off. Congress approved a succession of laws further restricting Chinese entry to the U.S. One law required Chinese immigrants who had left the U.S. to possess a certificate for reentry. Another denied entry to ethnic Chinese who had earlier migrated to Europe, Mexico, or the Philippines. In 1892 the Geary Act extended Chinese exclusion another ten years and required all Chinese legitimately in the United States to obtain a government-issued certificate from the Internal Revenue Service. This photo-passport had to be carried at all times; Chinese stopped without a certificate were subject to immediate and summary deportation unless a white witness confirmed they had resided in the U.S. before November 17, 1880. The law was challenged but upheld by the U.S. Supreme Court, with Justice Stephen Field dissenting.

In 1902 Congress made permanent the law excluding Chinese laborers from immigrating to the U.S.

But Chinese workers defied the exclusion laws. Though immigration restrictions were onerous, the poverty, war, and political turmoil that had driven Chinese men to seek a better life in California had not changed. Tens of thousands of immigrants, mostly Cantonese from the Pearl River Delta area of Kwangtung Province, pooled their family money and risked an arduous ocean voyage to come to the U.S.

Some tried to beat the Exclusion Act by debarking in Mexican ports and crossing the border into California. This practice led to lucrative smuggling operations, and the numbers grew so high that the Bureau of Immigration sent guards, known as Chinese Inspectors, to capture Chinese attempting to cross the hundred-and-eighty-mile stretch of the border near San Diego—the prototype of the Border Patrol.

The devastating 1906 San Francisco earthquake created an unusual opportunity for Chinese immigrants. The temblor and subsequent fire destroyed most marriage and birth certificates and other official documents. Since children of U.S. citizens were exempt from the Exclusion Act, many Chinese immigrants took advantage of the destruction of San Francisco records to enter the U.S. as "paper sons or daughters." U.S. citizens of Chinese descent, upon their return to the U.S. from sojourns in China, would claim to have offspring whose births matched the timing of their visits. This created "immigration slots" that could later be filled by a child—usually a son—who needed a "paper father" to legitimize entrance into the U.S.

The paper families were assisted by the *gam saan jong*, or Gold Mountain Firm system, which matched Chinese residents with claimed offspring arriving in California. At one point, there were as many as two hundred firms assisting in the immigration trade. Chinese immigrants considered the subterfuge a means of dealing with unfair immigration laws. Entire clans, villages, and regional organizations viewed the use of false identities as a means of beating the Bureau of Immigration at its own game.

On the long ocean voyage, "paper children" studied coaching books prepared for them months before that contained detailed descriptions of their paper families and villages. These books were necessary because the new immigrants faced harsh interrogation by officials at the immigration station on Angel Island in the San Francisco Bay.

From 1910 until it was closed in 1940, the immigration station on the small, forested island served as the point of entry for one hundred and seventy-five thousand Chinese immigrants. The walls of the dormitories are carved with Chinese poetry describing conditions on the island and the inmates' longings. From the ships, the new immigrants could see San Francisco, but their hopes were often dashed as they reached the dock. As one anonymous poet wrote:

> The Western styled buildings are lofty; but I have not
> the luck to live in them.
>
> How was anyone to know that my dwelling place
> would be a prison?

Though some would-be immigrants were not even allowed off the ships, most were ferried to the immigration station. The newcomers were separated by gender, race, and nationality, as Japanese "picture brides," Russian Jews, and Punjabis also went through Angel Island. Chinese women and men were kept in separate barracks, and husbands and wives were not allowed to communicate. Children under twelve were kept with their mothers, but teenage boys were locked in the men's dormitories. At any one time there were usually two hundred to three hundred men and thirty to fifty women in the barracks.

The Chinese newcomers were disqualified from entering the U.S. if rigorous medical screenings revealed they had certain maladies, including hookworm, ringworm, or trachoma. Immigrants from other countries did not have to undergo such exams.

The Chinese not only lived in separate quarters, they ate at different times from other immigrants and ate different food of poorer quality, including spoiled meats, wilted vegetables, and low-grade rice.

Half way up the hill on Island, in the
  building upstairs,

The imprisoned one has been separated from his
  people summer to autumn.

Three times I dreamed of returning to the
  native village

My intestines are agitated in its nine turns by
  the false Westerner.

I have run into hard times and am uselessly
  depressed.

There are many obstacles in life, but who will
  commiserate with me?

If at a later time I am allowed to land on the
  American shore,

I will toss all the miseries of this jail to the
  flowing current.

*Poetry, written in the classical Chinese style, was carved
into the walls of the Angel Island immigration station
by anonymous immigrants who wrote of loneliness, harsh
treatment, and aching memories of their homeland.*

This anonymous poem, translated by Him Mark Lai, is one of more than one hundred found carved into the walls of the former immigration station on Angel Island.

The poetry was rediscovered in 1970 by park ranger Alexander Weiss, just before the abandoned two-story wooden detention center was about to be destroyed. The poems were written in Classical Chinese style, following a strict poetic structure, with many references to legends and literary figures.

No one knows exactly when the poems were carved—they are almost all undated and unsigned, their anonymous authors not wanting to be identified by immigration authorities. But they describe the loneliness, anguish, and uncertainty of life on Angel Island for the tens of thousands of Chinese immigrants who were held there when the Exclusion Act was in effect.

This poem signed by Xu from Xiangshan describes the hardship that families faced in sending an immigrant to the U.S.:

Just talk about going to the land of the
    Flowery Flag and my countenance fills with happiness
Not without hard work were 1,000 pieces of gold dug up and
    gathered together.
There were words of farewell to the parents, but the throat choked
    up first.
There were many feelings, many tears flowing face to face, when
    parting with the wife.
Waves as big as mountains often astonished this traveler.
With laws as harsh as tigers, I had a taste of all the
    barbarities.

The first port of entry for many Chinese fleeing poverty, famine, and war in their homeland was the immigration station at Angel Island in San Francisco Bay, where they underwent grueling interrogations before they were permitted to travel the short distance to the mainland. Men and women, including married couples, were confined in separate barracks and not allowed to communicate.

Prior to their immigration hearings, Chinese inmates were forbidden outside visitors, and the authorities opened all their letters and gift packages to ensure they were not receiving coaching materials. Eventually, a detainee would be summoned before the Board of Inquiry, to be grilled in a sealed room by two inspectors and a stenographer; the inspectors used different interpreters, partly because of differing dialects, but primarily so interpreters would not be able to pass on any information helpful to the detainee. There were no established interrogation rules or procedures. Asking as many as six hundred questions in interrogations that lasted from one to three days, inspectors demanded detailed information: How many houses were in your village? How often do you receive a letter from your father? Where was the village cistern?

If answers matched the testimony of a detainee's relative in the U.S., immigration officials invited the father (or paper father) and someone from the immigrant's family association to Angel Island to assure that the potential immigrant's dialect matched the dialect spoken by his or her U.S. family.

To survive this grueling ordeal, the detainees organized a self-help group. The Angel Island Liberty Association, or Zi Zhi Hui, linked detainees and families in San Francisco, relying on Angel Island's Chinese kitchen staff to pick up coaching messages in Chinatown and, for a small fee, surreptitiously deliver them at mealtimes.

Angel Island was closed as an immigration station in 1940. In 1943 the Exclusion Act was repealed as a goodwill gesture to China, a wartime ally against Japan. The quota for Chinese immigrants, however, was only 105 per year until the mid-1960s.

The long practice of paper families would have ramifications years later.

Who Is a Citizen?

Even Chinese Americans able to prove they were born in the U.S. could not take their American citizenship for granted.

Wong Kim Ark was twenty-two years old in August 1895, when he arrived in San Francisco Bay aboard the steamship *Coptic*. The young cook was returning home after visiting China. He carried the necessary document to reenter the United States: a certificate of identity with his photograph and the signatures of three white witnesses who verified his birth in San Francisco. The customs official at the port admitted that Wong's "papers were all straight" but denied him reentry on the grounds that the young man's birth in California did not grant him U.S. citizenship.

Because the U.S. Constitution did not define "citizen," American jurists had adopted the British common law practice of assigning U.S. citizenship to any person born on United States territory. Race, however, impacted this practice. Courts in southern states, for example, refused to recognize the citizenship of free blacks born in the U.S., a position which the Supreme Court adopted in the infamous 1857 *Dred Scott* case.

The Fourteenth Amendment, added to the Constitution after the Civil War, defined citizenship for the first time by clearly stipulating that "all persons born or naturalized in the United States, and subject to the jurisdiction thereof, are citizens of the United States."

The Chinese Exclusion Act of 1882, in addition to a 1790 law restricting naturalization rights to "free white persons," already barred Chinese immigrants from naturalizing, but nativists attempted to extend the ban on citizenship to the U.S.-born children of Chinese immigrants. They argued that a child's citizenship derives from the nationality of the parents, regardless of where the child is born. In 1888 an attorney with the Department of Justice promoted the idea of bringing a test case to the Supreme Court to challenge birthright citizenship claims made by Chinese Americans.

They found their test case with Wong Kim Ark. Wong was the son of merchant Wong Si Ping and his wife, Wee Lee, who had lived in the United States for more than seventeen years. The younger Wong had visited China twice, once in 1890 and again in 1894, but had otherwise lived only in California.

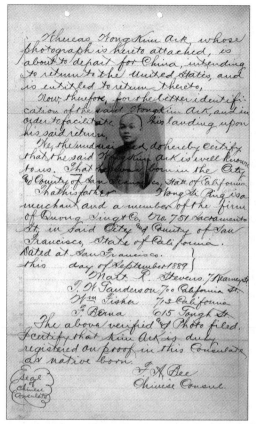

To enter the U.S. upon returning from a trip to China, Wong Kim Ark was required to show this document, signed by three citizens attesting to his birth in San Francisco. When a customs agent still refused to recognize Wong's U.S. citizenship, Wong took his case to the U.S. Supreme Court. In 1898 the Court determined that all people born on U.S. territory are citizens.

When Wong Kim Ark was denied entry into the country of his birth, the Chinese Consolidated Benevolent Association hired attorney Thomas Riordan, who had represented Chinese in other cases challenging exclusion laws. Riordan filed a petition for a writ of habeas corpus, arguing that Wong was being illegally detained.

Before the federal district court, government attorneys contended that birth in the United States did not automatically translate into allegiance to America, especially if immigrant parents did not instill in their children loyalty to the United States. They argued that citizenship should be determined by descent, to protect the nation from "the rag tag and bob tail of humanity, who happen to be deposited on our soil by the accident of birth, and whose education and political affiliations are entirely alien."

Although Judge William W. Morrow sympathized with the government's arguments (as a member of Congress, he had supported Chinese exclusion legislation), he ruled that Wong Kim Ark was a U.S. citizen and ordered his release. Morrow explained that to accept the government's arguments would mean "denationalizing" thousands of people who had been born in the United States to immigrant parents.

The government appealed to the Supreme Court.

U.S. Solicitor General Holmes Conrad, a Virginian who resisted the outcome of the Civil War, introduced a federalist argument to the government's case: states, not the federal government, had the right to define citizenship and its rights. He further argued that the Fourteenth Amendment was invalid because southern states had been forced to ratify it. And to top off his case, he added a cultural component: since Chinese immigrants were barred from naturalizing, that status should also apply to their American-born children.

Countering Solicitor General Conrad were Wong's attorneys, Maxwell Evarts and J. Hubley Ashton, two prominent northeastern lawyers who had represented other Chinese immigrants. Arguing that persons born in the U.S. had long been recognized as citizens, they also addressed the government's contention that the Fourteenth Amendment was invalid. They asserted that the principle of equality defined in the amendment would forestall a bloody civil war like the one recently ended.

On March 28, 1898, the high court ruled in Wong's favor. In a 6-2 opinion by Associate Justice Horace Gray, the justices determined that the framers of the Fourteenth Amendment had accepted the potential that children of Chinese immigrants would be granted birthright citizenship. Gray had written the Court's decision in an earlier case, *Fong Yue Ting v. United States*, that upheld broad congressional power to deport aliens at will. His *Wong Kim Ark* opinion was consistent in affirming the federal government's authority, in this case to define citizenship.

Wong Kim Ark had won the battle for birthright citizenship, but exclusionists and nativists continued to clamor for restrictions on the immigration and naturalization rights of Asians and Latinos. During World War II, the Native Sons of the Golden West would challenge the validity of the *Wong Kim Ark* decision in their quest to rid the country of Japanese Americans.

"Aliens Ineligible to Citizenship"

The Chinese Exclusion Act of 1882 cut off a large pool of unskilled workers for American farms and businesses. Soon after it passed, immigrants from Japan began arriving in California to fill the void. As their numbers increased in the late 1890s, so did agitation against them. In 1892 Denis Kearney and his Workingmen's Party led an anti-Japanese crusade, as they had done against the Chinese decades previously. They denounced the Japanese as "foreign Shylocks who are rushing another breed of Asiatic slaves to fill the gap made vacant by the Chinese who are shut out by our laws," asserting that "now Japs are being brought here in countless numbers to demoralize and discourage our domestic labor market and to be educated at our expense."

The vitriol of this rhetoric was out of proportion with the actual size of the Japanese population: the 1890 federal census recorded only 2,039 Japanese. The demand for agricultural labor was so high that California politicians found anti-Japanese agitation convenient to ignore.

By 1905, however, local and international developments had contributed to rising anti-Japanese sentiment. That year, Japan surprised the world by defeating Russia, then a leading military power, in the Russo-Japanese War. This victory fueled apprehensions about a potential American war with Japan and spurred Californians to question the loyalty of Japanese immigrants.

Three years later, President Theodore Roosevelt's administration negotiated the "Gentlemen's Agreement," under which the Japanese government voluntarily regulated immigration to the U.S. The agreement effectively cut off immigration of Japanese laborers to the United States.

Much to the dismay of anti-Japanese forces, however, the Gentlemen's Agreement contained a significant loophole: Japanese immigrants, known as Issei, could bring their families to the U.S. Consequently, thousands of Japanese women (many of whom were "picture brides" married by proxy in Japan to husbands living in the U.S.) immigrated to California and other western states. The continued arrival of Japanese and the growth of Japanese communities through the birth of a second generation, referred to as Nisei, further enraged exclusionists, who lobbied for a federal law cutting off all Japanese immigration. They eventually succeeded, in 1924.

Californians also passed a series of laws restricting or denying Issei property rights. In 1913 Republican Progressive attorney Francis J. Heney and California Attorney General Ulysses S. Webb authored a law, passed by the state legislature in two days, that barred "aliens ineligible to citizenship" from owning land and restricted leases to three years. Since legal Chinese immigration had ceased in 1882, the new Alien Land Law was directed almost exclusively against Japanese immigrants, though never explicitly naming them.

Issei navigated around the law by transferring land titles or leases into the names of their U.S.-born citizen children. In response, the Native Sons and Daughters of the Golden West and the American Legion qualified an initiative for the November 1920 ballot to forbid Issei from leasing land for any length of time, buying land in the name of their American-born children, or acting as guardians of property for their children. The initiative would also institute criminal sanctions for non-Japanese who were involved in transferring land ownership to Issei.

Proponents campaigned under the slogan "Save California from the Japs." They pushed a broad anti-Japanese agenda, including the revised Alien Land Law; a federal constitutional amendment denying citizenship to Nisei; exclusion of Japanese immigrants; and assurance that Asians would forever be barred from citizenship. To justify their racist proposals, they accused Japanese of having a high birthrate; of being spies, sex fiends, and rapists; and of "mongrelizing" white women. Almost all newspapers in the state supported the initiative, as did California's political leaders.

The smear campaign was successful. In 1920 California voters approved, three to one, the Alien Land Law initiative. The California Supreme Court ruled in 1922 that the provision prohibiting Issei parents from serving as guardians of property for their citizen children violated both the federal and state constitutions, but the U.S. Supreme Court in 1923 otherwise upheld the validity of the law. It would be another thirty-three years before voters repealed it.

Repatriados Forced across the Border

When Asian immigration to California generated a political backlash at the turn of the twentieth century, immigration from Mexico was numerically insignificant. From 1900 to 1909, Mexicans represented only .6 percent of total immigrants to the United States, increasing to 3.8 percent the following decade. It was easy to cross the southern border: one only had to pay a nickel to get a visa. As California industry and agriculture boomed, employers welcomed Mexican workers in the factories and fields.

During World War I, the U.S. government helped fill a labor shortage by facilitating the importation of Mexican laborers to work in the farms and ranches of private landowners. Many remained after the war, and the Associated Farmers, a conservative trade organization of commercial growers, continued to recruit Mexican laborers, assuming that since they were barred from joining the all-white AFL unions, they would be a more tractable labor force. By 1930, one and a half million people of Mexican ancestry lived in the U.S., about half of whom were U.S.-born.

But the welcome mat was suddenly pulled out from under Mexican workers when the stock market crashed in 1929. With the onset of the Great Depression, fortunes were lost, factories were shuttered, and millions found themselves out of work.

Under the banner of saving jobs for "real Americans," the federal government led a massive "repatriation" effort to scapegoat and deport Mexicans—with no distinction made for their legal status. The government's methods ranged from fear and intimidation to throwing people out of work and off relief rolls and eventually forcing more than a million people—an estimated 60 percent of them U.S. citizens—over the border.

Visa rules were tightened, reducing legal immigration to a trickle: the number of legal Mexican immigrants dropped from sixty thousand in 1925 to three thousand in 1931.

With the full consent of the AFL, many private companies refused to hire noncitizens. This blacklisting quickly extended to all people of Mexican origin, regardless of citizenship. George Clements of the Los Angeles Chamber of Commerce stated, "The slogan has gone out over the city and is being adhered to—employ no Mexican while a white man is unemployed. It is a question of pigment, not a question of citizenship or right." The sudden loss of jobs and income plunged many Mexican families into poverty.

In 1930 the Bureau of Immigration was under the auspices of the Department of Labor. President Herbert Hoover's secretary of labor, William N. Doak, launched a program of mass immigration raids in an ostentatious show of removing foreigners from the dwindling job market. Incited by this federal program, a hue and cry went up around California demanding expulsion of Mexicans. C. P. Visel of the Los Angeles Citizens Committee for Coordination of Unemployment Relief wrote to a federal official, "We can pick them all up through police and sheriff channels. You advise please as to method of getting rid. We need their jobs for needy citizens."

The AFL supported the "repatriation," as did veterans' groups (even though many Mexicans had served in the military) and nationalist organizations, such as the America for Americans Club, which called for permanently closing the border. The Hearst newspapers echoed the call. Counties dropped relief recipients from the rolls if they could not prove they were citizens, and many citizen children went hungry.

The public attacks and accusations spread fear and panic in California's Mexican American communities. Lacking jobs, with families to feed, and fearful of being arrested in raids, many Mexicans elected to leave "voluntarily."

An internal memo from Walter Carr, the Bureau of Immigration's Los Angeles district director, noted, "thousands upon thousands of Mexican aliens have been literally scared out of Southern California."

Immigration agents conducted random surprise inspections of boarding houses, restaurants, and poolrooms, entering without warrants and rounding up people based solely on the color of their skin. Rumors circulated in Mexican American communities prior to roundups, and the Spanish language newspaper *La Opinión* warned readers of the imminent raids. But no one was prepared for the mass raid on La Placita, the city plaza, a historic gathering place for Mexicans in downtown Los Angeles, on February 26, 1931.

On that winter afternoon, about four hundred people were relaxing on the benches in the sunny plaza. At three o'clock a large group of uniformed and plainclothes law enforcement officers, led by immigration agents in olive-drab uniforms, entered the square. Trucks cordoned off the area and police posted themselves at the entrances to prevent anyone from leaving. Panic swept through the crowd.

Officials forced everyone in the plaza to line up and produce identity documents. Those who had none were detained and shipped to Mexico without the opportunity to contact their families, forced to leave homes and property behind. Among them were citizens, legal residents, and veterans of the U.S. military. Radio announcer José David Orozco recalled "women crying in the streets when not finding their husbands."

The raid had been planned well in advance. Officials from the federal Bureau of Immigration had brought in agents from San Diego, San Francisco, and Nogales, Arizona. They enlisted the support of Los Angeles Police Chief R. E. Stackel and County Sheriff William Traeger. It took the federal government more than a week to coordinate the plan with local authorities.

In subsequent raids, government officials took stunned residents of Los Angeles's *colonias* and *barrios* to the train station in squad cars, trucks, and buses, often under armed guard. County administrators, calculating it would cost less to transport deportees to Mexico than to pay for a week's board in a detention facility, quickly organized "special trains" from the Southern Pacific station. Historian Carey Mc-Williams witnessed the departure of the first one: "The loading process began at 6 o'clock in the morning. *Repatriados* arrived by the truckload—men, women and children—with dogs, cats and goats, half-opened suitcases, rolls of bedding and lunch baskets."

Between 1931 and 1934, the Los Angeles Department of Charities launched fifteen special trainloads averaging one thousand *repatriados* each. The Los Angeles Board of Supervisors made careful arrangements with the railroads and shipping companies, calculating that it saved $347,468 in relief payments for one trainload. They did not take the human cost into the calculation.

Emilia Castañeda was born in Los Angeles in 1926. One day, when she and her brother came home from school, her father announced that the family had to leave for Mexico. "I don't remember what happened to our possessions, our furniture," Castañeda recalled. "The only thing my dad was packing was a trunk, what little belongings we had, and we were there at dawn. That I remember. It was real dark in the train station." Nine-year-old Castañeda was told by a county employee that she could stay if she said she was an orphan and would become a ward of the state. But the little girl insisted she was not an orphan, since she had her father.

Castañeda and thousands of other children were "repatriated" to a land they did not know. Because they had been punished for speaking Spanish in American schools, many spoke little if any Spanish and had problems coping with their new life.

From 1930 to 1939, Mexicans were 46.3 percent of all people deported from the U.S., yet they comprised less than 1 percent of population. "Sixty percent of those deported were U.S. citizens," according to historian Francisco Balderrama, who questions why so few outside of the Mexican community criticized the policy. He also notes that for decades, Mexicans were also largely silent about the forced deportation, preferring to tell the sad story in the musical laments of *corridos*, rather than in the halls of Congress or the courts.

Braceros: Back across the Border

With the start of World War II and the end of the Depression, the repatriation program ceased, and the pendulum swung swiftly in the opposite direction. America's entrance into the war created an acute labor shortage, as young men flocked to join the armed forces. In 1942 the U.S. government began negotiations with Mexico to bring workers from the impoverished Mexican countryside to work in U.S. agriculture and railroads. The Mexican government, which had been hit hard financially by the mass repatriation of families without jobs or benefits, insisted that the World War II–era contracts be directly with the U.S. government, not with individual private employers. Both governments agreed to solve their problems on the backs of the poorest Mexican workers, known as "braceros." The word comes from the Spanish *brazo*, arm, and is generally translated to mean "strong arms" or "working arms." On April 26, 1943, the United States and Mexico finalized the Bracero Treaty, under which the U.S. government became the braceros' official employer. Over the course of two decades, an estimated two million braceros would come to the United States. Many would leave with broken bodies and broken promises.

Agribusinesses welcomed the braceros as leverage against domestic workers' efforts to build unions, which had gained strength in widespread strikes and labor mobilizations in the thirties.

In its first year, the bracero workforce grew more than tenfold, from 4,203 to 52,098. The numbers increased steadily throughout the war, dwindled when GIs returned home, and then rose even higher during the Korean War. Despite the end of the war, Congress renewed the program three times in the 1950s. The flow peaked in 1956, with 445,000 workers. Almost half of them worked in California, providing about a quarter of the state's seasonal agricultural workforce.

Under the Bracero Treaty, workers were guaranteed steady wages, housing, and health services during the forty-five-day period of their work contracts. Ten percent of their gross wages would be deducted and put into a "savings fund," although many of the braceros were not told why this money was taken from their paychecks or how to claim it upon their return to Mexico.

After the allotted time of employment, braceros were required to return to Mexico for a new contract. Nonetheless, many stayed, which led the Immigration and Naturalization Service (INS) to round up Mexicans under a program called "Operation Wetback." By the mid-1950s, more than one million had been deported, crossing paths with new or returning braceros.

The U.S. government required growers who employed braceros to hire no fewer than one hundred workers. Therefore, the majority of agricultural laborers (railroads also employed a lesser number of braceros) worked for large growers. A wartime report showed that California agribusinesses and grower associations ordered 64,235 braceros annually, assuring themselves an inexhaustible supply of cheap, non-union labor. In 1957, 60 percent of seasonal hired workers were employed by a mere 5.2 percent of farms.

In 1942 the U.S. government started the bracero program to make up for the labor shortfall caused by World War II. Photographer Leonard Nadel said the workers at the border processing centers were treated "like livestock," herded into makeshift fumigation booths and sprayed with DDT.

More than 90 percent of braceros had no schooling or had only attended primary school. Many were peasants who worked as sharecroppers or laborers for landowners. In the early years, they were recruited from the states of San Luis Potosí, Zacatecas, Nayarit, and Durango. In later years, the majority came from states that were closer to the U.S. border. Many braceros had to bribe Mexican officials just to get on the list to participate in the program. Once they reached their destinations, they found the working conditions harsh, but challenging them meant risking deportation. They were often forced to work ten hours a day, six days a week, suffering abuse at the hands of foremen and enduring backbreaking stoop labor. Growers considered them a captive labor force; most came without their wives or families, which gave them more time to devote to farm work.

When union organizers tried to reach braceros, growers and their law enforcement allies met them with uncommon hostility. In Stockton, for example, labor contractors Loduca & Perry maintained a large labor camp for eight hundred braceros seven miles west of town. They surrounded the miserable settlement of wooden shacks with "No Trespassing" signs to keep the workers isolated. In the summer of 1961, two AFL-CIO organizers, Jefferson Poland and Fred Cage, tried to enter the camp to distribute leaflets in Spanish and English informing the braceros of their rights.

The owners and their foremen met Poland and Cage inside the gates and ordered them to leave. When they refused, they were grabbed, knocked to the ground, and thrown outside the camp. A few minutes later the two were dragged back into the camp and told they were under arrest for trespassing.

At their criminal trial, the union organizers argued that the Bracero Treaty guaranteed that workers could elect a spokesperson—either a bracero or a representative of a trade union—to negotiate with their employer. The workers had the right to meet with labor organizers on company property during non-working hours.

But San Joaquin County Judge Priscilla H. Haynes rejected the argument and found Poland and Cage guilty. In 1964, the U.S. Supreme Court refused to review their case, but U.S. Solicitor General Archibald Cox noted that negotiations were under way with Mexico to ensure that labor organizers could have access to the braceros' labor camps.

Pressure to repeal the bracero program began in the 1950s from farm labor organizations, civic and religious groups, and the broader trade union movement. In 1959 Secretary of Labor James P. Mitchell recommended measures to prevent the U.S. Employment Services (which then administered the bracero contracts) from undercutting wages and conditions for domestic workers.

In 1962 Congress brought braceros under minimum wage protections. This and other lobbying for improved working conditions made the program less profitable for growers. When the Bracero Treaty expired on May 30, 1963, agribusiness did not campaign for its renewal. The program officially ended on December 31, 1964. Without a contract, the workers who had sustained and built California agriculture during two wars returned to their villages, or disappeared into the nameless stream of migrant workers from the vineyards of Coachella to the lettuce fields of Salinas.

Decades later, a Mexican government commission revealed that most of the braceros had never been paid the 10 percent "savings" that had been taken from their wages under the Bracero Treaty. In 2002 attorney Bill Lann Lee filed a federal class action lawsuit on their behalf, seeking the funds due to them—an estimated half-billion dollars.

The suit named not only the Mexican and U.S. governments, but also the banks responsible for holding and disbursing the money. "We found that State Department officials were aware there was fraud and looting by Mexican bank officials and the government, but no one did anything for the braceros," Lee explained.

Seventy-five-year-old plaintiff Alberto Montes González, who picked cotton for several seasons, had not even realized that money was being taken out of his paycheck. "They always paid us in cash. It was a deal between the two governments."

Notre Dame sociologist Jorge Bustamante, former United Nations special rapporteur on immigrants' rights, said, "Every day that passes, I have less hope that the braceros will be compensated, because in a very short period of time there are not going to be any surviving braceros."

In October 2008, the Mexican government finally agreed to a one-time payment of thirty-five hundred dollars to each bracero who could prove he had worked in the program. The aging farmworkers searched for sixty-year-old contracts, pay stubs, and bracero ID cards, the documentation required to retrieve their withholdings.

The long overdue settlement did not help all of the estimated two million former braceros: many had died, others could not prove their wages had been withheld. Those who worked in the program after 1946 had to travel to Mexico to file their claim, and many were too ill or fragile to make the trip.

At the Mexican consulate in Fresno, eighty-six-year-old Cirilo Perez-Torres wondered if he would ever receive his reimbursement, since all of his documents had been destroyed in a flood in Guanajuato. "I remember everything," he said, "the field, the places, the crops. But they are not accepting my memories."

Though the bracero program ended in 1964, its fostering of a large, mobile, and vulnerable migrant workforce has continued to shape California agriculture.

Burial of the Alien Land Law

While the bracero program was gathering steam, one hundred and twenty thousand Japanese Americans were incarcerated in desolate concentration camps under President Roosevelt's wartime executive order. In 1945 many families, newly released from the camps, returned to their California hometowns to find landlords unwilling to rent to them. Worse, vigilantes in some towns threatened and attacked Japanese Americans to prevent them from reoccupying their former homes. Exacerbating these problems was a new state law appropriating two hundred thousand dollars to the state's Department of Justice to "investigate and vigorously enforce the Alien Land Law of 1920."

In 1944 the government sued Fred Oyama and his Issei father, Kajiro, who had purchased land in San Diego County in 1934. The title was in the name of Fred, who had been six years old at the time. In 1937 Fred's parents purchased additional land under their son's name. The state argued that the Oyamas had intended to violate the Alien Land Law. On October 31, 1946, the California Supreme Court issued its decision in *People v. Oyama*, upholding the reversion of the Oyamas' land to the state. The Oyamas appealed to the U.S. Supreme Court, which over two decades earlier had upheld most of the Alien Land Law.

Just five days after the state supreme court's decision, the California electorate voted on Proposition 15, the referendum to expand the 1920 Alien Land Law. The Japanese American Citizens' League (JACL), a civil rights group composed of Nisei, had assigned Mike Masaoka to lead the statewide campaign to defeat it. Surprisingly, California voters, a little over a year after the war with Japan, voted down the discriminatory measure.

On January 19, 1948, the Supreme Court in a 6-3 decision reversed the state court's decision in the *Oyama* case, invalidating a core component of the Alien Land

Law that outlawed aliens ineligible for citizenship from providing funds to purchase land for their American-born children.

The *Oyama* ruling said nothing about the legality of Issei owning land outright. So Sei Fujii, an Issei who owned and published the *Kashu Mainichi*, a popular Japanese-English newspaper in southern California, squarely challenged the Alien Land Law. Fujii, who had studied law at the University of Southern California, bought property in East Los Angeles and took title in his own name. The state promptly tried to confiscate the land. On April 17, 1952, in a 4-3 decision, the California Supreme Court ruled that prohibiting aliens ineligible for citizenship from owning land violated the equal protection clauses of both the state and federal constitutions. Writing for the majority, Chief Justice Phil S. Gibson ruled that although the state tried to connect property ownership with federal naturalization rights, the two were unrelated. Instead, Gibson declared, "the California Alien Land Law is obviously designed and administered as an instrument effectuating racial discrimination, and the most searching examination discloses no circumstances justifying classification on that basis."

At the same time, another test case was working its way through the judicial system. This one involved an extremely sympathetic plaintiff, Haruye Masaoka, an Issei widow with eight children. Mike Masaoka, who had led the campaign to defeat Proposition 15, was one of her sons. He had also helped organize and was the first to volunteer for the 442nd Regimental Combat Team, the all-Nisei unit that fought with distinction in Europe. Four of his brothers followed. The second eldest, Ben, was killed in combat in Italy, and the others were wounded; collectively, they earned more than thirty medals.

After the war, the family returned to Los Angeles. Mike Masaoka orchestrated the lawsuit with his mother as plaintiff. With two hundred and fifty dollars that Haruye received from the government after her son's combat death, the family bought a lot in Pasadena with the specific intention of challenging the Alien Land Law. James Purcell, the attorney who brought *Ex parte Endo*, a historic lawsuit challenging the incarceration of loyal Japanese Americans during World War II, volunteered to represent the Masaoka family.

Having already decided the *Fujii* case, the state supreme court summarily upheld a lower court ruling that the Alien Land Law was unconstitutional. After winning their test case, the Masaoka family sold the Pasadena property and used the proceeds to establish a scholarship with the JACL.

The *Oyama*, *Fujii*, and *Masaoka* decisions were fatal blows to the Alien Land Law. But because the 1920 version of the law was passed through an initiative, voters had to affirm its repeal. The final burial of the discriminatory legislation took place on

November 5, 1956, when California voters approved Proposition 13 by a two-to-one majority, repealing the Alien Land Law forty-three years after it was enacted.

Confessions of the Paper Sons

Another vestige of anti-immigrant sentiment, the Chinese Exclusion Act, was repealed in 1943, but it left California's Chinese American communities with long-standing and deep distrust of immigration officers, politicians, and the political process that had produced so many anti-Chinese laws. Historian Judy Yung asserts that the phenomenon of paper families deeply affected the second generation of Chinese Americans because they did not know their history and often had to maintain dual identities.

In addition to its psychological impact, the Exclusion Act had legal ramifications long after its repeal. Following World War II and the rise of the People's Republic of China, the State Department and the INS continued to view Chinese immigrants with suspicion, with the additional distorting lens of anti-Communism. To identify paper sons and daughters, the U.S. consulate in Hong Kong established an investigative unit of two hundred personnel; they demanded that Chinese applicants for immigration undergo blood tests, X-rays, and clinical examinations.

Once in San Francisco, the newcomers were still subject to intense scrutiny. In 1947 immigration officers in San Francisco detained for immigration fraud numerous Chinese Americans, including more than twenty U.S. servicemen returning from the war in the Pacific. Those detainees who could not prove their citizenship were detained and deported; one hung himself in the detention center.

California's Chinatowns once again became areas of government suspicion and scrutiny. The INS placed community organizations under surveillance and raided businesses, demanding immigration papers, licenses, and personal documents. After the federal government recognized the Chiang Kai-shek regime in Taiwan as the legitimate government of China and relations with the People's Republic cooled into nonexistence, the raids and interrogations took on an explicit anti-Communist tone. A State Department dispatch warning that security precautions had to be taken to "exclude Chinese Communist agents or criminal elements" led to a massive grand jury investigation in San Francisco. In 1956 the U.S. attorney ordered more than two dozen Chinese associations to submit all their records, including closely guarded membership rolls—within twenty-four hours—and subpoenaed six photography studios for negatives of all the photos of the associations' events and members.

The raids and investigations spread panic and alarm among Chinese residents and bred suspicion in the broader society, which began avoiding Chinatown's restaurants and tourist spots. The Chinese Consolidated Benevolent Association, following the community's long tradition of pursuing justice in courts, sued to quash the subpoenas. Their request was granted by Federal Judge Oliver H. Carter, who ruled on March 20, 1956, that the grand jury's broad search "had the effect of being a mass inquisition of the family records of a substantial portion of the Chinese population of San Francisco." The government did not appeal.

Finally, the government decided to offer a carrot along with its stick. In 1957 the INS instituted the "confession program." The government promised that Chinese who had entered the U.S. with fraudulent documents (i.e., as paper families) would not be prosecuted for perjury and could readjust their immigration status if they confessed.

The proposal deeply divided the Chinese community and caused great anguish for individuals and families. Many wanted to enter the confession program so that they could legitimize their status in the U.S. and bring additional family members from China. Moreover, they felt that since they might be under investigation for fraud anyway, this would be the best route to legal residency or citizenship. Others, still wary of a government that had ignored their rights for so long, were mistrustful. With no guarantee of citizenship, they did not want to walk into a trap. But if one person confessed, that confession implicated everyone who was named as a member of that family, whether they wanted to be part of the program or not. In some cases, whole villages had to decide whether to enter the program or continue under a cloud of suspicion.

Their skepticism was not unfounded. The Department of Justice had the discretion to prosecute—for crimes other than "paper family" documents—those who exposed themselves through confession. Most of those selected for prosecution were political dissidents who supported the People's Republic of China and were targeted as Communist subversives. Thus the program of seeking confessions and naming names in the guise of enforcing immigration laws also became a political witch hunt.

The confession program ended with passage of the 1965 Immigration Act, which expanded legal immigration from Asia. But during its years of operation, 13,895 persons had confessed, exposing more than 22,000 other people who were related to them by blood or paper.

Ballot Barriers

During the second half of the twentieth century, anti-immigrant sentiment manifested in restrictive language laws passed by the electorate, the legislature, cities, and towns. Like nineteenth-century anti-Chinese ordinances, most of the laws never mentioned specific ethnic groups, but their purpose was clear.

One of the first challenges to language-restrictive policies came in reaction to a late-nineteenth-century constitutional amendment. In 1891 A. J. Bledsoe, a Republican representing Humboldt County in the California State Assembly, introduced an amendment to the state constitution requiring English literacy to vote. This was a far cry from the debates at the first constitutional convention in 1849, where delegates decided that all California laws had to be written in both English and Spanish. But the leader of the anti-Chinese purge in Eureka argued that the language restriction was necessary to protect the state from uneducated immigrants. He asserted:

> If we do not take some steps to prevent the ignorant classes, who are coming here from Europe, unloading the refuse of the world upon our shores, from exercising the right of suffrage until they have acquired knowledge of our Constitution, our system of government, and our laws, it will soon come to pass that this element will direct in our politics and our institutions will be overthrown.

By 1894 California voters had approved an amendment to the constitution denying the franchise to those who could not write their names and read the constitution in English.

More than seventy years later, two Spanish-speaking citizens challenged Bledsoe's legacy. On August 24, 1967, forty-five-year-old Jesús Parra tried to register to vote in Los Angeles. A deputy registrar denied Parra's request but, sympathetic to his problem, suggested that he seek legal help from California Rural Legal Assistance (CRLA). Attorneys from the nonprofit legal services organization, formed just two years before, represented Parra as well as thirty-eight-year-old Los Angeles resident Genoveva Castro, who had unsuccessfully tried to register to vote three times. Parra and Castro were born in the United States but educated in Mexico.

CRLA attorneys argued that both citizens were literate in Spanish and had access to Spanish-language newspapers, periodicals, radio, and television programs providing ample information about local, state, and national issues and candidates on the ballot. The English literacy requirement was therefore an unconstitutional barrier preventing them from voting.

When *Castro v. State of California* reached the California Supreme Court in 1970, Justice Raymond L. Sullivan, writing for a unanimous court, acknowledged that "fear and hatred played a significant role in the passage of the literacy requirement" but, regardless of its origin, the issue before the court was whether the state had a legitimate interest in requiring voters to prove English literacy.

The court accepted that California had a compelling interest in ensuring that the state's eligible voters were capable of making informed electoral decisions. But the justices ruled that lack of literacy in English did not translate into political ignorance, and Spanish-literate voters could gain the information they needed from Spanish language media. It would be wrong, Sullivan wrote, to exclude from the franchise a group of citizens—Mexican Americans—who could address the discrimination they faced by voting and making their political voices heard. California's English literacy requirement thus was an unconstitutional violation of the Equal Protection Clause of the Fourteenth Amendment.

Sullivan concluded the opinion with a nod to history, commenting that it would be ironic if Castro and Parra, "who are heirs of a great and gracious culture, identified with the birth of California and contributing no small measure to its growth, should be disenfranchised in their ancestral land, despite their capacity to cast an informed vote."

The *Castro* decision was limited, in that the high court did not rule on the constitutionality of literacy tests for the franchise. The justices also specifically stated that their decision did not require the state to adopt "bilingual electoral apparatus."

It would be another five years before Congress expanded the Voting Rights Act to require the use of bilingual ballots in regions with a threshold percentage of foreign-language speakers. The law impacted numerous California counties with significant numbers of voters who were entitled to receive ballots and election information in Spanish, Chinese, Tagalog, and Vietnamese.

Lau's Language

In the fall of 1969, Kam Wai Lau enrolled her only child, six-year-old Kinney, in the first grade at Jean Parker Elementary School, on the edge of San Francisco's Chinatown. Just four years earlier, Congress had reformed federal law, opening up immigration to the U.S. from China and other countries that had been limited to strict quotas. Thousands of new Chinese immigrants arrived in San Francisco. Like almost three thousand other immigrant students in the San Francisco Unified School District, Kinney spoke Chinese as his primary language.

The school district was unprepared for this dramatic demographic change. Educators simply placed Chinese-speaking students in monolingual English-speaking classes, without any plan to teach them English. Nevertheless, school officials expected the immigrant students to keep up at grade level.

Frustration built among bored and confused students and their dissatisfied parents, who, lacking English-language proficiency, could only complain among themselves and to Chinatown activists.

One of those activists was Ling-chi Wang. In the summer of 1966, Wang, an immigrant from China enrolled in a graduate program in Near Eastern Studies at the University of Chicago, accompanied his girlfriend to San Francisco to visit her family. He got a job working with immigrants from Hong Kong in a summer youth program. "None of them spoke English," he recalled. "They were not able to find jobs; they were stuck. Some of the young people were dropping out of school because the San Francisco school district was not able to deal with their English-language problems....It was very clear to me that these young people had no chance in America." By the end of that summer, Wang had decided to stay in San Francisco and transferred to UC Berkeley. He founded the Chinatown Youth Service Center to provide an alternative for children and teenagers to gangs, crime, and drugs.

In February 1970 Wang organized a community meeting with school officials to discuss the problems of young Chinese immigrants. Parents and young people jammed into the auditorium of the Commodore Stockton Elementary School in the heart of Chinatown. Wang translated the questions of angry parents, who wanted to know why their children were not being taught English or at least studying other subjects in Chinese. He also translated the answers of school administrators, including Superintendent of Schools Robert E. Jenkins, who responded that fiscal limitations prevented the district from doing more.

Tensions escalated. Several Chinese students wearing "Yellow Peril" buttons had lined the rear of the auditorium, and one of them yelled that they were "tired of hearing the same useless answers over and over again." As angry insults filled the room, a firecracker hit Jenkins's chest and slid to the floor, unexploded. A barrage of firecrackers and eggs hit the stage, compelling Wang to escort the alarmed administrators out of the auditorium through a back door.

Wang realized he needed help convincing the school board to take action. He found an ally in Edward Steinman, a young attorney in the Chinatown office of the San Francisco Neighborhood Legal Assistance Foundation, where the firebrand lawyer was looking for ways to use his newly minted law degree for social change. Steinman knew that many of his clients, including Kinney Lau's mother, were dissatisfied with the school district. He recalled that Chinatown parents bitterly joked that there *was* bilingual education in Chinatown: the teachers spoke English and the students spoke Chinese.

Steinman met with Alan Nichols, president of the school board, who told him that although he sympathized with the plight of the Chinese-speaking students, other students had more pressing problems. The school board took the position that the district had no legal obligation to address the Chinese-speaking children's needs.

Steinman thought otherwise. On March 23, 1970, he filed a class action lawsuit in federal court on behalf of Kinney Lau and nearly three thousand Chinese-speaking students in San Francisco. He argued that the federal and state constitutions guaranteed the right to an education and that the district's acceptance of federal funds compelled it to help language-minority students learn English. The trial judge, however, accepted the district's argument that no constitution or law, whether federal or state, gave students the right to bilingual education. Although the school received federal funds for a Chinese bilingual program, there wasn't enough funding to serve all Chinese-speaking children. The Ninth Circuit Court of Appeals upheld the decision, ruling that it wasn't the district's fault that some students didn't understand English. The school's responsibility, the court determined, ended with providing Chinese-speaking students the same facilities, materials, teachers, and curriculum as other students. Meanwhile, nine-year-old Kinney Lau still had no opportunity in school to learn English.

Before Steinman asked the U.S. Supreme Court to review the case, the high court issued a ruling in a Texas suit, *San Antonio School District v. Rodriguez*, stating that even though students in wealthy areas had more educational advantages than students in poorer neighborhoods, the Equal Protection Clause was not violated as long as students in low-income areas received a basic education. With this recent precedent in mind, Steinman reframed his arguments: compelling Chinese-speaking students to attend monolingual English classes effectively denied them an education. Equality of curriculum, teachers, materials, and facilities did not matter to the Chinese students if they could not understand English and were not provided an opportunity to learn the language. Not taking their language into account had the same effect as intentionally denying these students an education.

In his brief to the high court, Steinman quoted U.S. Supreme Court Justice Felix Frankfurter that there is "no greater inequality than the equal treatment of unequals." Even the school district itself had acknowledged in the district court that "the lack of English means poor performance in school. The secondary student is almost inevitably doomed to be a dropout and become another unemployable in the ghetto."

By the time the case reached the Supreme Court, the federal government had issued regulations to help ensure the rights of language-minority students. According to Title VI of the Civil Rights Act of 1964, no program receiving federal funds could discriminate on the basis of race, color, or national origin. On July 10, 1970, just after *Lau v. Nichols* was filed in district court, the federal Department of Health, Education, and Welfare issued regulations directing school districts to "take affirmative steps to rectify the language deficiency" of non-English-speaking minority students.

Recognizing that a positive Supreme Court ruling could have national impact and improve the lives of hundreds of thousands of schoolchildren whose first language was not English, civil rights organizations, such as the Mexican American Legal Defense and Educational Fund (MALDEF) and the Puerto Rican Legal Defense and Education Fund as well as the National Education Association, filed briefs in support of the Chinese-speaking children. An assistant U.S. attorney general argued that the case affected "hundreds of thousands of Spanish-speaking children" and that school districts, by accepting federal funding, were compelled to provide a meaningful education to all students.

Writing for a unanimous court, Justice William O. Douglas ruled that since California required all children between the ages of six and sixteen to attend schools in which English was the basic language of instruction, and that since all students were required to prove proficiency in English in order to graduate from high school, there was no equality of treatment "merely by providing students with the same facilities, textbooks, teachers, and curriculum." Students who did not understand English, Douglas wrote, were effectively denied a meaningful education.

Focusing on the 1964 Civil Rights Act and avoiding the constitutional equal protection argument that Steinman had raised, the Court ruled that the district had to follow federal regulations since it accepted federal funds. School officials, therefore, had to guarantee that "students of a particular race, color, or national origin were not denied the opportunity to obtain the education generally obtained by other students in the system."

By the time of the judgment, issued nearly four years after the lawsuit was filed, Kinney Lau and his mother had moved from San Francisco. He would not benefit from the case bearing his name.

The landmark opinion said nothing about *how* the San Francisco Unified School District was to teach Chinese-speaking students English, only that it had to. The high court sent the case back to the district court to work out an implementation agreement.

The school district convened a citizens' task force composed of parents representing all major language groups in San Francisco. After holding community meetings and deliberating for eight months, the task force recommended bilingual and bicultural education. This meant that students with limited or no proficiency in English would be taught English but would learn other subjects in their native languages. In addition, these students would be taught about their cultural heritages.

Faced with pressure from the U.S. Department of Justice to approve a program by the beginning of the 1975 academic year, the school board approved the recommendations.

Even though the *Lau* decision did not mandate bilingual classrooms, it contributed significantly to the expansion of bilingual education. In 1975 the Department of Health, Education, and Welfare issued guidelines, known as the Lau Remedies, that set standards for school administrators to identify children needing language help, the programs to help them, and the qualifications of teachers. Schools risked losing their federal funding if they failed to provide these students bilingual education.

The following year, the California legislature passed the Chacon-Moscone Bilingual Education Act, giving public school students the right to be taught in a language they understood. The legislation also required bilingual-bicultural education in elementary schools where at least fifteen students spoke the same primary non-English language. In 1981 the legislature strengthened the Chacon-Moscone law, expanding schools' responsibilities to students with limited proficiency in English.

That was the height of bilingual education in California. But a backlash followed.

Bilingual Backlash

In 1987 California voters passed Proposition 63, a statewide initiative amending the state constitution to declare English the state's official language. The initiative came on the heels of the Immigration Reform and Control Act of 1986, a political battleground on which anti-immigrant rhetoric rose to new heights.

In the wake of Proposition 63, state legislators proposed new laws, including a draconian measure that would have mandated all government agencies—from motor vehicle offices to welfare and rehabilitation services—to communicate solely in English. Though that bill was defeated, several municipalities passed copycat local laws.

In southern California, English-only sentiment was strong in the growing suburbs of Los Angeles, where many Asian immigrants had settled after the 1965 changes to immigration laws. Local "English-only" ordinances proliferated like strip malls.

Monterey Park, a small city east of Los Angeles, had been the destination of Mandarin-speaking immigrants from Taiwan in the 1970s and 1980s; they were later joined by new residents from Vietnam and Hong Kong. In 1990 Monterey Park had the first Asian American majority population in the United States. Yet the newcomers were not always welcome, and Monterey Park became one of the first municipalities to pass an English-only law. One city councilwoman declared, "This is not a Chinese town. Why should Monterey Park be called the Chinese Beverly Hills?"

Nativist sentiment grew so virulent that modern-day vigilantes prowled Chinese neighborhoods in the dark of night, planting signs that read, "Will the last American to leave Monterey Park please bring the American flag?"

The city of Pomona, also in Los Angeles County, had quite a different profile. The fifth largest city in the county, its early growth was propelled by a prosperous citrus industry. By the late 1980s, its Asian population was still relatively small; yet in November 1988 Pomona passed an ordinance stating that at least half of any business sign with "foreign alphabetical characters" must be in "English alphabetical characters." The ordinance did not forbid signs in foreign languages per se, but prohibited signs that did not use the English alphabet. Therefore, signs entirely in Spanish or French would not be banned, while signs containing over 50 percent text in characters or script of Asian languages would not be allowed. It was a clear signal to the Asian community that their languages and cultures were not welcome in Pomona.

Though the ordinance was passed in the guise of a public safety measure—so police and emergency personnel could locate trouble spots—a memo from a city council member revealed a different motivation. It stated:

> Because of the liberalization of immigration policies, a heavy influx of Asian/Orientals have taken up residence in the United States, many of them in California. Their natural entrepreneurship has directed many of them into business ownership in many California cities, and those cities have been impacted by a proliferation of advertising and signs which consist of oriental characters. That practice has caused dissent and strife in some communities.
>
> In order to prevent the introduction of both racial and ethnic strife in our city, it is recommended that the City Council, by ordinance, require all signs to be in the English language, permitting only subtitles and explanatory language to be in foreign characters.

Conspicuously lacking in the legislative history was evidence of a real safety problem resulting from foreign-language signs. The city did not enact the ordinance at the request of the fire or police chief, or to address any other public safety problem. In fact, businesses were already required to post their addresses in Arabic numerals and the English alphabet, thereby making their locations easy for firefighters or police officers to find.

The Asian American Business Group challenged the ordinance, arguing that it not only violated the federal Equal Protection Clause, but also the constitutional right of free expression. Courts have ruled that some First Amendment protections must be afforded to commercial speech. While foreign-language business signs are a form of advertising, they are also a form of cultural expression.

U.S. District Court Judge Robert Takasugi agreed. He ruled on July 14, 1989, that the Pomona ordinance was an unconstitutional infringement on freedom of speech, stating:

> Since the language used is an expression of national origin, culture, and ethnicity, regulation of the sign language is regulation of content. A person's primary language is an important part of, and flows from, his/her national origin. Choice of language is a form of expression as real as the textual message conveyed. It is an expression of culture.

Judge Takasugi's ruling sent a message that local governments should not try to curtail the free speech and cultural expression of immigrant communities.

Ballot Language

A quarter-century after the landmark *Lau* decision, a wealthy Silicon Valley businessman qualified an initiative for the California ballot that threatened bilingual education in the state's public schools. Ron Unz publicly admitted that he had never set foot in a bilingual education classroom, yet his "English for the Children" ballot measure would impact more than one million California public school students with limited English proficiency.

The multimillionaire conceived of, financed, and directed the campaign to put Proposition 227 on the June 1998 ballot. The Unz initiative proposed to eliminate all bilingual education programs in more than one thousand school districts. Instead, students who could not speak English would be isolated and educated for one year in an English immersion program and then transferred into mainstream classrooms. The initiative would amend the state Education Code to take instruction out of the hands of local school districts, teachers, bilingual educators, and parents and force a "one size fits all" program on every public school in California.

Moreover, teachers who violated the initiative's requirement that instruction be "overwhelmingly in English" could be sued and held personally liable for financial damages.

Unz did not base his proposition on any scientific study of English-language acquisition, nor did he consult with expert educators who had studied the issue for decades. If he had, the initiative would have looked very different, as most bilingual educators agree that proficiency in a second language takes four to seven years.

Instead Unz based his initiative on what he perceived as widespread dissatisfaction with the school system. California, which during the postwar period had topped the nation in education spending and academic achievement, had by the mid-1990s dropped to forty-first in pupil spending. Reading and math scores were among the lowest in the country. Enrollment of Limited English Proficiency (LEP) students had doubled over the previous decade to 1.4 million; a third of first graders knew little or no English.

Dr. Laurie Olsen, who co-chaired Citizens for an Educated America, which opposed the initiative, warned that though Unz tried to distance himself from the nativist sentiment that created a groundswell of support for Proposition 227, supporters of the measure held a "reservoir of anger, distrust, and even hate focused on bilingual education, bilingual educators, and immigrants—particularly Spanish-speaking immigrants."

Olsen noted, "The sense that upholding English as the language of this nation is a stance of protecting a way of life—this outweighed every argument we could wage to try to defeat 227. This is what we were up against."

Proposition 227 passed overwhelmingly, with 61 percent of the vote.

The following day, students and parents filed a class action lawsuit, *Valeria G. v. Wilson*, in U.S. district court to block its implementation. Plaintiff Juana Flores, the parent of two daughters enrolled in bilingual classes in San Francisco schools, said through a translator, "Although I do not speak English well, I have been able to help my children with school. As parents, the more we are involved, the more children are going to see that education is important. If they take away bilingual education, they are going to take away our communication with the teachers, and we will no longer feel welcome at the schools, nor will we be able to participate in the school community."

Judge Charles Legge denied the request for an injunction, rejecting the parents' claim that the law prevented the school districts from complying with their obligations under the Equal Educational Opportunities Act and the Bilingual Education Act of 1974 (the law passed to implement *Lau*). The state began to implement the provisions of the new law the following month.

Ted Wang, an attorney with Chinese for Affirmative Action, which had helped bring the *Lau* case a quarter-century earlier, charged that "Proposition 227 set back education in California twenty-five years."

On the Ballot and the Border: No Safe Haven

> Guillermo Osorio López, 25, hypothermia, Pine Valley
> Evedo Osorio López, 19, hypothermia, Pine Valley
> Raul González Cruz, 29, hypothermia, Mount Laguna
> Pedro Orozco Gómez, 16, heat stress, Winterhaven

These are the names of just four of the hundreds of people who died in the first few years of Operation Gatekeeper. Their bodies were found in the scorched desert and frozen mountain passes between San Ysidro and Otay Mesa, along California's southern border.

The federal program started on October 1, 1994—just one month before Californians voted on Proposition 187, a ballot initiative to deny all education, health, and public services to undocumented immigrants. Both Operation Gatekeeper and Proposition 187 were political responses to the rabid anti-immigrant sentiment that proliferated in California in the 1980s and 1990s. And they both had dangerous—even deadly—consequences.

To understand the origins of these measures, it helps to look at southern California's recent history. The defense and aerospace industries there were particularly hard hit by the post–Cold War economic decline of the 1990s, and politicians sought scapegoats for the state's economic woes. California's demographics were dramatically shifting, as federal laws allowed for increased immigration from Latin America and Asia, as well as for the legalization of a large number of undocumented workers already in the United States.

The first California metropolis north of the Mexican border is San Diego, a city that underwent enormous growth after World War II, sprawling into suburbs and almost doubling in population. The city's economy was largely based on the defense industry and military bases. One of San Diego's mayors during its growth period was Republican Pete Wilson, who went on to become a U.S. senator and later governor of California. His base was in wealthy, white, Republican areas, and his political instincts were shaped by the polarized coexistence of the San Diego area's white, middle-class suburbs and the poor, largely Latino neighborhoods. The San Diego edition of the *Los Angeles Times* described northern San Diego County in 1988 as "a land unlike any other along the US-Mexico border…A place where squalid, plywood-and-cardboard shacks sit in the shadow of $1 million mansions, where the BMW and Volvo set rubs elbows at the supermarket with the dusty migrants fresh from the fields, where haves run routinely head-on into the have nots."

San Diego lies only a few miles north of San Ysidro, one of the most traveled crossings on the border. Delineated by the INS as the San Diego–Tijuana sector, it was one of the most porous areas of the border in the 1980s and early 1990s. A fence stretched about a mile from the port of entry, but it was in disrepair, with holes in some places big enough to drive a vehicle through. Throughout the day Mexicans gathered on the Tijuana side and waited for nightfall, when they would make their way to jobs in California's fields, factories, and restaurants. Some would tend the gardens, kitchens, and children of San Diego County's suburbanites.

The historian Oscar Martinez wrote, "Borders simultaneously divide and unite, repel and attract, separate and integrate." Nowhere is this more true than the fence that divides the U.S. and Mexico at the San Diego–Tijuana sector. As the *Los Angeles Times* described it:

> Until 1994, the San Diego sector commonly fielded fewer than one hundred Border Patrol agents per shift against several thousand border crossers lining the riverbanks and canyons. The sector recorded as many as three thousand arrests on busy Sundays. Every night was a potential riot, a journey into the battle theater of the absurd….Agents routinely used their vehicles to herd back crowds, speeding at them, churning up clouds of dust.

The border fence dividing the U.S. and Mexico became a focus of anti-immigrant forces in the 1990s. Under Operation Gatekeeper, the Clinton administration reinforced the fence with high-security cameras and sensors and beefed up the Border Patrol, making it the nation's largest law enforcement agency.

San Ysidro was also the site of what the INS called "banzai runs." In 1992 smugglers, known as *coyotes* or *polleros,* initiated risky methods to get their charges across the border. They would bring fifty or more migrants to the shoulder of the highway in San Ysidro and at a given moment orchestrate their run onto the freeway into southbound lanes. The migrants would weave in and out of heavy traffic, surprising and overwhelming the Border Patrol officers. The *coyotes* counted on most of the migrants getting through and running into the busy streets of San Ysidro, and then on to jobs in the strawberry fields in the Santa Maria Valley or the restaurant kitchens of Los Angeles.

In response to this wave of immigrants, new anti-immigrant organizations sprang up. Some were blatantly racist, like the White Aryan Resistance; others were milder in their approach but still took a nativist stance, like Americans for Border Control, which called for more armed guards, more fences, and citizen patrols on the border to keep out "the flood of illegals." Harold Ezell, while still serving as the INS western regional commissioner, founded the organization, stating, "Our borders are, indeed, out of control." Candidates for public office found they could get great mileage among white voters by echoing Ezell's charge.

In a 1991 *Time* magazine interview, Pete Wilson, by now the recently elected governor, blamed California's budget crisis (which had reached a deficit of $12.6 billion) on immigration. He claimed that California's generous welfare system served as a magnet for the undocumented, who were bankrupting the state.

In the summer of 1993, Wilson took out a full-page ad in the *New York Times* and other papers, framed as an open letter to President Clinton from the "People of California." It read, "Massive illegal immigration will continue as long as the federal government continues to reward it. Why even have a Border Patrol and INS if we are going to continue the insanity of providing incentives to illegal immigrants to violate US immigration laws?"

Wilson was not the only high-level politician to jump on the anti-immigrant bandwagon. In 1993 lawmakers from both parties in the California legislature introduced forty measures to deal with immigration. Even liberal Democratic Senator Barbara Boxer proposed posting the National Guard at the border.

The rhetoric worked. An August 1993 Field Poll showed that 74 percent of California's voters were convinced that illegal immigration was hurting the state.

In 1994 the xenophobia crystallized into Proposition 187, put on the ballot by a coalition of anti-immigrant groups called "Save Our State." The law would require state workers to deny help to anyone they knew or "reasonably suspected" of being "an alien in the U.S. in violation of federal law."

The measure had far-reaching implications. It proposed to exclude undocumented children from public schools, as well as state colleges and universities. It would deny undocumented families health care. It would prevent hungry families from getting any kind of public support.

"This law would turn teachers, doctors, and social workers into Border Patrol agents," charged Maria Blanco of MALDEF. But Pete Wilson, hoping that Proposition 187 would make him a contender for a future Republican presidential nomination, became its biggest booster. The centerpiece of his campaign, a TV ad, featured footage provided by the Border Patrol of Mexicans dashing across the border into the heavy traffic at San Ysidro. A narrator intoned, "They keep coming. Two million illegal immigrants in California. The federal government won't stop them at the border, yet requires us to pay billions to take care of them. Governor Wilson sent the National Guard to help the Border Patrol. But that's not all..."

At that point Governor Wilson appeared on screen, pledging to help "Californians who work hard, pay taxes, and obey the law."

The fight against the initiative was formidable. Immigrants' rights groups, civil rights organizations, and labor unions whose members were in the public sector (like the California Teachers Association, the Service Employees International Union, and the California Nurses Association) led an impassioned grassroots campaign against Proposition

187. Young people rallied, and high school students in major cities and rural areas staged walkouts. The Latino immigrant community mobilized with great fervor, registering new citizens to vote and conducting intensive voter education campaigns.

But it was not enough.

The initiative passed with nearly two-thirds of the vote, sending shock waves throughout the state—and all the way to Washington.

The day the election results were announced, civil rights groups filed suit in state court to block the education aspects of the proposition, and in federal court to challenge the health-care and social-services provisions and all other aspects of the initiative. The lawsuit charged that a state could not pass a law about immigration, which is governed by federal law. Judges in both lawsuits issued preliminary injunctions barring implementation of the law. Proposition 187 never went into effect because Gray Davis, Wilson's successor as governor, did not pursue the state's defense of the law.

Across the country, in Washington, DC, the popularity of Proposition 187 greatly concerned the Clinton administration. Buffeted by Republicans, and pressured by his own party's leaders in California to do something visible about illegal immigration, President Clinton included a massive infusion of funds for the Border Patrol in the 1994 Crime Act. The Border Patrol became the largest police force in the United States.

But the president needed a more powerful, high-profile effort to keep the Republicans from winning the political border wars.

Thus, Operation Gatekeeper was born. Phase I was launched a month before the November 1994 election. The timing was paradoxical. Both Clinton and Mexican President Raul Salinas had pushed hard for the North

Berkeley High School students were among the many who marched to oppose the xenophobic 1994 ballot measure Proposition 187, which would have turned teachers, doctors, and social workers into de facto Border Patrol agents. Backed by Governor Pete Wilson, the measure passed but was successfully challenged in federal court and never went into effect.

American Free Trade Agreement (NAFTA), and both governments lauded its imple-mentation in 1994. Immediately, commercial traffic across the border increased by 170 percent. The frantic, unrelenting political demand for more fences and armed guards at the border created a dilemma for Clinton. In its 1994 report, "Accepting the Immigration Challenge," his administration noted that "efforts to facilitate travel across the U.S.–Mexico border as part of NAFTA may conflict with the need to estab-lish closer controls on cross-border traffic to enforce immigration laws."

According to the INS, the goal of Operation Gatekeeper was to "restore integrity to the nation's busiest border." However, according to Claudia Smith, an attorney with the California Rural Legal Assistance Foundation (CRLA) who monitored abuse on the border, the goal was to move the problem out of public view. Using military tech-nology, the INS beefed up the border's infrastructure with blinding, stadium-style lights, infrared night scopes, high-powered vehicles, and helicopters. Border Patrol agents were provided with IDENT, a state-of-the-art computerized ID system, to keep a massive data bank of border crossers. And for photo opportunities, the agency built a brand-new, thirty-mile fence.

The program was designed to move the flow of immigrants away from the heav-ily populated San Diego area. The INS theorized that once the usual crossings were impenetrable, migrants would stop going across the border.

It did not work out that way. The same number of people crossed, but they tra-versed more isolated, more dangerous areas.

The program took its toll in migrant deaths. From 1994 to 2000, there were 305 deaths due to hypothermia, dehydration, and heat stroke; 175 deaths from drowning; 123 accidents (from vehicles and other hazards); and 14 reported homicides. Claudia Smith predicted, "As long as the strategy is to maximize the dangers by moving the migrant foot traffic out of the urban areas and into the mountains and deserts east of San Diego, the deaths will keep multiplying."

Because they were forced into unfamiliar and more dangerous terrain, border crossers had to hire smugglers, whose prices increased from about three hundred dol-lars to upwards of twelve hundred. In addition, because migrants ended up far from any city or transportation, they often had to pay several hundred more to a *raitero*, a smuggler who specialized in taking people from a remote area of the desert to a city where they could find work. The *coyotes* also devised new methods, including digging tunnels under the celebrated border fence and cramming passengers into the parade of NAFTA-generated semis streaming across the border day and night.

John Williams, chief for the San Diego sector of the INS, called Operation Gate-keeper "probably the single largest accomplishment in the Border Patrol's history." Yet as the number of apprehensions in San Ysidro dropped (from 46 percent of total apprehensions to 26 percent in 1998), the number in the eastern sections of California and beyond increased proportionately. All academic and government studies—including one by the federal government's General Accounting Office—agreed that the number of migrant workers on the U.S. side of the border did not decrease. The elevated danger and cost of border crossing were so onerous that many workers just stayed put in the U.S.

In the names of the Osorio López brothers, Raul Cruz, and sixteen-year-old Pedro Gómez—the young men who died crossing the border—CRLA attorney Smith and others filed a petition before the Inter-American Commission on Human Rights in 1999. The petition was eventually deemed inadmissible. From the inception of Operation Gatekeeper in 1994 to 2006, about three thousand migrants had died trying to cross the border, 472 in 2005 alone.

Most of their names are unknown.

— THREE —
AN INJURY TO ALL
THE RIGHTS OF WORKERS

"The working class and the employing class have nothing in common."
—Industrial Workers of the World mission statement, 1905

Allah-u Akbar! Allah-u Akbar! As the mourners snaked through the dusty roads between the vineyards of Delano, the sorrowful Muslim prayer rang out into the shimmering sunlight. The casket was draped with the red-and-black flag of the United Farm Workers (UFW). The thousands of marchers walking behind the coffin carried the UFW flag, banners with images of the Virgin of Guadalupe and Emiliano Zapata, rosaries, and guitars. They were farmworkers whose hands were calloused and torn from picking grapes, young Chicano students from UCLA and Berkeley, and national labor leaders from the AFL-CIO and the United Auto Workers.

The funeral procession made its way to Forty Acres, the UFW compound outside Delano, to bury twenty-four-year-old Nagi Daifullah, a Yemeni farmworker whose skull had been crushed by a blow from a Kern County sheriff.

Two days after Daifullah's funeral, sixty-year-old Juan de la Cruz was shot to death while walking a picket line in the same dusty vineyards.

This was the emerging face of the labor movement in California in 1973. The poorest workers—migrant farmworkers—were fighting against conditions that were familiar to generations of California laborers: starvation wages, unsafe conditions, child labor, and arbitrary hiring and firing. They were fighting with tools that were familiar, too: picket lines, boycotts, rallies, and marches. And they were subjected to the same tactics that had been used to suppress other workers: firing and blacklisting

UFW member Nagi Daifullah, a Yemeni immigrant, was killed by a deputy sheriff during the 1973 grape strike. His funeral procession, led by (left to right) Cesar Chavez, Congressman Don Edwards, and Dolores Huerta, wound through the dusty vineyards with images of the union eagle, the Virgin of Guadalupe, and former Egyptian president Gamel Nasser, a hero to Arab workers.

of union organizers, eviction from company-owned housing, assaults, arrests, jailing, and even murder.

They found solidarity among workers of all races. A 1965 grape strike, started by Filipino workers in the Agricultural Workers Organizing Committee, was joined within weeks by Mexican grape pickers affiliated with the National Farm Workers Association. They enlisted white, black, and Native American workers to *La Huelga* (the strike) and eventually the two unions merged into the United Farm Workers. When the growers brought in scabs from Texas, Mexico, and as far away as Yemen, the UFW organized the strikebreakers too. As UFW President Cesar Chavez said:

> The UFW is first and foremost a union. A union like any other union. A union that either produces for its members on the bread and butter issues or doesn't survive. But the UFW has always been something more than a union—we attacked that historical source of shame and infamy that our people in this country lived with. We attacked that injustice. And by addressing this historical problem, we created confidence and pride and hope in an entire people's ability to create the future.

The union movement in California had come full circle. The UFW melded the activism of the early days of the Industrial Workers of the World—when the workers' rights movement was a vehicle for the fight for freedom of speech and association—with the struggles of the first trade unions over working conditions and wages.

Though California's first workers' strike took place before statehood, by the early twentieth century employers had lobbied for, and local governments and the state legislature had enacted, laws tempering workers' power. Hoping to thwart the growth of unions, business leaders convinced the legislature to pass criminal trespass and vagrancy laws, which they used as tools against labor organizers; a law mandating "open shops," in which workers could not be required to be members of unions, provided easy access to strikebreakers. Employers also used criminal syndicalism laws and anti-picketing laws to thwart organizing efforts for decent wages and working conditions. In time, these regulations, ordinances, and statutes would be used against others as well: anarchists, socialists, and political dissidents of all kinds, peaceful protestors, and the poor and homeless.

Conversely, the labor movement's advocacy resulted in many laws that not only improved working conditions but benefited all Californians by guaranteeing freedom of speech in public places, freedom of association, due process, and the privacy rights of members of disfavored organizations.

The Wobblies: The Street Corner Is Our Union Hall

The first organization to connect the fight for civil liberties and the rights of organized labor, the Industrial Workers of the World—known as the IWW or the Wobblies—operated outside mainstream trade unions.

The origin of the nickname "Wobbly" is unclear. Some say it refers to a commonly used tool known as a "wobble saw," while others believe it was derived from a Scandinavian immigrant's mispronunciation of "IWW" as "eye-wobble-you-wobble-you." Whatever its origin, the sobriquet, first used in print by Harrison Gray Otis, the vehemently anti-labor publisher of the *Los Angeles Times*, stuck.

The IWW was founded in Chicago in 1905 by national figures including Eugene Debs of the Socialist Party, William D. "Big Bill" Haywood of the Western Federation of Miners, Joe Hill, and Mary Harris Jones, popularly known as Mother Jones. These militant organizers viewed the American Federation of Labor (AFL) unions as too narrow and tradition-bound to address the needs of the common worker. The IWW called for the formation of "one big union" dedicated to the "historic mission of the working class to do away with capitalism." Their statement of purpose declared:

> The working class and the employing class have nothing in common. There can be no peace so long as hunger and want are found among millions of the working people and the few, who make up the employing class, have all the good things of life. Between these two classes a struggle must go on until the workers of the world organize as a class, take possession of the means of production, abolish the wage system, and live in harmony with the Earth.

The Industrial Workers of the World, or Wobblies, fought for fair working conditions and free speech, organizing street-corner orations that were often broken up by law enforcement. As the initial speakers were arrested, many more came to take their places. IWW members filled jails from Fresno to San Diego.

The IWW distinguished itself from many AFL locals that banned Asian and Mexican members, inviting workers of all races, nationalities, and creeds to join. Many members of the IWW were immigrants from Mexico, China, Scandinavia, Ireland, Italy, and elsewhere.

The Wobblies who organized in California were from the "direct action," or "anarcho-syndicalist" wing of the IWW. They advocated strikes, demonstrations, and street-corner oratory, rather than participation in the electoral process. This may have been because many members of the western Wobblies could not vote: as migrant workers, they did not meet residency requirements, and many were not citizens.

The Wobblies found fertile ground among agricultural, dock, and railway workers in California. They were particularly successful among unskilled seasonal laborers, and many of their earliest members were Mexican farmworkers. By 1909 they had formed twenty locals in the state, from Sacramento in the north to Brawley in the south.

The IWW fought for free speech so its members could secure a public platform for attracting workers. "The street corner was our only union hall," one organizer explained.

Wobbly campaigns started with a worker standing on a street corner to speak, denouncing the greed of the bosses and exhorting the workers to unite and take action. When the first worker was arrested and taken to jail, another took his place. When that worker was arrested, another stepped up, and so on—until the jail cells were filled. When all the local members were arrested, the *Industrial Worker*, the IWW newspaper, summoned more workers from neighboring states to join them. Each man would demand a jury trial, further gumming up the works of the town judicial machinery, until free speech rights were acknowledged and the organizers let out of jail.

This tactic had been widely used in Washington, Oregon, and Montana, but organizers were unsure it would work in California. Though both the 1849 and 1879 California constitutions guaranteed the right of free speech, the 1909 California Supreme Court ruling in *In re May Thomas*, which upheld a Los Angeles anti-street-speaking ordinance, threatened to silence Wobblies who tested their rights in the Golden State.

This did not deter them. In 1910 the IWW took its street-corner campaign right to the center of the conservative San Joaquin Valley.

The city of Fresno was founded in 1872 as a station along the Southern Pacific Railway. By 1910 it was the seat of Fresno County and the financial and civic center of the agricultural San Joaquin Valley, with a population of twenty-five thousand.

The IWW chapter in Fresno, Local 66, was founded by Frank Little, self-described as "part American Indian, part hard-rock miner, part hobo." The chapter, largely composed of Mexican migrant farm and railway workers, held meetings above the Cosmopolitan Restaurant on Mariposa Street.

This militant, fast-growing chapter upset the city fathers, who preferred dealing with the "businesslike" AFL. Egged on by Chester H. Rowell, publisher of the *Fresno Morning Republican*, employers denounced the organization, claiming the initials IWW stood for "I Won't Work."

The local AFL also distrusted the Wobblies and their efforts to organize Mexican and Chinese workers, who were explicitly excluded from the traditional all-white craft union locals. In addition, the AFL was protective of its turf and did not appreciate competition from the upstart IWW.

In May 1910, Elmer Shean, a Wobbly free speech advocate and boilermaker, was arrested while speaking on the corner of Tulare and F Streets and charged with vagrancy. The police revoked the IWW's permit to hold street meetings and threatened to arrest any man without a job on vagrancy charges.

The Wobblies called a series of mass meetings in protest, and in August, Frank Little and his brother W. F. were arrested in front of the Fresno Beer Hall and thrown in jail for disturbing the peace.

Their arrests threw the IWW into action. *The Industrial Worker* put out the call: "All Aboard for Fresno! Free Speech Fight On!" A later edition exhorted, "We have got to win the streets of Fresno, we have got to show the Bosses that we mean business and unless we make it stick in the Raisin City, we are going to have trouble in other California towns." Men from as far away as Spokane, Portland, and St. Louis rode the rails to the sleepy Valley town to protect the right of free speech.

The *Fresno Morning Republican* said that if the IWW wanted a war, the city would be happy to oblige. Its rival paper, the *Fresno Evening Herald and Democrat*, declared, "For men to come here with the express purpose of creating trouble, a whipping post and cat-o'-nine tails well seasoned by being soaked in salt water is none too harsh a treatment for peace breakers." The AFL joined the fray, barring the Wobblies from the Labor Day picnic at Zapp's Park because the IWW wanted to carry red flags instead of Old Glory.

Almost as soon as Little was released from jail, he and a dozen other Wobblies were again arrested at their street-corner union hall for speaking without a permit. The city barred the IWW from meeting inside city limits, so the union relocated to a large rented tent at Palm and Belmont, just outside the city. As each wave of Wobblies rode into Fresno to give their street-corner orations, the police arrested them en masse.

The new trials began on December 8, and Frank Little was first on the docket. He conducted his own defense. The Wobbly leader dropped a bombshell: they couldn't arrest him for the crime of public speaking because the city had no law against public speaking.

Police Chief William Shaw was flabbergasted. The judge was, as well. But after his clerks researched seven volumes of Fresno city ordinances, the judge was forced to release Little and his twenty-five IWW comrades; the police chief instructed his officers that they could no longer arrest IWW members for public speaking.

The next night a lynch mob, frustrated by the verdict, descended on the jail. Though the deputies would not allow them to reach the Wobblies still behind bars, the vigilantes beat up IWW members who were visiting their comrades. The vigilantes then marched on the tent that was serving as the Wobblies' temporary headquarters, burned it to the ground, and brutally assaulted the IWW members assembled there. Police Chief Shaw let the mob have its way, claiming that since the tent was outside city limits he had no jurisdiction to stop the violence.

To ensure that they would have the law on their side for the next set of trials, on December 20, the city Board of Trustees unanimously approved the new law criminalizing public speeches, lectures, debates, or discussions in any public park, street, or alley within a forty-eight-block area.

The Wobblies found an unlikely ally in opposing the new ordinance. Local ministers realized that the new law did not exempt public Christian sermons—and that they were covered by the same prohibition as the godless radical union organizers!

Confidently, the Wobbly orators continued their street-corner protests, and the jails began to fill again. As they were booked, they gave the police aliases like Harrison Gray Otis, John L. Sullivan (the heavyweight boxing champion), and the ubiquitous

John Doe. By February 1911 one hundred men were inside the cramped jail. One evening as they protested loudly from inside the jail, shouting and singing labor songs, the jailer called out fire engines to subdue the crowd. The jailed Wobblies were hosed full force until the freezing water reached knee level.

Their treatment brought more Wobblies from Chicago, Denver, and St. Louis. In an attempt to avoid the railroad police, one group of Wobblies jumped from the train at the California border, crossing the Siskiyou Mountains on foot in a snowstorm. The determined band of workers trudged through Weed, Dunsmuir, Kent, and Red Bluff and were proceeding on to Chico when unexpected news arrived.

On March 2, 1911, fearing an invasion of the "hobo army," Fresno town fathers rescinded the ban on street speaking and released all of the remaining Wobbly inmates. A Wobbly leader sent a wire to the IWW headquarters in Chicago: "Complete Victory!"

Today, at the corner of Mariposa and I Streets, California Registered Landmark No. 873 commemorates "the first free speech fight in California and the first attempt at organizing the Valley's unskilled workers."

Turmoil among the Palms

The Wobblies occupied even less likely terrain in 1912, when the struggle moved to San Diego. By the turn of the century, the city of forty thousand was on the brink of an economic boom, with the chamber of commerce advertising for home buyers, businessmen, and workers. The San Diego Federated Trades and Labor Council, founded in 1891, organized workers in cigar factories, bakeries, and fisheries.

The prosperous enclave, fringed by palm trees and aqua waters, seemed an improbable battleground for the IWW. As legendary Wobbly Joe Hill put it, "There is much too much energy going to waste organizing locals in 'jerkwater towns' of no industrial importance. A town like San Diego for instance where the main 'industry' consists of 'catching suckers' is not worth a whoop in Hell from a rebel's point of view."

And yet a battleground it became.

San Diego IWW Local 245 was headquartered at 752 Fifth Avenue and met every Friday night at eight o'clock. They held rallies in downtown San Diego's Soapbox Row, on E Street between Fourth and Fifth Avenues. The union won a strike of mostly Mexican workers at the Consolidated Gas and Electric Company, securing union recognition and a raise to $2.25 a day. To the union's misfortune, the local lost members when many workers left to join the Mexican Revolution.

Some historians credit the proximity of the Mexican Revolution—both geographically and politically—with making San Diego the most vicious of the California free speech battlegrounds. A revolutionary movement in Baja California, led by brothers Ricardo and Enrique Flores Magón, peaked in early 1911 when the Magóns took control of the border town of Tijuana. When the Mexican *federales* retook Tijuana in June 1911, they chased many of the rebels across the U.S. border. The transplanted veterans of the Mexican Revolution found a new home in the San Diego IWW, and the chapter's anticapitalist rhetoric rose to a new level.

The city's elite feared that revolutionary turmoil across the border might threaten their balmy, prosperous enclave. Like their counterparts in Fresno, merchants and property owners petitioned the city council to ban street speaking in the downtown area as "a nuisance and detriment to the welfare of our city."

The merchants were whipped up in their anti-IWW fervor by a November 1911 visit from *Los Angeles Times* publisher Harrison Gray Otis, who joined the call for a ban on public speaking. In addition to his general anti-union vehemence, Otis owned land in Baja and did not want to lose it to the Mexican rebels. John D. Spreckels, the sugar baron who owned the *San Diego Union* and the *Evening Tribune*, feared the IWW would disrupt his plans for a railroad line to Yuma through Baja California.

On January 8, 1912, the council passed an ordinance restricting speech in forty-six square blocks in the center of town—including Soapbox Row—"for the immediate preservation of the public peace." Violation of the ordinance was punishable by thirty days in jail, a fine up to one hundred dollars, or both.

A diverse group of residents opposed the ordinance. Calling themselves the California Free Speech League, they enlisted church leaders, lawyers, and Socialists. The league called a demonstration for the evening of February 8, drawing an estimated five thousand.

But the protest quickly ended when the police moved in. Forty-one people, including three women, were arrested and jailed. Police Chief Keno Wilson proclaimed, "All these men have violated some law, whether they are street speakers or not, of that I am sure. So I am going to charge some with disturbing the peace and others with offenses which I shall figure out tomorrow."

The next day, scores more were arrested. The jail was bursting. Many were forced to sleep on concrete floors and subjected to police beatings when they complained. The protests continued for weeks. By March, the city and county jails were so crowded that some prisoners were transferred to Orange County. "They are singing all the time, and yelling and hollering, and telling the jailers to quit work and join the union. They are worse than animals," Chief Wilson complained.

Again, the Wobblies put out a call for supporters in the *Industrial Worker.* "On to California. Flood the jails of the Pacific Coast with unemployed. Come on the cushions; ride up on the top; stick to the brake beams; let nothing stop. Come in great numbers; this we beseech. Help San Diego win free speech." An estimated five thousand from across the country heeded the call.

Chief Wilson sent police to Sorrento, a railroad stop north of San Diego, with orders to arrest "all male vagrants and hoboes." The county board of supervisors even sent a mounted patrol to the county line to stop men who attempted to enter.

At the county line, vigilantes met the new arrivals with pickaxes, revolvers, blackjacks, and whips and forced them to sing "The Star-Spangled Banner" as they marched them to a cattle pen in San Onofre.

Backed by business interests, the vigilantes were formally organized into the Committee of 1000, dedicated to helping the police protect the city from the IWW. They published a warning letter in the *San Diego Union*:

> We the law abiding citizens of the commonwealth think that these anarchists have gone far enough and we propose to keep up the deportation of these undesirable citizens as fast as we can catch them, and that hereafter they will not only be carried to the county line and dumped there, but we intend to leave our mark on them in the shape of tar rubbed into their hair and that a shave will be necessary to remove it and this is what these agitators (all of them) may expect from now on, that the outside world may know that they have been to San Diego.

The editor of the liberal *San Diego Herald*, Abram R. Sauer, charged that the vigilante group included "not only bankers and merchants but leading church members and bartenders. The chamber of commerce and the real estate board are well represented. The press and public utility corporations, as well as members of the Grand Jury are known to belong."

Sauer was correct that the vigilantes had plenty of support in high places. The merchants' association and the chamber of commerce passed a resolution praising the actions of the Committee of 1000 in chasing the Wobblies out of San Diego.

The *San Diego Evening Tribune* editorialized: "Hanging is none too good for them and they would be much better dead; for they are absolutely useless in the human economy. They are the waste material of creation and should be drained off in the sewer of oblivion there to rot in cold obstruction like any other excrement."

With this encouragement from city officials and the press, the vigilantes stepped up their assaults. They kidnapped men out of the jail in the middle of the night and dropped them at the county line, where they were beaten and ordered never to return. The vigilantes also met trains coming south and dragged men out of the rail cars. As one Wobbly recalled:

> The moon was shining dimly through the clouds and I could see pick handles, ax handles, wagon spokes and every kind of club imaginable swinging

89

from the wrists of all of them while they also had their rifles leveled at us....They then closed in around the flat car which we were on and began clubbing and knocking and pulling men off by their heels....Afterwards there was a lot of our men unaccounted for and never have been heard from since. The vigilantes all wore constable badges and a white handkerchief around their left arms. They were drunk and hollering and cursing the rest of the night....We were forced to kiss the flag, and run a gauntlet. They broke one man's leg and everyone was beaten black and blue, and was bleeding from a dozen wounds.

The California Free Speech League publicized the assaults, generating widespread protests around the state. AFL locals in Los Angeles and San Francisco came to the support of the IWW, demanding an end to police violence. Anarchist leaders Emma Goldman and Ben Reitman went to San Diego. Goldman was on a national speaking tour and was anxious to address San Diego's labor militants. But as Reitman waited in the Hotel Montezuma for Goldman to begin her lecture, a group of vigilantes kidnapped him.

As soon as they crossed the city limits, his abductors started kicking and beating him. "'We could tear your guts out, but we promised the Chief of Police not to kill you,' they told me," Reitman later reported.

They stripped Reitman naked and with a lit cigar burned the letters IWW on his buttocks. They tarred him and, lacking feathers, rubbed sagebrush on his body. "One of them attempted to push a cane in my rectum. Another twisted my testicles. They forced me to kiss the flag and sing 'The Star-Spangled Banner,'" Reitman recalled.

Somehow Reitman got a message to Goldman, who quickly cancelled her talk and rushed to the train station. Vigilantes were waiting there for her. The train crew protected Goldman by refusing to allow the men on the train, and she made her way safely back to Los Angeles.

The attack on Reitman was so severe that Governor Hiram Johnson sent Attorney General Ulysses S. Webb to launch an official investigation, which quelled the vigilante activity. By the summer of 1914, the IWW was once again allowed to hold street meetings without police interference. In 1915 Emma Goldman returned to the city at the invitation of a liberal intellectual group, Open Forum. Her lecture on "The Enemy of the People" was received without incident. George Edwards, a member of Open Forum, remarked, "At last there is free speech in San Diego."

Publisher Otis's Open Shop

In the fall of 1910, Harrison Gray Otis sat behind his mahogany desk in the executive suite of the *Los Angeles Times* headquarters at First Street and Broadway in downtown Los Angeles and surveyed the city.

As publisher and editor of the largest news daily on the West Coast, and with massive real estate holdings in both California and Mexico, Otis sat at the apex of the Merchants and Manufacturers Association (M&M), a group of businessmen that held sway over the rapidly growing economy of southern California at the turn of the century. The city was renowned as the center of California's boom in agriculture, manufacturing, and real estate. To consolidate his leadership, Otis founded the Los Angeles Chamber of Commerce, whose goal was to attract new businesses, home buyers, and of course, workers to keep the wheels of industry turning.

Los Angeles, once a sleepy backwater overshadowed by San Francisco, had grown dramatically. At the turn of the century its population had reached 85,407. The census cited 1,415 manufacturing plants, with more than eight thousand workers. But the boom of the 1880s had already declined, and Otis did not want trade union demands to undermine his plans for the unfettered expansion of industry in southern California.

Otis became a champion of the open shop, a system wherein an employer could hire anyone—union member or not—at will. This was the employers' preferred method to keep unions out of the workplace, and to prevent unions from negotiating meaningful contracts.

Though Otis had warred with the unions since he climbed to the top of the Los Angeles business world, he had started out as a union man, even quitting his job as a "printer's devil" in Ohio at the *Rock Island Courier* when the owner would not allow a union. After stints with newspapers in Alaska and Santa Barbara, Otis became the editor of the *Los Angeles Times* in 1882, gaining full control of the paper in 1886. Initially, he maintained good relations with the Los Angeles Typographical Union. But as his fortunes changed, so did his worldview. Carey McWilliams wrote that Otis had "the fixed idea that he owned Los Angeles...and that he alone was destined to lead it to greatness."

His first major conflict with the unions came in 1890, when Otis and other publishers proposed a 20 percent wage cut for union printers. When the printers at the *Times* refused to accept it, he locked them out. By breaking the power of the strongest union at the paper, Otis established an open shop at the *Times* and used the paper as a platform for a long-term, vicious anti-union crusade.

With the M&M at the forefront, employers united to resist union organizing in every sector. They cancelled union contracts, locked out workers, and expelled union organizers. Employers brought in strikebreakers from other cities and shared a blacklist of union agitators who could not be hired anywhere in Los Angeles. The M&M—vociferously critical of boycotts by trade unions—even organized a boycott of their own: against employers who dared to negotiate with the unions.

In response, laborers—from theater workers to brewers—brought a string of actions in the spring of 1910. The most militant conflict pitted the Bridge and Structural Iron Workers union against the employers of the National Erectors Association. On June 1, with financial and organizing support from their union brethren in San Francisco, the metal workers launched the largest strike the city had ever experienced—more than fifteen hundred workers walked off the job. In retaliation, employers pressured the city council to pass a sweeping anti-picketing ordinance. Wherever union members took strike action, they were hit with injunctions, arrests, and police brutality.

The unions responded with increased organizing. The campaign against the open shop enlisted more than ten thousand new members in twenty-two new union locals. Membership in the Los Angeles Central Labor Council doubled.

In the pre-dawn hours of October 1, an explosion in Ink Alley, just outside the pressroom of the *Los Angeles Times*, destroyed the building and killed twenty employees. The police found more unexploded bombs at Otis's mansion on Wilshire Boulevard and at the home of M&M secretary Felix J. Zeehandelaar.

Otis immediately named the labor unions as the perpetrators of "the crime of the century." The *Times* headline the next morning (printed on a rival paper's equipment) screamed, "Unionist Bombs Wreck the *Times*." Police arrested a union printer, James B. McNamara, and his brother John J., secretary of the Bridge and Structural Iron Workers.

The charges against the union men brought widespread outrage from trade unionists around the country. Union leaders denounced the "fire-trap" in which Otis forced his employees to work and blamed the blast on a leaking gas main. AFL President Samuel Gompers claimed the charges against the McNamara brothers were a "frame-up" and mobilized a national defense fund that reached $236,000. Renowned attorney Clarence Darrow was enlisted to defend the McNamara brothers.

The Los Angeles County courthouse was jammed on December 1, 1911, the first day that the McNamaras appeared with Darrow. But union supporters were stunned by an announcement from the defense team: the brothers withdrew their plea of innocence. John pled guilty to the bombing and was sentenced to life in prison. James pled guilty to an explosion a year before at the Llewellyn Iron Works.

The impact of the confessions on the trade union movement was swift and severe. Otis used the brothers' confession to back his claims that trade unions were violent and dangerous to the prosperity of Los Angeles. Union membership declined precipitously; militancy waned and wages plummeted. The aggressive fight against the open shop came to an abrupt end.

By 1914, according to a report by the U.S. Commission on Industrial Relations, "The term 'open shop' in Los Angeles is wholly a misnomer. It is as tight a closed

A 1910 bombing killed twenty workers and destroyed the building that housed the Los Angeles Times, *published by the fiercely anti-union Harrison Gray Otis. The conviction of two union leaders thwarted union organizing and solidified support for the "open shop" policy for decades.*

shop town as San Francisco—with the lock on the opposite side of the door. Employers...frankly stated that they would not employ union men."

For the next quarter-century, the open shop held a tight grip on Los Angeles industry, thwarting all attempts at union organizing. By 1920 it had become a key component of the "American Plan," a strategy of the U.S. Chamber of Commerce and the National Association of Manufacturers to squelch the power of trade unions. Otis crowed that it was responsible for "the phenomenal industrial growth of Los Angeles."

The aftermath of the bombing also shaped the Los Angeles Police Department for decades to come. At the request of the M&M, the department had kept files on all trade union organizers and their supporters. Its 1913 annual report boasted that its dossiers "were said to be more complete than those of any city except New York."

Hop Pickers Wanted

After the gold rush, patterns of land ownership in California changed, and they became radically different than those in the rest of the country.

Rather than independent farms with multiple crops, California agriculture was based on the "factory in the field," as Carey McWilliams called it: large holdings producing single, specialized crops, dependent on seasonal labor. The huge, single-crop farms in California necessitated enormous amounts of labor during the harvest season, when workers would be mobilized quickly, work day and night, and then be let go just as quickly after the harvest. It was the beginning of a rural proletariat.

As California agriculture expanded from wheat to fruit orchards, vineyards, and vegetable farms, the "harvest tramps"—low-paid, temporary, and expendable—were a mainstay of its rapid growth. The IWW and other labor organizers branching out into the fields confronted a grim reality.

California growers were advertising nationally for workers, purposely trying to attract more workers than they needed, in order to force wages down and keep the workforce trapped and tractable. Many of the labor camps were intentionally kept filthy and unsafe to drive workers away before the season ended. Those who left early forfeited 10 percent of their wages.

Among these infamous farms was a hop ranch in Wheatland, north of Sacramento, owned by Ralph Durst. One of the state's largest employers, Durst advertised for workers throughout California and in Oregon and Nevada. He needed fifteen hundred for the 1913 harvest, and he attracted twenty-eight hundred.

Carey McWilliams described conditions at Durst's labor camp, where almost three thousand people, half of them women and children, resided:

> The lucky ones slept on straw or gunnysacks thrown on the floors of flimsy tents, rented from Durst at seventy-five cents a week. Others slept in the fields. There were nine outdoor toilets serving twenty-eight hundred people. The stench around the camp was nauseating, with women and children vomiting; dysentery was prevalent to an alarming degree. Between two hundred and three hundred children worked in the fields, and hundreds more children were seen around the camp in an unspeakably filthy condition; many, especially the younger ones, were dehydrated and sick.

Temperatures in the isolated, dusty camp often reached 105 degrees by noon. There was no sanitation or garbage disposal. There was no water in the camp, but one of Durst's cousins sold "lemonade," made from citric acid, for a nickel a glass.

The workers started picking at four o'clock in the morning and earned less than a dollar a day.

IWW organizers from Roseville and Yuba City set out to change the conditions at the Durst Ranch. Some were veterans of the Fresno fight; some were from San Diego, including Blackie Ford and Herman Suhr.

On August 3, Ford called a mass meeting to protest the camp conditions. Because many of the workers were immigrants—one report cited two dozen nationalities—interpreters translated into seven languages, including Japanese, Hindi, and Spanish. Tempers were running high: the previous night Durst had slugged Ford.

As he addressed the mass meeting, Ford took a sick baby from its mother's arms and proclaimed, "It's for the kids we are doing this." At the close of the meeting, the crowd sang a Wobbly favorite written by Joe Hill, "Mr. Block."

> Yes, Mr. Block is lucky; he found a job, by gee!
> The sharks got seven dollars, for job and fare and fee.
> They shipped him to a desert and dumped him with his truck,
> But when he tried to find his job, he sure was out of luck.

Children were clapping, and workers were laughing and tapping their feet, buoyed by the spirit of the song. At first they did not notice the Yuba County sheriff and his deputies making their way through the crowd.

Then a shot rang out. A deputy fired his rifle into the air, "to sober the mob," he later claimed. The workers panicked, and a riot began. Two hop pickers were killed—an Englishman and a Puerto Rican—along with a district attorney and a deputy who had accompanied Durst and the sheriff to the meeting. Numerous workers were injured and many others fled in fear. One observer recalled the "roads out of Wheatland being filled all that night with pickers leaving camp."

Governor Hiram Johnson sent four companies of the National Guard into the camp, where they arrested a hundred workers. In addition, scores of agents from the private Burns Detective Agency were deputized and led a "reign of terror" in the surrounding area. Hundreds of IWW members and sympathizers were arrested throughout the state; many were held incommunicado for months.

IWW organizers Ford and Suhr were charged with the murder of the district attorney. During the trial, when defense attorney Austin Lewis needed a witness, he'd write the name on a card and hand it to Wobblies in the courtroom. Brakemen and conductors on trains deemed Lewis's cards to be legitimate passenger tickets, allowing IWW members to travel around the state looking for witnesses.

The state-appointed special prosecutor was the attorney for the California Hop Growers' Association. During the trial, the song "Mr. Block" was read aloud by the prosecution and the songbook given to the jury. The local paper noted, "It was not the song itself that was so suggestive as it was the flaming red cover of the book wherein it was contained, *Songs to Fan the Flames of Discontent*." Ford and Suhr were convicted of second-degree murder and sentenced to life in prison. Durst went uncharged and unpunished.

The Wheatland Riot spurred an investigation by the state Commission on

Immigration and Housing that was highly critical of the growers and noted the positive role of the IWW organizers who brought together such a diverse group of workers for a common cause: "It is a deeply suggestive fact that these 30 men [IWW members], through their energy, technique and skill in organization, unified and dominated an unhomogeneous mass of 2,800 unskilled laborers" within two days. The commission recommended laws to improve the working and living conditions of migrant farmworkers; some changes were made but were short-lived.

This official recognition and a statewide campaign to free Ford and Suhr, supported by the AFL despite its misgivings about the "direct action" tactics of the IWW, eventually resulted in Ford and Suhr being released from prison in 1926; Ford was retried on murder charges and acquitted.

Frame-up

Unlike Los Angeles and the agricultural Central Valley, San Francisco had been a strong union town since its founding. The city boasted the first seaman's union and the first central trades council, established in 1863.

There was tension when, in 1916, on the brink of the U.S. entry into World War I, the Merchants and Manufacturers in San Francisco planned a parade down Market Street in support of military preparedness. The San Francisco Central Labor Council, opposed to its members becoming cannon fodder in a capitalist war, urged a boycott. The Building Trades Council went even further, denouncing the industrialists' march for war and their recent brutal attacks on striking miners and the "skulls of working men, women and children shot, murdered and burned to death." The businessmen then charged that the unions were unpatriotic, redubbing the IWW "Imperial Wilhelm's Warriors."

The Preparedness Day parade was the largest parade San Francisco had ever seen, attracting fifty thousand marchers and fifty bands. As they rounded the corner of Market and Steuart Streets, a bomb went off. Ten people were killed and forty wounded.

Within days, labor organizers Tom Mooney, his wife, Rena, his friend Warren Billings, and three others were charged with the crime. They were picked up without any evidence, and the police and district attorneys dropped all further investigation of the bombing.

Mooney and Billings were the perfect scapegoats for the anti-labor organizers of the Preparedness Day parade. The others, including Mooney's wife, were quickly acquitted or had their charges dropped.

Mooney, a molder by trade, was a well-known San Francisco labor leader. At the time, he was trying to organize a union among the workers of the United Railways, which operated the city's trams and streetcars. Three years earlier, he had been arrested—and acquitted—for illegal possession of explosives. Police suspected that he planned to destroy Pacific Gas & Electric transmission lines in the Carquinez Strait, in support of a strike against the electric company.

Billings had also been arrested during the electrical workers' strike, for transporting dynamite, and served two years in Folsom State Prison.

At the Preparedness Day bombing trial, District Attorney Charles M. Fickert presented eyewitnesses who testified they had seen Mooney and Billings at the scene of the explosion, carrying a suitcase containing a time bomb. Fickert counted on the jury to mistrust trade unionists because of the McNamara brothers' surprise confessions to the *Los Angeles Times* bombing just a few years earlier.

It worked. Judge Franklin P. Griffin sentenced Mooney to the gallows and Billings to prison for life. In 1918 Governor William Stephens commuted Mooney's death sentence to life imprisonment, two weeks before he was to hang.

The conviction of the popular labor leaders created a widespread outcry. Ten years later, Mooney was offered a deal: he would be set free if he admitted a connection with the bombing. Mooney replied defiantly, "I am not guilty of any crime. Why then should I be paroled and have all my movements mortgaged and restricted? I want to be free to take up my work where I left off twelve years ago."

In an affidavit on March 21, 1929—more than a decade after the verdict that sent Mooney and Billings to prison for life—a key witness recanted her testimony and admitted that the men had been framed by Fickert.

Labor leader Tom Mooney was framed and convicted for the bombing of a World War I Preparedness Day parade sponsored by the Merchants and Manufacturers Association. The main witness against him later recanted her testimony, but despite this and a worldwide outcry, Mooney spent more than two decades in San Quentin Prison before being released by Governor Culbert Olson.

The perjury admission generated a torrent of support for the wrongly convicted men. Nine of the ten living jurors wrote to Governor Clement C. Young supporting a pardon. Almost the entire prosecution team, including the chief of detectives, the captain of police, and the assistant prosecutor, also signed on to the request. The lone opposition in this group was voiced by D.A. Fickert, who was subsequently defeated in his reelection campaign.

Judge Griffin himself appealed to the governor. "I sentenced Mooney to death," he wrote. "Now I know that the wrong man was convicted and sentenced."

C. C. Reed, nephew of William H. Hyatt, an attorney with United Railways, stated that his uncle had explicitly told him that Mooney was framed because the company wanted him out of the way. Reed charged that United Railways President Patrick Calhoun had told his lawyers to hire detectives and pin the bombing on Mooney. Despite these revelations, Governor Young refused to pardon the men.

The years wore on and Mooney remained in prison. The Free Tom Mooney Defense Committee published an annual leaflet calling for his release. It pictured two photos of Mooney—the energetic young organizer at the time of his arrest and an increasingly haggard and frail old man who was rotting in prison. On August 14, the last day of the 1932 Olympic Games in Los Angeles, protestors staged a "Free Tom Mooney" demonstration at the Olympic stadium. Dressed in tracksuits, they ran around the arena in front of more than one hundred thousand spectators, carrying banners calling for Mooney's release. Six of the demonstrators were sentenced to nine months in jail for disturbing the peace.

Finally, the pressure paid off. Labor had helped elect Culbert L. Olson as governor in 1938, and he carried out his campaign pledge to pardon Mooney. The union organizer had spent twenty-two years in prison on a trumped-up charge.

Because he had a prior conviction, Billings was not released until the following year; he was officially pardoned in 1961.

The 1930s: We Want Work, We Want Food

The expansion of agriculture in California in the 1930s coincided with the Great Depression. As California became the country's leading food producer, first of wheat, then of oranges, avocados, lettuce, and grapes, growers throughout the state replicated the pattern of employing vast numbers of migrant laborers for seasonal work and laying them off when the last crop was picked. Workers struggled to make enough during the harvest season to last them through the rest of the year.

The concentration of farm and land ownership in the hands of the few increased as well. A 1930s U.S. Senate investigation revealed that more than half of gross farm profits belonged to a mere 10 percent of the owners. This same small percentage of owners hired more than two-thirds of the farmworkers, and their working conditions yielded a "shocking degree of human misery," the report stated.

The growers were highly organized: they fixed wages and coordinated recruitment and hiring to their economic advantage. They fought every attempt at worker organization, often with violence. In this they had the support of private vigilantes organized by their trade group, the Associated Farmers, and often of local law enforcement as well. The Associated Farmers was established by the growers in 1934 explicitly "to investigate the trouble which had been fomented by agitators who were more interested in the overthrow of our American system of government than in the welfare of the workers."

Though the name "Associated Farmers" invokes an image of hardworking rural men and women who till the land, *Fortune* magazine described the group as "dominated by big growers, packers, utilities, banks and other absentee landlords who are all-important in the state's farm system," such as the Bank of America, which owned 50 percent of the farmlands in central and northern California in the 1930s.

With close ties to law enforcement, the organization pledged every member to serve as a deputy sheriff. It kept an index-card file of "dangerous radicals," complete with side-view photographs and notes on strike activities, affiliations, and arrests, which it distributed to law enforcement agencies around the state.

McWilliams dubbed the group "Farm Fascists" and predicted, "Industrial agriculture in California will never permit the organization of farm labor without a fight to the finish."

The Associated Farmers launched a campaign to extend anti-picketing laws to rural areas and convinced local law enforcement to order "preventive arrests" of union organizers prior to the harvest seasons. Mirroring the ordinances that had been so effectively used by Otis and other Los Angeles employers, the rural anti-picketing laws were tailored to the particularities of agricultural organizing, where strikers and picketers had to cover huge expanses of land, rather than just one factory gate.

The conflict between the Associated Farmers and labor organizers created a volatile mood in the Central Valley. Between 1930 and 1939, a Senate investigative committee documented one hundred and forty strikes in California agriculture, half the national total. The strikes involved one hundred and seventy thousand workers, or 71 percent of the nation's agricultural workers. Since neither the AFL nor the CIO organized farmworkers, and a series of mass arrests and vigilantism had depleted the resources of the IWW, most of the labor actions were either spontaneous or coordinated by the Communist Party–led Trade Union Unity League (TUUL) and its agricultural arm, the Cannery and Agriculture Workers Industrial Union (CAWIU). McWilliams

A strike of eighteen thousand cottonfield workers throughout the San Joaquin Valley was sustained by a cohesive, multiracial coalition of union organizers. The strike ended when vigilantes attacked the Pixley union hall and the National Guard rounded up strikers into a stockade at the Tulare County fairgrounds.

observed, "Never before had farm laborers organized on any such scale and never before had they conducted strikes of such magnitude and such far-reaching social significance."

In 1930 two spontaneous strikes were called in the Imperial Valley: Mexican and Filipino workers in the lettuce fields and white workers in the packing sheds demanded an end to drastic wage cuts. The TUUL sent organizers into the valley and enlisted hundreds of workers. The workers sought an end to piecework, a wage of seventy-five cents an hour, and an eight-hour day, with time-and-a-half for overtime. They demanded sanitary working conditions, equal pay for women workers, and the abolition of child labor.

Eight union leaders were convicted under the California Criminal Syndicalism Act of 1919. Enactment of this law had been motivated by industrialists and owners of large agricultural holdings who, with fresh memories of the 1917 Bolshevik revolution, saw the IWW as the vanguard of a potential American Communist front. Politicians were quick to jump on the bandwagon, and legislators flooded both the assembly and senate with "anti-Red" bills, including the Criminal Syndicalism Act, which created the felony of promoting "any doctrine or precept advocating...unlawful acts or force and violence...as a means of accomplishing a change in industrial ownership or control, or effecting any political change." By this standard, the very Declaration of Independence would be considered illegal. Moreover, the question of what constituted an "unlawful act" became a convenient tool for the politically and economically powerful who wanted to squelch those that upset the status quo, like union organizers, strikers, or political reformers.

Though the law had been widely used against political radicals, this was its first use against farmworker organizers in California. All but one were sent to San Quentin.

During the pea season in the spring of 1933, more than three thousand pickers went on strike from Half Moon Bay to Hayward. That successful strike (wages were doubled from ten cents to twenty cents per hamper) was followed by strikes in the cherry orchards of Mountain View and Sunnyvale, the peach orchards of Merced and Sacramento, the grape vineyards of Lodi and Fresno, and the pear orchards of the Santa Clara Valley.

The largest strike of all involved eighteen thousand cotton pickers at a string of plantations throughout the San Joaquin Valley. With headquarters outside Corcoran, where five thousand pickers' families lived, the strikers were well organized. Under the leadership of Caroline Decker and other dedicated organizers, a multiracial coalition of workers set up committees to govern camp life and provide food, trained nurses, and decent, sanitary conditions. Then, vigilantes fired shots one night into a meeting at the union hall in Pixley. Two workers were killed and many more wounded. A funeral procession of three thousand marched through the streets of Bakersfield. Although eleven ranchers were arrested and tried for murder, they were acquitted after a brief trial.

The governor sent in the National Guard. Hundreds of strikers were rounded up and held in a stockade at the Tulare County Fairgrounds, effectively ending the strike. The growers used this strike to push for increased use of the Criminal Syndicalism Act against labor organizers and rank-and-file strikers.

The U.S. Senate's La Follette Civil Liberties Committee later called the actions of the Associated Farmers and the governor in the cotton strike "the most flagrant and violent infringements of civil liberties," citing their use of "espionage, blacklists, and strikebreaking which resulted in brutality…riots…bloodshed…and sheer vigilantism." For the rest of the 1930s, vigilante actions backed by the Associated Farmers continued unabated.

Laws of the Land

With the growers' escalated use of anti-picketing ordinances and the criminal syndicalism law, farmworkers needed increasingly sophisticated legal defenses. Using their connection to the Communist Party, the TUUL and CAWIU enlisted attorneys to assist the beleaguered agricultural strikers. The party sponsored a legal support organization, the International Labor Defense, and also secured assistance from the American Civil Liberties Union. The lawyers represented strikers and challenged the laws that were used against them.

ACLU attorney A. L. Wirin went to Madera County when he heard that 145 cotton strikers had been locked in a filthy jail for violating the local anti-picketing law: the ordinance prohibited a "procession" of automobiles on the highways without a sheriff's permit. Madera's sheriff, the inaptly named W. O. Justice, not only denied the strikers a permit, but at the request of the Associated Farmers, he deputized ranchers and granted them permits to carry guns "to prevent illegal coercion" by strikers. Sheriff Justice announced to the press that Madera County's anti-picketing ordinance would be "enforced to the limit—even if it means jailing the whole mob."

City parks were closed to all public meetings, and one park was intentionally flooded to block the strikers from meeting. Strikers jailed for violating the anti-picketing ordinance were held on two hundred and fifty dollars' bail; strike leaders were denied bail altogether. Wirin prepared habeas corpus petitions to secure their release. He also appeared before the board of supervisors and convinced them to rescind the ban on public meetings in parks. He filed a challenge to the anti-picketing ordinance in federal court, and in December 1939, a U.S. district judge in Fresno declared the ordinance unconstitutional.

Providing legal assistance to farmworkers in areas controlled by the Associated Farmers was a dangerous undertaking, as Wirin had discovered during a 1934 lettuce strike in the Imperial Valley. Wirin had obtained an injunction against the growers' interference with union meetings, but they ignored it and continued to break up meetings with violence. Vigilantes raided the labor camps, pelted the residents with tear gas, and burned their shacks to the ground.

On Tuesday, January 23, Wirin stopped for dinner at a hotel in Brawley before addressing a mass meeting of Mexican lettuce workers. A waiter told him that someone was waiting for him in the lobby. Wirin later described what happened:

> I was immediately seized by a dozen men, who dragged me outside and shoved me into a waiting car. A motorcycle officer cleared the way. I was thrown on the floor of the car, and was struck blow after blow with fists and clubs. Someone put his foot on my neck. They told me I was going to be killed. Soon the car stopped, and I was dragged out to receive more punishment. My suspenders were cut and my hands tied behind my back. A fire was started while I lay on the ground with my coat over my head. I pleaded that I was suffocating, but this only brought more blows. Then someone said, "Let's get the branding-iron before we drown him." After a while I was thrust back into a car and taken to American Legion headquarters. There

dozens of men turned their flashlights on me. This, someone said, was so all the Legionnaires would know me the next time I came to Imperial Valley. I was taken on a long ride, blindfolded and tied. I was turned loose in the desert eleven miles from Calipatria bare-foot and minus my personal belongings and twenty-five dollars.

Wirin filed a lawsuit in Los Angeles Superior Court seeking damages from Governor James Rolph Jr., the head of the state highway patrol, the police chief, and twenty-five John Does who "were Legionnaires and vigilantes."

As evidence, he submitted a National Labor Board report which indicated that "Constitutional rights had been openly disregarded by the law-enforcement agencies in the valley; the right of free speech and assembly had been wholly suppressed; excessive bail had been demanded of arrested strikers; the state Vagrancy Law had been prostituted and a Federal Court injunction had been flouted."

Wirin won.

In 1936 three thousand Salinas packing shed workers—most of whom were white—went on strike. Although the workers in the fields and in the sheds had been deliberately segregated by race, five hundred Filipino and Mexican field workers joined the labor action. The Filipinos had been victims of vicious vigilante violence during a strike two years earlier and were anxious to organize.

The Associated Farmers brought in Colonel Henry Sanborn, an Army Reserve officer and editor of the anticommunist magazine *The American Citizen*, to break the strike. They paid him three hundred dollars a month to "coordinate" law enforcement agencies and private vigilantes. Sanborn built a stockade around the packing sheds and lobbed over two hundred rounds of tear gas at the strikers, eventually breaking the strike. In an investigative report issued the following year, the National Labor Relations Board charged "inexcusable police brutality, in many instances bordering upon sadism."

By 1936, eighteen union organizers had been convicted under the state's criminal syndicalism law for their farm labor organizing. One of them was Caroline Decker, the dynamic leader of the Pixley cotton strike, who served time in Tehachapi State Prison. Their imprisonment severely hampered the CAWIU, and the strikes in the fields diminished.

Still, Wirin and other attorneys persisted in challenging the anti-picketing ordinances. In 1938 the court of appeal upheld the right to picket as an expression of free speech and granted a writ of habeas corpus to a picketer who had been jailed for contempt of a court order prohibiting peaceful picketing.

When the California Supreme Court refused to hear an appeal from the growers, the Associated Farmers put a statewide anti-picketing initiative on the ballot. But in 1940 the U.S. Supreme Court invalidated the law.

On the Waterfront

In the 1930s, the working conditions on California's busy docks were abysmal: men worked twenty-four hours a day, seven days a week, sometimes seventy-two hours at a stretch. They toiled at a furious pace and earned seventy-five cents an hour.

In a hiring process known as the "shape-up," hundreds, sometimes thousands of men swarmed onto the docks at dawn, desperate to be selected by the foreman for a day's work. "Sometimes four thousand men would report for the shape-up, but only one thousand men were hired," longshoreman Ed Paulson remembered.

Labor activist Elaine Black Yoneda recalled, "The first time I saw the shape-up, I thought a riot was going on."

The system fostered corruption, including kickbacks to the foremen. It also meant that men who got jobs didn't let them go. Men unloaded dangerous, heavy cargo from deep holds for days at a time without a break.

"If you started on a ship, you would work twenty-four to thirty hours straight," explained Germain Bulcke, who came from Detroit to work on the waterfront during the Depression. The straw bosses did not want anyone who fought for union rights or better conditions, said Bulcke, who was once thrown down the steps of a pier because of his organizing efforts.

Angry about these conditions, the longshoremen and other maritime workers called a strike in May 1934.

There had been previous dock strikes in San Francisco, and employers met each with fierce resistance. After a 1916 strike, maritime businesses and other employers organized an Industrial Association, which succeeded in getting anti-picketing legislation enacted. In 1919 the employers created the company-controlled Blue Book union to keep hiring on the waterfront under tight control.

But times were changing. The 1932 Norris–La Guardia Act guaranteed that workers could join unions of their choice. The following year, the National Industrial Recovery Act encouraged collective bargaining. The two federal laws spurred union organizing by the AFL-affiliated International Longshoremen's Association (ILA). Buoyed by national support from the Roosevelt administration, the popular *Waterfront Worker*, a mimeographed newspaper distributed by hand for a penny an issue, galvanized support for an impending strike.

At the 1934 ILA convention, dockworkers agreed on their demands: decent wages, a hiring hall, and a coastwide contract that would extend from Spokane to San Pedro.

During the 1934 maritime strike, militant dockworkers confronted police and defied employers who had imposed a company-controlled "Blue Book" union. The death of two union members led to the General Strike in San Francisco, which closed down the city for days.

On May 9, 1934, thirty-seven thousand West Coast longshoremen walked off the job, demanding one dollar an hour, a thirty-hour week, and an end to the shape-up.

T. G. Plant, the president of the Waterfront Employers, was in constant contact with local government and police. San Francisco Mayor Angelo Rossi announced, "Those who willfully strike for their own selfish ends, or for the overthrow of this government, will be met by the armed forces at my command who will be brought to bear to prevent them from carrying out their plan."

A *San Francisco Chronicle* headline warned, "Communist Plot to Take Over the City." The coverage in the Hearst-owned papers—the *Call-Bulletin* and the *Examiner*—was so anti-union that the strikers and other trade unionists called for a boycott, leading to a steep decline in those newspapers' circulation.

Over the next month, strikers and their supporters hunkered down for the long haul. Fellow trade unionists staffed the union halls and raised money for strikers' families. Elaine Black Yoneda mobilized lawyers and bail money from the International Labor Defense. Sympathetic cooks and restaurant workers set up a soup kitchen on the Embarcadero between Mission and Market Streets to feed the embattled workers.

The strike shut down the waterfront: not a ship was loaded, not a truck moved. The union action was costing San Francisco millions, and the chamber of commerce was clamoring for the reopening of the port.

On July 3 the employers, backed by the police and the mayor, declared, "The Port

Is Open." The streets were lined with patrol cars. Trucks carrying scores of strike-breakers rolled up to the Third Street docks, where a ship carrying rice was waiting to be unloaded. As the pickets tried to stop the scabs from entering the port, the police opened fire.

Bulcke recalled, "We jumped on the trucks and threw the rice and other goods into the street." In solidarity, the Teamsters stopped the trucks and tilted them on their sides. Police on horseback were thwarted by strikers with marbles.

"Bricks flew and clubs battered skulls. The police opened fire with revolvers. Clouds of tear gas swept the picket lines and sent the men choking in retreat. Mounted police were dragged from their saddles and beaten to the pavement. Nearby streets were filled with office and factory workers who poured red-eyed and gasping from the buildings into which tear gas had drifted," labor journalist Mike Quin reported. "The cobblestones of the Embarcadero were littered with fallen men. Bright puddles of blood colored the gray expanse."

Governor Frank Merriam called in the National Guard to protect the cargo. Declaring a state of martial law in the city, he said, "Among us a horde of irresponsible, professional agitators, mostly aliens, are trafficking shamelessly in the agonies of these stressful times. They are seeking revolution, not reform."

The following day, the docks were quiet for the Independence Day holiday. But the pitched battles resumed on July 5. Armed officers chased pickets up Rincon Hill.

Volunteering at the strike headquarters, Yoneda heard a sharp crack. What she first thought was a car backfiring, she soon realized, was shooting. The police hurled tear gas through the windows and shot into the crowd.

Bulcke, who was at the corner of Market and Steuart Streets, saw two police officers jump into an unmarked police car. "Four guys were lying in the street," Bulcke recalled. "I put one of them on my back and took him to the union hall at 113 Steuart Street. He was shot in the back." The man was Nick Bordoise, a volunteer cook in the union soup kitchen. He did not survive.

"Nick was a native of Crete, a culinary worker, a member of the Cooks' Union and the Communist Party," Mike Quin wrote. "His family as far back as he knew had been laborers. Loyalty to the struggles of labor was the familiar philosophy of his home life. All through the long strike he sweated cheerfully over a hot stove preparing meals for hungry pickets."

Howard Sperry, a striking longshoreman and World War I veteran, also lay dead. In honor of the two martyrs, the day became known as "Bloody Thursday."

On July 9, forty thousand maritime workers and their supporters marched the length of Market Street to Duggan's Funeral Parlor, in the Mission District, for a union memorial service. Streetcar drivers stopped their vehicles and stood in homage

Governor Merriam called in the National Guard to protect San Francisco from the striking dockworkers. From posts above the port, soldiers trained their weapons on the longshoremen.

as the procession passed. Thousands of spectators lined up to watch. The *San Francisco Chronicle* wrote that "the entire city gasped in amazement...Here they came as far as you could see in a silent, orderly line of march, a mass demonstration which transcended anything of the like San Francisco has ever seen...a mighty show of strength that amazed the citizens who packed the sidewalks and pressed out into the street."

The massive memorial march shifted public opinion about the strike. Even a member of the Industrial Association wrote, "It moved the entire community....[and] created a temporary but tremendous wave of sympathy for the workers."

Riding on the surge of public support, the longshoremen and their union supporters called for a general strike.

On the morning of July 14, San Francisco was quiet. No street cars clanged down Market Street. No jitneys lined up to drive people to work. Restaurants were closed. No gas was delivered into the city.

The 1934 General Strike shut down San Francisco for four days; virtually every union heeded the call. "An uncanny quiet settled over the acres of buildings. For all practical purposes not a wheel moved nor a lever budged. The din of commercial activity gave way to a murmur of voices in the streets," Quin wrote.

The *Chronicle* warned of a Bolshevik revolution: "a communist army planned the

During the 1934 General Strike, police raided and ransacked Communist Party offices, union headquarters, and left-wing bookstores. Though the officers later denied it, photos like this one provided evidence to the contrary.

destruction of the railways and highway facilities to paralyze transportation and later communication." Alarmed, the well-to-do fled the city.

The police took advantage of the General Strike to launch anti-Red raids. Squads descended on Communist Party offices, left-wing bookstores, and union halls. They raided the union soup kitchen and jailed men for vagrancy. They smashed windows, furniture, and typewriters in the Marine Workers Industrial Union Hall. They stormed an open-air meeting of the Workers Ex-Servicemen's League.

Five hundred people were arrested and held in a jail built for one hundred and fifty. Lawyers from the International Labor Defense represented them. During the trials, the police denied that they had destroyed any of the halls, claiming that the Communists had returned to the sites and smashed their own property to discredit the police. The police had to withdraw that claim when newspaper photos showed uniformed officers destroying property.

The Industrial Association, headed by John Francis Neylan, the attorney for the Hearst newspapers, created a team to coordinate with the police department and the press: agents rode in police cars and turned in reports that were printed in the Hearst dailies.

Though the General Strike could be sustained only for four days, the longshoremen stayed out for eighty days. As striker Pat Tobin recalled, "The decisive force in 1934 was the rank and file. In spite of every kind of scurrilous attack and red baiting, they stood by, stood fast and did not go back to work. The strike was never broken, even under tremendous pressure."

Harry Bridges emerged as the undisputed leader of the strike. Born in Melbourne, Australia, Bridges had gone to sea at age sixteen, inspired by Jack London. In 1922 he landed in San Francisco, where he got a job on the docks. He joined the Sailor's Union of the Pacific and, for a short time, the IWW. In the first month of the strike, he became chair of the Rank and File Strike Committee.

Bridges's tenacity and commitment to the formation of the union were key to the victory. While the East Coast president of the ILA, Joseph Ryan, had tried to force a premature settlement to the strike and had made attempts to separate the San Francisco strikers from other locals, Bridges remained steadfast. The schism eventually caused the West Coast longshoremen to disaffiliate from the ILA and forge their own union, the International Longshore and Warehouse Union (ILWU).

Bridges had an abiding faith in the rank and file, and the rank and file had an equally great faith in Bridges. Striker Bill Bailey remembers that the ship owners offered Bridges a hundred thousand dollars to leave town. "He asked the men, 'What should I do, should I take the money, give it to you for the soup kitchen and get the hell out of Dodge?' The men said 'No.'"

According to screenwriter and essayist Dalton Trumbo, during the strike Bridges gave all of his salary to the strikers. His salary as president of the ILWU was seventy-five dollars a week, no higher than the highest paid longshoreman.

In October the longshoremen and the employers agreed to arbitration. The arbitration led to signed contracts guaranteeing a thirty-hour week and a six-hour day. And even more significantly, the workers won the union hiring hall: an elected member of the union would assign men to work, guaranteeing that a foreman could no longer blacklist a worker for his union activities. As Roger Lyon, former editor of the ILWU newspaper *The Dispatcher*, noted, "Ultimately something very revolutionary came out of this strike. With the hiring hall, the longshoremen finally had control over their jobs, and they could equalize the jobs—it was a whole new system of job control. It was a visionary concept, but then it happened. No longer visionary, but a fact."

With waterfront contracts in hand, the union made a "march inland" to organize workers in the warehouses. Membership climbed to nine thousand by 1938.

The ILWU was one of few unions with an explicit prohibition against racial, re-ligious, and political discrimination. As African American longshoreman Cleophas Williams described it, "Our members include Americans, English, Russians, Negroes, Finns, Turks—every nationality in the world. Beyond any question the ILWU is the fin-est example of democratic trade unionism in America. Bridges insisted 'discrimination against Negroes is anti-labor and anti-American.'"

Under Bridges's leadership, the ILWU's organizing efforts expanded from basic economic goals to civil liberties and racial equality, positions that would become in-creasingly suspect during the McCarthy period. Dalton Trumbo wrote, "When con-fronted with such an organization, there are only two ways to destroy it: split the membership or eliminate the leader." In this case, Bridges was the obvious target.

The government tried three times to deport Harry Bridges. His first hearing, on charges of being a member of the Communist Party, was held on Angel Island in the summer of 1939. "I was such a dangerous character," Bridges quipped, "that they had to move my trial offshore."

Bridges was acquitted every time but was persecuted for decades by the FBI. He enjoyed tormenting the spies as well. Knowing his office was under government sur-veillance, he would type up nonsense poetry, tear up the paper and the carbon and put the scraps in different wastebaskets. He took delight in thinking that the FBI agents were staying up late trying to piece the papers together and trying to figure out what he was thinking.

The 1947 Taft-Hartley Act required union leaders to take anti-Communist oaths, causing deep divisions in the labor movement. Two years later, the Congress of Indus-trial Organizations (CIO), the major industrial union coalition, passed a resolution at its annual convention prohibiting union officers or board members from belonging to the Communist, Fascist, or "any totalitarian" party. Many ILWU leaders, who had vehe-mently refused to testify before congressional committees probing party membership, were angered by the resolution, claiming their First Amendment rights of freedom of speech and association would be violated. Ten left-wing unions were expelled from the CIO. Not wanting to suffer that fate, the ILWU voluntarily left the CIO.

Breaking the Color Bar

World War II brought a surge of shipbuilding to northern California, supported by an unprecedented infusion of billions of dollars in federal defense funds. The Bechtel Corporation (then Bechtel-McCone-Parsons) established Marinship, trans-forming the quiet Sausalito waterfront into an "instant shipyard." Wartime pro-duction buzzed around the clock at Moore Dry Dock in Oakland, Hunters Point in

San Francisco, and the Kaiser Shipyards in Richmond, which eventually became the largest shipyard in the world, employing almost one hundred thousand workers.

In just a few months, hundreds of thousands of workers were recruited, hired, trained, and put to work to meet the frantic wartime construction needs. Many had been on relief during the Depression and few had ever worked in the skilled trades of the shipyards. The ranks of shipyard labor swelled with women recruited from the South and Midwest, Chinese workers and African Americans from the South, who had been barred from many of the AFL craft unions, Mexican braceros, teenagers, and the elderly. In 1939 there were six thousand shipyard workers in the Bay Area; by 1944 that number had grown to almost a quarter-million. Young men of draft age could get a deferment for working in the vital defense industry. In just three months, from the end of 1943 to early 1944, Marinship filed over 5,010 deferment requests, most of which were granted.

During the war, almost half a million black workers moved to California; 90 percent of the black women and men employed in the shipyards were new migrants from the Deep South. The African American populations of Berkeley and Oakland doubled; in San Francisco the African American population quadrupled; and in Richmond, the African American population increased twentyfold.

But nowhere was the change as dramatic as in Marin County, where the African American population increased several hundredfold during the war. Previously all-white Marin County was the one place in the region where wartime housing for the new workers was not segregated. The county constructed new housing units—dormitories, apartments, and detached houses—in Marin City, just outside of Sausalito. Marin City was managed by Milen Dempster, the chief of project services for the county housing authority. Dempster, who had managed a federal migrant labor camp and run for governor on the Socialist Party ticket, insisted on an antidiscrimination policy. The units were rented on a first-come, first-serve basis, resulting in the most integrated wartime housing project in the country. Marin City residents also formed an active Double V club, an organization common in African American communities that was dedicated to a "double victory" over fascism abroad and racism at home.

Yet despite the promise of skilled jobs, high wages, and a role in wartime defense, the new African American workers faced a problem. Blacks were the largest group of minority workers in the shipyards, comprising 10 percent of the workforce, but the AFL craft unions that controlled 70 percent of the jobs, and all of the more skilled, higher-paid ones, were segregated. African American workers, though experienced and eager to work in the defense effort, were barred from the best jobs.

In 1941 a congressional committee found that a dozen trade unions involved in the defense industry banned Negroes from membership. Under threat of a march on

Washington by black workers to be led by A. Philip Randolph and C. L. Dellums of the Brotherhood of Sleeping Car Porters, President Roosevelt signed Executive Order 8802, barring race segregation in the defense industry. The order was later amended to establish the Commission on Fair Employment Practices, an agency that allowed employees to file official complaints against workplace discrimination. But a survey by *Fortune* magazine showed that almost half of the large national unions still discriminated against African Americans, in violation of Executive Order 8802, and in some cases in violation of their own union charters.

As a result, African American defense workers were excluded from training programs and consigned to unskilled labor. Many blacks were told they could not hold supervisory positions because southern white workers would not take orders from them.

In April 1941, the Pacific Coast shipbuilders signed a collective bargaining contract, known as the Master Agreement, with the Metal Trades Council of the AFL-affiliated unions. It was the first such contract in the nation. It guaranteed a pay scale (which was quite high, especially for those who had just come out of unemployment or the low-paying jobs of the Depression), bonuses for overtime and for swing or graveyard shifts, and decent working conditions. The Master Agreement also included a closed shop provision, requiring workers to be members of the appropriate union; in return, the unions agreed to a no-strike clause for the duration of the war.

The closed shop agreement ensured that at Marinship, Local 6 of the International Brotherhood of Boilermakers, Iron Shipbuilders and Helpers of America would control thousands of jobs.

To comply with the regulations of the federal government outlawing race discrimination, the Boilermakers created "auxiliary unions" for black workers. African Americans were required to pay dues but had no voice in the union; they could not participate in collective bargaining or even vote for their representatives. Despite complete lack of representation, they were bound by all the decisions of the union. This arrangement was carried out with the tacit consent of shipyard management.

The black shipyard workers rejected this segregationist arrangement. They organized the San Francisco Committee against Segregation and Discrimination, electing Marinship worker Joseph James as their president.

James, a talented New York singer, had come to San Francisco to perform in the all-black "Swing Mikado" at the Treasure Island Exposition in 1939 and settled in San Francisco's Fillmore District, a largely African American neighborhood with a lively arts scene. In 1942 James was hired as a welder's helper at Marinship; within a year he became a journeyman welder and a member of a "flying squad," a skilled team of troubleshooters.

In August 1943, James and his fellow workers were told they would have to join the all-black Auxiliary A-41. Irate, they declared they were not going to pay dues into a Jim Crow union and called for a boycott of the auxiliary. After three months, about half of the eleven hundred African Americans in the Boilermakers' jurisdiction refused to pay dues to the auxiliary.

On November 26, the Boilermakers told Marinship to fire four hundred and thirty black workers unless they paid their dues within twenty-four hours. That night, the Committee against Segregation and Discrimination voted unanimously to continue the boycott.

The next day, the union withdrew their work authorizations; the black workers could not enter the shipyard. Eight hundred African American workers gathered at the gate of the shipyard to condemn the mass firings. Though armed officers from the sheriff's department and the California Highway Patrol lined the roadway, the protest was orderly and there were no arrests. According to the San Rafael *Daily Independent*, it was "Marin's greatest labor demonstration and most critical situation to arise since the San Francisco General Strike of 1934."

At a meeting on Sunday, November 28, at a Fillmore District church, the committee voted to pursue legal action. The next day, James and seventeen other workers filed a lawsuit against the Boilermakers union and Marinship, seeking reinstatement and $115,000 in damages. They were represented by the National Lawyers Guild's Bernard Dreyfuss and the NAACP Legal Defense and Educational Fund's Thurgood Marshall, who went on to become a U.S. Supreme Court justice.

On February 17, 1944, the court ruled that the union's policy of "discriminating against and segregating Negroes into auxiliaries is contrary to public policy of the state of California." The decision barred the union from requiring blacks to join the segregated auxiliary and prohibited Marinship from laying off black workers who refused to pay dues to the auxiliary.

The shipbuilding company and the Boilermakers appealed to the California Supreme Court. On January 2, 1945, a unanimous court upheld the injunction against the union and the company. Chief Justice Phil Gibson wrote that it is "readily apparent that the membership offered to Negroes is discriminatory and unequal." The court noted that it was not prohibiting the closed shop, but that "an arbitrarily closed union is incompatible with a closed shop." This aspect of the ruling was welcomed by the plaintiffs, who did not want the case to be interpreted as opposed to unions or closed shop agreements, but solely against the racism of the labor unions.

The high court also ruled that the company had "full knowledge of the dispute and at least indirectly assisted the union in carrying out discrimination."

By the time the unions were desegregated, however, the war was over, and shipyard employment rapidly declined. When Marinship officially closed, in May 1946, there were few black workers—down from twenty thousand just a year before.

Joseph James said of the African American workers who now faced unemployment, "We need them, we use them, when we are through with them, we banish them." James left California after the war to resume his singing career in New York.

Historian Charles Wollenberg asserts that the legal legacy of the courageous black workers at Marinship is enduring, although they did not benefit in terms of financial gain: "In the midst of the national emergency...Marinship blacks even won the legal principle of equal membership in exclusive craft unions. But the precipitous decline of the shipyards caused an economic disaster from which the region's African American population never fully recovered."

President Roosevelt's executive order barring race discrimination in employment expired after the war, and a labor-supported initiative to create a state antidiscrimination law, Proposition 11, failed in 1946. It took a persistent effort by grassroots organizations, led by Oakland labor leader C. L. Dellums and two African American legislators, Augustus Hawkins and William Byron Rumford, to pass the Fair Employment Practices Act, which was signed into law by Governor Edmund G. (Pat) Brown in 1959.

Blood on the Grapes

In the 1960s, union membership grew and Congress passed numerous laws expanding the rights of workers that had been enshrined in the 1935 National Labor Relations Act, which guaranteed the right to form and join unions. Farmworkers, however, were specifically excluded from the law, and without legal protection or union contracts, they continued to endure poverty and degradation at the workplace.

A 1969 Senate Labor Committee reported that 95 percent of farm labor camps had no inside toilets or running water, and 99 percent were infested with rats and other vermin. Cesar Chavez testified, "Thousands of farm workers live under savage conditions—beneath trees and amid garbage and human excrement—near tomato fields which use the most modern farm technology. Vicious rats gnaw on them as they sleep. They walk miles to buy food at inflated prices. And they carry in water from irrigation pumps."

The sight of children working in the fields was still common on many farms, and those who hired child labor went unpunished. Babies born to migrant workers suffered a 25 percent higher mortality rate than the rest of the population; malnutrition among migrant worker children was ten times higher than the national rate. Farmworkers suffered two hundred and fifty times the rate of tuberculosis as the general population. They had the third highest accident and death rates, after miners and construction workers. A major cause of death was pesticide poisoning. In 1965 farmworkers' life expectancy was forty-nine years, compared to seventy-three years for the average American.

"Farmworkers are not agricultural implements," Chavez stated as he rallied workers in the fields, "They are not beasts of burden—to be used and discarded."

Just like longshoremen of an earlier generation, the UFW sought union recognition. With that crucial tool, other advances could follow.

When farmworkers struck the vineyards of the San Joaquin Valley in 1965, they faced an even more formidable enemy than their predecessors had when battling the Associated Farmers in the 1930s. By the 1960s, land ownership was even further consolidated in the hands of huge corporations—agribusinesses—that required large numbers of seasonal workers. Vineyards owned by Tenneco Oil Company, the Bank of America, Southern Pacific Railroad, and Safeway Stores reaped huge profits while farmworkers still earned the lowest wages in the state.

The first grape workers to walk out of the fields on September 8, 1965, were Filipino members of the Agricultural Workers Organizing Committee. They were soon joined by the National Farm Workers Association, whose membership was primarily Mexican and Chicano. The unions overcame past differences and merged into the United Farm Workers Organizing Committee.

From the very first days of the strike, on the eve of the grape harvest in Delano, growers posted armed guards in the fields and obtained court injunctions from friendly local judges to prevent strikers from picketing. In addition to scabs brought in from Mexico and Texas, state prison inmates were sent by Governor Ronald Reagan, who called the picketing grape workers "barbarians." As Chavez explained, "We found that the grower was but a small part of the opposition, for beside and behind him stood bankers, politicians, Birchers and pro-grower unions."

As a result, the UFW realized it could not win the strike on the picket lines alone. Drawing on lessons not only from labor history but from the civil rights movement, the union in 1967 called an international boycott of scab grapes. Farmworkers traveled thousands of miles across the United States to the large markets of New York, Boston, and Chicago to picket the supermarkets where grapes were being sold, and to ask fellow trade unionists and sympathizers to join the boycott. The UFW had always depended on other trade unionists for financial resources, food, training, and skills to build the UFW's capacity. In the grape strike, the support extended beyond the labor movement to religious groups, students, professional organizations, and the broader civil rights movement.

The boycott of table grapes took its toll on the growers' profits. In 1969 the

Dolores Huerta, UFW cofounder and vice president, was a leader of the 1965 grape strike, which led to the first union contracts with grape growers in California. The rallying cry "Huelga" (strike) and the union's black eagle symbol became known around the world through an international boycott of California grapes.

growers began to seek out other markets. President Richard Nixon, who called the grape boycott "illegal," sent grapes to South Vietnam as part of the "Food for Peace" program. The quantity that the U.S. government shipped was so large that in 1969, the impoverished, war-torn country of South Vietnam was the world's fourth largest importer of California grapes.

When the growers also attempted to ship grapes to Europe, ILWU members in major California ports initially refused to load the grapes onto the refrigerated cargo ships. But the growers invoked the Taft-Hartley Act's ban on secondary boycotts and sued the ILWU. A court ordered the ILWU to load the grapes or pay a fine of one thousand dollars a day.

In 1970, after years of pressure from the strike and boycott, one grower decided to break ranks: the first union contract in the vineyards was signed between the United Farm Workers and Lionel Steinberg, owner of a large grape vineyard in the Coachella Valley. Other growers soon followed suit, and by the end of the harvest, wooden boxes of California grapes were traveling across the country with the union label: the stamped red and black eagle of the UFW.

The union label on the boxes meant major changes for farmworkers. Their union contracts included a ban on child labor, the establishment of a fair basic wage, and safety and pesticide controls. The UFW sponsored the first health insurance plan for farmworkers, subsidized by the growers, and started five free clinics run by full-time medical workers. The UFW also began a cooperative auto shop and gas station, adult literacy and ESL programs, a bilingual radio station, and, to provide a home for aging Filipino workers who had not been allowed to marry in the U.S., the Agbayani Village retirement center.

People of color were in the leadership of the UFW, and the union took an explicitly anti-racist stance, opening membership to all who toiled to bring food to the table.

In 1973 the growers again attempted to crush the union. When the initial UFW three-year contracts expired, many of the growers signed backdoor "sweetheart" contracts with the Teamsters union, often without the vote of a single worker involved. In protest, UFW members set up picket lines outside the fields. A new wave of violence swept the vineyards as the Teamsters hired thugs at thirty dollars a day to harass the strikers with knives, baseball bats, grape stakes, and guns. Within the space of days, strikers Nagi Daifullah and Juan de la Cruz were killed.

The deaths sent a shock through the union and steeled the determination of the strikers.

"This is a war, this is a real war—all of the growers and right-wing elements…are trying to crush the farmworkers. We have to act like it's a real war," said Dolores Huerta, a founder of the UFW and its first vice president.

The strike ended in 1975 when Governor Edmund G. (Jerry) Brown signed the first farm labor law in California, the Agriculture Labor Relations Act. The law required—for the first time—that farmworkers be allowed to vote whether or not they wanted a union (and which union they wanted). Growers were bound by law to negotiate with the union that won the election.

Within the space of six months, the United Farm Workers won more than two hundred elections throughout California. With the UFW label stamped on the wooden grape boxes, the union spread out to organize in other crops, this time with the strength of the labor law behind them.

After the deaths of Nagi Daifullah and Juan de la Cruz, a reporter asked Chavez if the loss of life, the arrests, the beatings, the sacrifices of the strikers and the boycotters, and his own lengthy and life-threatening fasts for justice were worth the union contract. He replied, "If this is what it takes to build a strong union for good people, we are willing to do it. And in the end….We will win."

Workers Ahead

During the booming economy of the 1950s and 1960s, one in every three workers in California was in a union, including the majority of workers in the manufacturing sector, with contracts providing for decent wages, pensions, health benefits, and safe working conditions. But there were already moves afoot to turn the clock back on the hard-fought gains of laborers. In 1958 California's unions mobilized around the state to defeat a ballot measure to make California a "Right-to-Work" state, an institutionalized open shop policy.

In the 1960s and 1970s, industries in California began boarding up their gates, seeking cheaper labor across the border and as far away as the Philippines, Taiwan, and Thailand. Aerospace and auto plants closed, laying off tens of thousands of workers.

Though unions fought back against factory closures and widespread cuts in wages and benefits, they were hard pressed to deal with the employers' use of union-busting consultants, who advised them how to block union organizing drives by threatening closures, firing organizers, and holding mandatory closed-door meetings to intimidate employees. Union membership plummeted.

Permanent full-time jobs with good benefits in the manufacturing sector were replaced with temporary, part-time, low-wage jobs, often with few or no benefits, in the growing service industry. These jobs were often filled by immigrant workers who worked long hours in bad conditions, afraid to speak out or organize because of their undocumented status.

One method employers used to keep the workforce unorganized and divided was punishing workers for not speaking English. English-only rules proliferated in a wide range of workplaces: factories, hospitals, convalescent homes, hotels, and even government agencies.

The U.S. Equal Employment Opportunity Commission (EEOC) issued guidelines in 1980 stating that English-only workplace rules are a form of national-origin discrimination and therefore barred by the Equal Protection Clause of the Constitution and Title VII of the Civil Rights Act. Yet one of the first worksites to impose such a rule was the Southeast Los Angeles Municipal Court, in the suburb of Huntington Park. In 1984 Alva Gutierrez, a Latina court clerk, was fired from her job for speaking Spanish, based on a single complaint from a coworker.

According to the court administration, the rule was necessary to prevent a "Tower of Babel," to promote racial harmony and improve workplace morale.

Gutierrez challenged her dismissal, winning a favorable decision from the Ninth Circuit Court of Appeals. The opinion stated that the municipal court administration "failed to offer any evidence of the inappropriate use of Spanish." In fact, Judge Stephen Reinhardt wrote, "there is evidence indicating that racial hostility has increased between Hispanics and non-Spanish-speaking employees because Hispanics feel belittled by the regulation."

As for the employer's "Tower of Babel" claim, Judge Reinhardt added, "Since

Spanish is already being spoken in the Clerk's office to non-English-speaking Hispanic citizens, part of the 'Babel' that appellants purport to fear is necessary to the normal press of court business. Additional Spanish is unlikely to create a much greater disruption than already exists."

The United States Supreme Court vacated the decision based on a question of standing, as the plaintiff had left her position—not on legal grounds—and therefore the case cannot be cited as a precedent. Employees since then have often needed to take action at their own workplaces to strike down English-only regulations, as they did at the large, prestigious teaching hospital at the University of California San Francisco (UCSF).

In 1987 the hospital posted a new rule prohibiting employees from speaking any language other than English on the job, except during lunch, rest breaks, or when acting as translators for doctors or nurses. Workers were disciplined for speaking to each other in Spanish, Chinese, and Tagalog. Rene Zamora-Baca, a union employee who delivered food to patients' rooms, was overheard speaking Spanish to a woman on the housekeeping staff. He was reprimanded by his supervisor.

"I didn't think it was right to be afraid to speak Spanish—this rule is unfair and is used as a club by supervisors to keep people in line," Zamora-Baca said. He turned to his union steward, Yolanda Cortez, a hospital diet technician.

The workforce at UCSF was extremely diverse and included many immigrants who were employed in positions that did not require English proficiency. "They came to the U.S. in search of opportunity and freedom. Now they found those opportunities threatened by discriminatory policies at work," Cortez recalled.

The union filed discrimination charges with the EEOC, which upheld them. The university decided not to fight the ruling and abolished its English-only rule. The offensive notices come down and were replaced with a new flyer stating, "Oral reprimands or the suggestion that employees speak English as a courtesy shall be a violation of campus policy. Any employee who violates this policy may be subject to disciplinary action." The employees' actions forced the university to do a 180 degree turn. But immigrant workers were to face even more ominous threats.

La Migra on Trial

Raul Esquivel was nervous as he sat in the witness stand in the imposing U.S. district court in San Jose. The young foundry worker, who had immigrated from Mexico, was applying for citizenship. But that was not what brought him to the courtroom that day in February 1989. It was the sixth week of trial in *Pearl Meadows Mushroom Farm v. Nelson*, a massive class action lawsuit charging the Immigration and Naturalization Service (INS) with violating the rights of hundreds of Latino workers in scores of worksite raids conducted under the euphemism "Project Jobs."

It took great courage for Esquivel, struggling to raise a family in Vallejo, to testify about what had happened to him during a raid on the Benicia Foundry. He did not speak English and testified through an interpreter. The case was against a huge government agency, the one that would determine his future immigration status.

The presiding judge, Robert Aguilar, had been appointed to the federal bench by President Jimmy Carter. The son of Mexican farmworkers, he had risen from poverty to this lifetime appointment. During the lengthy trial, he was sitting in judgment of the INS—*La Migra*, an epithet that must have haunted his own childhood.

The lawyer representing Esquivel was also Mexican American. Mexican American Legal Defense and Education Fund (MALDEF) attorney Francisco Garcia was one of the lead counsel in this closely watched lawsuit. Trained at Harvard and Boalt Hall School of Law, Garcia, also a young father, was now facing off against the U.S. attorney and the INS.

And one of the lawyers sitting at the government table, under the strict guidance of U.S. Attorney Joseph Russoniello, was also part Mexican. Pat Bupara, a skilled trial attorney who had the aggressive, unrelenting style of his boss in questioning witnesses, was of mixed Mexican and South Asian origin.

Speaking through an interpreter, witness Esquivel explained how, during the raid on the foundry, an immigration agent had grabbed him by the waistband of his pants and harshly questioned him about his immigration status. Esquivel said he had tried to tell the agent that he was applying for amnesty for himself and his family. Garcia asked him, "And how did they respond?"

Esquivel clutched the side of the witness stand and answered, "He said, 'Fucking Mexicans lie every time.'"

John True, a staff attorney at the Employment Law Center, recalled looking around at the faces in the courtroom as Esquivel repeated the hateful words. True couldn't help wondering how Esquivel felt repeating the painful insult, and how the young civil rights attorney felt, and the half-Mexican prosecutor—and U.S. District Court Judge Aguilar.

One of the government attorneys objected, charging that the witness did not know enough English to understand what the agent had said.

Before he had a chance to complete his objection, Judge Aguilar cut him off: "Overruled."

The courtroom exchange revealed a lot about the changing demographics of

California in the 1980s, and the role that the immigration debate would play in shaping the future of the state's laws, employment patterns, and daily life.

The range of worksites that had been raided during Project Jobs revealed just how much the California economy depended on immigrant workers. The forty-four sites included poultry farms, where workers pulled out slimy innards from reeking chicken carcasses; mushroom farms, where they spent the sunlight hours in dank caves; factories; foundries; Mexican restaurants; and even a beauty college.

INS Director Alan Nelson said that the purpose of Project Jobs was to take "American jobs" and give them back to "Americans."

To do this, INS and Border Patrol agents fanned out across the country with a blare of publicity and systematically arrested thousands of individuals at their workplaces. In one week in California, they conducted more than thirty raids; thousands of workers were questioned, detained, and arrested. Many were deported.

After the raids, MALDEF phone lines lit up with calls from people all over the state complaining about the INS's tactics. Callers reported that only workers who appeared to be Hispanic were rounded up and questioned. INS agents insulted them with racial slurs, calling them "wetbacks," "*mojados*," and "tonks." When asked why INS agents referred to people as "tonks," one of them replied that the derogatory term originated in the sound of a flashlight hitting somebody's head—"tonk."

When MALDEF attorneys began investigating, they learned from employers that armed INS agents had entered factories and farms without proper warrants or consent. At some sites, they rounded up the entire workforce.

MALDEF and other civil rights groups filed the *Pearl Meadows* lawsuit, seeking an injunction to prevent the INS from entering private workplaces without warrants or voluntary consent and to prevent INS agents from using unlawful general warrants to seize workers.

By the time the case went to trial seven years later, tensions were still running high. The court had issued a preliminary injunction barring the INS from entering worksites without a warrant or consent. But there was evidence that the agency had continued warrantless raids years after the injunction.

In his opening statement, attorney True said that the effect of the high-profile raids was "to teach—in a highly visible and public way—the brutal lesson that even in the 1980s there are certain people in this country who do not have rights, who are not allowed dignity. There are people in this country that an official of our government may demeaningly refer to as a wetback, *mojado*, may insult, threaten, bully or beat."

The INS had continued the illegal tactics of Project Jobs, True asserted, and engaged "in unnecessary brutality, callous indifference to employee rights, and calculated aggression, all of which are designed to…strike fear into the hearts of workers as well as their employers and create an atmosphere in which most are simply intimidated from asserting their constitutional rights."

The trial took the better part of a year but resulted in a landmark ruling. The INS could no longer enter a workplace without a warrant or consent. Agents could not round up workers because they "looked Mexican."

Judge Aguilar vindicated the rights of Benicia Foundry worker Esquivel and the ninety-one others who had the courage to testify against the immigration agency.

FOUR

UNDER COLOR OF LAW

THE FIGHT FOR RACIAL EQUALITY

Negroes are not afraid of anything any more than anyone else. Negroes in the Navy don't mind loading ammunition. They just want to know why they are the only ones doing the loading! They want to know why they are segregated, why they don't get promoted.
—*Thurgood Marshall on the Port Chicago disaster, 1944*

Bridget "Biddy" Mason was a hardy woman. Born on August 15, 1818, most likely in Georgia, she had known slavery all of her life when in 1847 her owner, Robert Smith, a Mormon convert, decided to move his household from Mississippi to Utah. Mason made the seven-month, two-thousand-mile journey mostly on foot, while herding Smith's cattle, caring for her own three daughters (one of whom was an infant), and attending to the births of at least three children.

After a few years in Utah, Smith decided in 1851 to join a wagon train of one hundred and fifty Mormons bound for San Bernardino, where Brigham Young was initiating a Mormon way station. The thirty-two-year-old Mason once again journeyed across inhospitable territory, again likely on foot, to the Golden State.

Even though California entered the union as a free state, slavery existed within its borders. Slave owners who had arrived in California before September 1850 were allowed to keep their slaves as indentured servants. Hundreds of black slaves toiled in mines; others worked to buy their freedom. Some slaveholders, including Mason's owner, openly flouted the antislavery law because, as one of them said, "No one will put themselves to the trouble of investigating the matter." Some newspapers even posted advertisements for the sale of slaves.

The state legislature passed a Fugitive Slave Law in 1852, which allowed slave owners from other states to capture runaways who had escaped to California. Although the law lapsed in 1855, continual legislative efforts to pass a law prohibiting black immigration into the state sent chills through California's small black community. Many migrated to Canada, fearing they might otherwise be forced out of the state.

Having arrived in California, Robert Smith established a cattle ranch in the small town of Los Angeles. But in 1855, after a land dispute with Mormon leaders, he decided to move his household to Texas. Mason, however, did not want to go. While in Los Angeles, Mason's eldest daughter, seventeen-year-old Ellen, had fallen in love with Charles Owens, son of Bob Owens, a well-known African American resident of Los Angeles who ran a successful corral. Biddy Mason had shared with the younger Owens her fear about Smith's intended move to Texas. Owens told his father of the plan, and the two men determined to free Mason and her family.

In anticipation of their departure for Texas, the Smith party camped in a dusty canyon of the Santa Monica Mountains, waiting for another slave in the group to give birth. Along with at least one sheriff, Bob Owens and a band of his vaqueros surprised Smith. Owens petitioned for a writ of habeas corpus for Mason and her children. The sheriff spirited Mason and her daughters to the county jail, where he housed them for their own protection. In January 1856, their case went before District Court Judge Benjamin Hayes.

When confronted in court, Smith claimed that his slaves were members of his family, and that they were voluntarily going with him to Texas. Within the political and legal climate of 1856, it took determined courage for a slave to challenge a slaveholder in court. Not only was Mason bucking hundreds of years of slave-master power relations, she also confronted a legal barrier: California law prohibited the testimony of any person with half or more Negro blood (as well as Indians and Chinese) in court cases involving whites.

To get around the ban, Judge Hayes asked Mason to speak to him privately in his chambers. She told him, "I have always done what I have been told to do; I always feared this trip to Texas, since I first heard of it. Mr. Smith told me I would be just as free in Texas as here."

On the second morning of the trial, without informing her, Mason's attorney abandoned the case. When he was subpoenaed by the judge, the lawyer revealed that Smith and his attorney had bribed him a hundred dollars to drop the case. The sight of the bereft Mason and her children in the courtroom aroused the judge's sympathy.

Ruling that Smith had given up his right to ownership of slaves once he entered

California, the judge declared Mason and her daughters free.

Mason started working as a midwife and nurse in Los Angeles. After ten years, she had saved two hundred and fifty dollars and bought land amidst vineyards and vegetable gardens on Spring Street between Third and Fourth Streets, in the outskirts of the town. She parlayed her real estate holdings into wealth that was remarkable at the time for anyone, let alone a single African American woman. She used her wealth to feed and clothe the destitute in her neighborhood and helped to found the Los Angeles branch of the First African Methodist Episcopal Church.

In 1857, the year after Biddy Mason won her freedom, the United States Supreme Court ruled in

Despite a ban against slavery in the 1849 state constitution, many slaves brought into California after statehood, like Biddy Mason, remained in bondage. In 1856 a California judge granted Mason her freedom. She became a wealthy property owner and philanthropist in Los Angeles.

the infamous *Dred Scott* decision that slaves or descendants of slaves could not be U.S. citizens, and that blacks "had no rights which the white man was bound to respect."

That same year, an eighteen-year-old black man named Archy Lee made a very different kind of history in California. Lee had traveled overland from a Mississippi plantation with a man who claimed to own him, Charles Stovall. The trip was arduous; Stovall's oxen team gave out and the pair crossed the Sierra Nevada on foot. When they arrived in Sacramento in the fall, Stovall, low on funds and frail in health, hired Lee out for wages. Stovall also opened a private school, advertising in the local paper.

A small but active black community lived in northern California. Many free blacks had come to the state during the gold rush, settling later in the growing urban centers of San Francisco, Sacramento, and Stockton, where they became ministers, proprietors of small businesses, and laborers. Ships that docked in San Francisco's harbor brought many African American crew members. Shortly after the gold rush, the black community formed the Franchise League, perhaps the first civil rights group in the state, which broadened into the California Colored Convention in 1855. Subscriptions to Frederick Douglass's abolitionist newspaper *North Star* numbered fifty in San Francisco, a city with only one thousand African Americans.

When slave owner Stovall eventually decided he preferred life in Mississippi and planned to return with his slave to the plantation, he met great resistance from the African American community. Archy Lee was given refuge at Hotel Hackett, a Sacramento rooming house owned by free blacks. Stovall tracked him down and had him jailed. Immediately, one of the hotel proprietors filed a petition for a writ of habeas corpus to get Lee released.

The Sacramento courtroom of Judge Robert Robinson was packed with spectators—both black and white. There were no black lawyers in California, but the community had raised money for Lee's legal representation. One of his chief financial supporters was Mary Ellen Pleasant, herself a former slave, who had become one of the richest women in San Francisco. She had arrived from Nantucket in the gold rush years with fifteen thousand dollars in gold coins (a legacy she received after her first husband died) and wisely invested her money while continuing to work as a cook and domestic. She bought and began operating a fashionable boardinghouse bordering San Francisco's plaza that catered to the political elite.

Judge Robinson granted the writ, but as soon as Lee was released, he was re-arrested and led back to jail. His putative owner had succeeded in getting a new warrant from California Supreme Court Justice David Terry.

Though Lee's supporters were stunned, they eventually determined that going to the state supreme court might clarify the state's stance on slavery in California: state law permitted slaveholders "in transit" to maintain ownership of their slaves while in California. Lee's friends were confident they could prove that Stovall was not a transient and therefore could not claim ownership of Archy Lee. The atmosphere was tense. Of the three justices on the California Supreme Court, two were proslavery: Chief Justice Terry, who later served as a brigadier general in the Confederate army, and Associate Justice Peter H. Burnett, who, as California's first governor, had repeatedly proposed legislation to exclude free blacks from the state. Only Associate Justice Stephen J. Field, a Connecticut-born lawyer, opposed slavery.

The February 11, 1858, ruling may be one of the most curious and disturbing decisions in the court's early history. "In our view," Justice Burnett wrote, "a mere visitor is one who comes only for pleasure or health, and who engages in no business while here, and remains only for a reasonable time...If the person engages in business himself, or employs his slave in any business except attending upon his person or his family, he forfeits the character of visitor and his slave is entitled to freedom." The court recognized that Stovall was clearly not a "visitor" to California, as he had set up a school and hired Lee out for pay.

But in a surprising twist that outraged many Californians, Justice Burnett concluded that although Stovall was not entitled to claim Lee as his property, the court would nonetheless order Lee's return to Stovall because it was "the first case that occurred under the existing law....and under these circumstances we are not disposed to rigidly enforce the rule for the first time."

Lee's bid for freedom in a free state was thwarted.

The men of the Colored Convention were determined to liberate Lee. Word spread that Stovall planned to put Lee on a ship leaving San Francisco Bay. Volunteers from the African American community kept watch on the wharves. Stovall had hidden Lee on a small boat anchored off Angel Island, planning to transfer him at night to the Panama-bound *Orizaba*.

But this time the slave owner was thwarted. The black patrols had obtained a writ of habeas corpus from County Judge T. W. Freelon and alerted the sheriff of their plan. As Stovall's boat approached the ship, he was served with a warrant for holding a slave. Lee was taken into custody. The *Orizaba* sailed without them.

Tension was high as the case returned to court. One San Francisco newspaper counseled Judge Freelon that "there is in the life of every man a time to 'make his mark'" and called on him to free Lee and restore the state constitution from "the low estate into which it had fallen." The courtroom and the halls outside were packed with supporters and opponents of slavery.

Lee's new attorney was the well-known Quaker Edward D. Baker, an abolitionist orator and personal friend of Abraham Lincoln. Baker argued that the earlier state supreme court judgment should not hold, because it had not properly been brought as an appeal. He thundered, "[Chief Justice] Burnett said he would set aside the Constitution and the law because Stovall was ignorant of our law. God Almighty sets a premium on knowledge; the Supreme Court offers a reward for ignorance." Stovall's lawyer did not object. Judge Freelon overturned the earlier ruling and declared Lee's freedom.

A throng of supporters was waiting to parade Archy Lee through the streets of San Francisco. But as they left the courtroom, U.S. marshals seized Lee and took him back into custody. Stovall, assuming he might not prevail against Lee's prominent lawyer, had brought his claim to U.S. Commissioner George Pen Johnston, a southerner with a proslavery background.

Johnston surprised many by rejecting Stovall's claim that Lee was violating the National Fugitive Slave Law. The Kentucky-born Democrat, in a blow to Stovall and others who would import slavery to California, stated, "It seems a monstrous doctrine that on one affidavit [from Stovall, alleging Lee had escaped slavery in Mississippi] I should send a man off to be taken to another state as a slave...."

This time, Archy Lee was really free. The former slave was carried off like a hero. The community held a victory celebration and found a secure home for Lee at the fashionable boardinghouse of Mary Ellen Pleasant, who the following year helped finance John Brown's raid on Harper's Ferry.

Disagreements between the California Supreme Court justices who originally determined Archy Lee's fate lasted for decades. Though Chief Justice David Terry joined the Confederate army, he returned to California after the Civil War and settled in Stockton. In 1888 Justice Stephen Field, who by then was a federal judge, heard a case involving Terry's second wife, ruling against her. Months later, the two former colleagues met by chance in a railroad station, where Terry slapped Field. Field's bodyguard shot and killed the former chief justice.

A Century before Rosa Parks

By 1863 African Americans had won their right to testify in court, and a few years later, Mary Ellen Pleasant and Charlotte Brown exercised that right when they sued two San Francisco streetcar companies over segregation.

Charlotte L. Brown was well known in San Francisco's African American community: her mother, Charlotte Brown, born a free woman in Baltimore, had worked as a seamstress to buy the freedom of her husband, James. When the couple moved to San Francisco, James opened a stable and cofounded *Mirror of the Times*, one of the first African American newspapers in the state. An antislavery crusader, Brown also raised funds for Archy Lee.

As the sun was setting on April 17, 1863, Brown left her residence for a doctor's appointment on Howard Street. When the Omnibus Railroad car stopped on Filbert Street, she entered from the rear platform. There were only three other passengers, and she took a seat midway down the car. A conductor ordered her off. As Brown recalled, "I told him I had been in the habit of riding ever since the cars had been running. He answered, colored persons are not allowed to ride and I would have to get out."

Brown refused to leave. For three more stops, the conductor tried to eject her.

Finally, Brown recalled, "He took hold of me, by the left arm, somewhere. I made no resistance as he had taken me by the arm. I knew it was of no use to resist, and therefore I went out, and he kept hold of me until I was out of the car, holding on to me until I struck the walk."

Encouraged by her father, Brown sued the company for two hundred dollars. In response to the lawsuit, Omnibus Railroad justified its conductor's action by arguing that racial segregation was necessary to protect white women and children who might be fearful of riding side by side with an African American, an argument that was commonly used to justify segregation. But in November 1863, a San Francisco superior court judge rejected this reasoning and awarded Brown damages of five cents (the streetcar fare) plus legal costs.

Her success in court, though, did not immediately translate into change. Within days of the judgment, another streetcar conductor forced Brown and her father from a car. The tenacious Brown brought another lawsuit. And in October 1864, District Court Judge C. C. Pratt ruled that San Francisco streetcar segregation was illegal. He stated:

> It has been already quite too long tolerated by the dominant race to see with indifference the negro or mulatto treated as a brute, insulted, wronged, enslaved, made to wear a yoke, to tremble before white men, to serve him as a tool, to hold property and life at his will, to surrender to him his intellect and conscience, and to seal his lips and belie his thought through dread of the white man's power.

A jury awarded Brown five hundred dollars, a tenth of the five thousand she had sought in damages.

The judgment generated racist editorials in the San Francisco papers. And despite the legal victory, African Americans in the city still wound up walking to their destinations after streetcar drivers refused to stop for them.

One of them was Mary Ellen Pleasant. In 1866, three years after Charlotte Brown's lawsuits, a conductor on the North Beach Municipal Railroad refused to pick up the tall, middle-aged woman. She sued, and a jury awarded Pleasant five hundred dollars in punitive damages.

The streetcar company appealed the decision to the California Supreme Court. The high court ruled streetcar exclusion based on race was unlawful, but it also rescinded the damage payment to Pleasant, since there was no proof "to show willful injury," or any proof that the streetcar company had a policy of excluding blacks.

The lawsuits succeeded in changing the racist practice: no more stories about streetcar exclusion appeared in the local black press, which had reported all such incidents vigilantly. In 1893 the legislature enacted a statewide prohibition on streetcar segregation and exclusion.

Separate but Equal?

For nearly a century, California law allowed for and even mandated racial segregation in public schools.

In 1855 Paul K. Hubbs, state superintendent of public instruction, declared that segregation was the state's policy. "Whilst I foster by all proper means the education of the colored races," he explained, "I should deem it a death to our system to permit the mixture of the races in the same school." The education of children of color depended on their parents' capacity to pay for separate schools, or sympathetic white benefactors.

In 1859 Hubbs's successor, Andrew Jackson Moulder, argued that "to force African, Chinese and Diggers [a derogatory term for California Indians] into one school... must result in the ruin of the schools. The great mass of our citizens will not associate in terms of equality with these inferior races; nor will they consent that their children do so." Moulder was willing, though, to allow for separate segregated schools "for the inferior races...providing that the white citizens do not object."

By 1863 the state legislature had excluded children of color from white schools, threatening to withhold funding from any school that violated the law.

In 1872, after failing to get state legislation passed to outlaw segregated schools, African American leaders in San Francisco looked for a judicial remedy. They hired prominent attorney John W. Dwinelle to file a lawsuit on behalf of twelve-year-old Mary Frances Ward. Noah Flood, principal of the Broadway School, had refused to enroll the African American child in his all-white school. In 1874 the state supreme court ruled in *Ward v. Flood* that although Ward had a right to a public education, she did not have a right to attend the same school as white children. The justices saw no constitutional violation if African Americans were educated in segregated public schools on equal terms as whites. The court thus wrote into California law the "separate but equal" concept twenty-two years prior to the U.S. Supreme Court's decision enshrining that principle in *Plessy v. Ferguson.*

The silver lining to an otherwise dark judicial cloud was that the court mandated districts that didn't have segregated schools to allow all children, regardless of race, to attend a common integrated school. By the year following the *Ward* decision, school boards in San Francisco, Oakland, Sacramento, and Vallejo had eliminated segregated schools for African Americans. Mary Frances Ward began attending an integrated school.

In 1880 the legislature amended the General School Law of California, eliminating all references to race and requiring that "schools must be open for admission of all children." At the same time, the legislature repealed the law allowing districts to establish separate schools for African American and Indian children.

In 1888, seventy-two-year-old Edmond Wysinger tried to enroll his twelve-year-old son, Arthur, in a white public school in the Central Valley town of Visalia. S. A. Crookshank, a teacher, told the former slave to take his son to the "colored school." Wysinger sued for his son's admission to the Visalia School but lost in Tulare County Superior Court.

Despite the 1880 law, Visalia maintained segregated schools. The school district had operated a "colored" school since 1873, but it was not as well equipped and well maintained as the two-story Visalia School for white students, less than a mile away. Because it was difficult to secure teachers, the "colored school" year often began late and ended early.

In 1890 the state supreme court ruled in *Wysinger v. Crookshank* that the Visalia school district could not bar Arthur Wysinger from the white school on the narrow grounds that the legislature had denied local school boards the authority to establish segregated schools for African American children and had repealed sections of the Education Code requiring separate schools for African American and Indian children.

The court left open the possibility that political winds could shift again to allow segregation of students recently allowed to integrate: "If the people of the state desire separate schools for citizens of African descent, and Indians," the justices stated, "their wish may be accomplished by laws enacted by the law-making department of the government within existing constitutional provisions."

Reinforcing the notion that the court was not concerned with integration from a civil rights perspective, the justices pointed to an 1885 law that allowed for the segregation of Chinese, or "Mongolian," children.

That statute had grown out of a determined Chinese American family's attempt to enroll their daughter in an all-white elementary school in San Francisco.

In September 1884, Joseph and Mary Tape, Chinese immigrants who described themselves as "Christian, Americanized," had tried to enroll their eight-year-old daughter, Mamie, at the Spring Valley School. When the principal denied her admission, Mary McGladery Tape was determined to fight for integration. Tape, a Shanghai orphan brought to the U.S. by missionaries, sued the school board and also wrote a scathing letter to the *Alta*, which was published on April 16, 1885. The letter read in part:

> To the Board of Education—Dear Sirs: I see that you are going to make all sorts of excuses to keep my child out of the Public schools. Dear sirs, Will you please tell me! Is it a disgrace to be Born a Chinese? What right have you to bar my children out of the school because she is a Chinese Descend....May you Mr. Moulder never be persecuted like the way you have persecuted little Mamie Tape. I will let the world see sir What justice there is When it is govern by the Race prejudice men!

A municipal judge ruled in favor of Mamie Tape, basing his decision on the law requiring public schools to be open for admission of all children. On March 3, 1885, the state supreme court upheld the decision.

But when Mamie Tape showed up for class at the Spring Valley School, along with her family's attorneys, she was not allowed to enroll. The principal put her on a wait-ing list, claiming that she did not have the required vaccination certificate and that classes were already full.

While Mamie was waiting for admission, Superintendent Andrew Jackson Moulder, who twenty-five years earlier had argued for school segregation when serv-ing as state superintendent of public instruction, refused to admit her. He furiously lobbied for the passage of a bill to allow school districts to establish separate schools for "Mongolians." The legislature promptly passed a bill requiring all Asian children to attend segregated schools if they existed in a district.

Soon after the law went into effect, the San Francisco school board established a separate school for Chinese children on the outskirts of Chinatown. Mamie Tape and her brother Frank were among the first students enrolled.

Twenty years later, in May 1905, an unlikely alliance of trade unions and the business-dominated Native Sons of the Golden West, buttressed by the "Yellow Peril" hysterics of the press, formed the Oriental Exclusion League. The league successfully lobbied the San Francisco school board to segregate ninety-three Japanese public school students.

The Japanese government lodged a formal complaint. President Theodore Roos-evelt negotiated between the offended Japanese government and San Francisco lead-ers intent on segregation. In February 1907, Roosevelt invited San Francisco Mayor Eugene Schmitz and members of the San Francisco Board of Education to Washing-ton, DC, and convinced the local leaders to rescind previous segregation policies and allow Japanese children to attend public schools.

Native Americans were also subject to segregation. In 1893, not long after the *Wysinger* case in Visalia, the legislature had amended California's School Law to al-low districts to segregate Indian students. In 1921 the state further required Indian children to attend segregated federal Indian schools if one was within three miles of the child's residence.

In 1923, fifteen-year-old Alice Piper challenged the Big Pine School District in Inyo County for refusing to allow her to enroll at her local school because there was a nearby federal Indian school. On June 1, 1924, the California Supreme Court is-sued a mixed decision. The unanimous court ruled that the education of California children was the responsibility of the state, not the federal government. Therefore, the law compelling Indian students to attend schools run by the U.S. government was invalid. The court, however, judged constitutional the law allowing school districts to segregate Indians. It took nearly a decade for the state legislature to amend the School Law, in 1935, prohibiting segregation of Indian students.

"Inferiority Where None Exists"

While the School Law explicitly mandated segregation of African Americans, Native Americans, and Asians, the legislature never included Mexican Americans in the ranks of unwanted students. Under California law, Mexican Americans were considered "white." It was common practice, however, for districts with large Mexican American populations to engage in de facto segregation.

Gonzalo and Felicitas Mendez knew the sting of segregation.

Gonzalo, who had emigrated with his family from Chihuahua because of political unrest in Mexico, had worked all his life as a farm laborer. His wife, from Juncos, Puerto Rico, also was a migrant worker. Both were American citizens (Gonzalo naturalized in the early 1940s and Felicitas by virtue of her birth in Puerto Rico.) Known as one of the fastest orange pickers in Orange County, Gonzalo commanded a higher wage than many of his peers. His earnings allowed the frugal couple to save enough by 1944 to lease their own ranch, raising asparagus on forty acres in the rural Orange County community of Westminster. In many ways, they were living the American dream.

That fall, Gonzalo's sister, Soledad (Sally) Vidaurri, took her two children and Gonzalo's three children to enroll at the nearby 17th Street School.

An administrator refused to admit nine-year-old Sylvia Mendez or her brothers, Gonzalo Jr. and Geronimo, to the nearly all-white school, though he was willing to admit their lighter-skinned cousins. The Mendez children, the administrator explained, would have to enroll at the Hoover School, Westminster's "Mexican school," located a few blocks from the well-equipped 17th Street School.

At the time, Mexican Americans constituted the largest minority group in California and

Seven years before the U.S. Supreme Court repudiated the "separate but equal" doctrine, Gonzalo and Felicitas Mendez successfully sued Orange County school districts to end segregation of Mexican American students. NAACP attorney Thurgood Marshall used legal strategies from the Mendez case in Brown v. Board of Education.

more than 80 percent of southern California's agricultural labor force. Agribusiness leaders wanted to maintain this pool of workers; one Imperial Valley grower commented, "The schools teach Mexicans to look upon farm labor as menial. It only makes them dissatisfied and teaches them to read the wrong kind of literature."

In addition to economic motivations, racism contributed heavily to demands for segregation of Mexican American children. An educator in 1920 found that most whites wanted segregated schools because they viewed Mexicans as "a menace to the health and morals of the rest of the community."

School administrators in the 1920s had also justified segregation of Mexican American students for pedagogical reasons. They argued that segregated schools aided in "Americanization" programs that not only taught the presumably monolingual Spanish-speaking students English but also "American values," sanitation practices, and work habits. The expectation among many white policy makers and educators was that Mexican Americans would only fill vocational, industrial, and domestic service jobs; consequently, they need not be educated beyond the eighth grade.

This attitude had not changed much by the time the Mendez children were denied admission to the 17th Street School. James L. Kent, superintendent of the Garden Grove School District, near Westminster, believed that "Mexicans were inferior in personal hygiene, ability, and in their economic outlook." He listed "lice, impetigo, tuberculosis, generally dirty hands, face, neck and ears" as hygienic problems endemic among Mexican American children. He vowed that he would never allow a Mexican American child to enroll in the same school as a white child.

The differences between the "Mexican" and "white" schools in Westminster were typical of segregated schools throughout southern California: the Hoover School was a small frame building bordering a cow pasture; students there used hand-me-down books and discarded desks and other materials from the 17th Street School, where white students enjoyed new books and materials and ran on cultivated grass and playing fields.

Gonzalo and Felicitas Mendez were outraged when they learned that school officials had refused to enroll their children. The couple had taught their children that they had the same rights and responsibilities as other Americans. Like countless immigrants before them, the Mendezes, who had abandoned their own schooling early to support their families, recognized that education was key to ensuring a bright future. The rejection of their children at the 17th Street School was an ugly reminder of the racism underlying much of American life; only recently, they'd had another reminder: the Mendezes leased their land from a Japanese American family that was incarcerated because of wartime racism.

Instead of accepting segregation, Gonzalo and Felicitas Mendez decided to organize and advocate through the political system. They and other Mexican American parents convinced the Westminster school board to place on the local ballot a bond measure to raise funds for a new, integrated school. Voters, however, rejected the measure, and the school board did not pursue the funding. Still believing that a political remedy could be found, the Mendezes and others sent a letter to the school board asking that all parents who wanted their children transferred out of the "Mexican" school be allowed to do so. Not only did the board flatly refuse this request, it reduced the already small number of token transfers.

The stage was set for a judicial showdown.

Challenges to segregation of Mexican Americans were not unprecedented. In 1931 Mexican American parents in the small community of Lemon Grove, east of San Diego, had successfully convinced a local court to permit seventy-five Mexican American children to attend the local "white" school. In the 1940s, Los Angeles attorney David Marcus had won a lawsuit on behalf of Mexican Americans who challenged segregation in nearby San Bernardino public parks and swimming pools.

The Mendezes hired Marcus to represent them. He recommended that they join forces with a group of Mexican American World War II veterans, parents of students in the neighboring communities of Garden Grove, El Modena, and Santa Ana, who had also unsuccessfully petitioned their respective school boards to end segregation. On March 5, 1945, they filed *Mendez v. Westminster*, a class action suit on behalf of five thousand Mexican American children attending schools in four Orange County communities.

Gonzalo took a year off from work to organize the local Mexican American community around the case, accompanying Marcus on trips to the fields and citrus groves to persuade parents and their children to testify in court; he even offered to pay the transportation expenses and lost wages of anyone willing to testify at the trial in Los Angeles. He was motivated not only by the blatant injustice of segregation but also because he didn't want his "Sylvia, Gonzalo, and Geronimo growing up with hatred in their hearts for the children that went to the beautiful school."

At trial, Orange County Counsel Joel Ogle defended the four school districts, arguing that the U.S. Supreme Court's ruling in *Plessy v. Ferguson* legally justified segregation as long as separate facilities were equal. He further argued that there was a pedagogical need to segregate Mexican students in order to help them with the English language and to teach them American values and customs.

Marcus easily refuted the latter argument with testimony from the Mendez children, all of whom spoke English fluently. Other evidence revealed that school administrators did not base school assignments on English language proficiency tests, but rather on students' family names and skin color. Marcus used a novel strategy of calling on a social scientist, UCLA anthropology professor Ralph Deals, who testified that racial segregation in the Orange County schools harmed both Mexican American and white students because it reinforced stereotypes of inferiority and superiority, and that segregation hindered English-language acquisition because "the best way to learn any foreign language is to go among the people who speak that language."

Almost a year after the trial, U.S. District Judge Paul J. McCormick issued his opinion on February 18, 1946, in support of the Mendez family. McCormick dismissed the *Plessy* precedent by explaining that the "separate but equal" doctrine was inapplicable to California because the state had no law requiring segregation of Mexican American students; the *Plessy* ruling only applied to states in which state law imposed racial segregation. He then addressed the key issue of whether there was any educationally valid reason to segregate Mexican American children. He said that the "only tenable ground upon which segregation practices" could be justified was "the English-language difficulties of the children." He noted, though, that Mexican American children were not segregated for educational purposes.

Judge McCormick accepted the social science research as clear evidence that segregation hindered Spanish-speaking children from learning English. He elaborated by ruling that "commingling of the entire student body instills and develops a common cultural attitude among the school children which is imperative for the perpetuation of American institutions and ideals." He attacked segregation as fostering "antagonisms in the children" and suggesting "inferiority among them where none exists." Since no valid educational reason existed to justify racial separation, segregation violated the students' constitutional rights.

The school boards appealed. By this point, the *Mendez* case had attracted national attention as the possible suit in which a federal court would rule the "separate but equal" principle unconstitutional. That was the argument that the ACLU and National Lawyers Guild forwarded in friend-of-the-court briefs they filed in support of the Mendez family. They were joined by the American Jewish Congress, Japanese American Citizens' League, California Attorney General Robert Kenny, and a young NAACP attorney named Thurgood Marshall.

On April 14, 1947, the Ninth Circuit unanimously upheld Judge McCormick's decision but did not deliver the knockout punch invalidating the "separate but equal" doctrine. The *Mendez* case is nevertheless significant because it was the first time a federal court ruled that segregation of Mexican Americans in public schools violated not only state law but also the federal Constitution. It served as a precedent for federal courts in Texas (1948) and Arizona (1950) to rule *de jure* (government sanctioned) segregation of Mexican American school students unconstitutional. It also contributed to the passage of a bill signed by California Governor Earl Warren repealing all school laws requiring segregation.

The *Mendez* case was also an important trial run for strategies—such as the innovative use of social science research—and arguments successfully employed by Thurgood Marshall less than a decade later in the landmark *Brown v. Board of Education* case, in which the U.S. Supreme Court, led by Chief Justice Earl Warren, overturned *Plessy v. Ferguson* and ruled that "separate but equal" public schools were unconstitutional. David Marcus, the Mendez family lawyer, gave Marshall all of the documents from the *Mendez* trial.

Gonzalo Mendez died of heart failure in 1964, but Felicitas and her children lived to see a new school in Santa Ana dedicated in the fall of 1997: the Gonzalo and Felicitas Mendez School honored the couple who had helped end legal segregation of Mexican Americans.

Forbidden Love, Forbidden Marriage

In the spring of 1909, Gunjiro Aoki, a Japanese immigrant, and Helen Gladys Emery, the daughter of the archdeacon of the Protestant Episcopal Diocese of California, were like Romeo and Juliet. The couple had met through Aoki's brother, who worked for the archdeacon. They intended to marry.

Emery's family sought medical explanations for their daughter's love for the wavy-haired immigrant. Aoki's Japanese compatriots offered him a thousand dollars to break up with the sweet-faced twenty-one-year-old.

In Emery's hometown of Corte Madera, a crowd threw bricks at Aoki and threatened to tar and feather him. The young couple met with resistance in Portland and Tacoma. Finally, the mayor of Seattle gave them permission to marry there—under armed guard. When Emery left with her mother to marry Aoki, a mob met them at the train station, jeering and yelling, banging tin cans and throwing rotting flowers.

The couple faced not only societal disapproval but a legal barrier. The California legislature had passed an anti-miscegenation law in 1850 prohibiting marriages between whites and African Americans or mulattos. When anti-Asian prejudice increased with growing immigration from Asia, the legislature amended the law to ban marriages between whites and "Mongolians." The law imposed criminal penalties on civil and religious authorities who performed marriages between whites and people of other races.

Even a public health leader, Thomas M. Logan, a former president of the American Medical Association and the secretary of the California Board of Health, in 1871 had expressed the belief that evils were "likely to result from the combined intermixture of races and the introduction of habits and customs of a sensual and depraved people." Logan was referring to Chinese immigrants, but the stereotype of sexual perversity and promiscuity was also commonly assigned to African Americans and Japanese and Filipino immigrants.

Well into the twentieth century, many white Californians subscribed to the "polygenetic" concept of human development, believing that the human race had originated in several racially distinct ancestors. The white "race," according to the theory, was superior, and its purity should not be violated by mixture with "inferior races." California's anti-miscegenation law was silent on the subject of marriages between people of color of differing racial backgrounds.

In 1922 Congress passed the Cable Act, which invalidated a woman's American citizenship if she married an Asian immigrant. Federal law designated Chinese and Japanese immigrants "aliens ineligible for citizenship." The Cable Act was not repealed until 1936.

When immigration restrictions reduced the number of Chinese and Japanese coming to California, Filipino men began immigrating in greater numbers. Confused about whether Filipinos were "Mongolian," county clerks throughout the state were inconsistent in approving marriage licenses between Filipino men and white women. After a closely divided California appellate court ruled in 1933 that marriages between Filipinos and whites were legal because Filipinos were not "Mongolian" but of the "Malay" race, state lawmakers quickly passed a law invalidating marriages between Caucasians and Malays.

Filipino immigrants brought lawsuits challenging application of the anti-miscegenation law to them, but they did not dispute the fundamental fairness and constitutionality of the law. That did not occur until the late 1940s, when the Los Angeles county clerk denied a young couple a marriage license.

Twenty-five-year-old Andrea Perez and twenty-seven-year-old Sylvester Davis had dated for several months before deciding to marry. The post–World War II years looked promising to Perez, an immigrant from Mexico, and Davis, a veteran who had graduated from Los Angeles City College. They looked forward to a wedding mass celebrated in the Roman Catholic tradition in which they had both been brought up.

The couple climbed the steps of the building where the Los Angeles county clerk's office was located to obtain a marriage license. The county clerk, however, refused to issue them the license because Perez listed her race as "white" while Davis listed his as "Negro."

Perez and Davis were crestfallen, but not willing to abandon their commitment to each other. Perez contacted her former employer, attorney Daniel Marshall, and asked if he would represent them. He quickly agreed.

When the case reached the trial court, the county argued that the anti-miscegenation law was necessary to prevent the "Caucasian race from being contaminated by races whose members are by nature physically and mentally inferior to Caucasians." The county further reasoned that even if African Americans, Asians, and Native Americans were not by nature inferior to whites, the law was necessary to prevent the birth of children who would become "social problems." The county counsel deemed white people and persons of color who wanted to marry the "dregs of society."

Perez v. Sharp reached the California Supreme Court in 1948. The justices by a 4-3 vote struck down the anti-miscegenation law as arbitrary and unreasonable discrimination against certain racial groups. Although the vote was close, the passion motivating the majority was clear. Justice Roger Traynor wrote, "Marriage is something more than a civil contract subject to regulation by the state. It is a fundamental right of free men." Justice Jesse Carter called the ban on interracial marriage the "product of ignorance, prejudice, and intolerance."

The three dissenting justices, however, had their fingers on the pulse of popular opinion. Even after the ruling, it took eleven years and five attempts before the legislature removed the unenforceable anti-miscegenation provision from the books. This recalcitrance mirrored national attitudes toward interracial marriage: a year after the 1967 U.S. Supreme Court decision in *Loving v. Virginia*, which invalidated all existing anti-miscegenation laws in the country, a Gallup poll revealed that 72 percent of American adults disapproved of marriages between whites and people of color.

No Place to Be a Filipino

California was no stranger to racialized mob violence. The literal decimation of the native Californian population, from more than one hundred and fifty thousand to fifteen thousand in just a few decades, was due in part to lethal attacks. Carey McWilliams reports that the lynching of Mexicans in the 1860s in the southern part of the state was so common that newspapers scarcely bothered to report the details. In 1871 a mob of white and Latino vigilantes hung Chinese residents of Los Angeles from trees, gutters, and warehouse gates in the largest mass lynching in California history.

In the 1930s, this grim history continued when vigilantes again took the law into their own hands. Filipinos were the targets of a white mob in the agricultural town of Watsonville—with lethal consequences.

In many ways, Filipinos were an attractive labor pool. In 1898 the Philippines had become a colony of the United States with an educational system conducted in English, so that even those with just an elementary school education had a working knowledge of English. By 1930, approximately fifty thousand Filipinos lived in the

Under California's anti-miscegenation laws, Filipino men could not marry white women. Couples like the one pictured here had to go out of state to marry. The law was not changed until 1948.

United States, thirty-four thousand in California. The growers of the Pajaro Valley considered them prime workers for their crops: strawberries, sugar beets, blackberries, hops, and California's "green gold"—lettuce—because they were willing to do the backbreaking stoop labor that white workers disdained.

Filipino men could not legally marry white women in California, and federal immigration law severely restricted the number of Filipinas who could enter the country. This created a bachelor class of Filipinos, a transient army of workers who picked crops around the state. They lived in all-male labor camps and cheap hotels on the edges of Chinatowns in California cities.

Growers exploited Filipino workers, paying them rock-bottom wages. White workers resented them not only as economic competitors but because they socialized with white women. These two strains—rivalry at the workplace and in the dance halls—led to many violent attacks on Filipino workers.

In January 1930, as part of a statewide lobbying effort to pass a federal law barring Filipinos from the U.S.—similar to the Chinese Exclusion Act—the Northern Monterey Chamber of Commerce, headed by Judge D. W. Rohrbach, proposed a ban on Filipino labor. Filipinos were "disease carriers," Rohrbach declared, who were "but ten years removed from the bolo and the breech cloth." He added that it would be "better that the fields of Salinas Valley should grow into weed patches" than to allow Filipinos to stay.

The California State Federation of Labor endorsed the bill. On January 18, the Watsonville *Pajaronian* banner headline screamed, "State Organizations Will Fight Filipino Influx into the Country."

That night, Filipino workers leased a "taxi dance" hall seven miles southwest of Watsonville. A mob of white youths attacked the hall and tried to shut it down, but the Filipinos drove them away. The white teens formed "hunting parties," roaming the town, looking for fights, and shooting into Filipino labor camps. Though the police tried to keep a semblance of control, they were far outnumbered.

The Filipinos organized in self-defense against continuing mob violence, and they produced "The Torch," a broadsheet calling on fellow workers to fight the "Filipino-phobia" that was rampant in the valley.

By January 22, Watsonville police still could not control the white mobs. Santa Cruz County District Attorney W. M. Gardner ordered taxi dance halls closed. Hundreds of vigilantes raided Filipino living quarters, dragged residents into the street, beat them, and threw them off the Pajaro River bridge. A Chinese-owned apple drying business that employed Filipino workers was destroyed. Watching his town descend into mob violence, Watsonville Sheriff Nick Sinnott provided the Filipinos refuge in the city council chamber.

The hunting parties rampaged through the night. In the early hours of the morning, vigilantes fired bullets into a bunkhouse at the Murphy ranch. When dawn broke, twenty-two-year-old Fermin Tobera lay dead, shot through the heart.

A vigilante had left his shoe at the labor camp, which led to his arrest and the arrests of seven others. Several were sons of prominent families. Though they were charged with rioting and unruly conduct, they never faced murder charges for the death of Tobera. The district attorney never moved to recuse Judge Rohrbach from the case, despite his well-publicized anti-Filipino statements. The eight, convicted only of rioting, served thirty days in the county jail and were told to "refrain from agitation against the darker races."

The murder of Fermin Tobera shocked the Filipino community and reverberated all the way across the Pacific. The Philippine Resident Commissioner condemned the killing before Congress. After a funeral service in Watsonville, Tobera's body was sent home to Manila, where he received a martyr's welcome. The government laid him in state in the capitol and he was mourned by thousands.

His official death certificate simply read, "killed by some unknown person."

Deadliest Disaster

On the hot summer night of July 17, 1944, just before midnight, two military cargo ships exploded at the Port Chicago Naval Base, thirty miles northeast of San Francisco, sending a column of smoke and fire nearly two miles high. The *E. A. Bryan*, which was fully loaded with forty-six hundred tons of cluster bombs, depth charges, and other ammunition, was blown to bits. The only remnant of the giant *Quinault Victory* was its keel, which protruded from the water more than a thousand feet from shore. The explosion at Port Chicago, the deadliest disaster on U.S. soil during World War II, set off a chain of events that led to the desegregation of the entire U.S. military and the beginning of the civil rights movement.

The African American servicemen who loaded ships at Port Chicago with ammunition for the Pacific Theater worked around the clock. Hundreds of sailors were on the pier that night, and all of them died. Of the 320 fatalities from the explosion, 202 were African American. In the enlisted men's barracks at Port Chicago, black sailors from Chicago, New York, and other large urban centers lived with blacks from segregated rural Mississippi and Alabama. But no whites.

As Port Chicago veteran Joe Small explained:

> I went into the Navy in 1943. I left Great Lakes, Illinois, as an apprentice seaman and was shipped to Port Chicago, a naval ammunitions depot. Everybody above petty officer was white. All of the munitions handlers was black. We off-loaded ammunition from boxcars and loaded it on ships. We handled every type of ammunition that was being shipped overseas, from .30-caliber ammunition shells to five-hundred-pound bombs.

Small and his fellow sailors had gone through segregated boot camp. Very few blacks were allowed in combat. This had deeply frustrated nineteen-year-old Robert Routh from Memphis, who recalled, "To find yourself loading ammunition was a disappointment. We all wanted to be actually fighting. But we knew that what we did was essential to the war."

Working conditions at the segregated base were treacherous. The sailors worked twenty-four hours a day, in three shifts. Their equipment was substandard; many did not even have gloves.

According to Small:

> We were pushed by our officers. They bet between them as to what division would put on the most tonnage at any given time. We complained it would add danger to the already dangerous job. But we were assured that since there were no detonators in any of the shells or bombs, it was impossible for them to go off. None of us believed that.

More than two hundred African American sailors were killed when a munitions ship exploded at Port Chicago, northeast of San Francisco, in the deadliest disaster on U.S. soil during World War II. Those who refused to return to the lethal loading docks were court-martialed, but their defiance eventually led to the desegregation of the U.S. Navy.

A massive sea battle in the Philippines in the summer of 1944 escalated the U.S. military's need for heavy weaponry. As Port Chicago provided munitions for the entire Pacific Theater, loading assumed an even more furious pace. The *E. A. Bryan* had docked at Port Chicago on July 13, and by the 17th it was almost fully loaded. The *Quinault Victory* had just arrived that day. One hundred men went to work on the ship and were preparing it for the loading that was to start at midnight. Then the port exploded.

"It was the greatest fireworks you ever wanted to see," Robert Routh remembered. "With the second explosion, glass went everywhere. It was a combination of the glass and the concussion that destroyed my eyes." Routh was blinded by the huge blast and never regained his sight. The days and nights following the explosion were filled with horror. Routh recalled that many of the men had to collect the remains of fellow sailors from the ashes of the devastated pier. "You can imagine the psychological impact this had. My loss of sight was traumatic, but everyone had traumatic needs, physical or mental. And no help was given."

Although the white officers were granted thirty-day leaves, none of the black sailors were given leave or offered psychological counseling.

The Naval Court of Inquiry investigated the cause of the blast. It heard testimony from survivors, ammunition experts, and military personnel. Only five blacks were interviewed. No blame was placed on white officers for wagering over the speed of their units; the perilous practice was dismissed as good-natured fun. The naval court never officially established the exact cause of explosion. Just three weeks after the explosion, after the singed body parts, twisted metal, and smoldering debris had been cleared, the sailors were ordered back to work on a makeshift pier.

Initially, 258 men refused. When threatened with a court-martial, 200 went back to work. A lieutenant asked Joe Small if he would return to duty. He refused. Small recalled, "As I said that, someone back in the ranks said, 'If Small don't go, we won't go either.' From then on I was considered the leader." Small and 49 other sailors were charged with mutiny.

The deadly explosion had been widely covered in the national African American press, including the *Chicago Defender* and the *Pittsburgh Courier*. The NAACP mobilized its chapters around the country to pressure the Navy for a fair trial. Secretary of the Navy James Forrestal eventually agreed to allow NAACP Legal Defense and Educational Fund (LDF) staff attorney Thurgood Marshall to observe the trial. In the largest mass mutiny trial in U.S. Navy history, fifty African American sailors faced the seven white naval officers serving as judge and jury. The prosecutor, Lt. Commander James F. Coakley, argued that the sailors were cowards and guilty of treason. (Twenty-five years later, Coakley was the district attorney who prosecuted Black Panthers Huey Newton and Eldridge Cleaver.)

The trial lasted thirty-two days. The jury deliberated eighty minutes before finding all the sailors guilty of mutiny. They were sentenced to fifteen years of hard labor with a dishonorable discharge. Thurgood Marshall appealed the decision and pressed the sailors' case with First Lady Eleanor Roosevelt. The NAACP LDF published a pamphlet, "Mutiny: The Real Story of How the Navy Branded 50 Fear-Shocked Sailors as Mutineers," in which Marshall wrote, "I can't understand why, whenever more than one Negro disobeys an order, it's mutiny."

The appeal was rejected. The men stayed in prison. But their legacy did not end there. Because of the national publicity, the Navy altered its policy of segregated units. Shortly after the trial, the Navy desegregated training, shore facilities, and ships. Moreover, the military established new training and safety procedures for handling ammunition and explosions. For the first time, white sailors were assigned to Port Chicago to join African American sailors on the loading docks. Black sailors, some of whom had been at Port Chicago during the explosion, were assigned to ships at sea. After the war, the imprisoned sailors were released under a general amnesty, but their mutiny convictions have never been overturned. Their discharges did not entitle them to any veterans' benefits. Small explained, "I couldn't go to a VA hospital if I got sick. I lost my GI insurance. If I was to die under conditions that warranted a military funeral, I couldn't have it." The men who perished at Port Chicago accounted for 15 percent of all African American military deaths during World War II.

Housing: For Whites Only

Segregated residential areas have been part of California's social landscape since the American conquest. Ethnic neighborhoods checkered San Francisco in the gold rush era, with Chinatown being the most enduring. These enclaves developed not only out of people's desire to live with others who shared similar histories and cultural backgrounds, but also because of white hostility.

Private prejudice took on the color of legality through "restrictive covenants," agreements between white property owners not to sell to or allow non-whites or, in some cases, Jews to occupy residences. The first reported covenant involved San Diegans, who in 1892 tried to prevent a Chinese businessman the use of a laundry. In 1919 the California Supreme Court upheld the legality of a restrictive covenant preventing African American Alfred Gary from occupying a home in Los Angeles.

World War II created jobs in California aircraft manufacturing and shipbuilding plants and on military bases that attracted large numbers of African Americans, mainly to the Los Angeles region, the San Francisco Bay Area, and San Diego. From 1940 to 1950, the state's African American population more than tripled, from 124,306 to 462,172. This influx created housing crises in many cities. Government bodies, such as the public housing authority in the San Francisco Bay Area city of Richmond, created segregated housing for blacks. Restrictive covenants prevented African Americans from living outside a small section of South Central Los Angeles. But laws authorizing segregated housing began to erode in the mid-1940s.

In 1945 white property owners organized as the West Adams Improvement Association petitioned Los Angeles Superior Court Judge Thurmond Clarke to force fifty African Americans, including Academy Award–winning actress Hattie McDaniel, singer Ethel Waters, and actress Louise Beavers, from their homes in the Sugar Hill neighborhood of Los Angeles because they had violated covenants put in place by white property owners eight years earlier. The area of fading mansions had previously been an exclusive neighborhood of wealthy industrialists and bankers, but the Depression had compelled some to sell their homes. Beginning in the mid-1930s, African American professionals began buying houses in the area.

Loren Miller, a former journalist turned pathbreaking civil rights attorney, represented the African American homeowners.

Judge Clark addressed head-on the constitutionality of racially restrictive covenants, stating, "This court is of the opinion that it is time members of the Negro race are accorded without reservations and evasions the full rights guaranteed them under the Fourteenth Amendment of the Constitution. Judges have been avoiding the real issue too long. Certainly there was no discrimination against the Negro race when it came to calling upon its members to die on the battlefields in defense of this country in the war just ended."

The judge acknowledged that his decision was carefully worded to force "any higher court to pass on the constitutionality of all racial restrictive covenants before reversing the ruling."

While the Sugar Hill case, consolidated with other restrictive covenant cases, worked its way through the appellate process, the U.S. Supreme Court in the landmark 1948 decision *Shelley v. Kraemer* (which attorney Miller also litigated) struck down judicial enforcement of restrictive covenants as a violation of the Fourteenth Amendment. Just two weeks after this historic ruling, the California Supreme Court, citing *Shelley*, upheld Judge Clark's prohibition on judicial enforcement of restrictive covenants.

By the late 1950s and early 1960s, Governor Edmund G. (Pat) Brown and a majority of the state legislature favored racial integration. Within this political context, several important California laws took effect: In 1959, the Civil Rights Act, authored by Assembly Member Jesse Unruh, outlawed discrimination on the basis of race, color, religion, ancestry, or national origin in all business establishments. That same year, the legislature passed the Hawkins Act, named for pioneering African American legislator Augustus Hawkins, making it illegal for an owner of publicly assisted housing to discriminate.

White property owners persisted in defying and challenging these new laws.

In 1959 Seaborn and Jean Burks tried to buy a new home on Marietta Drive in San Francisco's hilly Miraloma neighborhood. Burks, a veteran and a small business owner, and his wife, a sixth grade public school teacher, offered the advertised price of $27,950. But because the couple was black, the tract's developer, the Poppy Construction Company, refused to sell to them.

Just two years earlier, San Francisco Giants star Willie Mays had faced similar discrimination. It took the intervention of San Francisco Mayor George Christopher and negative national press to convince a white homeowner to sell his house to the slugger. After Mays and his wife moved in, someone threw a bottle containing a racist note through their front window.

The Burks sued for damages under the new Unruh Act, but a superior court judge ruled against them. A coalition of civil rights groups organized to support the family's appeal. They faced an uphill battle because the lawsuit challenged a fundamental assumption that people had a right to sell their homes to whomever they chose.

The state supreme court agreed to hear *Burks v. Poppy Construction*, and Marshall Krause, a young ACLU attorney in his first appearance before the high court, represented the Burkses.

In a unanimous opinion written by Chief Justice Phil S. Gibson, the high court on March 26, 1962, upheld the constitutionality of the Unruh Civil Rights Act. The court dismissed the construction company's contention that the law did not apply to real estate transactions, ruling, "Discrimination on the basis of race or color is contrary to the public policy of the United States and of this state….Discrimination in housing leads to lack of adequate housing for minority groups, and inadequate housing conditions contribute to disease, crime, and immorality."

Despite the ruling, housing developers and realtors found ways to circumvent the law. In the early 1960s, the Southwest Realty Association in Los Angeles, for example, barred African American realtors from receiving the multiple listings, through which realtors share information about available properties. Developers often told would-be African American and Latino home buyers that a subdivision was suddenly sold out or that the bank working with the developer had frozen mortgage loans.

Inspired by the national civil rights movement led by the Reverend Martin Luther King Jr., activists publicly protested local segregation. In the summer of 1963,

Even after the U.S. Supreme Court prohibited "restrictive covenants" barring people of color from many neighborhoods like this one in Los Angeles, developers and white property owners in California resisted residential integration.

members of the Congress of Racial Equality (CORE) and other groups demonstrated at the Southwood Rivers housing development, built by developer Don Wilson in the Los Angeles suburb of Torrance. They accused Wilson of excluding African Americans. Wilson called the police, who arrested protestors for trespassing. Weeks of jostling among the developer, protestors, and the city followed. Demonstrators engaged in a "sit-out," blocking the driveway of the tract sales office. The city council passed an ordinance prohibiting individuals from being on the streets surrounding the development at night on weekends.

Eventually CORE agreed to limit its demonstrations in the tract to two pickets, one day a week, and the city dropped all charges against more than two hundred protestors.

Just weeks before the CORE protests, in the closing minutes of the 1963 state legislative session, lawmakers had passed the Rumford Act, named for William Byron Rumford, the first African American elected to public office in northern California. The law prohibited discrimination in most privately financed housing, and it outlawed racial discrimination by banks, real estate brokers, mortgage companies, and other financial institutions.

Thwarted by the legislature and the judiciary, California realtors and developers appealed directly to the electorate. In 1964 the California Real Estate Association, the Home Builders Association, and the Apartment Owners Association qualified Proposition 14 for the November ballot. The initiative, a state constitutional amendment, would repeal all fair housing laws and prohibit the state legislature from ever passing laws related to housing discrimination, thus locking into place racial discrimination in housing.

In November 1964, voters passed Proposition 14, two to one.

Wilfred and Carola Prendergast felt the impact of Proposition 14. In July 1964, when Carola rented an apartment on Burton Way in West Hollywood, she explained to the rental agent that her husband, an insurance agent, was working in San Francisco and would join her as soon as he received a transfer. A few months later, Wilfred moved into the apartment. On December 1, 1964, the Prendergasts received an eviction notice giving them one month to vacate. The rental agent had no problem renting to Carola Prendergast, who was white. But the eviction notice came suspiciously soon after the agent met her husband, who was African American. This was also immediately after Proposition 14 went into effect. The following month, the Prendergasts filed a lawsuit, *Prendergast v. Snyder*, challenging the constitutionality of Proposition 14.

Nearly three years later, the U.S. Supreme Court heard the Prendergasts' case and a companion case, *Reitman v. Mulkey*. Writing for the 5-4 majority, Justice Byron White upheld the California Supreme Court's judgment in both the *Prendergast* and

Reitman cases, agreeing that Proposition 14 embodied the right to discriminate on racial grounds in "the State's basic charter, immune from legislative, executive, or judicial regulation at any level of the state government," so that "those practicing racial discrimination need no longer rely on their personal choice. They could now invoke express constitutional authority, free from censure or interference of any kind from official sources."

The high court struck down Proposition 14 as a violation of the equal protection of the law guaranteed by the Fourteenth Amendment of the U.S. Constitution.

Alcatraz: This Is Indian Land

Beginning in 1953, the Bureau of Indian Affairs (BIA), under the direction of Commissioner of Indian Affairs Dillon Myer (who had overseen the incarceration of Japanese Americans during World War II), instituted a program to terminate the federal government's trust land responsibilities, breaking up reservations and assimilating Indians into urban areas. With the promise of job training and placement, financial aid, and housing, the BIA convinced more than eleven thousand Indians throughout the U.S. to leave their rural reservations and migrate to urban centers, including Los Angeles, Oakland, and San Francisco.

For Indians, the program was often disastrous. Thrust into an alienating urban environment, given little or no financial help or training, and faced with blatant discrimination, many of these newly urban Indians became disillusioned, resentful, and mistrustful of the government. A great number returned to their prior homes, but others stayed.

By the mid-1960s, approximately forty thousand Indians lived in the San Francisco Bay Area. Most were not native Californians.

By the late 1960s, American Indian activism had blossomed. In March 1969, Indians demonstrated outside the San Francisco federal building to protest BIA vocational training, which they complained had produced "ten thousand native mechanics and welders but only seven attorneys, four medical doctors, and two engineers." Native American students participated in strikes, along with other students of color, at UC Berkeley and San Francisco State University and advocated for Native American studies courses.

Indians were also angered by the terms of a law that President Johnson signed in September 1968 authorizing belated payment to California Indians for more than sixty-four million acres of land that were seized during the nineteenth century. The settlement worked out to roughly forty-seven cents an acre. This paltry sum embodied a century of broken treaties, exploitation, and injustice.

Native people, not only in the San Francisco area but throughout North America, found a focus for their outrage on Alcatraz, a sixteen-acre island in the middle of San Francisco Bay.

During the nineteenth century, Alcatraz had served as a fort and military prison where Hopi, Modoc, and Apache prisoners of war and Native people who refused to send their children to government boarding schools were incarcerated. The rocky island later entered American mythology as the home of a high-security federal penitentiary that held such infamous prisoners as gangster Al Capone. By 1969, however, the prison had been closed for six years. Alcatraz was excess government property with a skeleton staff of caretakers.

After three short-lived occupations, a group of young Indians led by former ironworker Richard Oakes, a twenty-seven-year-old Mohawk who was leader of San Francisco State University's American Indian student association, occupied Alcatraz.

Spirits soared around three o'clock in the morning on November 20, 1969, as nearly one hundred Indians, mostly students, landed and prepared to take over the island until the federal government ceded Alcatraz to Indian control.

Hand-painted, red-lettered messages quickly sprung up around the island: the slogans "Indians Welcome" and "Indian Land" were painted on a "Government Property" sign on a building that had once served as soldiers' barracks and later as apartments for prison guards. The message "Peace and Freedom. Welcome. Home of Free Indians" was emblazoned on the island's water tower.

Within twenty-four hours of the Indians' landing, the Coast Guard set up a blockade, but it backfired, generating publicity and sympathy for the occupiers. After four days, the Coast Guard lifted the blockade, and supporters ferried food and supplies to Alcatraz.

People across the country supported the effort, sending money, food, and supplies.

As news of the occupation spread, an estimated fifteen thousand Indians from throughout the country came to the island, some for brief sojourns, others intending to stay.

Nixon administration officials, facing political problems from recent revelations that U.S. soldiers had massacred innocent Vietnamese civilians in My Lai, were tentative about using violence to evict the Indians.

Three weeks into the occupation, federal officials floated ideas for Alcatraz: the National Park Service recommended that the island be part of a proposed Golden Gate National Recreation Area; California's Senator George Murphy, a former actor, proposed that Alcatraz be turned into an Indian National Park. The occupiers, however, remained steadfast in their demand that Alcatraz be deeded to American Indians. The federal government refused.

Native Americans took over Alcatraz Island from November 1969 till June 1971, protesting more than a century of broken treaties and mistreatment.

By early 1970, many of the original student occupiers had left Alcatraz to return to school. They were replaced by Indians from outside the area who did not always share the strategic objectives of the occupation.

Ed Castillo, a Cahuilla-Luiseño and one of the original occupiers, recalled, "We were all college students, literally every one of us, with one or two exceptions. We were very idealistic. The people who came after us were older, more cynical. Some had serious addiction problems. They began challenging Richard's [Oakes's] leadership. The challenges were verbal and physical."

On January 3, 1970, Oakes's thirteen-year-old stepdaughter, Yvonne, died in a fall while playing with other children in an abandoned building. Richard and Anne Oakes suspected that their daughter's death was not accidental. The grieving family left the island, never to return.

Nearly five months of negotiations with the government brought no resolution. In late May 1970, the government cut off water, electrical power, and phone service to the remaining seventy-five occupiers.

On the night of June 1, an eerie light glowed through the fog surrounding Alcatraz. Coast Guard officers discovered a fire consuming the former warden's residence and other nearby buildings. The government implied that the occupiers had set the fire, while those on the island accused the government of arson. Though the fire's

151

origin remained a mystery, it led to the decline of public support for the occupation. After nineteen months, only a handful of people remained on Alcatraz.

On June 11, 1971, armed U.S. marshals, FBI agents, and Government Services Administration security officers landed on the island. Confronted by the government police, the fifteen Indians there agreed to leave.

The takeover of Alcatraz had lasting symbolic and practical impact. The Nixon administration repudiated the decades-old tribal termination and assimilation program. On July 8, 1970, President Nixon publicly acknowledged that "The first Americans—the Indians—are the most deprived and most isolated minority group in our nation....It is long past time that the Indian policies of the federal government began to recognize and build upon the capacities and insights of the Indian people."

Congress passed laws returning land to native people. The budget of the Bureau of Indian Affairs grew by 225 percent. Scholarships for American Indian college students increased, as did funding for Indian health care.

"I think the occupation of Alcatraz Island was the seminal event in the modern movement of civil rights for American Indians," Ed Castillo stated. "It put Indians back in the history book in the twentieth century, and for that, it was worth it."

As Segregated as the Deep South

By the early 1960s, more than a century of socially sanctioned and judicially enforced residential segregation had branded racially distinct neighborhoods into cities throughout the state, particularly in sprawling Los Angeles County. From the Japanese American enclave of Gardena in the south and the African American ghetto of Watts in mid-county to the Mexican American barrio of Boyle Heights in the east and the white suburbs of the San Fernando Valley in the far northwest, it was not uncommon for a public school student in the Los Angeles Unified School District to attend a school that was ethnically and racially segregated.

Despite the 1954 *Brown v. Board of Education* decision outlawing "separate but equal" schools, some California schools, particularly in the southern part of the state, were as segregated as those in the Deep South. Although the civil rights movement focused on dismantling government-sanctioned segregation in the South, Californians continued to battle de facto segregation in the Golden State.

In 1963 Mary Ellen Crawford attended Jordan High School in Los Angeles's Watts neighborhood. The auditorium in the largely African American school had been condemned, and the school lacked basic equipment. But when the Los Angeles Unified School District announced plans for a million-dollar renovation of the school, activists complained that the result would be the "best segregated high school in the city." The NAACP and the United Civil Rights Committee brought a class action lawsuit representing Crawford and other African American students, calling for integration between Jordan and nearby South Gate High School, which despite being only a mile away was almost entirely white.

This proposal mobilized the white parents of South Gate, who submitted petitions to the school board protesting integration.

After Martin Luther King's Southern Christian Leadership Conference and the Student Nonviolent Coordinating Committee organized a two-mile march through downtown Los Angeles on June 24, 1963, to protest school segregation, Los Angeles school board member Charles Smoot charged, "These champions of equality come here to lend their support to local Negro demands that their race be given special status, special privileges, and special advantages over other races in this school system."

A few months after *Crawford v. Board of Education* was filed, Superior Court Judge Alfred Gitelson ordered the school board to end segregation at Jordan High. The board successfully delayed a trial for five years by pledging to desegregate and then presenting plans that impacted only a handful of the district's hundreds of thousands of students. By the time the case went to trial in 1968, it had expanded to cover 192 schools in predominantly African American and Mexican neighborhoods.

In 1970 Judge Gitelson issued a landmark ruling criticizing the district's "slavish adherence" to assigning students only to schools in their neighborhoods. The veteran jurist believed this policy perpetuated school segregation by reflecting residential segregation—*de facto* segregation. Citing a long list of the school board's omissions and actions, Judge Gitelson added *de jure* segregation—government-sanctioned segregation—to his description of the district's conduct. Charging that the school board's directives, which sounded as if they were in fact seeking integration, "were solely for public relations, to attempt to keep minorities pacified," he mandated integration by the 1971-72 academic year.

White politicians swiftly condemned the decision. Los Angeles Mayor Sam Yorty predicted that the decision would polarize the city. California Governor Ronald Reagan called the decision "utterly ridiculous," and Robert Finch, President Nixon's Secretary of Heath, Education, and Welfare, called it "totally unrealistic." Judge Gitelson was branded the "busing judge" and voted out of office. The school board appealed his order, delaying its implementation.

Several months after the ruling, Governor Reagan signed the Wakefield anti-busing measure, named after Floyd Wakefield, South Gate assembly member and owner of a sporting goods store. The law prohibited busing for any purpose without written parental permission. Immediately after Governor Reagan signed the bill, San

Francisco's school board filed a lawsuit with the state supreme court challenging the law's constitutionality.

In January 1971, the high court ruled that school districts were still legally responsible for desegregation. Although the new law only outlawed schools from busing students without parental consent, districts could still assign students to schools outside their neighborhoods. Parents could keep their children off school buses, but they were nevertheless responsible for transporting their children to their assigned schools. Justice Matthew Tobriner wrote that to create "a parental power to refuse consent to pupil assignments would beget a parental right to discriminate, and to do so in a context of social strife would enable many to exploit the right to inflict racial prejudice."

In reaction to the decision, Assemblyman Wakefield sponsored the Student School Assignment Initiative, which appeared on the November 1972 ballot as Proposition 21. The initiative prohibited assigning students to public schools on the basis of race, creed, or color and eliminated requirements that school districts keep records on racial imbalance and develop plans to eliminate such imbalance. When the initiative passed, it calcified school segregation tied to residential segregation.

Within forty-eight hours of the election, the ACLU petitioned the state supreme court to rule that the initiative violated the equal protection guarantees of the U.S. Constitution.

In January 1975, a unanimous California Supreme Court issued a mixed decision on the validity of Proposition 21. The high court ruled that school districts could take race into account when making school assignments for the purpose of integration. But districts no longer had to keep statistics on the racial and ethnic composition of school populations. Civil rights advocates were floored: without the data, it would be impossible to document racial segregation.

Meanwhile, the *Crawford* case was still winding its way through the courts. In 1976 the California Supreme Court vindicated Judge Gitelson's 1970 order, ruling that the Los Angeles school board had "in bad faith segregated its schools" and reaffirming its 1963 ruling in *Jackson v. Pasadena*, in which the court ruled that segregation itself was significant, regardless of whether the school district or state had *intentionally* caused it. By reiterating that the distinction between *de jure* and *de facto* discrimination "retains little, if any, significance for the children whose constitutional rights are at issue," the California Supreme Court set a stricter desegregation standard than the U.S. Supreme Court, which in a 1973 Colorado school segregation case had ruled that plaintiffs had to prove that the state had purposefully segregated students. The distinction between the two standards proved important years later in bringing the *Crawford* case to a close.

The California high court sent the *Crawford* case back to the lower court for implementation of court-ordered integration. That task fell to Superior Court Judge Paul Egly. He approved a plan covering eighty-five thousand children and calling for busing students across vast Los Angeles County.

Just days before busing was to begin, in September 1978, a flurry of judicial actions left the plan's future in doubt. Bustop, a group of largely white parents opposed to mandatory busing, petitioned Judge Egly to halt the plan. He refused, but Bustop received an eleventh-hour stay from the court of appeal just eleven days before the first day of school.

For four days following the appellate court ruling, attorneys for the NAACP Legal Defense and Educational Fund, the ACLU, the Los Angeles Center for Law and Justice, and the Integration Project worked nonstop on an appeal to the California Supreme Court. The court ordered that the plan be implemented as scheduled, on September 12. Bustop hurriedly petitioned U.S. Supreme Court Justice William Rehnquist to keep the buses from rolling.

Although he denied Bustop's request, Justice Rehnquist provided the group a political roadmap by suggesting that the state constitution be amended to prohibit busing.

State Senator Alan Robbins of the San Fernando Valley quickly introduced legislation for a constitutional amendment that freed school boards from any obligation to desegregate which exceeded federal standards. Since the U.S. Supreme Court had ruled in 1973 that only government-instigated segregation violated the Equal Protection Clause, California courts could only order desegregation if plaintiffs could prove that the school district intentionally segregated students. The amendment, which appeared on the November 1979 state ballot as Proposition 1, was approved by almost 70 percent of voters.

Though civil rights advocates challenged the legality of Proposition 1, a 1982 U.S. Supreme Court ruling upholding its constitutionality formally ended the judicial fight to desegregate Los Angeles public schools. The *Crawford* case, begun nearly twenty years earlier, was effectively dead.

During the 1980s and 1990s, the odds increased greatly that a low-income student of color in California would attend a school that was not only racially segregated but completely inferior. Consider this description from an 1862 petition protesting the conditions of San Francisco's black school:

> The air came laden—foul and unhealthful, study was disturbed by noise from a military band in the room above, and the plastering is broken and falling from the ceiling, so that the water from above runs through the floor upon the desks and floor of the schoolroom beneath.

Compare that description with the following 1999 statement of Shannon Carey, a teacher at Oakland's Stonehurst Elementary School:

> This January 24, the roof in my classroom leaked over half of my room.... The roof had been leaking for years—fourteen years, in fact—and yet not one repair was undertaken to prevent its eventual collapse. For three weeks, my 30 students and I wandered to four different locations, carrying our own desks and toting our own supplies....Our school does not have enough classrooms for all of its students, and a fifth grade class is permanently located on the auditorium stage. A class full of children sits cramped on the stage, trying to read novels, problem-solve, or conduct a science experiment while other students practice the trumpet, saxophone, and violin in the same space.

The conditions Carey described were not uncommon in California schools that served low-income children of color on the eve of the twenty-first century.

Another Round

Sweetie Williams and his family immigrated to California from American Samoa in 1999. His twelve-year-old son, Eliezer, attended seventh grade at San Francisco's Luther Burbank Middle School. When the elder Williams asked his son why he never did any homework, Eliezer responded that he had no textbooks to bring home. In addition to the textbook shortage, the school was plagued with vermin and roaches. Two of the school's three bathrooms were locked all day, every day, and the third was locked during parts of the day, leaving students with no open restroom.

Williams had not expected such conditions when he moved to California. "We've been told this is the land of opportunity," recalled the father of six, who worked as a baggage screener at San Francisco International Airport and served as pastor of the Samoan Full Gospel Church. "Our children are being deprived of that opportunity."

On May 17, 2000, the forty-sixth anniversary of *Brown v. Board of Education*, Eliezer Williams became the lead plaintiff in *Williams v. California*, a class action lawsuit on behalf of students attending eighteen California public schools. The lawsuit charged the state of California with failing to fulfill its constitutional mandate to guarantee the bare minimum infrastructure for a quality public education. In all but one of the schools cited in the suit, more than 90 percent of the student population was non-white.

As word about *Williams v. California* spread, more parents and students asked to join. In October 2001, a superior court judge allowed the lawsuit to be expanded beyond the initial eighteen schools to include every student in every substandard California public school.

Though the state's coffers were full, Governor Gray Davis preferred to spend money on a high-powered Los Angeles law firm, O'Melveny and Meyers, to defend the state, rather than fix the schools. Over a twenty-four-day period in 2001, corporate lawyers grilled witnesses ranging in age from eight to seventeen, sometimes for hours, trying to discredit their testimony about the unacceptable conditions in their schools, driving many children to tears.

The litigation continued for several more years, until Governor Gray Davis was recalled. Soon after taking office in 2004, the administration of newly elected Governor Arnold Schwarzenegger negotiated a settlement with the plaintiffs' attorneys, who were by then representing one million low-income students.

The settlement provided up to a billion dollars for school districts to purchase educational materials, to identify and fix deteriorating schools, and to ensure that all schools hired qualified teachers. The government also agreed to standards for teachers, access to textbooks, sanitary and safe campuses, and a parent-supported system to hold school districts accountable to those standards.

By the time of the settlement, Eliezer Williams was sixteen years old and about to begin his senior year at San Francisco's Balboa High School. Although he would not directly benefit from the lawsuit bearing his name, he was excited about its satisfying result. "Being a part of this case has taught me that people really can make a difference if they have the energy and desire to fight for equality," he commented. "I was determined to make things in my school better, and I know now that anyone can do something like this, not just me."

Backlash and Bakke

By the 1960s, California's famed public universities had a long history of low enrollment numbers for African Americans, Latinos, Native Americans, and Filipinos. To address this racial imbalance, the campuses that comprised the University of California system began to implement a variety of affirmative action programs to enroll and retain qualified minority students.

The year after the passage of the landmark 1964 Civil Rights Act, President Lyndon Johnson gave a speech at Howard University explaining why antidiscrimination laws were not sufficient to ensure racial equality:

> You do not take a man who for years has been hobbled by chains, liberate him, bring him to the starting line of a race, saying "you are free to compete with all the others," and still justly believe you have been completely fair.... We seek not just freedom but opportunity...not just equality as a right and a theory, but equality as a fact and as a result.

Later that year, Johnson signed an executive order mandating federally funded programs to take "affirmative action" to ensure equality in hiring and employment. The order was expanded to include gender in 1967.

The medical school at the University of California campus in the rural community of Davis, just west of Sacramento, became the flashpoint for a national debate about the constitutionality of affirmative action programs designed to diversify universities.

In 1970 the UC Davis medical school initiated an admissions policy to "enhance diversity in the student body and the profession, eliminate historic barriers for medical careers for disadvantaged racial and ethnic minority groups, and increase aspiration for such careers on the part of members of those groups."

In practice, UC Davis set aside 16 percent of its first-year medical school slots for economically and educationally disadvantaged applicants, specifically blacks, Latinos, Asians, and American Indians.

Allan Bakke was thirty-two when he first applied to the medical school, in 1972. The son of a mail carrier and a schoolteacher, both of Norwegian ancestry, he developed an interest in becoming a physician while serving in the Marine Corps. After leaving the military, he took night classes in chemistry and biology and volunteered in a hospital emergency room to prepare for a medical career.

All of the medical schools to which Bakke applied rejected him, most citing his age as the main reason. After he reapplied to UC Davis and was rejected a second time, Bakke hired Reynold Colvin to file a suit against the university, arguing that the medical school's fixed percentage of admissions for minorities violated federal and state equal protection guarantees as well as the 1964 Civil Rights Act.

The university's general counsel responded that the admissions program served two compelling and rational interests: encouraging minority physicians who would likely serve disadvantaged communities; and diversifying the medical school, enabling students and faculty to learn from the "ideas, needs, and concerns of minorities." He also pointed out that even in the absence of a special minority admissions program, Bakke would not have been admitted because his test scores were lower than those of other rejected applicants.

In March 1975, a superior court judge ruled that the admission program constituted a racial quota that violated the federal and state constitutions as well as the federal Civil Rights Act; he prohibited the university from using an applicant's race as a factor in admission.

It was a pyrrhic victory for Bakke, however, because the judge—stating that Bakke had not proved that he would have been admitted to the medical school barring the special admissions program—did not order the university to admit him.

Both the university and Bakke appealed the superior court decision directly to the state supreme court. In September 1976, the California Supreme Court announced its 6-1 decision that the medical school's affirmative action program was unconstitutional.

More than a dozen civil rights groups urged the university not to appeal. Believing that *Bakke* was not the best case to test the constitutionality of affirmative action programs, they feared that a negative decision by the U.S. Supreme Court would have an adverse, dramatic, and long-term impact on civil rights and race relations. But the university appealed.

Because of the importance of the case, a record fifty-eight friend-of-the-court briefs were filed, forty-two supporting the university (including one submitted by the federal government) and sixteen supporting Bakke. Former United States Solicitor General (and special prosecutor in the Watergate break-in investigation) Archibald Cox argued the university's case.

In the final days of its 1978 session, the Court announced the eagerly awaited judgment, one of the more complex judgments in the Supreme Court's history. Chief Justice Warren Burger and Associate Justices William Rehnquist, John Paul Stevens, and Potter Stewart agreed that the UC Davis admissions program violated the Civil Rights Act and that Bakke should be admitted to the medical school. Their opinion stated that any consideration of race in admissions, even as one of many factors, was unacceptable.

Associate Justices William Brennan, Thurgood Marshall, Byron White, and Harry Blackmun asserted that the medical school's program was not only constitutionally sound but that government programs could take race into account to remedy historic discrimination against a racial group.

With eight of the justices evenly split, the decisive vote in the *Bakke* judgment was that of Associate Justice Lewis Powell. The patrician Virginian and Nixon appointee explained that Supreme Court precedent had established racial classifications as inherently suspect and subject to the strictest judicial scrutiny, but that programs could survive that scrutiny if in pursuit of a "compelling state interest." Powell rejected the concept that redressing historical societal discrimination against minority groups was a "compelling state interest," but he did consider the need for a diverse student body to be compelling. Powell felt, however, that the UC Davis admissions program was not necessary to create a diverse student body.

Powell agreed with one group of his colleagues that the Davis program was unlawful and that Bakke should be admitted. However, he disagreed with this group that race could not be considered in admissions decisions. Consequently, he joined with the other four justices in reversing the California Supreme Court's decision that race could not be used as a factor in admissions decisions.

The immediate impact of the ruling was that Alan Bakke was admitted to the UC Davis medical school. The lasting impact of the *Bakke* judgment has been the continued and widespread use of affirmative action programs that do not employ rigid quotas for minority applicants; admissions officers could consider race as a factor in their decisions and use their expertise to determine the relative weight given to race in admissions decisions.

However, nearly twenty years after the *Bakke* decision, in a backlash against successful efforts to expand affirmative action programs, the regents of the University of California, spurred by Governor Pete Wilson and Regent Ward Connerly, a millionaire businessman from Sacramento, voted to end affirmative action in admissions, employment, and other activities beginning in the 1997 fall term. The following year, the number of African Americans admitted to the UC Berkeley law school dropped by 81 percent.

Governor Wilson and Regent Connerly did not stop there. Their next effort wreaked still further havoc on the state's efforts to achieve racial equality.

Putting Race on the Ballot

On November 5, 1996, veteran civil rights attorney Eva Paterson stood in a voting booth in her neighborhood in the Oakland hills. She scanned the long list of initiatives. When she came to Proposition 209, the "California Civil Rights Initiative," Paterson paused to read the description: "The state shall not discriminate against, or grant preferential treatment to, any individual or group on the basis of race, sex, color, ethnicity, or national origin in the operation of public employment, public education, or public contracting."

"I thought to myself, this sounded good. No discrimination based on race or gender. I literally had to catch myself from pulling the 'Yes' lever," Paterson remembered. She laughed wryly when she recalled that moment, because for the previous eighteen months, as co-chair of the California Civil Rights Coalition and a self-described "affirmative action baby," Paterson had spent seven days a week battling the measure. She had debated its champion, Ward Connerly. She had spoken all over the state at college campuses, church groups, and bar associations. She had responded to hundreds of press interviews—and yet, when she read the description of the "Civil Rights Initiative," it sounded appealing. It was meant to. Proposition 209's advocates counted on confusion to win the election. The measure was authored by two disgruntled white male academics—Glynn Custred of California State University, Hayward, and Tom Wood, executive director of the conservative California Association of Scholars—who believed they had been passed over in hiring decisions in favor of women of color. The initiative sought to amend the state constitution to outlaw affirmative action based on race or gender in education, hiring, and contracting in all state enterprises.

By the time it reached the public eye, Proposition 209 was carefully crafted to bolster the sagging political capital of Governor Pete Wilson. Wilson, whose popularity had soared on the wings of the anti-immigrant Proposition 187 two years earlier, was eying the Republican presidential nomination. "The measure was designed to mobilize voters with yet another racially divisive wedge issue, to elect politicians, not to protect equality," explained Dorothy Ehrlich, executive director of the ACLU of Northern California and another leader in the No on 209 campaign.

Before putting Proposition 209 on the ballot, Custred and Wood, joined by Governor Wilson and the state Republican Party, had sought the perfect public spokesperson for the campaign. They selected Connerly, a middle-aged African American man who adamantly opposed affirmative action, even though his own firm had won several lucrative state contracts through a minority-contracting program—nonetheless, a better public face for Proposition 209 than Custred and Wood. He was propelled into the media as the head of Californians Against Discrimination and Preferences, the parent of the Yes on 209 campaign. The campaign learned through extensive, and expensive, polling and focus groups that voters who supported equal rights and affirmative action could be confused by language that appeared to favor those values. Thus was born the title "California Civil Rights Initiative." Throughout the campaign, proponents masqueraded as civil rights supporters, although they had never participated in a march, a sit-in, or a freedom ride.

Money poured into the Connerly campaign from right-wing contributors, including media magnate Rupert Murdoch, far-right Pennsylvania publisher Richard Scaife, and donors from Newt Gingrich's political action committee in Georgia.

Though coalitions of civil rights, minority, and women's organizations formed in both the Bay Area and southern California to oppose the initiative, they were no match for the well-heeled, sophisticated tactics of Governor Wilson and the Republican Party. The No on 209 campaign could not raise high dollars from national sources; even President Bill Clinton, who liked to think of himself as the "first black president," was reticent, and the national Democratic Party was reluctant to back the opposition financially.

As the polls closed on election night, discouraging tallies came in. Except for six Bay Area counties and Los Angeles, Proposition 209 won throughout the state; the initiative passed by 54 percent. Early the next morning, civil rights attorneys walked up the steps of the federal building in San Francisco and filed a class action lawsuit, *Coalition for Economic Equity v. Wilson*, to stop the measure from going into effect.

UC Berkeley students, like these at Boalt Hall School of Law, were in the forefront of protests against Proposition 209, the 1996 ballot initiative that outlawed affirmative action in education, employment, and hiring.

Governor Pete Wilson blasted the suit for "thwarting the will of the people." Dorothy Ehrlich explained:

> We had a duty to rush to court to prevent this injustice—following in the footsteps of civil rights activists and lawyers who have gone before us. We did not do this out of disrespect for the rule of law, or for the vote of the majority. Rather we took this action out of respect for a cherished democratic principle. It is the principle that recognizes that sometimes the will of the majority—whether expressed at the ballot booth or in the halls of Congress—can deeply conflict with the constitutional guarantee that protects the rights of minorities. The Bill of Rights cannot simply be voted away.

The civil rights attorneys also argued that Proposition 209 was illegal because it would prohibit public employers from complying with federal law that encourages voluntary measures to remedy and prevent race and sex discrimination. The attorneys came armed with examples demonstrating that the measure had already caused great confusion throughout the state. Public employers from school boards, transportation agencies, and health clinics were genuinely stymied about how and whether to continue programs aimed at ensuring racial and gender equality. On December 23, 1996, U.S. District Court Judge Thelton Henderson issued a preliminary injunction barring enforcement of Proposition 209. His sixty-seven-page opinion stated:

The issue is not whether one judge can thwart the will of the people; rather the issue is whether the challenged enactment complies with our Constitution and Bill of Rights. Without a doubt, federal courts have no duty more important than to protect the rights and liberties of all Americans by considering and ruling on such issues, no matter how contentious or controversial they may be. This duty is certainly undiminished where the law under consideration comes directly from the ballot box and without the benefit of the legislative process.

Judge Henderson, who as a Justice Department attorney in the 1960s had protected civil rights activists in the South, immediately came under fierce attack. "It's the most garbage decision I've ever seen," charged Connerly. Republican House leader Tom DeLay called for the veteran judge's impeachment. Governor Wilson, Attorney General Dan Lungren, and Californians Against Discrimination and Preferences, represented by the right-wing Pacific Legal Foundation, appealed the decision to the Ninth Circuit Court of Appeals.

The Clinton administration finally decided to step in, and the U.S. Department of Justice filed an amicus brief arguing that Proposition 209 violated equal protection guarantees. But it was too little, too late. Had the national Democratic Party supported the No on 209 campaign with dollars and big-name endorsements, the measure might have been defeated at the ballot box. In April 1997, the appeals court overturned Judge Henderson's bold ruling.

The political impact of Proposition 209 was swift and stark. Governor Wilson identified thirty-one state-funded programs for elimination or curtailment, including summer science programs for elementary school students and hiring programs that ensured recruitment from minority communities. A 2008 report by the Tomas Rivera Policy Institute indicated that the number of Latino and African American law students enrolled in the University of California's three law schools declined by 28 percent between 1995 and 2006.

Flushed with the success of Proposition 209, Connerly took his campaign nationwide, putting similar measures on ballots from Washington to Michigan.

In July 1998, Paterson and other civil rights attorneys filed the first federal class action lawsuit aimed at showing the devastating impact of Proposition 209 on businesses owned by women and minorities; *Lucy's Sales v. Contra Costa County* was filed against the first local government in northern California to drop its affirmative action program in the wake of Proposition 209.

Lucy Lacy, an African American woman and owner of a supply company that had been certified by Contra Costa County as a minority- and woman-owned business, had repeatedly approached the county for business, but officials never even asked her to bid for a contract. "I can't even get my foot in the door," said Lacy. "All I want is a chance to compete, but the county's system is just closed off to anyone who's not in the 'good ole boys' network." Lacy's charges were borne out by the county's own statistics, which showed that businesses owned by white men received almost 99 percent of the $100 million in county annual contracts for goods and services each year. Despite the powerful showing, the plaintiffs lost the case. This was the first in a number of cases where affirmative action and antidiscrimination programs in employment, contracting, and education buckled under the weight of Proposition 209.

In 2003 Paterson again found herself in the voting booth facing a proposition about race authored by Ward Connerly. Like Proposition 209, this one, which appeared as Proposition 54 on the ballot, had a carefully chosen, well-tested, disingenuous name: the Racial Privacy Initiative. Proposition 54 promised a "color-blind" society by banning the collection of racial and ethnic data by any government agency in California.

But this time, the morning after the election was quite different. Proposition 54 was decisively defeated, 64 percent to 36 percent. Almost five million votes were cast against the measure; voters understood that the data was needed to track race discrimination, to prove it, and to take legal action against it.

Three years earlier, people of color outnumbered whites in the state for the first time. Californians who had fought race discrimination in the streets, the courts, and the halls of the legislature were now flexing their muscle at the ballot box.

— FIVE —

HOLDING UP HALF THE SKY

THE RIGHTS OF WOMEN

We are women clad in new power,
We see the weak. We hear their plea.
We march to set our sisters free.
— *Sara Bard Field, suffragist and poet, 1911*

Two decades after slavery was outlawed in the United States, a young woman from China was forced to sign the following "legal" contract:

> The contractee Xin Jin is indebted to her master/mistress for passage from China to San Francisco and will voluntarily work as a prostitute at Tan Fu's place for four and one-half years for an advance of $524 to pay this debt. There shall be no interest on the money, and Xin Jin shall receive no wages. At the expiration of the contract, Xin Jin shall be free to do as she pleases. Until then, she shall first secure the master/mistress's permission if a customer asks to take her out. If she has the four loathsome diseases she shall be returned within 100 days; beyond that time the procurer has no responsibility. Menstruation disorder is limited to one month's rest only. If Xin Jin becomes sick at any time for more than fifteen days, she shall work one month extra; if she becomes pregnant, she shall work one year extra. Should Xin Jin run away before her term is out, she shall pay whatever expense is incurred in finding and returning her to the brothel. This is a contract to be retained by the master/mistress as evidence of the agreement. Receipt of $524 by Ah Yo. Thumb print of Xin Jin the contractee. Eighth month 11th day of the 12th year of Guang-zu.

The four loathsome diseases for which Xin Jin could be returned for a refund were leprosy, epilepsy, conception, and "stone-woman," i.e., "inability to have carnal intercourse with men."

Some of California's earliest women residents were, like Xin Jin, young women from indigent families in China who were brought into the United States as indentured slaves and endured lives of unbearable suffering and isolation. This slavery went on for decades.

The contract, which Xin Jin was forced to sign, was merely a ruse to circumvent the Thirteenth Amendment's ban on slavery.

In the latter half of the nineteenth century, China was in great turmoil. Starvation and war enveloped the countryside, leaving millions in poverty. Many men traveled to the United States for jobs on railroads and farms. Others, attracted by the gold rush, set sail for "Gold Mountain," as Chinese referred to California.

Chinese women, however, did not come in great numbers across the Pacific. Most women were discouraged from traveling, and many could not travel because their bound feet made it hard for them to leave their villages, much less voyage abroad. In addition, men did not feel safe bringing their families with them, because of widespread anti-Chinese sentiment and violence in the United States. But once the men were here, anti-miscegenation laws barred them from marrying white women. They found themselves living lonely, long-term bachelor lives.

In 1852 San Francisco's Chinese population consisted of 2,954 men and 19 women. Enterprising men thought that importing women from China would be a lucrative way to ease these men's loneliness.

According to the 1860 census, of the 681 Chinese women in San Francisco, 583 were prostitutes. In the state capital of Sacramento, the census showed more than 90 percent of the town's prostitutes were Chinese, with a mean age of only twenty.

Many young women were also forced into prostitution in gold mining and lumber camps, as well as in agricultural areas. Historian Jean Pfaelzer discovered that white citizens in the Delta town of Antioch expelled all Chinese residents in 1876, alleging that Chinese prostitutes were exposing innocent teenage boys to moral depravity and disease.

The trade in Chinese prostitutes was initiated by certain tongs that had developed in San Francisco's Chinatown. Some of the tongs began as associations for immigrants from specific regions, towns, or villages, or with the same surname. Many had been formed to protect Chinese laborers in mining camps from having their wages withheld or from being lynched by vigilantes. Most associations grew into benevolent organizations or trade guilds.

However, as illegal trade in opium, women, and other goods grew between China and the newly prosperous California, some of the associations became involved in contraband trade and gambling. The Hip Yee Tong, for example, reportedly started trafficking in 1852. Over the next several decades it imported six thousand women, 87 percent of the Chinese women who arrived during that period. The trade in women brought the tong a profit of two hundred thousand dollars. About another tong, a former dealer in Chinese slaves told a newspaper reporter:

> You see the Hop Sing Tong fix it with the Custom House. They swore to the officers that the children were born here and went to China to visit. Some witnesses come and say they knew the girl who wants to land was born here, and they tell all about it. They say they know she is the same because they saw her when she went back to China. It was not hard to swear them in to this country.

Because the tongs profited greatly from trafficking in women, those who tried to stop the practice were met with threats, violence, and death warrants. Many others profited as well: the procurers who went to China to find the young women, the ship-ping companies, the "highbind-ers" (a term for Irish dockworkers that came to refer to underworld traders) who collected fees from them all. As historian Dorothy Gray notes, "American officials amassed fortunes...for winking at the slave and opium trades." White landlords made enormous profits by renting out elegant parlor houses and "cribs," the dingy, barren shacks where the newest—and oldest—wom-en were forced to ply their trade.

Most of the women were between the ages of sixteen and twenty-five when they were kid-napped, lured, or purchased from impoverished parents; many were as young as ten. One young woman wrote, "I was kidnapped in China and brought over here. The man who kidnapped me sold me for four hundred dollars to a

Women, like those pictured here, from destitute areas in south-ern China were sold or kidnapped and forced into prostitu-tion in San Francisco and remote gold mining areas. Many endured sexual slavery in the grimy back alleys of the city and died very young.

San Francisco slave-dealer and he sold me here for seventeen hundred dollars. I have been a brothel slave ever since."

As a letter from Wang Ah So to her mother poignantly reveals, some young women considered prostitution to be a filial obligation. On February 27, 1927, Wang wrote:

> Mother, you must be sure to take good care of yourself and not worry. The illness of your daughter is not very serious. In a few days probably there will be two or three hundred dollars sent you for New Years. Your daughter's condition is very tragic, even when she is sick she must practice prostitution [the literal translation from the Chinese is 'do business with her own flesh and skin']. Daughter is not angry with you. It seems to be just my fate.

A second letter relates:

> Next year I will certainly be able to pay off all the debts. Your daughter is even more anxious than her mother to do this. As long as your daughter's life lasts she will pay up all the debts. Your daughter will do her part so that the world will not look down on us.

The ship voyage was arduous, especially for those torn away from their families and homes. When they arrived in San Francisco, the young women and girls were taken to a barracoon, a long warehouse near the dock that had been turned into a makeshift barracks. The same name was used for holding pens for enslaved Africans on the East Coast and immortalized as a book title by Zora Neale Hurston. Those who had been promised to particular merchants were delivered to them. The others were stripped for inspection in full view of police and spectators and sold to the highest bidder. Girls and women who had been bought in China for $30 to $150 were sold for $500 to $3000. Some had been purchased as babies and raised to be prostitutes.

They were traded like any other commodity, as this bill of sale from Loo Wong to Loo Chee starkly attests:

> Rice, 6 mats at $2—$12
> Shrimps, 50 lbs. at 10 cents—$5
> Girl—$250
> Salt fish, 60 lbs. at 10 cents—$6
> Total—$273

In 1869 the *San Francisco Chronicle* reported on a cargo of Chinese women and girls as if they were a commodity market item:

> Each Chinese steamer now brings consignments of women, destined to be placed in the markets....The particularly fine portions of the cargo, the fresh and pretty females who come from the interior, are used to fill

special orders from wealthy merchants and prosperous tradesmen. A very considerable portion are sent into the interior under the charge of special agents, in answer to demands from well-to-do miners and successful vegetable producers.

The majority, however, remained in San Francisco's brothels. The tongs imposed a weekly tax of twenty-five cents. If the women did not pay, they were subject to whipping, torture by fire, banishment to brothels in the mining regions, and even death.

Their rates were based on age and attractiveness. Those who had reached puberty and were fortunate were sent to the cleaner and more comfortable parlor houses, which were often on the upper floors of Chinatown businesses and furnished with silk cushions, Chinese paintings, and bamboo decor. They housed between four to twenty-five "courtesans," who were often provided elegant clothing, jewelry, and perfumes. They attracted a higher class of clientele, all of whom were Chinese.

Those not so fortunate were taken to the cribs. They were, according to the *Chronicle*, "the refuse—consisting of boat girls and those who come from the seaboard towns, where contact with the white sailor reduces even the low standard of Chinese morals."

The cribs were flimsy shacks, some only twelve feet wide, on dimly lit, narrow Chinatown streets and grimy alleys. Six to twenty-four women were crammed into the bare, dark rooms furnished only with a washbowl, a bamboo chair, and a hard bed covered with matting.

The young women wore only short silk blouses or cotton pajamas, and only in cold rainy weather were they given black silk pants to cover their legs. They stood at the barred windows like the prisoners that they were, calling out to passing sailors, laborers, and teenage boys, offering sex for twenty-five cents. According to one male diarist of the time, the young women were "exposed like chickens in slatted cages. They looked glum and washed out to me." At least 90 percent of the young prostitutes suffered from some kind of illness.

Clauses in their contracts adding time for days taken off for menstruation or illness lengthened their enslavement. As Lucie Cheng Hirata notes, "In reality, the contract system offered very little advantage over the outright sale or slave system and was, in a number of ways, more brutal, because it raised false hopes."

Beatings and abuse were common; sexually transmitted diseases robbed the young women of their health. Ill treatment and poor health often shortened the prostitutes' "useful" life in the brothel to no more than six or eight years. Indeed, women who were broken, physically or mentally, were often encouraged to "escape" to mission houses. The less fortunate met a worse fate. They were taken to a "hospital" to die. A newspaper reporter described one such place:

When any of the unfortunate harlots is no longer useful and a Chinese physician passes his opinion that her disease is incurable, she is notified that she must die....Led by night to this hole of a hospital, she is forced within the door and made to lie down upon the shelf. A cup of water, another of boiled rice and a little metal oil lamp are placed by her side....Those who have immediate charge of the establishment know how long the oil should last, and when the limit is reached they return to the hospital, unbar the door and enter. Generally, the woman is dead, either by starvation or from her own hand.

Resistance was almost impossible. The young women were in a strange country, in debt and alone. They spoke little or no English and were treated with disdain by the white majority, who strolled just outside their windows, ogling or ignoring them. They were stigmatized and subject to racist assaults. Until churches started shelters for the women, it was virtually impossible for them to find a safe haven. When Protestant reformers such as Margaret Culbertson and Donaldina Cameron started their rescue work, brothel owners warned their prostitutes to stay away from the "white devils," who, they claimed, would "boil them, hang them up to dry and eat them."

Despite these gruesome warnings, some prostitutes did dare to run away. Their owners put bounties on their heads. While some succeeded in finding support from missionaries or police, most were recaptured and beaten by the highbinders. Others went mad and, in despair, committed suicide by opium overdose or drowning in the bay. A rare few earned enough to buy their freedom or married former customers and started new lives.

The Presbyterian Mission Home, located at 920 Sacramento Street in San Francisco, was the most aggressive of the missions. For sixteen years, its founder, Margaret Culbertson, went into brothels herself and led women to safety, often alone, sometimes with the assistance of police.

Her protégé and successor, New Zealand immigrant Donaldina Cameron, is said to have rescued fifteen hundred girls and women over three decades. Though her family warned her of the risks of rescue work, Cameron was deeply inspired by Culbertson and became her apprentice.

Unlike the many Christian missionaries who were primarily concerned with the perceived evils of Chinese custom, Culbertson and Cameron focused on the dangerous work of bringing women to safety. They faced many risks: shortly after Cameron started working at 920 Sacramento Street, a stick of explosives was found planted in the building. Had it been ignited, it could have destroyed the entire block.

Cameron became known as Lo Mo, "old mother," to the women, and Fan Gwai, "white devil," to the brothel owners, who would hide women if they heard Cameron was on the way. She often discovered prostitutes hidden behind panels in secret alleyways, and once in a boxlike enclosure between the floor and the ceiling of a two-story house. The San Francisco Police Department eventually established a special Chinatown unit, known informally as the Chinese Police, to help find and rescue the young women.

Though Cameron was less guilty than others of her time and class of religious rectitude, she and her missionary colleagues subjected the rescued women to strict codes of conduct and strong doses of Christianity and westernization.

It is to Cameron's credit that many of the girls and women she rescued returned to China. Some of the older ones, however, were too ashamed to go back to their ancestral homes. Several who stayed joined Cameron in saving other women from the cribs. Some were educated as teachers and nurses. One woman, Yoke Yeen, went to Stanford University and was reported to be the first Chinese woman to graduate from that school.

Laws against the slavery of prostitution, unlike the Emancipation Proclamation, were not based on concern for the welfare of women, or outrage over the institution of forced, contractual prostitution. Rather, they were based on the white Christian population's claim to moral superiority and the belief that Chinese prostitutes were debasing men and boys of the community.

In 1865 the San Francisco Board of Supervisors passed "An Order to Remove Chinese Women of Ill-Fame from Certain Limits in the City." That same year, the public health department expelled hundreds of prostitutes from San Francisco on the grounds that they were "offending public decency."

The Chinese Six Companies, an organization of prosperous Chinatown business-men who were battling the tongs for political dominance, offered to assist immigration officials in turning back ships from China carrying prostitutes. On June 1, 1868, the president of the Six Companies sent the legislature "A Petition to the State of California to Bar Prostitutes," outlining the negative effects of Chinese prostitution on the Chinatown community. As a result of pressure from the Six Companies, as well as growing anti-Chinese sentiment among the white population, the state legislature in 1870 enacted a law prohibiting Asian immigrant women from entering California unless they could prove they were not prostitutes.

In 1873 the legislature passed even tougher legislation, "An Act to Prevent the Kidnapping and the Importation of Mongolian, Chinese and Japanese Females for Criminal or Demoralizing Purposes." These laws reduced the number of arrivals. They also made the slave trade more expensive, as the procurer had to pay increased bribes to the customs officials. It now cost almost three thousand dollars to bring in a fourteen-year-old girl.

These laws, however, did not end the gruesome trade: they just pushed it deeper underground. The importers became more skillful at hiding their illicit cargo. One white madam wrote in 1898 that she had a Chinese slave who "came in with twelve-year-old girls, two dozen of them in padded crates, billed as dishware."

In 1876 the California State Senate held hearings on Chinese immigration, in which prostitution was a central issue. Hirata notes that "while sexual prejudice obscured the exploitative nature of prostitution as a business, a sense of racial superiority at first led whites to condone Chinese female slavery. Later when anti-Chinese sentiment grew, slavery was emphasized in anti-Chinese rhetoric."

The hearings featured doctors who warned about the transmission of venereal diseases from the prostitutes to white Californians, as if the diseases traveled only one way. A doctor with the San Francisco Board of Health claimed that a virulent strain of syphilis, originating in Chinese prostitutes, was infecting white boys as young as five.

California's anti-Chinese sentiment and laws had a national impact. In 1875 Congress enacted the Page Law, "forbidding the entry of Oriental contract laborers, prostitutes and criminals." The law nullified all of the contracts that had been "signed" between Chinese prostitutes and their procurers, stating that "the importation into the United States of women for the purposes of prostitution is hereby forbidden." The law also made it a felony to hold a woman for prostitution, with a penalty of up to five years in prison and a five-thousand-dollar fine.

Since the law made little distinction between women indentured to prostitution and others, it had the practical effect of preventing almost all Chinese women from coming to the United States, reducing the total number to about three hundred annually. Opposition to the enslavement of Chinese girls was put to use by advocates for the restriction and eventual elimination of Chinese immigration. After the Chinese Exclusion Act of 1882 was passed, the number of Chinese women immigrants fell to sixty-one annually. The lack of women immigrants greatly reduced the ability of California's Chinese community to expand, almost extinguishing it.

The most distressing questions of the period still haunt our history: Why was there not widespread opposition to the trafficking in young Chinese women? Were the parallels to African slavery not evident to the public at large? Was the practice somehow acceptable because it was kept out of the mainstream?

"How We Won the Vote"

Women won the right to vote in California in 1911, almost a decade before the Nineteenth Amendment granted universal suffrage to women throughout the United States. California became the "Sixth Star" in the banner created by West Coast suffragists, joining the suffrage states of Wyoming (which in 1869 became the first state to give the franchise to women), Colorado, Utah, Idaho, and Washington.

The movement making California the sixth star was fueled by dynamic, committed, and intelligent women who faced the daunting task of convincing a majority of men to give women the right to join them as voters. Most of the women who comprised this determined movement came from the urban upper middle class. They were influenced and inspired by the national suffrage movement launched in Seneca Falls, New York, in 1848.

In the late 1800s, California women lobbied the state and local governments, seeking changes in the law. Several women were so bold that they ran for office before they could even vote. San Francisco public school teacher Sallie Hart, for example, spent six weeks in Sacramento to win support for a bill that would allow women to serve as elected members of school boards. One senator described her as "going from seat to seat, like some blazing comet, shaking a kind of fascination from her twirled hair."

Laura de Force Gordon, who along with legal pioneer Clara Shortridge Foltz successfully lobbied the legislature to allow women to practice law, was nominated for the state senate by the Independent Party of San Joaquin County in 1871. In 1882 Marietta Beers-Stow ran for governor. A widow who had lost her entire inheritance (including her own writing desk) to her husband's creditors, Beers-Stow used her political campaign to expose the inequities of the probate court system. She called it the "highest court of prostitution," writing, "The Probate Court grows fat on the meat of the starving widow and children." In 1884 Beers-Stow took her political campaign national, running for vice president on a ticket with presidential candidate Belva Lockwood of Washington, DC.

Women's rights activists faced formidable opposition from men at all levels of society. The *San Francisco Chronicle* summed up the popular male opposition to women's suffrage in a poem published in 1870:

> Fiddle faddle! What's the use?
> You can't make her a man!
> Don't let her then be smirched and soiled
> By mingling in the fray,
> But keep her free from grosser acts
> To win her own sweet way.

The newspaper maintained the same argument in a more serious vein on its opinion pages. A July 16, 1871, editorial, "Shall Women Vote?" ridiculed the arguments of national suffrage leaders Elizabeth Cady Stanton and Susan B. Anthony and stated, "We have heard nothing in the points made by either of these ladies to lead us to the conclusion that either man or woman would be benefited by the extension of the privilege of voting to the latter."

The all-male legislature disparaged the women's campaign. When three hundred grassroots lobbyists claiming to represent fifty thousand women went to Sacramento to pressure the Committee on Public Morals about rights for women, the chair of the committee responded, "Well, you are no more than 50,000 mice! How many votes can you deliver? Go home and look after your own girls. They may be walking the streets for all you know!"

One of the women recalled, "At that, the male legislators all laughed heartily."

Infuriated by the lack of response from lawmakers, activists founded the Women's Suffrage Society in 1870. And knowing that the movement needed publicity and was not likely to garner support from the male-dominated newspapers, Emily Pitts Stevens had bought the *California Sunday Mercury*, which became the first publication in the West to advocate suffrage. From 1865 to 1870, Pitts Stevens hired women to set type for her journal, promoted the all-female Women's Cooperative Printing Union, and founded the Women's Publishing Company. On the first anniversary of the Women's Suffrage Society, the paper ran this poem:

> We ask a hearing; here we press our claim
> To our own birthright in a woman's name,
> Give us the Ballot; with it comes the power
> To right old wrongs; then consecrate this hour.

The president of the California Women's Suffrage Association, Ellen Clark Sargent, went to Washington, DC, when her husband, Aaron A. Sargent, was elected to the Senate. There, she became a friend of Susan B. Anthony and forged a link between suffragists in California and the nation's capital. Clark Sargent had greatly influenced her husband: Senator Sargent, who was the first person to utter the word "suffrage" in Congress in reference to women, later wrote the suffrage amendment to the U.S. Constitution. He also interceded with President Grant to secure the release of Anthony when she was jailed in 1872 for the federal offense of registering to vote.

California women succeeded in convincing legislators to put suffrage on the 1896 ballot. The referendum, Ballot No. 6, an amendment to the California constitution that would grant women the right to vote, lost badly—especially in San Francisco, home to the majority of voters, where twenty thousand men voted against it.

"The Liquor Dealers League, really the producers, proprietors and patrons of drink, defeated suffrage," explains women's historian Mae Silver. The Liquor Dealers League warned that if women got the right to vote, they would shut down the liquor industry—a convincing argument for many male voters. Silver points out that there were more drinking establishments in San Francisco than anywhere else in the state, and that the liquor lobby held sway over San Francisco politics.

But the women would not give up. Two days after their electoral defeat on November 3, 1896, they opened the State Woman Suffrage Convention in San Francisco's Golden Gate Hall "to plan for future." Though the movement was disrupted by any number of things, including, in 1906, the San Francisco earthquake and fire, in just a few short years the organizers regrouped for another try at the ballot.

Suffrage leaders organized women's clubs, such as the Friday Morning Club in Los Angeles. Although the purpose of these clubs was political, they followed the model of the existing women's social clubs of polite society. As Sylvie Thygeson described it, "You had these little afternoon gatherings of women, maybe six or eight women. You had a cup of tea. A little social gathering. While we were drinking tea, I gave a little talk and they asked questions about what was going on. We not only lectured for suffrage, but we also lectured for birth control and any of the things that belonged to women."

Another suffrage organizer, Jessie Haver Butler, wrote that when national leader Carrie Chapman Catt came to California, she took her "on the stump" throughout the state. "Many of the women were well-off so there was plenty of money around. They always met her at the train and escorted her to the hotel and all of us were there with her. Always they had these beautiful meetings."

Members of the College Equal Suffrage League even acquired the "Blue Liner," a flashy blue open roadster decorated with yellow streamers that they drove around California to spread the suffrage message. Aiming to mobilize support from men in small towns and rural outposts, they gave stirring speeches to miners, farmers, and ranch hands. Everywhere they went, crowds of men gathered to see the snazzy car.

There were also attempts to reach out to and mobilize working-class women. Selina Solomons was a Jew who dedicated her life to the suffrage movement, not a common activity for women in San Francisco's small Jewish community. Though she was from a highly educated family—her sister became a physician and psychologist and her brother was a cartographer of Yosemite—when her businessman father became addicted to absinthe, her mother struggled to raise the family on her own.

Solomons only had a high school education, yet she became a prominent writer and a speaker on women's issues. Solomons not only wrote the sole history of the suffrage campaign in California, "How We Won the Vote in California: A True Story of the Campaign of 1911," published by the New Woman Press, she also wrote a play, *The Girl from Colorado or The Conversion of Aunty Suffridge*, which she described as "an American Votes for Women comedy with a love interest."

Solomons was critical of the middle-class orientation of the suffrage movement. For example, in describing the founding of the Century Club, the first all-women's club in the state aimed at providing a political voice for women, she wrote, "In the

How We Won the Vote in California

By
Selina Solomons

Selina Solomons, a young Jewish suffragist in San Francisco, mobilized shop girls in the campaign for the right to vote. Her booklet How We Won the Vote *provides a rare look into the organizing of the campaign that secured women's suffrage in California almost a decade before the Nineteenth Amendment was passed.*

effort to attain social success, this club admitted to membership too large a number of merely fashionable women, and so swamped itself at the outset, and failed forever in the cherished purpose and aim of its founders."

Solomons also wrote of her experience going door to door, trying to summon votes for women in the 1896 campaign. She canvassed neighborhoods—both her own middle-class section of town and the area "south of the slot." This was the neighborhood south of Market Street, the main thoroughfare that separated the rich and poor. (Cable cars ran down the middle of Market Street, and the long slot through which they gripped the cable gave rise to the terms "north" and "south of the slot.") Solomons walked precincts inhabited by poor working people, mostly German and Irish immigrants. But she found the same response in both parts of town: the men opposed suffrage, and the women supported it.

She also noted the resentment some suffragists felt upon receiving numerous leaflets in foreign languages. They gritted their teeth, realizing that immigrant men could vote in the United States, while women could not vote in the land of their birth.

In February 1910, to reach working-class women, Solomons opened the Votes-for-Women Club in a loft at 315 Sutter Street, in downtown San Francisco. The club, festooned with suffrage-yellow paper flowers and banners, attracted shop girls and clerks. Equipped with a kitchenette, it provided nutritious dishes for a nickel each. Solomons hoped that the "girl who comes to eat, stays to read and talk."

The Votes-for-Women Club was popular with women workers, as well as downtown shoppers, and a look at its menu may explain why: on a typical day, it offered four kinds of soup—oxtail, tomato bisque, chicken, and clam chowder; five kinds of salads, all served with "mayonnaise and pure olive oil"; French artichokes; fried sand dabs; creamed codfish; "home-made cakes"; and "rich milk." At the bottom of the menu was another offering: "All Women Welcome to Our Rest and Reading Rooms—Afternoon Tea Served from 4 to 5 o'clock."

Solomons stocked the reading room with suffrage movement literature. She hosted lectures, forums, and cultural performances advocating votes for women. The club was run by volunteers, except for paid dishwashers and janitors. In a clever twist, Solomons started a dues-paying Men's Auxiliary to raise money for club maintenance.

One newspaper reported, "What Working Girls Do with Their 60 Minutes at Noon: Imbibe Votes for Women Arguments as Side-Dish to 'Just Home Cooking.'" A society woman was quoted as saying, "The other day I dropped in for luncheon and a pretty young girl who only an hour before had sold me a pair of gloves sat next to me." She was also surprised that "Miss Selina Solomons, the president of the Club, worked harder than any paid waitress would even think of doing."

Minna O'Donnell, also targeting her efforts at working-class women, organized support for women's suffrage from the Union Labor Party. Joining forces with Louise LaRue, a member of Waitresses Local 48, she formed the Wage Earners Suffrage League. Women from the waitress and laundry workers unions took the message to working-class San Francisco neighborhoods, influencing male trade unionists in the labor town.

When, in 1911, suffragists succeeded in getting another measure on the ballot, the movement developed an array of campaign materials: posters, leaflets, postcards, buttons, emblems—all in the blue and gold colors that symbolized their cause. "By the close of the campaign there was no yellow paper or cambric left in the stores of San Francisco or LA," Solomons recalled.

As the election neared, suffragists put up billboards: "Justice to California Women, Vote Yes to Amendment 4—Give Your Girl the Same Chance as Your Boy." These were countered by billboards reading, "Vote NO—Home-loving women do not want the ballot."

The *San Francisco Morning Call* and the *Los Angeles Herald* published positive editorials. The *Call* encouraged readers to "right this ancient wrong. Put a cross in the right place; the Yes Place. And put woman in her right place." But the powerful *Los Angeles Times* and *San Francisco Chronicle* opposed women's suffrage. When the *Chronicle* ran an ad full of misquotes and lies about national suffrage leaders, women went to the newspaper offices, threw copies of the paper to the ground, and demanded that the publisher recall the edition.

As the summer of 1911 wore on, the campaign went into full swing. In Los Angeles, Clara Shortridge Foltz, the first woman to practice law in the state, after having sued the dean of Hastings College of the Law to be admitted, held organizing meetings every Saturday in the Auditorium Theater. An indefatigable campaigner, Foltz traveled around the state to "towns, sheep ranches, and cross-roads mining camps." A suffrage rally on July 4 in a Los Angeles park was almost thwarted when the police threatened to invoke a city ordinance "forbidding political speeches in the park." The organizers got around the law by singing their message in the suffrage song "Beloved California," with its resounding line, "the vote will make us free!"

In the San Francisco Labor Day Parade, trade unionists heard national AFL President Samuel Gompers urge a vote for women's suffrage, and for another ballot measure calling for an eight-hour workday for women.

Shortly before election day, one of the suffrage movement's greatest champions, Ellen Clark Sargent, died. For the first time in California history, the flag was flown at half-mast to honor the death of a woman, and Governor Hiram Johnson spoke at a public memorial service in San Francisco's Union Square.

On election day, October 10, 1911, poll workers from the Votes-for-Women Club mobilized in great numbers. Suspecting that there would be fraudulent ballots, they organized more than one thousand men and women as poll watchers. Phoebe Apperson Hearst donated the use of the Dreamland skating rink in San Francisco as a central meeting place for the suffrage movement, providing a resting place and lunch for the volunteers. The *Chronicle* donated the use of the Scottish Rite hall to the opponents.

Election Day 1911 was a watershed. The vote was extremely close. In San Francisco, the early editions of both the *Chronicle* and *Examiner* declared suffrage had lost. Male voters in both San Francisco and Alameda Counties had voted against granting women the vote, and the conservative papers assumed that male voters outside the cities would do the same.

In the final tally, however, suffrage won by 3,587 votes. It was a bare 2 percent margin, but it was a vote that changed history.

The organizing efforts had paid off. Clara Shortridge Foltz's speaking tour around the state had won support from men outside of the major cities, tipping the balance for suffrage. Their support was memorialized in a poem from the College Equal Suffrage League entitled "Ode to the Farmers Who Voted a Majority for Us."

> Out of the dust of the street
> Came the denial;
> Out of the fumes of clubs,
> Scorn of our trial.
>
> But from the strength of the hills
> Men's voices hailed us;
> God bless our farmer-folk,
> Scarce a man failed us!

For the first time, a million women in California had the right to vote. Describing the wake she and her comrades held for the Votes-for-Women Club, Selina Solomons stated, "We gave free rein to our emotions in both manly and womanly fashion, with handshaking and back slapping as well as hugging and kissing one another." Later she recalled, "October 10, 1911, proved to be the greatest day in my life."

Women in Los Angeles were the first to exercise their right to vote. In a local election held on December 6, 1911, seventy thousand women went to the polls. Three months later, on March 28, 1912, women statewide had a chance to vote in the presidential primary.

California suffragists vowed to continue their fight on a national level. In 1915 they organized the Women Voters' Demonstration at the Panama-Pacific International Exposition, in San Francisco. More than ten thousand women attended from all over the United States and from as far away as China, Persia, and Italy. Organizers hung a banner from a tower declaring, "We demand an amendment to the Constitution of the United States enfranchising women!" They sent petitions to Congress and the president bearing the names of six hundred thousand supporters.

On the final day of the event, suffragists drove the famous Blue Liner through the gates of the exposition grounds, carrying four women, including poet Sara Bard Field, who composed this "Song of Free Women" for the occasion:

> We are women clad in new power,
> We see the weak. We hear their plea.
> We march to set our sisters free.
> Lo! Has rung the chime from Freedom's tower.
>
> No more we bend the knee imploring
> No longer urge our cause with tears.
> We have rent asunder binding fears.
> We are women strong for women warring.

Over the next decade, several California suffragists, including Charlotte Anita Whitney, who would later be convicted under the criminal syndicalism law for her radical ideas, traveled to the East Coast to help win passage of the Nineteenth Amendment.

On the back page of Selina Solomons's booklet about the campaign is a list of materials that could be purchased from the Votes-for-Women Club. Among the listings are flags in the national suffrage colors—blue and gold, two for a nickel—that say "California, the Next Suffrage State." The description reads, "Only a few of the above left over from the California campaign, order at once from..."—a fitting footnote to a successful campaign.

Women at Work

In the latter part of the nineteenth century, an Irish immigrant and teacher, Kate Kennedy, launched a lobbying campaign for "equal pay for equal work." Her efforts were partially successful when the state legislature adopted an 1874 law that mandated, "Females employed as teachers in the public schools of this state shall in all cases receive the same compensation as is allowed male teachers for like services."

At the time—and for many decades following—teaching was one of few professions open to women in California. Half of all teachers in Los Angeles in the 1870s were women, but before the 1874 law, their pay was less than that of their male colleagues.

Women in other professions soon followed Kennedy's lead. In 1878 Laura de Force Gordon and suffragist Clara Shortridge Foltz convinced the legislature to repeal the law that denied women admission to the bar. Foltz wrote, "The bill met with a storm of opposition such as had never been witnessed on the floor of the California senate. Narrow gauge statesmen grew as red as turkey gobblers mouthing their ignorance against the bill." The bill passed by two votes, and Gordon and Foltz became the first female practicing lawyers in California. And in 1890, the San Francisco Medical Society admitted its first woman member, Dr. Lucy Maria Field Wanzer.

The most enduring change occurred in 1879, when newly minted attorneys Foltz and Gordon drafted a constitutional revision that was adopted by the state constitutional convention. Article XX, Section 18, of the 1879 constitution stated, "No person shall, on account of sex, be disqualified from entering upon or pursuing any lawful business, vocation or profession." [The article was amended in 1970 and changed to Article 1, Section 8, which reads, "A person may not be disqualified from entering or pursuing a business, profession, vocation, or employment because of sex, race, creed, color, or national or ethnic origin."]

That section of the 1879 constitution was the basis for an important sex discrimination case just two years later. In 1881 waitress Mary Maguire was arrested for violating a San Francisco ordinance that prohibited women from "waiting on persons in a barroom from 6 PM to 6 AM in which liquor was sold." Maguire filed a writ of habeas corpus so that she could get out of jail, and the court granted her request stating that the ordinance was unconstitutional because it impermissibly disqualified women from pursuing a business that was lawful for men. The city argued that the law was necessary to protect against immorality. But the court ruled that the new constitutional provision did not contain any exceptions.

The court ordered Maguire released and struck down the ordinance, stating, "The language of the ordinance is plain, and its meaning unmistakable. It leaves nothing for construction. The words employed in this ordinance *incapacitate* a woman from following the business for which the petitioner was fined and *disable* her from doing so....Such legislation could only be considered an evasion of the Constitutional provision."

Despite the state constitution, women still faced fierce discrimination in many professions. When attempts were made to extend the equal pay argument beyond the professions, a 1911 Senate Report on Women in Industry declared the "natural inferiority of women" was the reason they were paid less.

A Bureau of Labor Statistics report documenting that a third of women workers were paid less than fifteen cents an hour catalyzed an energetic movement for a minimum wage for women and children. Katherine Philips Edson of Los Angeles, president of the California Federation of Women's Clubs, campaigned around the state for a change in the law. Meanwhile, women workers took the protest to the streets. In 1901 several hundred waitresses demanding higher wages went on a bitter strike that shut down almost two hundred San Francisco restaurants. In 1907 women laundry workers and assembly line workers at the Ghirardelli chocolate factory went on strike for better pay and an end to dangerous and unsanitary working conditions. In 1919 thirteen hundred women telephone operators struck for the right to bargain collectively.

At first, organized labor opposed the minimum wage legislation, fearing that government regulation would undermine their strength of collective bargaining. Under pressure from women workers, they changed their stance. In 1911, in the same election that brought the victory for women's suffrage, a law was adopted limiting the workday for women to eight hours (excluding labor on farms and in agricultural packing sheds). In 1913 the minimum wage law was passed.

Despite this enthusiasm, and the codification of sex equality in the California constitution, the state legislature, Congress, and the courts remained silent on women's rights for decades to come. But an astonishing experiment during World War II was to plant the seeds for a major change.

Rosie the Riveter

In 1940 President Franklin Delano Roosevelt called on the American people to provide a "Great Arsenal of Democracy" to support the allies of the United States against the rise of fascism in Europe. He asked everyone to join the war effort by "overproducing and overwhelming the enemy." Our European allies especially needed ships.

Industrialist Henry J. Kaiser heeded the call. Though he had never built a ship in his life, he opened a shipyard in Richmond, just across the bay from San Francisco, to supply liberty ships to Britain. The city gave Kaiser permits to transform the "boggy tideland" into a gigantic ship-building enterprise which, by the end of 1943, would launch seven hundred and fifty new ships.

The federal government poured so much defense contract money into California that one commentator called it the second gold rush. While southern California dominated the aircraft industry, northern California, especially the Richmond site, was the center of production for warships, tanks, and bombs and other armaments.

When the U.S. entered the war after the attack on Pearl Harbor, Kaiser expanded his operation. The four shipyards in Richmond became central to the war in the Pacific. A nearby Ford Motor Company factory was converted to manufacture armored tanks.

To meet the frantic production schedule, the shipyards operated twenty-four hours a day, every day except Christmas. To meet Roosevelt's demand for high, uninterrupted production, the AFL and the CIO signed a no-strike clause for the duration of the war. In addition, after C. L. Dellums, an Oakland labor leader, and A. Philip Randolph of the Brotherhood of Sleeping Car Porters threatened to organize a march of fifty thousand African American workers on Washington, Roosevelt issued Executive Order 8802, barring race discrimination in the government defense industry. But there was still a shortage of workers. For every soldier on the battlefield, it was estimated that seventeen people were needed on the home front. Where was the labor to come from?

As the demand for U.S. naval ships grew and male workers left for the front, defense contractors recruited women to fill their places. The first ten female workers were hired in 1942. Popularly known as "Rosie the Riveters," women eventually made up 25 percent of the shipyard workforce on the West Coast, more than twice the percentage of women in the defense industry nationwide. The Kaiser shipyards, where women worked around the clock alongside men, were the most productive in the United States.

The Kaiser Shipbuilding Corporation sent recruiters to the Midwest and the segregated South to meet a daily quota of one hundred and fifty new workers. Many midwestern farm girls and southern sharecroppers were anxious to join the war effort, and at the same time earn good wages and independence. Southern blacks, displaced by the mechanization of cotton, were anxious to leave the poverty and racial violence of the Jim Crow states. More than 1.2 million southern black workers headed west in a great migration; almost 90 percent of black employees in the Richmond shipyards were southerners.

Margaret Starks came from Arkansas to work in the shipyards in 1943. She later founded Richmond's first black newspaper, the *Richmond Guide*, and became an officer of the NAACP. It was "a long way from my cooking job in Pine Bluff," she recalled.

Women workers, popularly known and admired as Rosie the Riveters, filled a quarter of the shipyard jobs on the West Coast during World War II. Many African American women recruited from the South continued to endure segregated housing and racism in predominantly white Bay Area cities.

The women were paid the same wages as men in the shipyards, and in 1944, for the first time ever, union contracts included an "equal pay for equal work" clause. Special provisions were made to accommodate women workers. Round-the-clock child care was provided for seventy cents a day; public schools ran on double shifts. All-night cafeterias and take-out meal service helped women workers who did not have time to shop or cook for their families.

These women in the traditionally male workforce were not resented. Their efforts were admired, officially lauded, and even memorialized in popular culture. In 1942 a song in their honor hit the charts:

> While other girls attend their favorite cocktail bar
> Sipping dry Martinis, munching caviar
> There's a girl who's really putting them to shame
> Rosie is her name
>
> All the day long whether rain or shine
> She's a part of the assembly line
> She's making history, working for victory
> Rosie the riveter

Keeps a sharp look out for sabotage
Sitting up there on the fuselage
That little frail can do more than a male will do
Rosie the riveter…

What if she's smeared full of oil and grease
Doing her bit for the old Lend Lease…
Berlin will hear about, Moscow will cheer about
Rosie the Riveter!

Every day, a steady stream of workers arrived at the Richmond Greyhound Station. The new arrivals slept in movie theaters, parks, tents, and anywhere else they could find shelter. A nursery owned by a Japanese family that had been relocated to an internment camp was converted into a workers' dormitory. A public housing project, Atchison Village, became a defense housing project.

But although the assembly lines were racially integrated in accordance with Roosevelt's executive order, the town, housing, and children's facilities were segregated. The public housing in the new Atchison Village development was for whites only.

Betty Reid-Soskin, an African American "Rosie," worked as a file clerk in the segregated union hall of the Boilermakers Union in Richmond. "It's the one time in my life that I literally worked in a Jim Crow situation," she recalled. "All the black workers had 'trainee' or 'helper' stamped on their union cards, guaranteeing that they would not be in competition with white workers after the war."

The twenty-four-hour child care was quite an innovation, but it was available only to white families. Black parents, newly arrived from the South, had to rely on relatives, neighbors, or black churches while they worked night shifts on the assembly line.

Reid-Soskin recalls that the black workers who came to California from the segregated South despaired when they found the same segregation replicated in California. Many white southerners had jobs—better jobs, for the most part—at the shipyards, and brought their hostile racist attitudes with them. "Black workers came wanting something more and were disappointed," explained Reid-Soskin. "We African Americans were fighting and working for freedoms we wouldn't enjoy for another twenty years."

Yet there were also moments of great pride for African American workers. They built ships named for black leaders, the SS *Harriet Tubman*, the SS *George Washington Carver*, and the SS *Toussaint L'Overture*. Four ships were named after traditionally black colleges. The christening of the SS *Robert S. Abbott*, named for the publisher of the African American newspaper the *Chicago Defender*, was "the social event of the year," especially for African Americans who had migrated from Chicago. Lena Horne came to the launch. "We were so proud!" Reid-Soskin recalled.

Reid-Soskin hopes that the "conflicting truths" of the Rosie the Riveter period will be revealed. "I'm schizophrenic about the Rosie thing, because even now I have to qualify that I was a nontraditional Rosie," she said. "White women came out of the home for the first time, but African American women had been working since we came here on slave ships from Africa."

At the peak, the Richmond shipyards employed ninety-three thousand women. Many were trained as welders, electricians, and carpenters and for the first time earned a high enough wage to be independent. But all of this ended abruptly when the war was over: in 1945 the Richmond shipyards' female workforce was reduced to ten thousand. Military veterans were given priority for postwar jobs, and though some women remained in the workforce, their wages plummeted.

There was relief that the war was over, happiness that fathers, brothers, and lovers had come home safely. But many women, for the first time, had earned decent wages and learned new skills; the government-supported social infrastructure had provided them the means to work and raise a family simultaneously. Their dissatisfaction with the forced postwar return to the hearth became the seeds for the women's movement that was to follow.

Jutting out into San Francisco Bay, in a serene, leafy Richmond park where the bustling shipyards once operated, is the long, iron frame of a ship, its hull adorned with photographs and quotations from the women workers who served as the backbone of the shipbuilding industry during World War II. The anonymous quote at the end of this Rosie the Riveter monument reads: "You must tell your children, putting modesty aside, that without us, without women, there would have been no Spring in 1945."

A Pedestal or a Cage?

By the end of World War II, eighteen million women had jobs in the defense industry nationwide. Though women quickly lost these wartime posts, many persisted in finding a place in the workforce. In 1950, 30 percent of California women were working outside the home; by 1977, a majority of women in the state held part- or full-time jobs.

The influx of women into the workforce prompted President Kennedy in 1961 to create the President's Commission on the Status of Women, chaired by Eleanor Roosevelt. Its purpose was to "develop recommendations for overcoming discrimination in government and private employment on the basis of sex and to develop recommendations for services which will enable women to continue their role as wives and mothers while making a maximum contribution to the world around them."

Not surprisingly, the commission found hundreds of areas where women faced gross inequities, both in the workplace and in society at large. It made sweeping recommendations to overhaul the educational system, extend fair labor standards to jobs that traditionally employed women, provide child care, amend discriminatory social security laws, extend unemployment insurance to household workers, and grant paid maternity leave.

The commission documented what millions of American women had known for generations: sex discrimination impacts all areas of women's lives, from education, insurance, and taxes to divorce, pensions, and credit.

The Kennedy Commission did not endorse the measure that was to become the political centerpiece of the women's liberation movement—the Equal Rights Amendment—but it did propose the Equal Pay Act of 1963, the first federal law explicitly mandating women's rights at the workplace.

The following year, in a political fluke, women were added as a protected class in the proposed 1964 Civil Rights Act: working on the assumption that including gender as well as race in the bill's anti-discrimination provisions would alienate their fellow senators, a bloc of pro-segregationists hoped to jettison the entire bill. But their attempt was foiled. The resulting landmark legislation was signed by President Lyndon Johnson.

The 1964 Civil Rights Act established the Equal Employment Opportunity Commission (EEOC) to investigate complaints of discrimination in employment on the basis of race and sex. Aileen Hernandez, a magna cum laude graduate of Howard University who had been the Pacific Coast organizer of the International Ladies Garment Workers Union, was the first woman appointed to the commission. Recalling its earlier days she said, "The commission meetings produced a sea of male faces, nearly all of which reflected attitudes that ranged from boredom to virulent hostility whenever the issue of sex discrimination was raised."

This was frustrating but not surprising to Hernandez, who had picketed with the NAACP against segregation at the National Theater and had been personally congratulated by Eleanor Roosevelt for her leadership for women's rights. Hernandez described the era with a shiver. "When you opened the classified section of the *Los Angeles Times* or the *Chronicle*, there would be pages and pages of Help Wanted ads divided by sex. Of course, the ads under 'Women' were for low-paying clerical or sales positions. And the wages were always much lower than those for men."

Hernandez resigned from the EEOC in protest over the commission's inaction on claims of sex discrimination. She threw her intellect, advocacy, and prominence into the formation of the National Organization for Women (NOW), eventually becoming its president. "The torch has been passed to a new generation of women

Pioneering feminist Aileen Hernandez in a dress decorated with union labels in 1959, being admired by Governor Pat Brown (left). The union organizer went on to become the first woman appointed to the U.S. Equal Employment Opportunity Commission and the president of the National Organization for Women.

who are going to continue the struggle. We're talking about a new kind of society in which there really is full involvement of both sexes and all races and all colors and creeds. The struggle is for personhood and personhood is powerful," she said at the organization's founding.

NOW was part of a growing women's movement that lobbied for gender to be included in the state Fair Employment Practices Act along with race, religious creed, color, national origin, and ancestry. In 1970 the law was amended to bar discrimination against women.

In 1971 the spirit of barmaid Mary Maguire returned to the California courtroom. The Department of Alcoholic Beverage Control was about to revoke the liquor license of the owners of the Sail'er Inn because they hired women bartenders in violation of the California Business and Professions Code, which banned women from tending bar unless they owned the bar—or were married to the owner! Once again, the rationale for this law was the protection of women.

Herma Hill Kay, a petite, tough-minded attorney who went on to become the first woman dean of Boalt Hall School of Law at UC Berkeley, played a major role in the case. Her law school office overlooking San Francisco Bay is wall to wall with books; one whole shelf is filled with her writings. In terms of women's rights, she explained:

> Federal and state laws are intertwined, because when the United States
> Supreme Court speaks, it affects women around the country. However,
> California law is especially significant when it goes beyond the rights in
> federal law—as it did in the case of Sail'er Inn. In that case, the California
> Supreme Court did what the U.S. Supreme Court has never done, which is
> to determine "strict scrutiny," the most rigorous standard of judicial review,
> is the standard to look at discrimination against women. [Strict scrutiny, a
> legal standard that stems from the 1944 Korematsu decision, provides that
> courts must strike down laws that discriminate against people in "pro-
> tected" classes like race or sex, unless the state has a strong rationale for
> maintaining the law.]

Kay explained that one of her former students, feminist attorney Wendy Williams, was clerking for California Supreme Court Justice Raymond Peters when
the Sail'er Inn case reached the high court. "Wendy realized that this would be an
important case for strict scrutiny, but none of the parties had addressed the issue.
So she called me."

It might have seemed a straightforward decision to enter the case, except for one
thing—Sail'er Inn was a topless bar. If the women were to tend bar, they would have
to do it topless. "Of course," said the septuagenarian Kay with a twinkle in her blue
eyes, "the waitresses were already topless, but the bartenders made more money."

Kay wanted to enter the case and she enlisted the support of the Berkeley Women's
Law Student Association. "The students were torn about this," explained Kay, "and
we had a lengthy feminist debate as to whether it was worth it to join this case. You
can imagine the discussions, which went late into the night. Should our progressive
women's law association support women's liberation by advocating for the right of
women to serve drinks in a topless bar?"

In the end, because the women workers supported the litigation, the Women's Law
Student Association agreed to enter the case and made strict scrutiny the centerpiece
of its brief. It turned out to be a winning argument.

"The desire to protect women from occupational hazards was not a reason to
exclude them," the California Supreme Court ruled. But this time the court went
even further than the Maguire ruling, and further than federal law required at the
time. The opinion, by Chief Justice Raymond Peters, concluded that classifications
based on sex should be held to the highest standard—the standard of strict scrutiny—because "sex, like race and lineage, is an immutable trait, a status into which
the class members are locked by the accident of birth."

The opinion was an indictment of discrimination based on sex, race, ethnic origin,
and social class:

Women, like Negroes, aliens and the poor, have historically labored under severe legal and social disabilities. Like black citizens, they were, for many years, denied the right to vote, and until recently the right to serve on juries in many states. They are excluded from or discriminated against in employment and educational opportunities. Married women in particular have been treated as inferior persons in numerous laws relating to property and independent business ownership and the right to make contracts.

Echoing the demands of millions of women who had organized and marched for equality, Justice Peters stated that "exceptions cannot be based on popular notions of what is a proper, fitting or moral occupation for persons of either sex....[M]ere prejudice, however ancient, common or socially acceptable" is not a justification for discrimination.

The court also took on the age-old argument that these restrictions were for women's own good, stating, "Laws which disable women from full participation in the political, business and economic arenas are often characterized as 'protective' and beneficial. Those same laws applied to racial or ethnic minorities would readily be recognized as invidious and impermissible. *The pedestal upon which women have been placed has all too often, upon closer inspection, been revealed as a cage.*"[emphasis added]

Kay remembers that Justice Peters was happy to have the strict scrutiny argument before him. The Berkeley Women's Law Student Association legal argument "gave it the bite it ought to have," Kay added.

The California Supreme Court decision in *Sail'er Inn* came on May 27, 1971. Later that year, the United States Supreme Court ruled, in the case of *Reed v. Reed*, that women as a class have a constitutional right to equal protection. The high court ruled for the first time that classification based on sex was in violation of the Fourteenth Amendment, stating, "A sex classification must be reasonable, not arbitrary and must rest upon some ground of difference having a fair and substantial relation to the object of the legislation." The case was argued by Ruth Bader Ginsburg, then a professor of law at Rutgers University, on behalf of the ACLU. Thirty years later, she was the second woman to be appointed to the U.S. Supreme Court.

The stage was now set for the Supreme Court to do what the court in California had already so boldly done: make the standard of review in sex discrimination cases as close as possible to the strict scrutiny applied in race discrimination cases. But in the 1973 case of *Frontiero v. Richardson*, the high court fell one vote short of this. Instead, the all-male court adopted the looser standard of review that sex discrimination—in schools, Social Security, or other realms—should be looked at with "skeptical scrutiny."

At the time of these decisions, organizing around women's rights had reached a feverish pitch. Inspired by the civil rights struggle and the antiwar movement (and sometimes in response to the sexism encountered in those movements) women all over the state were creating their own organizations: child-care collectives, consciousness raising groups, caucuses within trade unions and professional associations, and political organizations. They worked to change their daily lives on both personal and political levels.

The impact of their organizing was seen when the California legislature approved the Equal Rights Amendment (ERA) soon after Congress passed it in 1972.

The ERA simply stated, "Equality of rights under the law shall not be denied or abridged by the United States or by any state on the basis of sex." Though it had been first introduced in 1923 by suffrage leader Alice Paul at the National Women's Party meeting in Seneca Falls, and adopted by both the Republican and Democratic Party platforms by the 1940s, Congress did not approve it as a potential amendment to the Constitution until 1972. The ERA needed to be ratified by thirty-eight states within seven years in order to become part of the Constitution. By 1979 it had failed, as it had only been ratified by thirty-five; though the deadline was extended until 1982, the measure never got the needed two-thirds majority.

Several states passed their own ERAs, but not California. Some argued that

Responding to demands from the growing women's movement, in 1970 the legislature passed a law barring sex discrimination in employment. Prior to that, "help wanted" ads were divided by gender and women were barred from many professions.

because of the state supreme court ruling in *Sail'er Inn*, California already had its own ERA and women in California did not need the legal protection that would be guaranteed by federal law.

Still, if the ERA had passed, there would be more certainty and less inconsistency in deciding sex discrimination claims. As political scientist Roberta Francis wrote, "If the ERA were in the Constitution it would influence the tone of legal reasoning and decisions regarding women's equal rights, producing over time a cumulative positive effect....Without the bedrock constitutional affirmation that equality of rights cannot be denied or abridged on account of sex, the political and judicial victories that women have achieved over the past two centuries are vulnerable to erosion or reversal, now or in the future."

In 1973 the California legislature created the Joint Committee on Legal Equality, modeled on the Kennedy Commission, whose purpose was to comb through the statute books and recommend changes to eliminate inequality between men and women. The committee's 1978 report identified four hundred discriminatory laws, many of them reflecting "a Victorian perspective of women as second-class citizens." Most of them were repealed; in one fell swoop, the legislature equalized workers' compensation allowances and death benefits; repealed the law that made husbands the sole managers of jointly owned property; and amended state disability insurance to cover pregnancy.

Vibrant new women's organizations, like Equal Rights Advocates and Tradeswomen, Inc., were established to open doors for women and to ensure they had equal opportunities and fair and safe working conditions in nontraditional jobs.

Each step of the way, women had to fight to make sure the laws were enforced. Court cases in California have dealt over and over again with the issue of sexual equality in education, sexual harassment, pensions, taxes, wages, insurance, property, divorce, and numerous other issues. In one case, a psychology instructor had to sue her college so that she could continue to teach during her pregnancy. In another, a welfare program offered job training to men over women and excluded women who had children.

In 1981 the legislature ruled that the standard of comparable worth (i.e., providing the same pay for dissimilar jobs of equal value) had to be used for setting salaries for state employees in female-dominated jobs. The lawmakers passed additional protections, but Governor George Deukmejian vetoed them. Despite earlier gains, a state task force reported in 1985 that California's labor force was still segregated by sex and that women earned only 60 cents for every dollar earned by men.

Divergent Views

In the 1970s, the rise of the women's liberation movement and growing participation of women in the workforce and the legal profession generated a new wave of litigation and legislation to advance women's rights.

In this great flowering of feminist thought and action, perhaps it was inevitable that there would be significant disagreements over the best course towards equality. Some feminists viewed the world as a place where women should have all of the rights and responsibilities of men. Anxious to tear down all barriers, they advocated for formal structural equality: women and men must be treated exactly the same. To prove discrimination, a woman would have to show that there was a man who was afforded better treatment, work conditions, benefits, salary, or promotional opportunities than she. History had shown, they argued, that treatment of women was often based on outdated stereotypes. Only by ensuring that women were treated exactly like men could one make certain that laws allegedly intended to protect women would not undermine the progress that women had made in their quest for equality. Many East Coast women's legal organizations, such as the National Women's Law Center and the NOW Legal Defense and Education Fund held this view.

Others, mostly from the West Coast (with the exception of New York's pioneering feminist author Betty Friedan) framed the issue in terms of equality of opportunity, as opposed to identical treatment. They argued that Title VII of the Civil Rights Act (the section that outlaws employment discrimination) reflected a male model and ignored the biological reality that only women get pregnant and bear children. According to these feminists, a woman's ability to bear children made her different—but not lesser—than her male counterparts. Attorney Patricia A. Shiu of the Employment Law Center, a project of the Legal Aid Society of San Francisco, explains that this model attempts to grapple with the limitations of Title VII, especially for poor women and women of color for whom there may be no white male for comparison. Seeking to design a new model for eliminating discrimination, one that recognized that what may be most advantageous and beneficial for men should not limit, much less define, the needs and reality of all women, West Coast feminists advanced a different legal strategy. In doing so, California led the way in making equal employment opportunity a reality for pregnant women workers.

Many West Coast–based women's and civil rights organizations, grounded in the trade union movement and communities of color, sought legal recognition that because only women could get pregnant, it was society's responsibility to ensure that women had equal employment opportunities consistent with their unique childbearing capacity. The Employment Law Center and Equal Rights Advocates advocated for laws that provided pregnant women with workplace accommodations and exemptions from unduly heavy lifting requirements proscribed by their physicians, and laws that prohibited employers from requiring both women and men with reproductive capacity to toil in toxic or unsafe workplaces.

In 1978 the state legislature passed the Pregnancy Disability Leave Act, which provided four months of job-protected leave for pregnant women. This law was enacted at virtually the same time that Congress amended Title VII by adding the Pregnancy Discrimination Act, which stated that providing special treatment for women constituted sex discrimination.

The question of whether laws recognizing different procreative roles of women and men would be a benefit or a burden came to the political forefront when Lillian Garland lost her receptionist job at California Federal Savings and Loan Bank (Cal Fed) after giving birth.

In 1982 Garland, an African American woman, became pregnant and notified her employer of her need for an unpaid pregnancy disability leave, as provided for under California law.

After delivering her child by Caesarean section, her doctor extended her leave so that she could recuperate fully from childbirth. When Garland attempted to return to Cal Fed after her leave, she was told that her job had been filled.

Garland found herself unemployed, with a newborn baby and no income. She was evicted from her apartment. The baby's father sued for custody.

"It was a cause I never thought about until it affected me," Garland said, "but once I was involved, it became my life. It wasn't fair that a woman basically had to choose between having a family and keeping her job."

Desperate, Garland sought help from the Employment Law Center. Patricia Shiu, already experienced in race, disability, and gender discrimination law, agreed to represent her. "All workers should be entitled to leave—and paid leave—to look after their children and families," said Shiu. "Race and class were infused in the debate. As women's rights attorneys, we should examine these issues from the bottom up, not the top down. We asked ourselves, 'What do the poorest paid, least powerful women workers need from the law?'"

In May 1983, the Department of Fair Employment and Housing filed an administrative claim against California Federal Savings and Loan, alleging it had violated the state Pregnancy Disability Leave law when it failed to reinstate Garland to her job. Just a few months later Cal Fed, joined by the Merchants and Manufacturers Association and the California Chamber of Commerce, filed a counteraction in U.S. district court arguing that the state law actually discriminated against men, because pregnancy leave benefits were available only to women.

Herma Hill Kay recalled that this case, *California Federal Savings and Loan Association v. Guerra*, the first pregnancy leave law to be considered by the U.S. Supreme Court, revealed the deep division between the East and West Coast feminists. The East Coast–based NOW and ACLU Women's Rights Project submitted amicus briefs urging extension (to men) or invalidation of the California statute. Equal Rights Advocates and other West Coast groups filed amicus briefs supporting Garland and the enforcement of the state law.

On January 13, 1987, in a decision by Justice Thurgood Marshall, the high court upheld the California law, ruling that states can require employers to provide job protection for pregnant workers. Marshall wrote, "[D]iscrimination is a social phenomenon encased in a social context....A realistic understanding of conditions found in today's labor environment warrants taking pregnancy into account in fashioning disability policies."

Justice Marshall said that he agreed with the lower court decision that the California law was intended "to construct a floor beneath which pregnancy disability benefits may not drop—not a ceiling above which they may not rise." Marshall opined that in complying with California law, employers would not treat pregnant women better than other disabled—presumably male—employees, because employers could also provide these employees with comparable benefits.

Shiu and Garland were elated. "I remember," Garland later said about a press conference announcing the decision, "that there was this group of girls walking past the Supreme Court building and asking, 'Who is that woman?' I heard them and went over to them and said, 'I am Lillian Garland and I won you the right to have a baby and keep your job.' The girl looked at me—and I'll always remember this—and said, 'Thank you so much.' I just started to cry."

Herma Hill Kay noted that the way the opinion was written "healed over the divisiveness" between the two schools of thought. Nonetheless, "the philosophical division still persists."

NOW lauded the decision as a "clear and crucial victory for women." Women's rights groups launched a campaign to educate men and women all over the country about the landmark decision. Shiu appeared on CNN and on the *Today Show* and other popular programs, often debating the merits of the California pregnancy law with employers. The decision became the impetus for the federal Family Medical Leave Act of 1993, providing all workers—women and men—four months of unpaid, job-protected leave to care for themselves or a family member with a serious health condition, or to bond with a newborn or newly adopted or foster child. According to Shiu, this had been the vision all along.

Shiu and others also lobbied for the California Family Rights Act (CFRA), a law allowing a worker to take leave to care for herself or a family member without losing her job or employment benefits—a measure that had been vetoed eight times by California governors. After the high court victory, Governor Deukmejian signed the bill into law, in advance of the federal law. Significantly, the combined California laws provide as much as seven full months of pregnancy disability and bonding leave, much greater than the federal law (which provides twelve weeks' leave), because they guarantee a pregnant worker an additional four months of leave during the period she is disabled by pregnancy, childbirth, or a related medical condition.

Attorney Pat Shiu (left) represented Lillian Garland (center) in the U.S. Supreme Court case that upheld California's law against pregnancy discrimination. The effort was supported by many feminists, including Betty Friedan (right), but opposed by others who thought that only identical treatment at the workplace would lead to equal rights for women.

A second case set the parameters for the rules that employers can use in the name of "worker protection."

Johnson Controls was a multinational corporation that produced chemicals for many industrial processes; it had several plants in California. Queen Elizabeth Foster, an African American woman in her late twenties, worked at a subsidiary of Johnson Controls, in a southern California plant that produced lead batteries. Because the plant dealt with toxic chemicals, the company instituted a "fetal protection program" banning women of childbearing age not only from jobs that exposed them to lead contamination, but from positions from which they could transfer to such jobs. The company required women workers of childbearing age to have a document certifying their inability to bear children in order to work in these jobs. Foster, who was neither pregnant nor planning to become pregnant, refused to give her bosses such a certificate and was fired.

Shiu agreed to represent her. She was joined by Beverly Tucker, a young attorney with the Department of Fair Employment and Housing, and the case became known as *FEHC v. Johnson Controls*.

When Shiu argued the case before the state court of appeal in 1989, she herself was pregnant. She remembers standing before the judges in her maternity clothes, arguing that the company's regulation—for women only—was tantamount to sex discrimination. She and Tucker provided the court with substantial medical evidence proving that the restrictions were of no benefit. From a fetal protection standpoint, fertile women, until they became pregnant, should be treated the same as fertile men.

Isabelle Katz Pinzler, an attorney with the ACLU Women's Rights Project, noted that both men and women are affected by high lead exposure and that the company's policies kept women from higher-paying positions. "What's wrong with these policies is that they assume that women can't and won't control their fertility, and that it's up to the company, not the woman, to balance the harm of not having a job against the harm of exposing a fetus to a dangerous substance."

The three-judge panel, ruling in 1990, unanimously agreed with Shiu's argument: discrimination based on fertility should be treated no differently from gender-based discrimination. Moved by the medical evidence, the court concluded that the Johnson Controls policy was grounded in unfounded and unscientific stereotypes of women, who were "unquestionably discriminated against....because only women are affected by its terms."

The court also noted that the company had erroneously assumed that all women employees would be potentially pregnant all the time and stated, "However laudable concern by businesses such as the company has for the unborn, they may not effectuate their goals in that regard at the expense of a woman's ability to attain work for which she is otherwise qualified."

Women employees at Johnson Controls in other states had also sued the company. *UAW v. Johnson Controls*, which consolidated the many state cases, including California's, was argued before the U.S. Supreme Court in October 1990 by California labor attorney Marsha Berzon, later appointed to the Ninth Circuit. Theodore Olson, who became solicitor general under President George W. Bush, argued on behalf of Johnson Controls. He was joined by the Merchants and Manufacturers Association and the California Chamber of Commerce. The 1991 decision by Justice Harry Blackmun struck down the company's restrictive fetal protection program, stating "women are not breeding mares."

The Fundamental Right to Choose

In 1850 California's first legislature passed an abortion ban, forbidding the procedure unless the woman's life was in danger. In 1858 the legislature passed an additional measure making it a crime to advertise, advise, or "hint" about how to obtain an abortion. Both laws carried stiff prison sentences.

For the next century, tens of thousands of women underwent illegal, back alley abortions leading to severe injury, illness, and death. By the 1960s, abortion was the main cause of maternal mortality in the United States; the *American Journal of Public Health* rated abortion as a public health problem for women as serious as cancer and heart disease. At that time, about one million abortions were performed in the U.S. annually. Of the estimated 125,000 in California, only 3 percent were done legally. The overwhelming majority of women who obtained abortions were married and, because of their economic circumstances or marital difficulties, did not want to have a child.

In 1961 Assembly Member John Knox introduced legislation to liberalize the abortion law. He later recalled that his fellow legislators pretty much ignored it, and it died without ever reaching the assembly floor.

The following year, Anthony Beilenson was elected to represent the Beverly Hills area in the assembly. When the freshman representative arrived in Sacramento in January 1963, he learned that Knox had introduced abortion reform bills in previous years and told Knox that he supported reform legislation. Knox already had a full legislative agenda, and a Catholic prelate in his Richmond district had been pressuring him to drop the abortion proposal. Though Knox was fully prepared to pursue the bill, he asked his new colleague to carry it.

In 1963 Beilenson proposed a bill to legalize abortions performed in hospitals by physicians when childbirth posed a substantial risk to the health of the mother, when the risk was high that the child would be born with a grave mental or physical defect, or when the pregnancy was the result of rape or incest. The law required that a medical committee approve a woman's request for an abortion.

"It's very difficult to believe, or to realize, that in those days even the major mainstream papers, like the *Los Angeles Times*, never printed the word 'abortion,'" Beilenson recalled. "They always used some euphemism such as 'illegal surgical procedure.'…it wasn't a topic of conversation. It was not a political issue. Nobody talked about it."

Though the bill was strongly supported by doctors who had performed abortions, veteran legislators warned Beilenson that his bill was a political kiss of death.

Indeed, in 1964 Beilenson's opponent tried to vilify the first-term assemblyman and conducted voter registration drives outside Catholic churches in Beilenson's district. Despite this, Beilenson was reelected by a larger majority than in his first election, and by a larger margin than any candidate in Los Angeles County that year. Rather than alienating him from voters, the abortion issue rallied new supporters, especially Republican women.

"I realized very quickly that this was a huge sort of underground issue which affected enormous numbers of people. When for the first time there was a sort of public platform for people to discuss it…it just exploded as an issue."

Beilenson recalled discovering how many lives the problem of illegal abortion had touched:

> I would give a talk in Eureka, or San Mateo, or wherever—I gave a lot of them around the state between '63 through early 1967—and people would come—women, of course—would come up to you after the talk and tell you about their experience with abortion. Their mother had one, they had one, their college roommate had one and lost her life having an illegal abortion. These were all regular…perfectly responsible people, who either themselves or their friends or their relatives had done something which was a felony."

As the issue became more open, public opinion shifted. By the late 1960s, three-quarters of all voters, and two-thirds of Catholic voters, agreed the abortion law should be liberalized.

In June 1967, when Beilenson's bill, the Therapeutic Abortion Act, finally passed the legislature, it was considered a major accomplishment of the session. Rather than being a political kiss of death, it had propelled Beilenson into legislative leadership, gaining him support for reelection to the assembly, then to the state senate and the House of Representatives.

The law finally allowed women to have legal, safe abortions. However, the procedure had to be approved in advance by a Therapeutic Abortion Board consisting of two obstetrician-gynecologists and a psychiatrist. ACLU attorney Margaret Crosby, whose later litigation protected the rights of indigent women and teenagers to have abortions, noted that the new law also sowed the seeds for unequal access. Only women with health insurance or private means could meet the requirement of obtaining approval by a committee of three physicians. Women in rural areas would have to travel great distances to reach a hospital that had a therapeutic abortion committee. The way the program played out shined a spotlight on the continuing hardship for indigent women. Ensuring women's—all women's—right to choose would take more organizing, more legislation, and more lawsuits.

Doctors at Risk

In May 1966, as the Therapeutic Abortion Act was winding its way through the legislature, nine San Francisco doctors were criminally charged with performing abortions. The doctors had performed the abortions in reputable hospitals, with consent of the hospitals' informal abortion committees, on women whose fetuses were in danger because they had contracted German measles during the first three months of their pregnancies.

When the state Board of Medical Examiners moved to suspend their medical licenses, the doctors went on the offensive—using their legal defense as a direct attack on the state law prohibiting abortions.

Attorney Herma Hill Kay organized an amicus brief with an impressive display of support: 225 deans of medical schools, heads of hospital gynecology and obstetrics departments, medical society leaders, and professors of medicine from across the country—including professors from every medical school in California—signed the brief. It argued that imposing the state's presence between a doctor and a patient violated the patient's right to the best medical treatment available. The outcry from the medical profession helped garner support for the Beilenson bill and eventually forced the Board of Medical Examiners to drop its efforts to suspend the medical licenses.

The case against another physician, obstetrician/gynecologist Dr. Leon Belous, resulted in the demise of the criminal abortion law. Dr. Belous had been on the staff of Cedars of Lebanon Hospital in Los Angeles since 1931 and was eminent in his field. In January 1967, six months before the Therapeutic Abortion Act was passed, Belous, a nationally known opponent of restrictive abortion laws, was convicted of conspiring to perform an abortion. He had referred a nineteen-year-old woman to a second doctor, who performed the abortion. Belous had previously watched the second physician do abortions, approved of his methods, and referred women whom he considered "absolutely desperate."

In 1969 the Society for Humane Abortion and other organizations filed an amicus brief in the California Supreme Court on behalf of Dr. Belous. Authored by women's rights attorney Norma Zarky, it was the first legal challenge to the constitutionality of criminal abortion laws anywhere in the country. Zarky, a 1939 law school graduate and the first woman president of the Beverly Hills Bar Association, argued that the state's century-old abortion law was an arbitrary invasion of the fundamental right of a woman to determine when to bear offspring, and that it impeded the right of a physician to prescribe for his patient in accordance with his best professional knowledge.

In addition, Zarky argued, the abortion law violated the First Amendment, since it was based on religious theory.

In an argument that presaged a key ACLU case two decades later protecting Medi-Cal funding for abortion, Zarky asserted that the law denied equal protection to all women by basing their ability to obtain an abortion on their financial status. Wealthier women, the dynamic attorney explained, have an easier time obtaining the psychiatric certification required for an abortion than women who cannot afford psychiatrists' high fees. She concluded that there was no compelling state interest strong enough to prohibit the performance of abortions by licensed physicians.

More than 175 medical professionals, including the dean of every medical school in California, signed the amicus brief: "These recorded facts bring us face-to-face with the hard, shocking—almost brutal—reality that our statute designed in 1850 to protect women from serious risks to life and health has in modern times become a scourge."

On September 5, 1969, the California Supreme Court became the first appellate court in the country to strike down a criminal abortion statute. Ruling that the criminal abortion statute was unconstitutionally vague and could not stand in the light of much improved medical practices, the 4-3 majority opinion acknowledged "the fundamental right of a woman to choose whether to bear children." Chief Justice Roger Traynor, Associate Justice Matthew Tobriner, and Justice Pro Tempore Fred R. Pierce joined the majority opinion authored by Justice Ray Peters. [Justice Pierce, presiding justice of the Third District of the State Court of Appeal, was assigned to hear the case after Associate Justice Stanley Mosk recused himself—because Dr. Belous had delivered his son!]

In 1972 the California Supreme Court, in *People v. Barksdale*, struck down sections of the 1967 Therapeutic Abortion Act. Evidence showed that requiring women to appear before a therapeutic abortion committee created huge disparities, and abortion access varied greatly in different regions of the state. The court determined that the constitution did not allow such vagaries. Not until 2002 did the legislature repeal the entire Therapeutic Abortion Act and replace it with the Reproductive Privacy Act, which established every Californian's right to control childbearing.

Advocates at Risk

While the medical profession was trying to adapt quickly to changes in the abortion law, a different kind of battle was going on in the streets and in living rooms and college dormitories. Advocates for reproductive rights were defying the laws against informing women about how to get an abortion. An early law amended in 1957—Section 601 of the Business and Professions Code—made it a felony to "willfully write, compose or publish any notice or any advertisement of any medicine or means for producing or facilitating a miscarriage, or abortion."

In 1969 Richard Orser, Pat Maginnis, and Rowena Gurner were convicted in San Mateo Superior Court for violating that law.

Richard Orser was born in Shaker Heights, Ohio, in 1943. As a college student, he volunteered for Planned Parenthood because he was concerned about overpopulation. When his roommate's girlfriend got pregnant, he helped the couple seek an abortion. Their search was fruitless, however, and he ended up as the best man at their wedding. His concern deepened when he worked at an Ohio state institution for the severely mentally disabled. There he came to know many young women who had been raped, impregnated, and forced to give birth, even though they could not care for their children.

When Orser moved to California to attend graduate school in psychology at Stanford, he was introduced to the nonprofit service organization Clergy and Counseling Service for Problem Pregnancies. "I heard of the three thousand girls who dropped out of school each year in Los Angeles because of pregnancy," Orser recalled. "I learned also of the many botched, quack, and self-induced abortions and the gruesome consequences that left women hemorrhaging or badly infected and unable to bear a wanted child—or, sometimes, dead."

The civil rights and anti–Vietnam War movements had fostered an explosion of questioning of the established order and exploration of new ideas. Students seeking alternative viewpoints launched "free universities" at many campuses. These were run in an egalitarian manner: anyone who had a special skill or interest could teach others. The counterculture Mid-Peninsula Free University offered classes from Plato to Acid Yoga to Haitian dancing. In 1968 Orser, by then a full-time psychology instructor at Redwood City's Cañada College, decided to offer a workshop at the Free University on how to obtain an abortion.

He placed a notice in the university catalog: "Anyone needing a competent physician to terminate an unwanted pregnancy (inexpensively) or other birth control aid, call 323-6802 between 10 and 11 PM. Call also if you are interested in legalizing abortion or in counseling those seeking abortion."

Orser knew he was filling an urgent need:

> One California hospital at that time was admitting ten cases of botched illegal abortions each day. Some of the women who came to me for information had already unsuccessfully attempted self-induced abortion by rolling down stairs, infusing solutions of Mr. Clean or other substances in their uteri. Women who had decided irrevocably to have an abortion and who were not able to find competent help, as through me, were very often apt to find tragedy or at the least a terrifying experience.

Many women—high school and college students, as well as older, married women—came to the workshops in the living room of Orser's rambling house on Clark Street in East Palo Alto, often accompanied by their boyfriends or husbands. He shared with them information on cost, alternatives in California (including going before the three-physician panel required by the Therapeutic Abortion Act), and ways to get safe clinic abortions in Mexico with competent physicians. He told the attendees that he could make arrangements for abortions in Mexico. Orser drew on the Association to Repeal Abortion Laws and the Clergy Counseling Service for Problem Pregnancies for much of his information. He accepted no money for the popular, informative sessions.

Orser and his colleagues meticulously researched the referrals to Mexican doctors. "We took trips to Nogales, Juarez, and other border towns to check out the doctors and make sure that the offices were clean and safe," he later explained. They discovered that these journeys were crucial to protect women from unscrupulous or unsafe abortion providers. "One doctor," he recalled with a grimace, "packed a woman's vagina with some kind of absorbent material after the procedure and instructed her to go to a specific doctor back in the States to have the packing removed. It turned out they were using the women to smuggle drugs."

Orser kept a metal box with file cards containing information on all the doctors and other contacts in Mexico. The handwritten cards included directions and information on what times of day were safe and what phone numbers and aliases to use. He would often make calls to Mexico, "complicated long distance calls in Spanish."

Orser was aware that what he was doing was not entirely legal, but the only precaution he took was to use a pseudonym, Conrad Alexoff. "The times were such that we felt invulnerable. So many people were involved, and we thought we were untouchable. We were totally unprepared for undercover operations." Orser realized later that he had "underestimated the wrath that the conservative Catholic district attorney of San Mateo held for the hippies, radicals, and freethinkers of the Free University."

One night in January, Deputy Barbara Schrier of the San Mateo County sheriff's department attended a session in Orser's living room, wearing a hidden recorder. She posed as a pregnant woman and asked his help seeking an abortion. After the group meeting, Schrier returned for a personal session with her "boyfriend" (another undercover officer), telling Orser (whom she knew as Conrad Alexoff) that she wanted to go to Mexico for an abortion and needed his help. Orser told her to call him later that evening, after he had time to make arrangements. A police transcript of the call reveals the conversation:

Conrad (Orser): Everything is all set…That is Nogales, Arizona. So you take the bus down to the border, from Tucson, and get off the bus, go to the phone booth, dial this number and ask for Pam…Tell her Conrad Alexoff referred you and she will send someone to pick you up.
Dep. Schrier: And she'll send someone to pick me up?
Conrad: Right, George, in a taxi probably.
Schrier: Who in a taxi?
Conrad: George.
Schrier: Then I'll lay 350 bucks on them and it's all cool.
Conrad: Not to the driver, to the doctor.
Schrier: Yes. Thank you, Conrad.

Five officers, who had been waiting impatiently at the local Dairy Queen for Orser to complete his phone call, burst into his home and arrested and handcuffed him. With his hands bound, Orser managed to toss the file box of contact information into the garbage and out of sight. Though the officers searched the house for two hours, they did not find the precious box.

They took him and his roommates to the county jail. Orser recalls that his roommates, who had nothing to do with his abortion information workshops, were not bitter about being arrested. They felt solidarity with him and just thought it was a "bummer" that he—and they—had been arrested.

Later that night, a police officer—realizing that the key evidence against Orser had not been located—went back to the house under the pretense that he had left his hat. Another roommate naively let him in. The officer found the box of contacts for the network of abortion providers.

The next day the headline in the San Mateo paper read, "Cañada College teacher arrested for abortion counseling." Orser was dismissed from his teaching position. Because he was such a popular teacher and his workshops were so widely supported by the students and faculty, no one at the college was willing to take his place. Finally the college brought in an outside professor. Orser recalled, "At the first class, he had to wear a bag over his head. He didn't want to be known on campus as the guy who replaced Richard Orser."

Immediately the nascent abortion rights movement swung into action. The Abortion Counseling Defense Fund sent out an appeal and received messages of solidarity and money from all over the country. Doctors pledged their support. Women wrote from Maine, Connecticut, and Michigan, enclosing a dollar or two and thanking Orser for his work. One apologized for her "small contribution" and explained that "my husband deserted me when he learned I was pregnant, and I couldn't even get a lead on an illegal abortion: I feel my efforts will make life better for good women in years to come."

In his stack of letters was one from a Texas attorney "working with the local chapter of Women's Liberation." Its author was Sarah Weddington, who three years later would win abortion rights for all U.S. women as the lead attorney before the Supreme Court in *Roe v. Wade*.

Orser was convicted of violating Section 601 of the Business and Professions Code. The state licensing board froze his teaching credential. Unwilling to give up the work that he knew was desperately needed, he founded the Problem Pregnancy Information Center, with offices at the University Lutheran Church in Palo Alto. To pay the bills, he took a job conducting psychological tests.

Around the same time, Patricia Maginnis, the founder and president of the Society for Humane Abortion, and her colleague Rowena Gurner reproduced a letter from an ob-gyn describing two safe methods of self-induced abortion and distributed it on thousands of handbills. Believing that no woman should have to go before a panel of doctors or prove that she was mentally unstable just to have an abortion, and emboldened by the enthusiastic response to the handbills, Maginnis stepped up her campaign and began offering workshops in self-induced abortion. The first class was held on July 27, 1966, in a San Francisco private home and drew a dozen women. Over the next few months, Maginnis and Gurner gave self-help abortion classes up and down the state. Attendance grew with each one, and the word spread. In Sacramento, sixty-five people attended; half of them had to stand for the entire five hours and another fifty were turned away for lack of space. Though undercover officers were spotted at several of the meetings, no arrests were made. Indeed, one police officer told Gurner, "No one will arrest you and Pat Maginnis. You're too hot."

Maginnis summed it up this way, "Police bully aborted women with crude harassment and interrogation but are cowards in enforcing a law being challenged. The most gross invasion of privacy is the use of police surveillance to control what should be a private matter between a woman and her physician."

Finally, after giving a class at a private home in Redwood City in February 1967, Maginnis and Gurner were arrested for violating the law against advertising abortion. They were convicted. Later on appeal, their case would be consolidated with Orser's.

ACLU attorneys Paul Halvonik and Charles Marson represented the three on appeal, arguing that the arrests were unconstitutional. "The [catalog and workshops] may deal with a topic some find revolting, unpleasant or offensive. But the First Amendment bars the state from inhibiting the flow of information and the expression of ideas, whether considered offensive by some people or not," their brief stated.

The appellate court agreed and reversed all three convictions, ruling that the law that prohibited distribution of information on how to get or induce an abortion was overbroad and that the information was protected by the First Amendment.

Thirty years later, Orser sat in his sun-filled living room in the Santa Cruz hills and surveyed stacks of court documents, transcripts, and letters of support. In his hands, he turned over a well-worn 3x5 file card, covered with handwritten addresses, phone numbers, and short descriptions. "Maria in Nogales, use name 'Garcia' and 'Sanchez.'"

He glanced at the card, looked up at the window, and said, "I will never know, but perhaps my work saved a life or two."

Article 1, Section 1

Through battles in the courts, in the streets, and in the legislature, women had secured the right to control their own bodies. Three years before the landmark Supreme Court decision in *Roe v. Wade*, abortion was legal in California.

In 1972 California voters passed the Privacy Amendment—Proposition 11— authored by Stanford constitutional law professor Anthony Amsterdam, adding the explicit right to privacy to the California constitution as Article 1, Section 1. That constitutional change was to become the basis for many key abortion rights victories. As attorney Margaret Crosby explained:

> The state constitutional right to privacy is one of the most important civil liberties Californians possess. The implicit federal privacy right has always been far narrower in scope than the explicit California guarantee. Because of the initiative, California has a doctrinally coherent broad right to privacy that protects from governmental interference a spectrum of fundamental choices about birth, death, bodily integrity, sexuality, and living arrangements, and regardless of whether these choices are traditional or nonconforming.

As a leading reproductive rights lawyer, Crosby used the California constitutional privacy provision in many creative ways to protect the right to choose over the next three decades, as anti-choice groups tried to make abortion inaccessible to the most vulnerable women in the state: the poor and the young.

Protecting the Most Vulnerable

In 1977, when the U.S. Supreme Court ruled that the government is not obligated to provide Medicaid funding for abortions, even though it pays for childbirth, Governor Jerry Brown assured women in California that Medi-Cal would continue paying for abortions, notwithstanding the withdrawal of federal funds.

However, anti-choice groups, emboldened by the federal action, succeeded in getting the state legislature to impose the same restrictions on Medi-Cal, eliminating funding for approximately 95 percent of abortions that had been eligible for Medi-Cal reimbursement. The state would provide abortion funding only if a physician certified that the pregnancy would cause the death of the mother, resulted from rape or incest, or would produce an infant suffering from one of five designated birth defects.

On behalf of a coalition of women's rights, welfare rights, and health organizations, Crosby and other women's advocates filed a lawsuit in state court, *Committee to Defend Reproductive Rights v. Myers*, challenging the funding cuts. The court of appeal upheld the legislature's cuts but stayed enforcement while an appeal went to the California Supreme Court. A dissenting opinion in the court of appeal addressed the hardship to indigent women in California: "Poor women must, as the price for medical care, bring unwanted children into their financially bleak worlds or, if they insist on exercising their constitutional right, seek their remedy from the unskilled and unclean in California's back alleys and byways."

Arguing that the court had not adequately considered California's express constitutional right to privacy, Crosby told the high court that the state cannot coerce poor women to give up their right to decide whether to bear a child as a condition of receiving medical benefits. The court also had not fully considered California's guarantee of equal protection, she noted, which precludes the state from denying the poor access to fundamental constitutional rights that are available to the more affluent.

California legalized abortion prior to the U.S. Supreme Court's landmark Roe v. Wade *decision, but activists have had to continually mobilize to protect women's right to choose.*

The high court by a 5-2 vote issued a stay, ordering doctors, clinics, and hospitals to continue providing Medi-Cal abortions pending resolution of the lawsuit. Because of Crosby's adept legal maneuvering, the legislature's funding cuts were never implemented while the case wound its lengthy way through the courts.

In 1981 the California Supreme Court issued its landmark decision ruling that the state's budget act, in restricting Medi-Cal funding for abortion but not for childbirth, violated the right to privacy guaranteed by the California constitution. Justice Matthew Tobriner wrote, "Once the state furnishes medical care to poor women in general, it cannot withdraw part of that care solely because a woman exercised her constitutional right to have an abortion."

Since the court relied solely on the California constitution, the state could not appeal the decision to the U.S. Supreme Court. But every year, for more than a decade, state lawmakers passed a budget act that included restrictions on abortion funding. Every year, Crosby had to go back to court to remind the state to abide by its responsibilities outlined by the California constitution and the state supreme court. Not until 1990 did a budget bill go to the governor that included full funding for abortion.

The second major target of the anti-choice forces was young women. In 1987 the legislature passed a law requiring teens under eighteen to obtain parental or judicial consent for an abortion. In doing so, it eliminated abortion from a broad category of sensitive health services available to California adolescents on a confidential basis, including HIV testing, treatment for sexually transmitted diseases, drug and alcohol addiction, mental health problems, sexual assault, and all pregnancy-related care, including childbirth.

Once again Crosby, this time joined by the National Center for Youth Law, went to court to challenge the restrictions. Knowing that the law would have disastrous effects on pregnant teenagers who would seek illegal, dangerous abortions or have to travel to states where they could get an abortion, the legal team marshaled pediatricians, public health experts, psychiatrists, and social workers from California and also from states where similar restrictive laws were already in effect.

The testimony in *American Academy of Pediatrics v. Lungren* was chilling. During a month-long trial in Judge Maxine Chesney's courtroom in San Francisco Superior Court, more than twenty witnesses spoke of the harm that could be done to young women's mental and physical health if they had to inform an unsupportive parent that they wanted an abortion. The court heard terrifying stories from other states of young women who had been thrown out of their homes, beaten, and even killed by a violent parent. Pregnant teenagers unable to travel to a courtroom, or to navigate the confusing and burdensome judicial system, would not be able to get a judicial bypass.

Judge Chesney ruled in favor of the women's health advocates, and her decision was upheld by the appellate courts, which meant that the law could not be enforced.

Still, the state insisted on appealing the case.

In 1997, in a 4-3 decision, the California Supreme Court ruled that the state had "failed to demonstrate adequate justification for the statute's intrusion upon a pregnant minor's right of privacy under the California Constitution," and struck down the 1987 law:

> No one would doubt the value to a pregnant minor of wise and caring parental guidance and support as she confronts a decision that will affect the rest of her life, assuming such support is available and the minor is willing to seek it. The statute at issue however…has its most significant impact in those instances in which a pregnant minor is too frightened or too embarrassed to disclose her condition to a parent (or to a court).

Since this ruling, lawmakers have repeatedly proposed bills designed to prevent or limit access to abortion. They authored measures requiring abortion reporting, monitoring "fetal pain," outlawing late term abortions, and requiring "informed consent." In 2005, 2006, and 2008, anti-choice forces, backed by church groups, mounted ballot campaigns to change the law requiring parental consent. Though they have been defeated every year, they continue to signal their determination to deny women the right to control their own bodies.

SIX

THE RIGHT NOT TO REMAIN SILENT

DISSENT

> There is a time when the operation of the machine becomes so odious, makes you so sick at heart, that you can't take part....And you've got to indicate to the people who run it, to the people who own it, that unless you're free, the machine will be prevented from working at all.
>
> —*Mario Savio, Berkeley Free Speech Movement, 1964*

On Liberty Hill, near the Port of Los Angeles, an official California landmark monument reads, "In 1923 the Marine Transport Workers Industrial Union 510, a branch of the Industrial Workers of the World (IWW), called a strike that immobilized 90 ships here in San Pedro. The union protested low wages, bad working conditions and the imprisonment of union activists under California's Criminal Syndicalism law. Denied access to public property, strikers and their supporters rallied here at this site they called Liberty Hill."

In 1923 an extended and bitter strike gripped the docks in San Pedro. Police and company goons assaulted strikers, and scores were injured, including thirteen-year-old Mae Sundstedt, whose legs were scalded by boiling coffee when hired thugs broke up a union meeting. The Los Angeles Police Department (LAPD) prohibited the striking longshoremen, many of them members of the IWW, or "Wobblies," from holding public meetings. In one night, six hundred men were jailed for the offense of "manifesting their sympathy with the strike" by cheering and singing.

As in other IWW strikes, workers traveled from afar to walk the picket line. One supporter who was moved to join them was Upton Sinclair. The renowned novelist and journalist mounted Liberty Hill and started to read aloud the First

Amendment of the Constitution in support of the workers' right to free speech and assembly. A police captain warned Sinclair to "cut out that Constitution stuff." Author Louis Adamic described the powerful scene:

> The patriots and their police chief longed for a riot, which, no matter what the truth of it, would be laid to the unrighteous Wobblies; while the latter were determined to avoid violence.
>
> Sinclair stepped upon an improvised platform....Someone lit a candle and held it up to him, that he might see the sacred texts. [He] was interrupted by a police sergeant and informed that he was under arrest—"suspected of criminal syndicalism."
>
> A gust of wind blew out the candle and the author of *Corydon and Thyrsis* walked down the dusty hill between two policemen, while the somber eyes of the stevedores flashed and the inarticulate crowd let out a cheer.

The future Pulitzer Prize–winning novelist was hauled off to jail.

The charge against Sinclair, "criminal syndicalism," was commonly used against strikers, Wobbly organizers, and other political dissidents. The criminal syndicalism

In 1923 author Upton Sinclair was arrested for reading the First Amendment to striking longshoremen in San Pedro. The police told him to "cut out that Constitution stuff." On his release, he founded the ACLU of Southern California.

law grew out of the post–World War I Red Scare that generated the 1919 Palmer Raids, in which the federal government rounded up hundreds of anarchists, socialists, and communists and deported many of them to Eastern Europe.

Sinclair described the result of his encounter with police on Liberty Hill: "I was arrested with three friends and held in jail 'incommunicado' for eighteen hours, for the offense of having attempted to read the Constitution of the United States, while standing on private property in San Pedro, with the written permission of the owner and after due notice to the mayor of the city and to the police authorities."

On his release, Sinclair wrote a public letter to the police chief, which was published in *The Nation* on June 6, 1923:

> All I can say, sir, is that I intend to do what little one man can do to awake the public conscience, and that meantime I am not frightened by your menaces. I am not a giant physically…I freely admit that when I see a line of a hundred policemen with drawn revolvers flung across a street to keep anyone from coming onto private property to hear my feeble voice, I am somewhat disturbed in my nerves. But I have a conscience and a religious faith, and I know that our liberties were not won without suffering, and may be lost again through our cowardice. I intend to do my duty to my country.

Sinclair wrote a play called *Singing Jailbirds* to spread the word about the Wobblies and the San Pedro strike. But an even more lasting legacy came out of Sinclair's action and arrest that night. Almost as soon as he was released from jail, Sinclair joined other free speech advocates to establish the American Civil Liberties Union of Southern California.

An Unlikely Felon

Although twenty-four other states adopted criminal syndicalism laws, all except California ceased to enforce them after 1921. California actively enforced the law until 1924. About five hundred people were arrested. A quarter of them, mostly IWW members, were imprisoned. During the 1940s, many of those convicted were pardoned, and in 1968 the U.S. Supreme Court belatedly ruled the law unconstitutional.

Although the criminal syndicalism law's main target was the IWW, one of its most illustrious and unusual victims was Charlotte Anita Whitney. On the crisp afternoon of November 29, 1919, as the fifty-three-year-old social worker and reformer walked in downtown Oakland after delivering a speech on race relations, the head of the police Loyalty Squad arrested her for violating the criminal syndicalism law.

Whitney's speech did not remotely touch on violence as a means for social change, but it was not her presentation that triggered her arrest. It was her well-known radical politics and her membership in the newly formed Communist Labor Party.

Whitney was an unlikely felon. Born into a wealthy and well-respected San Francisco Bay Area family, she could trace her ancestry to the *Mayflower*. She was the niece of Stephen Field, a member of both the California and the U.S. Supreme Courts. Whitney had been involved in social causes from women's suffrage and milk pasteurization to raising funds for victims of the 1906 San Francisco earthquake. She was the first president of the League of Women Voters of California, and she was active in pacifist work during World War I. Describing her political evolution, she once said, "Imperceptibly and unconsciously, I passed over the line, the invisible line, which divides mankind into two different groups, the group which stands for human exploitation and the group which stands for the fullness of life here and now, for human welfare."

Whitney's trial was highly charged. With the exception of one prosecution witness that the defense recalled in order to testify that the Communist Labor Party opposed terrorism, violence, and force, Whitney was the sole defense witness. When she took the stand, she acknowledged her membership in the Communist Labor Party. She explained that the party was not an instrument of terrorism or violence, and that it was not her purpose or that of the party to violate any known law. In his closing statement, the district attorney nonetheless asked the jury to "uphold the sacred tenets of Americanism and place with their verdict the seal of disapproval on the activities of the Communist

Born into a wealthy and prominent family, Charlotte Anita Whitney became a social reformer and political radical. In 1920 she was convicted of violating the state's criminal syndicalism law, merely for belonging to an unpopular political party.

Labor Party and its blood brother, the IWW…It is not only Anita Whitney on trial, but the dark doctrines of envy, murder, and terror."

The prosecution's scaremongering worked. The jury found Whitney guilty. She

was ordered to serve from one to fourteen years in San Quentin, a harsher punishment than if she had been convicted of manslaughter. Society women in the Bay Area vowed to accompany Whitney on a parade down Market Street in downtown San Francisco and escort her to the San Quentin gates, where they would demand to be imprisoned alongside her.

Whitney appealed her case to the U.S. Supreme Court, which in 1925 unanimously reaffirmed her conviction and upheld the constitutionality of California's criminal syndicalism law. Because of her social connections, however, she was free on bail before and after the Supreme Court ruled against her.

By 1927 an impressive group of Californians, including former Governor Hiram Johnson and Upton Sinclair, had called on Governor Clement C. Young to pardon the convicted radical. Whitney took the public position that she would not seek a pardon when more than five hundred others had been arrested for criminal syndicalism. Nevertheless, in 1927 Governor Young pardoned her, justifying his decision by explaining that sending the now sixty-year-old Whitney to prison would "revive the waning spirits of radicalism" by making her a martyr. Upon learning of her pardon, Whitney asked, "How can I be pardoned when I've done nothing wrong?"

Raising the Red Flag

Another byproduct of the Red Scare was a California law making it a felony to "display a red flag, banner or badge...as a sign, symbol or emblem of opposition to organized government or as an invitation or stimulus to anarchistic action or as an aid to propaganda that is of a seditious nature." Thirty-two states passed similar laws. California vigorously prosecuted trade union organizers, Communist Party members, anarchists, and other left-wingers who dared to display the red flag: between 1919 and 1921, five hundred people were arrested and slightly more than half were convicted. The penalty was six months to five years in prison.

But the arrest of a teenage counselor for flying a red flag at a children's camp in the foothills of the San Bernardino Mountains resulted in the first ruling from the U.S. Supreme Court protecting "symbolic speech" under the First Amendment.

Nineteen-year-old Yetta Stromberg, a student at the University of California and a member of the Young Communist League, was a counselor at the Pioneer Summer Camp in Yucaipa, about sixty-five miles east of Los Angeles. She taught campers "class-consciousness, the solidarity of the workers and the theory that the workers of the world are of one blood and brothers all." At the daily flag salute, Stromberg led the children in a pledge: "I pledge allegiance to the worker's red flag / And to the cause for which it stands: / One aim throughout our lives, / Freedom for the working class."

Rumors of the camp's teachings angered local members of the American Legion, who pressured the sheriff to do something about the nest of radicals in their midst. On August 3, 1929, the district attorney, the sheriff, members of LAPD's Intelligence Bureau, and several carloads of American Legionnaires raided the camp. Stromberg was arrested along with seven others. Three young campers were held as material witnesses.

Two attorneys from the ACLU of Southern California, Leo Gallagher and John Beardsley, volunteered to defend the accused. Gallagher, who was well known as a radical lawyer, was refused permission to see the prisoners and was physically attacked and choked by a San Bernardino deputy sheriff. Three other deputies who were in the office did nothing to stop the assault, nor did the Constitutional Rights Committee of the Los Angeles Bar Association act when the issue was brought to its attention.

After a nine-day trial, the jury returned guilty verdicts for all eight defendants. Judge Charles Allison gave the defendants the limit of the law: ten years for Stromberg, five years for the others. (An appellate court later reduced Stromberg's doubled sentence to five years.) Defendant Isadore Berkowitz, who chopped wood and did other odd jobs at the camp, did not appear at the sentencing. Severe injuries from being gassed on the battlefield during World War I had left Berkowitz physically and psychologically disabled. When he learned that he had been convicted, he was overcome by anxiety and grief. He hung himself the night before the sentencing.

Because the trial had been widely publicized, people all over the country rallied to Stromberg's cause. The supporters often found themselves harassed by law enforcement; a woman was fined seventy-five dollars for writing to the judge, advocating leniency. On the night of November 26, 1929, a group of supporters rented a hall in San Bernardino for a meeting about the trial. When they arrived, they found that the hall had been condemned at the instigation of the district attorney. As the evening's speaker addressed the crowd in the street, he was arrested, as were several others in the group before the night was over.

When the state supreme court refused to hear Stromberg's appeal, attorney Beardsley appealed her conviction to the U.S. Supreme Court. On May 18, 1931, in a 7-2 opinion written by Chief Justice Charles Evans Hughes, the high court overturned Stromberg's conviction and struck down California's red flag law. Justice Hughes wrote:

> The maintenance of the opportunity for free political discussion to the end that government may be responsive to the will of the people and that changes may be obtained by lawful means…is a fundamental principle of our constitutional system. A statute which….is so vague and indefinite as to permit the punishment of the fair use of this opportunity is repugnant to the guarantee of liberty contained in the Fourteenth Amendment.

The ruling in Stromberg's case was the first U.S. Supreme Court decision to strike down a state law because it restricted an individual's right to freedom of expression.

The case was sent back for a new trial in San Bernardino Superior Court. Attorney Beardsley presented a motion for dismissal. Although the American Legion and the anti-labor Better America Federation wanted to see Stromberg retried, the district attorney did not oppose Beardsley's motion. In October 1931, the case against Yetta Stromberg was finally dismissed.

The bold young counselor at the radical workers' camp had helped expand the protections of the First Amendment.

Tarred and Feathered

As politicians, police, and others in power continued to combat threats—or the appearance of threats—to the establishment during the 1930s, private citizens also took the law into their own hands. The Better America Foundation fomented a spate of vigilante attacks. Local groups, like the Committee of Safety in Santa Clara County, the Anti-Communist League of Imperial and San Diego Counties, and the Berkeley Nationals, also targeted leftists and union organizers. Organizing efforts among agricultural laborers had spurred the creation of the Associated Farmers, which strove to keep agribusiness free of radical politics and union organizing. The group's funds came from such "farmers" as the California Packing Corporation, the Southern Pacific Railroad, and the Spreckels Investment Company. In addition to these civic and business alliances, more secretive fascist organizations with anti-Semitic programs, such as the Silver Shirts, operated throughout the state.

During San Francisco's 1934 General Strike, women preparing food in Berkeley's Finnish Comrades Hall for striking longshoremen received a threatening phone call: "You'll make no sandwiches tomorrow." Later that day, scores of vigilantes wearing armbands of the Berkeley Nationals raided the Hall, smashing furniture, three pianos, and all the dishes.

In nearby Richmond, vigilantes invaded the home and studio of photographer Richard Prater, destroying his camera equipment. They aimed to silence Prater, who gave speeches on street corners about the rights of the unemployed.

In San Francisco, vandals broke into the headquarters of the International Workers Order, leaving behind broken school desks and shattered dishes. Eyewitnesses saw four police officers with the intruders.

And a yellowed file in the ACLU archives contains carbon copies of letters, legal briefs, and newspaper articles painstakingly retyped, bringing to life the chilling story of a 1935 vigilante attack in Santa Rosa.

Mrs. Beulah Heaney, a widow with five children, lived on a chicken ranch seven miles outside of Santa Rosa, an agricultural center fifty miles north of San Francisco. For nineteen years, she had never locked her door. She made her living selling poultry and eggs and taking in boarders, including Edward Wolff and his wife.

By the summer of 1935, Wolff, a fifty-one-year-old Kentucky native and Navy veteran, had lived in Sonoma County for eleven years. A restaurant proprietor who belonged to the chamber of commerce and Lion's Club and chaired the town's Christmas fund activities, Wolff had previously been a member of the Boilermakers Union and president of the Vallejo Trade and Labor Council. He had also worked for the presidential campaign of Franklin Roosevelt and Upton Sinclair's EPIC (End Poverty in California) campaign for governor. These political activities won him the animosity of many in the rural Republican county. Like his landlady, he was a member of the Utopian Society, an organization dedicated to Utopian socialism, which claimed half a million members in Depression-era California.

Around two a.m. on August 21, Mrs. Heaney was awakened by pounding on the door and the sound of pebbles and dirt being thrown against her roof. She saw the light of many flashlights play outside her window. A chorus of rough voices demanded to be let in. She opened the door, saw a mob of about fifty men, and was told, "We want Ed Wolff." She told them her children were asleep and asked for a warrant, while her daughter Beatrice tried to bar the door. Only when they threw her daughter to the ground did she relent and let them in. She smelled whiskey on their breath.

Several of the men held Mrs. Heaney and Beatrice against the wall while others swarmed through the house till they found Wolff hiding in a closet. They dragged him out and drove him to an isolated warehouse.

After the vigilantes left, Mrs. Heaney raced to town to report the incident to the sheriff, who told her that because she was "harboring a Communist," she "merited no protection."

Wolff was shocked at what he saw in the warehouse: a crowd of more than a hundred men, many armed. As makeshift identification, they had all tied handkerchiefs around their sleeves. The vigilantes surrounded Jack Green and Sol Nitzberg, who were covered with crankcase oil and feathers, looking "ready to drop."

Under the direction of a burly Irish immigrant, Fred Cairns, the men forced Wolff to kneel and kiss the American flag. To no avail, he protested that as a Navy man he should not bow or kiss the flag, he should salute it. He was beaten and told to be out of town by sundown the following day or face the same fate as Green and Nitzberg. While the crowd turned its attention to their tarred and feathered victims, Wolff took advantage of the dim light and distraction, tied a handkerchief to his sleeve to blend in, and edged out the door.

Jack Green, a sign painter who had lived in Santa Rosa for eleven years, and Sol Nitzberg, a chicken farmer, had been organizing apple pickers, an activity the Associated Farmers frowned upon. At ten o'clock that night, six men entered Green's office and forcibly took him to the Native Sons Hall. There, under the direction of Cairns, they struck him repeatedly and emptied his pockets. As Cairns threatened him with an army rifle, they asked him about the whereabouts of people on a list of "Reds" they wanted run out of town.

After a fruitless search for the men they'd asked Green about, the mob arrived at Nitzberg's home, throwing tear gas bombs into his house and forcing him to go with them to the warehouse. They threw Green and Nitzberg against hop bales and beat them repeatedly with brass knuckles, kicked them to the ground, and forced them to kiss the flag. Cairns threatened to inoculate them with syphilis germs and put "poisonous fluid" in their eyes, which were already stinging from tear gas. The vigilantes then shaved their victims' heads, yanked their shirts off, poured crankcase oil on their naked chests, showered them with chicken feathers, and forced them to walk the downtown streets of Santa Rosa for a quarter of an hour.

The Utopian Society wrote a letter to Governor Merriam demanding that he take immediate steps to effect the "apprehension and prosecution of the perpetrators of the outrages." They also wrote to California Attorney General Ulysses S. Webb and Sonoma County District Attorney W. F. Cowan. A group called the Citizens Constitutional Defense Committee formed to provide legal support. Carlos Spells of the Free Speech Forum (based in San Francisco) called on the sheriff to demand that he provide protection. The lawman refused on the grounds that the alleged victims "were all Communists and agitators" and threatened Spells with "great bodily harm and possible lynching" if he carried his investigation further.

Wolff announced to the press that he would return to Santa Rosa. "I believe that my return will be no more than my duty as a loyal American citizen whose service

Labor organizers Sol Nitzberg and Jack Green were kidnapped by vigilantes, beaten, tarred and feathered, and forced to walk through the streets of Santa Rosa. Law enforcement called them "communist agitators," and their attackers were never punished.

in the armed forces of this nation entitles him to defend the constitution against the foreign Hitlers and their entire subversive following," he told the *Labor Crusader* on August 27.

In October 1935, the ACLU filed a civil lawsuit in federal court, *Nitzberg and Green v. Cairns, et al.*, for twenty-five thousand dollars in damages for assault. The ACLU and others persisted in calling for criminal prosecution of the vigilantes. In August 1936, the pressure paid off. Attorney General Webb instituted belated criminal proceedings, charging the vigilantes with kidnapping, assault with a deadly weapon, assault by means of force likely to produce great bodily harm, and conspiracies to commit the foregoing offences.

But the jury, after sixteen minutes of deliberation, acquitted the vigilante leaders of all criminal charges, and the judge dismissed the charges against all the others. During the course of the trial, the ACLU received an anonymous letter saying that members of the jury were friends of the defendants.

The civil trial revealed the complicity of local law enforcement with the vigilantes. Four witnesses stated that a member of the Highway Patrol was part of the vigilante group that had questioned Green and "worked him over." ACLU of Northern California (ACLU-NC) Executive Director Ernest Besig pressed the Highway Patrol chief to discipline the officer, but no action was ever taken against him. Another defense witness testified that the police chiefs of Cloverdale and Healdsburg were present at the Native Sons Hall when Jack Green was brought before the mob. Still, no penalties were imposed on the attackers.

In the end, the only punishment that the ACLU could seek was the deportation of Cairns, who was an Irish citizen. However, the INS held that to be deported, Cairns had to be guilty of a crime involving moral turpitude and imprisoned for a term of one year or more. Cairns was granted citizenship in 1941.

The Red Squad

Although the Supreme Court had found the red flag law unconstitutional and prosecutions under the criminal syndicalism law effectively ended in 1924, government obstruction of Californians' political activities continued unabated.

When William Francis "Red" Hynes died at age fifty-five in Los Angeles on May 17, 1952, *The Nation* ran an obituary chronicling his reign of terror twenty years earlier as chief of the LAPD Red Squad. Before joining the LAPD in 1921, Hynes had worked undercover, infiltrating the IWW so successfully that he became secretary of a strike committee and editor of a strike bulletin. He later was the star witness in a trial that crippled the IWW in southern California.

In 1927 Police Chief James Davis named Hynes commanding officer of the Red Squad, and for ten years the unit spied on, harassed, censored, and physically abused political radicals in Los Angeles. Intelligence gathering was not a new activity for the LAPD: in 1913 the department crowed about maintaining dossiers on thousands of people. By 1928, the Red Squad had targeted leaders such as Frank Spector, local secretary of the International Labor Defense (ILD), a Communist Party–sponsored legal defense group; Louis Schneiderman, who would later become California Communist Party leader; and lesser-known individuals, including students and union organizers. In warrantless raids, the Red Squad searched and ransacked homes and businesses and confiscated books and money. Those arrested were, at times, held incommunicado for hours and denied access to attorneys. Some were beaten. Police turned over immigrants to immigration authorities for deportation.

Another of the Red Squad's typical tactics was to break up, often with violence, rallies organized by left-wing groups. In 1931, as the Depression drove millions out of work and into poverty, the National Unemployed Council designated February 21 as a national day of hunger marches, demonstrations, and petition campaigns in support of a Workers' Unemployment Insurance Bill then pending in Congress. In preparation, the Los Angeles Unemployed Council organized a February 10 march to City Hall. Thousands of demonstrators gathered on South Main Street, while a team of ten Red Squad officers dodged in and out of the crowd, searching for recognized activists. When the mid-day lunch siren sounded, twenty-five-year old Karl Yoneda held up a sign that read "Our Children Need Food." He later recalled, "At that, someone from behind cracked my head, "Bang," with full force, and I slumped to the pavement. I did not regain consciousness until the next afternoon in the Georgia Street Police Station emergency hospital holding cell. I was confined for forty-eight hours, knowing nothing of what happened to the other demonstrators."

Yoneda's friends from the ILD phoned every police station in Los Angeles, fruitlessly asking where he was jailed; it wasn't until Hynes called the ILD office to send someone to pick up the "dying Jap" that the ILD was able to post Yoneda's fifty-dollar bail and take him to a doctor.

Yoneda was convicted of "disturbing the peace" and served seventy-five days in jail. Several reputable Los Angeles citizens who were neutral observers of the rally were so outraged at the violent police attack against Yoneda that they protested to the governor, mayor, and police commission. But their indignation resulted in no official action.

The Red Squad regularly targeted the Cooperative Consumers League of Los Angeles, known as the Cooperative Center, the heart of left-wing activity in the city during the 1930s. Located in the Boyle Heights neighborhood, the center housed a bakery, café, and Jewish school. On February 18, 1931, after Red Squad officers had prevented people from entering Walker Auditorium for an address by William Z. Foster, national secretary of the Trade Union Unity League, the determined crowd migrated to the Cooperative Center, where police were also stationed. When the crowd demanded to be allowed into the center to hear Foster's speech, police began throwing tear gas bombs. By seven p.m., a gang of police officers was systematically destroying the center, breaking dishes in the kitchen, smashing chairs, windows, and light fixtures, and tearing down curtains and pictures in the main hall.

In July 1932, a federal judge granted an injunction restraining the LAPD from interfering with a meeting of the Friends of the Soviet Union. When the group held a meeting of several hundred people at Polytechnic High School several months later, the Red Squad completely ignored the injunction. Soon after the chair began addressing the group, the lights went out. He continued speaking in the dark, but a number of American Legionnaires had entered the auditorium, marching down the darkened aisles in lock step with their hands on each other's shoulders. They yelled, "There'll be no meeting here tonight; go on home," drowning out the chair, who asked for calm. Over thirty minutes passed while the Legionnaires continued their threats and orders. Eventually, someone detonated a tear gas bomb at the front of the auditorium. Hynes ordered the chair to dismiss the audience. When seventy-five uniformed police officers appeared on the scene, the audience cheered, thinking that the officers had arrived to protect their First Amendment rights. They were bitterly disappointed to learn that the police intended to aid the Legionnaires in forcing the audience to leave the hall.

The Red Squad's tactics were by now denounced by community leaders, including the Los Angeles Bar Association, the Ministerial Union of Los Angeles, and the Municipal League. After one incident, the Methodist Ministers' Association charged Hynes with "brutality, violating the Constitution, and attempting to build up a fascist dictatorship." Hynes retorted, "Who is [Methodist leader Dr. Edward P.] Ryland, to tell you we are violating the Constitution? He's no lawyer!" The police insisted that they had the right to declare meetings unlawful and prevent them from taking place. In August 1933, a municipal judge ruled that police interference in meetings violated the constitutional rights of individuals, who could receive damages as a result. The case was significant because, in theory, it obviated the need to obtain an injunction blocking the police from preventing or disturbing individual meetings.

Hynes's brutality even spread to suppressing agricultural workers' strikes outside Los Angeles. In 1936, two thousand celery workers who walked out of the fields in Los Angeles County seeking thirty cents an hour and a nine-hour day were greeted by fifteen hundred armed officers under Hynes's command. The police broke up the workers' procession, pursued strikers to their homes, and threw tear gas bombs into workers' shacks, where children were playing. The police attack was so fierce that the

Public Works and Unemployed Union of Santa Monica sent a letter to the White House protesting the Red Squad's "provocation and intimidation."

During his tenure on the Red Squad, Hynes would see three men serve as mayor of Los Angeles, but his fate was tied to the third, Frank Shaw. In 1938, after being exposed for public corruption, the disgraced Shaw was recalled from office, becoming the first U.S. mayor to be recalled. In his place, Los Angeles voters elected former judge Fletcher Bowron, who disbanded the Red Squad and demoted Red Hynes to the rank of patrolman with a humbling assignment in West Los Angeles, miles from the heart of the city. Hynes remained on the police force until 1943. After leaving, he worked a variety of jobs, including private bodyguard and aircraft plant security officer, an ignominious end to his glory days as chief of the Red Squad.

Although Mayor Bowron shut down the Red Squad in 1938, a decade later Police Chief William Worton resurrected the LAPD's spy team to investigate gangsters feared to be organizing vice in the City of Angels. It was under Police Chief William Parker, however, that the LAPD's intelligence-gathering infrastructure boomed. When Parker became chief in 1950, he transformed the Intelligence Squad from a five-person unit into a twenty-officer division overseen by a captain. Recognizing the power of knowledge, especially knowledge that could embarrass critics and political enemies, Parker declared that all intelligence files were the property of the chief of police.

Witch Hunting in Los Angeles

After World War II, the Cold War reigned: anyone who espoused sympathy with the Soviet Union—once an ally but now a threat—or with the Communist Party, or with left-wing ideas was suspect. The Korean War was looming, and Governor Earl Warren offered California as the first line of "civil defense" against the Red Menace (and, because of the founding of the People's Republic of China, the Yellow Menace as well). In 1946, Governor Warren smeared Henry Wallace, who had served as vice president under Franklin D. Roosevelt, with the following innuendo: "No, I do not say that Mr. Wallace is a Communist. I do not insinuate that he is. But I do say that leftist organizations that are attuned to the Communist movement have chosen him to muddy the political waters in our state."

FBI Director J. Edgar Hoover's career was also in ascendance. His long association with the FBI had begun under Attorney General Mitchell Palmer, who in 1919 ordered the infamous Palmer Raids.

For decades, Frank Wilkinson would be a target of both LAPD and FBI surveillance. Wilkinson, whose physician father was an elder in the Hollywood Methodist Church, was born into a privileged and prominent family. While at Beverly Hills High

School, he headed Youth for Herbert Hoover, supporting the Republican incumbent over Franklin Roosevelt because Hoover favored Prohibition. As an undergraduate at UCLA, Wilkinson was more interested in socializing with his fraternity brothers than studying, but he underwent a spiritual and political metamorphosis during a post-college trip to Chicago, New York, and the Middle East. While in Chicago, he visited social reformer Jane Addams's Hull House, where he witnessed poverty for the first time in his life. In New York, he stayed with the down-and-out in the Bowery. From there he traveled through North Africa and the Middle East, arriving in Bethlehem on Christmas Eve 1936. At the Church of the Nativity, where Jesus is believed to have been born, Wilkinson encountered hundreds of starving beggars. He emerged a left-winger and returned home an atheist and a zealous advocate for the poor.

Wilkinson channeled his newfound passion into work with the Los Angeles Housing Authority (LAHA), at the time one of the nation's largest public housing agencies and the first in California. During the early and mid-1940s, LAHA was dealing with a severe housing shortage because of incoming defense workers. Wilkinson's initial job was managing Hacienda Heights, the city's first integrated housing project, but the public housing advocate quickly rose to the position of assistant to the executive director and became the public face of LAHA.

In the early 1950s, Mayor Fletcher Bowron won the support of the city council to build ten thousand units of integrated public housing in areas like Chavez Ravine, a semi-rural, tight-knit, largely Mexican American community a few miles west of downtown. Real estate developers backed by the conservative *Los Angeles Times* opposed public housing, not only because they viewed it as a sign of "creeping socialism," but also because they wanted to exploit for profitable private development the real estate slated for public housing. In Wilkinson, these formidable opponents met their match. Armed with intimate knowledge about the condition of virtually every block of Los Angeles, Wilkinson organized "slum tours" for wealthy Westside residents and helped to produce a film about the deplorable housing conditions that many people of color in Los Angeles experienced. Plans to realize the vision of affordable housing began to look achievable.

On August 29, 1952, as Wilkinson was testifying as an expert witness in an eminent domain hearing to make way for thirty-five hundred public housing units in Chavez Ravine, an attorney representing two of Los Angeles's largest development companies asked him a question completely unrelated to his testimony on housing conditions: since 1929, what organizations, political or otherwise, had Wilkinson joined?

Taken aback, Wilkinson at first recounted his involvement with Youth for Hoover and other civic and religious groups. When the attorney pressed him to name the political organizations to which he belonged, Wilkinson refused to answer, "as a matter of conscience," and because to answer such questions might be self-incriminating.

By essentially invoking the Fifth Amendment, Wilkinson provided the enemies of the Chavez Ravine proposal just what they needed to feed to a scandal-hungry media and convince a fearful citizenry that Communists had infiltrated the LAHA. They not only red-baited Wilkinson but buried any hope of transforming Chavez Ravine into public housing.

Wilkinson now became a target of the state Committee on Un-American Activities, chaired by Senator John Tenney, a former officer in the left-wing Musicians' Union. A committee staff member tracked down Wilkinson at the Good Samaritan Hospital, where he had just undergone knee surgery. Armed with a subpoena and accompanied by a Los Angeles police officer and an FBI agent, he entered Wilkinson's room over nurses' objections. Wilkinson was still under the effects of sodium pentothal and did not respond to their shouts and attempts to pry open his eyes, so the men pinned the subpoena to his hospital gown. Ten days later, Wilkinson appeared before the committee and refused to answer questions regarding his political beliefs and affiliations. The Housing Authority fired Wilkinson and five other LAHA employees. Wilkinson's wife, Jean, lost her job as a public school teacher.

Later, during Mayor Bowron's brutal 1953 reelection campaign against Norris Poulson, Police Chief William Parker asserted in a televised hearing that Wilkinson was a subversive and that Bowron had defended him, tearing up intelligence files that Parker had been diligent enough to bring to the mayor's attention. Bowron lost the election, and with his defeat the public housing project slated for Chavez Ravine died. Newly elected Mayor Poulson collaborated with private real estate developers to work out a deal with Walter O'Malley, owner of the Brooklyn Dodgers, to purchase the land for a song. The deal nullified written promises guaranteeing the former residents of the Chavez Ravine community the right to move into public housing units.

But the persecution Wilkinson endured would inspire him to direct his energies toward exposing the witch hunters.

The Hollywood Ten

In 1946 Hollywood screenwriter Dalton Trumbo was at the top of his game. Metro-Goldwyn-Mayer signed him to a five-year contract and offered him the choice of an amazing three thousand dollars a week or seventy-five thousand dollars per script. It had been a meteoric rise for the former cub reporter from Colorado. He had started out as a reader at Warner Brothers just a decade earlier at sixty dollars a week. His more than two dozen screenplays since arriving in Hollywood included the hits

Kid from Kokomo in 1939, *Thirty Seconds over Tokyo* in 1944, and the 1940 film that brought him an Academy Award nomination, *Kitty Foyle*.

But in 1947 Trumbo received a summons that would turn his glamorous world upside-down forever. The House Un-American Activities Committee (HUAC) subpoenaed Trumbo and nine other motion picture writers and directors to testify about their membership in the Communist Party. The group, which included some of the most prestigious writers in the film industry, became known as the Hollywood Ten.

To understand the story of the Hollywood Ten, it is important to step back and look at the post–World War II Red Scare, the role of the motion picture industry in American culture, and the collision of the two.

Under Franklin Delano Roosevelt's New Deal, federal programs supported positive artistic depictions of labor struggles. Among the legacies of that period are murals of working people in public buildings like San Francisco's Rincon Annex Post Office and Coit Tower. This political consciousness also extended to Hollywood. Lester Cole, screenwriter for the *Romance of Ruby Ridge* and *Charlie Chan's Greatest Case*, recalled, "To show poverty, joblessness, hunger, and homelessness in movies not only awakened the consciousness of the millions who saw themselves represented realistically on the screen, but it…stimulated what was most dreaded by the producers who made the films—a sense of the dignity of the common man and woman, their courage and strength to fight back."

As Cole understood, however, it was not the writers but the Hollywood studio bosses who controlled films' content, and their goal was to make a profit. As MGM chief Sam Goldwyn once told a group of screenwriters, "If you want to send a message, use Western Union."

The Cold Warriors wanted to erase the beneficent image of the Soviet Union as a staunch ally of the United States that was popularized during World War II. And they wanted to destroy the mass-based people's art that Roosevelt's New Deal had fostered. Hollywood was in the crosshairs.

Heralding the triple threat of "the loyalty oath, the compulsory revelation of faith, and the secret police," Dalton Trumbo later designated the era as "the Time of the Toad." He cited nineteenth-century author Emile Zola as the source of this concept:

> Zola explained…his own method of inuring himself against newspaper columns. Each morning, over a period of time, he bought a toad in the marketplace, and devoured it alive and whole. The toads cost only three *sous* each, and after such a steady matutinal diet one could face almost any newspaper with a tranquil stomach, recognize and swallow the toad contained therein, and actually relish that which to healthy men not similarly immunized would be a lethal poison.

Trumbo placed the onset of the Time of the Toad as June 7, 1938, the establishment of HUAC by a congressional vote of 181 to 41.

For the first decade of its existence, HUAC was a "shabby and backstreet operation, specializing in anti-Semitic and racial insinuations," according to historian Garry Wills, who notes that "respectable congressmen avoided it." By the late 1940s, however, the committee became a vehicle for politicians who wanted to discredit the Roosevelt era. The committee asserted that Communists and fellow travelers had thoroughly infiltrated the Roosevelt and Truman administrations. In 1945, HUAC Chair John E. Rankin demanded that Truman "clean out the reds" in government. In 1947 Truman complied, ordering loyalty oaths for almost a quarter-million government employees. After that, as screenwriter Alvah Bessie described it, there was a "hurricane of suspicion, hysteria, fear, and witch-hunting that scourged the country."

The first chief investigator of the committee, Edward F. Sullivan, who had been a labor spy and fascist sympathizer, declared that "all phases of radical and Communist activities are rampant among the studios of Hollywood." By 1947, HUAC had declared its mandate to be "posing ideological tests for American artifacts, beginning with the movies." HUAC claimed that leading writers were placing subversive messages in Hollywood films and barring other writers who were unsympathetic to the Communist cause from working in the industry, via their union, the Screen Writers Guild.

The roots of the guild went back to 1933, when Yale-educated screenwriter Herbert Biberman founded the Hollywood Anti-Nazi League. The league attracted many anti-fascist writers, who organized a professional trade union. The guild's first president, John Howard Lawson, had been a volunteer ambulance driver in World War I (along with Ernest Hemingway and e. e. cummings). He sold his first movie script to Paramount in 1920 and worked on many political films, including *Blockade* (1938), about the Spanish Civil War, and *Counter-Attack* (1945), about the US-USSR alliance.

The motion picture industry originated in New York, but it settled in Los Angeles for two reasons—continuous sunshine and the open shop. The latter facilitated studio heads' setting up a puppet union, the Screen Playwrights. The two writers' unions held an election in 1938 to determine which would control contracts with the studios. It was a sweeping victory for the Screen Writers Guild. Immediately, studios began a red-baiting campaign. Guild leaders were accused of being "premature anti-fascists," and the *Hollywood Reporter* headlined the election story "Communist Takeover," in order to diminish the guild's influence.

The majority of HUAC subpoenas arriving in Hollywood in 1947 were addressed to screenwriters. The group that would become known as the Hollywood Ten had scripted or directed hundreds of Hollywood's best-known films. They were: Alvah

Bessie, who had been nominated for an Oscar for his 1945 film *Objective Burma*; Herbert Biberman; Lester Cole; director Edward Dmytryk; Ring Lardner Jr., who had won a 1942 Academy Award for *Woman of the Year;* John Howard Lawson; Albert Maltz; Samuel Ornitz; Adrian Scott; and Dalton Trumbo.

At the beginning of their hearings, the Ten took out a full-page ad in *Variety*, declaring that they would "use every legal means within our power to abolish this evil thing which calls itself the House Committee on Un-American Activities and to put an end, once and for all, to the uncontrolled tyranny for which it stands."

They were represented by attorneys Robert W. Kenny, former state attorney general under Governor Earl Warren; Charles Katz; Ben Margolis; Leo Gallagher (Yetta Stromberg's attorney); and Frank McTernan. They were backed by the star-studded Committee to Defend the First Amendment, whose members included leading celebrities of the day: Judy Garland, Lucille Ball, Frederic March, George S. Kaufman, Gregory Peck, and Burt Lancaster among them.

Many of the movie stars traveled to Washington for the hearings, drawing throngs to the Capitol. Newsreel and television cameras jostled for position with cheering fans as the committee members were supplied with thick dossiers on each man, filled with newspaper clippings, advertisements, Communist Party minutes and registration cards, and with lies, half-truths, unsupported rumors, and innuendo. The committee denied witnesses the right of cross-examination, or to see the evidence against them.

Invoking their First Amendment rights, the Ten refused to talk about other people's politics by "naming names," or to answer questions about membership in any party. Ring Lardner responded, "If I did, I couldn't look at myself in the mirror in the morning!" They told committee members that they were eager to talk about the importance of the Bill of Rights. As Bessie explained, they "were more than willing to talk to the committee, but the committee was not in the least interested in anything we had to say." Clashes between the writers and their congressional inquisitors became increasingly heated and hostile.

A mournful Bertolt Brecht, a registered alien subject to different laws, felt he had to answer the committee's questions. The inquisition so traumatized him that he sailed for Europe the following day.

His fellow German Thomas Mann, a naturalized U.S. citizen, offered to testify: "I have the honor to expose myself as a hostile witness. I testify that this persecution is not only degrading for the persecutors themselves but harmful to the cultural reputation of this country. [T]hat is how it started in Germany."

HUAC also heard from "friendly" witnesses, whom they treated with great courtesy and allowed to make personal statements before the committee. They included studio heads Jack Warner and Louis B. Mayer, actors Robert Taylor,

The witch hunters of the Cold War targeted progressive Hollywood writers and held them in contempt when they refused to testify before the House Un-American Activities Committee. The Hollywood Ten went to prison and were blacklisted by the movie industry for years to come.

Robert Montgomery, Gary Cooper, Adolph Menjou, and Ronald Reagan, writer Ayn Rand, and Ginger Rogers's mother, who claimed her daughter "had been forced" to speak this subversive line in a 1943 film by Dalton Trumbo: "Share alike, that's democracy."

The committee cited the Hollywood Ten for contempt and "refusal to divulge trade union and political affiliation." In April 1948, Trumbo and Lawson went on trial. The eight others stipulated that they would accept the same judgment imposed on the first two.

Both men were found guilty. "As far as I was concerned, it was a completely just verdict. I had contempt for the Congress," Trumbo stated.

Though their "crime" was only a misdemeanor, eight of the ten were sentenced to the maximum penalty—a year in jail and a thousand-dollar fine. (Herbert Biberman and Edward Dmytryk were sentenced by a different judge and received only six months each.)

The U.S. Court of Appeals for Washington, DC, upheld their convictions on June 13, 1949. When the U.S. Supreme Court refused to review the cases, lawyers for the Hollywood Ten were stunned. They had assured the screenwriters that the Court would never go along with the unconstitutional practices of HUAC. Only a few years earlier, in the Jehovah's Witness case of *West Virginia v. Barnette*, Justice Robert Jackson had written for the majority: "If there is one fixed star in our constitutional constellation, it is that no official, high or petty, can prescribe what shall be orthodox in politics, nationalism, religion, or other matters of opinion or force citizens to confess by word or act their faith therein." But since then, two liberal judges had died and been replaced by more conservative ones. And the Cold War atmosphere had deeply affected public and judicial opinions.

Alvah Bessie was sent to Texarkana, Texas, and discovered director Herbert Biberman in the cell next door. Ring Lardner and Lester Cole met with an even stranger coincidence at the federal prison in Danbury, Connecticut. New Jersey Congressman Parnell Thomas, the former chair of HUAC, had been convicted of embezzling government funds and was among their fellow inmates.

Twenty thousand people signed petitions calling for the Hollywood Ten to be paroled. Meanwhile, the movie industry was gripped by fear. Who would be the next to be accused of being subversive? The content of Hollywood films changed dramatically. Between 1947 and 1954, a glut of explicitly anti-Communist films was produced, including *The Red Menace, I Married a Communist* (whose main villain was ILWU leader Harry Bridges), and John Wayne's *Big Jim McLain*, which claimed to be an exposé of Communists in Hawaii. Budd Schulberg wrote and Elia Kazan directed *On the Waterfront*, a film Dalton Trumbo believed was "designed to justify stool pigeons and slander trade unionism."

The writers were betrayed by the very Hollywood they had helped to create. At the beginning of the HUAC hearings, Eric Johnston, president of the Motion Picture Association of America, had announced, "As long as I live I will never be a party to anything as un-American as a blacklist...We're not going to go totalitarian to please this committee." But a month later, Johnston was the spokesperson for fifty producers—and their financial backers—who gathered at the Waldorf Astoria in New York. Before a bank of cameras, they denounced the Hollywood Ten and volunteered to sever ties with all of them. "Their actions," the studio bosses declared, "have been a disservice to their employers and have impaired their usefulness to the industry."

A week later, Johnston accepted an award for the film *Crossfire*, the first major film to condemn anti-Semitism, which had been produced and directed by Adrian Scott and Edward Dmytryk, two of the men he had just banished from the movies.

The blacklist took the Hollywood Ten by surprise. On his release from prison, Lester Cole returned to Los Angeles to continue his script of *Zapata*, which was being directed by Elia Kazan. But Kazan dismissed him, and the scriptwriting was taken over by John Steinbeck. For the rest of the Ten, film jobs were just as few and far between. Many wrote under pseudonyms and others were forced to leave the film industry altogether. Cole explained, "We had to get ready to be a nobody." He became a short order cook and a warehouseman and wrote when he could, under assumed names. "We were pariahs," he said.

Biberman eventually made *Salt of the Earth*, the moving story of a militant miners' strike in New Mexico in 1954. No one in Hollywood would back it, so he produced it independently. Alvah Bessie got a job as the stage manager at the hungry i nightclub in San Francisco. He said it "would have been a good job for a writer, if they paid a decent salary." He was paid eighty dollars a week, which he supplemented by writing movie reviews for the *People's World* newspaper. He never again worked in Hollywood.

Trumbo moved to Mexico and sent scripts to Hollywood under assumed names. His screenplay for *The Brave One*, which he submitted under the name "Robert Rich," earned an Academy Award in 1956. In 1960, director Otto Preminger officially broke the blacklist by crediting Trumbo for writing the epic *Exodus*. That was followed by the hit *Spartacus* that same year. The film *Johnny Got His Gun*, based on Trumbo's 1939 antiwar novel, was honored at the Cannes Film Festival in 1971.

In total, HUAC summoned 324 movie industry figures to testify. Eventually hundreds of writers, actors, and other film workers were added to the "unofficial blacklist." Guilt by association was rampant. Actress Lee Grant, who was nominated for an Oscar for her role in *Detective Story*, was blacklisted for refusing to testify against her former husband, Arnold Manoff. Many who were blacklisted were left unemployed, impoverished, and isolated.

The blacklist held sway for decades. John Wayne, president of the Motion Picture Alliance, along with Roy Brewer, head of the craft unions (who had been expelled from the Communist Party in 1939 for trying to plagiarize another member's script), became "judge and jury," deciding who could work on films. Brewer later became a studio executive at Allied Artists. Ronald Reagan, then president of the Screen Actors Guild, kept tabs on left-leaning actors for the FBI.

The Screen Writers Guild, which had been at the forefront of opposing the tyranny of HUAC, was taken over by a new board so fearful of suffering the same fate as the union's founders that they completely rewrote the bylaws, determining that "no person shall be eligible to retain membership in the Guild or any of its branches, who refused to testify before HUAC."

HUAC held another round of movie industry hearings in 1951. Those who were called knew what was expected of them, and some even volunteered to testify so that they could apologize to the committee, recant their former stances, and prove their sincerity by identifying others with "suspect" political beliefs. Budd Schulberg and Elia Kazan told the committee that they had been duped by the "Communist conspiracy" and volunteered to help expose it. Edward Dmytryk, one of the Hollywood Ten, recanted. He had gone to England after being released from prison, but he returned to testify as a friendly witness. Lester Cole lambasted him as a "stool pigeon." Unlike the other members of the Hollywood Ten, Dmytryk went on to have an unimpeded Hollywood career.

But others continued to honor the First Amendment. Actor Zero Mostel offered to speak about his own politics but not about those of others. Writer Lillian Hellman told the committee she refused to cut her conscience to fit "this year's fashion." Paul Robeson, who not only refused to testify but gave a scathing speech before the committee, boldly branded the inquisitors "non-patriots." In doing so, he inspired others not to testify and is often credited with ending HUAC's stranglehold on the entertainment industry.

It was not until 1970 that the Screen Writers Guild repealed its ban on nontestifiers, after blacklisted writers Dalton Trumbo, Nedrick Young, Michael Wilson, and Carl Foreman had either won Oscars under assumed names or seen their names eliminated from the credits of Oscar-winning films.

Pianist and raconteur Oscar Levant once said, "Strip away the phony tinsel of Hollywood and you find the real tinsel underneath." In the case of the Hollywood Ten, what they found was toad meat.

Wilkinson Won't Plead the Fifth

It was not long after the second round of HUAC motion picture hearings that Frank Wilkinson was labeled a subversive, fired from his Los Angeles Housing Authority job, and abandoned by many of his friends and associates. He found work as a janitor on the graveyard shift in a Pasadena department store.

But soon, the Citizens Committee to Preserve American Freedoms, an organization formed to defend Californians targeted by witch-hunting committees, hired Wilkinson to work with subpoenaed individuals and explain their options for dealing with the potentially life-altering call to testify.

The hearings conducted by HUAC and its California counterpart, the senate Committee on Un-American Activities, were public inquisitions that left people prey to malicious gossip and personal vendettas. These committees purported to have an investigatory function, but in reality they served the practical purpose of putting hundreds of people on trial because of their suspected political beliefs without offering them the chance to confront their accusers or to defend themselves.

The Hollywood Ten were imprisoned for justifying their refusal to testify before

HUAC on the First Amendment. The only viable way to refuse to answer the committee's questions and avoid prison was to invoke the Fifth Amendment right against self-incrimination. The problem with this strategy was that, in the popular imagination, taking the Fifth Amendment was tantamount to an admission of guilt. HUAC had tried to smear the reputations of uncooperative witnesses by forcing them to invoke the Fifth Amendment.

Wilkinson and his colleagues at the Citizens Committee to Preserve American Freedoms believed that in order to refocus the public's attention on the unconstitutionality of HUAC and similar committees, uncooperative witnesses had to invoke the First Amendment, not the Fifth, as the basis for refusing to testify. The legal theory was that the First Amendment protection of free speech also protected the right *not* to speak, exactly because the fear of being hauled before a political testing committee like HUAC could chill a citizen's free and robust participation in the political arena.

However, since the Hollywood Ten had only recently failed with this argument, Wilkinson was unable to recruit a volunteer to test it. In December 1956, however, he found the ideal person: himself. That month he received a subpoena from HUAC for hearings to investigate the Los Angeles Committee for the Protection of the Foreign Born, an organization that Wilkinson had helped organize. Wilkinson was inspired by former Amherst College president Alexander Meiklejohn, a founder of the northern California ACLU, who stated: "The First Amendment seems to me to be a very uncompromising statement....No subordinate agency of the government has authority to ask, under compulsion to answer, what a citizen's political commitments are." Wilkinson refused to answer any questions at the hearing, even about his address. Instead, he told the committee, "I challenge, in the most fundamental sense, the legality of the House Committee on Un-American Activities. It is my opinion that this committee stands in direct violation of the First Amendment to the United States Constitution. It is my belief that Congress had no authority to establish this committee in the first instance, nor to instruct it with the mandate which it has."

Although the committee voted to recommend that Congress indict Wilkinson for contempt, it never did. Despite his best efforts to become the litigant in a potentially historic lawsuit challenging the very existence of HUAC, Wilkinson remained a free man.

In 1957 Wilkinson accepted a position with the Emergency Civil Liberties Committee (ECLC), a group formed six years earlier by well-known individuals like writers Carey McWilliams and I. F. Stone and philosopher Corliss Lamont in reaction to the national ACLU's cooperation with the FBI during the early 1950s. Through the ECLC, Wilkinson replicated on a national level the legal defense organizing he had been doing in Los Angeles. To Wilkinson's delight, ECLC shared his goal of eliminating HUAC completely.

Wilkinson did not have to wait long to again test his First Amendment challenge to HUAC. The opportunity arose in July 1958, not in southern California but in northern Georgia. As the civil rights movement was beginning to dismantle centuries of racist tradition in the South, HUAC announced it would conduct hearings in Atlanta, ostensibly to investigate Communist Party activities in the region but also, southern activists feared, to brand civil rights advocates as subversive. Carl Braden, a crusty former copy editor for the *Louisville Times*, summoned Wilkinson to Atlanta.

Within moments of entering his room at the Atlanta Biltmore Hotel, Wilkinson found a federal marshal knocking on his door and handing him a subpoena to testify before HUAC. Shocked, Wilkinson asked how the marshal knew he was at the hotel. The marshal said only that an FBI agent had called him the day before and explained that he was sending a subpoena by courier and that Wilkinson would be at the Biltmore at three o'clock.

At his second appearance before HUAC, Wilkinson again refused to answer any questions. This time, though, the House of Representatives voted 435-0 to find him in contempt of Congress.

Wilkinson had reason to hope that the Supreme Court would rule favorably in his case and that of Carl Braden, who was also held in contempt of Congress for refusing to testify at the same hearing. In June 1957, the high court had handed down decisions that seemed to foreshadow an end to political inquisitions and persecution. In *Yates v. United States*, the justices ruled that abstract advocacy (as opposed to direct action) could not be considered an effort to overthrow the government. And in *Watkins v. United States*, the Court ruled that a subpoenaed witness could not be held in contempt of Congress for refusing to testify about the Communist activities of others; and—ominously for HUAC—that Congress could not "expose for the sake of exposure" or "expose where the predominant result can only be an invasion of the private rights of individuals." These decisions, however, were not the most current relevant precedents when the Supreme Court heard Wilkinson's appeal. After President Eisenhower appointed two new justices, the ideological tilt of the court shifted to the right. In the 1959 decision *Barrenblatt v. United States*, the justices ruled 5-4 that a Vassar College instructor could be imprisoned for invoking the First Amendment to refuse to answer HUAC's questions.

That same majority voted in 1961 to uphold Wilkinson's and Braden's convictions.

Having exhausted all of his legal appeals, Wilkinson spent nine months in federal prisons. A few days before Wilkinson regained his freedom, in early 1962, Alexander

Meiklejohn, the scholar-advocate whose philosophy had inspired Wilkinson's First Amendment challenge, sent him a handwritten letter:

> Now that the immediate agonies are over, we can think more clearly about the great deed which you have done for your country, and for yourself.... Socrates...was jailed by the Athenians but he was not in a prison, because he had freely chosen to be there...That's true of you, too, Frank. Facing incarceration, you said, "Bad as that is, it is better than denying my own principles, and those of my country." And, by making that choice, you pre-served the freedom which, by submission to injustice and folly, you might have lost forever.

A Question of Loyalty

President Truman's 1947 executive order authorizing investigations into the "loy-alty" of every federal employee and applicant for federal employment impacted thou-sands of people. Truman's order also authorized the attorney general to create a list of "totalitarian, fascist, communist, or subversive groups." The government considered membership in or "sympathetic association" with any of the 123 organizations on the list to be evidence of disloyalty.

Individuals were spied on because they had years earlier expressed sympathy for militant labor leaders like Harry Bridges and Tom Mooney. Others were scrutinized because their relatives or neighbors were allegedly sympathetic to communism. And the government compiled dossiers for even flimsier reasons: one person's car was observed near the meeting place of a pacifist organization. A hearing board rea-soned, in declaring one employee to be a security risk, that "it is not enough that the employee shall be untainted; he must order his life with such positive knowledge as will absolutely negate the risk of guilt by association."

When politicians keen to exploit the Red Menace forced loyalty oaths on univer-sity scholars, the threat to academic freedom became urgent.

Near the end of the 1949 academic year, Edward Tolman, one of the country's most eminent psychologists, received notice that he would have to sign a new loy-alty oath. To receive his paycheck from the University of California (UC), he must swear that he did not support, believe in, or hold membership in any organization advocating or teaching the overthrow of the United States government by force or illegal means. The UC Regents instituted the oath to prevent the state legislature from scrutinizing the loyalty of university employees. The regents believed the oath, which they assumed would be uncontroversial, simply codified a longstanding policy barring Communists from university employment.

Though many professors considered the oath a threat to academic freedom, not all faculty members supported Tolman's call for its eradication. As a compromise, the UC Regents revised the oath in June 1949, requiring employees to deny membership in the Communist Party. Some faculty members were reluctant to sign, partly because the oath was linked with issuance of new employment contracts, and they resented the implicit coercion.

In late February 1950, the regents voted to fire any employee who did not sign the oath by April 30. Just a few months later, North Korea invaded South Korea, heightening anti-Communist sentiment and weakening support for the shrinking number of employees who refused to sign the oath. On August 25, 1950, the regents fired thirty-one faculty members who would not sign the oath. Tolman led a lawsuit for reinstatement. The professors argued that the oath violated the state constitution's requirement that the university be independent of all political or sectarian influences. They also pointed out that the state constitution prohibited any oath or loyalty test as a condition of public office or trust, except the oath of allegiance to uphold the constitution.

The California Supreme Court invalidated the oath on the disappointingly narrow grounds that only the state legislature (not the regents) had the power to require an oath of university employees. By that point, the regents had already voted to rescind it.

But the inquisitors were not done with troublesome academics.

In 1949 Phiz Mezey, a photographer and writer from New York who had made her way to San Francisco after graduating from Reed College in Oregon, was a professor in the journalism department at San Francisco State College (now San Francisco State University). Though the hiring committee had doubts about the twenty-three-year-old woman's ability to handle a class of returning war veterans, Mezey got the job, which included advising students who wrote and edited the school newspaper, the *Golden Gater*.

Administrators wanted the *Golden Gater* to focus on college life and present the school in its best possible light. But students were interested in the Korean War and other issues in the larger world. In the schism that developed, Mezey sided with the students and presented their perspective to the administration.

Arthur Duffy, one of the student editors of the 1950 summer-session *Golden Gater*, supported the Korean War and refused to run an antiwar article by a fellow student. Mezey, along with the paper's chief editor, urged Duffy to allow dissenting opinions in the paper, but because the *Gater* was student-run, Mezey felt she could not intervene directly. Disturbed by his lack of journalistic ethics, not to mention his failure to attend class or produce class assignments, Mezey gave Duffy a failing grade. Outraged, Duffy complained to administrators and insinuated that Mezey had "Communist leanings" and had failed him because he wrote editorials in support of the war.

Mezey explained to the dean that Duffy had failed to cooperate with the newspaper staff, saying he "held the view that his page was his private property." Duffy in turn went to the conservative, Hearst-owned *Call Bulletin* with his accusations; the paper ran a story headlined "Claim Anti-Red Student Penalized."

College administrators summoned Mezey to a meeting. To her surprise, a *Call Bulletin* reporter was also in the room. She was told to write a statement about the incident and to include the information that she was not a member of the Communist Party. Mezey refused. Instead, she wrote a letter to college president J. Paul Leonard asking, "No failures for classroom performance? Should I look into the backgrounds, families, and political viewpoints of my students before giving grades? I will not sign the loyalty oath now because I know that hereafter no teacher can adequately be protected under the law."

The loyalty oath that Mezey referred to had been devised by the state legislature during the UC oath controversy with the encouragement of Governor Earl Warren. Assemblyman Harold A. Levering, a former Chevy dealer from Santa Monica, authored the legislation containing the oath. Signers affirmed that they did not advocate overthrowing the federal or state government by force or violence or other unlawful means, and that they had not belonged to a group within the last five years that advocated such a thing, nor would they while employed by state government.

Senator Tenney proposed that all legislators show their patriotism by being the first "state employees" to sign the oath. The only legislator who voted against the bill was Contra Costa's Senator George Miller.

The new law required every state employee and everyone who received any money from the state to sign the oath by midnight on November 2, 1950, or lose his or her position. This meant that about a million public employees had to sign the oath or risk their livelihood.

Legislators—in particular Levering, Tenney, and Hugh Burns, a former undertaker from Fresno—proposed a flurry of bills to hunt down subversives. These included proposals to fire any public school employee "for the utterance of any treasonable or seditious words"; to require a loyalty oath of all public school teachers, lawyers, and businesses proprietors seeking state licenses or permits; to allow the Department of Education to investigate teachers; and to allow wiretapping of suspected subversives. Fortunately, most of these measures did not pass.

San Francisco State College became a hub of opposition to the Levering oath. At a meeting that overflowed a nearby Unitarian church, students, professors, and staff heard the church's eloquent Reverend Harry Meserve on the subject of who is truly loyal: "Is it the people who oppose the teachers' oath and refuse to sign because they believe in freedom of thought and expression, or the people who, in seeking an external conformity of all men to present policies, insist that they must sign the oath?"

At this meeting, several professors stood up to say why they would not sign. Frank Rowe, a modest, soft-spoken art professor, declared, "My reason for dissent is elementary. I'm loyal to the idea that freedom of speech, press, and assembly are the inviolable rights of all men." English professor John Beecher had served five years earlier as an officer on the *Booker T. Washington,* the only liberty ship with an integrated crew. "I am not going to sign this oath!" he told students. "Your education is at stake, and I think it is your fight too. I hope you will make this fight effective, memorable, and maybe pretty spectacular."

His declaration brought the students to their feet, while two unidentified men in suits in the back of the room whispered to each other and took notes.

When the November 2 deadline came, nine San Francisco State employees refused to sign. They were joined by public school teachers, child-care employees, bus drivers, school physicians and nurses, cafeteria workers, social workers, clerks, and other public employees. By November 3, a total of 890 Californians had refused to sign the oath.

A few days later, an ambitious young lawyer named Richard Nixon defeated Congresswoman Helen Gahagan Douglas, calling her a "fellow traveler" and the "Pink Lady." And art professor Frank Rowe found a dismissal notice on his desk, as did the other professors. Adding insult to injury, college administrators asked Rowe to brief his replacement. Rowe recalled:

> Several colleagues stopped me in the hall to tell me of the agony they had suffered. They agreed with me, they said, but just couldn't afford to lose their jobs. They assured me that their signing of the oath didn't mean that they would cease to work for its repeal. Curiously, all had hit upon a rationalization we were to hear many times—that they would be more effective against the oath it they worked against it from within the system.

The fired professors and sympathetic faculty organized the Joint Action Council for Repeal of the Levering Act, with Beecher as chair and Rowe as vice chair. Five professors sought legal assistance from the ACLU. But the ACLU board voted not to represent Beecher and Rowe, as they were officers of the Joint Action Council, which the board termed a "united front" organization, using the anti-Communist rhetoric of the times.

When fired language arts professor Eason Monroe tried to register as a lobbyist, to campaign in the state legislature against the Levering Act, Senator Burns told Monroe to "go back where you came from."

"I come from a small California town called Loyalton," Monroe replied dryly.

In 1952 Levering and Tenney proposed incorporating the loyalty oath requirement into the state constitution, and members of the Joint Action Council mobilized as never before. They wrote newspaper articles, distributed thousands of leaflets, sent mass mailings, and distributed press releases. They took scores of oath opponents to a hearing of the Assembly Committee on Constitutional Amendments. Rowe recalled, "The Assemblymen looked at the citizens who had carpooled from the Bay Area as though they were revolutionaries straight from the Kremlin. The people glared back."

John Beecher opened his testimony by saying the Levering oath was a conspiracy against the Constitution. The chair of the committee, Ernest Crowley, demanded, "Mr. Beecher, I'll ask you to withdraw that word 'conspiracy.'"

Beecher replied, "I am an

Non-signers of Levering Act of SF State University, 1950. Photograph by Hansel Mieth. During the McCarthy era, California enacted its own loyalty oath. Those who refused to sign, like the college employees pictured here, lost their jobs and were hounded by the FBI. Left to right: San Francisco State College employees Dr. Leonard Pockman and Charlotte Howard; Marguerite Rowe; San Francisco State employees Frank Rowe, John Beecher, Dr. Eason Monroe, Phiz Mezey, and Dr. Herb Bisno.

English teacher, and I choose words for their precise meanings. 'Conspiracy' is exactly what I mean. I will not withdraw the word." He was ejected from the hearing room, as his supporters in the audience booed and jeered. The amendment passed the committee, the assembly, and the senate, which did not even hold a hearing. The measure appeared on the 1952 ballot, and voters approved it by a two-to-one margin. The California Supreme Court upheld its constitutionality.

Through the good graces of muckraking author Carey McWilliams, a board member of the ACLU of Southern California, Eason Monroe was hired as the organization's executive director.

Rowe became an illustrator for a commercial ad agency, eventually heading up the advertising department of a large supermarket chain.

Phiz Mezey took a job at the Koret of California manufacturing plant. She was promoted to production manager, but when the FBI visited her supervisors, she was fired the same day. Mezey was under FBI surveillance for fifteen years. Agents talked to her neighbors, her employers, and even knocked on her door several times. "They would say, 'Hi Phiz, we know you got a rough deal. We just want to talk with you,'" Mezey recalled, but she always refused to speak with them.

A single mother, she had difficulty keeping a job because the FBI spooked her employers. Eventually she became a professional photographer. Her work, which includes photos of James Baldwin and Martin Luther King Jr., has been shown at the de Young Museum, the San Francisco Museum of Modern Art, and photo exhibits around the country.

In 1958, the U.S. Supreme Court dealt a blow to California's loyalty oaths. Lawrence Speiser, an ACLU attorney and veteran, challenged a property tax exemption requirement that veterans and churches sign an oath that they did not advocate the violent overthrow of the government. In a 7-1 ruling, the high court invalidated the oath as it related to property tax exemptions, because it placed the burden of proving loyalty on the taxpayer, rather than assuming loyalty. But an oath was still required of state employees.

In 1967 the California Supreme Court, in a lawsuit filed by Robert S. Vogel, a member of the Quaker Society of Friends, struck down the Levering Act as a violation of the First Amendment's guarantee of freedom of association. Thus ended a seventeen-year battle to eliminate an unconstitutional oath as a prerequisite for state employment in California. It is estimated that during that time, more than one million Californians signed the oath.

Following the ruling, the ACLU of Southern California filed a lawsuit on behalf of Executive Director Eason Monroe demanding his reinstatement at the university, and back pay. In 1971 ACLU staff attorney Fred Okrand added several other non-signers to Monroe's case. Though Monroe was not terribly optimistic, he mused, "Who knows, we may all be back at San Francisco State before the end of this century."

On December 31, 1971, the California Supreme Court ruled 6-1 that firing the teachers for refusing to take the oath was unconstitutional. Justice Matthew Tobriner stated:

> The nation's future depends upon leaders trained through wide exposure to that robust exchange of ideas which discovers truth "out of a multitude of tongues" rather than through any authoritative selection. The reinstatement of petitioner, and other similarly situated teachers, will serve to broaden, and thereby enrich the academic community by reintroducing into that community individuals with conscientiously held beliefs and ideals, beliefs which in the past have been excluded from the public schools simply because of public disapproval.

Reiterating the court's rejection of the loyalty oath, Justice Tobriner added, "The state can no longer justify continued exclusion from the public university community of all those who chose to rebel against this form of 'guilt by association.'"

The decision, however, awarded Monroe back pay and benefits only from the time of the 1967 ruling invalidating the loyalty oath, rather than from 1950, when he was fired.

Monroe returned to San Francisco State after an absence of twenty-two years. Sadly, he died of lung cancer before the academic year was out.

Mezey was rehired at San Francisco State in 1978, not in her previous position in the journalism department but in the School of Education.

In 1980 Frank Rowe wrote a personal history of those bleak times, *The Enemy among Us: A Story of Witch-Hunting in the McCarthy Era*, and he participated in a successful ACLU lawsuit in 1983 to prevent school districts from requiring teachers to sign the oath—which had been invalidated but remained on the books.

Pendulum Swings Slowly

Between 1951 and 1960, HUAC held at least one annual investigation in Los Angeles. The committee conducted San Francisco hearings in 1953, 1956, and 1957. William K. Sherwood, a Stanford University cancer researcher, was summoned to the 1957 hearings but committed suicide before testifying. "I will be in two days assassinated by publicity," he wrote. HUAC chair Francis E. Walter commented, "Well, it is certainly unfortunate that we couldn't interrogate him." Local newspapers ran angry editorials in response, and public opposition to the hearings began to grow. Even former President Harry Truman, alarmed at the virulent red-baiting in the 1952 elections, said, "McCarthyism is the corruption of truth, the abandonment of our historical devotion to fair play...and the unfounded accusation against any citizen in the name of Americanism or security...It is a horrible cancer that is eating the vitals of America."

In 1959 philosophy professor Arthur Bierman helped found San Franciscans for Academic Freedom and Education (SAFE) to support teachers who had been subpoenaed by HUAC. Bierman recalled that at first "it was practically impossible to get anyone to come out against [HUAC]. The fear was visceral. People would turn white. They would stutter." But within just a few weeks, SAFE had garnered an impressive list of endorsers, including religious leaders, labor officials, attorneys, professors, and Assembly Members Phillip Burton and John O'Connell. The ACLU's Ernest Besig offered the subpoenaed teachers legal help and provided SAFE media relations and connections with state and national legislators. Defense committees formed in Palo Alto, Hayward, and the greater East Bay. In late August, HUAC chair Walter announced that the committee was canceling its 1959 San Francisco hearings. It was the first time a HUAC inquisition had been cancelled.

Several months later, HUAC subpoenaed forty-eight northern Californians for three days of hearings in San Francisco. In contrast to the handful of professors who, a decade earlier, had dared to publicly oppose loyalty oaths, more than 165 San Francisco State College faculty members took out a full-page ad in the student newspaper denouncing the hearings. Three hundred UC Berkeley professors signed an anti-HUAC petition, as did two hundred at Stanford and one hundred at San Jose State University. Students at San Francisco State and UC Berkeley were particularly active in the anti-HUAC efforts, foreshadowing an era of student political activism around the civil rights and peace movements.

The hearings opened on May 12, 1960, in the ornate Board of Supervisors chambers at the top of a marble staircase in San Francisco City Hall. HUAC packed the room with members of the Daughters of the American Revolution, the American Council of Christian Churches, and other conservative groups, issuing them white entry cards and allowing them into the room before the general public.

Longshoreman and Communist organizer Archie Brown, who refused to have his patriotism questioned by the zealots on the committee, led the audience in singing "The Star-Spangled Banner" and was evicted from the hearing. Hundreds of students had gathered in the hallway, hoping to get into the room. As Brown was dragged out, he shouted, "Let those people in. This committee cannot come to San Francisco, announce its hearings, and then pack its attendance."

May 13 was, fittingly, a Friday. Late that morning, San Francisco Sheriff Matthew Carberry told protesting students that he would make sure afternoon admission into the hearing would be on a first-come, first-serve basis. But after the lunch break, Carberry was nowhere to be seen. When HUAC officials once again gave preference to entry card holders, students sat down outside the Supervisors' chambers and sang "We Shall Overcome."

Marshall Krause, a young attorney clerking for California Supreme Court Chief Justice Phil Gibson, met his wife for lunch that Friday and went to City Hall with her because she wanted to attend the hearing. He saw a police officer unfurling a fire hose and, without warning, turn the powerful spray on the protesting students, forcing them down the marble steps inside the City Hall rotunda.

Burton White, a UC graduate student, recalled that "at the shock of the water, everyone stood up. Some of the hardier males formed a wall with their backs to the water to form a shield of protection for the others. After the hosing stopped, the people sat down again."

Krause immediately told the offending officer the water attack was illegal. He was the first person arrested. Police officers grabbed him and, as he descended the slick stairs, tried to trip him.

"All of a sudden, the cops came pushing into a group of those sitting, trying to

Without warning, San Francisco police turned high-power fire hoses on students protesting a May 1960 hearing of the House Un-American Activities Committee in San Francisco's City Hall. The police attack on peaceful protestors drew national condemnation.

break them up," White recalled. "They swung their clubs freely and pushed the students all over a lobby and down the main floor....Cops came from the top and bottom of the stairs, dragging and punching and pushing and swinging their clubs." Police arrested sixty-four people, nearly half of whom were UC Berkeley students. None of them were convicted.

The unprovoked attack on peaceful protestors received national attention and outraged the public. The following day, five thousand people gathered outside City Hall to join the protest.

HUAC later produced a film entitled *Operation Abolition*, consisting of unsubstantiated narration combined with local television coverage of the protest, edited to blame the violence on "well-trained, hardcore Communist agents." *Operation Abolition* proved to be a popular draw with politically conservative groups throughout the country, but it also generated controversy at local screenings, converting new people to the anti-HUAC cause. In response to the inaccuracies, manipulations, and lies of *Operation Abolition*, ACLU-NC Executive Director Besig produced his own film,

Operation Correction, dissecting *Operation Abolition*. The ACLU hosted nationwide screenings.

One of the unintended effects of *Operation Abolition* was that it attracted students from around the country to the San Francisco Bay Area. Four years later, some of the newcomers participated in a pivotal movement at UC Berkeley that would inspire and motivate students on campuses throughout the nation.

Free Speech Movement

In 1941 the University of California built an administration building at the southern entrance to the Berkeley campus and named it in honor of university president Robert Gordon Sproul. Twenty years later, the university transformed the area in front of the imposing building into a wide, tree-lined pedestrian mall known as Sproul Plaza. In the early 1960s Berkeley students handed out political literature and collected funds for various causes at the entrance to the plaza on Bancroft Way.

Political waters had been coming to a boil in Berkeley since 1960, when the student government, dominated by conservative fraternities and sororities, wrested editorial control of the campus newspaper from progressive student editors. The following year, administrators banned SLATE, a student political party, and barred Malcolm X from speaking on campus.

Many students had volunteered in growing national and local civil rights actions. Dozens spent the summer of 1964 in Mississippi, where they witnessed and experienced racist intimidation and violence and joined civil rights groups like the Student Nonviolent Coordinating Committee (SNCC) and the Congress of Racial Equality (CORE). Awakened to racism in the South, students recognized it in their own backyard and organized pickets to protest job discrimination at local Lucky's supermarkets, the *Oakland Tribune*, and San Francisco's Sheraton Palace Hotel, where they staged a sit-in to the consternation of corsaged ladies attending a banquet. These protests did not sit well with the local business community.

On September 14, 1964, the first day of the fall semester, university administrators suddenly and, from the perspective of student activists, arbitrarily banned all non-campus-related political literature and activity. Students protested the policy, and on September 30, after negotiations had broken down, representatives of SNCC and CORE not only set up their tables but raised the bar by doing so just feet from Sproul Hall.

University officials instructed five students staffing the tables to report to Arleigh Williams, the dean of men, later that day. At the appointed time, undergraduates Arthur Goldberg, Sandor Fuchs, and Mario Savio spurred hundreds of students to protest outside the dean's office. Savio presented Williams with a petition signed by more than five hundred students who claimed that they too had staffed the outlawed tables. Savio demanded that everyone who signed the petition be treated exactly as the five who had been summoned to Williams's office and that any charges against the five students be dropped until the university had clarified its policy on campus political activity.

After Williams refused to agree to the demands, Savio announced that the protesting students would spend the night in Sproul Hall. For this, Chancellor Edward Strong indefinitely suspended eight student leaders. That night, the representatives of various campus political groups who occupied Sproul Hall dubbed their activities "the Free Speech Movement" (FSM).

The following day, Berkeley police arrested Jack Weinberg, a former student who was staffing a CORE table on Sproul Plaza. They drove a squad car onto the plaza, dragged Weinberg from behind the table, and shoved him into the back seat. Hundreds of students surrounded the police car, blocking its exit. Students climbed on top of the sedan and used it as an oratory platform, leaving police and campus officials dumbfounded. For the next thirty-two hours, several hundred people continuously surrounded the car, supplying sandwiches and milk to Weinberg (who remained in the back seat throughout) and listening to speakers on topics ranging from political philosophy to the campus ban on political activity.

When Chancellor Strong refused to meet with protestors, Savio led a hundred and fifty people into Sproul Hall. By late afternoon, nearly four hundred students had trapped two deans in their offices. Savio, a tall, intense, wiry-haired twenty-one-year-old who had spent the summer teaching in a freedom school in McComb, Mississippi, electrified the group. Students, he believed, were being treated as anonymous and interchangeable automatons, trained in what university president Clark Kerr called the "knowledge industry" to be complacent workers and managers in corporate America. Savio found the bureaucracy abhorrent. Tapped into the alienation and dissatisfaction of his generation, he quickly rose to leadership, becoming an icon.

By 5:30 the next evening, five hundred law enforcement officers from Berkeley, Oakland, Alameda County, and the California Highway Patrol, some carrying riot batons, had surrounded three sides of Sproul Plaza, while demonstration leaders negotiated with Kerr and Strong.

By 7:30, the negotiators had reached an agreement. The university would form a Committee on Political Activity, composed of students, faculty, and administration representatives, to develop recommendations for campus political activity. The university would lift its ban on political literature tables and advocacy. Disciplinary action against the eight suspended students would be decided by a faculty community on student conduct. The university would not press charges against Jack Weinberg.

For the next two months, FSM leaders and campus administrators clashed over the implementation of this agreement.

The situation came to a head on December 2. At a noon rally, Savio delivered what became a generation-defining speech, with this famous passage:

> There is a time when the operation of the machine becomes so odious, makes you so sick at heart, that you can't take part; you can't even passively take part, and you've got to put your bodies upon the gears and upon the wheels, upon the levers, upon all the apparatus and you've got to make it stop. And you've got to indicate to the people who run it, to the people who own it, that unless you're free, the machine will be prevented from working at all.

Folksinger Joan Baez sang "We Shall Overcome" as nearly a thousand demonstrators, many of them wearing FSM armbands, poured into Sproul Hall to occupy four floors of the building in protest of the administration's intransigence.

Sitting along the hallways, demonstrators sang, played cards, and studied. FSM leaders used walkie-talkies to talk with each other and set up a public address system to communicate with the press and others outside the building. As the seven o'clock closing time for the building neared, supporters delivered food. Some protestors watched films and others conducted Chanukah services. At one in the morning, the hallway lights were turned off and the demonstrators settled in for the night.

Just after three a.m., Chancellor Strong appeared with a bullhorn and announced that students had to leave the building or face disciplinary action. To buttress his request, about six hundred law enforcement officers from the Berkeley, Oakland, and university police departments, the Alameda County sheriff's department, and the California Highway Patrol had amassed outside Sproul Hall. About forty-five minutes after Strong made his announcement, the officers entered Sproul Hall, authorized by Governor Edmund "Pat" Brown, and began sweeping up protestors.

Demonstrators were prepared for the possibility of arrest and many refused to walk out, instead going limp and causing police to drag them down staircases and out of the building into awaiting police vehicles. It took more than twelve hours for 376 officers to arrest the 773 occupiers. At the time, it was the largest mass arrest in California history.

Although police cleared Sproul Hall, their rough treatment of protestors was a public relations disaster and further rallied students to the Free Speech Movement. A group of faculty members raised more than eight thousand dollars to free the students on bail.

FSM leaders called a successful campuswide student strike, resulting in perhaps half the student body either boycotting classes or not attending because sympathetic teaching assistants had cancelled classes. Picketers blocked campus entrances. More than five thousand people filled Sproul Plaza for a rally in which FSM leaders blasted President Kerr, Chancellor Strong, and Governor Brown. Kerr had opposed the UC loyalty oaths, but now the leaders of the Free Speech Movement viewed him as an agent of reactionary repression.

Kerr knew that dramatic action was necessary. He called a mass meeting in the Greek Theater, a 1903 amphitheater nestled into the hills east of the campus, cancelling classes so that all students and faculty could attend. He promised to announce a proposal "to inaugurate a new era of freedom under law."

On the cold morning of December 7, between sixteen thousand and eighteen thousand students, faculty, and staff poured into the amphitheater. They listened as Kerr explained new, liberalized political action rules.

As Kerr concluded his remarks, Savio jumped onto the stage to address the crowd. As he reached the rostrum, two university police officers grabbed him and dragged him off the stage. When several of his friends moved to help him, police pushed them aside and knocked them down.

Perhaps recognizing that Savio's detention would unravel any goodwill that his announcement might have created, Kerr commented after the meeting that a new start seemed "somewhat doubtful." He did not have to wait long to learn that he was right. About ten thousand people filled Sproul Plaza later that day and rejected his proposals by acclamation.

The following afternoon, three thousand FSM supporters sat for nearly three hours outside Wheeler Hall, listening to a loudspeaker hookup of the Academic Senate meeting that was taking place inside. The faculty voted 824 to 115 to support proposals not to restrict the content of on-campus speech or advocacy and to reject disciplinary action against any students or organizations for activities prior to the date of the senate meeting. The faculty vote endorsed what FSM leaders had requested from the beginning.

As Joseph Tussman, chairperson of the philosophy department, explained, "The question is: Should the university impose more restrictions on its students in the area of political activity than exist in the community-at-large? The senate said no."

When faculty members exited Wheeler Hall, the students who had been listening outside parted to make room and applauded. It was a perfect birthday present for Mario Savio, who turned twenty-two that day.

East L.A.: Student Blowout

In the early spring of 1968, Principal Reginald Murphy of Garfield High noticed leaflets circulating among his students that called for education reform, smaller class sizes, and more emphasis on Mexican American history in the curriculum. The leaflets also called on students at Garfield and three other high schools in East Los Angeles to join a walkout in support of these demands.

Despite years of attempts to desegregate and reform Los Angeles schools, those in Latino neighborhoods were still overcrowded, understaffed, and run down. Elementary school students were punished and ridiculed for speaking Spanish. Fewer than 5 percent of the district's teachers and only 1.3 percent of its administrators were Latino. Half of the students in East L.A. high schools did not graduate. The Vietnam War was raging, and the draft ravaged neighborhoods with high dropout rates, putting boys on the war front as soon as they left school. Few went on to college. Although Latinos represented one-tenth of California's school-age population in 1966, of the 26,083 students at UC Berkeley, only 76 were Latino. In the same period, 40 percent of the public school students in California sent to special programs for the "mentally handicapped" were Latino.

"Our schools in the Eastside were in such poor condition, as compared to their schools," recalled student leader Paula Crisostomo, referring to affluent white areas. "Brand-new schools in the valley and West Los Angeles were being put up…with swimming pools." Incensed that their schools were deteriorating while schools in white neighborhoods had outstanding facilities, student leaders formed the militant Brown Berets. They had honed their organizing skills in community training programs and church groups, and they had been inspired by the defiance and audacity of the United Farm Workers, the Black Panthers, and college campus protestors.

The high school students found an ally in Lincoln High history teacher and East L.A. native Sal Castro. Not only was he intimately familiar with the problems in the school system, he was frustrated that L.A.'s schools were still as inadequate as they had been when he was a student.

Students worked with the thirty-four-year-old Castro to conduct a survey of Chicano students and submitted the results—with a list of demands for change—to the Los Angeles school board. They were prepared to back up their demands with a widespread protest, a mass walkout. The password for the launch of the walkout— "blowout"—spread quickly among the teenagers. After a frustrating meeting with the school board, students were poised for political action.

On March 1, the word "blowout" reverberated through classrooms, and three hundred students walked out of Wilson High School. The following day, two thousand walked out of Garfield High; the next day they were joined by forty-five hundred more from nearby Lincoln and Roosevelt High Schools. By the end of the week, the *Los Angeles Times* reported that fifteen thousand students had joined the walkout. The teenagers carried signs reading "Chicano Power," "Viva la Raza," and a slogan borrowed from Emiliano Zapata and popularized by the United Farm Workers: "Viva la Revolución."

Tired of substandard schools, more than fifteen thousand Chicano high school students staged a walkout in March 1968. In May organizers, including teacher Sal Castro, were arrested for conspiracy, which sparked more protests.

Students were jubilant over the widespread response to the "blowout." But they were unprepared for the violent police reaction to their peaceful protest. As students picketed in front of the high schools, Los Angeles police officers descended, attacking them with clubs and fists. Officers armed for combat, with helmets and shields, identified student leaders and chased them through residential neighborhoods, where Mexican American families looked on in horror.

The blowout and the police response attracted national attention, spotlighting the bleak educational conditions in East L.A. Rubén Salazar, one of the few Mexican American reporters at the *Los Angeles Times*, delved into the educational, economic, and political problems of the Mexican American community and gave them wide exposure in the mainstream newspaper. The school board, stymied, finally agreed to discuss the students' demands. A March 26 meeting at Lincoln High School drew more than twelve hundred students, teachers, and parents. After a four-hour discussion, the board agreed not to take disciplinary action against students who had participated in the walkouts but offered little else. The students, again frustrated that no action was taken on the simple reforms they sought, stormed out of the meeting.

Not all the attention attracted by the blowout was helpful to the students' cause.

At the request of District Attorney Evelle Younger, the Los Angeles County grand jury began a secret investigation, using police informers to infiltrate the ranks of the student movement.

On Friday night, May 31, Sal Castro was preparing to chaperone the Lincoln High School prom when police burst into his home and took him into custody. Eliezer Risco y Lozado, thirty-one, editor of the militant biweekly *La Raza*, was arrested outside the newspaper offices; police raided the building and seized the paper's subscription list, files, and photo archive.

At two-thirty a.m., Carlos Muñoz, president of United Mexican American Students at California State University, Los Angeles, was writing a term paper while his two children slept upstairs. Police barged into his house. "'You're a Brown Beret,' they were telling me, 'you gotta have weapons.' They put the cuffs on me," Muñoz recalled. "They took them off again. They said, 'We're going to give you ten steps so that you can make a run for it.' I knew what they wanted me to do…I was scared for my life. I put my hands back up and said, 'You better cuff me and take me in.'"

Police raided the Brown Beret headquarters, where they confiscated membership lists, organizational files, and fliers. They also arrested nineteen-year-old David Sanchez, a Roosevelt High graduate who had served as chair of Mayor Sam Yorty's Los Angeles Youth Advisory Council.

After hearing testimony from fifty people and watching film footage taken during the walkouts, the grand jury had returned secret indictments against Castro, Risco, Muñoz, Sanchez, and nine other organizers on charges of criminally conspiring to create riots, disrupt the functioning of the public schools, and disturb the peace.

The midnight raids infuriated students. Many believed the arrests were politically motivated and that the government was using the grand jury indictments to quash the growing Chicano movement. Their concerns were validated when Los Angeles Police Chief Thomas Reddin told a local TV reporter, "Those who seek to conspire against the establishment are going to learn they are not immune from arrest." The political character of the arrests was sharply underscored by the timing of the indictment, just one week prior to the June primary, when District Attorney Younger was up for reelection.

Though the underlying criminal charges were misdemeanors, the conspiracy charge elevated the alleged crimes to felonies; an unusually high bail of ten thousand dollars was set for the defendants, who faced potential prison sentences of up to forty-five years. On June 13, three hundred people picketed in front of the LAPD; the following day two thousand demonstrated in front of the city jail in support of the "East L.A. Thirteen."

The brilliant and flamboyant attorney Oscar Acosta led the defense, making racism in the judicial system a pivotal point. "Not only do they discriminate against Chicanos," he said of the grand jury, "they are discriminating against all poor and young and minority persons." Acosta won the support of such luminaries as former Governor Pat Brown, future Los Angeles Mayor Tom Bradley, and UFW leader Cesar Chavez. He also enlisted support from the legal community. ACLU attorney A. L. Wirin filed suits against District Attorney Younger and Sheriff Peter Pitchess to prohibit prosecution of the East L.A. Thirteen, charging that they had been unfairly singled out because of their politics and organizational affiliations, in violation of their First Amendment rights.

When classes began in September, Sal Castro was barred from teaching at Lincoln High. Angry students and their parents picketed and held a sit-in, eventually pressuring the school board to allow the popular teacher to return to his classroom. It took more than two years for the charges against the East L.A. Thirteen to be dropped.

In August 1970, State Court of Appeal Presiding Justice Otto Kaus ruled that a grand jury indictment of conspiracy to disturb the peace could not be imposed on people exercising their fundamental First Amendment rights, because it would "make it dangerous to engage in certain constitutionally protected activities." Freedom of speech, the court stated, is not to be accorded "just grudging toleration—on the contrary, it is a national goal to be actively nurtured and encouraged."

La Voz de la Raza

The blowouts politicized a generation of Chicanos. Leaders of the student movement forged new organizations, including El Movimiento Estudiantil Chicano de Aztlán, whose acronym, MEChA, aptly means "matchstick" in Spanish. The Brown Berets spread to college campuses throughout the state. Students who walked out of class as high school juniors and seniors later picketed with farmworkers outside the sweltering vineyards of Coachella, joined the Poor People's March in Washington, DC, and with other students of color, led strikes at San Francisco State University, UCLA, and UC Berkeley to demand meaningful ethnic studies curricula.

In 1970 there was no end in sight to the Vietnam War and its continual drain of young men and resources from the impoverished rural communities of the San Joaquin Valley and the inner-city barrios of Los Angeles, San Diego, and San Jose. Mexican Americans were drafted at twice the rate Anglos were, and though they comprised only 5 percent of the U.S. population, they sustained 20 percent of all Vietnam casualties.

More than three hundred groups—with the Brown Berets and MEChA in the lead—formed the National Chicano Moratorium Committee and planned a massive march for August 29, 1970, in East Los Angeles. It was the first major mobilization of Latinos against the war.

The late summer day was stifling. Smog hung in the still air at ten in the morning as thousands of people gathered on Whittier Boulevard. Hundreds of volunteer monitors organized the enthusiastic crowd, leading spirited chants in English and Spanish and gently keeping demonstrators to the planned route. As the crowd marched toward Laguna Park, in the heart of East Los Angeles, many more protestors swelled their ranks, until more than thirty thousand people massed for the final rally.

But when the antiwar speeches started, hundreds of officers from the Los Angeles police and sheriff's departments, dressed in riot gear and equipped with guns, surrounded the peaceful crowd.

Rosalio Muñoz, a former UCLA student body president, was one of the first Chicanos to publicly resist the draft. He recalled, "When the police decided to stop the rally, they forced the crowd to the front, which was cordoned off by trucks and cars so marchers could not come in from the back. People were trapped there...and the kids were climbing off the stage. Then you saw the monitors coming around and trying to stop the cops. The cops started throwing tear gas, making it worse. And then the people started throwing things back."

Reporter Rubén Salazar, covering the march for Spanish-language television station KMEX, was inside the Silver Dollar Café when a tear gas canister fired by a

The Vietnam War took a disproportionate toll on Latinos: Chicanos were drafted at twice the rate of whites. The Chicano Moratorium, which mobilized thirty thousand people in East L.A. to protest the war, ended in a massive police assault on the demonstrators and the death of a beloved journalist, Rubén Salazar.

sheriff's deputy burst through the window. It hit Salazar in the head, shattering his brain. The groundbreaking journalist known as *la voz de la raza*—the voice of the people—was dead.

Salazar was one of three people killed during the moratorium. He was deeply mourned. Many believed his death was not random. He had written passionately about police brutality in East L.A., Mexican Americans' lack of representation on juries, and unwarranted police surveillance. In one article, Salazar had revealed that an officer who shot a Mexican American had been suspended twice before, once because he threatened a boy with a cocked pistol. In another, he had criticized a policeman who sprayed an apartment with gunfire during a murder investigation and killed two Mexican nationals. No weapons were found in the flat.

Pressure from the community and civil rights organizations led city officials to create a Blue Ribbon Committee to investigate Salazar's death. The result of the official inquiry: there was no cause for action against the deputy.

"Government Snooping in the Extreme"

Evidently unsure whether the Red Scare was over, Los Angeles Police Chief Ed Davis held a press conference charging that "Communists and Bolsheviks" had instigated the student walkouts and Chicano moratorium, "using the young Mexican Americans as prison fodder." Frank Martinez, an LAPD informant, later admitted that he had been assigned as an undercover agent to disrupt the Moratorium Committee. And undercover police officers posing as students "infiltrated" the 419-acre UCLA campus. They attended classes as well as meetings of university-recognized organizations, where they documented opinions expressed and compiled "intelligence reports" on professors and students.

Hayden White, a UCLA history professor, was active in campus antiwar organizing. In 1972 he brought a lawsuit against Chief Davis, claiming that it was illegal to use tax funds to spy on students and faculty.

The trial court, guided by narrow federal court decisions regarding surveillance, dismissed the case on the grounds that White did not suffer a specific harm. But when the case reached the California Supreme Court in 1975, the justices agreed unanimously that while intelligence gathering is a legitimate police activity, it must be strictly controlled in accordance with the Bill of Rights and the state constitution. To pass constitutional muster, a police department had to show a compelling reason why the surveillance was necessary and that there was no less intrusive means to achieve its goal.

Writing for the high court, Justice Matthew Tobriner explained that unlike prior cases restricting police surveillance because of the ban on illegal search and seizure, the UCLA case centered on the more unusual issue of the conflict between free speech and police spying. The court acknowledged that government activity that even indirectly inhibits the exercise of free speech could violate First Amendment rights:

> The censorship of totalitarian regimes that so often condemns developments in art, science, and politics is but a step removed from the inchoate surveillance of free discussion in the university; such intrusion stifles creativity and to a large degree shackles democracy.

> In the course of classroom debate some thoughts will be hazarded as trial balloons of new theories. Yet such propositions, that are tentative only, will nevertheless be recorded by police officers, filtered through the minds of the listening informers, often incorrectly misstated to their superiors and sometimes maliciously distended. Only a brave soul would dare to express anything other than orthodoxy under such circumstances.

The supreme court called such surveillance "government snooping in the extreme," and a violation of the right to privacy recently added to the California constitution.

Wilkinson's FBI File Tells All

Like UCLA professor Hayden White, Frank Wilkinson knew he was being spied on. But upon his release from prison in 1962, Wilkinson channeled his passion into burying HUAC and its staged inquisitions. Capitalizing on his booming baritone voice, charm, and natural talents as a raconteur, he crisscrossed the country giving rousing speeches. College students sought him out. It was not unusual for members of the American Legion or other virulently anti-Communist groups to picket his appearances or disrupt his speeches. But Wilkinson and the organization he had cofounded in 1960 with his friend Dick Criley, the National Committee to Abolish HUAC (NCAHUAC), remained the steadfast David to HUAC's Goliath.

NCAHUAC's work, coupled with shifting political attitudes ushered in by the civil rights and anti–Vietnam War movements, slowly eroded HUAC's seeming invincibility. HUAC's members contributed to the committee's demise as well. In 1968, J. Edgar Hoover supported committee chair Edwin E. Willis's suggestion that American urban "guerrillas," such as militant black activists, be put in concentration camps without trials, as Japanese Americans had been during World War II. Leading newspapers around the country began to editorialize against HUAC's smear tactics.

In the aftermath of the 1974 Watergate scandal, which brought new scrutiny to government repression of dissidents, HUAC was quietly put to death. In January 1975,

For thirty-eight years, the FBI spied on anti-HUAC activist Frank Wilkinson. In 1987 Wilkinson (left) posed with his attorneys Paul Hoffman (center) and Douglas Mirell (right) and a fraction of the 132,000 pages of his FBI files.

the House of Representatives voted to transfer the committee's jurisdiction to the Judiciary Committee, which was populated by liberals and moderates. When HUAC was at long last abolished, Massachusetts Representative Robert F. Drinan praised Frank Wilkinson, saying, "No account of the demise of the House Un-American Activities Committee would be complete without a notation of [his] extraordinary work."

Eighteen years after being released from prison, Wilkinson sued the FBI under the Freedom of Information Act, demanding the agency release its files on him. The lawsuit spanned eight years, but eventually the FBI handed over 132,000 pages documenting surveillance of Wilkinson by the FBI and other law enforcement agencies for thirty-eight years, beginning in 1942. At times, eight FBI agents were spying on Wilkinson on the same day. His phones were tapped without warrants. Agents were looking for evidence to prosecute him for violating the federal Smith Act, under which it was a crime to "knowingly abet, advise or teach the duty, necessity, desirability or propriety of overthrowing or destroying any government in the United States by force or violence" or to "be a member of, or affiliate" with any group or organization that advocated the overthrow or destruction of the government. Despite the concentration of resources focused on Wilkinson, no such evidence materialized.

The files also revealed that J. Edgar Hoover had targeted Wilkinson as part of the FBI's notorious COINTELPRO (COunterINTELligencePROgram), a systematic effort launched in 1957 to infiltrate, disrupt, and discredit domestic organizations that Hoover considered subversive. In April 1962, soon after Wilkinson was released from prison, Hoover informed FBI field offices that agents would receive special "incentive awards" for devising the best methods of disrupting Wilkinson's speaking engagements. The files showed that the FBI had distributed red-baiting flyers at Wilkinson's speaking engagements for more than two decades, as well as instigating protests by the American Legion and the American Nazis.

The FBI files also included a disturbing 1964 memo to J. Edgar Hoover from a Los Angeles FBI agent about an undisclosed source referring to a plot to assassinate Wilkinson. The memo documented Wilkinson's plan to speak to an ACLU group at a private home and said the FBI would "stake out" the residence. The FBI never told Wilkinson his life was in danger.

Assassination was not a far-fetched notion, given that in 1960 a firebomb had exploded on the stairs in front of Wilkinson's Los Angeles apartment, while two of his children were home. Fortunately, no one was injured. Despite constant surveillance, FBI records do not indicate who was behind the bombing or who painted a swastika on the building soon thereafter.

Snitches, Provocateurs, and COINTELPRO

When the growing movement in communities of color for self-determination and radical change threatened to disrupt the political status quo in the U.S., COINTELPRO became the FBI's weapon of choice. The Black Panther Party was in the leadership of that movement, and J. Edgar Hoover knew it.

By June 10, 1997, Elmer Gerard "Geronimo" Pratt had spent more than half of his forty-nine years in prison. But on that day, the former Black Panther leader left an Orange County courtroom a free man. Wrongfully convicted of a senseless murder, Pratt had made an arduous political and legal odyssey that drew support from Amnesty International, the ACLU, several members of Congress, Coretta Scott King, and even the world's most famous political prisoner, Nelson Mandela.

Born on September 13, 1947, Pratt was the youngest of eight children, raised by a proud and tough drayman and a devout mother in rural Morgan City, Louisiana, about a hundred miles southwest of New Orleans. He distinguished himself during two tours of duty in Vietnam, receiving two Bronze Stars and two Purple Hearts. He was commended for heroism for making repeated trips into a burning helicopter under the threat of enemy fire to rescue all of the occupants. But during his second tour of duty, Pratt began to see the war as another manifestation of American racism.

"In boot camp and advanced infantry training," he later recalled, "all we ever heard was 'gooks,' 'Buddha-heads,' 'slopes,' same way our daddies heard 'Krauts' and 'Japs.' You got to make people subhuman before you kill 'em."

Pratt received an honorable discharge with the rank of sergeant in the summer of 1968, just shy of having served three years, most of it in combat. A respected advisor in Morgan City encouraged the young veteran to travel to Los Angeles to meet Alprentice "Bunchy" Carter, one of the advisor's distant relatives, who was involved in the Black Panther Party for Self-Defense. The party, the elder explained, "got some good ideas" but needed help "organizing and defending themselves against the cops." One of Pratt's older sisters was returning to Los Angeles to resume a master's degree program, and they drove west together.

Three days after arriving in Los Angeles, Pratt met Bunchy Carter, the twenty-six-year-old Louisiana native who had founded the southern California branch of the Black Panther Party. The two became friends, and Pratt enrolled in UCLA's High Potential Program for minority students, where Carter was a year ahead of him. Through Carter, Pratt met Black Panther leader John Huggins and other party members. Drawn to the Panthers' platform for building pride in the black community, Pratt helped with the party's free breakfast, sickle-cell anemia testing, and clothing distribution programs. Carter gave Pratt the name "Geronimo ji Jaga," meaning Geronimo of the Jaga, a tribe of African warriors.

The Black Panther Party was formed in 1966 by Oakland activists Huey Newton, Bobby Seale, and David Hilliard in the aftermath of Malcolm X's assassination and violent clashes between police and African Americans in South Central Los Angeles. Inspired by liberation struggles of African, Asian, and Latin American countries, the Panthers advocated armed self-defense against police abuse. From its base in Oakland, the party grew to a nationwide membership.

In mid-December 1968, the Panthers flew Pratt to Oakland, where he participated in meetings of the Central Committee. Franco Diggs, a party elder at forty, dropped Pratt off at the Los Angeles airport. Upon his return to Los Angeles, Pratt learned that someone had shot Diggs three times in the head.

The following month, Bunchy Carter and John Huggins were shot dead on the UCLA campus, the climax of an internecine conflict between the Panthers and a black nationalist group called US (United Slaves).

Carter had left a taped message naming Pratt as his successor to lead the Los Angeles Panthers. The twenty-one-year-old Pratt was appointed to the party's Central Committee and First Cadre, the highest decision-making entity. In addition, he was named deputy minister of defense for the entire party. Pratt resisted, telling Panther leaders, "I don't want the job. I'm not from California. I don't even like California." But local Panther members counseled him to accept the post.

Someone else had expected to take over the southern California Panther leadership. Fifteen years Pratt's senior, Julius "Julio" Butler was a former Marine sergeant and Los Angeles County deputy sheriff who operated a hairdressing and cosmetology business. He had joined the party in 1968. Butler made it clear that he resented Pratt, whom he considered an untested outsider, and defied Pratt's orders. Others disagreed with Butler's assessment. "Of all the people in the Black Panther Party," former Panther Roland Freeman recalled years later, "Geronimo was the most effective. Julio wanted to be the leader, but the rank and file wanted Geronimo."

After two run-ins with the resentful Butler, one involving Butler's beating of a high school recruit, Pratt expelled him from the party.

In this politically charged and violent time, Pratt and other Panthers not only had to deal with internal conflicts but with the LAPD: the department's Urban Counterinsurgency Task Force regularly harassed black militants. In December 1969, just four days after police killed Black Panther leaders Fred Hampton and Mark Clark in Chicago, thirty LAPD officers and FBI agents surrounded the party's Los Angeles headquarters at Central Avenue and 41st Street. For more than four hours, beginning at 4:45 a.m., several Panthers held off the heavily armed lawmen. Pratt was not there, but he was responsible for fortifying the building with sandbags. Police fired five thousand rounds of bullets into the building, most of which lodged in the sandbags. Dynamite dropped from a police helicopter hit more sandbags on the roof. Three officers and six Panthers were wounded in the shoot-out, which from the Panthers' perspective was self-defense, but which the government considered guerrilla warfare.

By 1970 the Black Panther Party was beginning to implode. A rift developed between former Panther Minister of Information Eldridge Cleaver, who in 1968 fled the United States to avoid a prison sentence, and Minister of Defense Huey Newton. The two made pronouncements expelling each other from the party, and at one point Cleaver supporters tried to assassinate Newton. Pratt was caught in the middle. While recognizing and obeying Newton as the nominal leader of the party, he supported Cleaver.

That summer, Newton publicly and viciously expelled Pratt from the party, charging that Pratt's "devotion and allegiance was still to the ways and rules of the Pig Power Structure" and warning that any party member who attempted to aid or communicate with Pratt would be considered a part of the "conspiracy to undermine and destroy the Black Panther Party."

In mid-December 1968, while Pratt attended Panther meetings in Oakland, before he had risen to party leadership, Caroline Olsen was murdered on a tennis court in Santa Monica.

The crime was particularly senseless and brutal. On a chilly evening, the twenty-seven-year-old schoolteacher met her former husband, Kenneth, for a tennis date. Kenneth Olsen had just put coins in the court's timed lighting system when two young African American men approached the white couple and demanded money. The thieves took a total of eighteen dollars. Angered by the meager amount, one of the assailants ordered the couple to "lay down and pray." A few seconds later they shot Kenneth, who survived, and Caroline, who died.

Not long before the murder, Barbara Mary Reed, the elderly

Black Panther Party leader Geronimo Pratt, shown here in 1972 being taken to court, was wrongfully convicted of murder and spent twenty-five years in prison. Pratt and the Black Panthers were targets of the FBI's notorious COINTELPRO program.

white owner of the nearby Lincoln Hobby Center, reported to police that two young African American men had tried to enter her store. One had a pistol.

Santa Monica police detectives had Olsen and Reed review mug shots for nearly a year to no avail. At one point, Olsen picked a man out of a lineup, and police believed they had finally cracked the case until they learned that on the night of the murder the suspect was in Tracy, more than three hundred miles from the murder scene, in prison.

Trapping a Panther

The investigation appeared to be stalled until a surprising letter ended up with the LAPD. The letter, written by Julius Butler a few days after Pratt expelled him from the Black Panther Party, charged that Pratt had bragged about killing Caroline Olsen. Butler claimed that Pratt and other Panther leaders were threatening to murder him because he knew too much. He handed the letter to his friend DuWayne Rice, an

LAPD sergeant, on a Los Angeles street corner. It was in a sealed envelope with the words "to be opened in the event of my death."

Immediately after Butler handed Rice the letter and turned to leave, two men approached Rice, identified themselves as FBI agents, and demanded the letter, claiming it was evidence. When Rice refused to hand it over, the FBI contacted Rice's LAPD superiors. In October 1970, LAPD officers opened the nine-page letter leading to Geronimo Pratt's arrest.

Pratt was incredulous when he learned that he had been secretly indicted by the district attorney, on the basis of testimony from his former rival.

Police investigators received other leads about the Olsen murder but did not pursue them. As far as they were concerned, they had their man.

By the time of Pratt's trial, both Kenneth Olsen and Barbara Reed testified without hesitation, despite their earlier descriptions to the contrary, that Pratt was one of the men they had seen on the night of Caroline Olsen's murder. Prosecutors nevertheless faced a problem: the police could not match Pratt's gun to the bullets that killed Olsen. Julius Butler conveniently testified that Pratt had told him he had changed barrels on the gun. Under questioning from Pratt's attorney, Johnnie Cochran, Sergeant Rice admitted that Julius Butler was a police informant. Butler emphatically denied it.

Several Panther leaders could have vouched for Pratt's presence in Oakland during the Olsen murder, but by then Huey Newton had ordered his supporters not to help Pratt.

The jury deliberated for ten days to reach a guilty verdict. Upon hearing the decision, Pratt stood up in the courtroom and shouted, "You're wrong. I did not kill that woman!"

Pratt spent the first eight years of his sentence in solitary confinement in prison cells that consisted only of a concrete floor, a hole for a toilet, and a metal slab for a bed. He not only survived but earned the respect of prison personnel and fellow prisoners. One of his prison counselors wrote that Pratt was "remarkably free of rancor, bitterness, and self-pity. He has shown absolutely no hint of racial hatred attributed to him by the various law enforcement personnel responsible for his apprehension and prosecution. Pratt holds no animosity toward those individuals that contributed to his incarceration and states that they were as much a target and a victim of the situation as was he."

Exposing COINTELPRO

In 1976, a few years into Pratt's imprisonment, the U.S. Senate Select Committee to Study Governmental Operations with Respect to Intelligence Activities, headed by Idaho Democrat Frank Church, released a report that shocked the nation.

The Church report revealed that a primary goal of the FBI COINTELPRO program was to destabilize, undermine, and destroy an array of African American organizations, including the NAACP, the Southern Christian Leadership Conference, and the Black Panther Party.

In 1968, just two years after the party was founded, FBI director J. Edgar Hoover cited the Black Panthers as "the greatest threat to the internal security of the country" and ordered fourteen field offices to "submit imaginative and hard-hitting counterintelligence measures aimed at crippling the BPP."

Calling COINTELPRO a "vigilante operation," the Church report revealed covert FBI methods such as mailing anonymous accusations of infidelity to the spouses of targeted individuals, using informants to stir dissent, falsely labeling party members as informants, and encouraging street warfare between groups.

The Church committee reported that in Los Angeles the FBI aimed to exacerbate an existing conflict between the Panthers and the United Slaves (US). In 1970 agents at the FBI's Los Angeles field office sent a report to FBI headquarters explaining, "It is intended that US Inc. will be appropriately and discreetly advised of the time and location of BPP activities in order that the two organizations might be brought together and thus grant nature the opportunity to take her due course."

The committee also revealed why Newton had so suddenly expelled Pratt from the party. A Los Angeles COINTELPRO agent had sent a forged letter and other false information to Newton accusing Pratt of brutalizing and mistreating party members.

Additional documents revealed that in June 1970 the FBI had sent a report on Pratt, along with his picture, to FBI offices in New York, New Haven, Atlanta, Chicago, Sacramento, San Diego, and San Francisco, explaining that "constant consideration is given to the possibility of utilization of counterintelligence measures with efforts being directed toward neutralizing Pratt as an effective BPP functionary."

The year the Church report was released, Stuart Hanlon, a young law student who was working on Pratt's legal appeals, called U.S. Representative Paul N. "Pete" McCloskey, a Republican representing the Palo Alto area. The independent-minded congressman was deeply disturbed by Pratt's plight and helped the legal team unearth FBI records. Over the course of two decades, Pratt's legal team uncovered more and more evidence that, at the least, called for a new trial: the FBI admitted that a COINTELPRO mole had been a part of Pratt's initial defense team; a Freedom of Information Act request revealed that FBI agents had met with Butler thirty-three times before and after the Olsen shooting; an FBI wiretap log proved Pratt had spoken on the phone from an Oakland house at the time of the Olsen murder.

The momentum for a new trial grew.

After sixteen parole denials and four judicial refusals to reopen his case, Pratt and his attorneys had tempered hopes for justice when, in 1996, they filed a fifth petition for a writ of habeas corpus to reopen the case. Investigators with the Los Angeles district attorney's office, preparing to dispute this latest legal challenge, checked the district attorney's files on informers. In a locked drawer, they found three "Confidential Informant" cards for Julius Butler that proved he was an informant at least six months before Pratt's 1972 trial. The district attorney's office was bound by legal ethics to share this critical revelation with Pratt's lawyers, who saw it as the "smoking gun" evidence that proved Pratt's initial trial was tainted. Had the jury known Butler was a paid informant, his testimony would not have been as credible.

After nearly twenty-five years in prison, Geronimo Pratt finally had the opportunity to reopen his case. But since that would involve calling a sitting Los Angeles judge—Richard Kalustian, the former district attorney who prosecuted Pratt—as a witness, the presiding judge recused himself and the entire Los Angeles judiciary. The case was reassigned to Orange County Superior Court Judge Everett W. Dickey, a conservative Republican. Pratt's team was steeled for yet another disappointment.

The trial provided defense attorney Johnnie Cochran an opportunity to do something he had waited decades to do: put Julius Butler under oath and question him about his role in Pratt's case. On the witness stand for two days of testimony, the sixty-one-year-old Butler, now an attorney dressed in a well-cut gray suit, danced around Cochran's questions about his role as an informer for the LAPD and the FBI. While adamantly rejecting that the term "informant" applied to him, Butler admitted that he provided both the FBI and the LAPD with information about the Panthers.

Other witnesses further undermined Butler's credibility, including a retired LAPD captain who agreed that the characterization "agent provocateur" could fit Butler's role within the Black Panther Party.

In May 1997, Judge Dickey issued a ruling that left Pratt's team breathless. The conservative judge wrote that Julius Butler had committed perjury during Pratt's initial trial and that Butler had provided information to law enforcement officers on the Black Panther Party for at least three years before the trial. That information, which the judge wrote was "obviously relevant to his credibility as a witness," had been withheld from Pratt's defense team in 1972. In Judge Dickey's opinion, it could have "put the whole case in a different light, and failure to disclose it undermines confidence in the verdict."

The judge also dismissed the testimony of Kenneth Olsen and Barbara Reed, who in 1972 had identified Pratt as Caroline Olsen's killer. "The possibility of unreliability of cross-racial identifications of strangers based on a brief period of observation under stressful conditions has become so well known in the years since the Pratt trial that judges now almost always specially instruct a jury on the subject," Judge Dickey stated. The jury deciding Geronimo Pratt's fate in 1972 had received no such instructions.

Judge Dickey reversed Geronimo Pratt's conviction. On June 10, 1997, he ordered Pratt released from prison on twenty-five thousand dollars' bail, a symbolic amount that Johnnie Cochran suggested: roughly one thousand dollars for each year Pratt was imprisoned.

Los Angeles District Attorney Gil Garcetti appealed, but public opinion was against him. The *San Francisco Chronicle* editorialized that Pratt should be released as a "fitting rebuke to a witch-hunting era." The *Los Angeles Times* counseled Garcetti to "distance his office from the improper tactics of an earlier district attorney's office."

In February 1999, the court of appeal unanimously ruled that Pratt had been denied a fair trial. The following day, Garcetti announced that he would not pursue the case.

With the prospect of another criminal trial eliminated, Pratt and his attorneys filed a civil rights lawsuit charging that a conspiracy among federal and local law enforcement officials resulted in his wrongful conviction and life sentence. The City of Los Angeles, five retired LAPD officers, seven former FBI agents, and Julius Butler were named as defendants. In May 2000, a federal judge in Los Angeles approved a settlement of $4.5 million to Pratt for wrongful imprisonment: $2.75 million to be paid by the City of Los Angeles and the remaining $1.75 million to be paid by the FBI.

Are Peace Activists Terrorists?

Three weeks after the 9/11 attacks, U.S. Attorney General John Ashcroft directed states to establish "counter-terrorist task forces." In response, Governor Gray Davis and Attorney General Bill Lockyer set up the California Anti-Terrorism Information Center, or CATIC, whose mandate was to collect "terrorist-related" information and disseminate it to local law enforcement.

CATIC cast a broad net. A bulletin issued in April 2002, for example, advised law enforcement agencies to keep an eye out for "events involving Middle Eastern festivities," including the popular annual Afghan New Year's Festival at the Alameda County Fairgrounds in Pleasanton.

As advisories warning of violence and potential terrorist activities were disseminated up and down the state, many individuals and groups—whose only "crime" was that their views clashed with government policy—found themselves under surveillance.

One of them was retired phone company worker Barry Reingold. FBI agents questioned him after he had a heated debate in the confines of his San Francisco health club over the bombing of Afghanistan. Another was Kate Raphael, who volunteered with Jewish Women for Peace, handing out fliers in downtown San Francisco. When she opened her door to find the FBI, she told the agent, "If it's your job to investigate Islamic fundamentalist terrorists, then it's your job to know that they don't hang out with Jewish lesbians in San Francisco."

Like peace activists in many cities, members of Peace Fresno organized vigils and demonstrations in response to the Bush administration's threats in early 2003 to wage war in Iraq. The community group was open to all who were willing to do the hard work of mobilizing against the impending war.

On the morning of September 1, 2003, elementary school teacher Camille Russell, the president of Peace Fresno, was shocked to read an obituary in the *Fresno Bee*. Under the photo of a Peace Fresno member, whom she knew as Aaron Stokes, was an announcement that a member of the sheriff's department, Aaron Kilner, had died in a motorcycle accident. Russell put two and two together: Kilner was an undercover agent spying on the group.

"We were shocked and deeply disturbed to discover that one of our members—who had quietly participated in meetings, vigils, and demonstrations for several months—turned out to be a government spy," said Russell. For six months, the anti-terrorism unit of the Fresno County sheriff's department had infiltrated and conducted undercover surveillance of Peace Fresno. Initially, the department defended its covert intelligence: "For the purpose of detecting or preventing terrorist activities,

Activists in Peace Fresno, a nonviolent organization protesting the war in Iraq, were stunned to learn that their group had been infiltrated by the anti-terrorism unit of the sheriff's department. Many similar organizations, including Raging Grannies and Gold Star Mothers for Peace, also came under government surveillance after 9/11.

the Fresno County sheriff's department may visit any place and attend any event that is open to the public on the same terms and conditions as members of the public generally," Sheriff Richard Pierce stated.

But the sheriff came under harsh criticism. The *Fresno Bee* editorialized, "At a time when the sheriff is saying he needs more money for officers we question using detectives' time to monitor a political group like Peace Fresno with apparently no evidence of criminal activity. This certainly raises questions about the sheriff's priorities."

After California Attorney General Lockyer investigated the infiltration of Peace Fresno and concluded that its members' constitutional rights had been violated, Sheriff Pierce may have realized that he had overstepped his bounds. He announced he would not run for reelection, ending a forty-year career in law enforcement.

A 2005 Mothers' Day peace demonstration in Sacramento also came under surveillance—from an even more unlikely quarter, a branch of the military. The protest, organized by Raging Grannies, Code Pink, and Gold Star Mothers for Peace, drew fifty women, some of whom had lost family members in Iraq. The women gathered at the state Vietnam Veterans Memorial to sing, pray, and read a peace proclamation, all under the watchful eye of the California National Guard.

Lt. Col. Stan Zezotarski justified sending his troops to spy on the protestors, saying, "Who knows who could infiltrate that type of group and try to stir something up? After all, we live in an age of terrorism, so who knows?"

This ruffled Attorney General Lockyer. "You have to wonder how monitoring the activities of soldiers' widows and orphans advances the anti-terrorism effort," he said. His sentiments were echoed by State Senator Joe Dunn, who launched an investigation leading to the dismantling of the National Guard's intelligence program in November 2005. "At least for now, the Guard leadership won't be tempted to engage in domestic surveillance activities in California, which are barred by federal law," Senator Dunn said warily.

On April 7, 2003, antiwar protestors from Direct Action to Stop the War set up a nonviolent picket line at the Port of Oakland to highlight the role of two shipping companies that were transporting weapons to Iraq.

Without notice, Oakland police in full riot gear attacked demonstrators with wooden dowels and shot them with sting-ball grenades and shot-filled beanbags. As the protestors fled, the officers kept firing. Demonstrator Willow Rosenthal was shot in the back of the calf as she attempted to comply with a police order to disperse. Dockworkers at the port rushed to help the injured protestors. Fifty-eight people were wounded, including nine longshoremen. The *New York Times* described the clash as "the most violent between protestors and the authorities anywhere in the country since the start of the war in Iraq."

The protestors' response was two-pronged. Represented by the National Lawyers Guild and the ACLU, they filed a federal lawsuit, *Local 10 ILWU v. City of Oakland*, claiming that the Oakland police used excessive force in violation of their First Amendment rights. In addition they planned another demonstration at the port a month later. The May 12 protest was peaceful: as four hundred demonstrators marched to the gates of the port, the police did not repeat their assault.

In his thirty years at the ACLU, attorney Alan Schlosser had protected the rights of many demonstrators—from Iranian students to Vietnam vets, and he was intrigued by the widely divergent police responses to the two demonstrations. He filed a Public Records Act request to determine what went on behind the scenes of the first protest to make the police react so harshly to the nonviolent demonstrators. He learned that CATIC had sent out an advisory to the Oakland Police Department warning of "potential violence." "The Constitution itself was a victim on April 7, " said Schlosser, "just like our clients."

Government documents revealed that before the second demonstration, Oakland police officers posing as activists had infiltrated Direct Action to Stop the War, the group organizing the march. The undercover officers attended planning meetings and were even selected to plan the protest route.

After these revelations became public, a state Justice Department spokesman, Mike Van Winkle, told the *Oakland Tribune*, "You can make an easy kind of link that if you have a protest group protesting a war where the cause that's being fought against is international terrorism, you might have terrorism at the [protest]...You can almost argue that a protest against that is a terrorist act."

In November 2004, the injured demonstrators were awarded a two-million-dollar settlement and the city agreed to a new crowd control policy prohibiting the use of dangerous weapons—including wooden bullets, sting-ball grenades, pepper spray, and police motorcycles—against protestors. "By this agreement, Oakland became the first city in the nation where demonstrators will not have to incur the risk of serious injury from these weapons as the price of exercising their First Amendment rights to protest and assemble," said Schlosser.

These exposés of surveillance forced Attorney General Lockyer to order CATIC to stop gathering information or issuing bulletins on individuals or organizations engaged in peaceful expressive activity. The state agency issued new guidelines specifically stating that political protests—including civil disobedience—cannot be considered terrorist activities.

— SEVEN —

MIGHTIER THAN THE SWORD

THE RIGHT TO FREE EXPRESSION

> Banning books is so utterly hopeless and futile. Ideas don't die because a
> book is forbidden reading.
>
> *—Gretchen Knief, Kern County librarian, 1939*

When Kern County librarian Gretchen Knief returned home from her vacation in
August 1939, the familiar landscape was attracting national attention.

The rich agricultural San Joaquin Valley, where Knief lived, was the setting of
John Steinbeck's best-selling novel *The Grapes of Wrath:*

> The spring is beautiful in California. Valleys in which the fruit blossoms
> are fragrant pink and white waters in a shallow sea. Then the first tendrils
> of the grapes, swelling from the old gnarled vines, cascade down to cover
> the trunks. The full green hills are round and soft as breasts. And on the
> level vegetable lands are the mile-long rows of pale green lettuce and the
> spindly little cauliflowers, the gray-green unearthly artichoke plants.

Though the book had just been published in April, it was already in its seventh
printing. At the Kern County Library, six hundred readers had reserved it.

But Steinbeck had also described another facet of California's Central Valley.
His story of the hardworking, downtrodden Joads, who lost their Oklahoma land
and headed West, hoping to survive by picking fruit on abundant farms, exposed the
sordid underbelly of California agriculture. He wrote of the "harvest gypsies" who
"swarm the highways...nomadic, poverty-stricken, driven by hunger and the threat
of hunger from crop to crop, from harvest to harvest."

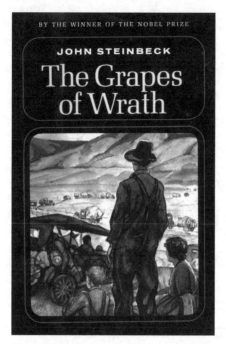

BY THE WINNER OF THE NOBEL PRIZE

JOHN STEINBECK

The Grapes
of Wrath

John Steinbeck's The Grapes of Wrath *was banned from the Kern County Library in 1939 because big farmers and county officials did not like the way the Nobel Prize–winning author depicted poverty and the plight of migrant farmworkers. The local librarian challenged the ban—and won.*

This powerful aspect of *The Grapes of Wrath* resulted in a surprise for librarian Knief. On her desk was an August 21 resolution from the Kern County Board of Supervisors ordering the book removed from the library shelves because "*The Grapes of Wrath* has offended our citizens by falsely implying that many of our fine people are shallow, ignorant, profane and blasphemous types living in a vicious filthy manner."

And who exactly were the "fine people" that the Kern County supervisors were trying so hard to protect?

Steinbeck's masterpiece grew out of his research for a series of articles in the *San Francisco News* about the mass migration of refugees from the Oklahoma Dust Bowl to California. Sensing that news articles would not attract enough attention to the plight of the wretchedly poor in the richest farmland of America, Steinbeck, a native of the agricultural Salinas Valley, set out to bring the migrants to life through his fiction.

At the end of the Joads' arduous trek to California, they find that jobs are scarce, pay is meager, and the squalid labor camps are crammed with thousands of other unemployed workers, as well as vermin and disease. Tom Joad joins a workers' strike for a living wage, realizing that "Hunger cannot be solved one person at a time, and hunger builds an angry response to exploitation. The great companies did not know that the line between hunger and anger is a thin line."

But the epic novel also is filled with hope and compassion. Not only does Tom take action and convince others to fight for a better life, but his sister Rose of Sharon—in one of the most unforgettable scenes in American literature—provides sustenance to a starving man with the milk from her breast.

It was a different group of "fine people" that the Kern County Board of Supervisors sought to protect by banning Steinbeck—the crew bosses, the labor contractors, and most of all, the large growers who exploited migrant workers for profit. Wofford

B. Camp, a prominent rancher and president of Associated Farmers of Kern County, called *The Grapes of Wrath* "propaganda of the vilest sort." Claiming to defend "our farm workers as well as ourselves when we take action against that book," he lobbied for the ban.

This is how Steinbeck depicted the Associated Farmers in *The Grapes of Wrath*:

> [T]he hostility changed them, welded them, united them—hostility that made the little towns group and arm as though to repel an invader, squads with pick handles, clerks and storekeepers with shotguns, guarding the world against their own people....The local people whipped themselves into a cold cruelty. Then they formed units, squads and armed themselves with clubs, with gas, with guns.

After their success in Kern County, the Associated Farmers launched a campaign to ban the book statewide, urging other counties to keep the novel out of libraries and schools. A photo in *Look* magazine showed Camp ceremoniously burning a copy of the book.

Steinbeck had anticipated the censors. He wrote in 1936, "When such a close-knit financial group as the Associated Farmers becomes excited about our ancient liberties and foreign agitators, someone is about to lose something."

Steinbeck was well aware that his writings would be considered inflammatory, but he wanted his book to be read widely. At his wife's suggestion, he had chosen the title from the lyrics of "The Battle Hymn of the Republic" to preempt the red-baiting he knew would greet its publication. He wrote to his editor at Viking, "The fascist crowds will try to sabotage this book because it is revolutionary. They'll try to give it the communist angle. However, the Battle Hymn is American and intensely so...if both words and music are there, the book is keyed into the American scene from the beginning."

Librarian Knief was dismayed by the ban. She wrote the board of supervisors:

> If that book is banned today, what book will be banned tomorrow? And what group will want a book banned the day after that? In the interest of a healthy and vigorous democracy, where everyone can speak his mind freely and without fear, and for the sake of the 600 readers in Kern County who wish to read the book, please rescind today's vote when you meet next Monday.

Noting this was the first instance of censorship in the library's history, Knief added, "[B]anning books is so utterly hopeless and futile. Ideas don't die because a book is forbidden reading. If Steinbeck has written truth, that truth will survive."

Scores of library patrons joined Knief's protest. A broad coalition, from religious leaders to trade unionists, registered opposition, as did the Workers Alliance, an organization of the unemployed.

On the morning of August 28, hours before the board's debate was scheduled to start, the Bakersfield courthouse was packed. Outside, pickets from the Workers Alliance carried banners urging the board to lift the ban.

When the debate began, members of the Associated Farmers denounced the book as "obscene." One pro-censorship speaker said, "You can't argue with a book like that; it is too filthy for you to go over the various parts and point out the vile propaganda it contains. Americans have a right to say what they please but they do not have the right to attack a community in such works that any red-blooded American man would refuse to allow his daughter to read them."

Opposing the ban, the Reverend Edgar J. Evans said the book was one of the most moving he had ever read and wondered if the censors objected not to the language but "the exposure of a sociological condition."

At the end of the meeting, the motion to rescind the ban lost, 2-2.

Librarian Knief did not give up. She distributed sixty copies of *The Grapes of Wrath* to other public libraries around the state.

The ban was not lifted until January 27, 1941.

Steinbeck's legacy and that of the Joads have long outlived the shortsighted ban on his novel. Steinbeck was honored with the Nobel Prize for Literature in 1962, and though it was awarded after the publication of his many other books, it is often presumed that the prize was really for *The Grapes of Wrath*.

The attempt by the Associated Farmers and their political henchman on the Kern County Board of Supervisors to ban *The Grapes of Wrath* provides a worthy introduction to the topic of censorship in California. During different eras throughout the state's history, censors have applied their scissors to works that threatened the powers that be.

Painting the Town Red

The Depression was tough on California artists. Already living on the economic edge, many promising painters, sculptors, and writers faced hardship as the financial crisis deepened.

Influenced by the public art of the bold Mexican muralist Diego Rivera and seeking to ease their financial burdens, several well-known San Franciscans, including painters Bernard Zakheim and Victor Arnautoff and poet Kenneth Rexroth, lobbied the government to provide work for local artists.

Their idea fell on sympathetic ears. Painter George Biddle, a personal friend and former Harvard classmate of Franklin D. Roosevelt, encouraged the president to provide relief for American artists through a federally funded program under the New

Deal. Though from a mainline Philadelphia family (his brother Francis later became Roosevelt's attorney general and would play a pivotal role in the internment of Japanese Americans during World War II) and a graduate of elite private schools, Biddle was also greatly influenced by the social realism of Diego Rivera, with whom he had traveled through Mexico. Biddle's proposal eventually resulted in the Public Works Art Project, a federal agency that sponsored literature, theater, and visual arts.

San Francisco painters and muralists embraced the program. The city's arts patrons were less enthusiastic. They were aware that in southern California, murals by Rivera's fellow Mexican artists José Clemente Orozco and David Alvaro Siqueiros had drawn the ire of authorities because of their political militancy and heretical content. In 1930 Pomona College trustees, joined by the local press, attacked the vivid *Prometheus* that Orozco had painted in the Pomona College dining hall, because of its daring depiction of the naked male body. Despite the outcry, the revolutionary mural remained because students rallied to Orozco's support. The fate of Siqueiros's *Tropical America*, painted in 1932 on an exterior wall of the Italian Hall on Olvera Street in Los Angeles, was not so felicitous. The mural depicted a crucified Mexican peasant, with an American eagle perching on the cross. Angry authorities had the mural whitewashed; only when the whitewash began to peel decades later was it rediscovered and restored.

The San Francisco artists' persistent lobbying eventually overcame elite fears about local public works projects. In 1933 the Public Works Art Project chose twenty-five painters to create murals on the interior walls of Coit Tower, on the theme "Aspects of Life in California—1934." At the time, no one imagined what a momentous year that would be for San Francisco—with the militant waterfront strike, the deaths of two strikers, and the General Strike. The federal arts administrator chose Arnautoff, who had worked with Rivera in Mexico City and Cuernavaca, to direct the project.

With government funds and the reluctant blessings of the elite San Francisco Arts Commission, work began on the murals in January 1934. Within a month, the artists learned that men armed with pickaxes had destroyed Rivera's celebrated mural *Man at the Crossroads* in New York's Rockefeller Center because the muralist refused to remove a portrait of Lenin. On hearing the news, the San Francisco Artists and Writers Union staged a sympathy protest at Coit Tower, drawing media attention. The Hearst-owned *Examiner* published an "exposé" of the subversive content of the Coit Tower murals, complaining that the news racks in Arnautoff's mural showed the left-wing *New Masses* and *Daily Worker*; a miner was depicted reading the *Western Worker* in a mural by John Langley Howard; and in the library scene by Bernhard Zakheim, a library patron was reaching for Karl Marx's *Das Kapital*. The worst offense, however, according to the *Examiner*, was Clifford Wright's drawing of a hammer and sickle over a window, accompanied by the slogan "Workers of the World Unite."

In 1953 a congressional inquiry supported by Vice President Richard Nixon investigated Anton Refregier's murals in San Francisco's Rincon Annex Post Office. The murals, like this painting of a workers' march, survived the inquisition and are on the National Register of Historic Places.

The *Examiner* ran a doctored photo of the hammer and sickle, making the image appear to be central to the mural, and urged the Arts Commission to stop the artists' subversive message. The photo ran on July 5, the same day police killed two workers in the waterfront strike, throwing San Francisco into turmoil. The Arts Commission inspected the murals, confirmed that they were in "opposition to the generally accepted tradition of native Americanism," and called a halt to the painting. Coit Tower was padlocked.

The doors were not opened again until after the dock strike was settled, more than three months later. The offending hammer, sickle, and slogan had been painted out. Even then, the critics were not appeased. An editorial in the *Stockton Record* proclaimed "Red Tint on Coit Tower."

Anton Refregier's murals at San Francisco's Rincon Annex Post Office faced even more severe opposition—a congressional inquisition.

In 1941 the U.S. Treasury Section of Painting and Sculpture (the successor to the Public Works Art Project) selected Refregier to create murals depicting California history on the walls of San Francisco's new post office. The artist, born in Russia, had come to the United States in 1920 to attend art school and then settled in Woodstock, New York; a celebrated painter, he had created large-scale public art for the 1933 Chicago World's Fair.

Refregier's San Francisco murals encircled the lobby of the large post office, which was located at the intersection where police had gunned down the two workers during the waterfront strike. His work seems imbued with the laborers' spirits, because he depicted California history through a working-class lens: Native Americans who tilled the land of the Spanish missions, miners who panned for gold, Chinese immigrants who built the railroads, and longshoremen—pictured both begging for work from a straw boss and marching for better working conditions.

Refregier's vision drew attacks from many quarters. First, the Catholic Church complained because a mural of a Spanish mission included a friar who was too fat. Refregier trimmed the cleric's waistline. In *Torchlight Procession*, depicting an 1867 workers' march, Refregier originally had a marcher carrying an "8 Hour Day" sign. When government authorities criticized the piece as too pro-labor, Refregier painted out the sign. The Public Buildings Administration, now controlled by Republicans who disparaged the New Deal, demanded that President Roosevelt's image be removed from the final panel, *War and Peace*. Though at first Refregier resisted, he later acquiesced by instead picturing the four freedoms—freedom from want and fear, and freedom of speech and worship—that Roosevelt had famously delineated in a 1941 speech. In 1948 the Veterans of Foreign Wars (VFW) objected to the inclusion of the longshoremen's strike. Under pressure from the VFW, the Public Buildings Administration covered the offending panel. Refregier wrote, "It was a most telling coincidence that on the day the men came to cover up this panel, I was at work on a mural depicting the burning of books by the Nazis."

Requests to alter the murals were not the only obstacles Refregier faced: the innovative muralist also received threats. In an unpublished account discovered by historian Gray Brechin in the Smithsonian, the artist wrote, "The stories in the Hearst press brought out gangs of hoodlums who were constantly under my scaffolding and I no longer worked after the sun set."

In 1952 Refregier wrote to the *Chronicle*'s art critic in defense of his murals: "We rejected long ago, while on the federal arts projects, the meaningless type of mural painting where the pioneer, dressed in Hollywood fashions, shaven and manicured, would be briskly walking along guided by a 'spirit' of one thing or another, its Grecian garments floating in the wind. This concept pays disrespect to the vitality, power, and labor of those who came before us."

The censors found a champion in an up-and-coming congressman from southern California, Representative Richard Nixon. Responding to a letter from an American Legionnaire complaining about the "Communist art" in the post office, Nixon promised that when the next round of elections produced "a change in the administration and a majority in Congress, I believe [there will be] a thorough investigation of this type of art in government buildings with the view to obtaining the removal of all that is found to be inconsistent with American ideals and principles."

That day came on May 1, 1953: Nixon was vice president, the Republicans were dominant in Congress, and Representative Hubert Scudder of Sebastopol proposed in a congressional hearing to take down the murals.

Representative Scudder opened the hearing by announcing that he had received complaints about the murals from the American Legion, the Daughters of the

American Revolution, the VFW, the Associated Farmers, and other organizations, and that he himself was concerned that the works by the "Moscow-born" Refregier "do not truly depict the romance and glory of early California history....[are] definitely subversive and designed to spread communist propaganda and tend to promote racial hatred and class warfare."

He objected specifically to the mural *Beating the Chinese*, depicting the Sandlot riots, in which an Irish worker forcibly cuts off a Chinese man's queue, and *The Waterfront—1934*, because it showed "strikes and other disturbances" that are not the "things that make California great."

California Representative Donald Jackson followed, and for forty-five minutes detailed Refregier's political associations and activities, including a reception he organized to honor Los Angeles painter Charles White, "a Negro artist." Representative Jackson admitted that he had never actually seen the Rincon Annex murals.

One critic from the American Legion argued that because the dominant color in three panels was red, "These murals are definitely subversive and designed to spread communistic propaganda."

Refregier had his defenders as well.

Congressman John Shelley (who became mayor of San Francisco a decade later), established his credibility by telling the committee he was a Catholic, a descendant of Irish pioneers, and a member of the Native Sons of the Golden West. "The cold factual portrayal of history...may be pleasing to some and repugnant to others, but if it is factual you cannot change history or a picture of history or a portrayal of it by saying, 'I do not like that.' Mr. Chairman, then we are definitely contributing to thought control and trying to build a Nation of Conformists."

Leading art critics and the directors of three San Francisco museums and two historical societies supported Shelley's testimony. The director of the San Francisco Museum of Art said the work was "high among the distinguished American murals of recent years." Sadly, one museum official said he had watched as many as eight hundred people using the post office, but "not one person even looked at the murals."

Five weeks after the hearing, the California State Senate passed a resolution urging Congress to take down the murals. The *Examiner* applauded the move, saying the murals should be removed if "loyal American citizens found them subversive."

But Representative Scudder's proposal did not get out of committee, and the murals remained.

In 1978 the post office was closed, but artist Emmy Lou Packard fought to save the murals, as she had earlier advocated to preserve the Coit Tower artwork. In 1979, the year Refregier died, his murals were declared an official San Francisco City Landmark.

In 1987 the Rincon Center was reopened as an office tower. The murals in the lobby were restored by artist Thomas Portue. In one of them, *San Francisco as a Cultural Center*, Refregier had included a depiction of ghostlike WPA artists painting and sculpting, their pale images fading into the background. It was a prescient commentary on the disappearance of the federally funded program that brought vibrant art to the public spaces of San Francisco.

Sex and the U.S. Mail

In the late 1940s, Ernest Besig, executive director of the ACLU of Northern California, began a voluminous correspondence with U.S. customs and postal authorities, challenging restrictions on publications that were banned from entering the United States, from Scandinavian erotic magazines and the works of Shakespeare in Russian to Communist Chinese publications. According to former ACLU-NC Legal Director Marshall Krause, Besig kept looking for materials that reasonably could be judged obscene, "but he never found any!" It was as if Besig presaged the remarks of U.S. Supreme Court Justice Potter Stewart in a famous 1964 decision: obscenity is hard to define, "but I know it when I see it."

In 1950 Besig found the book to challenge the censorship laws.

Henry Miller's *Tropic of Cancer* was first published in Paris in 1934. It was officially banned in the U.S. for three decades. The bawdy, stream-of-consciousness tale of a young man's sexual romp and personal angst was popular among intellectuals, bohemians, and American expatriates in Europe, but U.S. government officials kept it from readers in the author's homeland.

In 1950 Besig attempted to import both *Tropic of Cancer* and its sequel, *Tropic of Capricorn*, into the United States to initiate a test case. As he had expected, U.S. customs officials refused to relinquish the imported books. Besig sued in federal court.

At a non-jury trial in 1951, Judge Louis Goodman ruled against Besig, stating, "It is sufficient to say that the many obscene passages in the books have such an evil stench that to include them here in footnotes would make this opinion pornographic."

Besig appealed, but in October 1953 the Ninth Circuit Court of Appeals also declared the books obscene. Judge Albert Lee Stephens stated that they contained the "unprintable words of the debased and morally bankrupt" and "lacked literary merit."

Read All about It: Hoover and the Gay Magazine

While Besig was fighting to protect erotica in Miller's book, a gay publication in Los Angeles faced harsher scrutiny. In late 1952, members of Knights of the Clock, a Los Angeles group for mixed-race gay couples also involved with the Los Angeles chapter of the Mattachine Society, a national organization working for gay equality, came up with the radical idea of publishing a magazine for and by gay people. A diverse group including Martin Block, a Bronx-raised bookstore owner; Don Slater, a recent USC English literature graduate and his musician lover, Antonio Sanchez; Dale Jennings, a World War II veteran; African American accountant Merton Bird; lesbian couple Joan Corbin and Irma "Corky" Wolf; and Knights of the Clock and Mattachine member W. Dorr Legg formed "ONE Incorporated," the entity that would publish *ONE*, the first gay publication in the nation. After several issues, *ONE*'s staff boldly printed "The Homosexual Magazine" on the cover of each copy.

Postal officials confiscated the August 1954 issue to determine whether the publication was obscene. Jim Kepner, a *ONE* staff member, later speculated:

> I think the reason behind the post office's seizure…was an article in the previous issue suggesting that everybody knew J. Edgar Hoover was sleeping with Clyde Tolson, his close partner. That article attracted the interest of the FBI. Much later, through the Freedom of Information Act, we found a note from Hoover to Tolson saying, "We've got to get these bastards." There was also a note to the post office from Hoover urging them to check into *ONE*.

Around the time of the confiscation, FBI agents climbed the creaky stairs to *ONE*'s shabby second-floor offices on South Hill Street in downtown Los Angeles. Secondhand office furniture filled the two rooms. The agents demanded the address and phone number of the anonymous author who had written about Hoover and Tolson, claiming that the article bordered on libel. *ONE*'s editors were appalled. In a subsequent issue they wrote, "Is it not a commentary on the lack of understanding of even the most basic of American freedoms that members of a public agency should for a moment suppose that they would be permitted to tamper with freedom of the press? That *ONE* would ever stoop to compromising its writers, staff members, or subscribers is completely unthinkable."

FBI agents also questioned *ONE* staff members at their homes. Kepner recalled:

> They asked me if a couple of members of the staff were Communists and I hooted and said that they were very conservative. They were. I probably shouldn't have even told them that. I did say that I was a member of the Communist Party and that I had been kicked out for being gay. They wanted me to name people I had known in the party and what they did. I owed no thanks to the party for kicking me out, but I would never give information about individuals who were in the party, whom I still respected.

ONE staff contacted Eric Julber, a twenty-nine-year-old attorney just two years out of Loyola Law School, because he had successfully defended an African American victim of police abuse. They asked the young lawyer to convince the post office to return the confiscated copies of the magazine. Julber recognized that the post office's seizure was clearly government censorship, and he agreed to help. But before he could act, the solicitor general decided that the issue in question was not obscene, and the post office returned the copies.

At the time, subscribing to an openly homosexual publication, even one mailed discreetly in a plain envelope, was by no means an easy decision. Homosexuality was illegal in every state. Post office employees spied into the mail of suspected homosexuals, some of whom lost their jobs because they received gay publications.

Despite these real threats, by October 1954, *ONE* had 1,650 subscribers. Many of them never received their October issue. Los Angeles postmaster Otto K. Olesen seized that issue on instruction of the U.S. Postal Department in Washington, which banned the magazine under a law that forbade the mailing of any "obscene, lewd, lascivious or filthy" publication. "You Can't Print That" was the large headline on the cover of that issue, which included an explanation by attorney Julber of what constituted obscenity. In response to the government's censorship, the maverick staff of *ONE* sued Olesen.

As evidence that the October 1954 issue of *ONE* was obscene, federal authorities cited "Sappho Remembered," a melodramatic short story about a love affair between two women; a bawdy poem entitled "Lord Samuel and Lord Montagu" satirizing the arrests of several prominent British men on "morals" charges; and a small advertisement for a Swiss magazine that published gay pulp romances.

Julber defended *ONE* before Federal Judge Thurmond Clarke, who ruled that the October 1954 issue was "filthy and obscene" and that "the suggestion advanced that homosexuals should be recognized as a segment of our people and be accorded special privileges as a class is rejected."

After the Ninth Circuit upheld the ruling, Julber appealed to the U.S. Supreme Court, arguing that the publishers were denied equal protection because they were held to a higher standard than other publishers.

On January 13, 1958, in a one-sentence ruling, the Supreme Court announced that it had reversed the lower courts' rulings. The high court based its decision on *Roth v. United States*, a recent case in which "obscenity" had been defined as material, taken as a whole, whose dominant theme would seem, to "the average person, applying contemporary community standards," to appeal to "prurient interests." It was the first time that the Supreme Court had heard a case dealing explicitly with homosexuality, and the high court stated that homosexual content did not automatically define a publication as "obscene."

In the next issue of *ONE*, volunteer Don Slater wrote, "*ONE Magazine* has made not only history but law as well and has changed the future for all U.S. homosexuals. Never before have homosexuals claimed their rights as citizens."

Howl Puts Censorship on Trial

Lawrence Ferlinghetti arrived in San Francisco with the dream of opening a bookstore where poetry could thrive. During World War II, the military had sent the lanky New York poet to Nagasaki six weeks after the U.S. dropped a nuclear bomb there. When he was discharged he went to Paris, earning a doctorate in poetry at the Sorbonne.

In 1953, two years after settling in San Francisco, Ferlinghetti and his business partner Peter Martin founded City Lights bookstore—named for the Charlie Chaplin film—on a well-traveled corner between Chinatown and the Italian American enclave of North Beach, known for espresso shops and bars where artists congregated.

By 1956 City Lights and Ferlinghetti were part of a growing, revolutionary poetry scene. In the *New York Times Book Review*, Richard Eberhart noted, "The West Coast is the liveliest spot in the country in poetry today. It is only here that there is a radical regroupment of young poets. San Francisco teems with young poets." Eberhart made special note of Ferlinghetti's friend Allen Ginsberg, whose poetry was "a howl against everything in our mechanistic civilization which kills the spirit."

Ferlinghetti had published Ginsberg's poetry in a slim, black-and-white volume entitled *Howl and Other Poems*. The opening lines took the post–World War II literary world by storm:

> I saw the best minds of my generation destroyed
> by madness, starving hysterical naked,
> dragging themselves through the Negro streets at dawn looking for an
> angry fix,
> angelheaded hipsters burning for the ancient heavenly connection to the
> starry dynamo in the machinery of night,
> who poverty and tatters and hollow-eyed and high sat up smoking in the
> supernatural darkness of cold-water flats floating across the tops of
> cities contemplating jazz

While the authors and artists of San Francisco celebrated their newfound voices, law enforcement saw *Howl*, City Lights, and Ferlinghetti in a different light.

In June 1957, just a few years after City Lights opened its doors, two San Francisco police officers entered the bookstore and for seventy-five cents bought a copy of Ginsberg's forty-four-page *Howl and Other Poems*. That purchase (as well as an issue of a small-circulation literary publication, *The Miscellaneous Man*) was the basis for the arrest of Ferlinghetti and bookstore worker Shigeyoshi Murao for "willfully and lewdly printing, publishing, and selling obscene and indecent writing, papers, and books."

Captain William A. Hanrahan of the Juvenile Bureau explained, "We purchased each of these books and found them lewd. They are not fit for children to read." Ferlinghetti and Murao faced up to six months in county jail and a fine of five hundred dollars. The ACLU-NC bailed them out and took on their defense.

Ferlinghetti recalled, "I took it as just another expression of a police mentality that was very prominent in that decade. We didn't have a cent. If it hadn't been for the ACLU, we'd be out of business."

But if Ferlinghetti was a green-horn bookseller, attorney Al Bendich was even greener at the law. An impish, rosy-cheeked recent law school graduate, he had only been on the ACLU staff for a year when Executive Director Besig

In 1957 police arrested poet Lawrence Ferlinghetti for selling the Beat poet Allen Ginsberg's Howl *at his City Lights bookstore in San Francisco's North Beach. Ferlinghetti, pictured here, was acquitted and more than a million copies of the book are in print.*

asked him to join the legal team to defend the poet and his bookstore.

During the first round of the trial in August, San Francisco Municipal Court Judge Clayton Horn, sitting without a jury, dismissed the charges against Murao. The assistant district attorney stipulated that there was no evidence that the store employee knew the contents of *Howl* or had intended to sell obscene publications. Judge Horn also determined that *The Miscellaneous Man* would be ruled out as evidence against Ferlinghetti.

At the request of prominent criminal defense attorney Jake Ehrlich, who volunteered his services to the ACLU, Judge Horn ruled that he would permit literary experts to testify on the merits of *Howl*, and on the relationship of the alleged vulgar expressions in the book to the development of the poem's main theme.

Ehrlich, Bendich, and Lawrence Speiser formed the legal team that mobilized support for the poet and his bookstore. On a pad of lined yellow paper, attorney Ehrlich jotted down lists of prominent literary figures whom the defense would call to testify to the literary merit of the poem: the names of novelists Wallace Stegner,

James Baldwin, and John Steinbeck, poets Josephine Miles and Richard Wilbur, and Random House publisher Bennett Cerf were scrawled across the page.

Twenty-one San Francisco booksellers petitioned Mayor George Christopher to end police censorship of books, stating, "This sort of censorship has no place in a democratic society and is harmful to San Francisco's reputation as a center of culture and enlightenment."

The defense put nine expert witnesses on the stand and included letters from political novelist Eugene Burdick, poet Kenneth Rexroth, then literary editor of the *San Francisco Chronicle*, and editors from publishing companies and literary magazines across the country.

In closing arguments, Ehrlich read a poem by the sixteenth-century poet Christopher Marlowe that contained the same four-letter word cited by prosecutor Ralph McIntosh as evidence of *Howl*'s obscenity. Speiser read passages from the Bible, Balzac, Shakespeare, and James Joyce's *Ulysses* to show that they could all be compared to *Howl* for erotic content.

Attorney Bendich quoted the Bible, II Kings 18:27, as an example of great literature which would fall under the same ban if the prosecution's argument that mere dirty words and vulgar expressions "should be kept from decent homes." Bendich concluded by reminding the court that *Howl*, a poem of social criticism, was protected by the First Amendment unless it could be shown that the work presented a clear and present danger of a substantive evil.

The closely watched trial ended with a landmark ruling from Judge Horn, who wrote in his thirty-eight-page opinion, "In considering material to be obscene, it is well to remember the motto *Honi soit qui mal y pense*, 'Evil to him who thinks evil.'" Judge Horn noted:

> The theme [of *Howl*] presents unorthodox and controversial ideas. Coarse and vulgar language is used in treatment and sex acts are mentioned, but unless the book is entirely lacking in social importance, it cannot be held obscene...
>
> There are a number of words used in *Howl* that are presently considered coarse and vulgar in some circles of the community. In other circles such words are in everyday use. It would be unrealistic to deny these facts. The author of *Howl* has used these words because he believed that his portrayal required them as being in character. The People state that it is not necessary to use such words and that others would be more palatable to good taste.
>
> The answer is that life is not encased in one formula whereby everyone acts the same or conforms to a particular pattern. Would there be any freedom of the press or speech if one must reduce his vocabulary to vapid innocuous euphemism?

Life magazine called the decision a "Big Day for Bards at Bay" and anointed Ferlinghetti the "poetical pillar of the San Francisco spondee and trochee set." *Howl and Other Poems* quickly went into its fourth printing.

Back to the Tropics

In 1961 Ernest Besig was vindicated. U.S. Attorney General Robert Kennedy determined that *Tropic of Cancer* was constitutionally protected; he prohibited the post office and customs officials from blocking its distribution. But it was not the end of attempts to censor the book.

The year Kennedy lifted the ban, U.S.-based Grove Press published an American edition of the book and committed itself to assisting every bookseller that was prosecuted for selling it. By then, California officials were blocking book sales by invoking a state law that defined obscenity as matter that the average person, applying contemporary community standards, would believe appealed to "prurient interests," and materials which were "utterly without redeeming social importance."

In March 1962, San Diego booksellers Geraldine and Laurence McGilvery were charged with selling *Tropic of Cancer* to an undercover police cadet.

The McGilverys were acquitted by a superior court jury, who found them not guilty of selling obscene literature as defined by the statute. Judge Edward Schwartz told the jury he agreed with their verdict, concluding that it was in accordance with a U.S. Supreme Court ruling that "fundamental freedoms of speech and press have contributed greatly to the development and well-being of our free society and our indispensable growth."

However, a Los Angeles jury convicted Bradley Smith, a Hollywood bookseller, under the same statute for selling a copy of the same novel to a vice officer. The California cases were among seventy prosecutions nationwide for the sale of Miller's *Tropic of Cancer*.

The varied outcomes in different courts in different states created a dilemma for publishers, booksellers, and readers. To clarify the law, the ACLU decided to go on the offensive. In 1962 attorneys A. L. Wirin and Fred Okrand filed a suit on behalf of Los Angeles bookseller Jacob Zeitlin, manager of the Zeitlin and VerBrugge bookstore, and Los Angeles Community College English instructor Paul Ferguson. They claimed that the city's interpretation of the law denied them their right to sell and read the controversial book. They sought a judgment declaring sale of the book legal under California law and an injunction preventing the city attorney from prosecuting any bookseller who sold the novel.

Though lower courts ruled against the bookseller and professor, the California

Supreme Court took a different view, annulling the city's ban on *Tropic of Cancer* in 1963. The unanimous decision, written by Justice Matthew Tobriner, struck a decisive blow against official book censorship.

A year later, the U.S. Supreme Court issued a similar ruling in a Florida case, *Grove Press v. Gerstein.* Justice William Brennan wrote for the five-judge majority that "material dealing with sex in a manner that advocates ideas, or that has literary or scientific or artistic value or other form of social importance, may not be branded obscenity and denied the constitutional protection."

It seemed that the U.S. Supreme Court might do away with all obscenity prosecutions. But in June 1973, in another California case, *Miller v. California*, the high court again altered the standard, making criminal convictions for obscenity easier to obtain. In the majority opinion by Chief Justice Warren Burger, the Court lowered the standard of proof for prosecution from "utterly without redeeming social value" to "lacking serious literary, artistic, political, or scientific value."

The Court decided that instead of a national standard, the definition of obscenity would be set by "community standards." As Justice Burger explained, the Court saw no reason why "the people of Maine or Mississippi" had to "accept public depiction of conduct found tolerable in Las Vegas or New York City."

Since *Miller*, every case challenging censorship must show that the material in question has serious literary, artistic, political, or scientific value—a standard that has been interpreted in many ways over the decades.

The Power of the Press

Los Angeles Mayor Sam Yorty fumed when he opened the *Los Angeles Times* on November 19, 1968, and saw himself depicted in a political cartoon by Paul Conrad. At a press conference a few days earlier, the mayor had announced his desire that President-elect Richard Nixon appoint him Secretary of Defense. Conrad's drawing depicts medical attendants, equipped with a straitjacket, beckoning Yorty as he speaks on the telephone. In the caption the mayor says, "I've got to go now...I've been appointed Secretary of Defense and the Secret Service men are here!"

Mayor Yorty filed a libel suit against the paper, asking two million dollars in damages and contending that the cartoon maliciously implied that he was unfit to be Secretary of Defense and that he was insane if he believed himself to be qualified for the post. The mayor asserted he was under Nixon's consideration for a cabinet appointment.

ACLU attorneys A. L. Wirin and Fred Okrand, recognizing the danger to freedom of the press, submitted an amicus brief in support of the *Los Angeles Times*, arguing that if Mayor Yorty "is permitted to prosecute...or recovers damages, it will have a considerable inhibiting effect on what to many is the main purpose of the First Amendment: the right of, and the need for, the public to know and be informed in order that there may be true democratic government."

The real threat of the suit, the brief stated, is that "less sturdy or less affluent publications (the organs of small or unpopular groups, the voices of dissent) will be chilled and deterred from expressing opinions on important public matters."

To prove their point about the absurdity of Yorty's lawsuit, Wirin and Okrand delved into the history of political cartooning. They submitted to the court a Currier and Ives lithograph published

"I've got to go now...
I've been appointed Secretary of Defense and the Secret Service men are here!

Los Angeles Mayor Sam Yorty sued the Los Angeles Times *for libel when it ran this cartoon in 1968. Dismissing his claim, the judge noted the long history of political cartooning and its importance to freedom of the press.*

during the 1860 presidential election portraying "utopian supporters" marching with Lincoln to an asylum; the caption read "The Republican Party going to the Right House."

In 1970 State Court of Appeal Judge Macklin Fleming ruled out the possibility that the cartoon could be interpreted as a news report that Yorty was mentally ill. "From the cartoon," the judge wrote, "no reasonable person would assume more than that in the opinion of the *Los Angeles Times* the mayor was not qualified for the post of Secretary of Defense, President-elect Nixon would not appoint him, and it was foolish of the mayor to aspire to an appointment for which he was not qualified."

"The political cartoon has occupied a central position in the presentation of critical comment on events and personages of the times," Judge Fleming stated, adding "to penalize defendants for publishing this political cartoon would subvert the most fundamental meaning of a free press."

Mayor Yorty was not the only public official to try to thwart the sting of press criticism. In 1976 a San Francisco district attorney and two law enforcement officers filed a libel suit against the *San Francisco Examiner* and two reporters over a series of news stories about a Chinatown murder case.

Examiner staff reporter Raul Ramirez and freelancer Lowell Bergman wrote the series about the trial of a Chinatown youth accused of murder in 1972. Ramirez and Bergman questioned the law enforcement officials' use of a jailhouse snitch, Thomas Porter, as a key prosecution witness. Porter told the journalists that police officers had physically assaulted him to force his cooperation. After the articles were published, Porter changed his story again, saying he lied about the officers' behavior.

Reacting to the paper's allegations that police and prosecutorial misconduct had taken place, former Assistant District Attorney Pierre Merle and police inspectors Edward Erdelatz and Frank McCoy sued the reporters and the paper for libel. The Hearst newspaper's attorneys planned to represent only staff reporter Ramirez; they were ready to let freelancer Bergman hang out to dry. Ramirez rejected the arrangement. He and Bergman had worked together closely on the story, stood by its contents, and wanted a joint defense. Media Alliance, a media advocacy organization, mobilized support for the two reporters and secured lawyers to represent them.

In a 1979 trial presided over by Clayton Horn, the judge in the *Howl* case, a jury awarded a three-million-dollar judgment against the newspaper and the two reporters. Bay Area journalists were outraged.

The appeal took almost a decade, while the reporters continued working with a $1.8 million fine over their heads.

The California Supreme Court, in a November 1986 opinion by Chief Justice Rose Bird, reversed the judgment. The court, citing the reporters' extensive eighteen-month investigation and evidence that corroborated Porter's testimony, concluded that Ramirez and Bergman "did not possess a subjective awareness of probable falsity" at the time the articles were published.

The court also noted that the plaintiffs' charge that it was reckless for the reporters to believe statements by Porter, a prisoner with something to gain, was weakened by the fact that they themselves relied heavily on Porter's testimony.

The journalists' attorney Art Brunwasser, though thrilled with the reversal of the libel judgment, noted, "It is unfortunate that it took ten years to overturn the multi-million-dollar judgment which had no merit from the beginning. The existence of the judgment over a decade created a chilling effect on investigative journalism."

Ramirez left the *Examiner* to become an editor at the *Oakland Tribune* and later executive news editor for KQED Radio, a National Public Radio affiliate in northern California. Bergman went on to become an award-winning producer at *60 Minutes* and was featured in the film *The Insider* about his investigative work around the lies and corruption of tobacco companies.

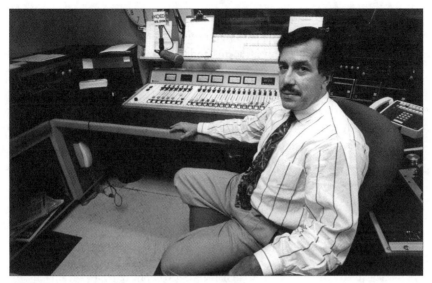

Raul Ramirez, then a reporter for the San Francisco Examiner, *was sued for libel by law enforcement officers angered by his coverage of a 1972 Chinatown murder trial. Ramirez and his codefendant, Lowell Bergman, faced a multimillion-dollar judgment, which the California Supreme Court reversed. Ramirez became the executive news producer at KQED Radio.*

Literary Greats Barred from the Classroom

V. I. Wexner was a dedicated reading teacher at Anderson Union High School, in rural northern California's Shasta County. "Many students are discouraged from reading," Wexner explained, "because the books available to them seem dull and uninteresting." He tried to remedy this problem by providing students a wide range of books—two thousand titles—by distinguished authors. Because of his infectious enthusiasm for books, his class, an elective, was one of the most popular in the school.

Among the selections he offered were works by Pulitzer Prize–winning author Richard Brautigan.

Wexner told the high schoolers that they should stop reading any book they found distasteful, embarrassing, offensive, or boring; no parents had ever complained about the veteran teacher or the books the students could read. So Wexner was perplexed when in 1978 the school board, contending that Brautigan's works were "full of obscenities and sexual references" inappropriate for their community, banned the award-winning author's books from classrooms and school libraries throughout the district. The board banished Brautigan's novels, including *Trout Fishing in America*, which *Book Week* had called "one of the most original and pleasing books to appear in the decade," and which the American Library Association had included in a list of titles particularly suited to young people.

Perhaps Wexner shouldn't have been so surprised. Eight years earlier, in 1970, the same school board had banned J. D. Salinger's classic *Catcher in the Rye*.

Wexner, a fellow teacher, three students, and Brautigan's publisher sued the school district in Shasta County Superior Court to get the books back on the shelves.

Unlike Steinbeck, who had stayed far away from the Kern County controversy three decades earlier, poet-novelist Brautigan was outspoken about the ban on his books. "I totally support those students and teachers at Anderson High School who wish to exercise their right of free speech as guaranteed to them by the Constitution of the United States," Brautigan wrote in an open letter. "What is at stake here is the freedom of teachers to teach and students to learn." Brautigan also focused on an unintended irony:

> On our Apollo 17 mission to the moon in December 1972, the astronauts named a crater after a character from one of the books that is forbidden to be taught at Anderson High School. I do not think it is the policy of the United States Government to name the geography of the moon after a character from a dirty book. The crater is called Shorty.
>
> The book is *Trout Fishing in America*. If *Trout Fishing in America* can get to the moon, I think it should be able to get to Anderson High School.

In 1981 Shasta County Superior Court Judge William Phelps, noting that he had read the books and found no reason to hear evidence on whether the works were obscene, granted a summary judgment to Wexner. The school board appealed.

In November 1988, the California Court of Appeal ordered the books returned to the library shelves and classrooms. In its twenty-eight-page unanimous decision, the court stated, "Book banning is the archetypical symbol of repression of free speech."

It is not only in rural areas that teachers and students have battled censorship.

In 1989 Wendy Coyle, an English teacher at San Francisco's Potrero Hill Middle School, started a literary magazine for her African American and Latino students who lived in a nearby public housing project.

The first edition of *The Potrero Hill Beat* was bursting with vivid images and raw emotions in the students' stories, essays, and poetry about difficult, real-life issues, including prostitution, drugs, gangs, and AIDS.

Fourteen-year-old Jaime Santa Maria wrote "Dear Somebody," a short story about drugs and suicide: "When I lived on Folsom, I used to see people do drugs. Sometimes I wanted to call the cops and turn them in for a reward. But my mom said they might do something to me. When she told me that my heart would stop."

On the afternoon that the literary magazines were about to be distributed, Coyle learned that school superintendent Ramon Cortines had confiscated seven hundred copies and locked them in a school storage room. "The message it sent to my students was," Coyle said, "'You don't belong.'"

Coyle's union, the California Teachers Association, filed a grievance with the school district, charging, "This is a blatant breach of academic freedom, and stifles the learning process of our students."

In a letter to Superintendent Cortines, the ACLU cited the California Education Code, which mandates that student-written material that is not "obscene, libelous or slanderous, or likely to incite others to commit illegal or disruptive acts" remain uncensored by school officials.

The superintendent withdrew his order and the student magazines came out of storage. *The Potrero Hill Beat* went on.

School censorship struggles bubbled up throughout the 1980s. In Bay Area suburbs, Christian groups wanted the Mount Diablo Unified School District and Livermore's Granada High School to ban, respectively, *Ms.* magazine and *The Chisholms,* a popular historical novel. In the Fresno County town of Laton, the school board tried to prevent the largely Latino high school student body from reading Rudolfo Anaya's *Bless Me, Ultima,* widely considered one of the finest pieces of contemporary Latino literature. Even in urban Oakland, school officials responding to a parent's complaint considered banning Alice Walker's celebrated novel *The Color Purple* the year after it won the 1983 Pulitzer Prize and the National Book Award.

In all of these cases, school administrators returned the literature in question to classrooms and library shelves after vigilant students, teachers, and parents advocated for the freedom to read.

Keyword: Censorship

The advent of the Internet brought censorship challenges to a new realm—cyberspace—but the players and the issues did not change: it was often religious fundamentalists who objected to material on the Internet on moral grounds, and librarians who protected the rights of people to read.

In 1999, in the leafy, middle-class suburb of Livermore, a parent known in court papers as Kathleen R. requested a court order to compel the public library to eliminate its policy of allowing uncensored use of the Internet. The suburban mother was upset because her twelve-year-old-son had downloaded a number of explicit pictures at the Livermore library, taken the disk to the home of a relative, and printed the images.

Ms. R.'s lawsuit against the library claimed that Internet access there was a "public nuisance." She sought to bar officials from spending public money on the library's computers, as long as minors or adults could use them to find sexual material considered "obscene" or "harmful to minors" under California law.

The ACLU stepped in to defend the library, arguing that both federal law and the First Amendment favor uncensored access to the Internet.

"The Livermore library's current policy allows each family to decide how its children should use the Internet without imposing one family's values on others," said ACLU attorney Ann Brick. "It is not the role of the public library to monitor or censor what children may read—that is the role of the parent." She added, "Parents have every right to supervise what their children access at home, but librarians have every right to provide constitutionally protected material to both children and adults. There is no way for the library to comply with the proposed court order without denying access to websites protected by the First Amendment."

Under federal law, Brick argued, libraries are immune from censorship suits because of their vital and longstanding role as an information resource for people of all ages and backgrounds.

In addition, Brick explained that using filtering software to prevent access to potentially offensive material, as some library patrons proposed, constituted a "prior restraint—a virtual gag order—that is prohibited by the First Amendment." The clumsy and ineffective blocking software censored speech based on arbitrary words or subjective views about what is offensive. For example, the sites of breast cancer and AIDS support groups were blocked; so was the work of poet Anne Sexton, because her name has the word "sex" in it. The website of the American Family Association, a conservative religious group, was blocked because it mentioned "homosexuality"—albeit in a disparaging context.

In 2001 the Alameda County Superior Court ruled in favor of the Livermore library, determining that all library users should have unfettered access to the Internet. The court was unwilling to treat the Internet differently from books, newspapers, or films in regard to First Amendment protections.

In 1997, forty years after the *Howl* trial, poet Lawrence Ferlinghetti joined the very first national challenge to Congress's early effort to censor the Internet—*ACLU v. Reno*—which resulted in a decision from the U.S. Supreme Court affirming that the First Amendment does apply to cyberspace.

The revered poet laureate of San Francisco became a plaintiff in the suit because, in his words, "This new law to censor the Internet would have a chilling effect on the First Amendment. It's upsetting and it's also un-American."

— EIGHT —

KEEPING THE FAITH

THE RIGHT TO RELIGIOUS FREEDOM

> If there is any fixed star in our constitutional constellation it is that no
> official, high or petty, can prescribe what shall be orthodox in politics,
> nationalism or other matter of opinion, or force citizens to confess by
> words or act their faith therein.
>
> —*U.S. Supreme Court Justice Robert Jackson,*
> Barnette v. West Virginia State Board of Education, *1943*

Charlotte Gabrielli was nine years old in 1936, when she was suspended from Fremont Elementary School in Sacramento. The bright little girl with brunette sausage
curls and a sweet smile was not suspended for misbehaving; in fact, she was trying to
obey her parents' instructions. Her parents, both deaf, were Jehovah's Witnesses. They
told Charlotte that in their religion, the "flag salute is a form of idolatry, forbidden
by the divine mandates." Like other Witness parents, they instructed their second
grader to show respect by standing quietly while her classmates recited the Pledge of
Allegiance, but not to join in the ritual.

When Charlotte was suspended, her parents advocated for her reinstatement, but
the principal and the school board refused. So the Gabrielli family's spiritual leader,
J. F. Rutherford, a former Missouri circuit judge and head of the International Bible Students' Association, or Jehovah's Witnesses, asked the ACLU to represent the little girl.

When the case came before Sacramento Superior Court Judge Peter Shields, Charlotte's attorney Wayne Collins argued that if students are suspended from public
school for not saying the Pledge, and their parents can't afford private school, then

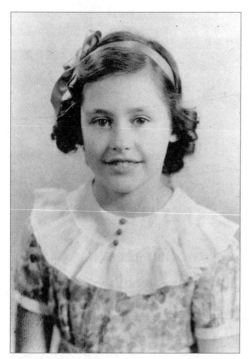

Jehovah's Witness Charlotte Gabrielli was suspended from her Sacramento elementary school in 1936 when she refused to say the Pledge of Allegiance because it was against her religion. The California Supreme Court upheld the compulsory flag salute, which was eventually banned by the U.S. Supreme Court.

it follows that the parents could be arrested for not sending their children to school. He explained that Jehovah's Witnesses in Nazi Germany were arrested en masse and forced into concentration camps because they would not pledge allegiance to Hitler. Jehovah's Witnesses prayed silently in the courtroom during the hearing.

In a similar Massachusetts case, non-saluting students were sent to reform school, prompting Nobel Prize–winning author Sinclair Lewis to write, "The gangs behind this compulsory flag salute nonsense are trying to turn that flag from the symbol of liberty into the symbol of tyranny, fascism, and death."

Judge Shields ruled that compelling a student to say the Pledge is unconstitutional if it conflicts with the child's religious beliefs. He based his decision on the California constitution, which guarantees "free exercise and enjoyment of religious profession and worship, without discrimination or preference," an even stronger guarantee of religious liberty than the First Amendment of the U.S. Constitution.

Judge Shields noted religious beliefs could not trump laws "necessary to the maintenance of the Government or the preservation of the public health, safety, or morals." Saluting the flag, he reasoned, did not come within any of these exceptions.

The Sacramento and San Francisco press applauded the decision, but the Veterans of Foreign Wars denounced it as "un-American and un-patriotic." Ordered by Judge Shields to allow Charlotte back in school, the school board refused and appealed the ruling. Attorney Collins argued in the state court of appeal that the flag salute is not a law but a custom, and violation of custom is not punishable. Patriotism can be taught by other methods, he insisted. The court of appeal unanimously agreed, and the school district once again appealed.

In 1938, the California Supreme Court upheld the compulsory flag salute, stating, "We see no violation of any article of the federal or state constitutions" and that "simple salutation to the flag and repetition of the pledge...tend to stimulate in the minds of youth...lasting affection and respect for and unfaltering loyalty to our government."

The court based its decision partly on the fact that, though Jehovah's Witness students had been suspended throughout the country, the U.S. Supreme Court had refused to grant hearings in similar cases because it found no basis to do so in federal law.

While the Gabrielli case was winding its way through the courts, a similar situation in Alameda County highlighted the regulations' arbitrary nature. Six-year-old Tessie Palmaymesa and her mother, also Jehovah's Witnesses, lived on the border of Oakland and San Leandro. Tessie's mother had enrolled her at Roosevelt School, in San Leandro, so she wouldn't have to cross a busy street. But when the principal there barred Tessie from class because she did not say the Pledge, her mother transferred her to Oakland's Morris Cox School, where she was allowed to leave the room during the flag salute. As the ACLU reported, "She returns when the exercise is concluded, and no one is hurt, not even the flag."

School officials in other locales were less enlightened. Following the *Gabrielli* case, students in Crescent City, Alhambra, and Fresno faced expulsion for refusing to salute the flag. Parents in Delhi and Modesto were arrested and charged with failing to send their children to school.

In June 1940 an event took place that affected Jehovah's Witnesses across the country. The U.S. Supreme Court ruled in a Pennsylvania case, *Gobitis v. Minersville*, that school boards could compel all students, including the Jehovah's Witnesses who brought the case, to salute the flag or face expulsion.

It was the beginning of World War II, and the 8-1 decision reflected the government's need to whip up enthusiasm for war and squelch any perceived slight to patriotism. The ruling by Justice Felix Frankfurter stated, "We live by symbols, and our flag is the symbol of national unity."

The single voice of dissent came from Justice Harlan Fiske Stone, who had supported conscientious objectors in World War I: "The essence of liberty is freedom of the individual from compulsion as to what he shall think and what he shall say, at least where the compulsion is to bear false witness to his religion."

When California schools opened the following autumn, the list of districts that expelled Jehovah's Witness students was staggering: Lodi, Redondo Beach, Selma, Alhambra, Crescent City, Delhi, Nevada City, Fresno, Benicia, Modesto, Lake County, Lassen County, San Bernardino, Antelope Valley, Tehama, Marin County, Napa, Chico, Hanford, Cajon, Twenty-Nine Palms, Los Alamos, Guadalupe, Orcutt, and Santa Maria.

In some districts, public school teachers were fired for not leading the Pledge in their classrooms.

California Attorney General Earl Warren exacerbated the problem by issuing an opinion that parents of expelled students "must furnish private instruction under the compulsory education law." Warren also stated that parents of children who did not salute could be jailed and their children made wards of the court. This had a devastating impact on Jehovah's Witness parents. Kathleen Cory, the divorced mother of a two-year-old and a five-year-old, was denied custody of her children by the Sacramento Superior Court solely because she was a Jehovah's Witness. The court of appeal, reversing the decision in 1945, ruled:

> The conclusion seems inescapable that appellant has been deprived of the custody of said children solely because she is a Jehovah's Witness, and, in the opinion of the trial court, the beliefs of the followers of that faith are inimical to the welfare of their children because they do not salute the flag and are unwilling to fight for their country.
>
> We have been cited to no case, and believe none will be found, wherein it has been held that the courts may deprive parents of the custody of their offspring because of a disagreement with such parents as to their religious views, at least as long as their teachings do not conflict with the laws of the land.

The ACLU documented two thousand schoolchildren expelled across the country and reported 355 violent incidents in forty-four states. From Mt. Shasta and Yreka in the north to Newhall and Elsinor in the south, vigilantes attacked Jehovah's Witnesses and drove them out of town, while police often turned a blind eye. Siskiyou County District Attorney Charles E. Johnson was quoted as saying, "They have no business on the streets peddling their publications if they contain seditious writing and attack other religions and organizations."

The situation got so bad in Los Angeles that District Attorney John F. Dockweiler, in July 1942, publicly excoriated mob violence against the Jehovah's Witnesses. His office filed a criminal complaint against a sailor in Hermosa Beach who assaulted a boy who stood at attention during a flag-saluting ceremony but refused to salute. That was the first criminal prosecution in California against any person charged with violating the rights of a Jehovah's Witness. "I am satisfied that the membership of this religious society have been the victims of lawless force and violence at the hands of over-zealous, self-styled patriots, who do not understand that true American patriotism calls for the protection, not the denial of the constitutional liberties of unpopular religious minorities in our midst," Dockweiler said.

On September 20, 1942, fifteen hundred Jehovah's Witnesses from Oregon and California gathered for a regional convention in Klamath Falls.

Members of the American Legion and the Veterans of Foreign Wars set up a war bond booth near the entrance to the convention hall, planted an American flag, and circled the hall with a sound truck exhorting the Witnesses to buy war bonds.

Someone threw a stink bomb into the main hall. Rocks flew through the windows, and a crowd of vigilantes heaved against the large sliding doors in the rear of the building, forcing their way inside. Another smoke bomb, tossed into the outer hall where women with infants were sitting, drove them into the main hall, where they were met by another stink bomb. As more than one thousand vigilantes attacked the Witnesses, the chief of police stood nearby and did nothing.

Three people were hospitalized, and many more suffered minor injuries. Banners and religious literature were seized and burned; the local headquarters of the Witnesses was destroyed. The vigilantes ransacked the convention hall, shattered plate glass windows, overturned scores of automobiles, and cut the telegraph wire that had been leased to carry a Witness leader's speech from Cleveland, Ohio.

This was just one of many instances where the police did not arrest the attackers; sometimes it was the police who were the assaulters. Such was the case with August Schmidt, a Jehovah's Witness in Redondo Beach. In a sworn statement to the district attorney, Schmidt described how uniformed police officer Charles Ellis threatened him and his wife, forced him to leave his home at gunpoint, and beat him with a blackjack all the way to the police station. Schmidt explained that when other officers at the station objected to the beating, Ellis "threw down his badge and gun on the desk and said, 'Tell the Chief he can get another man.' Then he hit me in the eye with his fist....The desk sergeant said, 'Why don't you quit? You've done enough.' Ellis replied, 'I'm mad enough I'd just as soon shoot up the whole bunch!' Then Ellis left."

The sympathetic desk sergeant released Schmidt without pressing charges and called a physician for him.

A grand jury returned an indictment against Ellis, charging him with two felonies: assault with a deadly weapon and assault with intent to do great bodily harm. At trial, he claimed that he had been acting in self-defense, because Schmidt had provoked him by stating that he would not salute the flag, and Ellis's attorney urged the jury to consider "patriotism" as a major defense. The jury found Ellis guilty of simple assault, a misdemeanor.

The furor against the Witnesses also took its toll on wartime draftees. In 1942, ACLU attorney A. L. Wirin and several Jehovah's Witnesses met with Major K. H. Leitch, the California director of the Selective Service. They challenged the arbitrary administration of the Selective Service Act by numerous local draft boards that denied Jehovah's Witnesses conscientious objector status. They cited the case of Harry Crutchfield, who, like all other Witnesses, considered himself a minister. His Oakland draft board nevertheless ordered his induction. Crutchfield refused and was convicted for violating the draft law. The ACLU argued that in a criminal prosecution for violation of a local draft board order, a defendant should be allowed to present evidence to a court and jury that the order was "arbitrary" or "capricious."

Ernest Strobel, a Jehovah's Witness, did receive conscientious objector status from his draft board, who deemed him eligible for noncombatant service and sent him to Fort MacArthur at San Pedro. But when he refused to salute the flag or put on a military uniform, other soldiers beat him so brutally that he lost consciousness and his clothes "were a mess of blood."

According to a letter from Strobel's lawyer to Secretary of War Henry Stimson, attackers dragged the bruised and bleeding man in front of three other Jehovah's Witnesses and "told them to look at the consequences if they refused to wear uniforms."

One of them was Herbert L. Weatherbee, who had explained to his Santa Barbara draft board that for religious reasons he could not wear the military uniform or participate in the war. His brother Kenneth later recalled that the draft board instructed Herbert to go to the induction center, where he would have an opportunity to explain his religious objection. However, when he arrived, the officer in charge said, "Mister, when you stepped across that threshold, you were in the army." Every day the soldiers would physically force the Witnesses to march to the parade ground and order them to salute the flag, which they refused to do. Weatherbee was beaten and thrown onto the hot vents of the stove in the kitchen where he was assigned to work.

When Weatherbee's family complained to California Congressman George Outland, the politician arranged for Wirin to meet with Weatherbee's mother. Wirin raised her concerns to the military. The Army claimed that "there was not the slightest evidence to bear out the statement that Private Weatherbee or any other soldier was beaten and forcibly put into uniform," and ordered him court-martialed for disobeying his superior officers and refusing to salute the flag. In March 1943 Weatherbee was sentenced by a military court-martial to life imprisonment with hard labor. The ACLU protested this harsh sentence, and in June the judge advocate general reversed the sentence and discharged Weatherbee from the military.

A newsletter from a conscientious objector organization reported that Strobel, who had been in the Army stockade and scheduled to be court-martialed, was also discharged because "his detention in the army stockade had caused a mental condition which made him unable to competently conduct his own defense at a court-martial."

On Flag Day, 1943, the Supreme Court admitted that it had made an error three years earlier, in the *Gobitis* ruling. Justice Stone, the lone dissent in *Gobitis*, had become chief justice in 1941. In the case of *Barnette v. West Virginia State Board of Education*, the Court reversed itself by a vote of 6-3. The decision, written by Justice Robert Jackson, became a landmark for asserting the rights of religious liberty. Jackson wrote, "If there is any fixed star in our constitutional constellation it is that no official, high or petty, can prescribe what shall be orthodox in politics, nationalism or other matter of opinion, or force citizens to confess by words or act their faith therein."

This stellar ruling, in the middle of wartime, vindicated the thousands of children who had heeded their parents and their religious convictions and had suffered dearly for it.

Although the U.S. was founded on the principles of religious diversity and freedom, those who stray from orthodox Christian beliefs are often subject to restrictions on their freedom of conscience. As with Jehovah's Witnesses, others who have suffered persecution in California were from minority religions—Native Americans, Black Muslims, and Sikhs—and some had no religion at all.

The Theological Heart of Peyotism

The town of Needles hugs the western border of the Colorado River, which separates the far eastern tip of San Bernardino County from Arizona and Nevada. On the evening of April 28, 1962, Jack Woody, Dan Dee Nez, and Leon B. Anderson gathered in a traditional hogan in the desert west of Needles. Members of the Navajo American Church of North America, the three men joined others for an all-night ritual central to their religion.

After police entered the hogan and announced that they were arresting all of the participants, one of them naively handed the officers a photocopy of the articles of incorporation of the Navajo American Church in a gold frame. The first part of the document read, "[W]e as a people place explicit faith and hope and belief in the Almighty God and declare full, competent, and everlasting faith in our Church things which and by which we worship God." Thus far, the statement differed little from mainstream monotheistic declarations of faith. The next sentence, however, distinguished the Church from other religions: "[W]e further pledge ourselves to work for unity with the sacramental use of peyote and its religious use."

The officers dismissed the religious claim and arrested Woody and the others for violating a California narcotics law banning the unauthorized possession of peyote.

Peyote buttons grow on the tops of small cacti native to the Rio Grande Valley of Texas and Mexico. When chewed or brewed in a tea, peyote buttons release mescaline, which induces hallucinations of kaleidoscopic colors and patterns. Peyote generates in many people feelings of openness and well-being and a heightened state of consciousness.

Members of the Navajo American Church blend the use of peyote with Christian theology. They believe that peyote is an embodiment of the Holy Spirit and that those who ingest it come into direct contact with God. Adherents direct prayers to peyote buttons, believing them to be objects of worship and symbols of protection.

The ceremony in which Woody and the other men were arrested was typical of Navajo American Church gatherings. It began at sundown on Saturday and was scheduled to end at sunrise the following day. An individual "sponsored" or convened the meeting as an expression of gratitude for good fortune or to seek guidance. The sponsor provided the peyote and breakfast the morning after the ritual. Befitting a solemn religious occasion, participants dressed formally in suits and dresses or ceremonial Indian garb. Although entire families attended meetings, only men consumed peyote. At an early point in the ritual, each man would take four buttons and chew them.

In November 1962, San Bernardino Superior Court Judge Carl Hilliard found the three Navajos guilty, imposed a prison sentence, and released them on probation. The court of appeal in San Diego upheld the convictions.

Rufus W. Johnson, a fifty-three-year-old former butler to Franklin D. Roosevelt and a decorated veteran of the all-black Buffalo Soldiers unit that fought in Italy during World War II, agreed to represent Woody and his codefendants before the state supreme court.

The Navajos claimed that the law infringed on their First Amendment right to the free exercise of their religion. The state argued that making an exception for adherents of the Navajo American Church to use peyote would open the door to fraudulent claims of religious uses. The court applied a test formulated by the U.S. Supreme Court: does the law create a barrier to the free exercise of religion, and if so, is there a compelling state interest for doing so? In a 6-1 decision, the high court ruled that the state could not constitutionally prosecute those using peyote in Navajo American Church rituals.

Writing for the majority, Justice Matthew Tobriner explained that forbidding the use of peyote was equivalent to removing the "theological heart of Peyotism." He stated that when balancing the heavy weight of denying the church members the free exercise of their religion against the "slight danger to the state and to the enforcement of its laws," the "scale tips in favor of the constitutional protection."

He was particularly perturbed by the state attorney general's argument that peyote "obstructs enlightenment and shackles the Indian to primitive conditions" and that the state had a responsibility to eliminate its use. In a pointed response, Tobriner explained, "We know of no doctrine that the state, in its asserted omniscience, should

undertake to deny to defendants the observance of their religion in order to free them from the suppositious 'shackles' of their 'unenlightened' and 'primitive' condition.'"
He concluded:

> In a mass society, which presses at every point toward conformity, the protection of self-expression, however unique, of the individual and the group becomes ever more important. The varying currents of the subcultures that flow into the mainstream of our national life give it depth and beauty. We preserve a greater value than an ancient tradition when we protect the rights of the Indians who honestly practiced an old religion in using peyote one night at a meeting in a desert hogan near Needles, California.

Black Muslims: Can the State Decide What a Religion Is?

The conflict over what constitutes a religion reached its height in the cases of Black Muslims in California. The controversy boiled over in Los Angeles in the sixties, with deadly consequences.

In 1960 Jesse L. Ferguson, a Black Muslim in Folsom Prison, tried to purchase a copy of the Q'uran. The warden refused. Prison officials confiscated other Muslim literature from Ferguson. A correctional officer described a religious scrapbook as "the usual 'Muslim' trash, advocating hatred of the white race, superiority of the black man." Prison officials destroyed it as "contraband."

The Nation of Islam, founded by Elijah Mohammed during the Depression, had a growing following among African American prisoners, who found meaning in the religion's assertion that Islam was the natural religion of African peoples, and that they should reject Christianity as the religion of black enslavement. The organization, which emphasized self-help and separation from the dominant white society, eventually gained a hundred thousand members, most from poverty-stricken inner cities.

When the warden confiscated his religious books, Ferguson tried to send a letter to a lawyer, but prison officials would not allow it. He then tried to mail a letter to his mother, asking her to forward it to a lawyer. Prison officials refused to send that letter as well, telling Ferguson the charges in the letter were untrue.

After Ferguson finally reached an attorney, the following year, he went to court claiming that Black Muslims' religious rights were being violated. The state constitution provides for the "free exercise and enjoyment of religious profession and worship, without discrimination or preference," Ferguson argued, and yet Black Muslim prisoners were denied a place to worship, Muslim literature, and visits from spiritual leaders. Prison officials broke up their religious meetings, often by force. In addition, several of the prisoners had been physically abused and segregated into a decrepit and filthy part of Folsom. As the state supreme court later noted, with unintended under-statement, "There appears to be considerable friction between the prison officials and the Muslim inmates as individuals and as a group."

On April 24, 1961, the California Supreme Court ruled against Ferguson. The legislature, it stated, gave control of prisons to the California Department of Corrections (CDC). The court noted that the general policy of the CDC was to encourage religious activities by inmates, but that the CDC director had determined that Black Muslims "were not entitled to be accorded the privileges of a religious group or sect." The State Advisory Committee on Institutional Religion had approved this policy in January 1961.

"It is apparent," the justices noted, "that the Muslim beliefs in black supremacy and their reluctance to yield to any authority exercised by someone who does not believe in their God present a serious threat to maintenance of order in a crowded prison environment."

The court also took it upon itself to define the religious beliefs of the prisoners. "According to their allegations, petitioners are members of a Muslim Religious Group. They believe in the solidarity and supremacy of the dark-skinned races, and that integration of white and dark races is impossible since it is contrary to the laws of God and nature."

Once they had decided that Black Muslims were a threat to the prison system, the court took the next logical step and ruled that the CDC's suppression was not unreasonable, and "not an abuse of [its] discretionary power" to manage the prison system.

While the Department of Corrections was claiming the beliefs of Black Muslims did not constitute a religion, University of California officials were banning a talk by Muslim leader Malcolm X, on the alleged constitutional grounds that they could not allow a religious leader to speak on a public university campus.

In June 1961, the NAACP chapter at UC Berkeley invited Malcolm X to speak there, on a nonreligious topic. Citing a section of the California constitution that required the campus to be "entirely independent of...sectarian influence," as well as regulations prohibiting the use of university facilities "for the purpose of religious worship, exercise, or conversions," officials barred Malcolm X from speaking on campus. Faculty members objected and sent a petition with 161 signatures to Chancellor Edward Strong, who responded by listing all the reasons the Black Muslim leader should not be allowed to speak on campus: the Black Muslim movement was religious; the Brotherhood was a religious sect; Malcolm X was a minister of the sect; the sect was evangelical and sought converts by proselytizing.

ACLU attorney Marshall Krause charged that using separation of church and state to justify banning Malcolm X from the UC Berkeley campus "perverts the meaning of the law and is a sham." Moreover, he noted, a year earlier the Episcopal bishop of San Francisco, James Pike, had given a major address on campus.

Despite intense negotiations with the NAACP and assurances that Malcolm X's talk would be nonsectarian, the university dug in its heels and refused to allow him to give his presentation.

Two years later, a new campus organization, SLATE, invited Malcolm X to speak. He finally gave his talk in Dwinelle Plaza on October 11, 1963, on the problem of racism in the United States.

In 1962 government authorities again challenged Black Muslims' legitimacy, with an even more serious outcome. For many years, the Los Angeles Police Department's Red Squad, under the leadership of Chief William Parker and his predecessors, had amassed files on individuals and organizations suspected of subversive activities. Mayor Sam Yorty, previously the head of the California legislature's Committee on Un-American Activities, knew about and wholeheartedly approved of the surveillance.

The LAPD also had the blessing of the FBI and its notoriously anti-Communist and racist director, J. Edgar Hoover, who ordered intensive surveillance and counterintelligence operations against Elijah Mohammed, head of the Nation of Islam, and Black Muslims nationally, on the pretext that the religious movement was a front for Communist agitation of blacks. In 1962 the LAPD targeted Mosque No. 27, in South Central Los Angeles.

On April 27, two LAPD officers approached two Black Muslims outside the mosque. The officers' manner was hostile; they refused to allow the two men to

In 1962 Los Angeles police opened fire on Mosque No. 27, killing Ronald Stokes, a Korean War veteran and personal friend of Malcolm X, and injuring dozens of others. Malcolm X is pictured here with William Rogers, who was shot and paralyzed, and later put on trial for assaulting police during the mosque attack.

explain their business in the area and manhandled them when they refused to answer questions. According to the police report, the two Muslims attacked the police officers. The officers, claiming self-defense, fired their service revolvers. On hearing the shots, members of the mosque ran into the street. There they saw several men lying on the ground, bleeding. The officers continued shooting, wounding five people: one Muslim was shot in the back and paralyzed from the waist down. Several policemen were injured in the melee. The secretary of the mosque, Korean War veteran Ronald Stokes, lay dead.

The death of Stokes shocked the Black Muslim community. Equally shocking was the arrest of several mosque members for assaulting law enforcement officers. A grand jury investigation dismissed Stokes's killing as "justifiable homicide." Los Angeles was tense; many feared a violent response to this armed assault on a religious institution. Elijah Mohammed dispatched Malcolm X from New York to support the members of Mosque No. 27 and bring national attention to the attack. Malcolm X had helped to establish Mosque 27. On May 5, at Stokes's funeral, which was attended by two thousand people, Malcolm X eulogized his old friend from Roxbury, Massachusetts. At a press conference the following day, he denounced the LAPD as "well-armed storm troopers" and called the shootout "one of the most ferocious inhuman atrocities" to take place in a "so-called democratic civilized society."

Eventually, Elijah Mohammed, fearing a police bloodbath against Black Muslims if Malcolm X and others continued their vitriolic public attacks on Mayor Yorty and the LAPD, recalled his emissary to the national headquarters in New York. Malcolm X, having witnessed the fury in the black community over the incident, protested his recall: "When our own brothers are brutalized or killed, we do nothing. We just sit on our hands."

His unease was justified.

Eleven Black Muslims were convicted of criminal charges, ranging from interfering with police officers to felony assault. The police officers who fired at members of Mosque No. 27 were never charged or disciplined.

Malcolm X's relations with Elijah Mohammed became increasingly strained, and in 1963 he left the Nation of Islam, eschewed black nationalism, and affirmed the brotherhood of all races. In 1965 Malcolm X was shot and killed in Harlem's Audubon Ballroom. The gunmen were revealed to be followers of Elijah Mohammed.

Logging Trucks through Sacred Land

In the early 1970s, Elizabeth Case began sacred work as a medicine woman among the Karuk Indians of the Klamath River area in northern California. Her work involved praying over medicines among old-growth fir, cedar, pine, and oak trees in the Chimney Rock area of the Siskiyou Mountains, federally owned land twenty miles inland of the Pacific Ocean and thirty miles south of the Oregon border.

For more than a thousand years, Yurok, Tolowa, and Karuk healers have gone to the Chimney Rock high country to receive spiritual power, guidance, and blessings that benefit all Native people in the region.

In the 1930s, the U.S. Forest Service began building logging roads in the area, one originating in Gasquet, in Del Norte County, and another further south, in the Humboldt County town of Orleans. In 1982 the agency announced its intention to connect the two legs of what they envisioned as a contiguous Gasquet-Orleans (G-O) road by paving a six-mile stretch that ran directly through the Chimney Rock area. The plan threatened not only the work of Elizabeth Case and other medicine men and women but the spiritual life of the Karuk, Tolowa, and Yurok tribes.

The Forest Service plan ran counter to a 1979 anthropological study the agency itself had commissioned, which explained that the local tribes' longstanding religious practices required the region to be private and devoid of visual and sound disturbances. The study concluded that any road "would cause serious and irreparable damage to the sacred areas" central to the religion of northwest California Indians, and it recommended that the G-O road not be completed.

The Forest Service attempted to mitigate harm caused by the road by designating "buffer zones" around significant religious sites, but admitted that an estimated seventy-two diesel logging trucks and ninety other vehicles would daily traverse the road within a half-mile of sacred areas. The felling of trees, allowed by another Forest Service plan, would desecrate the holy land.

It would be like "building an interstate through the Vatican," said Marilyn Miles, a Kickapoo attorney with California Indian Legal Services (CILS).

The Northwest Indian Cemetery Protective Association and several individuals, represented by CILS, sued in 1982 to bar the Forest Service from completing the G-O road. Federal Judge Stanley Weigel heard testimony from Native elders, including Sam Jones, a Yurok, who explained that his mother had instructed him to go to the high country for spiritual guidance before leaving for World War II. He survived, unharmed, some of the most bloody battles in the conflict and attributed his safety to the spiritual power of the high country. "It's always worked for us and has always worked for our people and if you destroy the center of the universe, I don't know what will happen," Jones testified.

In May 1983, Judge Weigel barred the Forest Service from implementing its plan. Citing the First Amendment's guarantee of religious freedom, the judge, who had in 1949 represented University of California professors who refused to sign loyalty oaths, stated, "religious beliefs need not be acceptable, logical, consistent, or comprehensible to others in order to merit First Amendment protection." The Ninth Circuit upheld Judge Weigel's decision.

The U.S. Supreme Court agreed to hear the government's appeal, and in April 1988 the high court issued its ruling. Justice Sandra Day O'Connor, writing for a five-judge majority, reasoned that "incidental effects of government programs, which may make it more difficult to practice certain religions but which have no tendency to coerce individuals into acting contrary to their religious belief," do not violate the First Amendment. O'Connor acknowledged that the road would hinder Indians from practicing their religion but believed it would not *prevent* them from doing so. She stated that even if the road were to virtually destroy the Indians' religion, there was no constitutional basis for them to object. Consequently, construction of the G-O road could move forward.

Justice William Brennan issued a stinging dissent, joined by Justices Thurgood Marshall and Harry Blackmun. Brennan pointed out that the G-O road would "virtually destroy a religion" but the Court nevertheless deemed it was not a "burden" to that religion. Brennan concluded that the majority ruling "sacrifices a religion at least as old as the Nation itself, along with the spiritual well-being of its approximately 5,000 adherents, so that the Forest Service can build a 6-mile segment of road that two lower courts found had only the most marginal and speculative utility."

The decision was a setback not only for Indians throughout the U.S. who sought protection of sacred lands, but for the religious freedom of all Americans. Recognizing that the outcome of the case impacted their religious freedom, Christian and Jewish organizations had submitted briefs in support of the tribes. Marc D. Stern, an attorney with the American Jewish Congress, called the decision one of the most disturbing for religious liberty in more than twenty-five years.

After their court defeat, G-O road opponents faced the daunting task of convincing the Forest Service to scrap its plan. Elizabeth Case and other activists demonstrated at the Forest Service's Eureka office. The elderly medicine woman explained to a Forest Service staff person, "Now our spiritual life is *our* life. That's the only life we got. That's our church life....They treat us like we're nothing. Same time we *do* fix the world. We *do* fix the world....Indian peoples fix the world. They do a lot of praying when they go up the mountain. If that quits, we won't have nothing. There won't be no anything."

In 1990 federal legislation rescued the sacred region. Congress passed a bill adding the G-O road high country to the Siskiyou Wilderness Area and barring logging and other development, including the completion of the G-O road. Although the legislation was enacted for environmental reasons and not for the sake of religious freedom, it prevented the G-O road from traversing the sacred area.

Elizabeth Case could continue fixing the world.

G-O road opponents at the Six Rivers National Forest headquarters in Eureka, May 1988. Left to right: Lyn Risling (Karuk/Yurok/Hupa), Byron Nelson (Hupa), Jimmy James (Yurok), Donna Martin in background (Yurok), Junie Mattice (Tolowa), Julian Lang (Karuk/Wiyot), and medicine woman Elizabeth Case (Karuk)

From Playground to Graduation: Including All Students

Long after Jehovah's Witness Charlotte Gabrielli affirmed her right not to recite the Pledge of Allegiance, other students carried on the fight for religious rights in school.

The graduates at Granada High School nervously assembled on tiered bleachers on a sunny summer day in 1983. Proud families filed into the stands. The high school band ran through the final rehearsal of "Pomp and Circumstance," and the principal checked the diplomas to make sure they were in the right order.

But the June 10 graduation ceremony in Livermore was far from routine. The middle-class suburb, surrounded by vineyards, ranches, and farmlands, was gripped by tension. Uniformed officers ringed the stadium, inspecting the handbags and camera cases of graduates' relatives. There were rumors of a bomb threat.

What had provoked this excessive show of law enforcement in this quiet, leafy town?

In the 1980s, radical religious activists viewed public schools as a battleground for the morals of youth. The rise of Christian fundamentalism had led to prayer circles before football games and in school courtyards, as well as pressure to include prayers in graduation ceremonies.

Just hours before the Granada High graduation ceremony was to begin, a battle raged in the California Supreme Court.

Leslie Bennett, Diane Brown, and ten other graduating seniors had objected to the inclusion of a Christian prayer in the ceremony. The prayer was composed by another graduate, Todd Ferro, who planned to read it at the celebration.

When they first learned about the prayer, Bennett and Brown had asked the graduation committee to eliminate it from the program. When that request was denied, they appealed to the school grievance committee.

"We felt the prayer violated the constitutional separation of church and state," explained Bennett. "I don't want to stop people from praying, but I don't think a prayer belongs in a graduation ceremony."

Their demand polarized the school and the community. During final exams, Brown and Bennett were harassed and jeered. "I've been called an atheist bitch, a freak, and scum by these so-called Christians. They yell it out in a crowd or hiss at me from cars as they pass by," said Bennett.

But Bennett and Brown had many supporters, including a local minister's wife, and teachers and administrators in other districts praised their actions.

At a heated school board meeting attended by more than one hundred students and parents, Brown made an eloquent plea. But the board voted 3-2 to include the prayer, and the next day, left with no other recourse, the students went to court.

ACLU attorneys Amitai Schwartz and Margaret Crosby filed *Bennett v. Livermore Unified School District* in Alameda County Superior Court, seeking an injunction to halt the prayer. With the graduation date looming, a hearing was set for the following day.

"State and federal constitutions erect a wall of separation between civil authority and religious activity," explained Crosby. "But the school board in Livermore proposes to breach that constitutional wall....Religious invocation is not rendered constitutional by the longevity of the custom, voluntary nature of the official event, ceremonial nature of graduation, or brevity of prayer," she argued.

The afternoon before the ceremony, Judge Raymond Marsh issued a preliminary injunction barring the prayer. With just hours to go, the board appealed his ruling to the state court of appeal, which upheld the injunction by a vote of 2-1. The board then appealed to the California Supreme Court, which refused to act before the Friday evening ceremony.

Despite threats and shaken nerves, the graduation went off without incident. Three hundred graduating seniors and their families heard a speech by English teacher Jim Willis reprimanding students for hypocrisy and unchristian behavior and warning them not to hiss or boo during the event.

They also heard a solo by Leslie Bennett and a poem by Todd Ferro, but no prayer. Both graduates—who hours before had been on opposite sides of the conflict—were cheered.

A small biplane, hired by the prayer's proponents, flew over the ceremony trailing a banner: "God Bless the Graduates."

The graduates had scattered to various colleges, universities, and jobs by the time Judge Marsh tried the case the following year. The courtroom was packed with reporters.

"Because matters of faith are deeply felt, any official government sponsorship of religion produces divisiveness in a community. This is why the framers of the Constitution put church-state separation as the first clause of the First Amendment; they feared that mixing religion and government would threaten a democracy, which depends on tolerance, reason, and compromise," Crosby argued.

Judge Marsh surprised many in the courtroom by delivering his ruling immediately after the oral argument. Quoting California Supreme Court Justice Rose Bird, Judge Marsh said, "There is no more important duty that a judge can have than to protect religious liberty." He ruled against the school board, rejecting its claim that attendance at graduation is voluntary. High school graduations are such an important societal event, he concluded, that it "ignores reality" to say students do not suffer coercion when they are forced to choose between violating their conscience and missing their own graduation.

The school board again appealed, and in 1987 a three-judge panel of the court of appeal unanimously upheld the lower court's ban on the prayer. "The practice of including a religious invocation at a graduation ceremony conveys a message of endorsement of the particular creed represented in the invocation and of religion in general," the court stated.

The court noted that the religious freedom provisions of the California constitution are "even more stringent than the U.S. Constitution" and explained that "the citizens of this country, and perhaps of this state in particular, are a people of highly diverse cultural, ethical, and religious backgrounds. The U.S. Supreme Court has consistently rejected any form of prayer, however inoffensive or nonsectarian, in the public schools."

The California Supreme Court refused to hear the school district's appeal, so the ban on prayer at graduation ceremonies went into effect in all public schools in the state.

"Some people unfortunately may see this as an attack on their very deep religious beliefs. It is not that at all. The people who wrote the First Amendment understood that religion is stronger when the government plays no part in it," Crosby reflected. "This decision is quite important in guaranteeing religious minorities the right to attend high school graduations—events of enormous personal and social importance—without feeling like outsiders."

Bennett, who attended Chabot College after graduation, remained perplexed over the controversy her objections to the prayer had evoked. "How could someone threaten to blow up two thousand people in the name of Christianity? That kind of hypocrisy makes me angry."

Institutionalized Religion

Another student who found himself at odds with a school policy faced even tougher odds—his school was part of the juvenile justice system. The Karl Holton Drug and Alcohol Abuse Treatment Center, a California Youth Authority institution near Stockton, held four hundred "wards." All were required to participate in Design for Living, a twelve-step program modeled on Alcoholics Anonymous (AA), five days a week for six months. Five of the twelve steps explicitly refer to God. Design for Living meetings included recitation of the Lord's Prayer and the mandatory workbooks were filled with references to God.

Youth Authority officials based eligibility for parole advancement on participation in the required class. The wards were warned that if they refused to participate in the program, they could lose good behavior points or be locked in their cells.

Despite these threats, in the summer of 1995, a seventeen-year-old ward told his teacher that he did not believe in a higher power and did not want to be in the program. The ward was labeled a "program failure" and expelled from Karl Holton. He was sent to the CYA segregation unit, the N. A. Chaderjian School, where he was locked in his cell twenty-three hours a day and barred from all vocational and educational programs.

A sympathetic teacher assisted the young man in seeking help from the Prison Law Office. Attorney Alison Hardy agreed to represent him. "CYA wards are being forced to adopt the religious beliefs of this program to gain access to educational and vocational opportunities. Our plaintiff sincerely believes that he must rely on his own inner strength and not a higher power to overcome addiction."

ACLU attorney Margaret Crosby, who co-counseled the case, explained, "The Constitution protects people's right to join AA voluntarily, to pray at meetings, and to believe that recovery requires a spiritual awakening and guidance from a Higher Power. But the Constitution also prohibits the government from coercing people to study, memorize, and believe religious ideas. The state cannot force young people to attend religious classes at a public school nor to adopt theistic concepts or suffer punishments."

CYA teachers and their union joined the suit. One teacher plaintiff, Harvey Martinez, said, "We understand the great need for substance abuse programs, particularly with young offenders. But there are many alternatives that are not based on religious principles."

In a court-approved settlement in the lawsuit, the CYA agreed to modify the Karl Holton center's substance abuse programs so that wards were no longer required to profess spiritual beliefs. The CYA revised all curricular materials to delete references to God and other religious concepts, and made attendance at AA meetings voluntary.

The young inmate who had risked the isolation ward and deferred release from prison to raise his objections to the religious program was vindicated. The CYA informed the Youth Offender Parole Board that the only reason he had been punished was that he had religious objections to the Design for Living program. "Our client cannot be stigmatized as a program failure for following his own religious beliefs," asserted attorney Hardy. He was soon released.

Five Sacred Symbols

The trickle-down effect of the Reagan and Bush administrations' War on Drugs, which led to a law-and-order climate and "zero tolerance" policies for weapons at schools, threatened the religious freedom of three young Sikh children in the San Joaquin Valley—and resulted in their suspension from elementary school for almost a full year.

One day in 1994, ten-year-old Rajinder Cheema was playing basketball in his schoolyard in the small, dusty Central Valley town of Livingston. When he took a jump shot, his T-shirt rose up on his thin frame, revealing a small, ceremonial knife, a *kirpan*, tucked in the waistband of his pants.

When a classmate asked him about it, Rajinder proudly explained that he had been baptized into his Khalsa Sikh religion, and that wearing the *kirpan* was one of the obligations of his religion.

The Khalsa Sikh faith, a five-hundred-year-old religion that originated in South Asia, has eighteen million adherents worldwide, many in the U.S. When Khalsa Sikhs are baptized, they undertake a religious duty to wear five sacred symbols: the *kirpan*, a comb, long hair, a steel bracelet, and special cotton undergarments. Each of the symbols—known as the "5 Ks,"—has religious significance. They must be worn at all times, even while bathing or sleeping.

But after Rajinder's young classmate told another friend, and that boy told a teacher, Rajinder was suspended from school for violating the district's zero tolerance policy for weapons. Rajinder's younger sister Sukhjinder, eight, and brother Jaspreet, seven, were also suspended. Three baptized Sikh adults who asked to talk with school officials were threatened with arrest if they entered school property wearing their *kirpans*.

Rajinder's mother was alarmed. She was a farmworker, raising three small children on her own. She was proud that they could speak English, were doing well

In 1994 Rajinder Cheema (right), pictured here with his brother and sister, was suspended from his elementary school in the agricultural town of Livingston for wearing a kirpan, one of the symbols of his Sikh religion, under his shirt. The school district claimed that the small, wrapped knife violated its zero tolerance policy for weapons.

in school, and were attentive to their religious studies. But when her children were suspended, she was at a loss. A Sikh community activist asked the ACLU to help her negotiate with the school.

Several school districts in California with substantial Sikh populations already had adopted explicit policies permitting baptized Sikh children to wear their *kirpans* to school. Other districts accommodated the practice without any specific policy. There had been no reports of Sikh-related school violence. As Stephen Bomse, an attorney who volunteered to represent the family, explained, "The *kirpan* is not a weapon, it is a religious symbol. Wearing it at all times is as important to Khalsa Sikhs as wearing a yarmulke is to Orthodox Jews."

The attorneys examined other districts' experiences and tried to create a workable solution. They proposed that the miniature *kirpans* be blunted and sewn tightly into their sheaths, which would be worn under the children's clothing, and not visible or removable. The Sikh community designed a small pouch to accommodate the school district's concerns. But the school district would not budge.

The year before, Congress had passed the Religious Freedom Restoration Act of 1993. The law was a direct response to a 1990 U.S. Supreme Court decision that drastically limited constitutional protection for religious freedom (*Employment Division, Department of Human Resources of Oregon v. Smith*). That decision had permitted states to enforce laws whose impact would prevent people from engaging in important religious activities, such as the ceremonial use of peyote, even though no specific group or religion was mentioned by name in the legislation.

The ACLU attorneys decided to invoke the provisions of the new religious freedom law to get Rajinder and his siblings back into school.

The ensuing months dragged on for the Cheema children, who, barred from attending school, were at home all day. Their mother hired a tutor, but they missed their teachers and their classmates. The first court ruling was disappointing—the school district's policy was upheld. As the summer vacation drew to a close, the children did not know whether they would be allowed back in school in the fall.

But on September 2, the Ninth Circuit Court of Appeals ruled that the school district had "a duty under the Religious Freedom Restoration Act to avoid all unnecessary burdens on the [students'] religious liberty." The court said that the district had to "make all reasonable efforts" to accommodate the religious beliefs and practices of the young Khalsa Sikh children, who had not attended school since January.

Noting that "the record is replete with evidence" that school safety concerns could be dealt with, the court instructed the school district to allow the children to wear *kirpans* that had been blunted and firmly sewn into their sheaths—the proposal that the school district had flatly rejected months before.

In September Rajinder, wearing a Batman T-shirt, a Sikh turban, and a concealed *kirpan*, returned to school. Unaware that he had made history, he was anxious to get his new spelling list and math problems, and meet his friends for a game of basketball.

— NINE —

THAT DARE NOT SPEAK ITS NAME

THE RIGHTS OF LESBIANS, GAY MEN, BISEXUALS, AND TRANSGENDER PEOPLE

We must destroy the myths once and for all, shatter them....And most important, every gay person must come out....Once they realize that we are their children, that we are everywhere, every myth, every lie, every innuendo will be destroyed.

—Harvey Milk, San Francisco supervisor, 1978

In 1950 in Seattle, twenty-six-year-old Phyllis Lyon met the first woman she'd ever seen carrying a briefcase. The trailblazer who so intrigued the wide-eyed associate editor of *Pacific Builder and Engineer* magazine was Del Martin, the newly hired editor of *Daily Construction Reports*. The two women became fast friends. Intelligent and adventurous, both had studied journalism. Lyon, a sharp and quick-witted Tulsa-born writer, had been an editor at the *Daily Californian*, the student newspaper at UC Berkeley, where she graduated in 1947. San Francisco native Dorothy Taliaferro (who went by Del) had also attended Berkeley and then transferred to San Francisco State College, where she wrote for the school paper and married a classmate, James Martin.

By 1950 Del Martin had divorced and was building a new life. After two years, Lyon and Martin acknowledged that their mutual affection extended beyond friendship. Together, they returned to San Francisco and, on Valentine's Day 1953, moved into an apartment on Castro Street in a largely Irish Catholic working-class neighborhood.

Although eager to meet other lesbians, Martin and Lyon were too shy to frequent bars, then the most popular gathering places for lesbians. When Rose Bamberger, a

Phyllis Lyon and Del Martin, two of the founders of the Daughters of Bilitis, the first U.S. organization for lesbians. It was founded in 1955, when being openly gay could result in arrest, harassment, and job loss.

Filipino American woman whom Lyon and Martin met through gay male friends, invited them to join three other lesbian couples to form a social group, they enthusiastically agreed.

The racially and economically diverse group of eight San Franciscans called their fledgling organization Daughters of Bilitis (DOB), an allusion to *The Songs of Bilitis* (1894) by Pierre Louÿs, which was in turn a tribute to Sappho, the ancient Greek woman known for her love poetry addressed to women. In 1955 the organization's cryptic name was appropriate, given the real dangers of being openly gay. Despite this, DOB's membership quickly expanded locally, then nationally. The group adopted a formal mission statement—"to encourage and support the Lesbian in her search for personal, interpersonal, social, economic, and vocational identity"—and worked towards the goals of educating the general public "to accept the Lesbian as an individual and eliminate the prejudice which places oppressive limitations" on her. Members of the organization participated in social science research, and the group promoted "changes in the legal system to insure the rights of all homosexuals."

DOB was the first formal organization working nationally for lesbian visibility and rights, but throughout California history owners and patrons of gay bars, civil service employees, gay men caught in entrapment schemes, and long-term committed gay couples contributed to the securing of legal precedents, legislative advances, and societal changes that resulted in greater freedom and equality for lesbians, gay men, and transgender people.

Ragtime Drag

As early as the gold rush, San Franciscans publicly acknowledged cross-dressing entertainers and male prostitution. Homosexual activity, however, was criminalized. In 1850 the state legislature made sodomy a felony. For more than seventy years, the maximum punishment was life imprisonment.

Criminalization of sexual orientation contributed to police harassment of men and women who did not conform to gender stereotypes. In November 1914, police arrested thirty-one Long Beach men who allegedly belonged to two private groups, the 606 Club and the 96 Club. The *Los Angeles Times* reported that the groups held weekly meetings in which members powdered their faces and wore kimonos. The paper dubbed club members "devils" and advocated "prominent publication of the name of every wretch convicted of a horrible enormity besides which ordinary prostitution is chastity itself." Then the *Times* did exactly that, publishing the names and occupations of those arrested, a common practice among California newspapers. This unwanted publicity contributed to the suicide of John Lamb, a forty-year-old banker and church officer, who swallowed cyanide on a San Pedro beach. In his suicide note he wrote, "I am crazed by reading the paper this morning."

The arrests resulted from the efforts of two freelance "vice specialists," W. H. Warren and B. C. Brown, whom the Long Beach police hired in the summer of 1914 to expose gay men. The Los Angeles Police Department had previously hired the two, who had no police training, and paid them for each arrest. While working in Los Angeles, Warren and Brown arrested dozens of men in what historians Lillian Faderman and Stuart Timmons believe may be the first documented instances of southern California police entrapping gay men. Typically, Brown and Warren loitered in public restrooms and bathhouses, attempting to get men to express a sexual interest. If one took the bait, an arrest quickly followed.

Most of those arrested either paid fines or went to jail. One man entrapped by Brown and Warren, however, fought back. Soon after the Long Beach arrests, Warren sat in the attic of a residential building, peering through a peephole into an apartment that Brown had rented from thirty-nine-year-old florist Herbert Lowe. Outside, another officer spied into the apartment through a window.

According to the police, Lowe entered his tenant's apartment, pulled the covers off the bed in which Brown was lying, and began kissing his body. The *Times* reported that the florist was startled by a noise outside and got up. The police rushed in and arrested him. The four officers on the scene testified that Lowe admitted to being a "social vagrant," the legal term applied to gay men, and offered them a fifteen-hundred-dollar bribe.

Lowe denied everything.

At trial, Lowe's attorney argued that the florist was a trusted community member, whereas his accusers, Brown and Warren, were carpetbaggers, little more than blackmailers "dripping with the blood of John Lamb," the Long Beach man who had killed himself.

The jury took less than thirty minutes to acquit Lowe.

Although Lowe was freed, the trial motivated the California legislature to pass a law designating oral sex a felony punishable by up to fifteen years in prison.

Sex and Security Risks

Beginning in 1947 and continuing throughout the 1950s, Cold War fears of communism bled into an equally ferocious alarm over homosexuality. Government leaders considered gay people security risks, not only because homosexuality was considered such a shameful secret that gay men and lesbians were vulnerable to blackmail, but also because they believed gay people lacked "emotional stability" and "moral fiber," and were therefore susceptible to manipulation by foreign powers. Harangued by Republicans who alleged that "sexual perverts" had infiltrated the government, the Truman administration instituted a federal anti-gay pogrom resulting in investigations, harassment, purges of suspected homosexuals, and federal policies excluding gay people from civil service jobs, military service, and naturalization rights.

In 1953 President Eisenhower issued an executive order specifically making "sexual perversion" (i.e., homosexuality) a basis for denying federal employment, and for firing employees under a security program that had initially targeted "subversives." In 1960 President Eisenhower issued another executive order, this time establishing the Industrial Security Program to protect the government from security threats posed by private sector employees working on government contracts; this order became the basis for barring homosexuals from the private sector defense industry.

Within this repressive political and social environment, small but determined organizations composed of what were then called "homophiles" formed to counter the prevailing anti-gay attitudes and laws of the era.

In 1951 a small group of politically aware gay men, some of whom had been involved with the Communist Party, met in a cozy home in the Silver Lake area of Los Angeles. They began a group based on the then radical idea that homosexuals were not criminals or mentally ill but were, instead, an oppressed minority that needed to organize for its rights and equal treatment under the law. According to Harry Hay, one of the founding members, the five original organizers established the group along the classic lines of revolutionary movements, with separate cells, or guilds, whose attending members would remain unknown to other cells:

> We allowed no photographs to be taken, and insisted nothing be put down in writing—no notes, no phone lists, or anything that could be used for blackmail or turned over to the FBI. We decided to call ourselves Mattachine after…medieval peasant monks who wore masks.…We too were forced to wear masks on the job and elsewhere. Paranoia was such at our early meetings that we had to promise total secrecy. Some newcomers were blindfolded and driven around in circles before being taken to meetings. Others came accompanied by members of the opposite sex as a cover for their safety.

From that core grew five separate Mattachine Society groups in Los Angeles. Within two years, there were chapters in San Francisco. In 1953, after a contentious, red-baiting general membership meeting, the Mattachine Society's founders resigned from the board, and Harold Call, a San Francisco journalist and businessman, took leadership of the organization, moving its headquarters to San Francisco. The group's political perspectives also shifted. Rather than promoting the identity of gay people as a distinct minority, Mattachine now focused on similarities to the mainstream as a means of reducing prejudice and discrimination against gay people. This was evidenced in a 1955 statement in the inaugural issue of *Mattachine Review*:

> We are not distinguishable from heterosexual people in any visible way… we are no more unreliable, unstable or dangerous than heterosexuals.…Our hearts are no less full of pride and honor at the sight of massed American flags because we are homosexual. We do not work less hard for America, or love her less, or support the Republican administration and policies less whole-heartedly because we are homosexual.

In January 1956, the new San Francisco–based leaders of Mattachine met with Phyllis Lyon and Del Martin, marking the beginning of cross-organizational homophile efforts. Martin and Lyon encouraged the Daughters of Bilitis to join Mattachine members in requesting their state legislators to change California's "sex laws." A few weeks later, the two DOB leaders traveled to Los Angeles to attend the annual Midwinter Institute organized by ONE, Inc., an offshoot of the Mattachine Society. They returned home enthusiastic about working in concert with the other homophile groups for social change. But not all members of DOB shared the leaders' eagerness for activism and educational programs; those who wanted DOB to be purely a lesbian social club quit. Lyon and Martin were nonetheless able to generate interest among other lesbians who shared their goal of "promoting the integration of the homosexual into society."

A year after founding DOB, Phyllis Lyon was the first editor of its groundbreaking monthly magazine, *The Ladder*. In the first issue, DOB president Del Martin wrote, "Nothing was ever accomplished by hiding in a dark corner. Why not discard the hermitage for the heritage that awaits any red-blooded American woman who dares to claim it?" Women throughout the world read *The Ladder*, grateful for the connection with other gay women.

DOB leaders were committed civil libertarians, rejecting member requests to take an anticommunist stance and instead favoring freedom of thought and political association.

Over the Memorial Day weekend in 1960, DOB hosted the first public gathering of lesbians in the United States: "A Look at the Lesbian," held at the Hotel Whitcomb, near San Francisco's Civic Center. Two hundred women attended, as did police from the city's "homosexual detail," who showed up to determine whether any of the women were wearing men's clothing. Del Martin told the officers to look at the conferees, all of whom wore dresses or skirts with blouses and stockings and heels. The officers left, but another man, an undercover CIA agent, spied on the gathering.

Although DOB and Mattachine actively promoted understanding of homosexuals during an era when being openly lesbian or gay had severe repercussions, neither they nor their members were the first in California to sue for equal rights. It was the owner of a San Francisco bar popular with gay men and lesbians who took this step.

"God Bless Us Nelly Queens"

During World War II, thousands of young men traveled through the port cities of Los Angeles and San Francisco. Although the military was relatively tolerant of gay people because it needed troops, officials nonetheless attempted to regulate soldiers' morals. They posted signs in bars that they suspected of being homosexual haunts, designating them out of bounds, and worked with police and state officials to keep military personnel out of gay and lesbian bars. This harassment continued in the postwar years.

The Black Cat, on the edge of San Francisco's North Beach neighborhood, was the focus of the first California Supreme Court ruling dealing with anti-gay animus. Poet Allen Ginsberg once called the Black Cat "maybe the greatest gay bar in America....Everybody went there, heterosexual and homosexual. It was lit up, there was a honky-tonk piano; it was enormous. All the gay screaming queens would come, the heterosexual gray flannel suit types, longshoremen. All the poets went there."

The bar's popularity in the 1950s and early 1960s was in part due to a charismatic drag performer, José Sarria, who sang parodies of operas and ended his performances by exhorting the crowd to stand and sing "God Bless Us Nelly Queens" to the tune of "God Save the Queen." Sarria interspersed his musical offerings with political education; he alerted gay and bisexual men about police entrapment and advised them to assert their constitutional rights if arrested on morals charges. In 1963 Sarria ran for the San Francisco Board of Supervisors. Although he didn't win a seat, he drew a significant number of votes and awakened the city's politicians to the fact that gay voters were a constituency not to be ignored.

The Black Cat was also well known to the State Board of Equalization (SBE), which was at the time the entity responsible for regulating bars and liquor licenses. SBE agents had spied on the Black Cat and concluded that it was "a hangout for persons of homosexual tendencies." On that basis, the SBE in 1949 revoked the liquor license of owner Sol Stoumen, invoking a law against using a business as a "disorderly house...for purposes injurious to public morals."

Angry about losing his successful business, Stoumen hired attorney Morris Lowenthal, who sued SBE chair George R. Reilly to get the license reinstated. Lowenthal cited the recently published Kinsey Report, which revealed that over one-third of American men had engaged in homosexual activity at least once since puberty. He argued that since so many men had same-gender sexual experiences, the "social taboo" against homosexuals was unwarranted. Lowenthal also raised the then unprecedented argument that homosexuals had a right to assemble openly.

Judge Robert L. McWilliams flatly rejected the freedom of assembly argument, stating:

> An occasional fortuitous meeting of such persons [homosexuals] at restaurants...is one thing. But for the proprietor of a restaurant knowingly to permit his premises to be regularly used "as a meeting place" by persons of the type mentioned with all of the potentialities for evil and immorality drawing out of such meetings is, in my opinion, conduct of an entirely different nature which justifies action on the part of the Board of Equalization.

The court of appeal unanimously upheld McWilliams's ruling. *Stoumen v. Reilly* reached the California Supreme Court in 1951. The high court unanimously reversed the earlier rulings and ordered the trial court to prevent the SBE from suspending Stoumen's liquor license. Chief Justice Phil S. Gibson ruled that there was "no evidence of illegal or immoral conduct on the premises or that the patrons resorted to the restaurant for purposes injurious to public morals." Mere patronage of the Black Cat bar by homosexuals was not evidence of wrongdoing. "Members of the public of lawful age have a right to patronize a public restaurant and bar so long as they are acting properly and are not committing illegal or immoral acts," Gibson concluded.

The decision was significant, at least in theory, because it articulated that the government could not prevent people from assembling simply because of their sexual orientation. On a practical level, however, the ruling was almost meaningless because it left open a loophole for state authorities to revoke liquor licenses if they could document even the most innocuous homosexual behavior on the premises.

In 1955 the legislature significantly undercut the practical significance of the *Stoumen* decision. Assemblyman Caspar Weinberger sponsored a bill that required the revocation of a liquor license if an establishment was a "resort for illegal possessors or users of narcotics, prostitutes, pimps, panderers, or sexual perverts." Bar owners could lose their licenses on the vague standard of "general reputation" in the community. The legislature also created a new agency, the Alcoholic Beverage Control Board (ABC), to oversee liquor licenses. Unlike its predecessor, the ABC did not deal with taxation and revenue but instead turned its complete attention to alleged vice. Just months after its formation, the ABC declared a "war on homosexual bars in San Francisco."

The ABC hired undercover agents to gather incriminating evidence, which could be as flimsy and subjective as effeminate mannerisms on the part of men or masculine behavior on the part of women. The regulating agency certainly considered same-sex propositioning, a felony in California at the time, as evidence of illegal and immoral activity. But otherwise, the vagueness of what constituted "immoral" and "illegal" opened the door for entrapment.

The *Stoumen* decision could not deter law enforcement officers intent on harassing gay people any more than it could deter licensing officials. One of the most dramatic early incidents took place in San Mateo County at a bar called Hazel's, owned by Hazel Nickola. On February 19, 1956, San Mateo County Sheriff Earl Whitmore shouldered his way through two hundred people gathered there. He jumped on the bar and shouted, "This is a raid!" Undercover agents identified patrons who had shown "homosexual behavior," and deputies took eighty-seven men to the county jail. Sheriff Whitmore explained that "the purpose of the raid was to make it very clear to these people that we won't put up with this sort of thing." Exactly what "this sort of thing" meant was not clear until the eighty-seven were charged with being "lewd and dissolute" persons and committing acts outraging public decency. The ABC revoked Nickola's liquor license, a decision upheld by the appellate court.

In a series of court decisions between 1957 and 1959, the judiciary validated the 1955 law allowing the ABC to revoke the liquor licenses of businesses judged to be "resorts for sexual perverts." But in 1959, the state supreme court heard the case of

Vallerga v. Department of Alcoholic Beverage Control. Albert L. Vallerga and Mary Azar owned Oakland's First and Last Chance Bar, which catered to lesbians and gay men. Morris Lowenthal represented Vallerga and Azar and argued that the 1955 law violated the bar owners' due process and placed an undue burden on them to determine the sexual orientation of their patrons. The high court agreed that the law was, indeed, unconstitutional. It was a pyrrhic victory, however, because the court suggested that the government could shut down any business "contrary to public welfare or morals."

In 1960 San Francisco businessmen reported to the district attorney that ABC administrators and police officers were demanding monthly payments not to raid gay bars. The press dubbed the revelation the "gayola" scandal, and an ABC investigator and police officer caught with marked bills pleaded guilty. In the wake of the scandal, the ABC and the police stepped up their harassment. Finally, the bar owners rebelled. In 1962 they formed the Tavern Guild in San Francisco, the first gay business association in the country, to protect themselves against police abuse. The guild retained an attorney and bail bondsman for people arrested in or near gay bars. It also published a brochure instructing patrons on their rights if arrested or questioned by police. In the 1950s, the Daughters of Bilitis had served a similar purpose, counseling women about their rights and securing legal representation for those arrested in lesbian bar raids.

In Los Angeles, police harassment of patrons and employees of gay bars was also a perennial problem. In 1948 the police department trumpeted to the press that it had records on ten thousand "known sex offenders." That same year, the Assembly Subcommittee on Public Morals for Southern California recommended that eight Hollywood bars be shut down because they were "gathering places for perverts." The committee also recommended banning the sale of alcohol to "unescorted women" in taverns, which could effectively close lesbian bars. The city council followed the committee's recommendations and passed laws targeting "degenerates in public places." After William Parker became police chief in 1950, arrests for "sex perversion" jumped by over 85 percent. Lesbians recall that police of the era accosted them simply for standing in front of a lesbian bar or looking too masculine.

In the first two weeks of 1967, officers of LAPD's Rampart Division raided five gay bars, beginning with another bar called the Black Cat, this one in L.A.'s Silver Lake neighborhood. At midnight on New Year's Eve, the Black Cat was filled with revelers. Balloons fell from the ceiling as the Rhythm Queens, a trio of African American women, sang a rock version of "Auld Lang Syne." Patrons exchanged New Year's kisses, which was enough of a crime for twelve undercover police officers inside the club to call on their uniformed colleagues outside. The officers forced their way into the bar, swinging billy clubs, injuring celebrants, and destroying furnishings and Christmas ornaments. Police arrested sixteen customers and employees and forced them to lie facedown on the sidewalk.

Officers chased patrons down the street to the nearby New Faces bar, knocked down the owner, and beat two of the bartenders unconscious. One of them, Robert Haas, was hospitalized with a ruptured spleen and then charged with assault on an officer.

A jury found six men guilty of lewd conduct because they had been seen kissing other men on the lips.

Another New Year's Celebration

One of the most galvanizing raids took place not in a bar but at a 1965 New Year's costume ball benefiting a San Francisco group called the Council on Religion and the Homosexual (CRH). CRH formed in 1964 after leaders at Glide Memorial Methodist Church, located in San Francisco's rundown Tenderloin neighborhood, contacted local homophile organizations about creating a ministry for young male prostitutes who congregated in the area. That led to a three-day retreat of fifteen members of

This couple braved a gauntlet of spotlights, police photographers, and uniformed officers to attend a 1965 New Year's fundraiser for a gay organization in San Francisco. Such harassment was commonplace throughout the 1950s and 1960s.

the Bay Area clergy and fifteen leaders of homophile groups, including Daughters of Bilitis founders Del Martin and Phyllis Lyon. They discussed issues such as theology and homosexuality, and attitudes of the clergy and homosexuals towards each other. By the end of the retreat, the group had formed CRH to continue the dialogue.

In late 1964, San Francisco gay and lesbian groups agreed to cosponsor a Mardi Gras–themed costume ball to raise funds for CRH at California Hall, two blocks from City Hall. Prior to the event, CRH ministers and attorneys met with the San Francisco Police Department's "Sex Crimes" detail. The police opposed the event and threatened to arrest anyone in drag. CRH emphasized that the affair was private, implying that police could not dictate dress codes. The meeting ended with police agreeing to allow the dance to take place, and CRH representatives believing that law enforcement would not interfere.

That understanding, however, crumbled when police blocked off all intersections leading to California Hall, set up floodlights in front of the building, gathered at the entrance, and took still photos and movies of everyone entering.

Despite this gauntlet, about five hundred courageous people went inside. Police then harassed the event organizers on many pretexts. Herb Donaldson, an attorney and legal advisor at the ball who later became a San Francisco Superior Court judge, recalled:

> The plainclothes police started coming in to make inspections. There was a fire inspection. There was a health inspection. I think it was about the fourth inspection when we said, "That's enough! If you want to come in, you're going to have to get a search warrant." We were cheek-to-cheek with the police. We were just standing there and they were standing there. They didn't believe we would stand them off

A group of uniformed officers with movie cameras pushed past the ticket table, running roughshod through the crowd on the dance floor, terrifying partygoers. Police arrested legal observer Donaldson and three other CRH volunteers for "obstructing an officer in the course of his duties," even though the police did not claim that anyone attempted to physically restrain them or prevent them from entering.

Police intimidation drove away hundreds of the expected fifteen hundred attendees, but in the long run the incident damaged the police. The following day, seven CRH-affiliated ministers held a press conference condemning law enforcement's behavior. The incident helped the general public realize that gay people were the targets of police harassment. San Francisco Mayor John F. Shelley demanded a full accounting of the incident from Police Chief Thomas Cahill.

Donaldson remembered that CRH ministers and their wives, "all dressed up in their Sunday 'go to church' clothes" at his criminal trial, which "was so important for the jury to see—to see the support."

The police insisted that the six uniformed and nine plainclothes officers were only at the event to enforce alcoholic beverage control laws and that they did not plan in advance to make any arrests. One officer, however, seriously undermined that argument when he admitted on cross-examination that prior to leaving the Hall of Justice he had prepared fifty numbered cards intended for police photographs of people arrested.

Municipal Court Judge Leo Friedman declared that the evidence was insufficient to support the charge of obstructing the police. It was clear, the judge stated, that the police were intent on disturbing the party. Suddenly ending the trial, he advised the jury to bring in a verdict of "not guilty," based on a motion of Donaldson's ACLU attorney, Marshall Krause. After ten minutes of deliberation, the jury announced its unanimous vote: not guilty.

The CRH ball and its aftermath ushered in a new era of gay activism to San Francisco. CRH issued a pamphlet entitled "A Brief of Injustices: An Indictment of Our Society and Its Treatment of the Homosexual," documenting employment discrimination, police harassment and entrapment, and anti-gay violence. The CRH incident also contributed to the formation of Citizen's Alert, a twenty-four-hour community hotline organized by Del Martin, for lesbians and gay men to report incidents of police abuse.

The CRH fiasco, as well as the "gayola" scandal a few years earlier, motivated the San Francisco Police Department to implement a community relations unit. Elliot Blackstone, a long-time advocate for such a program during his years on the San Francisco police force, was assigned to be the department's community relations officer for the Tenderloin neighborhood, one of the poorest in the city and a gathering place for homosexuals and gender nonconformists.

Three Years before Stonewall

California has been the site of transgender activity since at least the nineteenth century. (The term "transgender" encompasses people who do not conform to gender stereotypes, refuse to identify with a gender, or manifest a gender different from their birth-assigned sex. While some transgender people identify as lesbian or gay, not all do.) At the turn of the century, the Los Angeles Merchants Association even encouraged cross-dressing on All Fool's Night, the culmination of a weeklong commercial Carnivalesque celebration called La Fiesta. Bowing to religious leaders offended by the gender confusion of the event, the Los Angeles city council in 1898 not only banned All Fool's Night, but also passed an ordinance making it a crime for "a man to masquerade as a woman, or a woman as a man."

In 1922 the council revised the law, imposing a six-month jail sentence and five-hundred-dollar fine on anyone caught on the street dressed in clothes of the opposite sex. This gave police the legal basis to stop and harass women and men who did not conform to officers' notions of gender-appropriate clothing. The harassment continued even after Los Angeles municipal courts ruled, in two separate 1950 cases, that a woman could not be convicted for wearing men's slacks and coats and short hair unless there was further evidence of intent to conceal her identity.

Transgender people in California had been quietly organizing since the 1940s for recognition of their rights. Louise Lawrence, a male-to-female transgender person, began in the 1940s to live full-time as a woman in San Francisco. She learned of other transgender people in the U.S. and elsewhere and built a wide correspondence network. She worked with pioneering sex researcher Alfred Kinsey to educate social scientists about the needs of transgender people. Lawrence also mentored another transgender pioneer, Virginia Prince. Born in 1912 into an upper-middle-class Los Angeles family as Arnold Loman, Prince, who as an adult adopted the pseudonym Virginia Prince, began cross-dressing as a teenager. After earning a PhD in biochemistry, Prince moved to Oakland and worked at the UC San Francisco medical school. There she encountered transvestite patients. Feeling isolated about her cross-dressing, Prince contacted one of them, and they began meeting with other transvestites. Prince's wife filed for divorce, incorrectly believing her husband to be gay. The local press learned of the story and publicly identified Prince as a cross-dresser. Although the publicity was unwelcome, it spurred other cross-dressers to contact Prince, and they formed a small group in her home city of Los Angeles, to which she had returned.

In 1952 Prince and a group of transvestites that met in Long Beach published the newsletter *Transvestia: The Journal of the American Society for Equality in Dress.* Historian Susan Stryker considers the short-lived publication "arguably the first overtly political transgender publication in the U.S."

In 1960 Prince began publishing another iteration of *Transvestia.* The following year she formed the Hose and Heels Club, which soon changed its name to Phi Pi Epsilon, not only to mimic sororities but to reference the initials "FPE," an acronym for "Full Personality Expression."

These pioneering organizing efforts were a prelude to the more radical transgender political protests that erupted in 1966 in San Francisco's Tenderloin neighborhood. The mid-1960s were a time of transition for the Tenderloin. Urban renewal projects on the neighborhood's edge had brought tourism and convention-related hotel construction. City leaders wanted to polish the tarnished area, one of the most run-down in San Francisco.

At the same time, America's escalating involvement in the Vietnam War was bringing more military personnel to San Francisco. As they had during World War II and the Korean War, civic leaders and police cracked down on bars and prostitutes catering to soldiers and sailors.

Transgender people in the Tenderloin faced rampant discrimination and could not find jobs or decent places to live. Though nightclub managers hired male-to-female transgender people with talent and glamorous looks as drag performers, those jobs were few and far between. Lacking marketable skills and confronting discrimination, many male-to-female transgender people turned to street prostitution for economic survival. Police officers routinely harassed and arrested them. Many transgender people who lived in the neighborhood's seedy hotels were jailed for no reason, or on such flimsy charges as impersonating a female or obstructing the sidewalk.

In addition to adult transgender prostitutes, teenage hustlers of all genders worked the tough Tenderloin streets. To address their needs, Reverend Ed Havens of Glide Church formed Vanguard, a night ministry for young street prostitutes. Motivated by the then radical idea that, like racial minorities, sexual minorities were the targets of discrimination, Havens secured funding from the federal government's War on Poverty program to address the problems of the Tenderloin's transgender and youth prostitutes.

The spring and summer of 1966 were active in the city's lesbian, gay, and transgender communities. In April, the Society for Individual Rights, an early San Francisco gay rights organization, opened a community center in the Tenderloin as a locus for gay community activism and to organize residents to lobby for federal anti-poverty funds. In May, lesbian and gay activists gathered at the San Francisco federal building, at the edge of the Tenderloin, to protest the military's exclusion of gay people. In August, the Daughters of Bilitis convened its fourth biennial conference in San Francisco.

In the mid-1960s, police were known to allow prostitution, drug dealing, gambling, and other vice in the Tenderloin, if they were paid off. But in 1966, pressured by politicians, they targeted the Tenderloin for a prostitution crackdown.

That summer, the flashpoint for the Tenderloin's poor, disenfranchised, and dispossessed transgender people and young gay street prostitutes was a twenty-four-hour restaurant on the corner of Taylor and Turk streets. At Compton's Cafeteria, a diner where waitresses with paper doilies pinned onto their starched uniforms poured coffee for them, regulars gathered in the vinyl booths to gossip and talk. The police department's Elliot Blackstone recalled: "Compton's was a drag queen hangout. They'd buy coffee, then sit there for four or five hours. Compton's was losing money because of it." When Compton's management imposed a twenty-five-cent service charge on all orders, teens in the Vanguard program saw it as a thinly veiled attempt to keep customers like them out. They began picketing outside the restaurant.

Late on a hot August night, the collective rage of the Tenderloin's transgender women and street youth erupted. A boisterous group at one table upset the manager, who called in the police. An officer accustomed to harassing the restaurant's disempowered patrons grabbed the arm of a drag queen and tried to arrest her. Fed up with disrespect and police abuse, she threw coffee in his face.

Her action released the pent-up anger of the other patrons. They threw cups, saucers, silverware, and plates at the retreating officer, who called for reinforcements. The ensuing melee, which involved fifty to sixty people, spread into the street, with drag queens hitting police with their purses and kicking them with their high heels. Rioters broke restaurant windows and set fire to a nearby newsstand.

Susan Stryker explains that the riot at Compton's was "the first known instance of collective, militant queer resistance to police harassment in United States history." It took place three years before similar resistance by gay people and drag queens at New York's Stonewall Inn, the event many consider the birth of the movement for lesbian, gay, bisexual, and transgender equality.

"There was a lot of joy after it happened," explained Amanda St. Jaymes, who participated in the riot. "A lot of them went to jail, but there was a lot of 'I don't really give a damn. This is what had to happen.'"

In late 1966, Elliot Blackstone, by then the police department's liaison with the federally funded Central City Anti-Poverty Program, received a visit from a woman he later described as a "tall, football player–type female." The visitor was Louise Ergestrasse, a male-to-female Tenderloin prostitute, who explained to the burly officer that she and other transgender women traded sex for money because of employment discrimination. Ergestrasse demanded that Blackstone do something to reduce police abuse and help prostitutes out of sex work.

Together, they organized Conversion Our Goal (later changed to Transsexual Counseling Service). The group succeeded in reducing arrests under gender "impersonation" laws. With funding from the Erickson Educational Foundation, a philanthropy formed by a transsexual who was heir to a lead-smelting business, they connected clients to supportive social services and medical programs, including city-funded clinics that provided hormones to facilitate gender reassignment.

Behind Closed Doors

California vagrancy laws—specifically sections that addressed "soliciting or engaging in lewd or dissolute conduct"—long provided police with a vehicle for targeting individuals they believed to be gay or members of other marginalized groups. "Lewd vagrancy" convictions had significant consequences. In 1947 California required individuals convicted of "immoral conduct," including consensual same-gender sexual intimacy (even kissing and dancing), to register as sex offenders. Such "offenders" were not allowed to teach in public school, hold government jobs, or run for public office. They had to report their movements to police and submit to police surveillance.

Even more ominous, men arrested twice for public sexual behavior could be labeled "sexual psychopaths" and involuntarily committed to Atascadero State

Hospital, a maximum security hospital north of Santa Barbara. According to historian Nan Boyd, "Doctors were legally permitted to indefinitely hold any patient 'whose mental condition [doctors] believed would make him dangerous to be released.' Accused homosexuals could be committed to Atascadero without arrest or trial for a 90-day observation period, during which time hormonal and/or shock treatments might be imposed on the patient."

In 1952 Dale Jennings, a founder of the Mattachine Society, fought back. An undercover LAPD vice squad officer followed the muscular, thirty-five-year-old Jennings to his Echo Park home one evening. Jennings thought that the "big, rough-looking character" was a robber. According to Jennings, the officer made sexual advances, virtually forcing himself into Jennings's apartment before arresting him for "lewd vagrancy."

Jennings, a former USC theater student, challenged his arrest, a response that San Francisco attorney Herb Donaldson explained was unheard of at the time: "If you were arrested, your name could turn up in the newspaper." Donaldson's colleague Evander Smith added, "The police didn't have to deal with any trials from these cases because the clients were too embarrassed to be subjected to a jury trial, and the attorneys were too embarrassed to defend them. So they would either plead guilty and pay a fine or they'd waive a jury trial. When they waived the jury trial, they would most often be convicted by the judge, pay a fine, and be left with a police record."

Unlike the hundreds of men in California who had quietly pled no contest and paid fines to bury their arrests, Jennings insisted on a jury trial. Jennings recalled, "One of my prevailing thoughts was, 'I am not alone. Think of all the guys who have gone through this, completely alone. I must stand up for myself and for *them*....I knew that speaking out was of prime importance." The Mattachine Society hired attorney George Shibley, who a few years earlier had represented the young Mexican American defendants in the infamous Sleepy Lagoon murder trial. Shibley advised Mattachine leaders to organize a legal defense group, the Citizens' Committee to Outlaw Entrapment, to raise money and publicize Jennings's trial.

During the trial, Jennings was not ashamed to declare himself a homosexual, but he denied he was guilty of solicitation. He accused the vice officer of entrapment. The jury deadlocked, 11-1, with the one juror announcing he would vote a gay person guilty "until hell froze over." The judge dismissed the charges, and Jennings was freed.

Despite this important case, the first in the U.S. in which an avowedly gay man had successfully fought a lewd vagrancy charge, police continued to harass gay and bisexual men by charging them with the crime of asking someone to engage in "lewd or dissolute conduct," even though the conduct would take place between two consenting adults in private; the vagrancy law still allowed the police broad discretion in interpreting the phrase "lewd and dissolute conduct."

The law became more untenable after 1975, when the legislature passed a bill, sponsored by San Francisco Assemblyman Willie Brown, legalizing private consensual sex between adults. Brown had introduced this legislation every year since 1969. In 1975 Senate majority leader George Moscone of San Francisco championed it, and the legislative body split on a vote of 20-20. Moscone literally had the doors of the senate chambers locked until Lieutenant Governor Mervyn Dymally flew to Sacramento from Denver to break the tie.

Although the Brown Act took the government out of individuals' bedrooms, police still arrested gay people for meeting in public places and proposing consensual sex that was to take place in private. That began to change after the California Supreme Court heard the case of Don Barry Pryor.

On May Day 1976, Pryor met an attractive young man at a popular Los Angeles "cruising area." After Pryor entered the stranger's car and agreed to go home with him, the driver, an undercover police officer, arrested him.

Pryor challenged his arrest. The justices of the California Supreme Court agreed with Pryor's contention that the words "lewd" and "dissolute" were vague. Writing for the majority, Justice Matthew Tobriner pointed out that prior cases dealing with the law defined "lewd and dissolute" acts as "lustful, lascivious, unchaste, wanton, or loose in morals and conduct." Those definitions, though, were of no help because, as Tobriner pointed out, "some jurors would find that acts of extramarital intercourse fall within that definition; some would draw the line between intercourse and other sexual acts; others would distinguish between homosexual and heterosexual acts. Thus one could not determine what actions are rendered criminal by reading the statute or even the decisions which interpret it."

Although Tobriner agreed that the law did not meet "constitutional standards of specificity," he nonetheless did not rule the law unconstitutional. Instead, in a strange effort to specify the criminal behavior encompassed by the statute, Justice Tobriner defined criminal "lewd" and "dissolute" behavior to mean "touching of the genitals, buttocks, or female breast, for purposes of sexual arousal, gratification, or affront."

In upholding the law, the court faced an obstacle in the Brown Act, which decriminalized *private* sexual encounters. Clearly, it did not make sense to punish "solicitation" in a public place of a lawful sexual act that was to take place in private. The court decided that the law would only apply to individuals engaged in "lewd and dissolute" activity, as defined by the court, in a public place where someone might be offended.

Since a plainclothes undercover police officer usually would not qualify as a person who would be offended, it seemed that the court had put up a safeguard against inequitable treatment of gay men. Still, there was the problem of unfairly requiring gay and bisexual men entrapped in sting operations to register as sex offenders. By 1978 California was the only state to require individuals convicted of misdemeanor sex offenses to register with the police. On May 26, 1983, the state high court ruled that compulsory registration for individuals convicted under the "lewd and dissolute conduct" solicitation law constituted cruel and unusual punishment. But it was not until 1997 that the state allowed men convicted under the lewd vagrancy law to apply to have their names deleted from the sex offender registry.

No "Fag" or "Dyke" Teachers Allowed

In the early 1960s, longtime friends Marc Morrison and Fred Schneringer were both teaching in Orange County's Lowell Joint Unified School District. Schneringer was experiencing marital and financial problems, and he confided his troubles to Morrison. For a week in April 1963, their friendship manifested itself sexually. Their physical relationship never recurred, but Schneringer was troubled and reported to school district officials that his friendship with the forty-year-old educator had briefly turned sexual.

Morrison resigned from his job after administrators told him of Schneringer's confession. In March 1966, the state revoked the veteran educator's teaching certificates for violating the California Education Code's prohibition against "immoral or unprofessional conduct."

After Morrison unsuccessfully attempted to convince a trial court to reinstate his certificates, UCLA law professor Melville Nimmer took on the educator's case as a volunteer attorney for the ACLU of Southern California. The well-respected legal scholar argued that Morrison did not, under the law, do anything immoral or unprofessional and that his right to privacy had been violated. The homosexual contact that Morrison admitted had no reasonable bearing on his professional fitness, as was underscored when Schneringer was promoted to be a school principal.

Attorney Nimmer confronted the false stereotype that gay people were dangerous to children. He cited law-review articles pointing out that gay teachers posed no greater threat to children than heterosexual teachers. Nimmer also quoted a psychologist who concluded that "the assumption that [homosexuals] are somehow less in control of their impulses than are heterosexuals is the same kind of assumption that underlies white prejudice against Negroes or native-born prejudice against foreigners. In all these instances, the feeling is a reflection of fear based on lack of intimate knowledge of the people involved."

The appellate court rejected Nimmer's arguments and ruled that homosexual acts were immoral. Moreover, the court suggested that any sexual relationship outside of marriage, heterosexual or homosexual, was grounds for the state to rescind a teacher's credentials.

Morrison petitioned the state supreme court for review. On November 20, 1969, the court announced its 4-3 decision. Writing for the majority, Justice Tobriner explained: "Terms such as 'immoral or unprofessional conduct' or 'moral turpitude' stretch over so wide a range that they embrace an unlimited area of conduct. In using them, the Legislature surely did not mean to endow the employing agency with the power to dismiss any employee whose personal, private conduct incurred its disapproval." The law could only apply to evidence that Morrison was acting in an "immoral and unprofessional" manner on the job in a way that harmed his students and colleagues.

Tobriner found no evidence that Morrison's teaching record was blemished or that his brief, private, and consensual physical relationship had impacted his work.

Progress on the legal front did not protect gay teachers from virulent political attacks. In 1978, gay teachers were the target of a threatening voter initiative. The prior year, nearly 70 percent of voters in Florida's Dade County passed a referendum to rescind a measure protecting gay people from discrimination. That campaign was spearheaded by Save Our Children, a group of religious and political conservatives whose public face was former beauty queen, singer, and orange juice promoter Anita Bryant.

When news of the Florida election results reached gay bars and clubs in San Francisco, a spontaneous protest erupted. More than fifteen hundred people gathered at the intersection of Castro and Market Streets, the heart of the city's gay neighborhood. Holding candles and chanting, "Two, four, six, eight, gay is just as good as straight," the impromptu protestors marched up and down the hilly streets, growing in numbers until reaching Union Square at midnight. Surrounded by posh stores and hotels, the crowd held a rally. The main speaker was Harvey Milk, the garrulous, forty-seven-year-old owner of a camera store. A former stock analyst, he had moved to San Francisco from New York in 1972 and gone on to become an important political voice for San Francisco's surging gay population. Five months after the march, Milk was elected to the San Francisco Board of Supervisors, the first openly gay elected official in any major U.S. city. It was a huge symbolic victory for San Francisco's lesbian and gay community.

As the wiry, charismatic Milk was mobilizing gay political power in San Francisco, another California politician was banking on a gay issue to make him the Republican Party's 1978 gubernatorial nominee. John Briggs had been in the state assembly for ten years and the state senate for two, but few voters beyond his Fullerton district knew

San Francisco Supervisor Harvey Milk, the first openly gay elected official in a major U.S. city, exhorted lesbians and gay men to "come out" as a political strategy. He was assassinated at the age of forty-eight in San Francisco City Hall.

of him. The former insurance salesman presumed that attaching himself to a splashy anti-gay initiative would give him statewide name recognition and position him, like Florida's Anita Bryant, as a moral crusader.

Just two weeks after the Dade County vote, Briggs symbolically launched his initiative campaign in San Francisco, which he referred to as "the moral garbage dump of homosexuality in this country." His ballot measure would require school boards to fire or refuse to hire any individual who "advocated, imposed, encouraged, or promoted" homosexual activity. Under this broad language, a teacher could be fired for assigning a book by a gay writer, expressing any kind of support for the rights of gay people, or even attending a meeting on gay rights during non-work hours.

The initiative looked winnable. After the Dade County election, voters in St. Paul, Wichita, and Eugene had rejected equal rights for gay people. Backers of the California initiative gathered half a million signatures, nearly two hundred thousand more than necessary to qualify. The first statewide ballot initiative in the nation dealing with gay rights, it would appear on the November 1978 ballot as Proposition 6.

Briggs played on fear of gay people, claiming that "the only way they can get children is to recruit our children. I can't think of a better setting than the classrooms." He sponsored another initiative—to expand the death penalty—on the same ballot. He publicly linked both initiatives by printing leaflets with the image of a teenager lying in a pool of blood with the sensationalistic exhortation: "You can act right now to help protect your family from vicious killers and defend your children from homosexual teachers."

Gay community leaders throughout the state recognized that if Proposition 6 passed, anti-gay attacks would spread throughout the country and expand beyond schoolteachers. Memories of Cold War witch hunts had not faded, and lesbians and gay men acknowledged that the assault had to be met head-on.

Harvey Milk joined Sally Gearhart, an author and professor at San Francisco State University, where she was one of the first openly lesbian tenured faculty in the country, to co-chair the statewide campaign against the initiative. Milk turned the idea of homosexual recruitment on its head by stating at campaign rallies, "My name is Harvey Milk—and I want to recruit you. I want to recruit you for the fight to preserve democracy from the John Briggses and Anita Bryants who are trying to constitutionalize bigotry." Gearhart and Milk debated Briggs and proponents of Proposition 6 around the state.

Gay men, lesbians, and their allies, framing the initiative as a slippery slope towards attacks on other disfavored minorities, raised money, registered new voters (an estimated twenty-five thousand in Los Angeles) and canvassed door-to-door.

During the campaign, David Mixner, an aide to Los Angeles Mayor Tom Bradley, publicly acknowledged his homosexuality for the first time and organized political allies and Hollywood celebrities against the initiative. He used connections with closeted gay Republicans to broker a meeting with former governor Ronald Reagan and convince him that the initiative could violate privacy rights—which Californians just five years earlier had added to the state constitution—and unfairly target teachers.

Reagan issued a public statement cautioning that the initiative not only had "the potential for real mischief" but "the potential of infringing on basic rights of

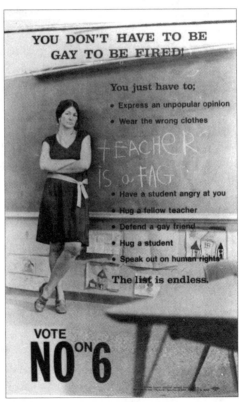

Lesbian and gay schoolteachers and their allies were the targets of Proposition 6, a 1978 voter initiative that would have barred public schools from employing them.

privacy and perhaps even constitutional rights." The former governor asked, "What if an overwrought youngster disappointed by bad grades imagined it was the teacher's fault and struck out by accusing the teacher of advocating homosexuality?...Innocent lives could be ruined."

The "No on 6" campaign trumpeted the statement in television and newspaper ads. Support for the initiative, as high as 61 percent, fell dramatically. Politicians and political candidates from both major parties, from liberal Governor Jerry Brown to conservative gubernatorial candidate Ed Davis, the former Los Angeles police chief with a history of anti-gay rhetoric and policies, publicly opposed Briggs. As support for his initiative crumbled, Briggs's rhetoric became more hysterical. He declared homosexuality a more "insidious threat" than communism and compared homosexuality to a "creeping disease" that "spread like a cancer throughout the body."

On election day, voters rejected the initiative by more than a million votes, 58 to 42 percent. Briggs even lost in Orange County, his home turf.

Just three weeks later, however, the jubilation over defeating the Briggs initiative turned to mourning.

Dan White, a former police officer and firefighter, had been elected to the board of supervisors by residents of the conservative, working-class southeastern section of San Francisco at the same time that Milk was elected. The clean-cut Irish Catholic did not share Milk's politics. During his first year on the board, White was the lone supervisor to oppose a measure introduced by Milk to prohibit discrimination against gay people in employment, housing, and public accommodations. Mayor George Moscone signed the legislation, signaling the growing political power of the city's lesbian and gay population.

Three days after voters defeated Proposition 6, White, whose only job was his part-time board position, resigned. Almost immediately, though, he changed his mind and asked Mayor Moscone to appoint him back to his position. Milk opposed White's plea, wanting to use the opportunity to build a progressive majority on the board. The mayor agreed.

On the morning of November 27, 1978, Dan White put on a tan, three-piece suit and left his Excelsior District home for City Hall. He snuck into the building through a small, ground-level side window. He went to the mayor's private office, pulled out his .38 caliber police revolver, and shot George Moscone four times. He then reloaded, crossed City Hall, and entered Milk's office. He shot his former colleague five times, twice in the head. Later that morning, White turned himself in.

News of the murders spread rapidly. That night, thousands of mourners filled Castro Street, each carrying a lit candle. Some carried pictures of the slain leaders. They marched down Market Street, a somber river of flickering lights flowing for miles toward City Hall. Forty thousand people gathered in front of the darkened, ornate rotunda. A loudspeaker broadcast a tape of a triumphant Milk, recorded just weeks earlier at the election night "No on 6" victory party, encouraging gay people to come out of the closet.

Six months later, the jury announced its verdict in Dan White's murder trial. White's attorney, Douglas Schmidt, played on the all-white, all-straight jury's sympathy by saying that White had been severely depressed and that the former police officer was not in his right mind the morning of the murders because he had consumed too many Twinkies. White, Schmidt argued, should be convicted of the lesser charge of manslaughter, not murder.

On May 21, 1979, the jury convicted Dan White of manslaughter. The verdict, as well as accumulated anger over ongoing police harassment, sparked five to ten thousand protestors to converge on City Hall that night. Shouting, "He got away with murder," "Remember Harvey Milk," and "We want justice," the protestors confronted police in riot gear.

Protestors set police cars on fire and broke City Hall windows. Police took revenge, descending on the Castro District and indiscriminately beating people. Officers stormed into the popular Elephant Walk bar in the heart of the neighborhood, smashed windows, and turned over tables, yelling "dirty cocksuckers" and "sick faggots."

The assassinations of Milk and Moscone did not stop the growth of gay political power in San Francisco. Milk's political aide Harry Britt, a former Methodist minister who in 1973 had left his wife and career in Dallas and moved to San Francisco, was appointed to fill the slain leader's supervisorial seat. But just a few years after Milk's assassination, another unforeseen tragedy impacted the gay community: Acquired Immune Deficiency Syndrome, or AIDS.

Pandemic and Panic

In the early 1980s, just as gay men and lesbians began to flex their political muscle, the AIDS pandemic hit gay communities throughout the world. Many gay leaders, as well as thousands of other Californians, died from AIDS at the prime of life.

During the early years of the crisis, it was unclear what caused the mysterious sickness or how the disease spread. By 1986, however, researchers understood that the human immunodeficiency virus (HIV) caused AIDS, and that the virus spread through intercourse or the exchange of blood. Although AIDS could impact anyone, it was still largely seen as a "gay disease." Public fears about transmission ran high.

Attempting to capitalize on heterosexuals' fears of AIDS and gay people, the Prevent AIDS Now Initiative Committee (PANIC), led by Lyndon LaRouche, a reactionary politician and erstwhile presidential candidate, qualified an ominous initiative for the November 1986 California ballot. Proposition 64 would require doctors to report to a central agency the names of all people infected with HIV. The most frightening aspect of the initiative, however, echoed the World War II incarceration of Japanese Americans and called for the quarantine and banishment of HIV-positive people.

Initial polling revealed strong voter support for Proposition 64.

David Mixner hired experienced organizers to lead a statewide campaign to defeat the proposition. They obtained endorsements from public health experts who condemned the initiative's false assumption that the HIV virus was spread through casual contact. The health professionals also blasted the penalties for testing positive for HIV, which they knew would discourage HIV testing and cause further spread of the disease. As the message spread that public health officials opposed the measure, support evaporated. Conservative Republican Governor George Deukmejian opposed it, calling it "wholly unnecessary and unwarranted." On election day, voters resoundingly rejected the proposition—71 to 29 percent.

Undeterred, LaRouche qualified an identical initiative to appear on the June 1988 primary ballot as Proposition 69. Voters rejected it, again with more than twice as many votes against it than for it.

But six months later, on the November 1988 ballot, voters faced not one but two more AIDS-related initiatives. Proposition 96, sponsored by conservative L.A. Sheriff Sherman Block, required HIV testing for anyone convicted of a sex offense or a crime in which blood or other bodily fluids could have been exchanged.

Also on the ballot was Proposition 102, championed by right-wing Representative William Dannemeyer. Having witnessed the defeat of the two LaRouche-sponsored initiatives that he supported, Dannemeyer sought to convince voters that his AIDS control plan was sound. Gone was the extreme policy of quarantines. But doctors would still be required to report the names of all HIV-positive patients. In addition, Dannemeyer's proposition required those testing HIV-positive to give health authorities the names of all their sexual contacts.

Dannemeyer found a sympathetic spokesperson: Paul Gann, who had spearheaded the immensely popular Proposition 13, which changed property taxation in California. Gann had contracted HIV from a 1982 blood transfusion during heart surgery.

Unwarranted fear had already generated housing and job discrimination against people with AIDS, HIV-positive people, and even those suspected of being HIV-positive. Dannemeyer's initiative would make such discrimination legal.

During the short time between the LaRouche and Dannemeyer initiatives, many of the key organizers and donors who had helped defeat the earlier propositions had died of AIDS. Already working to mobilize resources for community-based AIDS services, gay people were now hard pressed to find sufficient money and volunteers to defeat two statewide initiatives.

The "No on 102" campaign relied on persuasive public health messages. Dr. Laurens White, the distinguished president of the California Medical Association, reiterated his opposition to shortsighted, ineffective measures like Proposition 102. U.S. Surgeon General C. Everett Koop said that the initiative was not sound public health policy.

On election day, Proposition 102 was defeated two to one. But Sheriff Block's Proposition 96 passed.

Out of the Closet

Ten years earlier, on election night 1978, a joyous Harvey Milk had exhorted celebrants: "We must destroy the myths once and for all, shatter them....And most important, every gay person must come out....[O]nce they realize that we are their children, that we are everywhere, every myth, every lie, every innuendo will be destroyed." Milk knew that lesbians and gay men were being fired simply because of their sexual orientation.

So did Air Force veteran Robert DeSantis. The former seminarian had applied for a job with Pacific Telephone and Telegraph (PT&T) but was rejected because, he believed, a supervisor assumed he was gay.

PT&T had a reputation for anti-gay discrimination. Bernard Boyle knew why. After his coworkers at PT&T learned he was gay, they tormented him to the point that he resigned. Boyle's supervisor knew of the harassment but did nothing to stop it. PT&T employees Judy Lundin and Barbara Buckley faced similar treatment. Their colleagues insulted and bullied them after learning that the two telephone operators were in a relationship with each other. The two women were eventually fired.

Lesbians and gay men who were fired or not hired because of their sexual orientation joined with the Gay Law Students Association (a group of students at UC Berkeley's Boalt Hall School of Law and UC Hastings College of the Law) and the Society for Individual Rights (SIR) to fight PT&T's discrimination. After unsuccessful attempts to convince the California Fair Employment Practices Commission and lower courts to declare that anti-gay job discrimination was illegal, the coalition appealed to the state supreme court.

In 1979 Justice Matthew Tobriner, writing for a four-judge majority, explained that because PT&T had a state-sanctioned monopoly over nearly 80 percent of phone service in California, it operated more like a government entity than a private employer. The utility's monopoly status insulated it from the normal checks of the marketplace and forced consumers to subsidize its discrimination.

Consequently, under the equal protection guarantee of the state constitution, PT&T could not arbitrarily discriminate in employment.

Tobriner equated "the struggle of the homosexual community for equal rights, particularly in the field of employment" with political activity of the type that is covered by state labor laws that bar employers from forbidding employees to engage in it. "The aims of the struggle for homosexual rights, and the tactics employed, bear a close analogy to the continuing struggle for civil rights waged by blacks, women, and other minorities," he noted. In essence, being openly gay was a political act protected by state labor law.

In language that Harvey Milk would have applauded, Tobriner wrote that "one important aspect of the struggle for equal rights is to induce homosexual individuals to 'come out of the closet.'"

The supreme court sent the case back for trial. PT&T corporate attorneys stalled for several years. But in the mid-1980s, a sharp-eyed attorney for the plaintiffs discovered a pattern in the sea of PT&T's employment records: company interviewers marked the job applications of openly gay or suspected gay applicants with a specific letter code.

In December 1986, more than a decade after Robert DeSantis, Bernard Boyle, Judy Lundin, and Barbara Buckley initially sought justice, PT&T settled the case and agreed to pay the four plaintiffs and 250 other lesbians and gay men three million dollars, the largest anti-gay discrimination settlement to that point in U.S. history. PT&T also agreed to adopt a nondiscrimination policy covering gay people.

Still, the PT&T settlement did not protect lesbians and gay men in the private sector. The movement to realize that goal had begun in 1977, when members of the left-wing Bay Area Gay Liberation political group pushed for San Francisco to outlaw anti-gay discrimination. Matt Coles, a law student at Hastings, drafted the bill, introduced by newly elected Supervisor Harvey Milk, that was passed the following year.

Inspired by the San Francisco ordinance, advocates in Berkeley worked with Coles to write successful legislation for that city. Lesbian and gay leaders in Los Angeles also asked Coles to help craft an antidiscrimination law. The activists' ultimate goal was statewide antidiscrimination protection for lesbians and gay men under the state's Fair Employment and Housing Act (FEHA). "The FEHA was key to making people feel safe to be out," Coles later explained. "Once we could get a law passed protecting gay people, we could change the atmosphere and change social norms and move public opinion."

In 1979 the Los Angeles City Council passed an ordinance protecting lesbians, gay men, and transgender people from discrimination. By the mid-1980s, every major city in California had passed a similar law.

But the advocates still had not won a statewide law. In 1976 San Francisco Assembly Member John Francis Foran had introduced the first legislation to protect Californians from discrimination based on sexual orientation, and every year thereafter San Francisco Assembly Member Art Agnos had reintroduced it. Governor Jerry Brown was willing to sign such legislation, but the bills rarely even reached the assembly floor.

The tipping point came in 1984 as the business community began to realize that local antidiscrimination ordinances had not resulted in economic hardship. That year, the legislature finally passed a bill adding sexual orientation to the list of categories covered by the FEHA.

Governor George Deukmejian vetoed the bill, claiming there was no compelling evidence that gay people faced employment discrimination.

After the Deukmejian veto and Agnos's departure from the assembly to become mayor of San Francisco, Los Angeles Assembly Member Terry Friedman took over the annual introduction of the bill. Friedman's efforts were buoyed in 1986, the year of the PT&T settlement, when Attorney General John Van de Kamp issued a formal opinion that employment discrimination against gay people was unlawful in the private sector.

Before the 1990 election, Deukmejian's successor, Pete Wilson, had indicated in a *San Francisco Examiner* interview that he would approve a gay civil rights law. In September 1991, however, he vetoed such a bill. News of Wilson's veto spread quickly, and within hours massive protests erupted in Los Angeles, not only in the liberal enclaves of West Hollywood and Beverly Hills, but also in more conservative regions, such as the San Fernando Valley and the Orange County city of Anaheim. Protestors took over a runway at Los Angeles International Airport. The demonstrators' outrage fueled seventeen days of protests in the Los Angeles area, involving fifty thousand people.

In 1999 Governor Gray Davis signed legislation providing full protection for lesbians, gay men, and bisexuals from job discrimination and harassment under the Fair Employment and Housing law. Davis announced his approval of the bill just before speaking at a lesbian and gay presidential fundraiser in Beverly Hills. At the black-tie event, Davis crowed that the new law would "send a message across the country and around the world that we are determined to unleash the full potential of the human spirit here in California."

A Note in Her Locker

Alana Flores was an honor student at Live Oak High School in Morgan Hill, ten miles south of San Jose. But in her senior year, she attempted suicide.

For the previous three years, other students had harassed the attractive young woman because they believed she was a lesbian. The torment began early in her sophomore year when someone put a photo of a bound and gagged naked woman in Flores's locker. On the picture was a note with the message: "Die, die...Dyke bitch. Fuck off. We'll kill you."

Distraught, Flores took the photo and threatening note to the assistant principal, who dismissed her tears, saying, "Don't bring me this trash anymore. This is disgusting."

Students continued tormenting Flores. "Dyke" was scratched and then written in permanent ink on her locker. A student in a math class called her a "fucking dumb dyke" and made explicit sexual references to her without any repercussions from the teacher.

"After I graduated, I was no longer afraid," she recalled. "I was angry. I realized I was treated so unjustly that I had to do something about the corruption at Live Oak. I couldn't let this happen to anyone else."

In April 1998, Flores and four other former and current students in the Morgan Hill Unified School District filed a federal lawsuit accusing the district of refusing to protect them from almost daily anti-gay harassment. Joining Flores in the lawsuit was Freddie Fuentes. When he was in the seventh grade, a group of students had surrounded him one morning at a school bus stop, yelling, "Faggot—you don't belong here." They viciously hit and kicked him, leaving him writhing on the ground in

While they were students in the Morgan Hill Unified School District, Alana Flores (left) was threatened and harassed and Freddie Fuentes (right) was beaten, because other students thought they were gay. Flores was the lead plaintiff in a lawsuit holding school officials responsible for ending anti-gay harassment once they are aware of it.

pain. A school bus driver arriving on the scene ignored the injured student, allowed his attackers onto the bus, and left Fuentes behind. Fuentes was treated at a hospital with bruised ribs. Although school officials punished one of his attackers, it was Fuentes they transferred to another school.

One of the anonymous plaintiffs had dropped out of school because of harassment, reflecting the high percentage of lesbian and gay students who leave school because of abuse.

The lawsuit was significant because attorneys from the National Center for Lesbian Rights and the ACLU argued that discrimination based on sexual orientation is illegal, a claim that courts had not validated. The students' lawyers also argued that once school faculty and administrators learned of anti-gay harassment, they had a legal obligation to protect the students.

After the school district failed three times to convince judges to dismiss the lawsuit, it reached the Ninth Circuit Court of Appeals.

In an unprecedented ruling, the judges in April 2003 unanimously affirmed that school officials have a constitutional duty to proactively and effectively end anti-gay discrimination and harassment once they are aware of the problem.

After the ruling, the school district began settlement negotiations. In January 2004, the district paid the students and their attorneys over $1.1 million and instituted a comprehensive training program, mandatory for all faculty, staff, and administrators, focused on ending harassment based on sexual orientation and gender identity. In addition, the district agreed to implement an age-appropriate anti-discrimination training program for students and to adopt an explicit policy barring harassment on the basis of sexual orientation and gender identity.

While the *Flores* case was being litigated, the California legislature passed a bill introduced by Santa Monica Assembly Member Sheila Kuehl, the first openly gay California legislator. Kuehl's law provided protection from harassment to lesbian, gay, and transgender students in California's public schools. In 1999 Governor Gray Davis signed the bill into law.

The Family Circle

In 1997 State Senator Pete Knight cut off all contact with his son, David, when the thirty-seven-year-old Air Force fighter pilot told his father that he was gay. David was in a committed relationship with a man he had met through his uncle, the elder Knight's gay brother, who had died of AIDS.

The rejection that David Knight experienced, though painful, was not unusual. Many lesbians and gay men have been abandoned by their families. But the ostracism was even harsher for the Persian Gulf War veteran, because three years later his father launched a campaign to pass an initiative that would legalize discrimination against gay couples.

Proposition 22, known as the Knight Initiative, qualified for the March 2000 presidential primary ballot. The fourteen-word measure was deceptively straightforward. It stated, "Only marriage between a man and a woman is valid or recognized in California."

The proposition sent the message to California's four hundred thousand same-sex couples that their relationships were unworthy of state recognition. It threatened the progress that lesbians and gay men had made, through careful efforts since the 1960s, in eroding seemingly insurmountable barriers to legal recognition of their families.

One of the first victories had come in 1967, in the case of Ellen Nadler, a lesbian who sought custody of her five-year-old daughter. In an unprecedented decision, a California appellate court ruled that courts cannot consider a parent unfit solely on the basis of sexual orientation.

Yet throughout the 1970s and 1980s, lesbians who had given birth to children while in heterosexual marriages had to fight for custody of their children. In 1977 the custody struggle of Oakland resident Jeanne Jullion became a rallying point. Jullion's former husband, an Italian, challenged the thirty-two-year-old mother's right to custody of their three- and eight-year-old sons.

After a routine home evaluation, an Alameda County probation officer recommended that Jullion's sons live with their father, not because Jullion was an unfit parent but because of the stigma the county official believed the children would experience due to their mother's sexual orientation. The judge awarded custody to the father.

Lesbian community leaders rallied to help Jullion, raising money and publicizing the unfair standards that exalted heterosexual relationships and demonized gay families. Jullion spoke about her case at many public events, including the spontaneous San Francisco demonstration the night of Anita Bryant's anti-gay victory in Florida. "The vote in Dade County will translate to just this in our own lives," she told the crowd: "You can lose your kids, or your housing, or your job because you're gay. I don't believe I have to be straight to have rights in America."

On appeal, another judge awarded Jullion custody of her younger son but granted custody of the older child to his father. The court's order mattered little, however, because Jullion's former husband took the children to Italy and never returned. Three years passed before Jullion saw her children again and before she brought her youngest son back to the United States.

Prejudice against gay relationships was also manifest in immigration policies. In 1975 a gay couple challenged the Immigration and Naturalization Service (INS) for refusing to grant spousal status to the foreign same-sex partner of a U.S. citizen.

Anthony Sullivan, a former flight attendant from Australia, met rental car employee Richard Adams at a Los Angeles bar in 1971, and the two men quickly fell in love. In early 1974, two days before his visa was to expire, Sullivan married the friend of a friend to obtain a green card. However, the marriage was annulled so that Adams and Sullivan could pursue another legal avenue. On March 20, 1975, at the Metropolitan Community Church, a lesbian and gay Christian congregation, Sullivan and Adams solemnized their partnership through a "holy union," a religious ceremony performed by the denomination's founder, Reverend Troy Perry. "Our goal was to petition the INS for residency for Anthony on the grounds that the Holy Union should be recognized under the concept of freedom of religion," Adams later explained.

Soon after the ceremony, the couple read that the county clerk in Boulder, Colorado, was issuing marriage licenses to gay couples. Johnny Carson, host of *The Tonight Show*, confirmed the news when he joked about it. The couple boarded a plane to Colorado and married in Boulder on April 21, 1975.

Four days later, Adams petitioned the INS to classify Sullivan as his "immediate relative," thereby allowing his new spouse to remain in the country. The INS district director denied the petition, writing back on November 24, 1975: "You have failed to establish that a bona fide marital relationship can exist between two faggots." After the Board of Immigration Appeals upheld the petition denial, Sullivan and Adams sued the INS in federal court.

In February 1980, Judge Irving Hill ruled against the couple, stating that "marriage exists as a protected legal institution primarily because of societal values associated with the propagation of the human race," even as he noted that it would be unconstitutional to prevent heterosexual couples who were sterile or chose not to have children from marrying.

The couple waited nearly six years to learn that the Ninth Circuit Court of Appeals ruled against them. Writing for the majority, Anthony Kennedy, later appointed by Ronald Reagan to the Supreme Court, stated, "We do not find that the respondent's separation from his 'life partner' will cause him hardship, emotional or otherwise, sufficient to rise to the level of extreme hardship."

The lone dissenting judge, Harry Pregerson, vigorously disagreed, criticizing the government for not recognizing the "strain Sullivan would experience if he were forced to separate from the person with whom he has lived and shared a close relationship for the past twelve years." He continued, "This failure to recognize Sullivan's emotional hardship is particularly troublesome because he and Adams have lived together as a family."

After this defeat, the couple traveled in Europe. Sullivan was able to reenter the U.S., where he continued to live with Adams with no legal protection.

Over the next two decades, the government slowly came to recognize same-sex relationships. In 1981 Bill Kraus, an aide to San Francisco Supervisor Harry Britt, was inspired by a UC Berkeley staff member who was lobbying the university to provide health benefits for his same-sex partner. Kraus called a meeting of gay community and labor leaders to discuss how San Francisco could recognize same-sex partners. Matt Coles, the attorney who as a law student had authored San Francisco's antidiscrimination law, later recalled that the term "domestic partner" was born in that meeting. "We all hated it in the beginning," Coles said of the clinical-sounding name, "but nobody could think of anything better." The tall, lanky attorney drafted legislation for a city-recognized domestic partners' registry. The proposed ordinance required the city to make available to registered domestic partners of city employees all of the benefits automatically provided to the married spouses of heterosexual staff.

In 1982 the board of supervisors passed the ordinance. But after religious leaders lobbied against the law, Mayor Dianne Feinstein vetoed it.

Coles turned his focus to Berkeley, which in 1984 became the first city in the country to extend medical coverage and other benefits to the partners of lesbian and gay employees. The city of West Hollywood quickly followed.

By the early 1990s, Los Angeles, Santa Cruz, and Laguna Beach also provided benefits for the domestic partners of city employees. After several attempts to legislate such benefits in San Francisco, voters finally approved them nearly ten years after the initial domestic partnership law was vetoed. In 1995 state legislators began introducing modest bills providing limited statewide legal recognition of domestic partnerships. Four years later, the California legislature became the first state legislative body in the U.S to pass a law, without a court mandate, establishing a process for registering domestic partnerships. The law was narrow, mainly allowing for hospital visitation rights and authorizing health insurance for the domestic partners of public employees. In subsequent years, John Davidson and Jennifer Pizer of Lambda Legal, a civil rights group, drafted bills that expanded the law to include most of the rights and responsibilities of married heterosexual couples.

Even minimum legal protections for lesbian and gay relationships infuriated social conservatives like State Senator Pete Knight. In 1999 Knight put Proposition 22 on the ballot. With strong Mormon and Catholic backing, the campaign to pass the initiative amassed twice as much money as its opponents. This imbalance showed on election night. Proposition 22 passed, 61 to 39 percent.

But four years after the passage of the Knight Initiative, San Francisco Mayor Gavin Newsom authorized the county clerk to issue marriage licenses to same-sex couples.

The first couple to be married was Del Martin and Phyllis Lyon, just a few days after their fifty-first anniversary—on Valentine's Day, 2004. Dedicated civil rights activists witnessed the couple's City Hall wedding and were moved to tears as the eighty-three-year-old Martin and the seventy-nine-year-old Lyon, icons in the lesbian and gay community, exchanged vows.

Over the following four weeks, more than four thousand elated lesbian and gay couples from throughout the country lined up at San Francisco City Hall to be married. But the celebrations abruptly ended on March 11, 2004, when the state supreme court ordered city officials to stop performing same-sex marriages. Five months later, the high court invalidated the marriages.

That prompted San Francisco City Attorney Dennis Herrera and several civil rights organizations representing same-sex couples, including Martin and Lyon, to challenge state law. On May 15, 2008, four years after their City Hall wedding, Lyon and Martin witnessed the court's landmark 4-3 decision in *In re Marriage Cases*, a consolidated set of lawsuits dealing with the validity of same-sex marriage in California.

The California Supreme Court ruled not only that laws barring same-sex marriage violate the state's constitution, but that discrimination against lesbians and gay men would henceforth be subject to the most rigorous form of judicial review. It was the first state high court in the nation to rule that discrimination based on sexual orientation was as unconstitutional as discrimination based on race, sex, and religion.

Chief Justice Ronald George, author of the majority opinion, ruled that the "right of an individual to establish a legally recognized family with the person of one's choice" was protected by the state constitution's guarantee of privacy and personal autonomy.

Just as prior decisions recognized it was constitutionally impermissible to treat racial minorities as inferior and women as unequal to men, George explained, "we now similarly recognize that an individual's homosexual orientation is not a constitutionally legitimate basis for withholding or restricting the individual's legal rights."

On June 16, 2008, at 5:01 p.m., the precise moment that the supreme court's ruling went into effect, Del Martin and Phyllis Lyon were the first gay couple in San Francisco to be legally married. "It's something that has been due for a long time, and thank God it's here," glowed Lyon.

Weeks after the joyous, historic occasion, civil rights pioneer Del Martin died, on August 27, at the age of eighty-seven.

As they mourned Martin's death, advocates prepared to fight a ballot measure that would change the constitution and eliminate the newly won right of same-sex couples to marry. Proponents of the initiative, which appeared on the November 2008 ballot as Proposition 8, raised tens of millions of dollars, largely from Mormons, evangelical Christians, and Catholics.

Polling in the summer indicated that the initiative would fail, but support for it grew after a relentless barrage of pro-Proposition 8 television and radio ads falsely claimed that elementary school children would be forced to learn about same-sex marriage, and churches would lose their tax-exempt status for refusing to marry gay couples. This fearmongering masked the true intention behind the proposition: to take away the existing right of a minority group and to enshrine that discrimination in the state's governing document.

In June 2008, San Francisco Mayor Gavin Newsom officiated at the wedding of Phyllis Lyon (left) and Del Martin (right). A month earlier, the California Supreme Court had issued a landmark ruling invalidating the legal ban on same-sex marriages. Martin and Lyon were the first couple married in San Francisco after the decision went into effect.

"No on 8" campaign leaders raised funds to rebut the deceptive ads. Grassroots opponents of the initiative organized to counter the church-related groups that were working to pass the discriminatory measure.

But by election day the "Yes on 8" misinformation campaign had succeeded in convincing 52 percent of voters to legalize second-class status for same-sex couples. The four-point margin of victory was far lower than the twenty-two point margin for the Knight Initiative just eight years earlier. Societal acceptance of marriage equality was growing, especially among younger people. A post-election poll revealed that 57 percent of voters under the age of thirty-five rejected Proposition 8.

The passage of Proposition 8 sent shock waves of disappointment and anger through the gay community and its millions of supporters. Demonstrations and vigils, quickly organized via the Internet, proliferated not only in California but around the U.S. and in England, Australia, and Canada.

The National Center for Lesbian Rights, Lambda Legal, and the ACLU immediately filed a lawsuit in the state supreme court to nullify the measure. The civil rights groups argued that Proposition 8 eliminated the constitution's basic commitment to equality by taking away a fundamental right from just one group. They also pointed out that the measure thwarted the judiciary's exercise of its essential constitutional role of protecting the rights of minorities. According to the constitution, the lawsuit charged, such radical changes cannot be made by simple majority vote, but instead must first be approved by two-thirds of the state legislature and then passed by voters.

Leading organizations representing African Americans, women, Latinos, and Asian Americans as well as religious groups filed similar legal challenges, arguing that Proposition 8 threatened the equal protection of all Californians, not just lesbians and gay men.

The high court agreed to decide not only the question of the proposition's validity but also the legal status of the estimated eighteen thousand same-sex couples who had married between June 16 and November 4, 2008.

Reflecting on the passage of Proposition 8 and the work of securing equal rights, Kate Kendell, executive director of the National Center for Lesbian Rights, said, "In all civil rights movements, there are setbacks and stinging losses. But we must pick ourselves up and move forward. There is no other choice. It is the only way to create change."

— TEN —

BREAKING DOWN BARRIERS

THE RIGHTS OF PEOPLE WITH DISABILITIES

I was liberated from the thrall of crippling public policies by successful disability rights lobbying.

—*Author and advocate Paul Longmore, 1989*

Ed Roberts had lived in suburban Burlingame, south of San Francisco, all of his young life. In February 1953, the tall, gregarious fourteen-year-old returned from a Sunday afternoon baseball game feeling ill. The next morning, he awoke with a stiff body. That night he was admitted to the San Mateo County hospital. Two days later, hospital staff rushed the frightened young man to a respirator because he could not breathe. His lungs were not functioning. Paralysis had gradually set into his left side, a result of the poliovirus that had infected his body.

For the next few days, it was uncertain whether Roberts would live. He survived but was almost completely paralyzed from the neck down. He needed an iron lung to breathe.

The local Soroptimists, a women's civic group, funded special telephone service between Roberts's home and the local high school so that he could listen to classes. By his senior year, Roberts's mother, Zona, thought it would be good for her eldest child to attend one of his classes at school each week. Although the former athlete was uncomfortable with his classmates seeing him in a wheelchair, he acquiesced. He later recalled his first day back at school:

It was lunchtime; there must have been two hundred students, or it seemed like. They were all eating lunch around this court. So I started to get up, and every one of them turned to stare at me. My worst fear, and one of the reasons that I had not come out at all was that I was terrified of being stared at....And when I'd look up at them, they'd look away. And something remarkable occurred to me while I was there. The first thing was that it didn't hurt....The second thing that occurred to me was that maybe it wasn't all my problem, because when I looked back, they would look away....The third thing was, oh, it was like being a star! I think that was one of the more important times in my life, that I realized I could enjoy it....Actually, I could enjoy being stared at. If I thought of myself as a star, not just a helpless cripple.

Roberts developed from a lackadaisical C student into a straight-A high school scholar. But despite his academic performance, a school counselor told Roberts he could not graduate because he had not fulfilled driver's and physical education requirements. Zona Roberts unsuccessfully advocated with the principal to let her son graduate.

She then took her case to a friend on the school board. The board sided with the young man, and he received his diploma. The incident taught him a lifelong lesson: "You don't let people walk all over you; you do something about it. You fight for what you believe is right."

Unlike people of color, lesbians, and gay men, for whom the term "civil rights" means equal treatment, people with disabilities have sought acceptance of *differential* treatment through adaptive devices and services such as optical readers, sign-language interpreters, and architectural modifications. These accommodations are means to bring about equal access. The independent living movement for people with disabilities, unlike traditional rehabilitation services, does not focus on physical independence but rather on the right of people with disabilities to self-determination and the adaptive mechanisms necessary to live and participate in their communities, not in institutions.

In the 1960s and early 1970s, people with disabilities across the United States began organizing against the discrimination they faced daily—from inaccessible buildings to employment barriers. Californians with disabilities and their families and allies were central to the movement.

The "Rolling Quads"

Ed Roberts knew that a college degree was critical. He later explained, "The path to my future and to my working...was going to be education, totally. Because nobody was going to hire me the way I was. There was so much prejudice about disability." He attended College of San Mateo, where an American government class inspired him about the possibility for societal change through politics. He did well at the junior college and applied to UC Berkeley to complete his bachelor's degree.

In the early 1960s, the California Department of Rehabilitation aided individuals who had become disabled and helped retrain them to reenter the workforce. But a counselor from the department considered Roberts too disabled ever to work and denied state funds to cover his education. It took the vigorous advocacy of Roberts, his mother, and officials at the College of San Mateo to convince an upper-level official to reverse the counselor's decision.

Roberts was admitted to UC Berkeley, but at that time administrators were unaware he was disabled. The Dean of Men, Arleigh Williams, could not figure out where the university would house him. His iron lung, which weighed over six hundred pounds, would not fit in dormitory elevators, and other housing venues would not accept the disabled student.

Eventually, Dr. Henry Bruyn, a physician at Cowell Hospital, the university's medical facility, said Roberts could live there. This arrangement conformed to the prevailing conceptual framework of disability as a medical issue that the disabled person must overcome.

Students with disabilities had attended UC Berkeley before Roberts, but in 1962 he became the first student requiring assistance with essential functions (like getting in and out of bed) to attend the university. To mark this milestone, a local paper ran a story with the headline: "Helpless Cripple Attends U.C. Classes Here in Wheelchair."

The following year, six-foot-seven-inch John Hessler became the second disabled student to room at Cowell Hospital. Just after completing high school, Hessler had broken his neck in a diving accident that left him a quadriplegic. Because of his size, Hessler's parents could not care for him, and he had been living in a county hospital and taking a taxi to nearby Contra Costa College.

Over the next several years, other students with disabilities moved into Cowell.

In 1968 a counselor from the Department of Rehabilitation assigned to work with disabled students at UC Berkeley drew the ire of the very students she was supposed to help. She told Ed Roberts, who by then was pursuing a doctorate in political science, that he could not write his dissertation on the subject he had chosen. She tried to dismiss two students from the Cowell program because, in her view, they were not performing well enough academically. She threatened to cut off state funding to students who disobeyed her. The students in the program—nearly a dozen—recognized that if the counselor eliminated anyone from the program based solely on her own standards, all students in the program were threatened.

They advocated with her and her supervisor and eventually went to the media, generating critical stories in newspapers as far away as Sacramento. State legislators learned of the students' complaints and began to voice concerns. The counselor was reassigned.

To mark their victory, the group dubbed themselves the Rolling Quads.

The Rolling Quads focused on inaccessible classrooms, lack of transportation, and other barriers to their self-sufficiency. They successfully advocated with the city of Berkeley for curb cuts at street corners to accommodate wheelchair users, but they needed more resources to realize their vision. Led by John Hessler, they secured federal funds to make the campus accessible to disabled students. With a grant of eighty-one thousand dollars, the university in 1970 established a Physically Disabled Students' Program (PDSP), initially housed in an apartment above a fast food restaurant one block from the campus. The program, directed largely by people with disabilities, helped students find attendants, readers, and accessible places to live and provided wheelchair repair, transportation, personal counseling, financial advising, campus orientations, and preregistration. The program also counseled parents who were wary of allowing their previously sheltered children to attend the university.

PDSP's founders knew that they were creating an innovative and powerful model. Social workers around the state and nation heard about the program and interviewed its staff. Similar campus programs for students with disabilities developed in Riverside, Boston, Austin, and Long Island.

In the Berkeley area, non-students with disabilities also sought assistance from the program's staff. Applying their advocacy to the broader community, the campus activists secured government funding, rented a small Berkeley apartment for an office, and founded the Center for Independent Living (CIL) in 1972. The first such center of its kind in the country run by and for people with disabilities, CIL was constituent-driven, providing services like wheelchair repair and referrals to attendants as well as training and advocacy.

Ed Roberts (right) with Herb Willsmore (left) in UC Berkeley's Memorial Stadium in the late 1960s. Roberts was the first student with significant disabilities to attend the university and was a leader in the movement to secure equal rights for people with disabilities.

Creating National Policy

California's Department of Rehabilitation had a reputation for "creaming," or accepting individuals with mild disabilities who could easily be placed in jobs. In 1972 Congress passed a bill reauthorizing funding for state rehabilitation programs, stipulating that priority must be given to individuals with significant disabilities. The bill also authorized federal funding for independent living centers like CIL to prepare people with disabilities for employment and life outside of institutions.

President Richard Nixon vetoed the bill, not once but twice, spurring advocates across the country who had historically focused on a single disability, such as deafness or blindness, to form cross-disability coalitions.

Nixon eventually signed a watered-down version of the bill, the Rehabilitation Act of 1973. It included a simple but powerful provision, Section 504, which outlawed discrimination against people with disabilities in any federally funded program. This provision required public schools and other entities receiving federal funds to make their facilities accessible. Many members of Congress voted for the bill without recognizing the significant implications of Section 504.

Three years after President Nixon signed the bill, the Department of Health, Education, and Welfare (HEW)—the federal entity charged with implementing it—still had not issued any regulations, due to objections from universities and other federally funded institutions that balked at the costs of making their facilities accessible. HEW's regulations were vital because they would serve as guidelines for other federal agencies' implementation of the law: if HEW's guidelines codified "separate but equal" facilities, for example, other agencies could follow suit. When President Ford left the White House in 1977, HEW still had not adopted final regulations, despite a court order.

Disability rights advocates were hopeful that newly elected President Jimmy Carter would quickly implement Section 504. As a candidate, he had criticized Ford for not issuing regulations. Advocates were surprised and frustrated, however, when Joseph Califano, President Carter's HEW secretary, announced that he was establishing a task force to review implementation of Section 504. The task force did not include any people with disabilities or representatives of disability organizations. Activists also learned that Califano was considering ineffective regulations.

Rather than waiting for the task force's recommendations, the American Coalition of Citizens with Disabilities, an umbrella group composed of nineteen organizations, announced that if Secretary Califano did not approve strong regulations by April 4, 1977, advocates would launch a nationwide protest.

The April 4 deadline passed without regulations. The following day, demonstrators took over HEW offices in Washington, DC, and eight regional offices. More than seventy-five protestors occupied HEW's national office overnight, but agency officials ended the occupation, as they did in New York, by refusing to allow food into the building.

The San Francisco protest took a different turn. Organizers laid the groundwork for a prolonged occupation of the regional HEW office. Kitty Cone, a CIL staff member who had worked for years as a community and political organizer with the Socialist Workers Party, knew the importance of building a broad base of support. She drew on her experience to win endorsements from the Central Labor Council, the San Francisco Council of Churches, the San Francisco branch of the National Organization for Women, the NAACP, and other non-disability-based organizations ranging from the American Legion to the Communist Party.

Cone and other CIL staff organized committees—one to handle press, others to coordinate food and security—arranged for sign-language interpreters and sound equipment, and did extensive outreach to ensure a large turnout for a rally in front of the federal building on United Nations Plaza in San Francisco's Civic Center.

As the demonstration outside the San Francisco HEW office ended, CIL Deputy Director Judy Heumann, who used a wheelchair due to childhood polio, rallied protestors to tell the regional HEW administrator that "the federal government cannot steal our rights." More than a hundred people followed her into the imposing Beaux-Arts building.

At first HEW officials offered protestors cookies and punch; but once they realized that the activists were determined to stay, they announced that no food could come into the building, no outside calls could be made, and no one who left the building could reenter.

Protestors insisted on staying, many risking their health. Some needed ventilators, catheters, or specialized care. Others required attendants to assist them with basic life activities. Without this care, they could suffer extreme discomfort and pain, if not more serious health risks.

The demonstrators' disabilities, however, were a potent weapon to use against HEW. Several hours into the occupation, officials threatened them with arrest for trespassing. Protest leader Heumann responded, "Fine. Just know that one among us is hemophiliac and could bleed to death if you hurt him." Faced with a sure public relations disaster if they ejected wheelchair users and blind people from the building, federal police made no arrests.

Demonstrators took over the fourth floor of the federal building, sleeping on floors in offices, closets, and hallways. Protest leaders met in a large conference room to set strategy. The committees that had formed prior to the demonstration continued and new committees were charged with meals, cleanup, security, and religious services. Recognizing the need for mutual assistance to ensure the long-term viability of the sit-in, demonstrators helped each other with personal care.

The political groundwork that San Francisco protest organizers had laid prior to the demonstration paid off Mayor George Moscone ordered that food be allowed into the building, and the Black Panthers (who counted among their members protestor Bradley Lomax), delivered a huge pot of stew. News of the dramatic action spread through the community and others, including a lesbian-run café, blue-robed Catholic seminarians, McDonald's, and Safeway, donated and delivered food.

Three nights into the sit-in, federal police claimed they had received a bomb threat. That failed

In April 1977, activists across the country rallied to demand that the federal government implement a law barring discrimination against people with disabilities. (Top) Judy Heumann of Berkeley's Center for Independent Living speaks at the San Francisco demonstration. (Bottom) Heumann (left, holding sign) and Kitty Cone (right) protest outside the White House.

to get occupiers out of the building, so for several nights police harassed demonstrators in the middle of the night, waking and forcing them to roll up their sleeping bags, dress, and move their wheelchairs. Building occupiers, in turn, formed a security committee to monitor police and ensure people's health needs were met.

Initially unsupportive, federal employees grew to back the demonstrators' demands after learning more about their cause. Protestors serenaded federal workers coming into the building in the morning, and at night they kept up their spirits by singing civil rights songs such as the following (to the tune of "The Battle Hymn of the Republic"):

> I have seen the regulations that were drawn four years ago,
> To bigotry and discrimination it says a certain "No,"
> All that it's awaiting is the signature of Joe,
> And I hope to hell he signs it soon.

The 504 protest became a cause célèbre. Civil rights leaders Julian Bond and Jesse Jackson visited the building to lend moral support. The Butterfly Brigade, a volunteer patrol whose purpose was to prevent gay bashing, contributed walkie-talkies. The California Department of Health sent mattresses. San Francisco Representative Phillip Burton had portable phones designed for people in wheelchairs installed in the building, and Mayor George Moscone offered to install portable showers. These gestures led regional HEW director José Maldonado to complain, "We're not running a hotel here."

Ten days into the protest, Burton and Representative George Miller, from nearby Contra Costa County, held an ad hoc hearing of the House Education and Labor Committee in the HEW building to take testimony on discrimination against people with disabilities. Among those testifying was Ed Roberts, whom Governor Jerry Brown had appointed director of the California Department of Rehabilitation, the agency that years earlier did not want to fund his education. Roberts testified that the federal government's plans to water down Section 504 were a "blueprint for segregation."

Secretary Califano sent Gene Eiderberg, a low-level assistant, to testify on the department's plan. More than twenty years after the *Brown v. Board of Education* ruling outlawing segregated schools, Eiderberg explained that the proposed regulations allowed for "separate but equal" schools for children with disabilities. In addition, he said that the government's proposals gave schools and hospitals exemptions from otherwise mandatory wheelchair ramps and other physical plant modifications.

Heumann was furious, telling the aide, "We will not accept more segregation. When you erect buildings that are not accessible to the handicapped, you enforce segregation. There will be more sit-ins until the government understands this." After his testimony, Eiderberg withdrew to an HEW office. Burton followed him, kicked on the locked door, and demanded that he listen to the testimony of disabled activists.

Recognizing that West Coast pressure in Washington, DC, might be effective, Heumann led a delegation of nearly thirty Bay Area advocates to the capital, while dozens of their compatriots remained in the San Francisco federal building.

In Washington, Californians joined other disability rights activists to confront Secretary Califano and President Carter directly. Protestors arrived one midnight at the secretary's suburban home, where they formed a circle and lit candles in a silent vigil. Seven hours later, Heumann wheeled to the steps of the house and called, "Please open the door. I cannot get up your steps." An employee eventually answered the door and explained that Califano had left through the back door. The activists tried to confront Califano at his office, but guards blocked the entrance to the building. In frustration and anger, Heumann began ramming her wheelchair into the building's doors, and others followed suit. Dumfounded building guards, uncertain how to respond, kicked the wheelchairs.

The protestors also picketed the First Baptist Church, where President Carter worshipped. Carter eluded the activists by entering through a side entrance and leaving by a back door. When his car passed the protestors, he did not look at them.

Disappointed but undeterred, the advocates called on White House staff and members of Congress, including California Senator Alan Cranston, to support strong regulations. They eventually garnered enough congressional support to force a meeting with Carter's top domestic adviser, Stuart Eizenstat. Throughout the trip, the news media covered the activists' protests as a civil rights issue.

The political pressure paid off. On April 28, three weeks into the occupation of the San Francisco HEW building, Califano agreed to issue strong regulations to implement Section 504, thereby providing people with disabilities a significant civil rights law outlawing discrimination.

When San Francisco protestors heard the news, cheers rang through the building and spontaneous celebrations erupted. Rather than leave the building, they waited two more days for their compatriots to return from Washington, DC. Twenty-five days after the occupation started, the group triumphantly emerged, singing "We Have Overcome." They were greeted by cheers from several hundred supporters who joined the victory rally in United Nations Plaza.

Many disability rights advocates mark the 504 protests as the public birth of the disability civil rights movement. Kitty Cone later reflected:

> For the first time, disability really was looked at as an issue of civil rights rather than an issue of charity and rehabilitation at best, pity at worst. Many of us came to understand that problems we faced individually and that we had perceived as our own personal problems—such as inability to get into inaccessible buildings, or go to the university of our choice, or get around because of no transportation, or get a job—*weren't* our personal problems, they were societal ones.

Sharing Lessons, Building a Movement

After Califano issued 504 regulations, the federal government awarded CIL funds to train people with disabilities as well as the staffs of community service agencies and the Rehabilitation Service Administration in the western U.S. about the new regulations. Mary Lou Breslin, a friend of Kitty Cone's from the University of Illinois, was hired to conduct the trainings. The Kentucky native had coincidentally moved to the Bay Area and was running a job placement program for students with disabilities at UC Berkeley.

Around the same time, the Legal Services Corporation, a nonprofit created by

Congress to promote equal access to justice, provided CIL with funding to expand a paralegal project to assist people with disabilities.

Both of these efforts coalesced in the formation of a project within CIL, the Disability Law Resource Center (DLRC), headed by Bob Funk. A recent graduate from the UC Davis law school, he had lost a leg to the leprosy he contracted while a Peace Corps worker in Nigeria. DLRC continued the 504 training on the West Coast that CIL had been doing, expanded it to the Midwest, and provided materials and consultation to East Coast groups, thereby influencing nearly the entire country to reframe the issue of discrimination against people with disabilities as a civil rights issue.

In 1979 the U.S. Supreme Court issued its first decision dealing with Section 504, *Southeastern Community College v. Davis*, upholding a North Carolina community college's rejection of a deaf woman from its nursing program. Mary Lou Breslin recalled that in response to this negative decision, DLRC was "expected to perform the function of a national law center in disability, because there was such a huge need for it....The phones would never stop ringing—people were calling from all over the country and the world, wanting information on the issues because nothing existed."

DLRC Director Bob Funk, also recognizing the need for a national organization working in the judicial and legislative systems, negotiated with CIL leaders to transition

Staff of the Disability Law Resource Center in 1978. Bob Funk, founder of the center, which became the Disability Rights Education and Defense Fund, is in the front row, far left.

DLRC into an independent organization, to be called the Disability Rights Education and Defense Fund (DREDF), focused on disability policy and law.

"Our work was shaped by history," recalled Arlene Mayerson, a leading disability rights attorney and an early DREDF staff member. And indeed, the 1980 election of Ronald Reagan as president presented a new challenge. DREDF organizers knew that the former Hollywood star's call for government deregulation would create significant problems. To prepare, DREDF leaders convened a fall 1980 meeting involving former congressional staffers and government officials, as well as leaders from the NAACP Legal Defense and Educational Fund, the Leadership Conference on Civil Rights, the Mexican American Legal Defense and Educational Fund, and other civil rights organizations. For two days, twenty national leaders met in the San Francisco Holiday Inn, the only accessible hotel in that city at the time, so that DREDF staff could learn from the collective legislative, political, and judicial wisdom of the group; conversely, those not already knowledgeable about disability as a civil rights issue could learn from DREDF. Reflecting on the historic gathering, Mary Lou Breslin commented, "That meeting really laid the foundation for a decade of collaborative work....We worked on a legislative agenda that involved the civil rights community from the minute the meeting ended, practically."

The coalition-building and 504 trainings of the prior two years proved critical almost immediately: early in the Reagan presidency, Vice President George Bush started a government deregulation project, and Section 504 was an early target. By this time, DREDF had garnered support from the civil rights community to preserve Section 504 protections. The national network of grassroots activists that DLRC had built through its 504 trainings generated tens of thousands of letters to the administration, held vigils, and organized demonstrations. In addition, DREDF lobbyists in Washington, DC, shared an office with a friend of Bush's general counsel. Through that connection, they successfully lobbied the administration not to make any changes or cuts to 504 regulations.

Just Say No

Some fifteen years before these successes, in 1966, more than twenty-six thousand Californians lived in state mental hospitals. Among them were children with behavior problems, the indigent elderly, and alcoholics. Sixty percent were involuntarily committed. That year, Pasadena Assemblyman Frank Lanterman, Oakland Senator Nicholas Petris, and Stockton Senator Alan Short introduced bipartisan legislation to reform the state's antiquated laws governing the treatment of mental patients.

Their bill limited involuntary confinement to fourteen days, except for the "gravely disabled" or people demonstrably dangerous to themselves or others. It ended the system of automatically depriving mental patients of legal rights and provided them court hearings if they were held involuntarily for more than three days. Conservators would be required to make sure that gravely disabled individuals under their care received the services they needed. To ensure that no one was locked away and forgotten, the bill provided for yearly judicial review to determine if a patient still required a conservator. A representative of the California State Psychological Association called the legislation the "Magna Carta of the mentally ill." In 1967 Governor Ronald Reagan signed it into law as the California Mental Health Services Act.

This landmark law provided basic rights to the mentally ill, but by the late 1970s it was common for workers at California's mental hospitals to compel patients to take mind-altering drugs, known as psychotropics, including Thorazine, Prolixin, and Stelazine.

"You become confused, dissipated into the atmosphere around you. There is no you—no control or identity. Impulses control you, from sources you are unaware of. There is a total disintegration of yourself. You have no emotions. You do not feel human." This is how a college student who voluntarily entered the Napa State mental hospital described the effects of the drugs hospital staff forced her to take. Although the drugs could reduce hallucinations and delusions, their distressing and sometimes permanent side effects included shaking, apathy, restlessness, impotence, and painful muscular contractions. One potentially incurable side effect, known as tardive dyskinesia, causes persistent involuntary movement of the tongue, mouth, face, hands, and feet.

Patients were not informed about the potential for these negative impacts before being forced to ingest the drugs, and they often assumed that the side effects were symptoms of their mental illness. Hospital staff, however, were aware of the side effects. Some jokingly called patients' involuntary movements the Prolixin shuffle, the Thorazine shuffle, and the Stelazine stomp. Regardless of the extent of their medical training, psychiatric hospital staff administered psychotropics, with no uniform process to determine the need for and efficacy of the drugs, whether the treatment was the least restrictive intervention, or whether the patient was capable of consenting to the treatment.

Golden Gate University School of Law professor Mort Cohen was deeply disturbed that the state's mental hospitals routinely violated patients' rights in this way. The Brooklyn Law School graduate volunteered with the ACLU and in February 1978 filed a federal class action lawsuit, *Jamison v. Department of Health*, on behalf of patients at the Napa State Hospital, the largest mental hospital in California. The plaintiffs sought the right to refuse to take psychotropics.

Although he was one of the defendants, Dr. Jerome Lackner, director of the state Department of Health from 1975 to 1978, supported the patients' right to decline the drugs. In a declaration filed in the lawsuit, he explained the economic motivation for the use of the drugs: "The underlying political reality of the treatment of mentally ill patients is that cost considerations sometimes severely constrict the alternatives offered to patients....Thorazine, Prolixin, and Haldol are quite inexpensive compared with adequate staffing levels."

The case came before Judge William H. Orrick, who ordered the Department of Mental Heath to negotiate. In early 1979, the plaintiffs and the state reached a landmark settlement. The government agreed that patients *voluntarily* receiving evaluation and treatment at the state's public and private mental health-care facilities had the right to learn about the positive and negative side effects of psychotropic drugs before taking them. They also had the right to information about alternative treatments. After receiving this information, patients could refuse antipsychotic medications without fear that the hospital would use their refusal as grounds for initiating an involuntary commitment.

Although attorney Cohen was pleased that the state recognized the rights of voluntary patients to informed consent, he viewed the victory as only the first step. His next goal was to win the same right for *involuntary* patients.

It took another four years, but in May 1983 Judge Orrick approved a settlement ending the lawsuit. The first of its kind in the United States, the settlement provided that before drugs could be administered to them, involuntary patients must be given information about potential side effects and alternative treatments, and the opportunity to consent, except in emergencies.

"This agreement is a breakthrough for the rights of involuntary mental patients— by tradition a thoroughly disenfranchised group," said Cohen. "This is the first recognition that involuntary mental patients have the right to make some choices about their own treatment."

Each According to Her Needs

In 1972 Diane Lipton gave birth to triplets, two of whom died. Chloe, the surviving child, was born after only thirty weeks and had digestive and liver problems. Shortly before her first birthday, she was diagnosed with cerebral palsy, involving both cognitive and physical disabilities.

Eight months after the diagnosis, Lipton discovered a county-run center for people with severe disabilities near her home in El Cerrito, near Berkeley. She took Chloe there for physical therapy and a nursery program. When Chloe turned three, the Richmond Unified School District assigned her to the Cameron School for Orthopedically Handicapped Children, in El Cerrito.

In the 1970s, students with disabilities in the district, which served largely working-class communities in western Contra Costa County, were with very few exceptions only allowed to enroll in one of four schools solely for children with disabilities. Located in the El Cerrito hills with a view of the Golden Gate Bridge, the Cameron School was on the same block as the Castro School, one of the district's "regular" elementary schools. Despite this proximity, the only interaction between the two schools took place during a Halloween parade. Diane Lipton later speculated that because all of the students were in costume and children from both schools looked "freaky," the district allowed the disabled students to participate.

Prior to 1975, most American children with disabilities faced the same kinds of restrictions: they either did not receive a public education or were segregated into unequal schools and classrooms. But that year, Congress passed the Education for All Handicapped Children Act, which mandated that children with disabilities receive a free public education appropriate to individual needs and that schools integrate students with disabilities and their nondisabled peers as much as possible. This was the first federal law recognizing integrated education as the initial means of making people with disabilities full participants in society.

Soon after the law went into effect, Lipton attended a training session and learned that school districts were legally responsible to work with a disabled child's parents and teachers to develop an Individual Education Plan (IEP), a legally binding agreement. She also learned that parents who disagreed with the IEP or believed the school was not implementing it had due process rights through administrative hearings and civil courts. For Lipton, who had participated in the Free Speech Movement at UC Berkeley, the knowledge that she and her daughter had rights in the school district was revolutionary.

In the spring of 1979, the Richmond school district announced that it was cutting back on physical and occupational therapy for all students at the Cameron School because one of the state-funded therapists serving the district was being reassigned. Although Chloe's IEP called for her to receive occupational therapy three times a week, the district cut her therapy to one session per week.

Working with DREDF, Lipton unsuccessfully appealed the school district's decision. So she began organizing other parents who were angry about the cuts. DREDF filed complaints on behalf of each family with the Department of Education and soon discovered that the state had slashed similar programs throughout California. Inspired by the Richmond activists, other parents filed complaints.

Lipton and DREDF reported the situation to the federal Bureau of Education for the Handicapped (BEH), the agency responsible for oversight of special education programs receiving federal funds. At the same time, DREDF organized parents to lobby their congressional representatives and ask BEH to withhold California's funding.

Their action brought dramatic results. BEH withheld over seventy-two million dollars in federal money, a significant portion of California's funding for special education, until the state changed its policies regarding provision of therapies and streamlined its complaint process. "It was incredibly empowering," Lipton recalled. "It was like our first attempt to do something was so successful, we couldn't believe it."

Fresh from this victory, Lipton met with school administrators, teachers, and therapists for Chloe's annual IEP review. She requested that Chloe join a regular class daily at the Castro School for art, story time, social studies, lunch, and recess. Agreeing that it would benefit Chloe to participate in activities at the Castro School, the district administrator nonetheless refused to integrate her, saying it would be logistically difficult to move her from one school to another and that teachers and administrators at Castro were unwilling to accept the disabled child.

Lipton recognized it would be strategically important to build support for integration among other parents. But many parents feared that their children would be "dumped" into "regular" classes without appropriate supportive services, and that their kids would be subject to discrimination and derision. Lipton educated hesitant parents about the benefits of integrated education and gave examples of successful integration in other locales. Eventually some parents joined her advocacy effort.

Coincidentally, BEH had chosen to hold a public hearing in spring 1980 on California's compliance with the Education for All Handicapped Children Act. Parents seeking integration took the opportunity to submit evidence that the district was not complying with federal law. District administrators told the activist parents that their children would be integrated.

However, Chloe was still not allowed into the Castro School. Instead, the district focused on integrating the "highest functioning" class from the Cameron School. Even this experiment was disappointing because students with disabilities remained essentially segregated: only during lunch and recess were they allowed to interact with nondisabled students. Lipton filed a complaint with the Department of Education and BEH.

BEH concluded that the state had failed to provide an education to students with disabilities in the "least restrictive environment," and the following month, the district announced that it would move all Cameron students, including Chloe, to regular schools by the 1981 academic year.

Diane Lipton attended law school and eventually became an attorney at

DREDF, where she empathized with parents seeking help for their disabled children. In 1993 she put her knowledge, passion, and legal skills to work in support of the family and friends of sixteen-year-old Louise Fuller, a Bakersfield student with severe cerebral palsy.

Louise had integrated into her local elementary school, where she became close to a loyal group of nondisabled friends. But administrators assigned the blond teenager to a high school with a special education program, not to Foothill High, the school near her home that her friends attended.

Fueled by their bond with Louise and knowledge gained in their eighth grade study of the Constitution's promise of equality and the right to protest, Louise's friends began a campaign to bring her to Foothill High School.

They appealed to school officials, circulated a petition signed by nearly five hundred junior high and high school students, organized a picket around the school district office, held press conferences, and produced a video to build support for their cause.

On March 29, 1993, after eight hours of negotiation, Lipton and administrators from the Kern High School District reached an agreement that Fuller could attend high school with her friends the following academic year.

An Avid Student

Successes for Chloe Lipton and Louise Fuller, while significant, were local victories. A ten-year-old developmentally disabled Sacramento girl and her dedicated family won a landmark federal case that defined the legal test for integrating disabled students into California public schools.

Rachel Holland was born in 1982 in Sacramento. Her parents, Robert Holland, a small business owner, and Kim Connor, an analyst for the California State Senate, were initially unaware that their first-born child had any disabilities. Rachel was almost twenty months old before she was diagnosed with developmental disabilities. Her parents had enrolled her in a day-care program at the Shalom School, a private school they had helped to establish through the local Jewish Federation.

Rachel's parents fully believed that their local public school would be just as good as, if not better than, the Shalom School. "Our thoughts were that the school district would be like being in our mothers' arms," recalled Connor. So they were surprised by the challenges they encountered.

When Rachel reached kindergarten, the Sacramento City Unified School District assigned her to a class for children with severe disabilities at the Crocker Riverside School, in her neighborhood. Before Rachel started school, Connor visited her daughter's classroom and was disturbed by what she saw. It was a dreary space. Half the room was used for storage. There was not much equipment: no educational toys, no books, no artwork. There was, however, a three-sided wooden box, painted black, pushed against a wall. Connor asked the teacher about the box's purpose, and the instructor explained it was for "time out." When asked about curriculum, the teacher responded that the class was basically a behavior management program. Rachel's soft-spoken mother was deeply disappointed. She and her husband wanted their daughter to learn social independence skills and academics.

Connor noticed that the kindergarten classroom next door was alive with color-ful artwork, big toys, books, stimulating equipment, and costumes. In the inviting environment, children were talking and engaged.

Although Rachel's class was small, it included children who were not disabled but who had behavioral problems. Because some students yelled and acted out, children were not allowed to talk much in the classroom. That was particularly detrimental for Rachel. As part of her development, she needed to be encouraged to talk more. Students in Rachel's class wore progress charts around their necks. If they behaved well, the teacher gave them a cracker or a penny.

By the end of Rachel's first year at Crocker Riverside, it was clear to her parents that their daughter was not progressing. Urged by friends, the couple sent Rachel to a summer day camp run by their local synagogue. There, Rachel was not segregated, and she thrived.

Believing that Rachel would progress in a more stimulating setting, her parents advocated for an hour or more of daily interaction between their daughter's class and the classroom next door. School officials resisted. The family and the district went into mediation, which resulted in the district's agreeing to integrate Rachel, but no more than one hour per day.

Through the mediation, Connor and Holland learned other disturbing facts. Rachel was not allowed to join the rest of the school for morning recess or lunch because her teacher believed that Rachel's presence would have a regressive effect on other students. Holland and Connor also learned that Rachel's special education classmates were assigned segregated tables and were marched in and out of the lunch area separately.

As a professional public policy analyst, Connor was adept at doing research and she used her skill to examine laws regarding students with disabilities and to inves-tigate how other school districts integrated them. She learned that the Sacramento school district had a legal obligation to provide Rachel, to the maximum extent ap-propriate, an integrated education with nondisabled children. Segregation into spe-cial classes or schools was only an option if Rachel was so severely disabled that inte-gration would be unsuccessful even with special aides. Connor also discovered that just fifteen miles west of Sacramento, the Davis school district integrated children with disabilities beginning at preschool.

Armed with this knowledge, Connor and Holland invited professionals from the Davis school district to a series of IEP meetings so that they could discuss with their Sacramento counterparts how to integrate students with disabilities. The district proposed putting Rachel in a regular class for nonacademic activities—like art, music, lunch, and recess—and in a special education class at all other times. Under this plan, Rachel would shuttle at least six times a day between two classrooms. Holland and Connor found this proposal unacceptable. They realized that the district really did not want to integrate. "The district as a whole sent the message that kids with disabilities were not welcome," Connor recalled.

Reluctantly, they re-enrolled Rachel in the Shalom School. Rachel blossomed and developed an interest in painting and drawing. Connor explained, "She did very, very well. She learned to write her name. She made friends. She was invited to birthday parties."

Rachel's parents concluded that if the Shalom School could educate their cheerful, curly-headed child, so could the public schools that their tax dollars supported. They asked the district to place Rachel in a regular class at the Leonardo da Vinci School, an arts magnet school. The district refused. Administrators determined that Rachel's disabilities were severe and proposed moving her to a special day class at the Bear Flag Elementary School, outside of the family's neighborhood.

"We didn't want to be chased from our neighborhood school," Connor stated. She and her husband appealed the district's decision to the California Special Education Hearing Office.

During a fourteen-day hearing, Rachel's kindergarten teacher at the Shalom School testified that Rachel had developed academically, become more independent and more comfortable interacting with her peers, talked more, expanded her vocabulary, and improved her gross motor skills. Rachel's experience at the Shalom School clearly contradicted the district's assertions that Rachel was too severely disabled to take advantage of full-time placement in a regular classroom and that the costs of doing so would be too great.

In August 1990, the hearing officer determined that Rachel was a nondisruptive and motivated student who learned by modeling and imitating behavior. She ordered the school district to place Rachel in a regular classroom with supportive services, including an educational consultant and a teacher's aide. The hearing officer faulted the school district for not making an adequate effort to integrate Rachel and for overstating the costs of doing so.

The parents of Rachel Holland advocated for several years to integrate their daughter into Sacramento public schools. They won a federal lawsuit in 1994, and Rachel graduated from McClatchy High School in 2002.

The decision was a precedent for California and established the right of a developmentally disabled child to be integrated into a regular classroom.

Special education administrator Adolphus McGee expressed the district's disagreement with the order but said it would be carried out. Nevertheless, the district failed to hire an educational consultant to assist Rachel's teacher and appealed the hearing officer's decision.

Rachel's parents kept her in the Shalom School until the case was resolved.

Diane Lipton represented the Holland family in a December 1991 trial that took place before U.S. District Court Judge David F. Levi. Rachel's Shalom School second grade teacher, Nina Crone, testified that because she had never taught a child like Rachel, she was initially skeptical that her educational needs could be met in her class. But the educator's apprehension had soon disappeared. Rachel was a full member of the class. Her language and math skills were not at grade level, Crone testified, but that did not matter as much as her interaction with the other children. The real goal of the second grade, the instructor explained, is to help children with socialization, behavior, and communication. Using that metric, Rachel was doing fine.

"Rachel is very eager to come to class," Crone testified. "She practically pushes her father out the door in the morning….She really wants to be there. She wants to be part of the activities that we do in class. She gets a kick out of being with the other kids. She's very turned on. She wants to know what they're doing. She wants to do what they're doing."

In March 1992, Judge Levi ruled in favor of the Hollands, explaining that every child with a disability has a right to be educated in an integrated class and with supplementary aids or services. To determine whether a child could receive a satisfactory education in an integrated classroom, the jurist outlined criteria adopted from appellate courts in other parts of the country.

His decision reflected updated federal law. In 1990 Congress had reauthorized the Education for All Handicapped Children Act, renaming it the Individuals with Disabilities Education Act (IDEA) and mandating that each state establish procedures to maximize the integration of students with disabilities. Special education classes and segregated schools were appropriate only when a student's disability was so severe that education in a regular classroom with supplemental aids and services was impossible.

The school district appealed.

By this time, Judy Heumann, 504 protest organizer and a former leader of the Berkeley Center for Independent Living, was the U.S. Education Department's Assistant Secretary for Special Education and Rehabilitative Services. Heumann had personally known the sting of segregation. She had missed the first four years of elementary school because an administrator in her Brooklyn district would not admit her because she had polio. She convinced the U.S. Justice Department to intervene in Holland's case. Outlining the Clinton administration's position, Heumann explained, "We believe in inclusion for children with disabilities, and we will look for cases where we can be supportive….This case illustrated a much broader problem than just one affecting the Holland child. My hope is that there's a message in our becoming involved in cases like this."

In its brief to the Ninth Circuit, the Justice Department pointed out that only 3.16 percent of developmentally disabled children in California were being taught in regular classrooms during the 1989-90 school year. The government argued that "placement decisions must…be driven by the individual child's abilities and needs, and not by some label assigned to a child's condition."

On January 24, 1994, the Ninth Circuit upheld the district court decision and adopted Judge Levi's criteria for integration as law for the western U.S.

The school district appealed to the U.S. Supreme Court, but the high court refused to review the case. "This signals an end to the historic segregation and isolation of children with disabilities in the American public school system," said Lipton. Because the Court had upheld the appeals court decision, "the principles established in *Brown v. Board of Education* over four decades ago now apply to children with disabilities."

The school district had spent over a million dollars to keep Rachel Holland out of a regular classroom.

Her father explained his family's determination: "We didn't come in as spirited zealots—we 'backed in' by virtue of trying to get our daughter in a regular elementary class full-time."

In September 1994, eleven-year-old Rachel Holland entered Room 22 of the da Vinci School for the start of fifth grade. Her parents had fought the school district for more than five years to win her the right to an integrated education. About a month after she had settled into her new class, Rachel had an important guest. Judy Heumann visited the gregarious girl. One of Rachel's school friends asked the federal official, "How come it took so long for Rachel to get in this school?"

Heumann responded, "Sometimes it takes longer for adults to change than children."

Epidemic of Fear

> We are not claiming that the fears of the FBI agents were not real. We believe they were real: they were really scared that Dr. Doe has Kaposi's sarcoma.
>
> What historically has distinguished our court system is its ability to deal with real fears. What made the *Korematsu* case such a shameful incident in the history of our court system was not that the court went along with "slight" or "fringe" reactions, but that it did not separate itself from very real mass, irrational fears.
>
> If the FBI, as the nation's chief law enforcement agency, is able to simply dispose of Dr. Doe's claim by writing a check (a check that will be backed by other people's money) then the chief law enforcement agency of the United States will have been able to defy the Rehabilitation Act on the basis of irrational fear.
>
> We cannot allow that to happen. That is what federal courts are for.

With this dramatic argument, attorney Matt Coles, the director of the ACLU of Northern California AIDS/HIV Task Force, closed the trial in the case of *Dr. Doe v. Attorney General of the United States* in federal court on May 17, 1989.

The AIDS epidemic had hit San Francisco like a hurricane. In the mid-1980s the difficult-to-diagnose, multisymptomatic, then-fatal disease worked its way through the largely gay Castro District and beyond. AIDS was so new, so mysterious, and so deadly that it caused great fear. There was so little information about how it was spread that ignorance and panic replaced rational thinking. Many people feared they could catch AIDS from a handshake, a hug, or a cough on the bus.

Fear propelled several unsuccessful statewide ballot initiatives to quarantine and stigmatize people with AIDS.

As public health leaders and gay community advocates struggled to conduct widespread education campaigns to stem the epidemic and to preserve the rights of those who had the virus that caused AIDS, the death toll mounted. The *Bay Area Reporter*, a local gay newspaper, ran weekly obituaries: page after page of smiling young men who worked as teachers, musicians, accountants, who had come to San Francisco from Kansas, Michigan, Arkansas to find kindred souls, liberation, and love, were pictured on the flat newsprint, their portraits now draped in black.

By the late 1980s, the enlightened public health community began to influence public policy. But discrimination against those who had the mysterious disease still was rampant. The health-care profession itself was one of the arenas where anti-AIDS discrimination law was being tested and developed.

Dr. James Cullen, tall, elegant, and in the prime of his professional life, performed preemployment and annual physical exams for the FBI through a contract at San Francisco's Davies Medical Center, a hospital on the edge of the Castro District.

After Dr. Cullen had been working for the FBI for four years, an agent told him that the agency knew he had Kaposi's sarcoma, an AIDS-related cancer. The agent refused to disclose how the FBI knew about the soft-spoken physician's illness. California had already enacted a confidentiality law prohibiting disclosure of certain information about people with AIDS; the authors of the legislation were fully aware that in the prevailing atmosphere of mistrust and prejudice, people with AIDS could lose their jobs, their homes, and their livelihoods.

The FBI canceled agents' appointments with Dr. Cullen and threatened to terminate his contract. Dr. Cullen was taken aback. He knew from his own physician that he could work without risk of transmitting the HIV virus to his patients.

Long before the FBI took action against Dr. Cullen, another federal agency, the National Centers for Disease Control, had established guidelines for health-care workers with AIDS. The Centers for Disease Control was unequivocal in stating that doctors need not be restricted from patient contact unless they perform "invasive procedures" such as surgery. The routine physical exams that Dr. Cullen performed did not include invasive procedures.

Both the medical center and Dr. Cullen assured the FBI that his patients faced no medical risk. Still, the FBI sent its agents to other doctors.

At a loss, and fearful of losing his income, Dr. Cullen filed a suit against the FBI under the Rehabilitation Act, the decade-old law that banned federally funded programs from discriminating on the basis of disability or medical condition. The law was designed to prevent discrimination based on inappropriate fear of disabilities, including AIDS.

Dr. Cullen was represented by two attorneys who brought the right combination of experience to the case. Jo Anne Frankfurt of the Employment Law Center had a strong background in disability and job discrimination law, having represented many individuals under the Rehabilitation Act. Matt Coles was a pioneer in civil rights work for the lesbian and gay community, and the author of model domestic partnership laws and nondiscrimination laws for several California cities. The degree of discrimination against people with AIDS was so deep and widespread that the attorneys filed the case under a pseudonym—Dr. James Cullen became plaintiff "Dr. Doe."

The trial became a focal point not only because it could expand the scope of the Rehabilitation Act to include AIDS, but for educating the courts and the public about HIV, the cause of AIDS, and how it is transmitted. Attorney Frankfurt later recalled that Dr. Cullen was a shy man who never wanted to be the center of attention, but who was willing to bring his lawsuit to heighten public awareness about discrimination against people with AIDS.

Coles and Frankfurt put top health professionals on the stand to educate the judge about the ways HIV is and is not transmitted. Epidemiologist Dr. George Rutherford, director of the AIDS Office of the San Francisco Department of Public Health, testified that the risk of HIV transmission during a routine physical was "vanishingly small."

The attorneys also addressed the issue of privacy—knowing that it was key for people with AIDS, especially if they were in the health-care field, and could impact their livelihood. Frankfurt charged that the FBI took information about Dr. Cullen which "should have been his and left to him, and they used it in a way that hurt him substantially, both economically and emotionally."

"No employer—particularly our own government—should deem itself above the law in the use of confidential medical information. The FBI's actions were medically uninformed and morally reprehensible," she asserted.

"It is clear that the FBI violated Dr. Doe's constitutional right to privacy and that he was unfairly discriminated against solely because he has AIDS—despite the fact that he presents no health or safety risk to patients," Frankfurt told the court.

Although U.S. District Court Judge Charles Legge had imposed a temporary injunction against the FBI's action during the course of the trial, his first decision in the case was disappointing. He determined that the Rehabilitation Act did not give an individual the right to sue the federal government over discriminatory treatment; a suit could be brought only against institutions or programs that received federal funds. Judge Legge suggested that Dr. Doe file an internal administrative complaint with the Justice Department.

Coles and Frankfurt immediately appealed the ruling to the Ninth Circuit, telling the appellate court that lengthy administrative remedies like that suggested by Judge Legge would be inappropriate for people with AIDS. "The process can go on longer than a person with AIDS may be able to keep working," Coles argued.

Frankfurt added, "No employee who is fighting for life should also be forced to fight for a job."

The 2-1 ruling from the court of appeals was a strong endorsement for coverage of people with AIDS under Section 504 of the Rehabilitation Act. "If the FBI had been legitimately concerned about the risk of transmission, it would have inquired as to the character and effectiveness of the infection control procedures used, as it was required to do under the Rehabilitation Act," the court stated. The ruling also noted that the U.S. Supreme Court had previously held that a person with an infectious disease "is otherwise qualified for a position if he does not pose a significant risk of communicating the disease to others in the work place."

The decision, which came in July 1995, six years after the case was first filed, marked the first time a health-care worker had won such a case.

The court ordered the FBI to pay damages—to Dr. Cullen's estate. He had died of AIDS-related complications in 1992 at the age of forty-two. Before the order became final, however, the Supreme Court ruled that damages could not be ordered in a case against the federal government. Since Cullen had died and could not be reinstated to his job, the case ended in a technical win for the government.

Burn This Book

Paul Longmore was six years old when his family moved from New Jersey to Los Angeles. In 1955, when they settled in El Segundo, a town south of the Los Angeles airport, a sign at the entrance to the suburb declared, "El Segundo: A White Gentile Community." The same year, Longmore contracted polio.

He spent fourteen months at the Rancho Los Amigos rehabilitation hospital in Downey, twenty miles to the east, where he chafed at the military environment, the bad food, and the professional staff's lack of awareness that children like him did not appreciate being treated like medical specimens.

As the son of a Baptist minister, Longmore developed a healthy skepticism for ecclesiastic authority, and his experience at Rancho Los Amigos taught him to expand that skepticism to the medical community. Like many other leaders in the disability rights movement, Longmore learned to question authority and to make his own judgments for himself about his condition.

Longmore also learned that much was expected of children with polio. Rehabilitation professionals pushed children with polio to overcome their condition without acknowledging the far greater difficulties posed by societal prejudice and institutionalized discrimination against people with disabilities. Longmore later commented, "I am, from one perspective, a disabled overachiever, a 'supercrip.' That shouldn't surprise anyone. I had polio. The rehabilitation system drilled people who had polio in overcoming and then held us up as legendary exemplars of healthy adjustment to disability. American culture has lionized us for our alleged refusal to accept limitations."

From the age of nine, Longmore was fascinated with American history, especially the period leading to the Revolutionary War. He decided to become a history professor, but one of his undergraduate professors told the young scholar that no college would hire him because of his disability. Longmore recalled, "I felt like my teacher was not only discounting my abilities, but was counseling me to give in to discrimination." Undaunted, Longmore pursued a master's degree at Occidental College, where the chairperson of the history department repeated the prediction that Longmore would not get an academic job.

In 1971 Longmore was accepted into the doctoral program in history at the Claremont Graduate School, in a quiet area of the Pomona Valley. He applied for financial assistance at the Pasadena office of the California Department of Rehabilitation, but a counselor told him that the department did not fund doctoral studies. The state would happily train him to become a computer programmer, the counselor explained. Longmore secured his first year's tuition from a friend.

At the end of that year, Longmore applied for a fellowship but was not selected. When he met with selection committee members to ask why, they told him that no college would hire him, because of his disability.

Longmore had almost no resources to pay for school. He received less than two hundred dollars a month from Supplemental Social Security Income (SSI), a federal program for indigent people with disabilities. Living frugally on that income, he saved enough to pay for one course a year.

After unsuccessfully pursuing other sources of funding (including an appearance on the television game show *Tic Tac Dough*), Longmore again approached the Department of Rehabilitation. This time, a counselor said the state would fund the equivalent of tuition at a California public university. Since tuition at the Claremont

Graduate School was triple that of a public university, the department's support allowed Longmore to take two classes a year.

As Longmore inched towards his PhD, a Department of Rehabilitation counselor told him that the agency planned to close his case, regardless of whether he completed his degree, because it was taking him too long. Longmore pushed back, explaining that he could not graduate in a timely manner because the department would not pay his full tuition. The counselor eventually admitted that staff were pressured to close cases to boost the department's performance statistics.

This admission was not news to Longmore—it was common knowledge among people with disabilities that the department closed cases to make itself look effective—but Longmore used the admission in his advocacy. He quoted the beleaguered counselor in a letter to his representative in the state assembly, who interceded with the department, which soon reversed its decision.

Longmore had little time to savor this victory before confronting another institutional Catch-22. Because polio had left him without the use of his arms and with limited use of his right hand, he hired attendants to help him with eating, showering, and dressing. He also often used a ventilator because of severe spinal curvature. By October 1988, the cost of his aides and ventilator came to over twenty thousand dollars a year. He met these expenses through a combination of government programs. California's In-Home Support Service Program paid for his assistants, while Medi-Cal paid for the ventilator, but only as long as he earned less than three hundred dollars a month or had no more than eighteen hundred dollars in savings.

The income threshold was so low because the federal government defined "disability" as the complete inability to engage in substantial gainful activity. This archaic definition originated in attempts to prevent nondisabled workers from feigning disability to qualify for welfare relief. By the time Longmore reached graduate school, it was clearly outdated. It did not take into account dramatic technological advances making it possible for people with disabilities to work, or the changing architectural environment and slowly evolving societal attitudes that made it easier for them to access and keep jobs. Even after federal courts directed the Social Security Administration (SSA) to use a less rigid definition of "disability" and to guarantee benefit recipients due process rights, the SSA refused to comply.

These policies devastated people's lives. In 1978, twenty-seven-year-old Lynn Thomson, a quadriplegic with muscular dystrophy, was receiving $390 monthly from SSI. The San Fernando Valley resident decided to earn extra money as a night telephone dispatcher for a health-care service company. After Thomson dutifully reported her meager earnings, the SSA informed her that she owed them ten thousand dollars in overpayments because of her extra income. The SSA said it would withhold her benefits until she reimbursed the government. In addition, the SSA threatened to cut off her Medi-Cal health coverage and attendant services, without which she would be forced into a nursing home. Thomson contested the SSA's decision, and a long battle with the bureaucracy followed. Anxious about her survival, Thomson took her own life, leaving a recorded message explaining that her experience with the SSA had driven her to suicide.

The lingering definition of "disability" as the complete inability to work trapped Longmore between a rock and a hard place. To have any chance at a competitive academic job, he needed experience as a teaching assistant or part-time college instructor. However, if he accepted a teaching position, he would earn more than the paltry three hundred dollars a month allowed by the SSA. Even more foreboding was the prospect of actually securing a long-term faculty position, which would disqualify him for federal support but not provide enough income to pay for his ventilator and attendants.

In 1986 Congress provided people with disabilities some relief by passing the Employment Opportunities for Disabled Americans Act, which allowed people with disabilities to work and still receive government assistance. The timing was providential for Longmore. In 1984, more than twelve years after he began his doctoral program, he completed his PhD.

But he still faced another bureaucratic obstacle.

In 1988 the Huntington Library, a respected research institution in San Marino near Longmore's southern California home, offered him a fellowship to continue his academic research on George Washington. In addition, that fall the University of California Press, a leading academic publisher, planned to release *The Invention of George Washington*, a book Longmore adapted from his dissertation. The bad news was that the SSA considered both fellowships and publishing royalties to be a special category of income. Consequently, if Longmore accepted the fellowship or received any book royalties, he would be disqualified from some or all of the government assistance he depended on to survive.

Longmore protested, writing President Reagan and other federal officials. But Dorcas Hardy, commissioner of Social Security, would not alter her position.

"When I read the commissioner's…warning that SSA would punish me if I received any royalties from my book," Longmore later recalled, "something in me reached a breaking point. Years of finding myself trapped and thwarted by this system, years of feeling demeaned and degraded by it, came to a head. I said to myself, 'I've had enough.'"

Longmore knew dramatic action was necessary. He decided to burn his book in a public protest.

On October 18, 1988, Longmore and nearly four dozen supporters gathered in front of the federal building in downtown Los Angeles with signs reading, "We want to work! Why won't the government let us?" and "Jobs. Not tin cups." Others circled the sidewalk in front of the building in a picket line, chanting disability rights slogans. Television cameras rolled, and reporters took notes.

Longmore explained the reason for the demonstration. He then set his book on fire. Recalling how this felt, he later said:

> I somberly watched the fire consume my book. I had planned the protest. I had rehearsed how to burn the book. I had even thought about what sort of expression I should have on my face. But I could never have prepared for the emotional effect on me of the act itself. I was burning my own book, a book I had spent ten years of my life laboring over, a book that had earned me my PhD in history, a book I felt proud of and, in fact, loved. It was a moment of agony.

A few months after the protest, Representative Robert Matsui learned of Longmore's dilemma. Matsui was carrying a bill in the House of Representatives to eliminate lingering work penalties in the Social Security program, and he added a provision that would solve Longmore's problem. It would allow social security recipients to earn book royalties, fellowships, research grants, and speakers' honoraria and keep

In October 1988, historian Paul Longmore protested federal work disincentives for people with disabilities by burning a copy of his book The Invention of George Washington.

their benefits. The SSA ultimately agreed that people with disabilities could earn book royalties and honoraria and still receive benefits, but those awarded grants and fellowships could not.

After decades of struggle against discrimination, bureaucratic obstacles, and legal barriers, Longmore realized his dream of becoming a university history professor. In 1992 the San Francisco State University history department hired him as an assistant professor. Within six years, he was promoted to the rank of full professor.

"I was liberated from the thrall of crippling public policies by successful disability rights lobbying," Longmore insisted. "No matter how hard I worked, I could never have succeeded without the removal of work penalties. What tore them out of my way was the political tenacity and perseverance of our disability rights community. I got this far because of the achievements of the disability rights movement."

A Floor, Not a Ceiling

Many disability rights advocates believed that the historic 1990 Americans with Disabilities Act (ADA) would usher in a new era. This landmark civil rights law protects people with disabilities in employment, government services, public accommodations, and transportation. However, in a series of 1999 cases, the U.S. Supreme Court ruled that the ADA does not protect people whose disabilities can be alleviated through medications, prosthetic devices, or aids. Consequently, federal courts denied ADA protection to people with amputations, cancer, epilepsy, insulin-dependent diabetes, bipolar disorder, and heart conditions.

It was up to state governments to codify more expansive protections. Well before the ADA, California had strong antidiscrimination laws protecting people with disabilities. In 1974, for example, the legislature added them to the groups covered by the Fair Employment and Housing Act (FEHA). And in its 1982 *American National Insurance Co. v. Fair Employment and Housing Commission* ruling, the California Supreme Court had defined "disability" broadly. In that case, insurance agent Dale Rivard sued his employer, which had fired him because of his high blood pressure. The question before the high court was whether hypertension is a disability. The court decided it is.

Attorney Prudence Kay Poppink, who argued the *American National Insurance* case before the state supreme court, was no stranger to discrimination. In the early 1970s, she had been one of the few women admitted to UC Hastings College of the Law, where some of the male students called the small quota of women the "dyke mafia."

Poppink took a job with the Employment Law Center, where she represented people with disabilities who experienced discrimination. Disability rights law was a new field at the time, and Poppink was key in securing the right of individuals to bring lawsuits alleging illegal discrimination under Section 504 of the Rehabilitation Act. She later worked for the California Fair Employment and Housing Commission, overseeing enforcement of the FEHA and crafting state legislation expanding and clarifying the law. She then became an administrative law judge with the commission, adjudicating cases of alleged employment and housing discrimination.

In the late 1990s, Poppink worked with California State Senator Sheila Kuehl on legislation to clarify who would be protected by the FEHA provisions related to disability. Kuehl introduced legislation explicitly stating that California's antidiscrimination laws apply to anyone with a condition or disorder that limits a major life activity, such as walking, seeing, hearing, speaking, breathing, learning, working, or self-care. In contrast, the ADA applies only to people with conditions that "substantially" limit a major life activity. Without Kuehl's legislation, tens of thousands of Californians with disabilities would be left unprotected from discrimination in employment, education, and public accommodations. During an assembly hearing on her bill, Kuehl explained that "California disability law provides protections independent from the ADA" and that the ADA "provides a floor of protection to Californians with disabilities, but not a ceiling."

The proposed statute insured that mitigating factors, such as medication, prosthetics, and assistive devices, could not be taken into consideration when determining whether a condition limits a major life activity, unless the mitigation itself limits a person's ability to engage in a major life activity.

Undergoing breast cancer treatment at the time, Poppink testified in favor of the bill.

Disability rights advocates muted publicity about the bill, knowing that business and insurance lobbies would object to the measure for cost reasons. Without fanfare, it sailed through the legislature. In honor of Poppink's three decades of advocacy, Senator Kuehl named the legislation the "Prudence Kay Poppink Act." On September 30, 2000, Governor Gray Davis signed it into law.

Six weeks later, Prudence Kay Poppink, who some call the "mother of disability law in California," died of complications from breast cancer. She was fifty-six years old.

— ELEVEN —

THE WRONG SIDE OF THE LAW

CRIMINAL JUSTICE

> I lived in New York in Harlem, Chicago's South Side, and believe it or not
> I have never been as harassed as I was in Los Angeles....I just have this
> deadly fear of the Los Angeles police.
>
> —*Assembly Member Mervyn Dymally, 1966*

When former County Supervisor Frank Shaw first ran for mayor of Los Angeles in 1933, the *Los Angeles Times* questioned his capabilities. Soon after that election, Shaw endeared himself to the newspaper's publisher by reappointing James Davis as chief of police. The *Times* appreciated Davis's efforts to silence labor organizers during the paper's management clashes with workers. However, a competing daily, the *Los Angeles Record*, wrote: "It is an axiom with Davis that constitutional rights are of benefit to nobody but crooks and criminals, and that no perfectly law-abiding citizen ever has any cause to insist upon 'constitutional rights.'"

In 1937 Mayor Shaw won reelection, but his regime soon unraveled because of a pious businessman's investigations into graft and corruption.

Clifford Clinton, the square-jawed son of missionaries, owned the popular chain of Clifton's Cafeterias. At the urging of crusading County Supervisor John Anson Ford, Judge Fletcher Bowron appointed Clinton to sit on a county grand jury investigating corruption linked to city hall. Clinton had earned a reputation as a fair dealer by providing meals at his restaurants for a penny during the height of the Depression. As a founder of CIVIC (Citizens Independent Vice Investigating Committee), a five-hundred-member group of church and business leaders formed to investigate corruption in local government, he took his position seriously. He hired private investigator

Harry Raymond, a former chief of police in San Diego and nearby Venice. Raymond uncovered damning evidence that city leaders, including Mayor Shaw, had colluded with gangsters to profit from gambling, prostitution, and narcotics operations. Organized crime had paid off the mayor and his cronies, who in turn demanded that the police and even the judiciary turn a blind eye to their illegal activities.

Rather than being lauded for his civic virtue, Clinton found his cafeterias assessed an additional sixty-seven hundred dollars in taxes and his application for a license to open a new restaurant rejected. The harassment continued when several "patrons" sued him after they claimed to have contracted food poisoning in his restaurants. Vandals hurled stink bombs into his establishments and sent his family threatening letters. The *Times* joined in the persecution by implying that Clifton's Cafeterias were akin to "slum soup lines." On the evening of October 27, 1937, Clinton's home, on the corner of Western Avenue and Los Feliz Boulevard, was bombed. The blast destroyed the basement and ground floor but did not injure Clinton or his family, who were asleep. Refusing to be intimidated, Clinton vowed, "I'll never stop now."

Clinton was not the only target of official wrath. Chief Davis ordered his officers to spy on the Boyle Heights home of private detective Harry Raymond. Days before Raymond was scheduled to testify before the grand jury in late January 1938, a bomb exploded when he started his car, blowing out the engine, destroying his garage, and breaking windows for blocks around. He commented to his rescuers, "What a rotten way to get a guy." Despite the one hundred and fifty pieces of metal, glass, and wood embedded in his body, Raymond survived.

Raymond testified before the grand jury from a wheelchair. One of his next-door neighbors identified LAPD Captain Earle Kynette and another officer as the men that had planted the bomb. Kynette headed the LAPD Intelligence Squad, also known as the Metropolitan Squad.

The Metropolitan Squad surveilled and created dossiers on individuals whom the mayor and the police department considered political enemies. The squad kept voluminous reports on such figures as Clinton; Supervisor John Anson Ford, who had run for mayor against Shaw; Representative Jerry Voorhis; and Assemblyman Sam Yorty, who would later be elected mayor.

Chief Davis initially denied that Kynette and the Metropolitan Squad had any connection with the bombing. The police chief even went so far as to assign Kynette to investigate the crime. The Metropolitan Squad leader suggested that Raymond might have planted the bomb himself. The evidence against Kynette and the Metropolitan Squad, however, was too great to ignore, and a grand jury indicted Kynette and two other officers on four felony counts. The three men were incarcerated without bail.

When confronted with the mountain of evidence against him during a ten-week trial, Kynette pleaded the Fifth Amendment. The jury convicted Kynette of attempted murder, assault with intent to commit murder, and the malicious use of explosives, and he was sent to San Quentin. The judge said, "I have listened to the evidence in this case carefully and I really believe you are as guilty as the jury found you. I have no misgivings as to the justice of the verdict."

As the trial came to a close, the city council eliminated the ninety-thousand-dollar fund that Mayor Shaw had requested to maintain the spy squad and other LAPD undercover work. Following the verdicts, the council passed a resolution calling

In 1938 Earl Kynette, head of the LAPD Metropolitan Squad, was convicted of attempted murder, assault with intent to commit murder, and the malicious use of explosives. The squad harassed and kept files on political opponents of Mayor Frank Shaw. Kynette is pictured here reading the Constitution.

upon the mayor, the chief of police, and members of the police commission to resign immediately, in order "to clear the way for putting the administration of the police department under men who will use that department solely for the public good and who will let the personnel of that department perform their legitimate duties with efficiency and self-respect."

Chief Davis resigned, but Mayor Shaw refused. In 1938 Los Angeles voters recalled the corrupt politician.

The previous year, Los Angeles voters had amended the city charter in an attempt to keep the LAPD independent of politics. The result was unrivaled authority for the chief of police. With no mandatory retirement age, a chief could serve as long as he wanted, unless convicted of extreme malfeasance. A few years earlier, the police and firefighters' union had successfully convinced Los Angeles voters to give police officers similar rights. The new voter-approved charter instituted a one-year statute of limitations to bring charges against a police officer. Only a Board of Rights consisting of three police officers could judge and fire a fellow officer. And the accused officer could choose his judges from the names of six ranking officers randomly drawn. The police chief could only decrease penalties against his employees.

Although nominally governed by a police commission appointed by the mayor, the LAPD in reality was accountable to no one but the chief. In the decades following the 1937 charter amendment, the LAPD evolved as a bastion of power unto itself.

At the same time that these structural changes resulted in unprecedented power for the LAPD, the city's population was changing. Although civic leaders of the 1920s and 1930s had promoted Los Angeles as the "white spot," Mexican Americans, African Americans, and Asian Americans were now settling in the Los Angeles Basin in large numbers.

Before the Shaw scandal, the LAPD's role in upholding business interests had been obvious, as they broke up strikes and persecuted political leftists. After the scandal, the LAPD shifted its focus from harassing trade unionists and radicals to waging a "war on crime." Mexican American and African American communities were the targets of this new focus.

Twentieth-Century Vigilantes

Between 1875 and 1947, sixty-three people were lynched in California. Nearly half were Latino, Indian, Chinese, or African American. Like the San Francisco vigilantes of the 1850s, many lynch mobs claimed a lenient criminal justice system had motivated their extralegal killings. And they often had the cooperation, if not outright participation, of the police.

In 1933 Governor James Rolph Jr. validated a San Jose mob that brutally killed two men accused of kidnapping and murdering the popular heir to a local department store, calling the lynching "the best lesson California has ever given the country."

Police arrested seven people in association with the lynching, but despite eyewitnesses and photos of the violence, no one was ever convicted.

Mob violence with official acquiescence took an ugly racist turn during World War II. Jazz clubs were all the rage and the "zoot suit" was a popular fashion. The high-waisted, pleated, baggy pants that tapered to narrow cuffs, accompanied by a long jacket—sometimes plunging to the knees—with wide lapels and shoulder pads especially appealed to youth. Men wore their hair long, tapered to a "duck tail" at the nape. Although young people of all races wore the zoot suit, the fashion became associated with Mexican Americans. And for many Mexican Americans, the zoot suit symbolized a rebellion against their second-class status. This generation had witnessed the "repatriation" in the 1930s of thousands of Mexicans and Mexican Americans when their labor was no longer needed, and they had experienced firsthand the sting of legalized racism that flew in the face of the democratic principles the country was defending in World War II.

But for many outside the Mexican American community, the zoot suit represented gangsterism.

On May 31, 1943, a fight broke out near downtown Los Angeles between a dozen white sailors and a group of zoot suit–clad young Mexican Americans. One sailor was struck to the ground unconscious, his jaw broken. Three years before, Los Angeles had built a million-dollar naval armory and training facility in Chavez Ravine, bordering neighborhoods populated by Mexican American families. (Once slated for public housing, Chavez Ravine is now the home of Dodger Stadium.) Resentful of the privileged, all-white Navy trainees and personnel invading their neighborhoods, young residents had taunted the sailors.

Three days later, a group of about fifty sailors left the armory intent on settling the score. Armed with homemade weapons crafted from broom handles and dumbbells, they snuck past the sentries. As they made their way towards downtown L.A., they began searching bars, restaurants, and other businesses for young men sporting the offending zoot suit. At the Carmen Theater, they turned on the houselights and discovered several twelve- and thirteen-year-old boys dressed in the jazzy attire. The sailors beat and stripped the adolescents and then set their zoot suits on fire. They continued marauding until the shore patrol and police rounded them up. The executive officer of the armory arranged for the men who were taken to the police station to be released without charges.

For four more nights, sailors, soldiers, marines, and civilians wreaked havoc downtown and in East L.A. and South Central. They searched for Mexican Americans and pummeled those they found. White mobs stopped streetcars, pulled young Mexican Americans, African Americans, and Filipino Americans from their seats, threw them into the streets, and beat them.

Time magazine summed up the police action: "to accompany the [servicemen's] caravans in police cars, watch the beatings, and jail the victims." A mob leader told the press, "We're out to do what the police have failed to do. We're going to clean up this situation...."

William Eastlake, an Army sergeant who was on leave in Los Angeles and witnessed the riots, wrote, "I could find nothing to distinguish the behavior of our soldiers from the behavior of Nazi storm troop thugs that roved Berlin in mobs bent on beating up outnumbered non-Aryans....I found the zooter on most occasions outnumbered two hundred to one, except in their enforced segregated districts."

After five nights of continuous rioting, Clarence Fogg, the naval commander for southern California, declared all of downtown Los Angeles out of bounds to naval personnel. Although violence spread to the surrounding communities of Watts, Long Beach, and Pasadena for the following two days, the mass rioting subsided after Commander Fogg's order.

After a week of rioting, police had arrested more than six hundred Mexican Americans and African Americans, but only a handful of the thousands of vigilantes.

Los Angeles County Supervisor Roger Jessup reflected the views of the city fathers, commenting, "All that is needed to end lawlessness is more of the kind of action as is being exercised by the servicemen—if this continues zooters will soon be as scarce as hen's teeth." The Mexican ambassador in Washington sent a formal inquiry to Secretary of State Cordell Hull regarding the violence. As the rioting reached a crescendo, Governor Earl Warren appointed a citizens' committee chaired by Joseph T. McGucken, auxiliary bishop of Los Angeles, to research the causes of the rioting and to make recommendations. The McGucken committee squarely blamed race prejudice for the vigilante action:

> It is significant that most of the persons mistreated during the recent incidents in Los Angeles were either persons of Mexican descent or Negroes. In undertaking to deal with the cause of these outbreaks the existence of race prejudice cannot be ignored....The guilty must be punished regardless of what clothes they wear—whether they be zoot suits, police, army, or navy uniforms. The streets of Los Angeles must be made safe for servicemen as well as civilians, regardless of national origin. The community as well as its visitors must learn that no group has the right to take the law into its own hands.

Recognizing the damage done to downtown businesses by the military's off-limits orders and the possible denial of future military contracts, the local press and city officials steadfastly insisted that racial prejudice had played no role in the rioting. A *Los Angeles Times* editorial opined, "We have the largest Mexican colony in the United States here and we enjoy fraternizing with them....We have paid homage and honor to the Californians of Mexican descent among us....We like Mexicans and we think they like us." The *Times* blamed the rioting on zoot suit gangs.

The LAPD's hostile attitude toward Mexican American and African American communities continued, spiked by several high-profile incidents. In July 1946, a riot nearly broke out at the corner of Central Avenue and Adams Boulevard after a Highway Patrol officer shot a fleeing black suspect in the back and killed him. In what became dubbed the "Bloody Christmas" incident, drunken officers at the Central Station mercilessly beat young Chicano men in custody on Christmas Day 1951. This was one of the rare instances in which the LAPD meted out punishment to its own, firing two officers and reprimanding thirty-six others.

In the early 1950s, half the Watts residents who responded to a survey reported that Los Angeles police had forced them to line up, frisked them, and slapped and kicked them for no apparent reason. Resentment smoldered among the city's black residents into the 1960s before igniting in a week of violence.

From Watts to Eulia Love

By the early evening of August 11, 1965, South Central Los Angeles had cooled down to 75 degrees from temperatures in the nineties earlier in the day. Despite the lingering yellow-gray film of smog blanketing the city, residents sat on porches, steps, and curbs, enjoying the summer night. About seven p.m., an African American motorist on Avalon Boulevard noticed an erratically driven 1955 gray-white Buick, and he signaled to California Highway Patrolman Lee Minikus, telling the officer that the driver might be drunk. A few minutes later, Minikus stopped twenty-one-year-old Marquette Frye on Avalon Boulevard near 116th Street. Frye, who had moved to Los Angeles eight years earlier from Wyoming, was driving with his twenty-two-year-old stepbrother, Ronald, who had recently been honorably discharged as an airman second class. The Air Force veteran had only been in Los Angeles for two days.

The Frye brothers had been celebrating Ronald's new life as a civilian with some young women friends and were heading home for dinner. Marquette Frye admitted that he and his brother had enjoyed a few screwdrivers but insisted he was not drunk. He attempted good-naturedly to convince the officer not to ticket him and cooperated with Minikus's instructions to prove his sobriety by walking a straight line. Still trying to charm his way out of arrest, he joked, "Now, would you like me to walk it backward? Although Frye believed he had passed, Minikus judged differently and radioed for another officer to join him. A small crowd gathered. They poked fun at the trim young man dressed in Italian shoes, tailored sport shirt, and brimmed hat. They joked with the officer, too. A friend of the Frye family went to tell Frye's mother, Rena, who lived a block away, that her stepson was being arrested.

A few minutes later, Minikus's partner arrived and Marquette Frye realized he would be arrested. He insisted on his sobriety and said that he would not go to jail. More Highway Patrol officers pulled up, along with Los Angeles police. The crowd swelled, growing so large that it blocked one lane of traffic on busy Avalon Boulevard. As he jostled with Minikus, who brandished a baton, Frye declared, "You'll have to kill me before you take me to jail!" Meanwhile, as a CHP officer tried to keep Ronald Frye from helping his brother, another officer thrust a riot baton into Ronald's ribs. The same officer then hit Marquette above his left eye and jabbed him in the stomach. Minikus clenched Marquette in a headlock and led him to a patrol car.

By this time, Rena Frye had arrived. Believing that her stepson would receive further abuse in the police car, she jumped on Minikus's back, trying to pull him away from Marquette. A CHP officer pulled Rena away, pushed her against a patrol car, handcuffed her, and shoved her into the rear seat. Ronald was arrested as well.

More law enforcement officers arrived bearing shotguns and riot batons to keep the growing crowd, now in the hundreds, away from the car transporting the Fryes to jail. In the crowd was twenty-one-year-old Joyce Gaines. Minutes earlier, she had been getting her hair done at a nearby beauty parlor. Still wearing pink curlers and a beautician's smock, she walked four blocks up Avalon Boulevard and worked her way to the front of the crowd, where she saw the Fryes being driven off. She was about to return to the beauty parlor when someone grabbed her arm and pulled her backward. Someone in the crowd had spat on a CHP officer and he decided that it was Gaines. A struggle ensued as CHP and LAPD officers tried to handcuff the young woman and put her in a patrol car. The smock she wore made her appear to be pregnant, and word quickly spread that the police were beating a pregnant woman.

As the police cars sped away, angry young people in the crowd broke off into small groups and for several hours stoned cars and attacked white motorists driving near the intersection of Avalon Boulevard and Imperial Highway. Police in riot gear pushed their way into the crowd, indiscriminately striking out with batons and fists.

The following day, John Buggs of the L.A. Human Relations Commission and Rev. H. Hartford Brookins, pastor of the First African Methodist Episcopal Church of Los Angeles and chair of the United Civil Rights Committee, met with LAPD Deputy Police Chief Roger Murdock in an attempt to quell further violence. Buggs had told young people in the area that if they promised not to "start anything" the police would not be in the area that night. Murdock, however, would not negotiate, telling the two black leaders, "We know how to put down a riot, and we are going to handle it our own way. We have already decided what we are going to do, and what you have got to say isn't going to change it."

This attitude reflected the leadership of Chief William Parker. Early in his career with the LAPD, Parker had been assistant to disgraced Chief James Davis. By 1965 the no-nonsense South Dakotan, who resembled the farmer depicted in Grant Wood's *American Gothic*, had served as chief of police for fifteen years. He had reorganized the LAPD along paramilitary lines and believed that the police were a thin blue line protecting law-abiding citizens from "forces of evil."

Chief Parker's leadership was just one factor contributing to the resentment experienced by the city's African American population. Proposition 14, a voter initiative repealing fair housing laws, had passed just nine months earlier. Between 1963 and 1965, the LAPD had killed sixty African Americans; twenty-seven of them were shot in the back. In 1962 the LAPD had raided the Los Angeles Black Muslim mosque in a hail of gunfire, killing one member and paralyzing another for life.

Los Angeles City Councilman Billy Mills, who lived in South Central and had worked as a probation officer between 1957 and 1960, recounted that "a very common entreaty for instruction to a Negro motorist is 'Nigger, get out of [that] car.'" Mervyn Dymally, South Central's assemblyman during the early 1960s, shared Mills's assessment of the LAPD's treatment of African Americans, commenting, "I lived in New York in Harlem, Chicago['s] South Side, and believe it or not I have never been as harassed as I was in Los Angeles....I just have this deadly fear of the Los Angeles police."

Despite having won his office with help from black voters, Mayor Sam Yorty ignored appeals to hear the black community's grievances, so their leaders appealed to the U.S. Commission on Civil Rights. When, in June 1962, the California Advisory Committee to the commission held hearings in Los Angeles, Mayor Yorty suggested that the hearing was communist-inspired. Chief Parker insisted that the police were the beleaguered minority, and that a communist-instigated campaign was the source of police brutality complaints. "I do not believe that there is any difficult problem existing in the relationship between the Los Angeles Police Department and the Negro community," he said.

The night after the Fryes' arrest, violence turned more destructive. Rioters set cars on fire and threw rocks and asphalt chunks at firefighters. Looting had started the night before and now spread, and some businesses were set on fire. The police attempted to sweep the area, marching down Avalon Boulevard.

Violence, looting, and arson bled almost unabated into a third day along the Avalon Boulevard–Imperial Highway corridor and spread into the nearby Watts neighborhood, the fires adding to the 92 degree midday heat.

By Friday, August 13, Police Chief Parker was comparing his LAPD officers to soldiers fighting the Viet Cong. Deputy Police Chief Murdock said that the way to handle the perceived guerilla warfare was "to put as many people as we can in jail." By late that afternoon, violence had spread to three separate areas: a mile of Avalon Boulevard from Century Boulevard to Imperial Highway; Watts; and the commercial area around Manchester and Broadway.

State authorities alerted Governor Edmund "Pat" Brown, who was vacationing in Greece, and he returned home immediately. Meanwhile, Lieutenant Governor Glenn Anderson ordered National Guard troops into the riot areas.

Friday the 13th saw the first fatality. At about six-thirty that night, the sound of sirens and crashing glass prompted Leon Posey Jr., a lean twenty-one-year-old, to step outside a barbershop on Broadway. He was hit in the back of the head by a .38 caliber bullet. Posey was taken to nearby Oak Park Hospital but died because no anesthetist would enter the riot zone, and therefore no doctor could perform a potentially life-saving operation.

On Saturday, Governor Brown imposed a curfew over a 46.5-square-mile area from the cities of Gardena and Compton in the south to the Santa Monica Freeway in the north, and from the cities of Vernon, Huntington Park, and South Gate in the east to Crenshaw Boulevard in the west. No unauthorized person could be on the streets after eight p.m.

That evening, close to fourteen thousand National Guardsmen, police, and sheriffs deputies were on duty. Troops with machine guns were stationed at major intersections in South Central, and the National Guard set up roadblocks at key intersections and fired upon panicky motorists unaware of the obstacles. National Guard Lt. Colonel Robert Dove commented on the chaos:

> The type of people that give you trouble are not the type of people most of the time that were hurt....It took a couple of days to learn under what circumstances people should or should not fire....This is the sad thing about these shootings. You shoot some of the wrong people. Fifteen percent cause all the trouble, but the 15 percent hide behind the 85 percent, and you harass the 85 percent trying to find the 15 percent that you can't get.

A drunk driving arrest in August 1965 sparked pent-up resentment against police brutality, resulting in several days and nights of violence in Watts and neighboring areas of South Central Los Angeles. Nearly four thousand people were arrested; thirty-four were killed; more than one thousand were injured. Property damage was an estimated $40 million.

Police swept the vast riot zone. The LAPD opened the previously shuttered Lincoln Heights jail to accommodate the growing number of arrestees, who were locked in large cells holding eighty to a hundred or more. Some were injured, with bruises, cuts, and burns. Bathrooms were inadequate, and bunks had no mattresses.

Police arrested nearly four thousand people, the biggest mass arrest in American history. It was difficult to secure legal representation for the huge number of arrestees. ACLU attorney A. L. Wirin said, "Never in the four decades of its existence has the ACLU of Southern California been confronted with so grave a challenge to civil liberties as posed by the criminal prosecutions in the aftermath of the Watts incident."

On Monday, August 16, five days after Marquette Frye's arrest, the Los Angeles Hall of Justice began processing the thousands of adults and juveniles who had been arrested. The vast majority (more than 2,400 adults) were charged with burglary and theft. Among the nearly 2,250 accused of felonies, charges against 700 were dismissed. Of the remaining, 800 were found guilty of misdemeanors, 350 were found innocent, and 350 (or 16 percent of those initially arrested) were convicted of felonies.

By the time the violence ended, thirty-four people had been killed; more than a thousand were injured, and property damage was an estimated forty million dollars.

As the embers of burned businesses cooled, Governor Brown appointed a seven-member commission to investigate the causes of the riot. Chaired by former CIA director John McCone, with attorney Warren M. Christopher (who later served as secretary of state under President Clinton) as vice chair, the McCone Commission conducted a series of hearings and staff investigations at breakneck pace. The commission accepted Chief Parker's analysis and issued a report blaming the riots on criminals within the black community and secondarily on black leaders who, they said, had fueled black resentment because of "imagined slights" like Proposition 14. The commission assiduously denied the existence of racial problems and, more specifically, a long history of police misconduct as a spark for the riots.

Despite overwhelming testimony from African Americans and civil rights advocates, McCone flatly refused to admit to the possibility of brutality by the LAPD; accusations of police brutality were simply a means of undermining the rule of law and eroding society into a state of chaos, he reasoned.

After the riots, National Guard Captain Richard W. Baer commented:

> The attitude of the law enforcement agencies toward the Negro population had a distinct adverse effect on the battalion. There were many instances of negative attitudes toward everything Negro, police officers making such statements as "Shoot the SOBs!" "Rough them up every time you get the chance!" and similar statements soon gave our men the impression that the Negro was an enemy to be destroyed in every way.

On June 23, 1967, with memories of the Watts insurrection still smoldering in the city's psyche, LAPD officers were involved in another violent street confrontation. Unlike the conflict in Watts, this clash involved largely middle-class whites and took place in Century City, nestled between Beverly Hills and wealthy Westwood.

President Lyndon Johnson was attending a five-hundred-dollar-a-plate fundraising dinner at the swank Century Plaza Hotel that night, and ten thousand demonstrators had amassed to protest the Vietnam War. Lines of police officers created a bottleneck in front of the hotel, effectively forcing marchers from four street lanes to one. Other officers blocked the intersection in front of the initial marchers.

Nine stories above, Los Angeles Police Chief Thomas Reddin, who had succeeded William Parker after the longstanding chief died of a heart attack, stood at a hotel window looking down on the demonstrators. He noticed a "bulge" in the crowd and, believing that an assault on the hotel was imminent, ordered his officers to disperse the protestors.

Waiting near the hotel, a phalanx of thirteen hundred riot-helmeted officers carrying guns and nightsticks was poised to take action. After Chief Reddin issued his order, officers announced over a distorted loudspeaker system that the march was an illegal assembly and the demonstrators must disperse.

Many marchers did not hear or understand the instructions. But those who did had nowhere to go. They were boxed in by the police guarding the hotel to the west, thousands of marchers to the south, a steep embankment and railed construction zone to the east, and a police blockade to the north.

A line of officers started pushing the crowd. Police then began striking demonstrators, knocking many of them down.

No one in the crowd had provoked the police or made any movement toward the hotel, so it was a shock when officers began attacking the marchers, among whom were children, elderly people, and people with visible disabilities.

For nearly ninety minutes, Los Angeles police officers beat, kicked, and verbally abused hundreds of peaceful protestors. More than five hundred people later submitted statements about police abuse to the ACLU and the demonstration organizers.

In the years following Watts and Century City, the LAPD, under the leadership of Chiefs Ed Davis and Daryl Gates, continued to alienate African Americans and others. ACLU of Southern California Executive Director Eason Monroe described "a new and dangerous escalation in what appears more and more to be open warfare between the citizens of the barrios and ghettos and the police."

In 1969 the U.S. Civil Rights Commission lamented that, four years after the Mc-Cone report, "few changes have been made in…the handling of civilian complaints alleging misconduct by law enforcement personnel."

Ten years later, the shooting death of Eulia Love would, for many, come to symbolize the LAPD's abuse of power. On January 3, a Southern California Gas Company employee tried to collect twenty-two dollars for an unpaid bill from the South Central Los Angeles widow. He threatened to turn off her gas. She attacked him with a shovel, and he fled. He returned, however, with two LAPD officers. Distraught and furious, she wielded a kitchen knife when she confronted the men. The two officers shot her with twelve rounds of ammunition.

Incidents like this flared up over the years, but no real reform resulted. Not until the world witnessed the brutal beating of a Los Angeles motorist did any real change come about.

The Whole World Watches

Shortly after midnight on March 3, 1991, husband-and-wife California Highway Patrol officers Melanie and Tim Singer pursued a white 1988 Hyundai sedan speeding on the Foothill Freeway. After the driver exited into the Lake View Terrace area of the northeast San Fernando Valley, the Singers radioed for help, and LAPD officers Laurence Powell and Timothy Wind joined the chase. The driver finally pulled over near a Tastee Freez on Foothill Boulevard in a multiracial neighborhood of working-class homes. The Singers used their loudspeaker to order the twenty-five-year-old African American driver, Rodney King, out of the car. He exited and got down on the ground, surrounded by twenty-seven law enforcement officers, at least ten of whom had guns aimed at him.

LAPD Sergeant Stacey Koon, the ranking officer on the scene, believed that King did not follow directions to exit the car immediately. Because of King's muscular build, Koon jumped to the conclusion that he was an ex-convict who had worked out while in prison. Koon later said he believed King was high on PCP.

Officer Powell bent down to handcuff the prone King. Koon then shot King with a Taser gun, sending fifty thousand volts of electric shock through his body. Powell used his two-foot-long, solid aluminum police baton like a baseball bat and took "power swings" at King's face, head, and knuckles, forcing screams of pain. Powell later acknowledged the beating but claimed he attacked only after King charged him. Melanie Singer, however, recounted that King was on his knees when Powell began hitting him.

King remembered that Koon told him, "You better run now, nigger, 'cause we're gonna kill you." At that point, King tried to get up and Koon screamed orders at Powell and fellow LAPD officer Timothy Wind: "Hit his joints, hit his wrists, hit his elbows, hit his knees, hit his ankles." Wind and Powell hit King fifty-five times within eighty-one seconds. Another officer, Theodore Briseno, ground his foot onto King's neck. King was curled into the fetal position, trying to protect himself.

At least thirty-one law enforcement officers from the LAPD, CHP, and the L.A. Unified School District, as well as residents and others in passing vehicles, witnessed the beating. King lay face down in the street, his feet and hands hog-tied, before an ambulance transported him to the Pacifica Hospital emergency room.

Fifteen minutes later, Powell sent a message to a fellow officer over the LAPD's Mobile Digital Terminal system: "I haven't beaten anyone this bad for a long time." But Powell's official report mentioned nothing of the beating, only that King was taken to the hospital for treatment of abrasions and contusions on his face, arms, legs, and torso.

Similarly, Stacey Koon recounted that King's injuries amounted only to a split lip and minor facial cuts due to "contact with asphalt." In reality, the officers had broken King's cheekbone and ankle. The police beating resulted in permanent injuries to the bones that held King's right eye in its socket, eleven fractured bones at the base of his skull, a serious concussion, and facial nerve damage.

Although the incident horrified the many witnesses, the law enforcement version of the event—that King had resisted arrest and charged the officers—might have been accepted as reality, had it not been for George Holliday. The burly plumber, who lived in the Mountainback apartment complex overlooking Foothill Boulevard, had videotaped almost three minutes of the beating.

Ramona Ripston, ACLU-SC Executive Director, commented, "The only thing aberrant about the King beating is that it was filmed."

After television stations worldwide aired the videotape, local and national leaders began calling for Chief Daryl Gates's resignation. Gates had little choice but to recommend that Koon, Powell, Wind, and Briseno face felony charges. For two of the officers, this was not the first instance of documented violence. Ted Briseno was suspended for sixty-six days without pay after kicking and beating an arrestee in 1987. Lawrence Powell had broken a man's arm in 1989, and the city had paid seventy thousand dollars in a settlement and admitted that Powell used excessive force.

A grand jury indicted all four officers for assault with a deadly weapon and unnecessarily beating a suspect. In addition, Koon and Powell were charged with filing false police reports. Gates then fired Wind, who was still a probationary officer, and suspended the other three.

Mayor Tom Bradley and Chief Gates appointed the Independent Commission on the Los Angeles Police Department, headed by sixty-five-year-old powerhouse attorney Warren Christopher, who had been the vice chair of the McCone Commission that investigated the Watts riot. The commission's mandate was broad and included making recommendations about citizen complaints and disciplining of police.

After hearing from nearly eight hundred individuals, including police officers, expert witnesses, organizational representatives, and private citizens, the commission issued a 228-page report in July 1991. Unlike the McCone Commission twenty-five years earlier, the Christopher Commission concluded that "there is a significant number of officers in the LAPD who repetitively use excessive force against the public and ignore the guidelines of the department regarding excessive force." The commission also found that the problem of excessive force was "aggravated by racism and bias." They faulted management and the police commission, which not only failed to discipline or fire several hundred problem officers who had "repeatedly misused force" but often promoted these same officers. Calling the Rodney King beating a landmark event, the commission recommended that Chief Gates and current police commission members resign.

Gates, who had served as chief for more than thirteen years, announced his retirement date as June 1992. The same month as Gates's intended departure, the Christopher Commission's reform recommendations—which included giving the police commission the right, with approval of the city council, to fire the police chief—appeared on the ballot as Proposition F. In the weeks preceding the chief's retirement and the vote, another critical event took place: delivery of the verdicts in the cases against LAPD officers Stacey Koon, Laurence Powell, Timothy Wind, and Ted Briseno.

The officers' attorneys had successfully convinced a Los Angeles judge to grant a change of venue, to the overwhelmingly white suburb of Simi Valley, in southern Ventura County. About four thousand law enforcement officers lived in the region, where tract homes overlooked orchards and strawberry fields. Upon learning that the King trial would be conducted in his county, the head of the local NAACP commented that the prosecution "would be better off going to Mississippi."

The officers' defense attorneys portrayed King as a wanton criminal who defiantly resisted arrest. The officers used appropriate force to protect law-abiding citizens from criminals like King, argued the defense.

After seven days of deliberation, the jury reached verdicts on April 29, 1992. Beginning at three-thirty that afternoon, the court clerk announced "not guilty" ten times; the jury had found none of the officers guilty of any of the charges. The only point of debate, which had taken six days of discussion, was an assault charge against Powell. The jury eventually split on this question, and the judge quickly declared a mistrial on that issue. Police officers throughout Los Angeles celebrated.

To most people who had seen George Holliday's video, the verdicts were unbelievable. And the verdicts sparked the brittle tinder of accrued resentment in South Central. With shouts of "No justice, no peace!" thousands poured into the streets. As the arrest of Marquette Frye had, almost twenty-seven years earlier, the acquittals of the officers ignited three days of violence and destruction, once again centered in South Central but this time spreading into the neighboring Pico-Union and Korea-town districts.

Like his mentor Chief Parker, Chief Daryl Gates was ineffective during the critical early hours of violence, when some residents of South Central stoned vehicles driven by non-blacks. At the time, Gates was in posh Brentwood attending a fundraising event to defeat Proposition F. Because he had earlier ordered that several police divisions, including the 77th Division in South Central, be under his direct command, it was unclear who was in charge during his absence.

By the end of three days of turmoil, 58 people were dead, 2,383 were injured, and property damage amounted to nearly eight hundred million dollars.

Soon after the rioting ceased, the L.A. Police Commission assembled another independent commission, headed by former FBI and CIA director William Webster, to investigate the riots. The commission concluded that the LAPD's slow response to the violence after the verdicts was attributable "first and foremost to the performance of the chief of police and his command staff." The department's initial reaction, the commission concluded, was characterized by "uncertainty, some confusion, and almost a total lack of coordination." Gates called Webster and an advisor to the commission "liars."

Although the four officers charged with the Rodney King beating had not been convicted, structural changes impacting the police department were made. In June 1992 Los Angeles voters passed Proposition F two to one, to amend the city charter to adopt the Christopher Commission's recommendations. It was now possible to fire a police chief. The chief's tenure was limited to two five-year terms, and the city had a mandate to create a system to track problem officers. A police commission watchdog unit would oversee the disciplinary process.

In 1992 Stacey Koon, Laurence Powell, Timothy Wind, and Ted Briseno were tried in federal court for violating King's civil rights. Two years after the beating, a federal jury found Wind and Briseno not guilty. They found Koon and Powell guilty. The two were sentenced to eighteen months in federal prison, the most lenient sentence allowed.

"Thou Shalt Not Kill"

At the dawning of April 21, 1992, Robert Alton Harris became the first person to be executed by the state of California in a quarter-century.

Up until the very last moment, judges from San Francisco to Sacramento to

Washington, DC, were in a tug of war over Harris's fate. Harris's defense team, which had worked round-the-clock since the execution date had been set a week earlier, filed motions in state and federal courts in the hours leading up to the scheduled execution.

At 3:45 a.m., prison guards, having been told all the stays were exhausted, strapped Robert Harris into one of the two chairs in the gas chamber. There he sat for twenty minutes, awaiting his death. Then, at 4:01 a.m., following a new stay of execution from the Ninth Circuit Court of Appeals, the guards unstrapped him and took him back to the holding cell.

Outside the gates of San Quentin, hundreds of death penalty opponents kept an all-night vigil. For months they had mobilized protests throughout the state, and on the eve of the scheduled execution they marched across the Golden Gate Bridge to the massive stone prison. As the waves of San Francisco Bay lapped against the prison walls, they heard prayers from ministers, rabbis, and Native American spiritual leaders. The protestors carried tombstone-shaped placards marked with the names of the 502 people who had been executed in California, and signs that read simply, "Thou shalt not kill."

At 5:45 a.m., word came from the U.S. Supreme Court with an undisputed air of finality: "No further stays of Robert Alton Harris' execution shall be entered except upon order of this court."

Witnesses were rushed back into the gas chamber viewing area at 6 a.m. "We were on double-time. There was no question that there was an attempt to get this done as soon as possible," said witness Michael Tuck, a Los Angeles television reporter.

The cyanide pellets were dropped at 6:05 a.m. At 6:21, Robert Harris was pronounced dead by a prison physician.

Harris had been convicted and sentenced to death for the 1978 murders of two teenagers, John Mayeski and Michael Baker, in San Diego. He had been born with organic brain damage resulting from fetal alcohol syndrome. This condition was exacerbated by brutal childhood beatings. But a jury never had the opportunity to consider these mitigating circumstances in deciding Harris's sentence.

This medical evidence was, however, known to Governor Pete Wilson, the only person authorized to grant clemency. At Harris's clemency hearing in Sacramento, a week before the execution, experts in psychiatry from UCLA and UC San Diego explained to the governor that a person with fetal alcohol syndrome cannot make the kinds of mental judgments that are defined as "premeditation," a criterion for determination of first-degree murder. In addition to the scientists' testimony, a plea for Harris's life was made by his spiritual advisors: his cousin Reverend Leon Harris, who was a Baptist minister, deputy sheriff, and state-certified drug and alcohol counselor from Mobile, Alabama; and Reverend Earl A. Smith, the chaplain at San Quentin.

But the clemency pleas, the protests, and the voluminous legal pleadings fell on deaf ears. California was ready to resume state killing.

Capital punishment had been included in the California Penal Code since 1872. At that time, county sheriffs conducted executions, often in a public square with an enthusiastic audience of townspeople. In 1891 the law was amended to limit executions to the two state prisons, San Quentin and Folsom. José Gabriel was the first person to be hanged at San Quentin, on March 3, 1893.

The gas chamber, which replaced the hangman's noose in 1937, operated for the next three decades. Among those put to death during those years was Caryl Chessman, who wrote four books while on death row and whose 1960 execution for robbery, kidnapping, and rape—while there was uncertainty about his guilt—brought worldwide notoriety to California. Governor Pat Brown, a death penalty opponent, had stayed Chessman's execution several times, but allowed it to proceed in 1960. Governor Brown, who commuted the death sentences of twenty-three condemned

Drawing by artist Howard Brodie of the San Quentin gas chamber execution of Aaron Mitchell in 1967.

"It would be very difficult for anybody to see the contortions and not presume they were conscious. I don't think anything can prepare you for that."
— *former Mississippi prison warden*

Aaron Mitchell was the last person executed in San Quentin's gas chamber before the California Supreme Court declared the death penalty cruel and unusual punishment in 1972. State executions were halted until 1992, when Robert Harris was executed.

men, agonized over the death penalty while he was in office and later condemned it as "barbaric." In his 1989 book, *Public Justice, Private Mercy: A Governor's Education on Death Row,* the former governor wrote, "Beyond its horror and incivility, [the death penalty] has neither protected the innocent nor deterred the wicked."

On April 8, 1967, Aaron Mitchell became the 194th and last person executed in the gas chamber until 1992. For the next quarter-century, state and U.S. Supreme Court rulings outlawed the death penalty.

The California Supreme Court declared on February 18, 1972, in *People v. Anderson,* that the death penalty violated the state constitution because it constituted cruel and unusual punishment. Because of the ruling, one hundred and seven inmates were taken off death row and resentenced to life imprisonment. In a rapid response, by November that same year voters had passed an initiative promoted by law enforcement interests that reinstated the death penalty.

Justice Stanley Mosk commented, "The people of California responded quickly and emphatically...to callously declare that whatever the trends elsewhere in the nation and the world, society in our state does not deem the retributive extinction of a human life to be either cruel or unusual."

The judge lamented the voters' decision, stating, "I prefer values more lofty than those implicit in the macabre process of deliberately exterminating a human being [but that] does not permit me to interpret in my image the common values of the people of our state."

Also in 1972, the U.S. Supreme Court ruled in *Furman v. Georgia* that the death penalty was not being applied in a constitutional manner because capital punishment standards varied widely from state to state. As one of the majority justices, Potter Stewart, stated, "These death sentences are cruel and unusual in the same way that being struck by lightning is cruel and unusual." The decision put a moratorium on the death penalty throughout the country, including California's newly passed initiative, until states devised death penalty practices that conformed to constitutional standards.

In 1976 the U.S. Supreme Court, in *Gregg v. Georgia*, reinstated the death penalty, ending the moratorium on executions. The high court determined that new statutes in Georgia, Florida, and Texas could end the arbitrary nature of capital punishment by offering "guided discretion" for imposing the ultimate penalty. In 1977 California enacted its new death penalty law, authored by State Senator George Deukmejian, to reinstate the death penalty for first-degree murder when "special circumstances" existed. These special circumstances included: murder for financial gain, murder by a person previously convicted of murder, murder of multiple victims, murder with torture, murder of a peace officer, and murder of a witness to prevent testimony.

The revised Penal Code also included a new alternative: life imprisonment without the possibility of parole, which could be applied instead of the death penalty for certain crimes, including kidnapping for ransom, extortion, or robbery. In 1977 Governor Jerry Brown—like his father, Governor Pat Brown, a death penalty opponent—vetoed the bill, but the legislature narrowly overrode his veto, by one vote.

That same year, Governor Brown appointed Rose Bird to the California Supreme Court—the first woman to serve on that court. He not only appointed her to the court but, in a controversial move, to the position of chief justice. Bird was accustomed to being a groundbreaker. She had been the first woman public defender in Santa Clara County and the first woman cabinet member in California, serving as Brown's secretary of agriculture. In that position, she presided over the Agricultural Labor Relations Board—an innovative state forum that for the first time gave farmworkers an official voice against growers. Her pro-labor stance angered many powerful agribusiness and corporate leaders. Her appointment to the supreme court ignited their fury.

Like Governor Brown, Chief Justice Bird opposed the death penalty. She voted against capital punishment every time it came before her, a total of sixty-four times. During her tenure, the court overturned sixty-one death sentences.

The year after Bird's appointment, State Senator John Briggs, a right-wing demagogue from Orange County, put an initiative on the ballot expanding the number of crimes punishable by death.

It was one of the first "anti-crime" measures to go on the state ballot, and its campaign was characterized by vitriolic accusations that Bird and her liberal colleagues on the supreme court were responsible for a rise in violent crime in California. Voters passed Briggs's initiative by 67.5 percent. (The other Briggs initiative on the same ballot, a measure that would have barred openly lesbian and gay men from teaching in public schools, failed.)

Also on the ballot was Rose Bird's confirmation as chief justice. Gun Owners of California founder Senator H. L. Richardson organized an effort to oust her. She retained her seat, but 48.3 percent of the electorate voted against her. This was the first of seven attempts to remove the chief justice during her eight years on the court.

According to civil rights attorney Amitai Schwartz, that election was a "turning point on criminal justice" which led to the so-called "war of the Rose," the successful 1986 campaign to oust not only Chief Justice Bird but her colleagues Joseph Grodin and Cruz Reynoso from the court. A formidable anti-Bird coalition had coalesced into the spuriously named Crime Victims for Court Reform, which was backed by big money from California business. In addition, Governor George Deukmejian, prosecutors, and sheriffs publicly campaigned against her. San Diego Sheriff John Duffy ordered his two hundred deputies to distribute campaign literature against the chief justice.

New York Times columnist Tom Wicker wrote on September 14, 1986:

> [T]he death penalty is only the trumped-up excuse for the anti-Bird campaign—the actual purpose of which clearly is to put a conservative majority on the California Supreme Court...And a deeper motive of the business groups—big contributors include the Independent Oil Producers Agency and the Western Growers Association—was suggested when Crime Victims for Court Reform issued a paper charging the Bird court with being "anti-business."

As actor and abolitionist Mike Farrell noted, Bird's opposition to the death penalty was merely "the club they used to punish her for her other trespasses."

The unprecedented removal of the three justices by popular vote meant that conservative Governor George Deukmejian could handpick their replacements. Not surprisingly, the governor selected justices that favored business and the death penalty. For chief justice, he chose his former law partner, the most conservative member of the court, Justice Malcolm Lucas.

Court of Appeal Justice J. Anthony Kline, who served with Bird in the Brown administration, said that the removal of the three justices changed the face of the California judiciary, noting, "The defeat of Rose Bird was significant because it created a new danger in this state, the danger of politicizing a judicial branch that had not been subject to political pressures."

About every five years since Briggs's successful initiative, another initiative has gone before voters to expand the number of crimes punishable by the death penalty. All of them have passed.

Nearly six years after Rose Bird was ousted, the state executed Robert Harris. Perhaps the only positive change that came out of his execution was that it shined a light on the horrors of the gas chamber. Just days before Harris's execution, Michael Laurence, a member of his defense counsel and the director of the ACLU of Northern California Death Penalty Project, filed a federal lawsuit, *Fierro v. Gomez*, on behalf of California's death row inmates, seeking an end to the gas chamber.

October 25, 1994, was the opening day of the trial in Judge Marilyn Hall Patel's courtroom, on the eighteenth floor of the metal-and-glass federal building towering over San Francisco's Tenderloin District. For three weeks, journalists and other eyewitnesses to executions joined toxicology experts, neurologists, prison officials, and legal scholars to testify about the gas chamber. Thousands of pages of written testimony, including declarations from Nazi concentration camp survivors who had witnessed mass deaths by gas—the same gas that was used in San Quentin's death chamber—supplemented the witnesses on the stand.

Drawing on the expert testimony presented by scientists about the severity and duration of pain during gas chamber executions, the court concluded that inmates remain conscious for several minutes and suffer intense pain.

"The gas chamber is inhumane and has no place in a civilized society," Judge Patel ruled in October 1994. "The gas chamber is widely viewed as an antiquated mode of execution, causing a slow, painful, and inhumane death." Declaring it "cruel and unusual," in violation of the Eighth Amendment, she ordered the Department of Corrections to shut the gas chamber down.

This landmark ruling was the first in U.S. history to hold any method of execution unconstitutional.

But it did not end California's death penalty, it only changed the method of execution. Two years later, William Bonin was executed inside the former gas chamber at San Quentin—by lethal injection.

The Penal Colony

For California's first thirty years, only one state penitentiary existed—San Quentin Prison, built like a granite fortress jutting into San Francisco Bay on the tip of Marin County. San Quentin housed both men and women until a women's prison was built in 1933 at Tehachapi. In 1880 another state prison was built, at Folsom. Over the following century, while the state population climbed from under one million to almost twenty-six million, only ten new prisons were built.

During the 1960s and 1970s, California Department of Corrections Director Ray Procunier emphasized rehabilitation of prisoners. Other states looked to California as a model of prison reform. That all began to change in the 1980s, when a new emphasis on law and order, combined with the national War on Drugs, filled prisons to capacity. In 1982 California voters passed Proposition 8, marketed to the voters as the Victims' Bill of Rights. This wide-ranging initiative was a prosecutor's garden of delights. In addition to allowing crime victims to testify at sentencing hearings, the new law lengthened sentences and eviscerated state court rulings that had banned illegally obtained evidence in criminal trials. A practical result of the initiative was the exponential growth of the inmate population of California's state prisons.

"The broader political message of the sweeping victory of Proposition 8," according to veteran ACLU lobbyist Francisco Lobaco, "was that law and order forces could use the initiative process as a tool to further their political desires to stay in office. No longer did they have to go through the complex legislative process with crime bills; they could go directly to the voters."

The legislature, Lobaco reasons, is a deliberative body that rarely goes to extremes when enacting laws. But with the initiative

These early prisoners were housed at San Quentin, the first and only state prison during California's first three decades.

Due to the War on Drugs, California prisons currently house more than twice the population they were intended to hold and do not provide basic health care. The inmate population is disproportionately African American and Latino.

process, he notes, "all you need is a million dollars to get a million signatures, and you can put your popular law-and-order measure on the ballot."

"There is always going to be somebody with money," he adds. "And once a crime bill goes before the voters, it will almost definitely be passed."

The record proves Lobaco right. Since the passage of the "Victims' Bill of Rights," almost all initiatives in the realm of criminal justice have reduced the rights of the accused, extended sentences, and created more prisons. Between 1984 and 2000, California constructed forty-three more prisons, including high security "max" and "supermax" institutions. By the end of the millennium, California had the nation's largest prison system.

In what USC geography professor Ruth Wilson Gilmore calls an "archipelago of concrete and steel cages," California's prisons now dominate remote towns up and down the state, from Pelican Bay in the far north to Blythe in the southernmost desert region. But by 2000, there were one hundred and seventy-three thousand inmates, which stretched the facilities far beyond their capacity. Ninety-three percent were men; two-thirds were Latino and African American. The majority were from big cities, with 60 percent from Los Angeles alone. These stark figures reveal the bleak lives of those abandoned behind prison bars: the overwhelming majority are poor; many are unemployed; many are drug addicts—almost half of California's prisoners were locked up for violating a drug law. Prison suicide and recidivism are twice the national average. Lobaco calls the ever expanding, overcrowded prison population "a time bomb."

The law-and-order mentality that swept the nation under the administrations of Ronald Reagan and George H. W. Bush and their War on Drugs reached a feverish peak in California in 1994. Anti-crime hysteria infected the capital, making rational policy debate on crime issues virtually impossible.

That year the legislature held a special session to focus specifically on crime. "Hundreds of anti-crime bills were introduced, many of them draconian in scope and intent," says Lobaco, who witnessed the stampede by lawmakers. By the end of the session, more than two hundred and thirty bills affecting criminal law had been enacted, including enhancement of penalties for sex-related crimes, rollback of prisoners' rights, obstacles for journalists wishing to interview inmates, and Megan's Law, which mandated that information about sex offenders be available to the general public. More than a hundred of these new laws increased penalties. Very few focused on crime prevention or rehabilitation. Lobaco recalls it as "the worst year for the rights of the accused."

The prior year, twelve-year-old Polly Klaas had been kidnapped from her Petaluma home during a slumber party and murdered. The brutal crime shocked the state and the nation—President Clinton referred to Polly Klaas in his State of the Union address. Her accused killer, Richard Allen Davis, a repeat felon with prior kidnapping convictions, confessed almost as soon as he was arrested.

The child's murder spurred the passage of a bill that had been proposed several times but stalled in the legislature. The National Rifle Association (NRA) supported the bill and others like it around the country with money and publicity, dubbing it with the catchy nickname of "three strikes and you're out." The measure mandated a life sentence for any felony committed by a person with two previous convictions for a violent or serious felony. But few politicians bothered to read the fine print: they were focused on public opinion polls, which showed that in the wake of the Klaas murder, 80 percent of Californians favored the bill.

In fact it was what Vincent Schiraldi, the director of the Center on Juvenile and Criminal Justice, called "governance by hyperbole," the harshest sentencing law in the nation. Civil rights advocates tried to warn about the bill. "Everyone talks about punishment and retribution," said the ACLU-SC's Ramona Ripston. "A huge percentage of people in prison are just languishing. There's nothing to help them overcome their problems." But their voices were drowned out by the popular law-and-order rhetoric.

The measure flew through the legislature with overwhelming bipartisan support; only a handful of legislators dared to speak against it. Even politically popular, well-established, liberal Speaker of the Assembly Willie Brown said, "I'm not standing in front of this train."

On March 7, 1994, Governor Pete Wilson signed the bill into law. That same day, Mike Reynolds, a Fresno photographer whose daughter had been murdered, submitted enough signatures to qualify a virtually identical Three Strikes initiative, Proposition 184, for the November ballot. "Once the legislature had passed the Three Strikes law, there was no need for an initiative—it was not going to amend or improve the law in any way. But the ballot measure was used by many—notably the prison guards' union—as a political rallying point," explained ACLU-NC Executive Director Dorothy Ehrlich, a leader in the campaign to defeat the measure.

The California Correctional Peace Officers Association (CCPOA) contributed $101,000 to gather signatures to qualify the initiative.

Over the previous decade, the CCPOA had become a key player in California politics. The organization was established in 1957 but prior to the 1980s was not influential in state politics. But the number of correctional officers grew along with the prison population, and under the aggressive leadership of Don Novey, the union expanded to one of the largest in the state. Sheer numbers made it one of the most powerful political forces in California; by 1992 the CCPOA was the state's second largest political action committee (PAC), contributing over a million dollars to state legislators' campaign coffers, with large sums going to gubernatorial and district attorney contests as well.

The CCPOA's political agenda reflected the interests of its members—not only in improving their working conditions and raising their salaries (which it did quite effectively), but in expanding the prison system. Measures that extended prison terms or restricted private prisons were good for the CCPOA.

One of the CCPOA's most effective political strategies was funding and promoting the victims' rights movement, a strategy that included establishing organizations like the Doris Tate Crime Victims Bureau and Crime Victims United of California. The latter group, a PAC, received over 95 percent of its start-up expenses from the CCPOA.

In the law-and-order climate, and with the avid support of the CCPOA and its affiliated victims' rights groups, the Three Strikes measure passed overwhelmingly, winning 70 percent of the vote.

The immediate impact was life sentences for thousands more nonviolent offenders, like Michael Garcia, who stole a package of chuck steaks from a Pomona market after his stepmother's Social Security checks were stopped and he lost his temporary job fixing trucks. He had no money and was desperate to feed his family. Like Garcia, many of these new prisoners had not physically harmed anyone. Their third strikes were not violent felonies. Yet they are now behind bars for life in the ever expanding California prison system. Many of them are young. By 2000, California taxpayers were paying more for prisons than for institutions of higher education.

By the turn of the millennium, overcrowding in California prisons had reached crisis proportions.

A pair of lawsuits filed in 2001 by the Prison Law Office charged that the lack of adequate medical and mental health care violated the constitutional ban on cruel and unusual punishment. One federal judge called the medical treatment of prisoners "horrifying" and "shocking"; another court ruling found the system to cause an "unconscionable degree of suffering and death," noting that an inmate in California's prisons needlessly dies every six to seven days due to grossly deficient medical care. Though the lawsuits succeeding in getting the federal courts to monitor health care in the thirty-three adult prisons, by 2006 the attorneys determined that severe overcrowding made it impossible to reform the prison health-care system, and in 2008 the federal courts convened a three-judge panel to come up with solutions. "Overcrowding is dangerous for the prisoners, for the Corrections officers, and for the public," argued attorney Michael Bien.

Criminalization of the Poor

"The law, in its majestic equality, forbids all men to sleep under bridges, to beg in the streets, and to steal bread—the rich as well as the poor."

Anatole France was not speaking about California law when he made this incisive statement in 1902, but he may as well have been. Since its earliest days, California has criminalized poverty. In 1855 the legislature passed the "Greaser law," which allowed for up to ninety days of hard labor for "the issue of Spanish and Indian blood...who go armed and are not known to be peaceable and quiet persons, and who can give no good account of themselves." Mexicans and Indians were jailed simply because they were nonwhite and poor. Over the decades, new iterations of the vagrancy law would be used against other marginalized groups, including political dissidents, Dust Bowl refugees, women, lesbians, and gay men—and always, the poor.

In 1936, at the height of the Depression, Los Angeles Police Chief James Davis established the "bum blockade," a border control program to keep out, as he put it, the "refuse of other states." He sent 135 officers to California's borders with Arizona, Nevada, and Oregon to greet would-be migrants with the questions: "Any work? Any money?" If the answers were negative, the LAPD offered two choices: go back home or face thirty to eighty days of hard labor for violation of vagrancy laws.

What authority did the LA police chief have to enforce the law in other counties? At least one person thought he had none. The sheriff of Modoc County not only refused to deputize the fourteen LAPD officers Davis sent to the far northeastern corner of the state but told them, "You have violated all the rules of decency."

At the height of the Depression, California enforced "vagrancy" laws against Dust Bowl migrants, and the LAPD stationed officers at the state's borders to prevent poor people from coming into California.

During the wave of agricultural strikes in the 1930s, the police, often joined by vigilantes backed by the Associated Farmers, raided labor camps to arrest union organizers as "vagrants." During the celebrated 1934 General Strike in San Francisco, police used the vagrancy law to arrest more than five hundred people—cramming them into a jail built for one hundred and fifty—to drain the resources of the union. Conviction carried jail time and up to a thousand-dollar fine.

During World War II, unaccompanied women were the targets of vagrancy laws. San Francisco and Los Angeles were departure ports for military personnel heading to the Asian theater, and the cities' bars and dance halls were lively meeting places. It was common practice for police to "vag" women in bars, public dance halls, or simply on the streets, forcing them to take venereal disease tests and holding them without bail for three to five days while they awaited the test results. The San Francisco Special Women's Court continued all criminal cases for three days pending test results. In general, male suspects were not tested, much less accused of promiscuity or arrested on the casual claim they had given someone a sexually transmitted disease.

For decades, arbitrary police use of the state's vagrancy law went unchallenged. The law's demise came about largely through the determined effort of one man who was incensed about being stopped on the street by police for no reason.

In 1975 Edward Lawson had just moved to San Diego. One balmy night he decided to walk home from a friend's house. But a police officer who thought the lanky, dreadlocked African American man looked suspicious in the predominantly white neighborhood stopped him and demanded his I.D. When Lawson refused to produce any, he was arrested and charged with violating the Penal Code section that required an individual to provide "credible and reliable" identification to a police officer who has reason to be suspicious. This law was used disproportionately against poor people and gave police wide discretion to arrest whomever they deemed "undesirable."

Over the next eighteen months, Lawson was stopped fifteen times. Each time, he documented the arrest, took the officer's badge number, and grew more irate. Since he was unsuccessful in fighting the individual charges against him, he decided to sue the police department to strike down the law, which he noted was "primarily used against black and brown people and youth—and that is a lot of people in California." Initially, Lawson had difficulty interesting local lawyers or media in his case, so he represented himself. The state courts ruled against him, but when the Ninth Circuit validated his complaint, the legal community and the press began to pay attention. One of those who believed in Lawson's constitutional complaint was Mark Rosenbaum, a young ACLU-SC attorney who had cut his legal teeth while on the team representing Daniel Ellsberg when he was prosecuted for leaking the Pentagon Papers to the *New York Times* at the height of the Vietnam War.

The ACLU was interested in Lawson's case because it highlighted racism in the criminal justice system. "Most officers used race as an index of suspicious conduct," recalled Rosenbaum.

In 1982 Lawson's suit reached the U.S. Supreme Court, where Rosenbaum argued that California's vagrancy law violated the Fourth Amendment's guarantee against unreasonable searches and seizures and the Fifth Amendment's protection against self-incrimination.

Lawson's argument was bolstered by two earlier decisions. In 1962 the high court had ruled that a California law criminalizing narcotics addiction violated the Eighth Amendment's prohibition against cruel and unusual punishment. Individuals could not be arrested merely for their *status*—as a drug addict—in the absence of criminal behavior.

A decade later, the Supreme Court struck down a Jacksonville, Florida, ordinance targeting "rogues and vagabonds" because it was too vague. Writing for a unanimous court, Justice William O. Douglas stated that such laws allow for discriminatory law enforcement. (The plaintiffs in that case were interracial couples who believed racism motivated their arrests.)

Justice Douglas wrote, "Of course, vagrancy statutes are useful to the police. Of course, they are nets making easy the roundup of so-called undesirables. But the rule of law implies equality and justice in its application. Vagrancy laws of the Jacksonville type teach that the scales of justice are so tipped that even-handed administration of the law is not possible."

In Lawson's case, the court did not reach the Fourth and Fifth Amendment claims, but in a 7-2 decision, it struck down the anti-loitering statute as too vague. Writing for the majority, Justice Sandra Day O'Connor stated that the law "contains no standard for determining what a suspect has to do in order to satisfy the requirement to provide a 'credible and reliable' identification." Echoing Justice Douglas in the Jacksonville case, O'Connor said that this gave too much weight "to the moment-to-moment judgment of the policeman on his beat" and could lead to "harsh and discriminatory enforcement by local prosecuting officials."

Crisis in Homelessness

During the years that Edward Lawson was fighting to strike down the state's vagrancy law, two new conditions emerged that made California's poor even more vulnerable to police action. Both were connected to Ronald Reagan.

When Reagan was California's governor in the 1970s, patients' rights advocates led a movement to close the state's large psychiatric institutions, many of which had become warehouses where patients spent their entire lives isolated from family and community. The science of mental health had shown that people with psychiatric illnesses could improve more quickly if they were not shut away in dehumanizing mental hospitals, but instead received supportive, community-based services. Governor Reagan favored hospital closures as a budget-saving measure. However, he denied funding for essential community-based assistance. Consequently, thousands of patients were sent into communities that lacked both resources and intent to care for them. Many people found themselves on the streets, ill equipped to cope with life outside of a hospital.

Just a few years later, when Reagan became president, his administration slashed federal funding for housing. In 1976 the government had funded two hundred thousand new units of subsidized housing, but by the end of the Reagan administration, a decade later, that number was down to nothing. The lack of public housing created a huge increase in the number of poor families who could not afford a place to live.

The poor and the mentally ill who had nowhere to go ended up on the streets. They often found themselves not only without homes, but unable to exercise their civil rights. Lacking addresses, homeless people are disenfranchised in many ways:

they cannot register to vote; they are often ineligible for food stamps or public assistance; they may lose their children.

Though the state vagrancy law had been invalidated, cities and counties passed local ordinances in the name of public health or public safety, prohibiting sleeping in public, sleeping in vehicles, encampments, panhandling, and loitering. In reality, most of these laws were aimed at pushing homeless people off the streets and into jail—or simply out of town and out of sight.

A study by the National Law Center on Homelessness and Poverty showed that between 1982 and 1992 there were more than one thousand cases challenging anti-homeless practices and laws. Many of these lawsuits merely tried to preserve the fundamental rights of homeless people.

Los Angeles was the epicenter of laws targeting the homeless. As in many other large cities, the downtown Skid Row area had become a gathering area for the indigent during the Depression. Rescue missions and soup kitchens had set up shop in the area to provide food and shelter for the massive numbers of unemployed. In the 1970s, the city redevelopment agency had designated the forty-block area around Skid Row as a place for the homeless—largely to keep them out of other neighborhoods—and many services were concentrated in the area. According to homeless rights attorney Gary Blasi, the growth of the homeless population, many of whom suffer from mental illness and addiction, reflects the failure of society's institutions: local schools, foster care, health and mental health services, and the juvenile and criminal justice systems.

In May 1987, Police Chief Daryl Gates, at the urging of the local business association, ordered all Skid Row residents to leave within seven days. Those remaining would be subject to arrest. On the night of May 30, forty officers swept through Skid Row, seized shopping carts that contained medications, personal photographs, warm clothing, and important documents; destroyed makeshift cardboard and tarp shelters; and threatened to arrest anyone who did not leave. As the mass removal was taking place, residents and advocates shouted, "Shame, shame, shame, the whole world's watching." The following day, street sweepers removed everything that remained on the grimy sidewalks.

Though an estimated one thousand people had been arrested, City Attorney James Hahn declared, "I'm not going to prosecute individuals for not having a place to stay. I simply will not prosecute people for being poor." The *Los Angeles Times* supported him. "Men and women on Skid Row have lost jobs, houses, apartments, families, and all too often futures," the paper editorialized. They "need safe shelter, not jail cells."

L.A.'s strategy of using the police to solve homelessness has been replicated in many other California towns and cities. In 1990, in the Orange County town of Santa Ana, police swooped down on the civic center area, arrested sixty-four people, handcuffed them, and marked their arms with ID numbers. After being held for hours at the police station without food and water, they were driven to the edge of town and told not to return, echoing earlier police attacks on Wobblies.

In 1993 San Francisco Mayor Frank Jordan instituted the Matrix program, slapping people with a seventy-six-dollar fine for "sleeping, camping, urinating in public or otherwise disturbing the quality of life." At the time, the city's homeless population was estimated at between eleven thousand and sixteen thousand, but there were shelter beds for fourteen hundred—13 percent at best. One advocate, echoing Anatole France, noted, "Homeless people have no choice but to carry on life-sustaining activities—to sleep, eat, sit, stand—in public."

In the first three months of Matrix, police arrested thirty-two hundred people. One of them was Thomas O'Halloran, a widower and police officer's son who had worked at the phone company for twenty-five years and raised eight children. After he depleted his life savings on medical expenses for his wife, who died in 1991, O'Halloran found himself homeless. Unsuccessful in the city's lottery to get a shelter bed, he stayed on the streets.

At noon on August 12, O'Halloran sat on a bench in Civic Center Plaza reading a book, his shopping cart with all his possessions nearby. A police officer issued him a ticket for "camping." He could not pay the seventy-six-dollar fine, so his arrest went to warrant, and he was afraid he would be jailed.

O'Halloran and the Coalition on Homelessness sued the city in federal court to halt the Matrix program. Judge Lowell Jensen, a Reagan appointee and former Alameda County district attorney who had made his name by prosecuting Black Panthers, denied the homeless plaintiffs' request to stop the arrests.

The Ninth Circuit Court of Appeals ruled the case moot because San Francisco's new mayor, Willie Brown, pledged to dismantle the Matrix program and dismiss the citations.

Out of the 3,200 arrested under Matrix, only 145 were ever found guilty of any crime.

Celestus Blair, a homeless man who peaceably asked passersby for charity, was arrested in San Francisco five times in one year under a section of the state Penal Code that made it a misdemeanor to approach others on public sidewalks for the "purposes of begging or soliciting alms."

Blair challenged the statute as a violation of his First Amendment rights and turned to the ACLU for help. "It is ironic that this city, whose namesake is St. Francis, would deprive the poor of their right to seek alms," ACLU volunteer attorney Michael Hallerud told the U.S. district court.

In 1992 Judge William Orrick found that Blair, who by then had become a city bus driver, should not have been arrested. The judge stated:

Begging can promote the very speech values that entitle charitable appeals to constitutional protection. A request for alms clearly conveys information regarding the speaker's plight. Begging gives the speaker an opportunity to spread his views and ideas on, among other things, the way society treats its poor and disenfranchised. This can change the way the listener sees his or her relationship with and obligations to the poor.

Judge Orrick noted that the law also violated equal protection guarantees because it prohibited only approaches accompanied by a request for personal charity. "One may approach and speak at will to solicit directions or the time of day, request signatures for a petition, or any other number of common occurrences without running afoul of this statute," he wrote.

Courts throughout the country cited Judge Orrick's groundbreaking decision to invalidate anti-begging laws. But just as the ruling went into effect, San Francisco voters passed an anti-begging ordinance, Proposition J, which outlawed "aggressive panhandling" but was ambiguous about the line between protected speech and criminal behavior. Its passage had a ripple effect, and soon San Diego, Anaheim, and Beverly Hills passed anti-panhandling ordinances, most punishable by six months in jail and a five-hundred-dollar fine.

Homeless people in Los Angeles, like this mother and child, are subjected to laws prohibiting sleeping in public, loitering, panhandling and sleeping in vehicles—laws intended to push the poor off the streets and out of public view.

"No city in the U.S. has been able to significantly reduce chronic homeless populations solely through policing," asserts Gary Blasi. "We need to provide real alternatives to living in streets or jails. Until the root causes of homelessness are addressed, homelessness cannot be criminalized out of existence."

Charges Dismissed

Abuses of power occur throughout the criminal justice system, from penal institutions to law enforcement to the law itself. The judicial system is not immune to this syndrome. The tale of the Sleepy Lagoon murder trial is a case in point.

Tension filled Los Angeles in the summer of 1942. Just a few months earlier, the federal government had forced Japanese Americans from the city because of wartime hysteria. Soon thereafter the local papers began running stories about Mexican American juvenile delinquency and crime. (The zoot suit riots would take place the following year.) The violent and mysterious death of José Díaz set into motion a series of events resulting in the largest mass trial in California history.

José Díaz lived with his family in a bunkhouse on the Williams ranch in what was then rural Los Angeles and is now the city of Maywood. Quiet and reserved, the twenty-two-year-old farmworker with a pencil-thin moustache enjoyed jazz. On the evening of August 1, he wavered about attending a birthday party for his neighbor Eleanor Delgadillo Coronado at her parents' home, also on the Williams ranch. Díaz was to report for induction into the Army two days later and had a lot on his mind. At the last minute he decided to go to the birthday celebration. It started slowly, but after the four-piece band had waited almost an hour, there were enough couples to dance. Around eleven o'clock guests ejected about twenty angry young men from nearby Downey who had crashed the party.

Around the time that the party crashers left the Delgadillo home, a group of Mexican Americans from the 38th Street neighborhood in nearby Vernon had congregated at the reservoir on the Williams ranch. Legalized segregation barred Mexican Americans from public swimming pools (or restricted their use to one day a week, usually the day before the pool was to be drained and cleaned). Young Mexican Americans used the reservoir, which the press dubbed "Sleepy Lagoon" after a popular Harry James song of the time, as a swimming hole. At night, the grassy banks and poplar-filled area around the reservoir became a lovers' lane.

Soon after nineteen-year-old Henry "Hank" Leyvas, his girlfriend, and half a dozen of their friends from Vernon arrived at the reservoir, a fight erupted between them and another group who happened upon them. Outnumbered, Leyvas and his friends returned to their neighborhood to marshal support for retaliation. When they got back to Sleepy Lagoon, they heard music from the nearby party at the Delgadillo home. Thinking that their attackers might be at the party, they went there. A fight broke out between the 38th Street group and the party guests.

After the fight broke up, the injured and stunned Delgadillos and their remaining company discovered José Díaz in the middle of the road, several yards away from the Delgadillo house. He was lying face up with his pockets turned inside out. Díaz arrived at Los Angeles General Hospital just past three a.m., and the attending physician diagnosed the would-be soldier's injuries: a cerebral concussion, abrasion and large swelling above his nose, two stab wounds near his diaphragm and breastbone, and a broken finger. Ninety minutes later, Díaz was dead.

The next day, headlines blared that "Mexican Boy Gangs" had killed Díaz. Governor Culbert Olson issued orders to eliminate youth gangs. In response, the LAPD put on a show of force. With sheriff's deputies, police officers conducted a three-day sweep of Mexican American communities, stopping young people in cars at major intersections and taking more than six hundred into custody. The criteria for arrest were flimsy: police charged many with "suspicion" of having committed a crime. While the local press lauded the police, hundreds of innocent young people were caught in the dragnet, fingerprinted, and booked.

Young Mexican Americans were used to run-ins with law enforcement. By the time of the Sleepy Lagoon arrests, the LAPD had a history of "field interrogations," which typically consisted of police stopping cars with Mexican American passengers and ordering everyone out while the officers searched the vehicles for contraband. LAPD officers frequently arrested groups of young Mexican Americans who gathered on street corners or in front yards and charged them with vagrancy or suspicion of a crime, then held them in custody for three days and released them when there was no evidence of wrongdoing. These arrests had material consequences. One young man reported, "My mother had to mortgage the furniture to get enough money to bail me out—and I lost my job 'cause I was in jail for seventy-two hours. It's like that with the police—they arrest you, beat you up, hold you three days—and you lose your job." The "overarresting" of Mexican Americans artificially inflated crime statistics for that population, thereby leading police to focus on the "criminal" Mexican American community.

In a Los Angeles County grand jury hearing on "Mexican American juvenile delinquency," Lieutenant Edward Duran Ayers of the sheriff's department's Foreign Relations Bureau acknowledged that economic discrimination and segregation contributed to crime among Mexican Americans, but stressed a biological determinism that compelled Mexicans to violence. Ayers linked Mexican Americans to Aztecs who practiced human sacrifice and had a "total disregard for human life." While acknowledging that a "great majority of the Mexican people here are law-abiding," he asserted that "the hoodlum element as a whole must be indicted as a whole."

Police Chief Clemence Horrall praised Ayers's analysis as "an intelligent statement of the psychology of the Mexican people, particularly, the youths."

In this climate, police arrested Henry Leyvas and twenty-three other young men from the 38th Street neighborhood for conspiracy to murder José Díaz.

Police booked Leyvas under a false name, presumably to hinder his family and attorney from locating him. Despite this ruse, Leyvas's attorney found him handcuffed and nearly unconscious in an interrogation room with blood covering his shirt and mouth.

Police obtained "confessions" through intimidation and force. When the entire group appeared en masse before the grand jury, they were dirty, demoralized, and bruised. The grand jury indicted all twenty-four for first-degree murder. The Sleepy Lagoon murder trial, *People v. Zammora*, would be the largest mass trial in California history (Zamora's name was misspelled in court records).

Mexican American activist Josefina Fierro de Bright and LaRue McCormick of the International Labor Defense, the left-wing group that had provided legal representation for ILWU strikers and other trade union organizers in the 1930s, founded the Citizens' Committee for the Defense of Mexican American Youth to build support for the defendants and to protest the prosecutor's prejudicial tactics. McCormick secured George Shibley, a progressive attorney who brought much-needed experience to the legal team.

Judge Charles William Fricke, a former L.A. district attorney, presided over the trial. During his quarter-century tenure as a judge, he had developed the nickname "San Quentin Fricke" because he sentenced more people to the state penitentiary than any other judge in California history.

There was not enough space in the courtroom to seat all the defendants with their attorneys. Judge Fricke dealt with this by seating the young men alphabetically in two rows opposite the jury, far from their counsel at the defense table. He denied the defense request to allow the defendants to cut their hair, siding with the prosecution's assertion that the youths' appearance was evidence of their character and that haircuts might render them unidentifiable by witnesses.

In what was called the Sleepy Lagoon murder, twenty-four young Mexican American men were charged with killing a man in 1942. Among many trial irregularities, the judge separated defendants from their attorneys because the courtroom was not large enough for them to be seated together.

After defense attorney Shibley learned that members of the jury had read local newspaper coverage, which had sensationalized the defendants as the "goons of Sleepy Lagoon," he subpoenaed jurors to question them, but Judge Fricke ruled against his motion for a mistrial. Judge Fricke also ridiculed the defense counsel in front of the jury, calling one attorney a "ventriloquist's dummy" and describing another's statement as "absolutely unworthy of any respectable member of the bar."

The prosecution never provided any physical evidence that the defendants had murdered or conspired to murder José Díaz. There was no evidence that anyone had actually killed him. An autopsy indicated that Díaz's injuries could have been caused by repeated falls on the rocky road. In lieu of evidence, the prosecution built its case on the theory that Leyvas and his friends had conspired to kill someone in retaliation for the attack at Sleepy Lagoon.

After a thirteen-week trial, the jury deliberated for six days. On the cold morning of January 13, 1943, the Sleepy Lagoon defendants knelt in the prisoners' room to pray before entering the courtroom to hear the verdicts. The jury found Leyvas and two others guilty of first-degree murder; nine others were found guilty of second-degree murder; five were found guilty of assault; and five were found not guilty. Living up to his nickname, Judge Fricke sentenced Leyvas and the others convicted of first-degree murder to life imprisonment at San Quentin. The verdicts shocked the defendants, and many in the courtroom wept openly.

After the convictions, the Citizens' Committee for the Defense of Mexican American Youth, now called the Sleepy Lagoon Defense Committee (SLDC), raised funds for an appeal and publicized the miscarriage of justice. Under the leadership of National Chair Carey McWilliams and Executive Secretary Alice Greenfield McGrath, the committee recruited labor, religious, political, and community leaders. Singer Nat King Cole and actors Anthony Quinn, Rita Hayworth, and Orson Welles supported the SLDC's work. Charlotta Bass, publisher of the *California Eagle*, the largest African American newspaper in southern California, was an early and vocal advocate. The SLDC framed the case within the long history of anti-Mexican prejudice and argued that the verdicts and ongoing discrimination against Mexicans worked against the domestic and international solidarity necessary to win World War II.

District Attorney Clyde Shoemaker, the lead prosecutor in the trial, accused the SLDC of being a communist organization and threatened to revoke the tax-exempt status of a Unitarian Church if it allowed an SLDC conference to take place on church property.

When defense attorney Shibley was drafted into the Army, the committee secured left-wing powerhouse attorney Ben Margolis Jr. to lead the Sleepy Lagoon appeal. On October 4, 1944, the Second District Court of Appeal unanimously reversed the convictions of the seventeen young men. The judges explained that they had reviewed all six thousand pages of the court transcript as well as the fourteen hundred pages of appeal briefs and concluded, "Our examination of the record in this case convinces us that there is a complete lack of evidence from which the jury could properly find or infer that the appellants formed a conspiracy of the kind and type or for the purposes claimed by the prosecution." The court added that there was no evidence that any of the defendants had murdered or even assaulted Díaz.

The appellate court also severely criticized Judge Fricke, complaining that the former prosecutor had allowed hearsay and other inadmissible evidence, and that Fricke's unorthodox seating of the defendants far from their attorneys had deprived them of their constitutional right to effective counsel. The appellate court cited numerous other instances of Judge Fricke's judicial misconduct, including his disallowing testimony that police officers had beaten the defendants into making self-incriminating statements, and "erroneously den[ying] defense attorneys' motions to admit evidence that helped their clients and ma[king] contradictory rulings on the same points of law, depending on whether the ruling helped or hindered the prosecution."

On October 23, 1944, Los Angeles Superior Court Judge Clement D. Nye dismissed all charges against the young men convicted of murdering José Díaz, and the eight defendants who were still imprisoned were released later that same day.

The appellate decision in *People v. Zammora* had the practical long-term effect of ending mass trials in California, as the judges ruled that if a courtroom was not big enough to allow defendants to sit with their attorneys, then a larger courtroom had to be found.

Murgia [sic] Motion

The fight against abuses in the criminal justice system is daunting. But sometimes, against tremendous odds, those who dare to challenge wrongdoing not only vindicate themselves but change the law, and the practice of law.

When the massive grape strike polarized the Central Valley in 1973, growers secured court injunctions to keep United Farm Workers (UFW) pickets far from their property, so far that their voices could not be heard by the strikebreakers working in the vineyards. The injunctions also limited the number of picketers, leaving them isolated and vulnerable, especially in the early morning darkness when the crews started work, to attacks by thugs the growers had hired and the rival Teamsters union. The UFW challenged the injunctions in court and was determined to continue picketing on the dusty county roads adjacent to the fields while their challenges were pending.

Every time the UFW set up a picket line, armed law enforcement officers threatened, arrested, and hauled them to jail, often using excessive force and shouting racial slurs at the nonviolent strikers. The arrests became so routine and the numbers so large that police brought empty school buses to the fields to take arrestees to the county jail. As happened with the Wobblies decades before, each time strikers were pulled away from the lines, more volunteers took their place.

Some strike leaders well known to the police were targeted for arrest. One was Lupe Murguia, a gentle, mustachioed father of eight who had joined the union at the start of the first grape strike, in 1965. A seasoned organizer, Murguia served as a picket captain, directing crews of strikers in the predawn hours. In the early days of the strike, Murguia later recalled, a sheriff had rammed the side of his Valiant and "with a more direct hit would have killed me and a young striker riding with me." Over the course of the harvest season, Murguia was arrested almost three dozen times.

Murguia recalled that one early morning at the height of the strike, he and several other picket captains were organizing in front of the Giumarra Vineyards in Kern County when sheriff's deputies arrived and taunted strikers. The deputies told Murguia they were arresting the picket captains for breaking the injunction, and he was again led off the line. When he called another organizer to take his place, he recalled, "all hell broke loose when the sheriffs attacked the strikers," and the new picket captain was beaten with billy clubs.

UFW attorneys challenged the convictions of Murguia and five other well-known activists on the grounds that they had been unfairly singled out for prosecution. Kern County law enforcement authorities had "engaged in a deliberate, systematic practice of discriminatory enforcement of the criminal law against UFW members and supporters," they charged. The case, *Murgia v. Superior Court* (court records misspelled "Murguia") went all the way to the California Supreme Court.

In a unanimous opinion written in 1975 by Justice Matthew Tobriner, the court ruled that "if a particular defendant, unlike similarly situated individuals, suffers prosecution simply as the subject of invidious discrimination...[this] becomes a compelling ground for dismissal of the criminal charge, since the prosecution would not have been pursued except for the discriminatory designs of the prosecuting authorities."

The court based its ruling on the 1886 U.S. Supreme Court ruling in *Yick Wo v. Hopkins*, which determined that a seemingly neutral San Francisco ordinance outlawing wooden laundries was targeted only and unfairly at Chinese laundrymen. Justice Tobriner stated, "Neither the federal nor state Constitution countenances the singling out of an invidiously selected class for special prosecutorial treatment whether that class consists of black or white, Jew or Catholic, Irishman or Japanese, United Farm Worker or Teamster."

UFW organizers were thrilled, after having their rights so brutally ignored in the vineyards and on the picket lines, to be vindicated in the state's highest court. UFW member Alberto Escalante remembered hearing about the ruling and thinking, "Though Lupe would be the first to shrug off the idea that he's ever been anything other than just another guy, many of us consider him a hero and a champion for the rights of the people."

Escalante's words were prescient. The 1975 ruling was enshrined as the Murgia [sic] motion, which has become widely used in criminal defense law; a defense attorney can move for dismissal of criminal charges upon a showing of selective prosecution for improper purposes.

Criminal defense attorneys have used the Murgia motion in a variety of innovative ways to uncover and illuminate bias in the criminal justice system, protecting the rights of political radicals, women, and gay men far from the dusty Kern County vineyards.

Escalante added, "This quiet, unassuming hero" helped create a means to "continue to protect the rights of those who, for whatever reasons, have been illegally singled out and arrested simply because they're recognizable, believed to be one of the leaders, or simply because the sheriff or policeman doesn't like who they are."

Driving While Black or Brown

On a pleasant June evening in 1998, Curtis Rodriguez, a criminal defense attorney from San Jose, was driving with fellow attorney Arturo Hernandez on Highway 152 to Merced, at the northern end of the San Joaquin Valley. On a ten-mile stretch of highway frequented by migrant farmworkers and lined with orchards and artichoke fields, they noticed a large number of California Highway Patrol vehicles flagging down cars. One after another, they saw vehicles stopped by the side of the road, and passengers—all of whom appeared to be Latino—standing on the highway.

Distressed, Rodriguez and Hernandez decided to document the CHP stops. On their return trip, Hernandez took photos while Rodriguez concentrated on obeying the speed limit and all traffic laws, to avoid giving the CHP any excuse to stop them. Hernandez kept the camera in easy reach on top of the dashboard.

Despite their precautions, a CHP officer followed them and signaled Rodriguez to pull over. The officer said he had stopped them because Rodriguez's car "had touched the line" in the middle of the road and because his headlights were on—even though drivers are advised to turn on their headlights on that section of highway.

"The officer told me he was going to search the car for weapons," Rodriguez recalled. "I refused permission for the search. Since I am an attorney, I know my rights.

The officer had no probable cause to search the car, so I did not give my consent to search. Unfortunately, the officer refused to respect my legal rights. He ordered me out of the car and searched it, without my permission.

"Of course, he found nothing illegal. After checking our licenses and insurance papers, he ordered us back in the car. We sat waiting twenty more minutes and then, finally, he told us we could go. He didn't issue me a ticket, because I didn't do anything wrong."

Later the officer claimed that he thought the camera—on the dashboard the whole time—was a gun, and that he feared for his safety.

Rodriguez and Hernandez found themselves caught in the same dragnet they had tried to document. They were two of the tens of thousands of innocent motorists who have been stopped, searched, and treated like criminals based on nothing more than their skin color and a law enforcement officer's hunch. They were victims of racial profiling; their offense is commonly known among African Americans and Latinos as driving while black or brown, or DWB.

Racial profiling is the use of race by law enforcement to any degree when making decisions about whom to stop, interrogate, search, or arrest—except when there is a specific suspect description.

Racial profiling has historic precedents in California. In the early days of statehood, black men like Archy Lee were presumed to be runaway slaves; Indians and Latinos were commonly pursued as horse thieves.

Despite the civil rights movement and the passage of antidiscrimination laws, many law enforcement officers still view people of color, especially young men, suspiciously. The stories of biased police encounters are legion and are heard every day on street corners, in barber shops, in juvenile detention centers, and at elegant functions hosted by minority professionals. The practice became even more common with the onset in the 1980s and 1990s of the War on Drugs.

In 1986 the U.S. Drug Enforcement Agency rolled out a federally funded highway drug interdiction program known as Operation Pipeline. The program trained officers at highway patrol agencies to make "pretext stops"—pull drivers over for minor traffic violations and search their cars—based on a racially biased profile of drug couriers. LAPD Chief Daryl Gates had already institutionalized the practice of stopping people on a pretext in order to conduct a search: he called it "proactive policing."

Thousands of CHP officers were trained in Operation Pipeline practices. Officers were instructed to look into cars for drug indicators, such as fast food wrappers, maps, hand tools, cell phones, and pagers. These innocuous items suddenly became cause for suspicion. The officers were also trained to use race as a factor in determining who seemed to be a likely drug courier, and to look for nervous body language and "mismatched occupants." CHP officers were instructed to use "consent searches," the practice of seeking permission to search a vehicle even when there is no evidence of criminal activity, if they saw any of these indicators.

Despite the fact that African Americans and Latinos are not any more likely than whites to be carrying drugs or other contraband, they became the main targets of Operation Pipeline.

The increasing number of racial profiling stops and searches stemming from Operation Pipeline and local police departments' adoption of similar tactics began to reach crisis proportions. Law enforcement stops of high-profile celebrities and stories from other states about pretext stops escalating into violence against innocent drivers were of great concern. Though widely ignored in the mainstream media, the issue became a major topic of talk shows on Latino radio stations and the subject of scalding editorials in the African American press.

Because no law enforcement agency kept statistics on the races of drivers who were stopped, questioned, searched, or cited, the evidence remained anecdotal. In order to document the problem for skeptical politicians and white journalists, the ACLU started a statewide hotline for people to report their experiences of racial profiling. A black radio station in Los Angeles publicized the hotline, and within an hour so many people had called that the phone line temporarily crashed. Soon DWB stories poured in from all over the state: the African American president of the local bar association stopped in Oakland; the Latino appliance repairman and his white wife on the freeway near Hayward; the dreadlocked guidance counselor in San Mateo; and the Filipino-Chinese high school class officer in Vallejo.

A coalition of civil rights organizations formed to win passage of legislation to bar racial profiling and mandate the collection of racial data on law enforcement stops and searches. Assemblyman Rod Pacheco, the first Latino Republican elected to the California legislature in nearly a century, introduced the bill. A former prosecutor who had been named legislator of the year by many law enforcement organizations, Pacheco gave a passionate speech on the assembly floor about his own experience with racial profiling when growing up in East Los Angeles.

Pacheco's bill passed with overwhelming bipartisan support. But Governor Gray Davis, a Democrat who had been elected with widespread backing from minority voters, stunned these supporters with a veto, claiming there was "no evidence the practice is taking place statewide." Instead of mandating data collection, Governor Davis urged police agencies to do so voluntarily.

"The veto was an insult to people of color in California," said Michelle Alexander, director of the ACLU-NC Racial Justice Project. Similar bills were enacted in other states; Davis was the only sitting governor to veto one.

Four months after the veto, not a single major law enforcement agency had followed the governor's invitation to voluntarily collect data. A group of determined legislators reintroduced the bill. On the floor of the legislature, State Senator Martha Escutia and Assemblyman Edward Vincent recounted how police had stopped them for no reason—in Vincent's case, when he was working as a probation officer. Governor Davis still refused to change his position.

When efforts stalled in Sacramento, attorney Curtis Rodriguez filed a federal class action lawsuit against the CHP, seeking data on stops by the Highway Patrol and an end to racial profiling. During the course of the lawsuit, the court ordered the CHP to collect data for six months. The data verified Rodriguez's initial instincts. In the area of the Central Coast where Rodriguez had first observed the mass stops, the numbers revealed that Latino drivers were three times as likely, and African Americans twice as likely, to be stopped as white drivers.

Although the results of the CHP survey jolted a few local police departments to begin examining their own practices, fewer than fifty of the three hundred and fifty law enforcement agencies in California collected data voluntarily. Yet limited as it was, the data uncovered patterns of racial profiling by police in big cities, small towns, and rural areas. The Oakland Police Department survey showed that African Americans were three times as likely to be searched as whites. In San Diego, Sacramento, and Stockton, Latinos and African Americans were more than twice as likely as whites to be searched in the course of an ordinary traffic stop.

Rodriguez v. California Highway Patrol was settled in 2003, prohibiting pretext stops and racial profiling, and mandating that the CHP maintain data on the race and ethnicity of the drivers that are stopped and searched.

Despite the historic settlement, there was still no uniform law in California to track racial profiling, and the practice—though exposed—continued. After 9/11, momentum for change slowed down to a halt, and racial profiling took on a different shade.

— TWELVE —

BEHIND BARBED WIRE

WORLD WAR II REMOVAL AND INCARCERATION

> But in addition to the physical confinement, there was the fence around
> our spirit, and this imprisonment of the spirit was the most ravaging part
> of the evacuation experience.
>
> *—Hiroshi Kashiwagi recalling World War II incarceration, 2000*

The forced exclusion and incarceration of more than one hundred and twenty thousand Japanese Americans during World War II was one of the worst violations of
civil liberties in American history. Eighty-three percent of the targeted Japanese were
California residents, and the majority were American-born citizens, known as Nisei.
Their incarceration, as well as that of German and Italian aliens and kidnapped South
Americans, was unprecedented in U.S. history. Racism, fear of immigrants, vigilantism, dissent, and the collapse of the criminal justice system crystallized in this tragic
episode. The mass incarceration also presaged civil liberties challenges during the
Cold War, the Vietnam War, and the Bush administration's "war on terror."

In 1942, twenty-three-year-old Fred Korematsu was motivated by love, not constitutional principles, when he defied military exclusion orders that required all
people of Japanese ancestry to leave their homes on the West Coast and enter government camps. The Oakland-born welder planned to marry his Italian American
fiancée and leave California. He underwent plastic surgery to alter his appearance. He
assumed the name "Clyde Sarah" and created a fictional identity as a Spanish-Hawai-
ian orphan. Despite his efforts, local police detected him. He was jailed and eventually sent to one of the ten concentration camps where most West Coast Japanese
Americans were forced to stay until 1945.

Korematsu's romantically inspired civil disobedience transformed into a quiet but steadfast belief that the government had violated his fundamental rights as an American. His determined challenge of the military's exclusion orders resulted in one of the most infamous cases in the history of the U.S. Supreme Court and led to a forty-one-year legal and political odyssey.

The incarceration of Japanese Americans did not occur in a political or legal vacuum. More than seventy years of anti-Asian, and specifically anti-Japanese, attitudes and beliefs translated into policies and laws that resulted in internment.

Decision Making after Pearl Harbor

By 1941 more than half of the Japanese Americans in the Pacific Coast states were U.S. citizens of school or college age. In contrast to the public portrayal of Japanese as unassimilable and threatening, Japanese Americans, especially the Nisei, were studiously Americanizing themselves. They attended public schools, where they learned of constitutional values; they established or joined Christian churches; and they developed American community institutions.

Hours after the Japanese military bombed Pearl Harbor on the morning of December 7, 1941, President Franklin D. Roosevelt signed an emergency proclamation authorizing the Justice Department to arrest Japanese, German, and Italian aliens.

The FBI wasted no time. Agents began rounding up immigrant (Issei) leaders of the Japanese American community that night.

On December 15, 1941, Secretary of the Navy Frank Knox told reporters, "The most effective fifth column work of the entire war was done in Hawaii, with the possible exception of Norway." There was no proof to verify this accusation of espionage and sabotage.

A few weeks later, on January 25, 1942, a Pearl Harbor investigating committee headed by Supreme Court Justice Owen J. Roberts issued a widely publicized report blaming military leaders in Hawaii—Army commander Lt. Gen. Walter C. Short and naval commander Adm. Husband E. Kimmel—and charging them with "dereliction of duty." The report also made the unfounded charge that "Japanese spies on the Island of Oahu" included "persons having no open relations with the Japanese Foreign Service," a statement that implied Japanese American espionage. Not until after the war was it revealed that no evidence existed to back up this assertion.

Knox's statement and the Roberts Report fueled fears and rumors that Japanese in California were part of a fifth column of Japanese militarists.

On January 27, two days after publication of the Roberts Report, Lt. Gen. John

L. DeWitt, head of the Western Defense Command, met with California Governor Culbert Olson, who joined California Attorney General Earl Warren, Los Angeles Mayor Fletcher Bowron, and other political leaders to demand that all Japanese Americans be removed from the state.

A few weeks later, Attorney General Warren turned the lack of sabotage into a negative in a February 21, 1942, statement before a congressional committee:

> I am afraid many of our people in other parts of the country are of the opinion that because we have had no sabotage and no fifth column activities in this state since the beginning of the war, that means that none have been planned for us. But I take the view that this is the most ominous sign in our whole situation. It convinces me more than perhaps any other factor that the sabotage that we are to get, the fifth column activities we are to get, are timed just like Pearl Harbor was timed.

DeWitt, haunted by the blame placed on his colleague Lt. General Short, argued in a report to the secretary of war that Japanese and "other subversive persons" be "evacuated" from the Pacific Coast. He asserted, "Racial affinities are not severed by migration. The Japanese race is an enemy race and while many second and third generation Japanese born on United States soil, possessed of United States citizenship, have become Americanized, the racial strains are undiluted." Following that logic, he concluded that "along the vital Pacific Coast over 112,000 potential enemies, of Japanese extraction, are at large today."

Secretary of War Henry L. Stimson and Assistant Secretary of War John J. McCloy, in a February 11, 1942, meeting with President Roosevelt, argued for relocation of all Japanese Americans, aliens and citizens, from "restricted areas" on the West Coast. Roosevelt agreed. His only caveat was to "be as reasonable as you can."

Attorney General Francis Biddle initially opposed the full-scale removal of American citizens as unconstitutional, and he considered the removal of Japanese aliens, who were barred from citizenship, to be unwise. In early February 1942, Biddle said, "There is no reason in the world why loyal persons, either aliens or Americans of foreign birth, should not be employed by American industry."

Among those who ignored his counsel were government agencies. In early February, the Los Angeles city government dismissed nearly one hundred Japanese American employees. That same month, the State Personnel Board resolved not to hire naturalized citizens born in enemy nations or their citizen descendants. All current employees in the targeted groups would be investigated. To his credit, Attorney General Warren issued an opinion that the resolution was unconstitutional and a violation of civil rights. Nonetheless, the board issued a ten-page questionnaire to all Japanese American state employees. The questionnaire requested information about past visits to Japan, knowledge of the Japanese language, and association with Japanese organizations. It was a formal prelude to the mass dismissal of Nisei state employees.

On February 19, 1942, President Roosevelt issued Executive Order 9066, authorizing the secretary of war "to prescribe military areas…from which any or all persons may be excluded." Congress promptly passed Public Law 503, which criminalized violations of the executive order.

On March 2, 1942, DeWitt designated southern Arizona and the western halves of Pacific Coast states as "Military Area No. 1." He announced that all Japanese Americans would have to leave the area. Twenty-two days later, he announced that all German and Italian aliens and all persons of Japanese ancestry living in Military Area No. 1 were subject to a curfew requiring them to be in their homes between eight p.m. and six a.m.

Uprooting Communities

Rumors circulated in Japanese American communities about police searches. Sadako Kashiwagi, a Nisei who grew up on a farm in Penryn, northeast of Sacramento, remembered hearing that Japanese had to get rid of contraband, like knives, cameras, pictures, Japanese-language books, and cultural artifacts. "My father was an avid reader and had a great respect for books," she recalled. "We had a fireplace in the farmhouse and he took all the books and maps and just threw them into the fireplace. I just couldn't believe it."

Initially, Japanese Americans could "voluntarily" settle anywhere outside Military Area No. 1. The governors of interior states, however, objected to this migration, fearing the arrival of masses of dislocated Japanese Americans. DeWitt consequently changed his mind, and on March 27 ordered that Japanese were subject to government-controlled removal to hastily constructed camps.

Many Japanese Americans only had days to arrange for the disposition of their homes and property. Some relied on friends to store possessions. Others sold their belongings at rock-bottom prices to unscrupulous buyers, who, knowing that the Japanese had to leave, would not pay market value. The government allowed the Japanese to take only what they could carry.

In the spring of 1942, Japanese Americans with government-issued tags attached to their clothes lined streets throughout California and boarded buses and trains transporting them to temporary "assembly centers," twelve of which were in the state. These hurriedly converted fairgrounds, livestock pavilions, and racetracks housed the excluded Japanese Americans for several months, until the Army constructed more permanent camps. Privacy was at a premium in communal restrooms, showers, and mess halls.

The majority of Japanese Americans who were incarcerated were under twenty-five or over fifty years of age, like this elderly man and his grandchildren in Hayward waiting for a bus to a War Relocation Authority camp.

Violet Kazue de Cristoforo was running a Japanese-language bookstore in Fresno with her husband, Shigeru Matsuda, when they and their two young children were forced into the Fresno Assembly Center. De Cristoforo, who was pregnant with a third child, recalled life in a tarpaper shack, where the 110 degree heat and stench were unbearable: "The floors were built right on top of the racetrack. And there was the manure, and there were cracks in the floor, so that every bit of summer heat, every minute of the day when you're in the barracks, pushed the smell up."

California's Concentration Camps

On March 18, 1942, the Roosevelt administration created a civilian agency, the War Relocation Authority (WRA), to administer the ten long-term camps constructed in

At Manzanar, the camp newspaper was "free" even though its readers were not. Roy Takeno, the Free Press *editor, stands outside the newpaper's office.*

desolate areas of California, Arizona, Wyoming, Colorado, Utah, Arkansas, and Idaho. Once again, the government forced Japanese Americans to move.

The government claimed that this unprecedented action was a military necessity: the military reasoned that some Japanese would be likely to engage in sabotage, and there was no time to distinguish loyal Japanese Americans from the disloyal. The military also argued that detention was necessary to protect Japanese from vigilante violence.

The WRA constructed two camps in California: Tule Lake, near the Oregon border in an arid, high-desert valley, and Manzanar, north of the town of Lone Pine in the haunting Owens Valley, on the eastern edge of the Sierra Nevada.

Built at the foot of Mount Whitney, the highest point in California, Manzanar was home to more than ten thousand Japanese Americans, mainly from southern and central California. Like the other nine WRA camps, Manzanar was surrounded by barbed wire. From elevated watchtowers, armed guards surveyed the one-square-mile camp, which was composed of thirty-six blocks. Typically, each block had fourteen barracks built of wood and tarpaper. Each barrack was divided into four small apartments. Every block had a mess hall, separate latrines for men and women, and laundry rooms.

Yuri Tateishi, a Riverside-born Nisei, recalled arriving at Manzanar at night:

> The floors were boarded, but they were about a quarter to a half inch apart, and the next morning you could see the ground below. What hurt the most…was seeing those hay mattresses. We were used to a regular home atmosphere, and seeing those hay mattresses—so makeshift, with hay sticking out—a barren room with nothing but those hay mattresses. It was depressing, such a primitive feeling….You felt like a prisoner.

Twenty-three-year-old Tom Watanabe was living in the Boyle Heights neighborhood of Los Angeles when he and his family were sent to Manzanar. He remembered:

They assigned us to a barracks with three other families....people I never met in my life. Four families in one room. No partition or nothing. The room was twenty by twenty. In that particular room there was my wife, my two sisters, myself, the other families, almost twelve people. All we had was room enough to walk by. Up in Manzanar it's 100 degrees during the day, but at night it's cold as hell. And we had to use our blankets for partitions, to divide off privacy for our family.

Conditions at the Tule Lake camp, in the shadow of a bluff called Castle Rock, were similar. Hiroshi Kashiwagi, a Nisei

Conditions at hastily constructed camps were primitive. Here, new arrivals at Manzanar stuff hay into bags to create makeshift mattresses.

who grew up in the rural towns of Loomis and Penryn, east of Sacramento, was nineteen when he arrived at Tule Lake with his mother, younger brother, and younger sister. His father languished in a distant sanatorium, ill with tuberculosis. Kashiwagi recalled:

> Tule Lake...it was a prison. Physically there were the barbed wire fence and the guard towers manned by MPs with rifles and machine guns; many of the soldiers were veterans of the war in the South Pacific and were still quite nervous. We didn't dare go near the fence for fear of being shot at, and there were instances of that. But in addition to the physical confinement, there was the fence around our spirit, and this imprisonment of the spirit was the most ravaging part of the evacuation experience.

Resistance!

Soon after the Kashiwagi family entered the Tule Lake camp in 1942, it became a vortex of anger, intimidation, fear, and hysteria.

Problems began in early 1943. At the encouragement of the Japanese American Citizens' League (JACL), a national civil rights organization founded by young Nisei in 1930, the War Department decided to form an all-Nisei combat team, recruited

Hiroshi Kashiwagi was nineteen years old when he and his family were forced to live in the Tule Lake camp, which eventually became the site for Japanese Americans whom the government considered disloyal or uncooperative.

from Hawaii and WRA camps. While the War Department was attempting to implement this plan, Lt. Gen. DeWitt argued against it. He told the House Naval Affairs Subcommittee that "a Jap's a Jap. They are a dangerous element, whether loyal or not. There is no way to determine their loyalty....It makes no difference whether he is an American! Theoretically he is still a Japanese, and you can't change him."

Despite DeWitt's heated rhetoric, WRA officials enthusiastically assisted the War Department. The military recruitment process would not only prove that a large number of Nisei were eager to don U.S. Army uniforms and fight fascism, it would also provide the WRA with a means to pursue its goal of resettling internees outside of the camps.

To identify military recruits, the WRA devised a clumsy and ill-advised questionnaire, ambiguously titled "Application for Leave Clearance." Rather than administering the questionnaire only to draft-age Nisei men, the WRA initially chose to compel all internees over seventeen, male and female, Nisei and Issei, to complete the questionnaire. Two questions in particular generated confusion, anger, and frustration. One question read: "Are you willing to serve in the armed forces of the United States on combat duty, wherever ordered?" The second question, an ominous foreshadowing of the loyalty oaths that proliferated during the Cold War, read: "Will you swear unqualified allegiance to the United States of America and faithfully defend the United States from any or all attack by foreign or domestic forces, and foreswear any form of allegiance to the Japanese emperor, or any other foreign government, power, or organization?"

Some Nisei men were wary of answering "yes" to the first question, unsure whether it would mean automatic induction into the Army.

The second question also posed problems. If Nisei were to "foreswear" allegiance to Japan, that would imply they had once been loyal to Japan, a distasteful if not unacceptable option. For Issei, who were denied naturalization rights, a positive answer could mean renouncing their Japanese citizenship, leaving them literally without a country. Kashiwagi recalled:

> We refused to register [complete the loyalty questionnaire]. There were a lot of us who resisted. At the same time, the Army came in and they had a Nisei representative recruiting volunteers so we thought it was one and the same thing. So we resisted as long as we could. There were so many questions, 'What happens if…?' There was great confusion….For the family, the decision was very unanimous. My mother's first concern was to keep the family together. Her great fear was that if we registered, we would be drafted and sent to the Army.

Since the loyalty questions were part of an "Application for Leave Clearance," some internees feared that positive answers to both questions would result in eviction from camp, regardless of whether they could support themselves in the hostile world outside. The WRA demanded either "yes" or "no" answers, denying internees the opportunity to voice their complex reactions to these questions. The government interpreted responses of "no" to either question as evidence of disloyalty.

Camp administrators stonewalled residents' requests for clarification. The frustration they generated was exacerbated by a series of unsatisfactory mass meetings with Army recruiters whose pat answers were useless to internees trying to understand the reasoning behind the questionnaire.

Masses of irate Tule Lake internees refused to complete the loyalty questionnaire. Hiroshi Kashiwagi's experience was not atypical:

> I took the position that I was an American thrown into prison whose loyalty was now being questioned. In a prison situation, my response could only be negative, so I boycotted the order. Of course, those who refused were placed in the same group as those who answered "No-No" to the questions and segregated as disloyal Americans.

Many requested patriation to Japan to avoid completing the suspect government document. Kashiwagi remembered:

> Block 42, a neighboring block, was one of the first ordered to register. Most of the young men there had signed up for repatriation to Japan….As a reprisal, the Administration picked them first to register. When no one appeared on the designated day, the authorities took action. Around 5 o'clock in the afternoon, the mess bells rang out urgently and alarmingly, announcing the arrival of the soldiers to round up the recalcitrant evacuees. The

young men who already had their suitcases packed were forced at bayonet point onto the Army truck. Everyone was outraged and emotions ran high. Mothers, girlfriends, brothers, and sisters were tearfully bidding good-bye to the young men who were being taken to the county jail outside of camp. This show of force by the Administration was meant to break down the resistance.

Tensions flared not only between the incarcerated and the administration but between camp residents who saw merits in the WRA program and those who considered anyone friendly to the administration to be traitors.

Protests in the camps over the questionnaire led Secretary of War Stimson to segregate those who answered the loyalty questions negatively. In June 1943, the WRA designated Tule Lake as the camp for everyone who answered "no," as well as "troublemakers" from all of the camps. Those considered "disloyal" arrived at the desolate Modoc County outpost in September and October 1943.

On November 1, 1943, more than five thousand internees demonstrated when Dillon Myer, head of the WRA, visited Tule Lake. A human barricade surrounded the administration building for three hours while Meyer and other WRA officials heard from community leaders, incensed over inadequate food and inept and racist management.

Three days later, the camp director, Raymond Best, called in the Army to subdue a group of internees who had attempted to prevent a truck, driven by whites, from leaving the camp. Tule Lake farm laborers were striking over safe working conditions and compensation for injured workers. The internees believed that the truck carried food to strikebreakers who were being paid one dollar an *hour*, rather than the prevailing wage of twelve dollars a *month* for Tule Lake farmworkers. The Army took control of the camp, enforced a strict curfew from seven p.m. to six a.m., arrested many protestors, and used tear gas to disperse crowds. The camp commandant ordered all Tule Lake internees to report to a mass outdoor assembly on November 14.

Not a single person attended.

The Army declared martial law and conducted warrantless searches of all living quarters to ferret out the leaders of the insurgency. The military arrested suspected subversives and imprisoned them in the camp stockade.

Eight months later, in July 1944, ACLU of Northern California Executive Director Ernest Besig visited Tule Lake to interview internees in preparation for a test case challenging the process whereby Japanese American citizens had been judged disloyal and sent to the camp. What he discovered shocked him.

He learned that since the November declaration of martial law, eighteen citizens (out of an initial group of over one hundred arrested men) had been imprisoned without charges in Tule Lake's concrete stockade. The WRA and Army denied prisoners visits from their wives or children, and their mail was censored. The WRA even built a wall to prevent the men from waving to their families.

Morgan Yamanaka, one of the young men in the stockade, later recalled:

> There was no rhyme or reason as to who ended up in the stockade, who was released, at what point they were released. Somehow, my name and my brother's were on that list…when they made a sweep from one end of camp to the other. The fellows who stayed in, approximately 2-3 months longer than I did, were known leaders within various units within Tule Lake organizations. What the hell was I? I was the captain of a fire department and not involved in any formal activity within the camp. In my case and my acquaintances' cases, the majority of the hundred plus people in the stockade were in there for the same reason I was—we didn't know. We were given the classical third degree—shoved into a dark room with a spotlight so we couldn't see.

Yamanaka also recalled midnight raids, one in particular: "I remember it was snowing, truly cold….[T]hey surrounded us with soldiers in uniforms with heavy army coats…and they had a machine gun aimed at us, and we stood in the snow for three, four, five hours in our underwear and *zoris* (sandals)."

This incident motivated some of the prisoners to launch a six-day hunger strike.

Besig also heard allegations that police beat internees with baseball bats during the November 4 protests. Besig was only at Tule Lake for two days before the camp

For nine months, men were jailed without charges in the Tule Lake stockade. For a time, the camp was under martial law.

director ordered him out. He learned after his departure that two sacks of sugar had been poured into his gas tank before he left. Decades later, records revealed that Roger Baldwin, the executive director of the national ACLU based in New York, had given his approval to camp authorities for Besig's ouster.

Returning from his Tule Lake visit, Besig wrote to Secretary of the Interior Harold Ickes, cataloging the unlawful conditions at the camp. Soon thereafter, the eighteen men remaining in the stockade were allowed visitors for the first time in eight months, and the wall erected to prevent the prisoners from waving to their families came down.

Besig enlisted Wayne Collins, a young San Francisco attorney, to secure the prisoners' release. In August the wiry lawyer drove nearly four hundred miles, from San Francisco to Tule Lake. He told WRA officials that he intended to bring habeas corpus proceedings to free the imprisoned men. Faced with this possibility, the WRA quietly released the eighteen men from the stockade. But conditions continued to deteriorate.

Challenging Wartime Orders

While conditions at the Tule Lake camp were declining, the curfew orders, forced exclusion, and detention of Japanese Americans were being challenged in court.

The JACL, the only collective voice for Japanese Americans during the war, advised cooperation with the government as the most effective way to demonstrate loyalty. Because of this counsel, as well as the deference Japanese Americans and most Americans of the time paid to the government, it was difficult to identify plaintiffs willing to fight the government's actions. A handful of Japanese Americans, however, stepped forward. Ernest and Toki Wakayama challenged exclusion orders and orders prohibiting Japanese from leaving assembly centers without permission. Although the Wakayama case would not become a landmark suit, two other cases, those of Fred Korematsu and Mitsuye Endo, which dealt respectively with exclusion and detention of Japanese Americans, picked up where the Wakayamas left off and reached the U.S. Supreme Court. Two other wartime cases reached the Supreme Court. Minoru Yasui, a Portland attorney, challenged military curfew orders imposed against Japanese Americans, and the case of Gordon Hirabayashi, a pacifist and a student at the University of Washington, focused on both the curfew and exclusion orders.

Ernest and Toki Wakayama were, in many ways, ideal plaintiffs. Hawaii-born Ernest, a former post office employee, was a World War I veteran, served as secretary of the Republican precinct club in Hawaii for eight years, and was the acting adjutant of his American Legion post. In California, he served as the secretary-treasurer of the fishermen's union on Terminal Island. After Pearl Harbor, Wakayama unsuccessfully tried to convince government officials that Japanese fishermen would donate their boats to the military.

Toki, her husband's junior by twenty years, was a former beauty queen from Riverside and was pregnant with the couple's first child.

Upon his arrival at the Santa Anita assembly center, a converted racetrack, Ernest Wakayama noticed internees making camouflage netting. He encouraged them to stop their work because it was a violation of the Geneva Convention to use prisoners of war as laborers in the war effort. For this advocacy, assembly center administrators labeled him a troublemaker.

In June 1942, Ernest Wakayama and three others were indicted for participating in an "illegal" meeting: the four were accused of holding a meeting in which the Japanese language was spoken, despite the fact that at the time there was no written order barring the use of Japanese. The gathering that the government considered illegal was a civic meeting to discuss assembly center business. Because the majority of attendees understood Japanese more easily than English, the meeting chair asked participants to speak in Japanese.

Wakayama contacted Edgar Camp, an attorney he knew through his previous union work, who in turn engaged attorney A. L. Wirin of the ACLU of Southern California. Wirin not only challenged the criminal charges lodged against Wakayama but the Wakayamas' very incarceration at the assembly center, filing writs of habeas corpus disputing the constitutionality of the military's exclusion orders. Wirin amended the petition several weeks later to challenge directly the argument of military necessity that the government had used to justify the removal and incarceration of Japanese Americans. The Wakayamas denied that such necessity existed. Meanwhile, at the request of Attorney General Biddle, the U.S. attorney's office in Los Angeles dismissed the indictment against Wakayama and the three others for conducting the "illegal" meeting.

In February 1943, a year after President Roosevelt issued Executive Order 9066, the federal district court in Los Angeles ordered writs of habeas corpus for the Wakayamas, the first writs issued by a U.S. court in a constitutional challenge to the military orders since the declaration of war.

In the meantime, Ernest and Toki Wakayama had been transferred to Manzanar, where Ernest participated in protests over the suspected theft of food by a camp administrator. Wakayama later told his eldest son that while at Manzanar he received death threats not to pursue his habeas corpus action. The elder Wakayama asked the camp director for protection but was refused. Facing the imminent birth of his first child and threats from which he could not escape, and discouraged by the government's violation of the freedoms he had fought for in World War I, Ernest Wakayama in early 1943 asked his attorneys to drop his case and instead applied for patriation to Japan. With this development, the U.S. attorney pressured Wirin to withdraw the lawsuit. Wirin agreed. Publicly, however, the ACLU explained that the Wakayamas withdrew their challenge because they had requested a transfer to the camp at Rohwer, Arkansas, to be united with family and to be closer to their nephew who was serving in the Army at nearby Camp Shelby.

Attorneys working for the WRA, the Justice Department, and the War Department considered the four Supreme Court cases—those of Fred Korematsu, Mitsuye Endo, Minoru Yasui, and Gordon Hirabayashi—to be interrelated, and they developed legal strategies to defend the spectrum of restrictions—curfew, exclusion, and detention—singling out Japanese. They knew that at any point in the legal proceedings in any of these cases, a court might rule on the constitutionality of Executive Order 9066, and the entire basis of the government's program would be undermined.

WRA attorneys were keen on upholding the curfew and exclusion orders as a means of justifying the internment program. The War Department wanted its "military necessity" argument vindicated. The Justice Department, however, was ambivalent.

WRA attorney Edwin Ferguson said, "The keystone of our defense in any litigation will be the proof of facts showing disloyalty or possibility of disloyalty among the Japanese to an extent justifying the special precaution of detention."

The problem was that no such evidence existed.

On the afternoon of May 30, 1942, three weeks after the military forced Japanese Americans to leave Fred Korematsu's hometown of San Leandro, a police officer stopped the young welder. Korematsu was waiting on a street corner for his fiancée, Ida Boitano. During the brief period when Lt. General DeWitt allowed Japanese to leave the West Coast voluntarily and move to other parts of the country, Korematsu and Boitano intended to marry out of state and move somewhere in the Midwest, where they hoped, as Korematsu said, to live "as normal people." But plastic surgery had done little to transform his appearance, and the short window of opportunity closed before the couple could save enough money to leave California.

Ernest Besig, searching for a test case to challenge the exclusion orders, visited the thin, soft-spoken man in jail. Besig did not sugarcoat the legal and political road ahead: he explained that virulent and pervasive anti-Japanese sentiment coupled with judicial deference to wartime military decisions made their prospects grim. Nevertheless, Korematsu agreed to serve as a plaintiff.

The *Korematsu* lawsuit generated controversy within a divided ACLU. The national board of the civil liberties organization, based in New York, split over how

Fred Korematsu (third from left), shown here with his family in their Oakland nursery, defied government orders that all Japanese Americans leave the West Coast to be incarcerated in desolate camps.

to respond to the government's unprecedented actions against Japanese Americans. One group argued that the president's executive order was unconstitutional. Another faction, composed of Roosevelt loyalists and legal conservatives, believed that the government had a right "to establish military zones and to remove persons, either citizens or aliens, from such zones when their presence may endanger national security, even in the absence of martial law."

After a vote of the ACLU national advisory committee supported the latter group, the national ACLU adopted a policy forbidding local branches from sponsoring cases challenging the constitutionality of Executive Order 9066. If suits were to be brought under the ACLU's name, they could only challenge implementation of the executive order as racially discriminatory against Japanese.

"I am amazed and shocked at the attitude by New York," Besig wrote to the national office. "I for one do not intend to be faithless to the commitments we have made with Korematsu. This office just doesn't do business that way. I think the Board has one helluva nerve suddenly to change its opinion and give it retroactive effect."

The forced removal of Japanese Americans was not just a theoretical injustice to Besig. His Nisei secretary was among those who were forced to leave San Francisco.

The American Friends Service Committee also protested the treatment of Japanese Americans, and more than two hundred religious, political, intellectual, and academic leaders from throughout the country, ranging from John Dewey and Norman Thomas to W. E. B. Du Bois and Reinhold Niebuhr, sent a letter to Roosevelt objecting to the unconstitutionality and unfairness of mass incarceration. The signers argued for civilian hearing boards to determine loyalty.

Besig was not a member of the California bar and could not serve directly as Korematsu's attorney, so he recruited Wayne Collins to represent Korematsu. On June 20, 1942, Collins and fellow attorney Clarence Rust filed a wide-ranging demurrer in federal court in San Francisco attacking Executive Order 9066, Public Law 503, and the exclusion order as violating fundamental due process and equal protection rights.

A federal judge denied the attorneys' motion, so the only legal issue in Korematsu's September 1942 criminal trial was whether the young Nisei had violated DeWitt's exclusion order. Within that narrow legal framework, Collins predicted Korematsu would be found guilty, and he set his sights on arguing in the appellate court the constitutional issues raised by the case.

Nonetheless, the chain-smoking attorney had his client testify, to prove to Judge Adolphus St. Sure the sincerity of the young man's beliefs and possibly secure a lighter sentence. The earnest, open-faced Korematsu explained that he had to drop out of Los Angeles City College for lack of funds and return to Oakland to work in his family's nursery. He described volunteering for military service but being rejected for medical reasons. He nevertheless proclaimed his willingness to serve in the military. He established that he had never been to Japan, did not claim dual citizenship, did not read Japanese, and had only an elementary command of the language. He confirmed his attempt to assume another identity by altering his draft card and undergoing plastic surgery.

Judge St. Sure was clearly impressed with Korematsu's genuineness, but he felt obliged to rule that Korematsu was guilty of violating the military's exclusion orders and placed him on five years' probation. St. Sure set bail at twenty-five hundred dollars, which Besig immediately posted. Korematsu was technically free, pending his appeal. As he left the courtroom, however, a military police officer seized him and escorted him to the Tanforan Assembly Center, in South San Francisco, where his family was interned. From Tanforan, Korematsu was transferred to Topaz, the camp at Abraham, Utah.

After a unanimous Ninth Circuit Court of Appeals upheld the constitutionality of the military's exclusion orders against Japanese Americans, Korematsu's only option was to bring his case to the U.S. Supreme Court.

"A Loaded Weapon"

The Supreme Court ruled 6-3 against Korematsu in 1944. A year and a half earlier, in *United States v. Hirabayashi*, the justices had unanimously upheld the constitutionality of the curfew orders imposed against Japanese. They accepted the government's arguments that people of Japanese ancestry, including Nisei citizens, had "attachments" and ethnic affiliations to the Japanese enemy and therefore as a group could be a greater danger than people of other ethnic backgrounds.

Although the Court in *Hirabayashi* acknowledged that distinctions between citizens based on ancestry were by their very nature "odious to a free people," they reasoned that the danger of espionage and sabotage trumped equality.

Writing for the six-justice majority in *Korematsu v. United States*, Justice Hugo Black concluded that it was not "beyond the war power of Congress and the Executive to exclude those of Japanese ancestry from the West Coast war area at the time they did." Conceding that exclusion was much more severe than a curfew, Justice Black justified the court's decision on the "apprehension by the proper military authorities of the gravest imminent danger to the public safety."

Black concluded by rejecting claims that the military's orders were grounded in racial prejudice; instead, he wholly accepted that military authorities considered the need for action against Japanese Americans to be great, and "time was short."

But three justices, who eighteen months earlier had upheld curfew orders in *Hirabayashi*, criticized the forced exclusion of Japanese Americans.

One dissenter was Justice Owen Roberts, who had chaired the government commission investigating the bombing of Pearl Harbor. The commission's report had spread the false notion that espionage by Japanese Americans contributed to the surprise attack. Roberts pinpointed Korematsu's dilemma: he was forbidden to remain in the "zone in which he lived" unless he submitted himself to "military imprisonment" in an assembly center (which Roberts argued was a "euphemism for a prison"). The justice flatly stated that Korematsu's was a "case of convicting a citizen as a punishment for not submitting to imprisonment in a concentration camp based on his ancestry, and solely because of his ancestry, without evidence or inquiry concerning his loyalty and good disposition towards the United States."

Justice Tom Murphy, in his dissent, targeted the inherent racism of the military's orders. In the earlier *Hirabayashi* decision, Murphy had characterized the military's curfew on Japanese Americans as teetering on the "very brink of constitutional power." In his *Korematsu* dissent, he stated that the forced exclusion of Japanese Americans in the absence of martial law fell into "the ugly abyss of racism." Murphy argued that the government's claim of military necessity failed the judicial test that any deprivation of constitutional rights must be "reasonably related to a public danger that is so 'immediate, imminent, and impending' as not to admit of delay and not to permit the intervention of ordinary constitutional processes to alleviate the danger." As he pointed out:

> Nearly four months elapsed after Pearl Harbor before the first exclusion order was issued; nearly eight months went by until the last order was issued; and the last of these [Japanese Americans] was not actually removed until almost eleven months had elapsed. Leisure and deliberation seem to have been more of the essence than speed. And the fact that conditions were not such as to warrant a declaration of martial law adds strength to the belief that the factors of time and military necessity were not as urgent as they have been represented to be.

Murphy methodically refuted all of the unsubstantiated claims of Japanese American disloyalty articulated in DeWitt's *Final Report, Japanese Evacuation from the West Coast, 1942*, a lengthy document that the government used to bolster its arguments defending the military's wartime banishment and detention program.

Murphy asserted that the main reasons for the exclusion appeared to be "largely an accumulation of much of the misinformation, half-truths and insinuations that for years have been directed against Japanese Americans by people with racial and economic prejudices—the same people who have been among the foremost advocates of the evacuation."

In a final salvo to the majority, Murphy called the Court's decision "legalization of racism."

The final dissenter, Justice Robert Jackson, acknowledged that wartime military leaders in a geographic region under military control must not be "held within the limits that bind civil authority in peace." Nevertheless, Jackson argued that the Constitution should not be distorted to approve any action that the "military may deem expedient." In distinguishing between military and judicial reasoning, Jackson stated:

> A military order, however unconstitutional, is not apt to last longer than the military emergency....But once a judicial opinion rationalizes such an order to show that it conforms to the Constitution or rather rationalizes the Constitution to show that the Constitution sanctions such an order, the Court for all times has validated the principle of racial discrimination in criminal procedure and of transplanting American citizens. The principle then lies about like a loaded weapon ready for the hand of any authority that can bring forward a plausible claim of an urgent need.

Jackson concluded his dissent with a cautionary note that the judicial system was limited in its powers to restrain the military and that the "chief constraint upon those who command the physical forces of the country…must be their responsibility to the political judgments of their contemporaries and to the moral judgments of history."

By the time of the decision, Korematsu had relocated to Detroit, where he was working for a company that manufactured airplane hangars. Upon learning of the ruling, Korematsu wrote to Besig, "What happened in [the] Supreme Court is a great disappointment. I know everything possible was done in fighting the case. Even tho we lost, I can't express my appreciation of thanks for all the fighting the ACLU and you have done for me. Will you please give my thanks and regard to Mr. Collins."

Justice Jackson's comment about the moral "judgments of history" proved prescient. Fred Korematsu would wait forty years to be legally vindicated.

"The Power to Detain"

Mitsuye Endo was a clerical worker in the Sacramento office of the Department of Motor Vehicles when, within days of Executive Order 9066, the state of California instructed its 314 Nisei employees to stay home indefinitely. On April 2, 1942, the State Personnel Board informed all Nisei employees that they were immediately suspended and that formal charges would be filed against them. Eleven days later, all Nisei employees received identical statements of the charges that they were citizens of Japan, that they could read and write the Japanese language and had attended Japanese schools conducted by Buddhist church officials, and that they were members and officers of Japanese organizations that were "violently opposed to the Democratic form of Government of the United States and to its principles."

To add insult to injury, the board further charged that the dismissed Nisei would be physically unable to perform any service to the state because of their forced exclusion.

Rumors had circulated earlier in the year that the state would fire all Nisei workers. Attorney Saburo Kido, president of the JACL, recruited a former colleague, San Francisco lawyer James Purcell, in case the rumors proved to be true. By the time of the dismissal, all of the fired employees were confined in assembly centers. Recognizing the injustice of firing all Nisei state employees on such spurious charges, Purcell and Kido decided to act.

Purcell administered a questionnaire to more than one hundred former state employees to find the most sympathetic plaintiff who could challenge the unlawful detention of a state employee.

He found his plaintiff in Mitsuye Endo, whose answers to the questionnaire exuded "Americanism": she did not speak or read Japanese, had never been to Japan, was raised a Methodist, and had a brother in the Army. "I was very young, and I was very shy," Endo recalled. "In fact, when they came and asked me about it, I said, 'Well, can't you have someone else do it first?' It was awfully hard for me. I agreed to do it at that moment, because they said it's for the good of everybody, and so I said, 'Well, if that's it, I'll go ahead and do it.'" Purcell never met Endo in person; he obtained permission to represent her by correspondence.

On July 12, 1942, Purcell filed a habeas corpus petition in federal district court in San Francisco asking the court to compel Milton Eisenhower, director of the WRA, to show cause why Endo should not be released.

The *Endo* case posed the most serious legal problem for the government because Executive Order 9066 allowed *exclusion* but not indefinite *detention* of Japanese Americans. On the same day as the first hearing in the *Endo* case, the WRA began issuing temporary regulations allowing internees to apply for leaves to accept jobs or to attend schools outside the restricted military area.

Purcell argued before Federal Judge Michael J. Roche that detention of Japanese Americans violated due process and was beyond the military's power without congressional authorization. "So far as I know," Purcell asserted, "there has never been a decision of the Supreme Court of the United States upholding the right of a military commander to hold a citizen...without a hearing." He also argued that the power to exclude Japanese from military areas "certainly doesn't contain in it the power to detain after exclusion."

Deputy U.S. Attorney Alfonso J. Zirpoli argued that the court should accept as fact the government's assertions about its inability to distinguish loyal from disloyal, as well as the potential for sabotage. He urged the court to tread lightly in opposing actions that the executive branch and military deemed necessary. Despite the fact that the WRA had announced temporary regulations allowing for limited leaves from camp only that day, Zirpoli argued that Endo had not availed herself of administrative means of gaining her freedom.

Almost a year later, Judge Roche signed a brief order declaring that Endo was not entitled to a writ of habeas corpus because she had not sought to secure her release under WRA regulations.

By the time the *Endo* case reached the U.S. Supreme Court (the same day that the *Korematsu* case was argued), the government agreed that it was beyond the WRA's power to detain citizens who were not charged with disloyalty or subversion.

On December 18, 1944, Justice William O. Douglas, writing for a unanimous court, declared that President Roosevelt's executive order did not authorize the detention of loyal Japanese Americans, but he suggested that temporary detention for the purpose of preventing espionage and sabotage could be authorized. Justice Murphy, in a concurring opinion, condemned the incarceration, commenting that "detention in Relocation Centers of persons of Japanese ancestry regardless of loyalty is not only unauthorized by Congress or the Executive but is another example of the unconstitutional resort to racism inherent in the entire evacuation program....[R]acial discrimination of this nature bears no reasonable relation to military necessity and is utterly foreign to the ideals and traditions of the American people."

While the *Endo* and *Korematsu* cases wound their ways through the federal court system, other Nisei challenged their continued exclusion from California. In July 1944, Oakland native George Ochikubo, a thirty-three-year-old dentist, sued to prevent Charles H. Bonesteel, DeWitt's successor as western defense commander, from enforcing the exclusion orders. Joining the lawsuit were twenty-four-year-old Ruth Shizuko Shiramizu, widow of a Nisei Purple Heart awardee, and twenty-six-year-old Masaru Baba, an honorably discharged Army veteran. A. L. Wirin represented them and argued that mass exclusion of Japanese Americans was no longer a military necessity, a point that the military itself had privately acknowledged months earlier in an internal memo.

The Roosevelt administration, however, decided to postpone ending the mass exclusion orders until after the November 1944 presidential election. On December 17, 1944, the day before the Supreme Court announced its *Endo* decision, the War Department lifted orders excluding Japanese Americans from the West Coast, effective January 2, 1945. The WRA also announced that all "relocation camps" would be closed by the end of 1945. Although the government rescinded mass exclusion, it maintained exclusion orders against specific individuals.

The government responded to the *Ochikubo* lawsuit by lifting exclusion orders on Shiramizu, the widow, and Baba, the veteran, but issuing an individual exclusion order against Ochikubo. The military justified Ochikubo's continued exclusion in part on his advocating, in the Topaz camp, that internees not complete the loyalty questionnaire until the administration clearly explained the two controversial questions and guaranteed that their civil liberties would be restored.

In late February 1945, Federal Judge Pierson Hall heard arguments in Ochikubo's case. Wirin argued that exclusion proceedings did not allow the excluded individual to cross-examine witnesses or to know, let alone refute, any evidence. Additionally, Wirin claimed that the military had no power to exclude civilians since the civil courts were open.

Military officials falsely and misleadingly testified that there were no fixed criteria to determine who should be excluded on an individual basis. The opposite was true. By not disclosing the factors used to determine individual exclusion orders, the military avoided admitting that according to its own review process there was no evidence to merit designating the Oakland dentist for individual exclusion.

In June 1945, Judge Hall ruled that military authorities could not enforce exclusion orders, but could only turn in an individual who violated those orders to the local U.S. attorney for criminal prosecution. The government appealed the decision, but the case became moot after the Army issued a proclamation on September 4, 1945, following Japanese surrender, revoking individual exclusion orders against Ochikubo and some six thousand Japanese Americans and aliens, including Germans and Italians, who had been forbidden to return to their West Coast homes.

Trials on the Way Home

Although most Japanese Americans could return home in 1945, several thousand internees at the troubled Tule Lake camp faced complicated problems that not only prevented them from leaving the camp but called into question their very citizenship.

On July 1, 1944, President Roosevelt signed unprecedented legislation allowing a U.S. citizen to renounce citizenship during wartime. Within the dysfunctional and demoralizing environment of Tule Lake, this new law had proved potent. The camp was already home to disillusioned and bitter Issei who desired to return to Japan, as well as militant Kibei (Nisei educated in Japan) who experienced bankrupt promises of democracy in the United States and saw their future in Japan. They formed three "patriotic" organizations, one for young men, another for women and girls, and a third for older men.

Tule Lake administrators, for a time, allowed Japanese ultranationalism and pro-Japanese propaganda to flourish through these groups, which used violence, intimidation, and fearmongering to bully thousands to follow their program of renunciation. For months, these groups conducted early morning military-style drills and belligerently championed Japan. They filed spurious letters requesting applications for renunciation and then told the surprised recipients that the government was demanding that they renounce their citizenship. They formed goon squads, threatening non-renunciants that their relatives in Japan would be physically harmed.

Exploiting internees' fears of facing hostility and economic insecurity outside of the camp, the pro-Japan zealots told Tule Lake residents that if they did not renounce their U.S. citizenship they would be thrown out of the camp to fend for themselves. The pro-Japan groups also played on filial loyalty and fear of family separation. This was often reinforced by parents who compelled their teenage and young adult children to renounce their citizenship, believing that their families would be separated if all members did not renounce. Hiroshi Kashiwagi recalled:

> Many of the people who were brought in from the other camps talked and told us that all the aliens in Tule Lake would be separated from their children and be deported to Japan and that citizen children better request repatriation to prevent separation from their parents and to avoid getting in trouble when families got to Japan....My mother became so alarmed she repeatedly insisted that we apply for repatriation. I delayed. There was much agitation in the Block for repatriation, and it broke out into open hostilities....I realized that I had to send in an application [for repatriation] for my own safety as people who had refused to apply were being called "White Japs" and "Inu" (dog) and a number had been beaten up by unidentified gangsters.

Adding to the psychological pressure was the fear generated by camp informers who reported to the ultranationalists. Tensions heightened after the July 1944 murder of Yaozo Hitomi, who had openly criticized the pro-Japan groups. By March 1945, when Justice Department renunciation hearings at Tule Lake came to a close, more than five thousand Nisei, including minors, had renounced their citizenship.

In September 1945, the Justice Department announced its intention to deport them. But many, like Kashiwagi, had changed their minds in the intervening months. "Soon after we signed the papers, we knew it was a mistake because there was no sense doing it," the soft-spoken Nisei recollected. "But I think we were under a lot of group pressure, and we weren't thinking straight."

In November 1945, a group of Japanese Americans who had renounced their citizenship filed a mass habeas corpus petition, *Abo v. Clark*, in San Francisco federal court for release from Tule Lake and prevention of their deportation. The same group filed an additional suit seeking to have their renunciations cancelled and to have the court affirm their U.S. citizenship. Unable to identify a single attorney willing to assist the renunciants, Wayne Collins took on the massive case himself.

The suit charged that the renunciations resulted from coercion by both the government and pro-Japan groups, which the government knowingly permitted to carry on a campaign of violence to force loyal American citizens to renounce their citizenship. A federal judge immediately signed an order directing the government to show cause why writs of habeas corpus should not be issued. The government had to confront the problem of what to do with the thousands of renunciants whom Justice Department officials had assumed would be deported to Japan. In response, the Justice Department, on January 6, 1946, began holding "mitigation hearings" at Tule Lake. A renunciant who could prove duress at the time of renunciation would be freed from detention. No special consideration was given to children under twenty-one at the time of renunciation.

Because the mitigation hearings were costly and time consuming, the Justice

Department reviewed only 2,000 cases, even though more than 3,000 people requested hearings. Of those who received hearings, all but 449 were released. When Tule Lake closed in March 1946, the government moved the remaining renunciants to a Justice Department internment camp at Crystal City, Texas. However, release orders for some of the men came through right up to the time of their departure, and they were rescued from the Texas-bound train.

Rejecting the government's arguments that the remaining *Abo* plaintiffs were alien enemies, U.S. District Court Judge Louis Goodman on June 30, 1947, ordered their release and canceled their deportation. They had been in camps for more than five years.

Because the mitigation hearings only dealt with deportation, the question of citizenship remained open. The government consequently created the term "native American aliens" to describe the renunciants, because their citizenship status was uncertain.

Judge Goodman validated the renunciants' citizenship. He criticized the government for accepting the renunciations, asserting that officials were "fully aware of the coercion" at Tule Lake by pro-Japan zealots, and knew of "the fear, anxiety, hopelessness and despair of the renunciants." Goodman concluded, "It is shocking to the conscience that an American citizen be confined without authority and then while so under duress and restraint for his Government to accept from him a surrender of his constitutional heritage." The government appealed.

While the *Abo* case was working its way through the federal court in San Francisco, a second set of Nisei successfully petitioned the federal court in Los Angeles to invalidate their renunciations. Unlike *Abo*, which charged that *both* the government and ultranationalists in Tule Lake contributed to the mass renunciation, the four plaintiffs in this case, a minor and the wives of Issei, accused only the ultranationalist groups. In 1949 Ninth Circuit Judge William Denman ruled in their favor, but the decision applied only to the four named plaintiffs.

A year and a half later, the Ninth Circuit handed down its decision in the *Abo* mass renunciants' case. Although Denman agreed that the oppressive conditions at Tule Lake were in large part caused by government officials, he claimed that the lower court had erred in not giving the government an opportunity to show that specific renunciants would have acted similarly regardless of the coercive conditions. The cases of nearly all of the adults were consequently sent back to the lower court to enable the government to prove that specific renunciants acted freely and voluntarily.

Denman's decision evidenced the momentum gained by the Cold War in the time between his rulings in the two renunciation cases. He stated, "In a cold war already existing when the cases were tried and now with the hot war in Korea, the federal courts should be more vigilant than ever that the massing of 4,315 plaintiffs in two suits does not conceal the facts as to such enemy minded renunciants."

Facing the prospect of thousands of trials that would take years to complete, the Justice Department developed an administrative process to deal with renunciants' cases. The government required them to supply an affidavit explaining their renunciation; if nothing in the Justice Department's files was sufficient to overcome the plaintiff's arguments, the attorney general would not oppose a court judgment canceling renunciation.

Collins and his secretary prepared and filed thousands of affidavits, including one for Hiroshi Kashiwagi.

Even with the streamlined process, it wasn't until May 20, 1959, more than thirteen years after the initial lawsuit to regain citizenship was filed, that U.S. Attorney General William P. Rogers announced that the review of the renunciation cases had been completed and that more than four thousand Nisei had regained their citizenship. Despite this claim, some renunciants waited until the mid-1960s for their U.S. citizenship to be secured.

Other "Enemy Aliens"

Japanese Americans were not the only ethnic group targeted during the war. The government designated German and Italian immigrants who had not become U.S. citizens "enemy aliens." President Roosevelt's orders immediately after the bombing of Pearl Harbor directed the FBI to arrest and detain any alien that the government considered dangerous to the United States.

The orders set in motion plans that the government had devised years before. After England and France declared war on Germany in September 1939, President Roosevelt authorized the FBI to compile what became known as the "Custodial Detention" list, composed of "potentially dangerous" individuals to be detained or placed under surveillance in case of war. The FBI used organizational membership records, subscription lists, and informers (who often shared gossip, rumors, and at times, lies) to compile its lists of "subversive" individuals considered dangerous because of their relationship to Axis organizations or because they could aid espionage and sabotage.

Eddie Friedman was a German immigrant on one of the FBI lists. On the evening of December 8, 1941, less than forty-eight hours after the bombing of Pearl Harbor, Friedman and his wife, Liesl, were delivering hors d'oeuvres and Viennese pastries, hand-made by Friedman's employer, to a party hosted by a wealthy German immigrant in San Francisco.

Friedman and his wife had immigrated to San Francisco from Germany two years earlier. The job of selling and delivering pastries was a far cry from his prior work as an attorney in his native Hamburg. But at forty-seven, the new immigrant needed a job. So when a Viennese couple in San Francisco asked him to sell their homemade cookies and pastries door-to-door, he reluctantly agreed.

After delivering food that December evening, Friedman and his wife returned to their apartment above a garage on the corner of Pierce and Sacramento Streets and were surprised to find three burly FBI agents. They arrested him.

It must have been déjà vu for the former lawyer. Just three years earlier, two Gestapo agents had arrested Friedman, and he was sent to the Oranienburg-Sachsenhausen concentration camp outside of Berlin because he was a Jew. Then, Liesl Friedman had implored her husband's friends in the legal community to convince the local Nazi party leadership to release Friedman. They succeeded.

His stay in an American internment camp was not so short.

He was held without charges at Fort Lincoln in Bismark, North Dakota, a camp for German, Japanese, and Italian enemy aliens as well as prisoners of war, one of four such camps run by the Justice Department that held thousands of people. The Jewish prisoner's fellow inmates included German sailors who decorated their rooms with swastikas and pictures of Hitler.

For months, Friedman wrote to government officials, charitable organizations, and public figures ranging from Edward Ennis, head of the Justice Department's Alien Enemy Control Unit, to First Lady Eleanor Roosevelt pleading for release from the camp. In February 1942, he wrote to the National Refugee Service, "I came here to be saved from Nazi persecution, and now, what fateful irony, this land of freedom just locked me together with the same people she gave me shelter against."

Like that of the other enemy aliens interned at Fort Lincoln, Friedman's fate was determined by a hearing board composed of local citizens. Internees were not allowed legal representation, nor were they allowed to confront witnesses or see evidence gathered by the FBI against them. The U.S. attorney, however, allowed witnesses to testify on behalf of the enemy aliens. The hearing board then recommended to the attorney general whether the internee should be released, paroled under Immigration and Naturalization Service supervision, or remain interned.

When Friedman appeared before his hearing board in February 1942, the local U.S. attorney questioned him about his connections to Germany. Friedman responded, "My brother hanged himself in a concentration camp. My uncle died in a camp. They would not give him his pills." He explained he had no family left in Germany.

In late March 1942, Friedman received the government's decision. He was paroled, but only on the condition that he not return to San Francisco. General DeWitt had by then designated the western areas of the Pacific Coast states Military Area Number 1, from which he could exclude anyone.

Once again, Liesl Friedman fought for her husband's return. She advocated with the U.S. attorney in San Francisco, the local Immigration and Naturalization Service parole officer, and finally with the officer in charge of Fort Lincoln for her husband's unconditional release.

On April 24, 1942, more than four months after his swift removal from San Francisco, Friedman received the good news that his parole to his adopted hometown was approved. He arrived in San Francisco four days later.

By World War II, Italians were the largest immigrant group in the United States, with significant populations living in California. Italian aliens were also on the FBI's Custodial Detention List.

Filippo Molinari, who worked as a San Jose sales representative for the San Francisco–based Italian newspaper *L'Italia*, recalled his arrest and subsequent imprisonment by the FBI:

> I was the first one arrested in San Jose the night of the attack on Pearl Harbor. At 11 p.m., three policemen came to the front door and two at the back. They told me that, by order of President Roosevelt, I must go with them. They didn't even give me time to go to my room and put on my shoes. I was wearing slippers. They took me to prison…and finally to Missoula, Montana, on the train, over the snow, still with slippers on my feet, the temperature at seventeen below and no coat or heavy clothes!

On January 25, 1942, the military designated the coastal areas of California (generally the area west of Highway 1 or Highway 101) and also entire towns, like Pittsburg, on the Sacramento–San Joaquin Delta northeast of San Francisco, off-limits to all enemy aliens. Four days later, the attorney general announced that enemy aliens living in the restricted area had to move out within a month; ten thousand Italian Americans were forced to relocate.

The order disproportionately impacted tight-knit Italian fishing communities in Monterey, Half Moon Bay, Santa Cruz, and San Francisco. Many Italian immigrants, particularly women like seventy-six-year-old Santa Cruz resident Celestina Stagnaro Loero, had not naturalized and consequently had to move. The round-faced native of Riva Trigoso sadly called the February evening in 1942 when two Justice Department officials visited her the *mala notte*, or "bad night." The agents told her that within two days she would have to leave the clapboard house that had been her home for more than forty-one years, or risk arrest. Two of the diminutive woman's sons, as well as two of her grandsons, had enlisted in the Navy, so a granddaughter living next door had to translate the bad news.

The livelihood of California's Italian fishermen, who operated 80 percent of the state's fishing fleet, was severely damaged, if not eliminated, by wartime restrictions and requisitions. In late January 1942, the attorney general issued orders that prohibited "enemy alien" fishermen from taking out their boats and banned them from the vicinity of the wharves. The next month, the Coast Guard buttressed the attorney general's order and barred all "enemy aliens" from fishing in bay and coastal waters. Among them was the father of baseball star Joe DiMaggio.

The Army and Navy requisitioned the boats of Italian American citizens for the war effort.

In early February, Attorney General Biddle issued orders requiring all enemy aliens to register at local post offices and obtain a Certificate of Identification—a pink identity booklet which included a photo and fingerprint—that they had to carry at all times. They were also subject to a curfew from eight o'clock at night until six in the morning and forbidden to travel outside a five-mile radius from their homes.

Enemy aliens could not possess "contraband" such as guns, cameras, and short-wave radios. Law enforcement officials searched homes, sometimes repeatedly. The Justice Department considered the legal requirement that there be probable cause for a house to be searched to be met merely if an alien lived there, regardless of whether the house was owned by a U.S. citizen.

By May 1942 the government had removed Japanese Americans in California from their prewar homes, so the focus of enforcement fell on Italians and Germans. DeWitt persisted in demanding that Italian and German aliens be removed from the Pacific Coast states, but the Justice Department and President Roosevelt resisted the idea, fearing the political and economic consequences on the war effort. There were also racial considerations. In April 1942, Attorney General Biddle wrote to the president, "You signed the original executive order permitting the exclusion so the Army could handle the Japs. It was never intended to apply to Italians and Germans." In May 1942, the War Department dropped the idea of the mass exclusion of Italians and Germans. On Columbus Day 1942, the government lifted restrictions on Italian Americans.

Historian Rose Scherini suggests that restrictions were lifted because the Roosevelt administration wanted to encourage the goodwill of Italian American voters in the congressional elections the following month. In addition, the Army planned to invade Italy in the spring and wanted to improve morale among Italian Americans, the largest ethnic group in the armed forces during the war.

After Italy surrendered in October 1943, the government released most Italian men from Justice Department camps.

Kidnapped South Americans

Following the Japanese attack on Pearl Harbor, the U.S. government prodded four-teen Latin American countries to deport to the United States more than six thou-sand people. Four thousand were German, including Jews who had fled Europe; two thousand were Japanese, and nearly three hundred were Italian. Hemispheric security was the stated reason for the program, but other motivations spurred the action. In the case of Germans, the United States sought to remove German eco-nomic and political power from the region, but also to exchange German Latin Americans for Americans held prisoner behind enemy lines in Europe. In the case of Japanese, the United States wanted hostages to exchange with Japan for Ameri-can citizens. South American leaders, especially those in Peru, were eager to expel Japanese immigrants and their families.

These forced migrants were arrested in their home countries, placed on ships bound for the United States, stripped of their passports and, upon arriving in the United States, arrested as illegal immigrants and detained in Justice Department camps.

In 1942 and 1943, the United States and Japan engaged in prisoner of war exchanges that included more than eight hundred Japanese Latin Americans. The United States considered the Japanese Peruvians still interned in the United States at the end of the war "illegal aliens" and began deportation proceedings. The Peru-vian government refused to readmit any of them, even if they were Peruvian citi-zens or married to Peruvian citizens.

The United States government ultimately shipped more than a thousand for-mer Peruvians to war-ravaged Japan, a nation most had never seen before. More than three hundred Japanese Peruvians remaining in the United States fought their deportation in court.

Wayne Collins took on their case in federal court in San Francisco, charging that the Japanese Peruvians had been kidnapped, brought to the U.S. against their will, and imprisoned in internment camps by the U.S. immigration service. The court stopped the deportation program, but the Japanese Peruvians remained in legal limbo.

In 1950 the Peruvian government indicated that it would give individual consideration to Japanese Peruvians who wanted to return. But the majority had rebuilt their lives in the U.S. In 1954 the federal government allowed the Japanese Peruvians who remained in the United States to become naturalized U.S. citizens. Three hundred did.

"Not Justified by Military Necessity"

In 1942 the Federal Reserve Bank in San Francisco conservatively estimated that Japanese Americans lost $400 million because of forced exclusion and incarceration. In 1948 President Truman signed the Japanese Evacuation Claims Act, which provided limited compensation for property losses. The statutory limit for claims was twenty-five hundred dollars, and individuals were given eighteen months to file.

More than two decades passed before Edison Uno, a Nisei JACL activist, introduced a resolution at the organization's 1970 national convention calling for federal legislation requiring monetary payments to Japanese Americans who were interned and for a $400 million fund for Japanese American community projects. Uno had been incarcerated with his family at the camp in Crystal City, Texas, and was an early advocate of educating the public about the realities of the incarceration. Although the JACL national council adopted the resolution, the matter did not move forward immediately. In 1970 the idea of monetary redress seemed an unachievable goal and former internees were not psychologically or politically able to pursue the project. Emotional wounds from the war had not healed.

But advocates from the Japanese American and civil rights communities pressured President Gerald Ford to revoke Executive Order 9066 on February 19, 1976 (the thirty-fourth anniversary of the order) and acknowledge that the forced exclusion of Japanese Americans was wrong. Later the same year, the JACL national council unanimously approved a resolution calling for payments of twenty-five thousand dollars to all excluded and incarcerated Japanese Americans (or their heirs), along with a community trust fund. The council urged that the JACL pursue federal redress legislation.

JACL leaders approached Senators Daniel Inouye and Spark Matsunaga of Hawaii and Representative Norman Mineta of San Jose about redress legislation. The congressmen advised redress proponents to advocate first for a federal commission charged with investigating the exclusion and incarceration program and issuing a government report. Such a document would be crucial in future advocacy for redress.

Although JACL leaders thought that a commission would delay redress legislation, the organization supported the proposal. Their decision spurred the creation of two other organizations. The National Council for Japanese American Redress (NCJAR) opposed the JACL strategy. The group pursued redress through a class action lawsuit that ultimately reached the U.S. Supreme Court but was unsuccessful. Among the significant results of NCJAR's lawsuit, however, was an admission

In 1981 Hiroshi Kashiwagi (bottom, second from left) testified before the Commission on the Wartime Relocation and Internment of Civilians (top), a presidential committee which concluded that the wartime incarceration of Japanese Americans resulted from racism, wartime hysteria, and a failure of political leadership.

by U.S. Solicitor General Charles Fried that racism, not military necessity, had motivated the government in 1942 to exclude and incarcerate Japanese Americans. Another organization, the National Coalition for Redress and Reparations (NCRR), consisted mainly of grassroots activists who worked to educate and unite Japanese Americans and Asian Americans around a common redress goal and to link the redress movement to broader civil rights struggles.

On July 31, 1980, President Jimmy Carter signed legislation creating the Commission on Wartime Relocation and Internment of Civilians, whose mandate was to review Executive Order 9066 and its impact on American citizens and permanent resident aliens, to review the military orders requiring the relocation and detention of these groups, and to recommend appropriate remedies.

Between July and December 1981, the commission conducted eleven hearings in ten cities throughout the United States, including Los Angeles and San Francisco. NCRR organized testimony from Japanese Americans at these well-attended hearings, which became a public forum for former internees to acknowledge the injustice of their wartime incarceration and to articulate, often for the first time, their memories of the war years.

In February 1983, the commission released its unanimous findings in a 467-page report entitled *Personal Justice Denied.* It concluded that Executive Order 9066 was "not justified by military necessity" and found that the wartime exclusion and incarceration program resulted from race prejudice, wartime hysteria, and a failure of political leadership. The commission also acknowledged that "a grave injustice was done to American citizens and resident aliens of Japanese ancestry who, without individual review or any probative evidence against them, were excluded, removed and detained by the United States during World War II." According to the commission's estimate, the total income and property losses suffered by Japanese Americans was between $810 million and $2 billion (in 1983 dollars).

The commission's recommendations included a formal governmental apology, a presidential pardon to the three men convicted of curfew or exclusion violations, funding for an educational and humanitarian foundation to sponsor research and public educational activities, and payments of twenty thousand dollars to each surviving internee.

Meanwhile, a redress movement for California state workers was moving through the legislature. On February 19, 1982, the fortieth anniversary of Executive Order 9066, freshman Assemblyman Patrick Johnston, from the San Joaquin Valley, introduced legislation to provide monetary redress to 314 surviving Japanese Americans who were wrongfully terminated as California state workers in 1942. On August 17, 1982, Governor Jerry Brown signed the bill, thereby providing the first monetary redress from any governmental body to Japanese Americans. The following year, Los Angeles County, the city of Los Angeles, the city and county of San Francisco, and the counties of Alameda, Placer, Sacramento, San Joaquin, and Santa Clara passed similar legislation.

Using the federal commission's recommendations as a guide, Japanese American Congressmen Spark Matsunaga, Daniel Inouye, Norman Mineta, and Robert Matsui and their allies introduced redress bills from 1983 through 1987. During that period, Japanese Americans strategically framed redress not as a Japanese American problem but as a larger constitutional issue. They created a broad-based coalition of civil rights, labor, and religious groups and successfully lobbied members of Congress to support redress. In September 1987, the House of Representatives passed the legislation, and the Senate followed seven months later.

Up to that point, the Reagan administration had been poised to veto it.

Redress supporters, however, reminded President Reagan that as an Army captain he had participated in a 1945 medal ceremony for Kazuo Masuda, a Nisei soldier killed in Italy. When Masuda's family tried to resettle in Santa Ana after the war, vigilantes threatened them. The community refused to allow Masuda's body to be buried in the local cemetery. Responding to this racism, the Army had sent a high-level delegation to Santa Ana to present the Distinguished Service Cross to Masuda's family. As a soldier, Reagan had accompanied General Joseph Stilwell in this military group. Prompting him to recall this incident was key in swaying him to approve the legislation.

On August 10, 1988, President Reagan signed the Civil Liberties Act of 1988, which provided a formal governmental apology and payments of twenty thousand dollars to Japanese Americans who were excluded and incarcerated, and created a Civil Liberties Public Education Fund to help the public grasp the experience of Japanese Americans who were interned during World War II.

Japanese Latin Americans who had been kidnapped were not recognized in the law. In 1996 attorneys filed a lawsuit, *Mochizuki v. United States*, on their behalf to be included in the Civil Liberties Act's provisions. In 2000 a settlement was reached. The government would apologize to the Japanese Latin Americans and give them five thousand dollars in redress (a quarter of what Japanese Americans received) in exchange for dropping the lawsuit. Some Japanese Peruvians, however, rejected the settlement and continued to pursue redress equal to that given to Japanese Americans.

Edison Uno, the man who had initially proposed redress nearly twenty years before passage of the Civil Liberties Act, did not live to see his vision become reality. The thin, bespectacled college administrator died of a heart attack in December 1976, at the age of forty-seven.

Righting a Great Wrong

In 1947 Dr. Stetson Conn, a civilian historian for the Department of the Army and later the Army's chief military historian, analyzed evidence available during the war and concluded that there was "little support for the argument that military necessity required a mass evacuation."

More than three decades later, Aiko Yoshinaga-Herzig, a researcher for the Commission on Wartime Relocation and Internment of Civilians, her husband, John (Jack) Herzig, and Peter Irons, a lawyer and political science professor, uncovered proof that during the war the government had purposefully suppressed, altered, and destroyed evidence related to Japanese American loyalty and instead presented to the U.S. Supreme Court "lies" and "intentional falsehoods."

These were strong charges, but the evidence was compelling.

Among the revealing documents was correspondence from the Justice Department's Edward Ennis to Solicitor General Charles Fahy regarding a January 26,

1942, Office of Naval Intelligence report on Japanese Americans. Written a few weeks after the Pearl Harbor bombing, the report concluded, "In short, the entire 'Japanese Problem' has been magnified out of its true proportion, largely because of the physical characteristics of the people [and] should be handled on the basis of the *individual*, regardless of citizenship, and *not* on a racial basis." Troubled by the report, Ennis had written Fahy that "the Government is forced to argue that individual selective evacuation would have been impractical and insufficient when we have positive knowledge that the only Intelligence agency responsible for advising General DeWitt gave him advice directly to the contrary." Ennis asked whether the Justice Department had an affirmative duty to advise the Supreme Court, which was considering the *Hirabayashi* curfew case, of the report; to Ennis, anything less could approximate suppression of evidence.

Despite Ennis's apprehensions, Solicitor General Fahy chose not only to disregard the report but to contradict it.

Yoshinaga-Herzig also discovered that the War Department had purposely altered a military report used as evidence in the wartime Supreme Court cases. In April 1943, General DeWitt had rushed copies of his *Final Report, Japanese Evacuation from the West Coast, 1942* to the War Department. This was the report in which he argued that the removal of Japanese Americans was necessary because "it was simply a matter of facing the realities that a positive determination could not be made, that an exact separation of the 'sheep and the goats' was unfeasible." DeWitt failed to elaborate why.

Secretary of War John McCloy was disturbed because DeWitt had admitted just a few months earlier, in a confidential memo, that there was sufficient time to determine individual loyalty while Japanese were under military control in assembly centers. If time was not an issue and DeWitt still insisted that it was impossible to determine individual loyalty, the underlying racism of DeWitt's orders was clear. The government had already argued before the Ninth Circuit in all of the wartime cases that military necessity required the Japanese to be removed en masse because the Army lacked adequate time to determine individual loyalty. If the U.S. Supreme Court was aware of DeWitt's belief that time was not an issue, the justices could, understandably, question the credibility of the government's arguments.

To deal with this problem, McCloy had enlisted a member of DeWitt's staff and a War Department legal staff member to craft a revision finessing the offending language.

Yoshinaga-Herzig discovered one remaining copy of the original version of DeWitt's report. The differences between the two versions were thereby revealed. The researchers also discovered documents revealing that the Justice Department and the solicitor general knew that the FBI and Federal Communications Commission (FCC) had refuted DeWitt's claim, in the *Final Report*, that Japanese Americans had radio contact with Japanese submarines in the Pacific. The FCC had personally informed DeWitt both before and after the exclusion orders that not a single report of suspect radio transmissions was verified.

Some Justice Department officials felt compelled to inform the Supreme Court about the evidence contradicting DeWitt's report. John Burling, a department attorney, wrote to Solicitor General Fahy that "We are now…in possession of substantially incontrovertible evidence that the most important statements of fact advanced by General DeWitt to justify the evacuation and detention were incorrect, and furthermore that General DeWitt had cause to know, and in all probability did know, that they were incorrect at the time he embodied them in his final report."

The solicitor general suppressed this crucial information from the Supreme Court.

Four decades later, armed with this dramatic new evidence, professor Irons contacted Fred Korematsu, Gordon Hirabayashi, and Minoru Yasui, presented them with the new findings, and asked whether they wanted to reopen their wartime cases and challenge their convictions. After learning of the government's mendacity, Fred Korematsu thought for a moment before simply stating, "They did me a great wrong."

All three men agreed to appeal their convictions, and the bearded professor set out to find attorneys in San Francisco, Portland, and Seattle, the sites of the three original trials, to represent them. He believed that attorneys of Japanese ancestry should lead this fight. Through Yasui, Irons met Dale Minami, a dynamic young San Francisco attorney who was involved in the redress movement. Minami, in turn, identified Don Tamaki, Lorraine Bannai, and other attorneys, most of whose parents and grandparents had been incarcerated. All volunteered their services.

Because Korematsu, Hirabayashi, and Yasui had exhausted all available legal appeals and served their sentences, they had to rely on an obscure and rarely used legal procedure called a petition for writ of error *coram nobis* to reopen their cases. This procedure allows an individual to seek reversal of a criminal conviction based on evidence of governmental misconduct resulting in a fundamental injustice.

On January 19, 1983, the attorneys filed their petition on behalf of Fred Korematsu in the U.S. district court in San Francisco. Victor Stone, the Justice Department attorney responding to the *coram nobis* cases, brought up the possibility of presidential pardons, but the three Nisei refused, since pardons would absolve the government from acknowledging that the laws and military orders resulting in the men's convictions were unconstitutional. Korematsu commented, "We should pardon the government." With the option of presidential pardons rejected, the case moved forward.

On November 10, 1983, Federal Judge Marilyn Hall Patel ruled from the bench before a packed federal courtroom and granted Korematsu's petition vacating his conviction. In issuing her ruling, Judge Patel acknowledged that Executive Order 9066, Public Law 503, and DeWitt's exclusion orders were "based upon and relied upon by the government in its arguments to the court and to the Supreme Court on unsubstantiated facts, distortions and representations of at least one military commander, whose views were seriously infected by racism." In a later written opinion, Patel called the government's response to the *coram nobis* petition "tantamount to a confession of error," and she commented that "there is substantial support in the record that the government deliberately omitted relevant information and provided misleading information in papers before the court."

More than four decades after police arrested him on a San Leandro street, Fred Korematsu was vindicated. In 1942 it was love for a woman that had compelled him to stand up for his freedom. But forty years later, it was love for the Constitution that inspired him to ask for justice. It was late in coming. But it was satisfying.

EPILOGUE

> History teaches us that in times of war, we have often sacrificed fundamental freedoms unnecessarily. The executive and legislative branches, reflecting public opinion formed in the heat of the moment, frequently have overestimated the need to restrict civil liberties and failed to consider alternative ways to protect national security. The challenge is to identify excess when it occurs and to protect constitutional rights before they are compromised unnecessarily.

Fred Korematsu addressed these words to the U.S. Supreme Court. But not in 1943, when he defied the forced removal of Japanese Americans from the West Coast.

Korematsu made this statement in 2003, as part of a legal challenge to the Bush administration's "war on terror" policy of indefinitely detaining people without charges and without representation.

Korematsu's friend-of-the-court brief was filed in the cases of *Khaled Odah v. United States, Shafiq Rasul v. George W. Bush*, and *Yasir Hamdi v. Donald Rumsfeld*. One was on behalf of six hundred people from forty-four different countries who were being held at the U.S. prison in Guantanamo Bay, Cuba. The others were on behalf of two U.S. citizens whom the U.S. government had designated "enemy combatants." Each of the plaintiffs had been held without formal charges, without a fair hearing, without access to counsel, and without any meaningful judicial review.

Fred Korematsu's involvement invoked the warning that U.S. Supreme Court Justice Robert Jackson had made when he dissented in the 1944 *Korematsu* ruling: "The Court for all time has validated the principle of racial discrimination in criminal procedure and of transplanting American citizens. The principle lies about like a loaded weapon, ready for the hand of any authority that can bring forward a plausible

In 1998, half a century after the U.S. Supreme Court ruled against him, Fred Korematsu received the Presidential Medal of Freedom, one of the nation's highest civilian honors, from President Bill Clinton. In 2003 Korematsu submitted a brief in support of a challenge to the Bush administration's program of indefinitely detaining people without charges or representation.

claim of an urgent need."

* * *

On September 11, 2001, hijackers slammed planes into the World Trade Center, tumbling the massive structures and killing thousands. In the days, weeks, and months that followed, while the nation mourned, the Bush administration unleashed a "war on terror" that jeopardized the rights of tens of millions.

The loaded weapon had been fired.

Racial profiling, government spying, and the silencing of dissent took their toll on immigrant communities, libraries, and peace activists throughout California.

Before the dust cleared from the smoldering embers of the twin towers, the Bush administration requested and Congress passed a 342-page law entitled the "Uniting and Strengthening America by Providing Appropriate Tools Required to Intercept and Obstruct Terrorism Act," a long title fitting for an enormous sweep of legislation. Its acronym is easy to remember: The USA Patriot Act.

Representative Peter DeFazio described the precipitate activity on Capitol Hill on October 25, 2001: "The final version of the Patriot Act was rewritten between midnight and 8 o'clock in the morning behind closed doors by a few unknown people, and it was presented to Congress for a one-hour debate and an up-or-down vote."

The sweeping provisions included secret surveillance and searches (known as the "sneak and peek provision"), widespread access to personal records (including library, insurance, medical, and financial information), and the suspension of the rights of the accused, especially noncitizens who could be arrested and subject to deportation for belonging to or providing material support to any organization that the government deemed "terrorist."

Congress had rejected many of these same proposals in the months and years prior to 9/11, recognizing they violated the Constitution. But in the chilling atmosphere, lawmakers were eager to go along with the Bush administration.

Only one senator voted against this massive, dangerous bill—Russ Feingold. In casting his nay vote, the Wisconsin Democrat said, "Congress will fulfill its duty only when it protects both the American people and the freedoms at the foundation of American society. So let us preserve our heritage of basic rights. Let us practice as well as preach that liberty. And let us fight to maintain that freedom that we call America."

The Bush administration quickly stifled those who questioned the rush to revoke civil liberties in the name of national security. Speaking before the Senate Judiciary Committee, Attorney General John Ashcroft attacked those who raised concerns: "Your tactics only aid terrorists for they erode our national unity and diminish our resolve...[T]o those who scare peace-loving people with phantoms of lost liberty, my message is this: They give ammunition to America's enemies and pause to America's friends. They encourage people of good will to remain silent in the face of evil."

With rhetoric that succeeded during the Palmer Raids and the Red Scare of the previous century, the federal government again equated the right to dissent with supporting "the enemy," this time a vague, sprawling, boundaryless, timeless, and terrifying enemy: "terrorism."

Disappeared in the U.S.A.

Soon after the attack on the World Trade Center, the federal government arrested thousands of Arab, Middle Eastern, and South Asian men. Even the most diligent immigration and constitutional lawyers initially found it almost impossible to get information about the detainees. No one knew their names, their countries of origin, the charges against them, or even where they were being held. Only when their families contacted lawyers and civil liberties groups did knowledge about those detained come to light. The exact number of detainees is not known, although civil rights attorneys estimate that more than five thousand people were locked up.

None of them were found to have any connection to the 9/11 terrorist attacks.

The government followed the initial roundup a few months later with the National Security Entry/Exit Registration System (NSEERS), which required tens of thousands of men between the ages of sixteen and thirty-five who were in the United States on temporary visas from twenty-five countries—primarily Middle Eastern and South Asian nations—to register, and be fingerprinted and photographed

When the U.S. government demanded after 9/11 that tens of thousands of men from twenty-five countries register and be fingerprinted and photographed, many worried that they would be deported or sent to internment camps.

at INS offices. If they failed to show up, they were subject to criminal penalties and deportation.

Attorney Jayashri Srikantiah, director of the immigrants' rights clinic at Stanford University Law School, remembers "awful images of young men who had done nothing wrong lining up outside the INS offices to report." She represented two Pakistani teenagers who were attending school in the Silicon Valley town of Cupertino. The seventeen- and nineteen-year-old boys voluntarily registered in San Jose. The older brother was detained, arrested, and sent to the Yuba County jail for allegedly overstaying his visa by a matter of days. The younger brother was required to miss school every third Wednesday to re-register with the INS. The government told them they had fallen out of visa compliance. Eventually they were deported to Pakistan.

More than eighty-three thousand men and boys, predominantly Muslim and including students, businessmen, and visitors legally in the United States, registered with the INS.

Srikantiah accused the government of "targeting people based on religion, ethnicity and race, not individualized suspicion." This alienated the very communities that the government should have involved in its investigation. It was precisely because the government and police had not developed meaningful relations with California's Arab and Muslim communities that they had to resort to ethnic-based sweeps.

In the end, NSEERS resulted in deportation proceedings against 13,740 men nationwide, none of whom were charged with terrorism.

As part of the Bush administration's "war on terror," thousands of Arab, Middle Eastern, and South Asian men were arrested and detained. Many, like this Iranian in Sacramento, were kept behind bars for months without anyone knowing where they were or why they were being held.

Because the NSEERS program proved cumbersome, the government replaced it with a more targeted program of FBI interrogations, "Project Interview," which focused on Middle Eastern men, particularly Iraqis and Iranians, including U.S. citizens. One senior government official told the *New York Times* that this is "the largest and most aggressive program we've ever had."

The FBI descended on the Iranian community in southern California, home to the largest population of Iranians outside of Iran, "Little Kabul" in Fremont, and other immigrant communities. They conducted interrogations at FBI offices, workplaces, homes, and even local cafés, peppering selected residents with questions like: How often do you go to a mosque? When do you visit the Middle East? Do you know Saddam Hussein? Who did you vote for in the Iraq elections?

Once again, men were jailed and deported for minor immigration infractions—like overstaying a visa or neglecting to let the INS know about a change of address—that would have been ignored prior to 9/11. Like NSEERS, "Project Interview" uncovered no terrorists.

Muslim, Arab, South Asian, and Middle Eastern citizens and residents who saw their family members, neighbors, and friends whisked away by government agents, held in detention indefinitely, and subjected to secret hearings, harassment, violence, and deportation lived in constant fear and anxiety. "Some people in the community were afraid there was going to be internment," attorney Srikantiah recalled.

Although the programs never replicated the mass internment of Japanese Americans during World War II, California's Muslims had reasons to fear the government, even after the detention and deportation programs eased.

In October 2007, Michael Downing, commanding officer of the Los Angeles Police Department's Counter Terrorism/Criminal Intelligence Bureau, revealed in congressional testimony that the LAPD intended to create a database to map the city's Muslims in an effort to "identify and counter violent extremism."

The news sent shock waves through the community. Muslim leaders, along with civil liberties organizations, immediately sent a letter of protest to the LAPD. The mapping project unfairly targeted Muslims based on their religion and ethnicity, they wrote, and "increases the inaccurate perception among the larger community that Muslims are doing something suspicious that merits investigation."

The groups told the LAPD that religious profiling is as "unlawful, ill-advised and deeply offensive as racial profiling." Moreover, the mapping project engendered fear and distrust in the Muslim community, hampering—rather than enhancing—legitimate law enforcement efforts.

Only after the outcry did the department agree to drop the plan.

Trickle-Down Profiling

It was not only government profiling that Middle Easterners and South Asians had to face. The war on terror encouraged the "delegation of national security to private individuals," according to civil rights attorney Shirin Sinnar.

Arshad Chowdhury, a twenty-six-year old MBA student, experienced that firsthand. The Connecticut-born son of Bangladeshi immigrants, Chowdhury had worked directly across the street from the World Trade Center until April 2001. That alone made him more than willing to submit to multiple security checks at San Francisco International Airport in October 2001. But he was puzzled when, just as his flight to Detroit was about to leave, his name was announced over the loudspeaker.

In full view of more than two hundred passengers, Chowdhury was surrounded by four police officers, two FBI agents, and staff members of Northwest Airlines. As the minutes wore on, Chowdhury worried that he would miss his flight and asked the agents if he could go on another. One agent replied, "If we do find something, you're not going anywhere, buddy."

Chowdhury was finally cleared, but Northwest staff still would not let him board. Airline agents escorted him to a US Air flight.

In April 2002, the Council on American-Islamic Relations (CAIR) conducted a statewide poll among its California members in which 87 percent of respondents said they knew of a Muslim who had faced discrimination since 9/11. The same poll showed, however, that three-quarters of the Muslim respondents reported that they still felt welcome in California. Later that year, in a poll conducted by New California Media, a coalition of ethnic media outlets, 56 percent of Arab, Iranian, Pakistani, Asian-Indian, and Afghan California residents felt they had been victims of racial or ethnic discrimination following 9/11.

According to the Hate Crimes index compiled by the California Department of Justice, hate crimes against people of "other ethnicity or origin"—mostly anti-Arab acts—tripled between 2000 and 2001.

Contemporary Blacklists

Tom and Nanci Kubbany thought that Arcata, a friendly college town on the redwood coast near the Oregon border, would be a good place to raise their three children. In order to qualify for a mortgage, Tom worked two jobs. The couple saved as much as they could, rented a small place, paid off old debts, and found a friendly mortgage broker. But one day the broker stopped returning their calls. The Kubbanys had no idea why.

When they finally reached her, the mortgage broker reluctantly told them that they had been denied a loan because their credit report showed that Tom was on a government terrorist watch list. Tom and Nanci were incredulous. Tom was born and raised in Michigan and had no connection to any terrorist group. Dismayed, they contacted the Lawyers' Committee for Civil Rights (LCCR) in San Francisco.

An LCCR probe revealed that a finance officer thought she had found Tom's name on the "Specially Designated Nationals and Blocked Persons" list maintained by the Office of Foreign Assets Control (OFAC). Tom was not on the list, but his middle name, "Hassan," appeared there because it also happened to be an alias used by one of Saddam Hussein's sons, Ali Saddam Hussein Al-Tikriti. Tom had never been to Iraq, and was thirty years older than Saddam Hussein's son. Clearly, this was a mistake. The family was distraught. "It was surreal," Tom said. "It's like everything stopped. Like, wait a minute, this is silly, this is a joke, you know."

But the Kubbanys did not get the mortgage.

An investigation by the LCCR revealed that the OFAC list contained more than six thousand entries. The presence of common Muslim and Spanish names—"Abdul," "Ortega," "Hassan," and "Patel"—on the list made it inevitable that many people would be caught in its web. That most of these names are prevalent in already vulnerable immigrant communities increased the likelihood of discrimination, especially by untrained merchants, mortgage brokers, and bank tellers.

Another set of blacklists, maintained by the Transportation Security Administration (TSA), is commonly known as the "no-fly list." The TSA actually keeps two lists, one of individuals who are completely prohibited from flying, the other of passengers who are required to undergo additional searches and questioning before they are allowed on a plane.

The lists are like a "black box," explained immigration attorney Srikantiah. "The names and information came from many government agencies. It is still unclear how names got on the list." Even more chilling is the fact that there is "no mechanism to get your name off—or to even verify that it is on the list."

Two veteran California peace activists discovered that their names were on the list only when they tried to board a plane for Boston at the San Francisco airport in 2002. An airline agent detained them, saying that their names might be on a secret federal list. They were only allowed to fly after being questioned and cleared by San Francisco police officers. Their experience—and that of more than three hundred others at the San Francisco airport since 9/11—indicated that although the airlines had access to the list, passengers could not even verify whether their names were on it.

The "no-fly" and OFAC lists are just two of the blacklists that the government maintains at the Terrorist Screening Center, a clearinghouse for names of people who are on the multitude of government watch lists for terrorist activity. The lists are expansive and include the names of people who attend political demonstrations and religious services, and people whose names sound or are spelled like those of suspected terrorists.

Although the lists originated prior to 9/11, President Bush's Executive Order 13224, issued when he declared a "national emergency to deal with the terrorist threat," greatly expanded their scope and volume. By 2007 the combined watch lists of the Terrorist Screening Center were reported to include more than seven hundred and twenty thousand names—four times as many as three years earlier. The inspector general of the Justice Department reported that the Terrorist Screening Center had "significant weaknesses" that produce a high error rate and a slow response to complaints from citizens. Nonetheless, according to a 2007 investigative report in the *Washington Post*, twenty thousand new names were added each month.

Freedom-Fighting Librarians

The Patriot Act gave the FBI virtual carte blanche to search library and bookstore records and to determine the reading habits of millions of people, in violation of their First Amendment rights.

In 2003 Karen Schneider, chair of the Intellectual Freedom Committee of the California Library Association, explained that librarians were infuriated by the new surveillance. "It doesn't matter if it's one or ten thousand inquiries," she said of potential FBI demands. "Once you start down this slippery slope of gagging people and cloak-and-dagger secrecy you remove such an important check in the checks and balances of intellectual freedom versus national security that there's bound to be abuse."

California librarians came up with ingenious ways to protect the public's freedom to read.

In the Yolo County seat, Woodland, City Librarian Marie Bryan began ripping up records by hand rather than provide them to the government. Eventually, the Woodland library bought a new shredding machine.

In South Pasadena and Monterey Park, librarians posted notices reading, "Attention Library Patrons: The FBI has the right to obtain a court order to access any records we have of your transactions in the library, a right given to them in Section 215 of the USA Patriot Act."

A 2003 California Library Association survey showed that 78 percent of its members shredded documents; 73 percent deleted computer files and log-in data; and 41 percent, anxious to be ready before the FBI knocked on their library doors, changed policies concerning patron confidentiality and retention of records to ensure that their patrons' reading habits did not end up in a government dossier.

The Patriot Act subjects librarians to criminal prosecution if they even reveal they have been contacted by the FBI, but the dogged librarians figured out a way to get around that, too. Santa Cruz Library Director Anne Turner explained, "In my standard oral report to the board, I say we've not been contacted by the FBI in the last month. The month I don't say it the board will know I have been contacted, because, of course, I am not allowed to tell them."

"Libraries have always made it safe for people to look for information in a private way," said Berkeley Public Library Director Jackie Griffin. "There's a fundamental idea here that if you look at a site about terrorism or look at a site about how to make a bomb or you look at a site that's about any of these ideas, somehow that's bad in and of itself. People have the ability to look and to judge and to find out for themselves. Our best defense against terrorism is to have a well-informed public."

Even if Californians never enter a library, they are subjected to an even more widespread government spying program just by browsing the Internet on their home or office computers.

Big Brother's Listening

Mark Klein was a communications technician for AT&T for more than twenty-two years.

In 2002 the site manager at Klein's downtown San Francisco office told the computer expert to expect a National Security Agency (NSA) agent. When the agent arrived, Klein directed him to a room, where the agent interviewed a management-level technician. A few months later, Klein noticed a room being built next to the switch room where phone calls are routed. The manager who had been interviewed by the NSA was installing equipment. The regular technician was not allowed to enter the room.

Klein was instructed to install a special kind of routing equipment in the newly constructed room. Though he did not know it at the time, the same equipment was being installed at the behest of the NSA at phone company sites in Los Angeles, San Jose, and San Diego.

Klein decided to blow the whistle: "Based on my understanding of the connections and equipment at issue, it appears the NSA is capable of conducting what amounts to vacuum cleaner surveillance of all the data crossing the Internet—whether that be people's email, web surfing, or any other data," he later told a congressional investigative committee.

Klein's revelations were echoed in December 2005, when the *New York Times* revealed that the NSA had been conducting warrantless wiretapping of domestic phone calls and emails under its Terrorist Surveillance Program, with no judicial supervision or warrants. The NSA authorized intercepts based on a "reasonable basis to conclude" that one party was connected to "terrorists."

A few months later, in May 2006, *USA Today* reported that shortly after September 11, 2001, the giant telecommunications corporations AT&T and Verizon had provided the NSA with the personal calling patterns of millions of customers, including phone numbers called and the times and dates of the calls. This was done without their customers' knowledge or consent, in violation of both federal and state law. A source who, like most in the *USA Today* exposé spoke on the guarantee of anonymity, said the goal was to create a "database of every call ever made" within the country.

The Electronic Frontier Foundation and the ACLU filed lawsuits in state court in California on behalf of a wide cross-section of telephone users, including former Congressman Tom Campbell and nationally syndicated columnist Robert Scheer of the *San Francisco Chronicle*, against AT&T and Verizon for illegally handing over customer records to the spy agency.

Charging that the phone company giants violated the explicit privacy guarantee of the California constitution as well as the state Public Utilities Code, the suits sought a court order to stop the wholesale delivery of Californians' phone records to the government. The privacy provision of the California constitution was passed with the "precise purpose of prohibiting data sharing of this type," asserted ACLU attorney Ann Brick.

In July 2008, President Bush signed legislation granting retroactive immunity to telecommunications companies that had acted at the government's behest to supply private customer information. As it had with every other lawsuit attempting to block post-9/11 constitutional violations, the administration invoked "national security" to trump all legal arguments.

Crossing the Line: Rendition and Torture

In fall 2007, the U.S. Senate held hearings to confirm former Judge Michael Mukasey for the post of U.S. attorney general. Senators asked the nominee about waterboarding, an interrogation technique that simulates drowning.

Mukasey declined to say whether it was illegal.

Many listening to the hearings could not believe that Mukasey did not repudiate the practice, which has been considered a form of torture since the Spanish Inquisition.

Yet the nominee for the highest law enforcement office in the United States refused to say that this brutal practice should be prohibited. California Senator Dianne Feinstein, a leading Democrat and a member of the key Judiciary Committee vetting Mukasey, voted in favor of his nomination despite the fact that the War Crimes Act of 1996 made "cruel, inhuman and degrading treatment," even outside the U.S., a federal crime.

The Bush administration also ignored this law, when authorizing "extraordinary rendition," the practice of kidnapping people of any nationality anywhere in the world and secretly sending them to undisclosed locations where "harsh methods of interrogation" might include the searing of flesh and waterboarding.

A 2006 *New Yorker* article revealed that San Jose, California-based Jeppesen Dataplan Inc., a subsidiary of the Boeing Corporation that specializes in high-priced private flight services to exclusive clients, was aiding the government with extraordinary rendition.

A former Jeppesen employee disclosed that a company executive had stated at a private meeting, "We do all of the extraordinary rendition flights—you know, the torture flights. It certainly pays well. [The CIA] spare no expense. They have absolutely no worry about costs."

Since the war on terror began, the U.S. government has, through its extraordinary rendition program, transported at least one hundred and fifty foreign nationals to countries like Jordan, Egypt, Afghanistan, and Morocco, where, official State Department reports indicate, torture is "routine."

For at least seventy of these rendition flights, Jeppesen provided the aircraft, flight crews, logistical support route and weather planning, fueling, maintenance, customs clearance, and even ground transportation.

Jeppesen flew Binyam Mohamed, an Ethiopian, from Pakistan to Morocco. While in CIA custody, he was blindfolded, shackled, and strapped to a plane seat. He was detained in a secret location in Morocco for eighteen months, where interrogators routinely beat him unconscious, broke his bones, cut his genitals, and poured hot liquid into his open wounds.

In May 2007, the ACLU, representing Mohamed and two other victims of the extraordinary rendition flights, filed a lawsuit in U.S. district court in San Jose seeking to end the company's participation in the torture flights. Citing the Alien Tort Statute, the plaintiffs charged that Jeppesen's actions violated the United Nations Convention against Torture and Other Forms of Cruel, Inhuman or Degrading Treatment, which the U.S. ratified in 1992.

Claiming national security, the government sought to dismiss the case, and the court agreed. The ACLU appealed. Soon after taking office, President Barack Obama ordered all U.S. government entities to end the use of torture and ordered the closure of secret overseas prisons. However, officials in his Justice Department maintained the previous administration's "state secrets" position in the *Jeppesen* case.

In April 2009, President Obama declassified Bush administration memos that attempted to justify brutal CIA interrogation techniques including waterboarding, keeping suspects naked, awake for as long as eleven days, or in stress positions, and slamming them into walls.

That same month, human rights groups submitted a petition signed by a quarter-million people calling on Attorney General Eric Holder to appoint a special prosecutor to examine torture and other government abuses.

On April 28, 2009, a three-judge panel of the Ninth Circuit Court of Appeals unanimously reversed the lower court's *Jeppesen* ruling. "According to the government's theory, the judiciary should effectively cordon off all secret government actions from judicial scrutiny, immunizing the CIA and its partners from the demands and limits of the law," Judge Michael Hawkins stated, rejecting the government's arguments. Citing an earlier U.S. Supreme Court decision, he continued, "As founders of this nation knew well, arbitrary imprisonment and torture under any circumstances is a 'gross and notorious...act of despotism.'"

ACLU attorney Ben Wizner said the plaintiffs in the *Jeppesen* case may be "the first torture victims to really have their day in court."

At the Crossroads

More than half a century ago, muckraking journalist and historian Carey McWilliams observed:

As a people, we have never liked to ponder the meaning of shabby episodes in our nation's history during which a majority of Americans have, momentarily at least, forgotten the meaning of the Bill of Rights, knuckled under to the noisy tirades, and demonstrated a shocking opportunism. Once the disgraceful episodes have abated, it is most embarrassing to those whose silence or approval made them possible to be reminded of what happened; they avert their eyes from the sordid record and do not like to be told who did what, where and when.

Invariably, a conscious effort is made, usually furthered by the media, to make the episode appear less shameful than in fact it was, and, also to convince a later generation that it could not happen again.

What if, rather than whitewashing these "shabby episodes" of our history, we used them to guide us through contemporary troubles and challenges?

Common threads connect past outrages with those of today. When the federal government authorizes torture under the guise of "harsh interrogation techniques," it manifests the same contempt for the rule of law that allowed the vigilantes of Downieville to lynch a Mexican woman and the vigilantes of San Francisco to forcibly banish their political enemies. When the attorney general accuses civil libertarians of aiding terrorists, he displays the same disregard for dissent that was the foundation for the wholesale dismissal of government workers who refused to sign California's McCarthy-era loyalty oaths.

Muslim, Middle Eastern, and South Asian communities targeted for government surveillance and roundups in the wake of 9/11 responded by exercising their constitutional rights, like this woman at a San Jose peace rally.

When librarians resist FBI searches of their patrons' records, they fight the same suppression of knowledge and disrespect for the First Amendment as the publishers and booksellers who defended *The Grapes of Wrath* and *Howl*.

And the government's questioning, detention, and deportation of Muslims and

Arab Americans solely on the basis of their ethnic backgrounds and religious beliefs hauntingly echoes the incarceration of one hundred and twenty thousand Japanese Americans during World War II.

Our contemporary era may seem more dangerous, more ominous than past times of crisis when civil liberties were threatened.

And yet, even in these times—or especially in these times—it is vital to remember the lessons of history, from eras when Californians faced fearsome obstacles.

Many stood up for their rights and dignity during perilous times, risking loss of livelihood, social stigma, arrest, imprisonment, and even life itself.

When we witness prisoners at Guantanamo being denied access to courts, it is inspiring to recall nineteenth-century Chinese immigrants who were detained without charges on an island in the San Francisco Bay.

When Muslims, South Asians, and Middle Easterners are considered suspect just because of their ethnicity, we can take heart from the African American and Latino community leaders who denounced segregation and racial profiling.

For every determined striker, suffragist, or demonstrator, there were ten times as many "accidental fighters," who were caught up in the maelstrom of repression and fought back: Filipino and Latino farmworkers excluded from the protection of labor laws; Japanese American families incarcerated on a trumped-up charge of "military necessity"; lesbians and gay men denied marriage rights; people with disabilities shut out of classrooms and workplaces.

It is not easy to stand up against the politically powerful who demonize dissent and exploit the climate of fear. As in the past, dissent is equated with disloyalty. Immediately after the attacks on the World Trade Center, public opinion was overwhelmingly behind the government's severe national security measures. Only the most steadfast were willing to question the suppression, in the guise of national security, of civil liberties. But with little regard for the consequences to themselves, they did speak out.

The Japanese American Citizens' League (JACL) did not protest the incarceration of Japanese Americans during World War II and, in fact, encouraged Japanese Americans to cooperate. But on September 12, 2001, the JACL—the oldest Asian American civil rights organization in the country—issued a press release warning the government not to forfeit civil liberties in response to the terrorist attacks, and denouncing discrimination against Arab and Muslim Americans.

In the weeks and months following 9/11, the ACLU had a "Know Your Rights" brochure translated into Arabic, Urdu, Hindi, Farsi, Punjabi, and Somali and distributed more than twelve thousand multilingual copies to grocery stories in California that serve largely Arab, South Asian, Middle Eastern, and Muslim customers.

The California Library Association launched an advertising campaign to expose and oppose provisions of the Patriot Act that violate freedom of speech and press.

And, as in previous times of repression, new fighters stepped forward. At first they came largely from the targeted communities. The Council of American-Islamic Relations, the Asian American Bar Association, and the Muslim Lawyers Association brought together advocates who specialize in civil rights and immigration law to train Muslim community leaders about their legal rights in the face of rapidly changing federal laws and policies.

This resistance influenced public opinion, and support for vulnerable communities emerged from unexpected quarters. When the FBI launched "Project Interview," the interrogation program that focused on Middle Eastern, South Asian, and Muslim men, several northern California police departments—including those in San Francisco, San Jose, and Oakland, along with the San Mateo County Sheriffs Office—declined to participate, realizing that the program was causing anxiety and fear in the communities they were charged to protect.

When Attorney General John Ashcroft proposed deputizing local police to enforce immigration law, the California Police Chiefs Association protested, arguing that to be effective partners with their communities, they "must not be placed in the role of detaining people based on a change in their immigration status."

Gradually, public opinion shifted. A poll by the Public Policy Institute a year after 9/11 showed that there were more Californians (51 percent) concerned about restrictions on civil liberties than that the government would fail to enact strong anti-terrorism laws (41 percent).

Encouraged, activists organized up and down California, city by city, and convinced fifty-three local governments and eleven counties to pass resolutions opposing the Patriot Act.

On February 16, 2006, the California senate voted in favor of a resolution opposing key provisions of the Patriot Act. The resolution determined that "no state resources will be used to collect information based on residents' activities that are protected by the First Amendment, or to scoop up personal records without a direct connection between the records sought and suspected criminal activity." The resolution also stated that government security measures "should be carefully designed and employed to enhance public safety without infringing on the civil liberties and rights of innocent persons in the state of California and the nation."

In 2007 the San Jose Human Rights Commission passed a resolution condemning the involvement of one of that city's companies, Jeppesen, in the extraordinary rendition program.

But even with these developments, huge challenges remain.

In 2005 the ACLU surveyed 103 California police departments about their knowledge of restrictions on political surveillance delineated in a manual issued by the state attorney general's office. Of the 90 percent of departments that responded, not one had a policy or training manual that referenced the attorney general's guidelines. Only six departments had restrictions on surveillance. One department, Westminster, responded that it had never heard of the manual until it received the ACLU survey, and then the staff searched for it…on the Internet! The Torrance police department suggested that responding to the survey "could assist those who are considering or planning to engage in terrorist activities."

Organizations like the ACLU, the National Lawyers Guild, the Council on American-Islamic Relations, Veterans for Peace, the American Friends Service Committee, and even the environmental group Greenpeace find themselves on a national terrorism database, spied upon and infiltrated simply because they have stepped forward to defend civil rights and liberties. Private law firms that provided pro bono counsel to prisoners at Guantanamo were rebuked by a Justice Department official for "defending terrorists."

In the face of these challenges, organizing to defend civil liberties continues. As Dale Minami, lead counsel in the successful case to overturn Fred Korematsu's conviction, explained at a UC Berkeley symposium in 2003, building organizations that work for justice in the face of threats, blacklisting, and political smears is the best way to ensure civil rights and liberties.

As a new generation of fighters steps forward—immigrants, peace activists, student protestors, Gold Star Mothers, and Iraq Veterans against the War—we must ensure that their stories are told as well—to the public, to policy makers, and to future generations.

$$\bullet \quad \bullet \quad \bullet$$

Once a remote Spanish outpost, California is now one of the largest and most diverse of the United States. Since the gold rush, what has happened in California has rippled across the country.

As Judge Marilyn Hall Patel reminded us in 1984 when she took the courageous step of overturning Fred Korematsu's wartime conviction:

> Korematsu stands as a constant caution that in times of war or declared military necessity our institutions must be vigilant in protecting constitutional guarantees.

> It stands as a caution that in times of distress the shield of military necessity and national security must not be used to protect government actions from close scrutiny and accountability.

It stands as a caution that in times of international hostility and antagonisms, our institutions, legislative, executive and judicial, must be prepared to exercise their authority to protect all citizens from the petty fears and prejudices that are so easily aroused.

Her words are a beacon in the post-9/11 era, as are those of artist Anton Refregier, who painted California's history on the murals in San Francisco's Rincon Annex Post Office. He warned us not to "recreate history in a false image—where the pioneer dressed in Hollywood fashions, shaven and manicured, would be briskly walking along guided by a 'spirit' of one thing or another, its Grecian garments floating in the wind." Rather, he called on us to respect "the vitality, power and labor of those who came before us."

The history of those who shaped civil liberties in California—from the beginning of our state until today—must not be ignored or forgotten, if we are to ensure the rights of those who come after us.

SOURCES AND BIBLIOGRAPHY

Archival Sources

ACLU News (Newspaper of the ACLU of Northern California), 1936–present.
Open Forum (Newspaper of the ACLU of Southern California), 1924–present.
California Historical Society, San Francisco, CA: ACLU-NC; Women's Suffrage; Santa Rosa Outrage, 1935—news clippings, court papers, and letters from ACLU-NC files; Howl Trial, 1954—news clippings, court papers, notes and papers from ACLU-NC files; Japanese American incarceration.
California Loyalty Oath Digital Collection, Wendell M. Stanley papers. Bancroft Library, Univ. of California, Berkeley, bancroft. berkeley.edu/collections/loyaltyoath/index. html (Jan. 6, 2009).
California State Archives, Sacramento, CA: San Quentin and Folsom Prisons; Oral Histories (state legislators).
California State Library/History Room, Sacramento, CA.: Early California history.
Disability Rights Education and Defense Fund, Berkeley, CA: Integration of students with disabilities—news clippings.
Labor Archives and Research Center, San Francisco State University, San Francisco, CA: Women's Trade Unions; San Francisco General Strike.
National Archives and Records Administration, San Bruno, CA: Case file, Wong Kim Ark; Case file, *Archy Lee v. Stovall*; Case file, *James v. Marinship*; World War II, Commission on Fair Employment Practices; House Joint Resolution 2111 (removal of Refregier murals from Rincon Annex Post Office, hearing before the Subcommittee on Public Buildings and Grounds Committee on Public Works, House of Representatives. *Congressional Record*, May 1, 1953).
ONE Institute, Los Angeles, CA.
San Francisco Public Library/History Room, San Francisco, CA: Loyalty Oath; Hollywood Ten; House Un-American Activities Committee/San Francisco Hearing.
Southern California Library for Social Studies and Research, Los Angeles, CA: Black Panther Party.
UCLA, Los Angeles, CA: ACLU-SC Archives; Sleepy Lagoon Trial/Zoot Suit Riot; Chicano History.

Personal Archives:
Jo Anne Frankfurt: *Dr. Doe v. FBI* case files; clippings; trial notes and correspondence.
Aileen Hernandez: *The First Five Years: 1966–1971.* NOW: National Organization for Women, report by President Aileen Hernandez and the National Board of Directors.
Phiz Mezey: *The Repeal*, Newsletter of the Federation for Repeal of the Levering Act, San Francisco, CA.
Richard Orser: Letters; court documents, flyers, etc. Society for Humane Abortion newsletter, San Francisco, CA, 1967.
John True: *Pearl Meadow Mushroom Farms v. INS* trial notes and correspondence.
Frank Wilkinson: clippings, correspondence, flyers.

Interviews
(All interviews conducted by the authors, except where noted.)
Mary Lou Breslin, Senior Policy Advisor, Disability Rights Education and Defense Fund.
Ann Brick, staff attorney, ACLU-NC.
Ed Chen, U.S. District Court Magistrate Judge; former staff attorney, ACLU-NC.
Matt Coles, Director, National ACLU LGBT and AIDS Project; former staff attorney, ACLU-NC.
Kim Connor, disability rights activist.
Kitty Cone, disability rights activist.
Margaret Crosby, staff attorney, ACLU-NC.
Herb Donaldson, San Francisco Superior Court Judge.
Dorothy Ehrlich, Deputy Executive Director, National ACLU; former Executive Director, ACLU-NC.
Lawrence Ferlinghetti, poet, publisher, owner of City Lights Bookstore, San Francisco (interviewed by Elaine Elinson and Eric Fournier).
Ann Forfreedom, feminist writer and historian.
Dr. Marcia Gallo, historian and author.
Aileen Hernandez, labor leader, first woman member of the EEOC, former president of NOW.
Hiroshi Kashiwagi, poet, playwright, former internee at Tule Lake.
Herma Hill Kay, attorney, first woman dean of Boalt Hall Law School.
John Knox, former member of the California State Assembly.

Marshall Krause, former Legal Director, ACLU-NC.

Jeff Lanzman, historian, museum attendant, Colton Hall Museum, Monterey.

Herb Levine, Executive Director, Independent Living Resource Center, San Francisco.

Francisco Lobaco, Director, ACLU California Legislative Office.

Paul Longmore, disability rights activist, history professor, San Francisco State University.

Felicia Lowe, filmmaker; Angel Island Immigration Station Foundation.

Waverly Lowell, archivist, former Director of National Archives, Northern California Collection.

Jan Masaoka, granddaughter of plaintiff in challenge to the Alien Land Law.

Arlene Mayerson, Directing Attorney, Disability Rights Education and Defense Fund.

Phiz Mezey, photographer, former journalism professor, San Francisco State University.

Dale Minami, lead attorney, *Korematsu v. U.S.*

Susan Mizner, Director, Mayor's Office on Disability, San Francisco.

Mimi Okrand, widow of Fred Okrand, former Legal Director, ACLU-SC.

Richard Orser, abortion rights activist, defendant in *People v. Orser.*

Raul Ramirez, News and Public Affairs Director, KQED-FM; former reporter, *San Francisco Examiner* (interviewed by Elaine Elinson and Eric Fournier).

James Rawls, historian, author, professor, Diablo Valley College.

Betty Reid-Soskin, Park Ranger, World War II Home Front National Historic Park; Black Women Stirring the Waters.

Ramona Ripston, Executive Director, ACLU-SC.

Amitai Schwartz, appellate attorney.

Pat Shiu, attorney, Employment Law Center.

Gary Duane Sowards, death penalty attorney.

Ken Stein, Mayor's Office on Disability, San Francisco.

Edward Steinman, lead attorney, *Lau v. Nichols*; professor of law, University of Santa Clara Law School.

Dana Van Gorder, Executive Director, Project Inform; former aide to San Francisco Supervisor Harry Britt; Northern California No on 64 campaign coordinator.

Edgar Wakayama, son of Ernest Wakayama, who challenged WWII incarceration.

Ling-chi Wang, UC Berkeley emeritus professor of ethnic studies, community activist.

Kenneth Weatherbee, brother of Herbert Weatherbee, Jehovah's Witness during WWII (interviewed by James N. Pellechia and Jolene Chu).

Frank Wilkinson, Director Emeritus of National Coalition Against Repressive Legislation

(NCARL); founder and former Executive Director, the Committee to Abolish HUAC.

Judy Yung, author; Emerita Professor of American Studies, UC Santa Cruz.

Bibliography

Chapter One: Staking Our Claim

Beilharz, Edwin A., and Carlos U. López, eds. *We Were 49ers!: Chilean Accounts of the California Gold Rush.* Pasadena, CA: Ward Ritchie Press, 1976.

Blew, Robert W. "Vigilantism in Los Angeles, 1835–1874." *Southern California Quarterly* 54:1, 11–30.

Carranco, Lynwood. "Chinese Expulsion from Humboldt County." *Pacific Historical Review* 30:4, 329-340.

Coblentz, Stanton A. *Villains and Vigilantes: The Story of James King of William and Pioneer Justice in California.* New York: Wilson-Erickson, 1936.

Ellison, William Henry. *A Self-Governing Dominion: California, 1840–1860.* Berkeley: Univ. of California Press, 1950.

Fernandez, Ferdinand F. "Except a California Indian: A Study in Legal Discrimination." *Southern California Quarterly* 50 (June 1968), 161–175.

Fisher, James A. "The Struggle for Negro Testimony in California, 1851–1863." *Southern California Quarterly* 51 (1969), 313–324.

Gunther, Vanessa Ann. *Ambiguous Justice: Native Americans and the Law in Southern California, 1848–1890.* East Lansing: Michigan State Univ. Press, 2006.

Hagaman, Wallace R. *Chinese Temples of Nevada City and Grass Valley, California, 1868–1938.* Nevada City, CA: The Cowboy Press, 2003.

Heizer, Robert F., and Alan F. Almquist. *The Other Californians: Prejudice and Discrimination under Spain, Mexico, and the United States to 1920.* Berkeley: Univ. of California Press, 1971.

Hurtado, Albert L. *Indian Survival on the California Frontier.* New Haven, CT: Yale Univ. Press, 1988.

———. *Intimate Frontiers: Sex, Gender and Culture in Old California.* Albuquerque, Univ. of New Mexico Press, 1999.

Ignoffo, Mary Jo. *Gold Rush Politics: California's First Legislature.* Sacramento: California State Senate, and Cupertino: California History Center and Foundation, 1999.

Longstreet, Stephen. *The Wilder Shore: A Gala Social History of San Francisco's Sinners and Spenders, 1849–1906.* Garden City, NY:

Doubleday and Co., 1968.

Mullen, Kevin J. *Let Justice Be Done: Crime and Politics in Early San Francisco*. Reno: Univ. of Nevada Press, 1989.

O'Meara, James. *The Vigilance Committee of 1856 by a Pioneer California Journalist*. San Francisco: J. H. Barry, 1887.

Pfaelzer, Jean. *Driven Out: The Forgotten War against Chinese Americans*. New York: Random House, 2007.

Richards, Leonard L. *The California Gold Rush and the Coming of the Civil War*. New York: Alfred A. Knopf, 2007.

Secrest, William B. *Juanita: The Only Woman Lynched in the Gold Rush Days*. Fresno: Saga-West Publishing Co., 1967.

Senkewicz, Robert M., S.J. *Vigilantes in Gold Rush San Francisco*. Stanford: Stanford Univ. Press, 1985.

Stanley, Gerald. "Senator William Gwin: Moderate or Racist?" *California Historical Quarterly* 50:3.

Stevenson, Robert Louis. *The Old Pacific Capital—Monterey/The New Pacific Capital—San Francisco (1880–1883)*. Monterey: Old Monterey Preservation Society, 2005.

Swisher, Carl Brent. *Stephen J. Field: Craftsman of the Law*. Washington, DC: The Brookings Institution, 1930.

Williams, Mary Floyd. *History of the San Francisco Committee of Vigilance of 1851: A Study of Social Control on the California Frontier in the Days of the Gold Rush*. Berkeley: Univ. of California Press, 1921.

Court Cases

People v. Hall, 4 Cal. 399 (Cal. 1854).

Fong Yuen Ling, Sam Yuen, Yin Tuck and Ah Yung v. Mayor and Common Council of the City of Los Angeles, 47 Cal. 531 (1874).

Wing Hing v. City of Eureka, 1886.

Chapter Two: In a Strange Land

Anderson, Lydia. *Immigration*. New York: Franklin Watts, 1981.

Andreas, Peter. *Border Games: Policing the U.S.–Mexico Divide*. Ithaca: Cornell Univ. Press, 2000.

Anzaldua, Gloria. *Borderlands/La Frontera: The New Mestiza*. San Francisco, Aunt Lute Books, 1987.

Balderrama, Francisco E., and Raymond Rodriguez. *Decade of Betrayal: Mexican Repatriation in the 1930s*. Albuquerque: Univ. of New Mexico Press, 1995.

Biegel, Stuart. "Bilingual Education and Language Rights: The Parameters of the Bilingual Education Debate in California Twenty Years After *Lau v. Nichols*." *Chicano-Latino Law Review* 14 (Winter 1994), 48–60.

Bustamante, Jorge. "Characteristics of Migrants," "Some Thoughts on Perceptions and Policies," "Mexico–United States Labor Migration Flows." In *Migration between Mexico and the United States: A Binational Study*. Washington, DC: U.S. Commission on Immigration Reform, 1998, utexas.edu/lbj/uscir/binpap-v.html (Jan. 21, 2009).

Chan, Sucheng. "The Making of the Quintessential Scholar-Activist." *Amerasia Journal* 33:1, 121–137.

Chavez, Leo. R. *Covering Immigration: Popular Images and the Politics of the Nation*. Berkeley: Univ. of California Press, 2001.

Crawford, James. "The Campaign against Proposition 227: A Post Mortem." *Journal of Bilingual Education* 21:1.

Fung, Robert, ed. *Proceedings of the Conference on the 50th Anniversary of the 1943 Repeal of the Chinese Exclusion Acts*. San Francisco: Chinese Historical Society of America, 1993.

Galarza, Ernesto. *Merchants of Labor: The Mexican Bracero Story*. New York: McNally and Loftin, 1964.

García, Juan Ramon. *Operation Wetback: The Mass Deportation of Mexican Undocumented Workers in 1954*. Westport, CT: Greenwood Press, 1980.

Grebler, Leo, Joan W. Moore, and Ralph C. Guzman. *The Mexican-American People: The Nation's Second Largest Minority*. New York: The Free Press: 1970.

Guttentag, Lucas. *The Rights of Passage: Immigrants, Civil Liberties and Public Policy*. New York: American Civil Liberties Union, 1994.

Healy, Patrick J., and Ng Poon Chew. "A Statement for Non-exclusion." San Francisco: Chinese Historical Society of America, 1905.

Hess, Gary R. "The Forgotten Asian Americans: The East Indian Community in the United States." *Counterpoint: Perspectives on Asian America*, ed. Emma Gee. Los Angeles: Asian American Studies Center, UCLA, 1976, 413–422.

Hing, Bill Ong. "No Place for Angels: In Reaction to Kevin Johnson." *University of Illinois Law Review* 559, 2000.

Ichioka, Yuji. *The Issei: The World of the First Generation Japanese Immigrants, 1885–1924*. New York: The Free Press, 1988.

Koch, Wendy. "U.S. Urged to Apologize for 1930s Deportations." *USA Today*, April 5, 2006.

Lai, Him Mark, Genny Lim, and Judy Yung. *Island: Poetry and History of Chinese Immigrants on Angel Island 1910–1940*. Seattle: Univ. of Washington Press, 1991.

Light, Ken. *To the Promised Land.* New York: An Aperture Book (in association with the California Historical Society), 1988.

Locklear, William R. "The Celestials and the Angels: A Study of the Anti-Chinese Movement in Los Angeles to 1882." In *Anti-Chinese Violence in North America,* ed. Roger Daniels. New York: Arno Press, 1978.

Luzzaro, Susan. "If You Don't Run You Don't Get Hit," *San Diego Reader,* Feb. 22, 2001.

Martin, David A., and Peter H. Schuck, eds. *Immigration Stories.* New York: Foundation Press, 2005.

Martinez, Oscar J. *Border People: Life and Society in the U.S.–Mexico Borderlands.* Tucson: Univ. of Arizona Press, 1994.

McClain, Charles J. *In Search of Equality: The Chinese Struggle against Discrimination in Nineteenth-Century America.* Berkeley: Univ. of California Press, 1994.

——— and Laurene Wu McClain. "The Chinese Contribution to the Development of American Law." In *Entry Denied: Exclusion and the Chinese Community in America,* ed. Sucheng Chan. Philadelphia: Temple Univ. Press, 1991.

McPherson, Stephanie Sammartino. *Lau v. Nichols: Bilingual Education in Public Schools.* Berkeley Heights, NJ: Enslow Publishers, 2000.

McWilliams, Carey. *North from Mexico: The Spanish-Speaking People of the United States.* 1949. Reprint, New York: Greenwood Press, 1968.

Moquin, Wayne, and Charles Van Doren, eds. *A Documentary History of the Mexican Americans.* New York: Bantam Books, 1971.

Nevins, Joseph. *Operation Gatekeeper: The Rise of the "Illegal Alien" and the Making of the U.S.–Mexico Boundary.* New York: Routledge, 2002.

Ono, Kent A., and John M. Sloop. *Shifting Borders: Rhetoric, Immigration and California's Proposition 187.* Philadelphia: Temple Univ. Press, 2002.

Pfaelzer, Jean. *Driven Out: The Forgotten War against Chinese Americans.* New York: Random House, 2007.

Reel, James. "Men with Guns." *Sojourners,* July–August 2003.

Reimers, David M. *Still the Golden Door: The Third World Comes to America.* New York: Columbia Univ. Press, 1992.

Rodriguez, Rey M. "The Misplaced Application of English-Only Rules in the Workplace," *Chicano-Latino Law Review* 14:61.

Roy, Eric. "Righting an Old Wrong" *VOANews.com* September 29, 2003, alternet.org/story/16859.

Salyer, Lucy. *Laws Harsh as Tigers: Chinese Immigrants and the Shaping of Modern Immigration Law.* Chapel Hill: Univ. of North Carolina Press, 1995.

Sandmeyer, Elmer Clarence. *The Anti-Chinese Movement in California.* 1939. Reprint, Urbana: Univ. of Illinois Press, 1991.

Schlosser, Eric. "In the Strawberry Fields." *Atlantic Monthly* 276:5.

Shorris, Earl. "Raids, Racism and the INS: The Trial of La Migra." *The Nation,* May 8, 1989.

University of California, Los Angeles, Asian American Studies Center. *Letters in Exile: An Introductory Reader on the History of Pilipinos in America.* Los Angeles: UCLA Asian American Studies Center, 1976.

Urrea, Luis Alberto. *The Devil's Highway.* Boston: Back Bay Books, Little, Brown and Co., 2004.

Valenciana, Christine. "Unconstitutional Deportation of Mexican Americans during the 1930s: A Family History and Oral History." *Multicultural Education,* Spring 2006.

Yu, Connie Young. "The Chinese in American Courts." *Bulletin of Concerned Asian Scholars* 4:3 (special edition).

Film and Video

Carved in Silence. Produced and directed by Felicia Lowe. National Asian American Telecommunications Association, 1988.

The Chinatown Files. Produced by Amy Chen and Ying Chan. Second Decade Films, 2001.

Separate Lives/Broken Dreams. Produced by Jennie Lew and Yvonne Lew. Chinese American Citizens Alliance, 1993.

Court Cases and Documents

Ho Ah Kow v. Nunan, 12 Fed.Cas. 252 (No. 6546) (C.C.D. Cal. 1879).

Look Tin Sing v. United States, 21 F. 905 (C.C.D. Cal. 1884).

Yick Wo v. Hopkins, 118 U.S. 356 (1886).

Fong Yu Ting v. United States, 149 U.S. 698 (1893).

United States v. Wong Kim Ark, 169 U.S. 649 (1898).

Bracero Treaty: For the Temporary Migration of Mexican Agricultural Workers to the United States, effected August 4, 1942, 56 Stat. 1759 (1942), E.A.S. 278; as amended April 26, 1943, 57 Stat. 1152 (1943), E.A.S. 371 (1943).

Oyama v. California, 332 U.S. 633 (1948).

Haruye Masaoka v. People, 39 Cal. 2d 883 (1952).

Sei Fujii v. California, 38 Cal. 2d 718 (1952).

Poland v. California, *cert. denied,* 377 U.S. 939 (1964).

Castro v. California, 2 Cal. 3d 223 (Cal. 1970).

Lau v. Nichols, 414 U.S. 563 (1974).

Zamora-Baca v. UCSF, *EEOC* Charge No. 370-88-0851, June 28, 1988.

Asian American Business Group v. City of
Pomona, 716 F. Supp. 1328 (C.D. Cal. 1989).

Gutierrez v. Municipal Court, 838 F. 2d 1031
(9th Cir. 1988), *vacated as moot,* 490 U.S.
1016 (1989).

Pearl Meadows Mushroom Farm v. Nelson, 723 F.
Supp. 432 (N.D. Cal. 1989).

Gregorio T. v. Wilson, 59 F. 3d 1002 (9th Cir.
1995).

Pedro A. v. Dawson, Case No. 965089 (Cal. Super.
Ct., San Francisco City & County, filed
Nov. 9. 1994), *appeal dismissed by* Pedro A. v.
Dawson, Case No. A094151 (Cal. 1st Dist.
Ct. App., dismissed Oct. 3. 2001).

Cruz v. United States, 219 F. Supp. 2d 1027 (N.D.
Cal. 2002).

Valeria G. v. Wilson, 12 F. Supp. 2d 1007 (N.D.
Cal. 1998), *aff'd* 307 F. 3d 1036 (9th Cir.
2002).

Victor Nicholás Sanchez et al. v. United States
("Operation Gatekeeper"), Petition 65/99,
Inter-Am. C.H.R., Report No. 104/105,
OEA/Ser.L/V/II.124, doc. 5 (2005).

Chapter Three: An Injury to All

Beesley, David. "Communists and Vigilantes in
the Northern Mines." *California History* 64:2.

Bulosan, Carlos. *America Is in the Heart.* 1946.
Reprint, Seattle: Univ. of Washington Press,
1973.

Chatfield, LeRoy, comp. *Cesar Chavez: The
Farmworker Movement 1962–1993.*
Sacramento: Si Se Puede Press, 2005, at www.
farmworkermovement.org (Jan. 21, 2009).

Clark, Thomas Ralph. *Defending Rights: Law,
Labor Politics and the State in California,
1890–1925.* Detroit: Wayne State Univ. Press,
2002.

Daniel, Cletus. *Bitter Harvest: A History of
California Farmworkers, 1870–1941.*
Berkeley: Univ. of California Press, 1981.

———. "In Defense of the Wheatland Wobblies."
Labor History 19:4.

Delaney, Ed, and M. T. Rice. *The Bloodstained
Trail: A History of Militant Labor in the United
States.* Seattle: The Industrial Worker, 1927.

Frost, Richard H. *The Mooney Case.* Stanford:
Stanford Univ. Press, 1968.

Genini, Ronald. "Industrial Workers of the
World and Their Fresno Free Speech Fight,
1910–1911." *California Historical Quarterly*
53 (Summer 1974), 101–114.

Graham, Frank P., and A. Philip Randolph,
eds. *Farm Labor Organizing, 1905–1967: A
Brief History.* New York: National Advisory
Committee on Farm Labor, 1967.

Gray, James. "The American Civil Liberties
Union of Southern California and Imperial

Valley Agricultural Labor Disturbances,
1930, 1934." Dissertation, UCLA, 1966.

Issel, William, and Robert W. Cherny. *San
Francisco, 1865–1932: Politics, Power, and
Urban Development.* Berkeley: Univ. of
California Press, 1986.

Kushner, Sam. *Long Road to Delano.* New York:
International Publishers, 1975.

LeWarne, Charles. "On the Wobbly Train to
Fresno." *Labor History* 14:2, 264–289.

Matthiessen, Peter. *Sal Si Puedes: Cesar Chavez and
the New American Revolution.* New York: Dell
Publishing, 1973.

McWilliams, Carey. *Factories in the Field: The Story
of Migratory Farm Labor in California.* 1939.
Reprint, Boston: Little, Brown, 1971.

———. *Fool's Paradise: A Carey McWilliams
Reader,* ed. Dean Stewart and Jeannine
Gendar. Berkeley: Heyday Books, 2001.

Meynell, Richard B. "Little Brown Brothers, Little
White Girls: The Anti-Filipino Hysteria of
1930 and the Watsonville Riots." *Passports*
22, 1998.

Miller, Grace L. "The I.W.W. Free Speech Fight:
San Diego, 1912." *Southern California
Quarterly* 54:3, 211–238.

Quin, Mike. *The Big Strike.* 1949. Reprint, New
York: International Publishers, 1979.

Schwartz, Harvey, ed. *Harry Bridges: An Oral
History of the Origins of the ILWU and
the 1934 General Strike, A Centennial
Retrospective.* San Pedro: Harry Bridges
Institute, 2001.

Seldes, George. *Freedom of the Press.* New York:
Bobbs-Merrill, 1935.

Selvin, David. *A Place in the Sun: A History of
California Labor.* San Francisco: Boyd and
Fraser Publishing, 1981.

———. *Sky Full of Storm: A Brief History of
California Labor.* San Francisco, California
Historical Society, 1975.

———. *A Terrible Anger: The 1934 Waterfront and
General Strikes in California.* Detroit: Wayne
State Univ. Press, 1996.

Shanks, Rosalie. "The I.W.W. Free Speech
Movement, San Diego 1912." *Journal of San
Diego History* 19:1.

Starr, Kevin. *Endangered Dreams: The Great
Depression in California.* New York: Oxford
Univ. Press, 1996.

Trumbo, Dalton. *Harry Bridges: A Discussion of the
Latest Effort to Deport Civil Liberties and the
Rights of American Labor.* New York: League of
American Writers, 1941.

Villalobos, Charlotte Benz. "Civil Liberties in
San Diego: The Free Speech Fight of 1912."
Master's Thesis, San Diego State College, 1966.

Weintraub, Hyman. "The I.W.W. in California,
1905–1931." Master's Thesis, UCLA, 1947.

Wellman, David. *The Union Makes Us Strong: Radical Unionism on the San Francisco Waterfront.* Cambridge: Cambridge Univ. Press, 1997.

Winter, Ella. "More Trouble in Salinas." *New Republic* 80 (1934).

Wollenberg, Charles. *Marinship at War: Shipbuilding and Social Change in Wartime Sausalito.* Berkeley: Western Heritage Press, 1990.

———, ed. *Photographing the Second Gold Rush: Dorothea Lange and the Bay Area at War, 1941–1945.* Berkeley: Heyday Books, 1995.

Film and Video

Golden Lands, Working Hands. Written and directed by Fred Glass. San Francisco: California Federation of Teachers, 1999.

Harry Bridges: A Man and His Union. Directed by Berry Minott, narrated by Studs Terkel. San Francisco: MW Productions, 1992.

Audio

The ILWU and the San Francisco General Strike. Produced by Danny Beagle and Robert Gabriner. Berkeley: KPFA Radio, 1974.

Court Cases

In re May Thomas, 10 Cal.App. 375 (1909).

In re Application of Mooney, 10 Cal. 2d 1, 10-15 1937, and People v. Billings, 34 Cal.App. 549 (1917).

James v. Marinship Corp., 25 Cal. 2d 721 (1944).

Bridges v. United States, 346 U.S. 209 (1953).

Chapter Four: Under Color of Law

Aguirre, Frederick. "*Mendez v. Westminster School District*: How It Affected *Brown v. Board of Education.*" *Journal of Hispanic Higher Education* 4, Oct. 2005.

Alexander, Michelle, and Elaine Elinson. *Driving While Black or Brown: The California DWB Report.* San Francisco: American Civil Liberties Union of Northern California, 2001.

Allen, Robert. *The Port Chicago Mutiny: The Story of the Largest Mass Mutiny Trial in U.S. History.* Berkeley: Heyday Books, 2006.

Almaguer, Tomás. *Racial Fault Lines: The Historical Origins of White Supremacy in California.* Berkeley: Univ. of California Press, 1994.

Arriola, Christopher. "Knocking on the Schoolhouse Door: *Mendez v. Westminster*, Equal Protection, Public Education, and Mexican Americans in the 1940s." *La Raza Law Journal* 8:2, 166+.

Ball, Howard. *The Bakke Case: Race, Education and Affirmative Action.* Lawrence, KS: Univ. Press of Kansas, 2000.

Beasley, Delilah L. *The Negro Trailblazers of California.* 1919. Reprint, San Francisco: R and E Research Associates, 1970.

Bragg, Susan. "Knowledge Is Power: Sacramento Blacks and the Public Schools, 1885–1860." *California History* 75:3, 214–221.

Branch, Taylor. *At Canaan's Edge: America in the King Years, 1965–68.* New York: Simon and Schuster, 2006.

Bunch, Lonnie G. III. "A Past Not Necessarily Prologue: The African American in Los Angeles." In *20th Century Los Angeles: Power, Promotion, and Social Conflict,* ed. Norman M. Klein and Martin J. Schiesl. Claremont: Regina Books, 1990.

Chandler, Robert J. "Friends in Time of Need: Republicans and Black Civil Rights in California during the Civil War Era." *Arizona and the West* 24:4, 319–340.

de Graaf, Lawrence. "The City of Black Angels: Emergence of the Los Angeles Ghetto, 1890–1930." *Pacific Historical Review* 39:3, 323–352.

———, Kevin Mulroy, and Quintard Taylor, eds. *Seeking El Dorado: African Americans in California.* Los Angeles: Autry Museum of Western Heritage in association with Univ. of Washington Press, 2001.

DeWitt, Howard. "The Watsonville Anti-Filipino Riot of 1930: A Case Study of the Great Depression and Ethnic Conflict in California." *Southern California Quarterly* 61, Fall 1979, 281–302.

Ettinger, David S. "The Quest to Desegregate Los Angeles Schools." *Los Angeles Lawyer*, March 2003, 55+.

Fleming, Maria. "A Tale of Two Schools," In *A Place at the Table: Struggles for Equality in America,* ed. Maria Fleming. New York: Oxford Univ. Press in association with Southern Poverty Law Center, 2001.

Fortunate Eagle, Adam. *Alcatraz! Alcatraz!: The Indian Occupation of 1969–1971.* Berkeley: Heyday Books, 1992.

Franklin, William E. "The Archy Case: The California Supreme Court Refuses to Free a Slave." *Pacific Historical Review* 32, May 1963, 137–154.

Gonzales, Juan. *Harvest of Empire: A History of Latinos in America.* New York: Viking, 2000.

Hayden, Dolores. "Biddy Mason's Los Angeles, 1856–1891." *California History* 68:3, 86–99.

Heizer, Robert F., and Alan F. Almquist. *The Other Californians: Prejudice and Discrimination under Spain, Mexico and the United States to 1920.* Berkeley: Univ. of California Press, 1971.

Hudson, Lynn M. *The Making of "Mammy Pleasant": A Black Entrepreneur in Nineteenth-Century San Francisco.* Urbana: Univ. of Illinois Press, 2003.

Johnson, Jason. "Slavery in Gold Rush Days: New Discoveries Prompt Exhibit..." *San Francisco Chronicle,* Jan. 27, 2007.

Johnson, Troy R. *We Hold the Rock: The Indian Occupation of Alcatraz, 1969 to 1971.* San Francisco: Golden Gate National Parks Association, 1997.

Lapp, Rudolph M. *Archy Lee.* Berkeley: Heyday Books, 2008.

———. *Blacks in Gold Rush California.* New Haven: Yale Univ. Press, 1977.

———. "Negro Rights Activities in Gold Rush California." *California Historical Society Quarterly,* March 1966.

Lopez, Ian Haney. *Racism on Trial: The Chicano Fight for Justice.* Cambridge, MA: Belknap Press of Harvard Univ. Press, 2003.

Magagnini, Stephen. "Fortune Smiled on Many Black Miners." *Sacramento Bee,* Jan. 18, 1998.

Malcomson, Scott. L. *One Drop of Blood: The American Misadventure of Race.* New York: Farrar, Straus and Giroux, 2000.

McWilliams, Carey. "The Evolution of Sugar Hill." *Script* March 1949: 24+.

———. *North from Mexico: The Spanish-Speaking Peoples of the United States.* 1949. Reprint, New York: Greenwood Press, 1968.

Melendy, Brett H. "California's Discrimination against Filipinos, 1927–1935." In *Racism in California: A Reader in the History of Oppression,* ed. Roger Daniels and Spencer C. Olin Jr. New York: The Macmillan Co., 1972.

Meyer, Stephen Grant. *As Long as They Don't Move Next Door: Segregation and Racial Conflict in American Neighborhoods.* Lanham, MD: Rowman and Littlefield, 2000.

Moisa, Ray. "The BIA Relocation Program: Some Personal Recollections." *News from Native California* 2:2, 8–11

Muñoz, Carlos Jr. *Youth, Identity, Power: The Chicano Movement.* New York: Verso, 1989.

Ogletree, Charles, J. *All Deliberate Speed: Reflections on the First Half Century of Brown v. Board of Education.* New York: W.W. Norton and Co., 2004.

Osumi, Megumi Dick. "Asians and California's Anti-Miscegenation Laws." In *Asian and Pacific American Experiences: Women's Perspectives,* ed. Nobuya Tsuchida. Minneapolis: Asian/Pacific American Learning Resource Center and General College, Univ. of Minnesota, 1982.

Pfeifer, Michael J., "Race and Lynching in the American West in the Early Twentieth Century," presented at the British Association of American Studies meeting at Keele University, Staffordshire, UK, April 7, 2001, academic.evergreen.edu/p/pfeiferm/home.htm (Jan. 06, 2009).

Pilling, George. "The Wysingers of Visalia: Visalian Changed Education in California." *Valley Voice,* Oct. 5, 2005.

Robinson, Toni, and Greg Robinson. "*Mendez v. Westminster:* Asian-Latino Coalition Triumphant?" *Asian Law Journal,* 2003, 101–123.

Rosales, Arturo F. *Chicano! The History of the Mexican American Civil Rights Movement.* Houston: Arte Publico Press, 1996.

Ruiz, Vicki L. "'We Always Tell Our Children They Are Americans': *Mendez v. Westminster* and the California Road to *Brown v. Board of Education.*" *College Board Review,* Fall 2003, 21–27.

Rustin, Bayard. *Down the Line: The Collected Writings of Bayard Rustin.* Chicago: Quadrangle Books, 1971.

Schwartz, Bernard. *Behind Bakke: Affirmative Action and the Supreme Court.* New York: New York Univ. Press, 1988.

Seligson, Tom. "Isn't It Time to Right the Wrong?" *Parade Magazine,* Feb. 6, 2005.

Showalter, Michael P. "The Watsonville Anti-Filipino Riot of 1930: A Reconsideration of Fermin Tobera's Murder." *Southern California Quarterly* 71 (Winter 1989), 341–348.

Steinberg, Stephen. *Turning Back: The Retreat from Racial Justice in American Thought and Policy.* Boston: Beacon Press, 1995.

Takaki, Ronald. *A Different Mirror: A History of Multicultural America.* Boston: Little, Brown and Co., 1993.

Terkel, Studs. *The Good War: An Oral History of World War Two.* New York: Pantheon Books, 1984 (includes an eyewitness account of the Port Chicago explosion and trial by African American sailor Joseph Small).

Volpp, Leti. "American Mestizo: Filipinos and Antimiscegenation Laws in California." *U.C. Davis Law Review* 33:4.

———. "Divesting Citizenship: On Asian American History and the Loss of Citizenship through Marriage." *UCLA Law Review* 53:2.

Wallovits, Sonia Emily. *Filipinos in California.* Los Angeles: Univ. of Southern California, 1966.

Welke, Barbara Y. "Rights of Passage: Gender-Rights Consciousness and the Quest for Freedom, San Francisco, California, 1850–1870," in *African American Women Confront the West, 1600–2000,* ed. Quintard Taylor and Shirley Ann Wilson Moore. Norman: Univ. of Oklahoma Press, 2003.

Wheeler, B. Gordon. *Black California: The History of African-Americans in the Golden State.* New York: Hippocrene Books, 1993.

Williams, Jean Kinney. *Bridget "Biddy" Mason" from Slave to Businesswoman.* Minneapolis: Compass Point Books, 2006.

Wollenberg, Charles. *All Deliberate Speed: Segregation and Exclusion in California Schools, 1855–1975.* Berkeley: Univ. of California Press, 1976.

———. "Ethnic Experiences in California History: An Impressionistic Survey." *California Historical Quarterly* 50:3.

Film and Video

Alcatraz Is Not an Island. Executive Producer: Millie Ketcheshawno (Myskoke); Director: James M. Fortier (Métis-Ojibway). Diamond Island Productions, 2001.

Mendez v. Westminster: For All the Children/Para Todos los Niños. Produced by Sandra Robbie. KOCE Foundation, 2002.

Court Cases

Charlotte Brown cases (Cal. 12th Jud. Dist., San Francisco City & County): The Hall of Justice and City Hall were destroyed in the earthquake and fire of 1906 and Superior Court records were almost completely lost. Case numbering was restarted at 1 after the 1906 disaster.

Ex parte Archy, 9 Cal. 147 (1858).

Pleasants [sic] v. North Beach and Mission Railroad Company, 34 Cal. 586 (1868).

Ward v. Flood, 48 Cal. 36 (1874).

Tape v. Hurley, 66 Cal. 473 (1885).

Wysinger v. Crookshank, 82 Cal. 588 (1890).

Alice Piper et al. v. Big Pine School Dist. of Inyo County, 193 Cal. 664 (1924).

Mendez v. Westminster, 64 F. Supp. 544 (S.D. Cal. 1946), aff'd, 161 F. 2d 774 (9th Cir. 1947).

Davis v. Carter, 31 Cal. 2d 870 (1948).

Perez v. Sharp, 32 Cal. 2d 711 (1948).

Shelley v. Kramer, 334 U.S. 1 (1948).

Burks v. Poppy Construction Co., 57 Cal. 2d 463 (1962).

Jackson v. Pasadena City School Dist., 59 Cal. 2d 876 (1963).

Prendergast v. Snyder, 64 Cal. 2d 877 (1966).

Reitman v. Mulkey, 387 U.S. 369 (1967).

Regents of University of California v. Bakke, 438 U.S. 265 (1978).

Crawford v. Board of Education, 458 U.S. 527 (1982).

Coalition for Economic Equity v. Wilson, 122 F. 3d 692 (9th Cir. 1997).

L. Tarango Trucking et al. v. Contra Costa County et al., Case No. 3:98-cv-02955-WHO (N.D.

Cal. filed Jul. 29, 1998).

Williams v. California, Case No. 312236 (Cal. Super. Ct., San Francisco City & County, filed May 17, 2000) (Settlement December 2004).

Chapter Five: Holding up Half the Sky

Asbury, Herbert. *The Barbary Coast: An Informal History of the San Francisco Underworld.* New York: Thunder's Mouth Press, 1933.

Beasley, Delilah L. *The Negro Trailblazers of California.* 1919. Reprint, San Francisco: R and E Research Associates, 1970.

Beebe, Rose Marie, and Robert M. Senkewicz, eds. *Testimonios: Early California through the Eyes of Women, 1815–1848.* Berkeley: Heyday Books and The Bancroft Library, 2006.

Cary, Eve, and Kathleen Willert Peratis. *Woman and the Law.* New York: National Textbook Co., 1977.

Colman, Penny. *Rosie the Riveter: Women Working on the Home Front in World War II.* New York: Crown Publishers, 1995.

Cooney, Robert P. J. *Winning the Vote: The Triumph of the American Woman Suffrage Movement.* Santa Cruz: American Graphic Press, 2005.

Craig, Mary Lynde. "Is Legislation Needed for Women?" Presentation to the Woman's Parliament of Southern California, Los Angeles, Oct. 11, 1903. Women's Legal History Project, Stanford Law School.

Cushman, Clare, ed. *Supreme Court Decisions and Women's Rights: Milestones to Equality.* Washington, DC: Congressional Quarterly Press, The Supreme Court Historical Society, 2001.

Davis, Reda. *California Women: A Guide to Their Politics, 1885–1911.* San Francisco: California Scene, 1967.

Egelko, Bob. "And *Privacy.*" *California Lawyer,* Aug. 2008.

———. "California's Secret ERA." Unpublished article, 1983.

Egli, Ida Rae, ed. *No Rooms of Their Own: Women Writers of Early California.* Berkeley: Heyday Books, 1992.

Englander, Susan. *Class Conflict and Coalition in the California Women's Suffrage Movement, 1907–1912: The San Francisco Wage Earners' Suffrage League.* Lewiston, NY: Mellen Research Univ. Press, 1992.

Francis, Roberta W. "Reconstituting the Equal Rights Amendment: Policy Implications for Sex Discrimination." Special Session on Women and Politics, American Political Science Association Conference, San Francisco, Aug. 29, 2001.

Gluck, Sherna, ed. *From Parlor to Prison: Five*

American Suffragists Talk about Their Lives.
New York: Octagon Press, 1976.

Gray, Dorothy. *Women of the West.* Millbrae, CA: Les Femmes, 1976.

Gullett, Gayle. *Becoming Citizens: The Emergence and Development of the California Women's Movement, 1880–1911.* Urbana: Univ. of Illinois Press, 2000.

Hernandez, Aileen C. "E.E.O.C. and the Women's Movement (1965–1975)." Written for a Symposium on the Tenth Anniversary of the United States Equal Employment Opportunity Commission, Rutgers Univ. Law School, Nov. 1975.

———. Speech to National Organization for Women, September 1977.

———, and Letitia P. Sommers. *The First Five Years.* Chicago: National Organization for Women, 1971.

Hirata, Lucie Cheng. "Free, Indentured, Enslaved: Chinese Prostitutes in Nineteenth Century America." *Signs: Journal of Women on Culture and Society* 5:1, 3–29.

Hurtado, Albert L. *Intimate Frontiers: Sex, Gender and Culture in Old California.* Albuquerque: Univ. of New Mexico Press, 1999.

Kay, Herma Hill. "From the Second Sex to the Joint Venture: An Overview of Women's Rights and Family Law in the United States during the Twentieth Century." *California Law Review* 88:6.

———, and Martha West. *Text, Cases and Materials on Sex-Based Discrimination.* Egan, MN: Thomson West, 2006.

Lewin, Tamar. "Battery Producer Loses a Bias Case." *New York Times,* March 3, 1990.

London, Jack. "South of the Slot." *Saturday Evening Post* 181, May 1909.

Moore, Shirley Anne Wilson. *To Place Our Deeds: The African American Community in Richmond, California, 1910–1963.* Berkeley: Univ. of California Press, 2000.

Pinzler, Isabel Katz. *With Liberty and Justice for Women: The ACLU's Contributions to Ten Years of Struggle for Equal Rights.* New York: American Civil Liberties Union, 1982.

Rosen, Ruth. *The World Split Open: How the Modern Women's Movement Changed America.* New York: Viking, 2000.

Royce, Sarah. *A Frontier Lady: Recollections of the Gold Rush and Early California.* Lincoln: Univ. of Nebraska Press, 1977.

Sargent, Shirley. *Solomons of the Sierras: The Pioneer of the John Muir Trail.* Yosemite: Flying Spur Press, 1989.

Seagraves, Anne. *Soiled Doves: Prostitution in the Early West.* Hayden, ID: Wesanne Publications, 1994.

Silver, Mae, and Sue Cazaly. *The Sixth Star: Images and Memorabilia of California Women's Political History, 1868–1915.* San Francisco: Ord Street Press, 2000.

Solomons, Selina. *How We Won the Vote in California: A True Story of the Campaign of 1911.* San Francisco: The New Woman Publishing Co., 1912.

Sproul, Kate. *Women and Equality: A California Review of Women's Equity Issues in Civil Rights, Education and the Workplace.* Sacramento: California Senate Office of Research, 1999.

Yellin, Emily. *Our Mothers' War: American Women at Home and at the Front during World War II.* New York: Free Press, 2004.

———. "Rosie: A Legend on the Home Front," *Common Ground,* Fall 2007.

Yung, Judy. *Unbound Feet: A Social History of Chinese Women in San Francisco.* Berkeley: Univ. of California Press, 1995.

———. *Unbound Voices: A Documentary History of Chinese Women in San Francisco.* Berkeley: Univ. of California Press. 1999.

Film and Video
Of Lost Conversations and Untold Stories. Produced by Betty Reid-Soskin. Richmond, California: National Park Service, 2007.

Court Cases
In re Maguire, 57 Cal. 604 (1881).
People v. Belous, 71 Cal. 2d 954 (1969).
Ballard v. Anderson, 4 Cal. 3d 873 (1971).
Sail'er Inn v. Kirby, 5 Cal. 3d 1 (1971).
People v. Barksdale, 8 Cal. 3d 320 (1972).
People v. Orser, 31 Cal.App. 3d 528 (1973).
Geduldig v. Aiello, 417 U.S. 484 (1974).
Committee to Defend Reproductive Rights v. Meyers, 29 Cal. 3d 252 (1981).
California Federal Savings and Loan Association v. Guerra, 479 U.S. 272 (1987).
Johnson Controls, Inc. v. California Fair Employment & Hous. Comm'n, 218 Cal. App. 3d 517 (1990).
United Auto Workers v. Johnson Controls, Inc., 499 U.S. 187 (1991).
Am. Acad. of Pediatrics v. Lungren, 16 Cal. 4th 307 (1997).

Chapter Six: The Right Not to Remain Silent
Barrett, Edward L. *The Tenney Committee: Legislative Investigation of Subversive Activities in California.* Ithaca, NY: Cornell Univ. Press, 1951.

Basinger, Jeanine. *American Cinema: One Hundred Years of Filmmaking.* New York: Rizzoli, 1994.

Bessie, Alvah. *Inquisition in Eden.* New York: MacMillan, 1965.

Bloom, Hannah. "The Passing of 'Red' Hynes." *The Nation*, Aug. 2, 1952, 91–92.

Buhle, Mari Jo, Paul Buhle, and Dan Georgakas, eds. *Encyclopedia of the American Left.* Urbana: Univ. of Illinois Press, 1992.

Caughey, John. "Farewell to California's 'Loyalty' Oath." In *Los Angeles: Biography of a City*, ed. John Caughey and LaRee Caughey. Berkeley: Univ. of California Press, 1976.

Cole, Lester. *Hollywood Red: The Autobiography of Lester Cole.* Palo Alto, CA: Ramparts Press, 1981.

Donner, Frank J. *Protectors of Privilege: Red Squads and Police Repression in Urban America.* Berkeley: Univ. of California Press, 1990.

Gardner, David P. *The California Oath Controversy.* Berkeley: Univ. of California Press, 1967.

Goines, David Lance. *The Free Speech Movement: Coming of Age in the 1960s.* Berkeley: Ten Speed Press, 1993.

Goldman, Emma. *Living My Life.* 1939. Reprint, New York: Penguin Books, 2006.

Hellman, Lillian. *Scoundrel Time.* New York: Bantam Books, 1977.

Henstell, Bruce. *Sunshine and Wealth: Los Angeles in the Twenties and Thirties.* San Francisco: Chronicle Books, 1984.

LaVally, Rebecca. *200 Significant Statutes and Constitutional Amendments of the 20th Century.* Sacramento: California Senate Office of Research, 1999.

Murphy, Kim. "Surveillance Case Sheds Light on McCarthy Era." *Los Angeles Times*, Oct. 18, 1987.

Olsen, Jack. *Last Man Standing: The Tragedy and Triumph of Geronimo Pratt.* New York: Doubleday, 2000.

Paddison, Joshua. "Summers of Worry, Summers of Defiance: San Franciscans for Academic Freedom and Education and the Bay Area Opposition to HUAC, 1959–1960. *California History*, Fall 1999, 188–201.

Pomerantz, Charlotte, ed. *A Quarter-Century of Un-Americana, 1938–1963.* New York: Marzani and Munsell, 1963.

Rorabaugh, W. J. *Berkeley at War: The 1960s.* New York: Oxford Univ. Press, 1989.

Rosenfeld, Seth. "Reagan, Hoover and the U.C. Red Scare: The Campus Files." *San Francisco Chronicle* special report, June 9, 2002.

Rowe, Frank. *The Enemy Among Us: A Story of Witch-Hunting in the McCarthy Era.* Sacramento: Cougar Books, 1980.

Rubens, Lisa. "The Patrician Radical: Charlotte Anita Whitney." *California History* 65:3, 158–171.

Schlosberg, Mark. *The State of Surveillance: Government Monitoring of Political Activity in Northern and Central California.* San Francisco: American Civil Liberties Union of Northern California, 2006.

Sherrill, Robert. *First Amendment Felon: The Story of Frank Wilkinson, His 132,000-Page FBI File, and His Epic Fight for Civil Rights and Liberties.* New York: Nation Books, 2005.

Trumbo, Dalton. *The Time of the Toad: A Study of Inquisition in America by One of the Hollywood Ten.* Los Angeles: Hollywood Ten, 1949.

———. *Additional Dialogue: Letters of Dalton Trumbo, 1942–1962*, ed. Helen Manfull. New York: M. Evans and Co., 1970.

Weinstein, Henry. "Rich Life on Behalf of Poor: 1st Amendment Activist Frank Wilkinson…" *Los Angeles Times*, Jan. 29, 2006.

Whitten, Woodrow. "Trial of Charlotte Anita Whitney." *Pacific Historical Review* 15 (Sept. 1946), 286–294.

Wilkinson, Frank. "Revisiting the 'McCarthy Era': Looking at *Wilkinson v. United States* in Light of *Wilkinson v. Federal Bureau of Investigation. Loyola of Los Angeles Law Review* 33 (Jan. 2000), 681–698.

Film and Video

Berkeley in the Sixties. Produced and directed by Mark Kitchell. First Run Features, 1990.

Chicano! History of the Mexican American Civil Rights Movement. Executive producer, José Luis Ruiz. National Latino Communications Center and Galán Productions, in cooperation with KCET Los Angeles, 1996.

The Front. Directed by Martin Ritt, written by Walter Bernstein. Sony Pictures, 1976.

Hollywood on Trial. Produced by James Gutman, directed by David Halpern. Corinth Films, 1989.

Miller, Kazan and the Blacklist: None Without Sin. Directed by Michael Epstein. American Masters Series/PBS, 2003.

Court Cases

Whitney v. California, 274 U.S. 357 (1927).

Stromberg v. California, 283 U.S. 359 (1931).

Nitzberg and Green v. Cairns [Silva M.A. Green v. Cairns], 1936.

Lawson v. United States, 176 F. 2d 49 (D.C. Cir. 1949).

Pockman v. Leonard, 39 Cal. 2d 676 (1952).

Wilkinson v. United States, 365 U.S. 399 (1961).

Castro v. Superior Court, 9 Cal.App. 3d 675 (1970).

Monroe v. Trustees of the California State Colleges, 6 Cal. 3d 399 (1971).

In re Pratt, 112 Cal.App. 3d 795 (1980).

Wilkinson v. Federal Bureau of Investigation, 33

Loy. L.A.L. Rev. 681 (1999–2000).
Local 10, ILWU v. City of Oakland, Case No. 3:03-cv-02962-TEH (N.D. Cal. filed Jun. 26, 2003).

Chapter Seven: Mightier Than the Sword
Brechin, Gray. "Politics and Modernism: The Trial of the Rincon Annex Murals." In *On the Edge of America: California Modernist Art*, ed. Paul Karlstom. Berkeley: Univ. of California Press, 1996.
Conrad, Paul. *Conartist: 30 Years with the* Los Angeles Times. Los Angeles: Los Angeles Times Publishing, 1993.
Egendorf, Laura K., ed. *Censorship: Current Controversies*. San Diego: Greenhaven Press, 1999.
Ginsberg, Allen. *Collected Poems: 1947–1980*. New York: Harper and Row, 1988.
———. *Howl and Other Poems*. 1966. Reprint, San Francisco: City Lights Books, 1994.
Heins, Marjorie. *Sex, Sin and Blasphemy: A Guide to America's Censorship Wars*. New York: The New Press, 1993.
Jewett, Masha Zakheim. *Coit Tower: Its History and Art*. San Francisco: Volcano Press, 1983.
Kappel, Tim. "Trampling Out the Vineyards: Kern County's Bar on *The Grapes of Wrath*." *California History*, Fall 1982.
Karolides, Nicholas J., Margaret Bald, and Dawn B. Sova. *100 Banned Books: Censorship Histories of World Literature*. New York: Checkmark Books, 1999.
Leonard, Arthur S. "Obscenity and Community Standards" and "The Right to Mail Homosexually Oriented Publications." In *Sexuality and the Law: An Encyclopedia of Major Legal Cases*, ed. Arthur S. Leonard. New York: Garland Publishing, 1993.
Lingo, Marci. "Forbidden Fruit: The Banning of *The Grapes of Wrath* in the Kern County Free Library." *Libraries and Culture* 38:4, 351–379.
Miller, Henry. *Tropic of Cancer*. New York: Grove Press, 1961.
Morgan, Bill, and Nancy J. Peters, eds. Howl *on Trial: The Battle for Free Expression*. San Francisco: City Lights, 2006.
Murdoch, Joyce, and Deb Price. *Courting Justice: Gay Men and Lesbians v. the Supreme Court*. New York: Basic Books, 2001.
Steinbeck, John. *The Grapes of Wrath*. 1939. Reprint, New York: Penguin Books, 1992.
———. *The Harvest Gypsies: On the Road to the Grapes of Wrath*. Berkeley: Heyday Books, 1988.

Court Cases
Besig v. United States, 208 F. 2d 142 (9th Cir. 1953).

People v. Ferlinghetti, Case No. B27585 (Munic. Ct., San Francisco City & County, decided 1957).
ONE Inc. v. Olesen, 355 U.S. 371 (1958).
People v. Smith (Municipal Ct., Los Angeles Judicial Dist., conviction for sale of Tropic of Cancer, 1962); *aff'd*, 161 Cal.App. 2d Supp. 860 (Appellate Dept., Superior Ct., Los Angeles County, 1958); *rev'd*, Smith v. California, 361 U.S. 147 (1959) OR Smith v. California, 361 U.S. 147 (1959).
Attorney General v. Book Named "Tropic of Cancer," 345 Mass. 11 (1962).
Zeitlin v. Arnebergh, 59 Cal. 2d 901 (1963).
Grove Press, Inc. v. Gerstein, 378 U.S. 577 (1964).
Yorty v. Chandler, 13 Cal.App. 3d 467 (1970).
McKamey v. Mt. Diablo Unified School District, Case No. 215577 (Cal. Super. Ct. Contra Costa County, filed 1981, decided 1983.
McCoy v. Hearst Corp., 42 Cal. 3d 835 (1986).
Wexner v. Anderson Union High Sch. Dist. Bd. of Trustees, 209 Cal.App. 3d 1438 (1989).
Kathleen R. v. City of Livermore, 87 Cal.App. 4th 684 (2001).

Chapter 8: Keeping the Faith
Alderman, Ellen, and Caroline Kennedy. *In Our Defense: The Bill of Rights in Action*. New York: Avon Books, 1991.
Clegg, Claude Andrew III. *An Original Man: The Life and Times of Elijah Muhammad*. New York: St. Martin's Press, 1997.
Emenhiser, JeDon. "The G-O Road Controversy: American Indian Religion and Public Land." sorrel.humboldt.edu/~jae1/emenLyng.html (Jan. 6, 2009).
Falk, Donald. "Where the G-O Road Stands Now." *News from Native California* 2:3, 8–9.
Gendar, Jeannine. "Environmental Issues" *News from Native California* 7:1, 8–9.
King, Daniel P. "Religious Freedom in the Correctional Institution," *Journal of Criminal Law, Criminology, and Police Science* 60:3, 299–305.
Knight, Frederick. "Justifiable Homicide, Police Brutality or Governmental Repression? The 1962 Los Angeles Police Shooting of Seven Members of the Nation of Islam." *Journal of Negro History* 79, 1994.
Lang, Julian. "The No-GO March." *News from Native California* 2:3, 4–7.
Margolin, Malcolm. "G-O Road Update: The Journey to Washington." *News from Native California* 1:6, 10–11, 16.
Nabokov, Peter. "The G-O Road 'Principle.'" *News from Native California* 2:3, 7–8.
Peters, Shawn Francis. *Judging Jehovah's Witnesses: Religious Persecution and the Dawn of the*

Rights Revolution. Lawrence: Univ. Press of Kansas, 2000.

Smith, Christopher E. "Black Muslims and the Development of Prisoners' Rights." *Journal of Black Studies* 24:2, 131–146.

Theodoratus, Dorothea J. "G-O Road: Northwest California Religion Case to be Reviewed by Supreme Court." *News from Native California* 1:5, 4–5.

Film and Video
Knocking. Produced by Joel Engardio and Tom Shephard. The Independent Lens, PBS, 2007.

Court Cases
Gobitis v. Minersville, 21 F. Supp. 581 (E.D. Pa. 1937).

Gabrielli v. Knickerbocker 12 Cal. 2d 85 (1938).

West Virginia State Board of Education v. Barnette, 319 U.S. 624 (1943).

In re Ferguson, 55 Cal. 2d 663 (1961).

People v. Woody, 61 Cal. 2d 716 (1964).

Bennett v. Livermore Unified Sch. Dist., 193 Cal. App. 3d 1012 (1987).

Lyng v. Northwest Indian Cemetery Protective Association, 485 U.S. 439 (1988).

Employment Division, Oregon Department of Human Resources v. Smith, 494 U.S. 872 (1990).

Cheema v. Thompson, 67 F. 3d 883 (9th Cir. 1995).

Martinez v. California Youth Authority, Cal. Sup. Ct. San Joaquin County, filed Dec. 13, 1994, settled May 12, 1995.

Chapter Nine: That Dare Not Speak Its Name
Boyd, Nan Alamilla. *Wide Open Town: A History of Queer San Francisco to 1965.* Berkeley: Univ. of California Press, 2003.

Caldwell, John. "Legally Wed in Colorado, 1975: Pioneering Gay Couple …Stood up and Demanded to Be Recognized." *The Advocate*, March 30, 2004.

Clendinen, Dudley, and Adam Nagourney. *Out for Good: The Struggle to Build a Gay Rights Movement in America.* New York: Simon and Schuster, 1999.

D'Emilio, John. "Gay Politics and Community in San Francisco Since World War II." In *Hidden from History: Reclaiming the Gay and Lesbian Past*, ed. Martin Bauml Duberman, Martha Vicinus, and George Chauncey Jr. New York: New American Library, 1989.

Eskridge, William N. Jr. "Privacy Jurisprudence and the Apartheid of the Closet, 1946–1961." *Florida State University Law Review*, Summer 1997.

Faderman, Lillian, and Stuart Timmons. *Gay L.A.:*

A History of Sexual Outlaws, Power Politics, and Lipstick Lesbians. New York: Basic Books, 2006.

Gallo, Marcia M. *Different Daughters: A History of the Daughters of Bilitis and the Rise of the Lesbian Rights Movement.* New York: Carroll and Graf, 2006.

Howarth, Joan W. "First and Last Chance: Looking for Lesbians in Fifties Bar Cases." *Southern California Review of Law and Women's Studies*, Fall 1995.

Hurewitz, Daniel. *Bohemian Los Angeles and the Making of Modern Politics.* Berkeley: Univ. of California Press, 2007.

Jullion, Jeanne. *Long Way Home: The Odyssey of a Lesbian Mother and Her Children.* San Francisco: Cleis Press, 1985.

Knight, David. "My Father Is Wrong on Gays"; *Los Angeles Times*, October 14, 1999, B11.

Leonard, Arthur S. *Sexuality and the Law: An Encyclopedia of Major Legal Cases.* New York: Garland Publishing, 1993.

Martin, Del, and Phyllis Lyon. *Lesbian/Woman.* 1972. Reprint, Volcano, CA: Volcano Press, 1991.

Marcus, Eric. *Making Gay History: The Half-Century Fight for Lesbian and Gay Equal Rights.* New York: Harper Collins, 2002.

Murdoch, Joyce, and Deb Price. *Courting Justice: Gay Men and Lesbians v. The Supreme Court.* New York: Basic Books, 2001.

Patterson, Richard North. "California's Prop. 22: Psychodrama as Public Policy." *San Jose Mercury News*, Feb. 28, 2000.

Shilts, Randy. *The Mayor of Castro Street: The Life and Times of Harvey Milk.* New York: St. Martin's Press, 1982.

Stryker, Susan. *Transgender History.* Berkeley: Seal Press, 2008.

Ullman, Sharon R. *Sex Seen: The Emergence of Modern Sexuality in America.* Berkeley: Univ. of California Press, 1997.

White, C. Todd. *Pre-Gay L.A.: A Social History of the Movement for Homosexual Rights.* Champaign: Univ. of Illinois Press, 2009.

Williams, Walter L., and Yolanda Retter, eds. *Gay and Lesbian Rights in the United States: A Documentary History.* Westport, CT: Greenwood Press, 2003.

Film and Video
Screaming Queens: The Riot at Compton's Cafeteria. Produced by Victor Silverman and Susan Stryker in association with Independent Television Service and KQED, 2005.

The Times of Harvey Milk. Produced by Richard Schmiechen, directed by Rob Epstein. Telling Pictures, 1984.

Court Cases
Stoumen v. Reilly, 37 Cal. 2d 713 (1951).
Vallerga v. Dep't of Alcoholic Beverage Control,
53 Cal. 2d 313 (1959).
Nadler v. Superior Court, 255 Cal.App. 2d 523
(1967).
Morrison v. State Board of Education, 1 Cal. 3d
214 (1969).
Jullion v. Ceccarelli, Case No. 49874-4 (Cal.App.
Dept. Super. Ct., Alameda County, June 8,
1977).
Gay Law Students Association v. Pacific
Telephone and Telegraph, 24 Cal. 3d 458
(1979).
Pryor v. Municipal Court, 25 Cal. 3d 238 (1979).
Sullivan v. INS, 772 F. 2d 609 (9th Cir. 1985).
Flores v. Morgan Hill Unified School Dist., 324 F.
3d 1130 (9th Cir. 2003).
In re Marriage Cases, 43 Cal. 4th 757 (2008).
Strauss v. Horton, Case No. S168047, Supreme
Court of California (2009).

Chapter Ten: Breaking Down Barriers

Breslin, Mary Lou. "Cofounder and Director of
the Disability Rights Education and Defense
Fund, Movement Strategist." Oral history
conducted 1996–1998 by Susan O'Hara.
Regional Oral History Office, The Bancroft
Library, Univ. of California, Berkeley, 2000.
Brown, Mareva. "Friends Protest." *Bakersfield
Californian, Oct. 15, 1991,* A9.
Cone, Kitty. "Political Organizer for Disability
Rights, 1970s–1990s, and Strategist for
Section 504 Demonstrations, 1977." Oral
history conducted in 1996–1998 by David
Landes, Regional Oral History Office,
The Bancroft Library, Univ. of California,
Berkeley, 2000.
Cooper, Claire. "Pals Keep Disabled Teen on the
Go." *Sacramento Bee,* Nov. 28, 1993, A1.
Dawson, Dee-Anne. "Disabled Pupil Loses School
Pick." *Bakersfield Californian,* May 16, 1991.
———. "Making a Case for Louise." *Bakersfield
Californian,* May 15, 1991, D1.
Heumann, Judith. "Pioneering Disability Rights
Advocate and Leader in Disabled in Action,
New York; Center for Independent Living,
Berkeley; World Institute on Disability;
and the U.S. Department of Education
1960s–2000." Oral history conducted by
Susan Brown, David Landes, Jonathan Young
in 1998–2001. Regional Oral History Office,
The Bancroft Library, Univ. of California,
Berkeley, 2004.
Landau, Julia. "The Richmond Case Study: Ending
Segregated Education for Disabled Children."
In *Stepping Stones: Successful Advocacy for
Children,* ed. Sheryl Dicker. New York:
Foundation for Child Development, 1990.

Lipton, Diane. "Parent, Special Education
Advocate for the Center for Independent
Living's Disability Law Resource Center, and
Attorney for the Disability Rights Education
and Defense Fund, 1979–2002." Oral history
conducted by Denise Jacobson in 2001.
Regional Oral History Office, The Bancroft
Library, Univ. of California, Berkeley, 2004.
Longmore, Paul K. *Why I Burned My Book and
Other Essays on Disability.* Philadelphia:
Temple Univ. Press, 2003.
———, and Lauri Umansky, eds. *The New
Disability History: American Perspectives.* New
York: New York Univ. Press, 2001.
Roberts, Edward V. "The UC Berkeley Years: First
Student Resident at Cowell Hospital, 1962."
Oral history conducted by Susan O'Hara in
1994. In "University of California's Cowell
Hospital Resident Program for Physically
Disabled Students, 1962–1975: Catalyst for
Berkeley's Independent Living Movement,"
Regional Oral History Office, The Bancroft
Library, Univ. of California, Berkeley, 2000.
Roberts, Zona. "Counselor for Physically Disabled
Students' Program, Mother to Ed Roberts."
Oral history conducted in 1994–1995 by
Susan O'Hara. Regional Oral History Office,
The Bancroft Library, Univ. of California,
Berkeley, 2000.
Scotch, Richard K. *From Good Will to Civil
Rights: Transforming Federal Disability Policy.*
Philadelphia: Temple Univ. Press, 2001.
Shapiro, Joseph P. *No Pity: People with Disabilities
Forging a New Civil Rights Movement.* New
York: Times Books, 1994.
Zukas, Hale. "National Disability Activist:
Architectural and Transit Accessibility,
Personal Assistance Services." Oral history
conducted in 1997 by Kathy Cowan and
Sharon Bonney. In "Builders and Sustainers
of the Independent Living Movement in
Berkeley III," Regional Oral History Office,
The Bancroft Library, Univ. of California,
Berkeley, 2000.

Court Cases
Southeastern Community College v. Davis 442
U.S. 397 (1979).
American National Ins. Co. v. Fair Employment
and Housing Comm., 32 Cal. 3d 603 (1982).
Jamison v. Farabee, Case No. 78-0445-WHO (N.D.
Cal. Apr. 26, 1983) (consent decree).
Sacramento City Unified Sch. Dist. v Rachel H.,
14 F. 3d 1398 (9th Cir. 1994).
Doe v. Attorney General, 44 F. 3d 715 (9th Cir.
1995).

Chapter Eleven: The Wrong Side of the Law
Adler, Patricia Rae. "The 1943 Zoot Suit Riot:

Brief Episode in a Long Conflict." In *The Mexican Americans: An Awakened Minority,* comp. Manuel P. Servín. Beverly Hills: Glencoe Press, 1974.

Adrian, Erin. "Rose Elizabeth Bird: Choosing to Be Just." Palo Alto, CA: Stanford Women's Legal History Biography Project, 2002 (womenslegalhistory.stanford.edu (Jan. 8, 2009).

American Civil Liberties Union of Southern California. *Day of Protest, Night of Violence: The Century City Peace March.* Los Angeles: Sawyer Press, 1967.

Blasi, Gary. *Policing Our Way out of Homelessness.* Los Angeles: UCLA School of Law, 2007.

———, Michael Dear, and Jennifer Wolch. "5 Steps to Get out of Skid Row." *Los Angeles Times,* Dec. 31, 2006.

———. *A Reality Based Approach to Ending Homelessness in Los Angeles.* Los Angeles: Inter-University Consortium against Homelessness, Univ. of Southern California, 2007.

Boyarsky, Bill, and Penelope McMillan. "Won't Prosecute Homeless Who Are Arrested—Hahn." *Los Angeles Times,* May 30, 1987.

Branch, Taylor. *At Canaan's Edge: America in the King Years 1965–68.* New York: Simon and Schuster, 2006.

Brown, Edmund G. (with Dick Adler). *Public Justice, Private Mercy: A Governor's Education on Death Row.* New York: Weidenfeld and Nicolson, 1989.

Cummings, Judith. "Hope, Too, Is Transient in Camp for Homeless." *New York Times,* June 22, 1987.

Conot, Robert. *Rivers of Blood, Years of Darkness: The Unforgettable Classic Account of the Watts Riot.* New York: William Morrow and Co., 1968.

Davis, Mike. *City of Quartz: Excavating the Future of Los Angeles.* New York: Vintage Books, 1992.

Domanick, Joe. *Cruel Justice: Three Strikes and the Politics of Crime in America's Golden State.* Berkeley: Univ. of California Press, 2004.

———. *To Protect and to Serve: The LAPD's Century of War in the City of Dreams.* New York: Pocket Books, 1994.

Escobar, Edward J. *Race, Police, and the Making of a Political Identity: Mexican Americans and the Los Angeles Police Department, 1900–1945.* Berkeley: Univ. of California Press, 1999.

Eulau, Heinz. "The Sleepy Lagoon Case." *New Republic,* Dec. 11, 1941, 795–796.

Fagin, Leonard. "Deinstitutionalization in the USA." *Bulletin of the Royal College of Psychiatrists* 9, June 1985.

Fogelson, Robert M., comp. *The Los Angeles Riots.* New York: Arno Press and The New York Times, 1969.

Friend, Tad. "Dean of Death Row." *New Yorker,* July 30, 2007.

Gilmore, Ruth Wilson. *Golden Gulag: Prisoners, Surplus, Crisis, and Opposition in Globalizing California.* Berkeley: Univ. of California Press, 2007.

Griffith, Beatrice. *American Me.* Boston: Houghton Mifflin, 1948.

Gooding-Williams, Robert, ed. *Reading Rodney King, Reading Urban Uprising.* New York: Routledge, 1993.

Hafetz, Jonathan L. "Homeless Legal Advocacy: New Challenges and Directions for the Future." *Fordham Urban Law Journal* 30, 2003.

Horne, Gerald. *Fire This Time: The Watts Uprising and the 1960s.* Charlottesville: Univ. Press of Virginia, 1995.

Jones, Solomon James. *The Government Riots of Los Angeles, June 1943.* San Francisco: R and E Research Associates, 1973.

Lopez, Ian Haney. *Racism on Trial: The Chicano Fight for Justice.* Cambridge, MA: Belknap Press of Harvard Univ. Press, 2003.

Mantley, Rick, ed. *Hard Times* 1:3.

MacDonald, Heather. "The Reclamation of Skid Row." *City Journal,* Autumn 2007.

MacLean, Pamela. "The Strong Arm of the Law." *California Lawyer* 22:11.

Mazón, Mauricio. *The Zoot-Suit Riots: The Psychology of Symbolic Annihilation.* Austin: Univ. of Texas Press, 1984.

McCarthy, Thomas. "Report from Los Angeles." *Commonweal,* June 25, 1943, 243–244.

Meier, Matt S., and Feliciano Rivera, eds. *Readings on La Raza: The Twentieth Century.* New York: Hill and Wang, 1974.

Ogletree, Charles J. Jr., and Austin Sarat, eds. *From Lynch Mobs to the Killing State: Race and the Death Penalty in America.* New York: New York Univ. Press, 2006.

Owens, Tom (with Rod Browning). *Lying Eyes: The Truth Behind the Corruption and Brutality of the LAPD and the Beating of Rodney King.* New York: Thunder's Mouth Press, 1994.

Pagán, Eduardo Obregón. *Murder at the Sleepy Lagoon: Zoot Suits, Race, and Riot in Wartime L.A.* Chapel Hill: Univ. of North Carolina Press, 2003.

Schiraldi, Vincent, and Peter Sussman. *Three Strikes: The Unintended Victims.* San Francisco: Center on Juvenile and Criminal Justice, 1994.

Stoner, Madeleine R., *The Civil Rights of Homeless People: Law, Social Policy and Social Work Practice.* New York: Aldine de Gruyter, 1995.

Court Cases

People v. Zammora [sic], 66 Cal. App. 2d 166 (1944).

Furhman v. Georgia, 408 U.S. 238 (1972).

Murgia [sic] v. Municipal Court, 15 Cal. 3d 286 (1975).

People v. Harris (1981) 28 Cal. 3d 935, 948 [171 Cal. Rptr. 679, 623 P. 2d 240].

Kolender v. Lawson, 461 U.S. 352 (1983)

Blair v. Shanahan, 775 F. Supp. 1315 (N.D. Cal. 1991).

California v. Powell, Case No. BA035498 (Cal. Sup. Ct., Los Angeles County, Apr. 30, 1992).

Gomez v. District Court, 503 U.S. 653 (1992).

Fierro v. Gomez, 865 F. Supp. 1387 (N.D. Cal. 1994).

Joyce v. San Francisco, 846 F. Supp. 843 (N.D. Cal. 1994)

Coleman v. Wilson, 912 F. Supp. 1282 (E.D. Cal. 1995).

Rodriguez v. California Highway Patrol, 89 F. Supp. 2d 1131 (9th Cir. 2000).

Plata v. Schwarzenegger, Case No. 01-1351 (N.D. Cal.) (Pending).

Coleman v. Schwarzenegger, Case No. 90-0520 (E.D. Cal.) (Pending).

Chapter Twelve: Behind Barbed Wire

Bannai, Lorraine K. "Taking the Stand: The Lessons of Three Men Who Took the Japanese American Internment to Court." *Seattle Journal for Social Justice,* Fall/Winter 2005.

Bernstein, Joan Z, chair. *Personal Justice Denied: Report of the Commission on Wartime Relocation and Internment of Civilians.* Washington, DC: U.S. Government Printing Office, 1983.

Christgau, John. *"Enemies": World War II Alien Internment.* Ames: Iowa State Univ. Press, 1985.

Chuman, Frank F. *The Bamboo People: The Law and Japanese-Americans.* Del Mar, CA: Publisher's Inc., 1976.

Daniels, Roger. *Concentration Camps, North America: Japanese in the United States and Canada during World War II.* Malabar, FL: R. E. Krieger, 1981.

———. *The Politics of Prejudice: The Anti-Japanese Movement in California and the Struggle for Japanese Exclusion.* Berkeley: Univ. of California Press, 1977.

DiStasi, Lawrence. *Una Storia Segreta: The Secret History of Italian American Evacuation and Internment during World War II.* Berkeley: Heyday Books, 2001.

Irons, Peter. *Justice at War: The Story of the Japanese American Internment Cases.* New York: Oxford Univ. Press, 1983.

———, ed. *Justice Delayed: The Record of the Japanese American Internment Cases.* Middletown, CT: Wesleyan Univ. Press, 1989.

Kashiwagi, Hiroshi. *Swimming in the American: A Memoir and Selected Writings.* San Mateo: Asian American Curriculum Project, 2005.

Maki, Mitchell T., Harry H. L. Kitano, and S. Megan Berthold. *Achieving the Impossible Dream: How Japanese Americans Obtained Redress.* Urbana: Univ. of Illinois Press, 1999.

Muller, Eric L. *American Inquisition: The Hunt for Japanese American Disloyalty in World War II.* Chapel Hill: Univ. of North Carolina Press, 2007.

Robinson, Greg. *By Order of the President: FDR and the Internment of Japanese Americans.* Cambridge, MA: Harvard Univ. Press, 2001.

———, and Toni Robinson. "*Korematsu* and Beyond: Japanese Americans and the Origins of Strict Scrutiny." *Law and Contemporary Problems* 68:2, 29–55.

Tateishi, John, comp. *And Justice for All: An Oral History of the Japanese American Detention Camps.* New York: Random House, 1984.

tenBroek, Jacobus, Edward N. Barnhart, and Floyd W. Matson. *Prejudice, War and the Constitution.* Berkeley: Univ. of California Press, 1954.

Tule Lake Committee. *Second Kinenhi: Reflections on Tule Lake.* San Francisco: Tule Lake Committee, 2000.

Weglyn, Michi Nishiura. *Years of Infamy: The Untold Story of America's Concentration Camps.* 1976. Reprint, Seattle: Univ. of Washington Press, 1996.

Yackle, Larry W. "Japanese American Internment: An Interview with Fred Korematsu." *Public Interest Law Journal,* 1993.

Yamamoto, Eric, et al. *Race, Rights and Reparation: Law and the Japanese American Internment.* Gaithersburg, NY: Aspen Law and Business, 2001.

Zia, Helen, ed. *Here, in America? Immigrants as "The Enemy" during World War II and Today.* San Francisco: National Japanese American Historical Society, 2005.

Film and Video

Of Civil Wrongs and Rights: The Fred Korematsu Story. Written, directed and produced by Eric Paul Fournier. PBS and National Asian-American Telecommunications Association, 2000.

Rabbit in the Moon. Produced and directed by Emiko Omori. Wabi-Sabi Productions, 1999.

Unfinished Business: The Japanese American Internment Cases. Written, directed, and produced by Steven Okazaki. Mouchette Films, 1986.

Court Cases

Toki Wakayama v. United States, No. 2376-H, and Ernest Wakayama v. United States, No. 2380 (S.D. Cal. Feb. 4, 1943).

Ex Parte Endo, 323 U.S. 283 (1944).

Korematsu v. United States, 323 U.S. 214 (1944).

Ochikubo v. Bonesteel, 60 F. Supp. 916 (S.D. Cal. 1945).

Inouye et al. v. Clark, 73 F. Supp. 1000 (S.D. Cal. 1947), reversed on other grounds, 175 F. 2d 740 (9th Cir. 1949).

Abo v. Clark, 77 F. Supp. 806 (N.D. Cal. 1948), *rev'd in part, aff'd in part, sub. nom.* McGrath v. Tadayasu Abo 186 F. 2d 766 (9th Cir. 1951).

Korematsu v. United States, 584 F. Supp. 1406 (N.D. Cal. 1984).

Mochizuki v. United States, 43 Fed. Cl. 97 (Fed. Cl. 1999).

Epilogue

Asian Law Caucus. "Sixty Years after the Internment: Civil Rights, Identity Politics and Racial Profiling." Transcript of forum sponsored by Asian Law Caucus and UC Berkeley School of Law, April 17, 2003.

Cauley, Leslie. "NSA Has Massive Database of Americans' Phone Calls." *USA Today,* May 11, 2006.

———, and John Diamond. "Telecoms Let NSA Spy on Calls." *USA Today,* Feb. 6, 2006

Center for Constitutional Rights. *Maher Arar: Rendition to Torture.* New York: Center for Constitutional Rights, 2007.

Chomsky, Noam. *9-11.* New York: Seven Stories Press, 2001.

Cole, David. *Enemy Aliens: Double Standards and Constitutional Freedoms in the War on Terrorism.* New York: The New Press. 2003.

———, and James X. Dempsey. *Terrorism and the Constitution: Sacrificing Civil Liberties in the Name of National Security.* New York: The New Press, 2006.

Cuddy, Bob. *Caught in the Backlash: Stories from Northern California.* San Francisco: American Civil Liberties Union, 2002.

De Sa, Karen. "Caught in the Aftermath: Hard Life of a September 11 Detainee." *San Jose Mercury News,* Aug. 12, 2002.

Didion, Joan. *Fixed Ideas: America Since 9/11.* New York: New York Review of Books, 2003.

Egan, Timothy. "A Nation Challenged: Civil Liberties." *New York Times,* Dec. 21, 2001.

Ehrlich, Dorothy. "Patriotism v. the USA Patriot Act." *San Francisco Chronicle,* July 4, 2005.

Finan, Chris. *From the Palmer Raids to the Patriot Act: A History of the Fight for Free Speech in America.* Boston: Beacon Press, 2007.

Harris, Maya. "Making Torture Possible." *Los Angeles Daily Journal,* June 21, 2007.

Klein, Mark. "Wiretap Whistle-Blower's Account." *Wired,* April 7, 2006.

Kramer, William, ed. *After the Attacks.* New York: Open Society Institute, 2002.

Leone, Richard C., and Greg Anrig Jr., eds. *The War on Our Freedoms: Civil Liberties in an Age of Terrorism.* New York: The Century Foundation, 2003.

Linfield, Michael. *Freedom under Fire: U.S. Civil Liberties in Times of War.* Boston: South End Press, 1990.

Mayer, Jane. "Outsourcing: The CIA's Travel Agent." *New Yorker,* Oct. 30, 2006.

Minow, Mary. "The USA Patriot Act and Patron Privacy on Library Internet Terminals." *California Libraries* 11:11.

Nakashima, Ellen. "Terrorism Watch List Is Faulted for Errors." *Washington Post,* Sept. 7, 2007.

Reza, H. G. "Southland Muslim Groups Sue FBI over Surveillance." *Los Angeles Times,* Sept. 19, 2007.

Roy, Sandip. "Unlikely Target of War on Terror Still Has Faith in America." *Pacific News Service,* May 1, 2003.

Sanchez, Rene. "Librarians Make Some Noise over Patriot Act." *Washington Post,* April 10, 2003.

Schlosberg, Mark. *The State of Surveillance: Government Monitoring of Political Activity in Northern and Central California.* San Francisco: ACLU of Northern California, 2006.

Serrano, Susan Kiyomi, and Dale Minami. "*Korematsu v. United States:* A 'Constant Caution' in a Time of Crisis." *Asian Law Journal* 10:1, 37-50.

Sinnar, Shirin. *The OFAC List: How a Treasury Department Watchlist Ensnares Everyday Consumers.* San Francisco: Lawyers' Committee for Civil Rights, 2007.

Solomon, Alisa. "Things We Lost in the Fire." *Village Voice,* Sept. 11, 2002.

Srikantiah, Jayashri. "No-Fly List Risk." *Los Angeles Daily Journal,* July 1, 2003.

Stanton, Sam, and Emily Bazar. "Liberty in the Balance." Four-part series, *Sacramento Bee,* Sept. 2003.

Stone, Geoffrey R. *Perilous Times: Free Speech in Wartime from the Sedition Act of 1798 to the War on Terrorism.* New York: W.W. Norton, 2004.

Terkel, Studs. "The Wiretap This Time." *New York Times,* Oct. 29, 2007.

Yamamoto, Eric, and Susan Kiyomo Serrano. "The Loaded Weapon." *Amerasia Journal* 28:1, 51-62.

Court Cases

Korematsu v. United States, 584 F. Supp. 1406 (N.D. Cal. 1984).

Chowdhury v. Northwest Airlines Corp., 226 F.R.D. 608 (N.D. Cal. 2004).

Hamdi v. Rumsfeld, 542 U.S. 507 (2004). (The amicus brief of Fred Korematsu was submitted simultaneously on behalf of the petitioner in this case and in two related cases, Odah v. U.S., and Rasul v. Bush.)

In re National Security Agency Telecommunications Records Litigation (N.D. Cal. Aug. 14, 2006).

Mohamed et al. v. Jeppesen Dataplan, Inc., Case No. 5:07-cv-02798-RS (filed 2007).

General

Administrative Office of the Courts. "Striving for Justice: Yesterday, Today and Tomorrow." San Francisco: Judicial Council of California, 2005.

Chafe, William H., and Harvard Sitkoff, eds. *A History of Our Time: Readings on Postwar America.* New York: Oxford Univ. Press, 1999.

Coodley, Lauren, ed. *The Land of Orange Groves and Jails: Upton Sinclair's California.* Berkeley: Heyday Books, 2004.

Foner, Eric. *The Story of American Freedom.* New York: W. W. Norton, 1998.

Glasser, Ira. *Visions of Liberty: The Bill of Rights for All Americans.* New York: Arcade Publishing, 1991.

Halberstam, David. *The Fifties.* New York: Fawcett Columbine, 1993.

Knutson, Robert Logan. "The American Civil Liberties Union in Northern California." Master's Thesis, UC Berkeley, 1950.

Kutulas, Judy. *The American Civil Liberties Union and the Making of Modern Liberalism, 1930–1960.* Chapel Hill: University of North Carolina Press, 2006.

LaVally, Rebecca. *200 Significant Statutes and Constitutional Amendments of the 20th Century.* Sacramento: Senate Office of Research, 1999.

McWilliams, Carey. *California: The Great Exception.* 1949. Reprint, Berkeley: Univ. of California Press, 1998.

Rawls, James J., and Walton Bean. *California: An Interpretive History.* New York: McGraw-Hill, 2003.

Starr, Kevin. *California: A History.* New York:

Modern Library, 2005.

Walker, Samuel. *In Defense of American Liberties: A History of the ACLU.* Carbondale: Southern Illinois Univ. Press, 1999.

Walters, Dan. *The New California: Facing the 21st Century.* Sacramento: California Journal Press, 1992.

Zinn, Howard. *Disobedience and Democracy: Nine Fallacies on Law and Order.* New York: Random House, 1968.

———. *A People's History of the United States, 1492–Present.* New York: Harper Perennial, 2003.

Websites

ACLU (National), aclu.org (Jan. 8, 2009).

ACLU of Northern California, aclunc.org (Jan. 8, 2009).

ACLU of Southern California, aclu-sc.org (Jan. 8, 2009).

Archival material from early San Francisco, sanfranciscomemoirs.com (Jan. 8, 2009).

California Historical Society, californiahistory.net (Jan. 8, 2009).

"The Council on Religion and the Homosexual," lgbtran.org/Exhibits/CRH/Exhibit.aspx?P=I (Jan. 8, 2009).

Digital History, digitalhistory.uh.edu (Jan. 8, 2009).

edwardlawson.com/SupremeCourt.html (June 3, 2009).

GLBTQ, www.glbtq.com/social-sciences/prince_vc.html (Virginia Prince, June 26, 2009)

Online Archive of California, oac.cdlib.org (Jan. 8, 2009).

Oakland Museum of California, museumca.org (Jan. 8, 2009).

"Report of the Debates in the Convention of California, on the Formation of the State Constitution," lcweb2.loc.gov/ammem/cbhtml/cbhome.html (Jan. 8, 2009).

Sullivan, Andrew, and Richard Adams, www.geocities.com/WestHollywood/Stonewall/1676/1975Marriages/ImmigrationCase.html (June 8, 2009).

Virtual Museum of San Francisco Archives, 1846–1864, sfmuseum.org/hist1/index.html (Jan. 8, 2009).

Women's Legal History Biography Project, Stanford Law School, law.stanford.edu/publications/projects/wlhbp/articles.html (Jan. 8, 2009).

CREDITS AND PERMISSIONS

Introduction
Map of California by Mapping Specialists

Chapter 1: Staking Our Claim
1849 California Constitution courtesy of
California State Archives, Office of the
Secretary of State, Sacramento.
Yosemite Miwok/Paiute woman courtesy of
California State Parks, 2009.
Chinese miner panning gold courtesy of
Ed Parsons, Main Street Shop, Sonora,
California.
"Hanging of the Mexican Woman," from *Hunting
for Gold*, by William Downie, courtesy of
the California History Room, California
State Library, Sacramento, California (Neg.
8735).
Hounds attack on Chileans courtesy of The
Bancroft Library, University of California,
Berkeley (AP2 C4 V.43:553).
Execution of Casey and Cora courtesy of San
Francisco History Center, San Francisco
Public Library (Neg. # 8490).
Los Angeles Chinatown, Calle de los Negros,
1884, courtesy of Security Pacific Collection,
Los Angeles Public Library.
Anton Refregier mural of the Sandlot riots, photo
by Elaine Elinson.

Chapter 2: In a Strange Land
Yick Wo Laundry courtesy of the ACLU of
Northern California.
Poetry at Angel Island immigration Station,
photo by Bruce Judd, courtesy of
Architectural Resource Group, 2001.
Women and children at the Immigration Station
on Angel Island courtesy of California
Historical Society (FN-18240).
Wong Kim Ark identity document (Records of
the U.S. District Courts, Record Group 21)
courtesy of National Archives and Records
Administration–Pacific Region, San Bruno,
CA.
Braceros being processed by authorities at
Mexican border, photo by Leonard Nadel,
courtesy of Smithsonian Institution,
National Museum of American History.
"La Linea" (The Line), U.S. Mexico Border, photo
© by Ken Light, courtesy of Ken Light.
Berkeley High School student protests against
Proposition 187, photo by David Bacon,
courtesy of David Bacon.

Chapter 3: An Injury to All
Nagi Daifullah funeral procession, photo by
Sam Kushner, courtesy of Labor Archives
and Research Center, San Francisco State
University (People's World Collection, Box
13, Folder 2).
IWW Solidarity sticker courtesy of Labor
Archives and Research Center, San Francisco
State University (Ephemera Collection).
Los Angeles Times building after bombing, 1910,
courtesy of Security Pacific Collection, Los
Angeles Public Library.
Tom Mooney in prison courtesy of The Bancroft
Library, University of California, Berkeley
(Mooney, Thomas POR 7).
Striking cotton workers, photo by Paul Taylor,
courtesy of The Bancroft Library, University
of California, Berkeley (BANC PIC 1945-
007:4-PIC).
National Guard in San Francisco during 1934
ILWU strike courtesy of ILWU archives.
Dockworkers confronting police during 1934
General Strike courtesy of ILWU archives.
Police ransacking the Workers School, 1934,
courtesy of San Francisco History Center,
San Francisco Public Library (AAD-5004).
Dolores Huerta photo by Harvey Richards,
courtesy of Estuary Press.

Chapter 4: Under Color of Law
Biddy Mason courtesy of Security Pacific
Collection, Los Angeles Public Library.
Felicitas and Gonzalo Mendez courtesy of the
Mendez family.
Interracial couple Francisca and Jose Navalta
courtesy of Anita Navalta Bautista, Filipino
American National Historical Society.
WWII sailors at Port Chicago courtesy of Percy
Robinson.
"This tract is exclusive and restricted," Los
Angeles, courtesy of the Southern California
Library for Social Studies and Research.
Alcatraz during Native American occupation,
photo by Michelle Vignes, courtesy of The
Bancroft Library, University of California,
Berkeley.
UC Berkeley protest against Proposition 209,
photo by David Bacon, courtesy of David
Bacon.

Chapter 5: Holding up Half the Sky
Chinese prostitutes in San Francisco, courtesy of

San Francisco History Center, San Francisco Public Library, (AAB-7004).

"How We Won the Vote in California," *cover,* courtesy of San Francisco History Center, San Francisco Public Library (324.3 So47).

"Rosies," WWII shipyard workers, 1943, photo by Emmanuel Joseph, courtesy of African American Museum and Library at Oakland, CA.

Aileen Hernandez, courtesy of Aileen Hernandez.

Non-traditional employment demonstration in San Francisco, photo by Cathy Cade, courtesy of Cathy Cade and Labor Archives and Research Center, San Francisco State University (Union Wage Collection, Box 2, Folder 6).

Lillian Garland with Pat Shiu and Betty Friedan © Bettmann/Corbis.

Pro-choice demonstration, photo by Rick Rocamora, courtesy of Rick Rocamora.

Chapter 6: The Right Not to Remain Silent

Upton Sinclair courtesy of the ACLU of Southern California.

Charlotte Anita Whitney courtesy of The Bancroft Library, University of California, Berkeley (Whitney, Charlotte Anita – POR 6).

"Vigilante Acquitted" (from 1984 Historic Edition of *ACLU News*), *ACLU News* archives, courtesy of the ACLU of Northern California.

Free the Hollywood 10 protest, photographer unidentified, courtesy of Labor Archives and Research Center, San Francisco State University (People's World Collection, Box 5, Folder 9).

Non-signers of Levering Act of SF State University, 1950, photo by Hansel Mieth, courtesy of Collection Center for Creative Photography, University of Arizona, © 1998 The University of Arizona Foundation.

HUAC-era hosing of demonstrators at San Francisco City Hall courtesy of San Francisco History Center, San Francisco Public Library (Oversize Box 32).

"Free Saul Castro" protest, photographer unidentified, courtesy of Labor Archives and Research Center, San Francisco State University (People's World Collection, Box 11, Folder 6).

Chicano Moratorium, photo by Allen Zak, courtesy of Labor Archives and Research Center, San Francisco State University (People's World Collection, Box 11, Folder 6).

Frank Wilkinson courtesy of UCLA Charles E. Young Research Library Department of Special Collections, *Los Angeles Times* Photographic Archives, Copyright © Regents of the University of California, UCLA Library.

Geronimo Pratt courtesy of UCLA Charles E. Young Research Library Department of Special Collections, *Los Angeles Times* Photographic Archives, Copyright © Regents of the University of California, UCLA Library.

Peace Fresno demonstration courtesy of Howard K. Watkins (www.watkinsphotoarchiveproject.com).

Chapter 7: Mightier Than the Sword

Cover for *The Grapes of Wrath,* illustration created by Elmer Hader for the Viking Press 1939 edition.

Anton Refregier mural at Rincon Annex, photo by Elaine Elinson.

Lawrence Ferlinghetti, courtesy of San Francisco History Center, San Francisco Public Library (AAD-2815).

Sam Yorty cartoon by Paul Conrad, 1968, reprinted with the artist's permission.

Raul Ramirez, photo by Rick Rocamora, courtesy of Rick Rocamora.

Chapter 8: Keeping the Faith

Charlotte Gabrielli, age 9, 1936, courtesy of California Historical Society (FN 28804).

Mosque 27 courtesy of UCLA Charles E. Young Research Library Department of Special Collections, *Los Angeles Times* Photographic Archives, Copyright © Regents of the University of California, UCLA Library.

Malcolm X and William Rogers, 1963, courtesy of *Herald Examiner* Collection, Los Angeles Public Library.

G-O Road opponents courtesy of Heyday Institute.

Cheema children photo by Adrian Mendoza courtesy of the *Modesto Bee.*

Chapter 9: That Dare Not Speak Its Name

Phyllis Lyon and Del Martin courtesy of Phyllis Lyon.

Couple attending the CRH Ball, photo by Ray "Scotty" Morris, courtesy of The Bancroft Library, University of California, Berkeley (2006.029-PIC).

Harvey Milk, photo by Robert Pruzan, courtesy of Gay, Lesbian, Bisexual, Transgender Historical Society.

"No on 6" ad courtesy of Gay, Lesbian, Bisexual, Transgender Historical Society.

Alana Flores and Freddie Fuentes, photo by Gigi Pandian, *ACLU News* archives, courtesy of the ACLU of Northern California.

Phyllis Lyon and Del Martin with San Francisco Mayor Gavin Newsom, photo by Liz Mangelsdorf, courtesy of National Center for Lesbian Rights.

Chapter 10: Breaking Down Barriers
Ed Roberts and Herb Willsmore, courtesy of The Bancroft Library, University of California, Berkeley (UARC PIC 2800 H:007).

Judy Heumann, photo by HolLynn D'Lil, courtesy of HolLynn D'Lil.

Judy Heumann and Kitty Cone, photo by HolLynn D'Lil, courtesy of HolLynn D'Lil.

Disability Law Resource Center staff, courtesy of Disability Rights Education and Defense Fund (DREDF).

Rachel Holland, at graduation and childhood photo, courtesy of the Holland Family.

Paul Longmore courtesy of UCLA Charles E. Young Research Library Department of Special Collections, *Los Angeles Times* Photographic Archives, Copyright © Regents of the University of California, UCLA Library.

Chapter 11: The Wrong Side of the Law
Earle Kynette, 1938, courtesy of *Herald Examiner* Collection, Los Angeles Public Library.

National Guard in Watts Riots, Los Angeles, CA., courtesy of San Francisco History Center, San Francisco Public Library, ©AP Images.

Aaron Mitchell execution drawing by Howard Brodie, courtesy of Howard Brodie.

Early San Quentin prisoners, San Quentin Mug Book Page SQ7892–SQ8462, courtesy of California State Archives, Office of the Secretary of State, Sacramento.

Prisoners at California State Prison, Sacramento, photo by Max Whittaker, courtesy of Max Whittaker/*The New York Times*/Redux Pictures.

Depression-era migrants photo by Dorothea Lange, Farm Security Administration, courtesy of Labor Archives and Research Center, San Francisco State University (People's World Collection, Box 1, Folder 9).

Homeless woman with child courtesy of *Making Change* (Los Angeles newspaper for and by homeless people).

Sleepy Lagoon defendants, 1942, courtesy of *Herald Examiner* Collection, Los Angeles Public Library.

Chapter 12: Behind Barbed Wire
Elderly man and grandchildren, photo by Dorothea Lange, courtesy of National Archives (#210-GC 160).

Ray Takeno, photo by Ansel Adams, courtesy of Library of Congress (LC-A35-T01-4-M-4).

Men stuffing mattresses at Manzanar, CA. courtesy of San Francisco History Center, San Francisco Public Library/© Bettman/Corbis.

Hiroshi Kashiwagi courtesy of the Kashiwagi Family Collection.

Tule Lake stockade, photo by R. H. Ross, courtesy of John and Reiko Ross.

Fred Korematsu with family courtesy of Karen Korematsu.

Hiroshi Kashiwagi testifying before redress commission courtesy of Isago Isao Tanaka.

Epilogue
Fred Korematsu with medal of freedom, photo by Shirley Nakao, courtesy of Shirley Nakao.

Post-9/11 demonstration, photo by Maria Archuleta, *ACLU News* archives, courtesy of the ACLU of Northern California.

Sacramento jail, photo by Paul Kitagaki Jr., courtesy of *Sacramento Bee*/ZUMA.

San Jose peace rally, photo by Rick Rocamora, courtesy of Rick Rocamora.

INDEX

ABOUT THE AUTHORS

Elaine Elinson was the communications director of the ACLU of Northern California and editor of the *ACLU News* for more than two decades. She is a coauthor of *Development Debacle: The World Bank in the Philippines,* which was banned by the Marcos regime. She is a book reviewer for the *San Francisco Chronicle* and the *Los Angeles Review of Books,* and her articles have been published in the *Nation, Poets and Writers, Truthdig, Woman's Day,* and numerous other periodicals. She is married to the journalist Rene CiriaCruz and they have one son.

Stan Yogi managed development programs for the ACLU of Northern California for fourteen years. He is the coauthor, with Laura Atkins, of the award-winning biography for young readers *Fred Korematsu Speaks Up.* He is the coeditor of two books, *Highway 99: A Literary Journey Through California's Great Central Valley* and *Asian American Literature: An Annotated Bibliography.* His work has appeared in the *San Francisco Chronicle, MELUS, Los Angeles Daily Journal,* and several anthologies. He is married to nonprofit administrator David Carroll.